THE SKUAS

To John Coulson

THE SKUAS

by Robert W. Furness

Illustrated by

JOHN BUSBY

T & A D POYSER

Calton

© *Robert W. Furness 1987*

ISBN 0 85661 046 1

First published in 1987 by T & A D Poyser Ltd
Town Head House, Calton, Waterhouses, Staffordshire, England

British Library Cataloguing in Publication Data
Furness, R.W.
  The skuas.
  1. Catharacta.
  I. Title
  598'.33   QL696.C488
  ISBN 0–85661–046–1

Text set in Monophoto Ehrhardt, printed and
bound in Great Britain by Butler & Tanner Ltd, Frome and London

Contents

5

List of photographs

List of Figures

List of Tables

Acknowledgements

Brown Skuas presented themselves for study from the moment when the first load of stores was sent ashore. The pair in whose territory the hut was built were the first to be noted; they watched closely, removed all small and portable objects, stole sandwiches and left the building site only to chase off other intruders. By contrast, three pairs of Black Backed Gulls Larus dominicanus *nesting 100 metres from the site abandoned their eggs within two days of the party's arrival. All the skuas soon lost the little timidity which they at first possessed; a pair not otherwise engaged would accompany the observer as he moved within its limits, leaving him at the territory boundary to be escorted by the next pair. Boundaries could in this way be ascertained clearly, and the territory significant to a pair could be defined as that area within which the birds were prepared to escort the observer. A hide was in one case erected near to a nest site in an attempt to secure photographs of nest-building, but it was never possible to enter the hide without the full knowledge of the birds, who would sit patiently outside, occasionally peering in through the flap to see what I was doing. The presence of the hide seemed to exercise their curiosity more than the undisguised presence of the observer.*

Stonehouse (1956)

First and foremost, I must acknowledge my debt to all those who have studied skuas in the past, whose work has made this book possible. The papers on skua biology by Bernard Stonehouse, Bob Burton, Euan Young and Malte Andersson have been sources of particular delight and inspiration.

Although I have tried to deal with all of the skuas, inevitably the coverage is uneven. Partly this is due to the fact that some skuas have been studied in great detail while others have received little serious attention. It also follows from my limited experience. My interest in skuas was first aroused by my biology teacher, Peter Mawby, who took me to Foula in the summer of 1971 as a member of a seabird ringing expedition. I have to thank Peter for encouraging me to take a scientific interest in skua biology by persuading me to sit in a hide on a 'Bonxie' club site for several days on end! Since 1971 I have returned to Foula each year to continue fieldwork with skuas, particularly the Great Skua, known locally in Shetland as the 'Bonxie'. I would have preferred to refer to the Great Skua as the

Bonxie throughout this book, but this evocative local name is not well known outside Britain, so I have generally used the more formal name.

Between 1973, when I was allowed to do my Zoology degree second year project on Foula, and the end of my PhD in 1977, I spent over four months of each year on Foula. My work on Great Skuas in this early period was supervised by Dr John Coulson, and I am deeply grateful to him for his skilful, patient, and caring guidance and criticism. The long visits to Foula were made particularly enjoyable by the hospitality of the islanders, and my understanding of skua biology was greatly enhanced by long conversations with the late Alastair Holbourn, who first led me into the fruitful field of historical writings, and the late Mima Gear, who had a detailed knowledge of the island's birds that could only be gained from a lifetime's outdoor experience. My work was greatly aided by long term ringing and censusing of seabirds on Foula that had been running for many years before my first visit. This was under the direction of ornithologists such as Christopher Mylne, Tony Land, Bob Dickens, Ted Jackson, John Gittins, Tony Mainwood and Peter Mawby, who were all involved in leading expeditions of young people organised by the Brathay Exploration Group. I am most grateful to 'Brathay' for accommodation on Foula and the assistance that numerous members of expeditions gave in ringing skuas, collecting prey remains and pellets, counting and mapping breeding seabirds on Foula.

I particularly thank Rob and Ann, John and Isobel Holbourn, for permission to work on Foula and for generously helping to organise the logistics of my fieldwork. Many individuals have helped me with fieldwork in Shetland, and particularly prominent amongst these have been David and Gillian Okill, Garry Heath, Kenny Ensor, Mark Tasker, and Ian Burrows. I am grateful to Richard Caldow, Bridget Furness, Anne Hudson, Sandra Muirhead and David Thompson both for help with my fieldwork in Shetland and for allowing me to quote from their PhD thesis material. Other items of unpublished information were freely provided by Mike Richardson and Pete Ewins of the NCC, Shetland, John Croxall, Jim and Sheila Gear, John Scott, Kate Thompson, Euan Young, and staff of the British Museum (Natural History), Tring. The British Trust for Ornithology made available national ringing recoveries of skuas. I thank John Cooper and Roy Siegfried of the FitzPatrick Institute for African Ornithology for giving me the opportunity to visit Gough Island on two occasions to study the Tristan Skua.

Many people provided photographs of skuas for me to select from, and I thank them all. I have tried to include photographs that illustrate particular points rather than necessarily those of highest technical standard. It has been a delight to have John Busby draw skuas to complement the text; his style captures their character exceptionally well.

Susan Anderson and Kenneth Ensor read the whole book in draft, and suggested many improvements, while John Cuthbert, Jeremy Greenwood, John and Isobel Holbourn commented helpfully on particular chapters. Kenneth Ensor and Susan Anderson drew many of the figures and helped with proof reading. Susan also printed many of the photographs, helped me with fieldwork, and allowed skuas of a variety of species to attack her, and bravely defended me from particularly aggressive ones while I measured eggs or chicks; her support has been invaluable.

ROBERT W. FURNESS

Introduction

... and many other fowles, among which I noted the nature of one, which we called an Allen; who (like the great fishes, which eate up the small, or like some great men, which devoure all the labours of the poore) when some smaller birds have gotten any thing then he leaveth not beating of them, till they have cast up what they have eaten, which he laying hold of devoureth up; and so with little meate in their gorges, and few feathers on their backes, he leaveth them to get more, not for themselves but for him.

Poole (1625)

The skuas (Family Stercorariidae) are close relatives of the gulls (Family Laridae). Skuas are characteristically and widely known as pirates and predators, although many birdwatchers have never seen one, since all the skua species are generally uncommon and their breeding sites remote. For some lucky birdwatchers a vivid memory is the sight of a skua on passage in the autumn flying rapidly after a flock of terns or Kittiwakes. Having selected a victim the skua accelerates and, after prolonged aerial contortions reminiscent of a First World War dogfight, the skua forces its victim to drop or regurgitate its food. While the victim makes its escape, the skua catches the stolen food in mid air and hurries after another flock with fast winnowing wingbeats.

The experience described above differs little from the first documented description of this characteristic behaviour, by Poole (1625), and used to head this chapter.

SKUA SYSTEMATICS

The skuas have been classified in many different arrangements of species and subspecies, grouped into one or two genera. The reasons for this are discussed later (Chapter 2) but on the basis of current knowledge I favour the following classification.

Family STERCORARIIDAE

Genus *Stercorarius* (small skuas) – three species:
1. *Stercorarius parasiticus*   Arctic Skua (Parasitic Jaeger)
2. *Stercorarius pomarinus*   Pomarine Skua (Pomarine Jaeger)
3. *Stercorarius longicaudus*   Long-tailed Skua (Long-tailed Jaeger)
    (*S. longicaudus* is divided into two subspecies: *longicaudus* and *pallescens*)

Genus *Catharacta* (large skuas) – three species:
1. *Catharacta skua skua*   Great Skua ('Bonxie')
    Catharacta skua hamiltoni   Tristan Skua
    Catharacta skua lönnbergi   Brown Skua (Subantarctic Skua)
    Catharacta skua antarctica   Falkland Skua
2. *Catharacta maccormicki*   South Polar Skua (McCormick Skua)
3. *Catharacta chilensis*   Chilean Skua

Partly because the classification of skuas has been rather confused, there are several alternative names for some of the taxa. This classification has a number of features that invite further consideration. It has been argued that the Pomarine Skua shares a number of features with the large skuas and bridges the gap between the groups and requires that all skuas are placed in a single genus. Also, the fact that the Great Skua has been breeding in the North Atlantic for only a very short time (in an evolutionary sense) raises the question of its origins from the Antarctic or subAntarctic. *Catharacta skua* is the only species of vertebrate (other than introduced commensals of man such as house mice, and perhaps man himself) that has a breeding distribution in both the Arctic/subArctic and the Antarctic/subAntarctic. While the Great Skua appears on morphological, anatomical and behavioural grounds to be most similar to the Brown Skua and Falkland Skua, the South Polar Skua is the only southern skua regularly to migrate north of the equator, and so might yet be a contender as the closest relative of the Great Skua. Should this prove to be the case, then the classification outlined above would clearly have to be changed again.

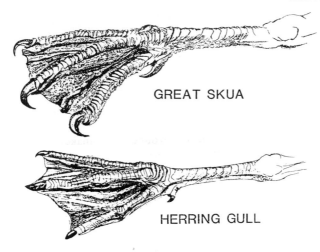

Fig. 1   *Skua and gull legs compared.*

Skuas possess a unique combination of strong hooked claws on the toes and swimming membranes between the toes (Fig. 1), thus combining the characters of birds of prey and seabirds. They also have hard scales, or scutes, on the legs, similar to those on birds of prey but contrasting with the soft fleshy skin on the legs of gulls. The shape of the leg, however, is gull-like. Skuas also have well developed supra-orbital salt glands which allow them to drink seawater when freshwater is unavailable, though all skuas are very fond of drinking, and bathing in, freshwater. The bill is strong and hooked, with a prominent distal nail on the upper mandible which is rounded and smooth by comparison with the same part of a gull's bill (Fig. 2). Elongation of the two central tail feathers is hardly

GREAT SKUA   HERRING GULL

Fig. 2   *Comparison of the bills of skuas and gulls.*

detectable in the large skuas, but is very pronounced in the small skuas (Fig. 3).

The two skua genera show rather different wing shapes (Fig. 4; Photos 1 and 2) and plumage patterns. The large skuas have broad blunt wings while the small skuas have narrow, pointed and long wings. The large skuas are generally brown, with some rufous or golden markings and a conspicuous white wing flash consisting

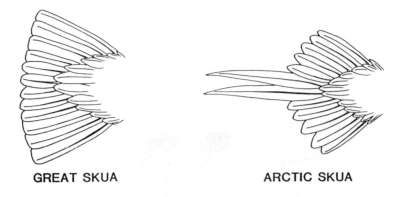

GREAT SKUA   **ARCTIC SKUA**

Fig. 3   *Tail shapes in adult Great Skuas and Arctic Skuas.*

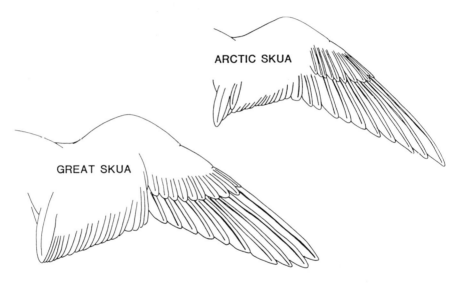

Fig. 4   *Wing shapes of* Catharacta *and* Stercorarius *skuas.*

of exposed white lower parts of the primaries, most obvious on the underwing, and hidden when the wing is closed.

PLUMAGE POLYMORPHISM

The South Polar Skua has two adult plumages, although this polymorphism is not well known and has in the past been confused by the fact that the plumage fades through the season due to the high ultra-violet radiation during the Antarctic

1. South Polar Skua in flight, showing the rounded wings and tail typical of large skuas. This bird is a pale phase individual, photographed near Cape Hallett, Northern Victoria Land, Antarctica. Photo: J. G. Pascoe

summer, and also by the confounding presence of the monomorphic dark Brown Skuas in some parts of the South Polar Skua range. Until recently it was often not appreciated that these were two distinct species, and much confusion resulted. The two colour phases of the South Polar Skua occur as dark-bodied or light-bodied individuals, but this polymorphism may be rather different from that well known in the small skuas. The Arctic Skua shows continuous variation in plumage from totally sooty brown through many intermediate stages to extreme pale phase, in which the entire belly, breast and neck are white or cream coloured and the wings, tail, back and crown of the head are dark brown. In both the South Polar Skua and the Arctic Skua there is a cline in the proportions of the colour phases: in the South Polar Skua the proportion of light birds increases towards the interior of the Antarctic; with the Arctic Skua the proportion of light birds also tends to increase with latitude, though some anomalies exist. Some of the explanations put

2. *A male Long-tailed Skua in flight, showing the more pointed and narrower wings of the small skuas and much elongated central tail feathers.* Photo: J. de Korte.

forward for these patterns and for the existence of the polymorphic plumage will be considered later (Chapter 9).

Both the Pomarine Skua and Long-tailed Skua show the same plumage polymorphism as the Arctic Skua, but the frequency of dark phase Long-tailed Skuas is extremely low. Even at the southern extreme of their breeding range in Scandinavia, where about half the Arctic Skuas are of the dark phase, only light phase Long-tailed Skuas are known. A very few dark Long-tailed Skuas have been seen at breeding sites, and all of these have been in Greenland, so belong to the subspecies *S. l. pallescens* (Chapter 2). The dark morph of the Pomarine Skua is rather uncommon, and occurs at a frequency of 5–20% in most breeding localities with rather little evidence of clinal variation in relation to latitude or of any other consistent pattern of geographical variation in the proportions of the colour phases (Chapter 9).

EVOLUTIONARY ADAPTATIONS

Many of the differences between skuas and their close relatives, the gulls, may be related to the evolution of skuas as 'seabirds of prey'. While several such explanations have been suggested, proving that these ideas are correct is generally impossible, and disproving them is often difficult. Thus, for example, female skuas are larger than their mates. In gulls, as in most birds, it is the male which is the larger sex. The 'reversed sexual size dimorphism' seen in skuas is best known in birds of prey and is usually explained in that instance in terms of the relative feeding efficiency of the sexes and the different roles of male and female birds of prey in feeding and guarding the chicks. If this is the explanation, then perhaps the ecological equivalence of skuas as seabirds of prey explains why they too have evolved a reversed sexual size dimorphism, and one that is in the opposite direction to that found in their closest relatives, the gulls (Chapter 5).

Similarly, one explanation for the observed tendency for skuas to be dark in plumage while gulls are generally light coloured, is that dark plumage is less conspicuous so allows skuas to approach potential victims of their attacks with less chance of being detected. This 'aggressive camouflage' hypothesis assumes that an ability to sneak up on victims undetected is advantageous for a klepto-parasite (Chapter 8), and suffers from the difficulty that the relative conspicu-ousness of light or dark birds is rather dependent on the background against which they are to be viewed and on the prevailing light conditions. The question of which plumage is the more conspicuous is still open to argument. Answering these and other questions demands a knowledge of the detailed life history of skuas. It also requires that direct experimental tests or field observations of the points in question should be made. For example, if skuas show no division of labour while chick rearing, then the larger size of females cannot easily be explained as an adaptation to defend the brood better, but this is more likely to be a correct explanation if female skuas spend more time attending the chicks while the males do most of the foraging for the family.

There are many aspects of the biology of skuas which are of particular interest. The Arctic Skua is probably the only species of bird in which individuals may exist solely by kleptoparasitism (the stealing of food from other species) at all times of the year, and even obtain sufficient return from the practice to allow them to breed and rear young fed on the prey caught by other species, and intended for their chicks. Yet Arctic Skuas are equally at home breeding far inland on the Arctic tundra, where their ecology is very different from that at coastal seabird colonies. *Catharacta* skuas also show considerable adaptability in response to their environment (a characteristic of course which skuas share with their close relatives, the gulls). This diversity of life styles can be related to the wide variety of environmental and ecological conditions exploited by skuas. Thus their mating system is usually, as in most birds, one of monogamous pairing, and because skuas are long-lived this can lead to lifetime mate fidelity. However, under certain circumstances we can find females paired with two males who share the same territory and nest. This is a form of polyandry. We can also find situations where skuas indulge in polygyny, with one male mated to two females (Chapter 10). Feeding behaviour can also show great flexibility within a skua species; in some situations pairs feed totally within their breeding territory, while in some they feed totally outwith the territory (Chapter 7). In some situations pairs feed only during the day, but in a few places pairs feed only at night and spend the day sleeping. Relating the differences in life style to the prevailing ecological conditions is a fruitful tool in the study of evolutionary ecology and one to which skuas are particularly well suited.

ECOLOGICAL RELATIONSHIPS

While skuas provide a fruitful group for the study of evolutionary adaptations and the way in which species can adapt to a variety of different ecological niches, skuas also provide a number of problems for the conservationist as well as a useful marine top-predator that can act as a marine environment canary. Skuas accumulate high levels of certain pollutants (Chapter 14), but also have a bad reputation among islanders in remote areas, where great skuas in particular are often accused of attacking sheep and other livestock (Chapter 15). Certain skua populations have suffered intense persecution as a result, while others have adapted to man's activities in such a way that their numbers have greatly increased, and this too can be a problem where the enlarged numbers of skuas may pose a threat to other wildlife populations (Chapter 16).

The aim of this book is to outline our knowledge of the ecology of skuas and to consider some of the interesting questions which this raises. While the intrinsic interest and many unique attributes of skuas have resulted in several studies of all sorts of aspects of their biology, there have been rather few direct tests of hypotheses relating to their evolutionary ecology. In most cases the studies that have been made in this context have answered few questions but uncovered many more. We can conclude at this early stage that there is abundant scope for future research into the ecology of skuas, particularly with regard to the evolution of ecological differences between populations.

Rather little is known about Long-tailed, Pomarine and Chilean Skuas, whereas Arctic Skuas have been the subject of much detailed genetical and ecological research, and some aspects of Great and Brown Skua ecology are very well known. I have not attempted to give each species equal coverage in this book, but rather have chosen to highlight aspects of skua biology where the available knowledge provides insights into the role of skuas in ecosystems, including their interactions with man (as pests or in problems of conservation) and the adaptations they show to their ways of life.

CHAPTER 2

Early history and classification of skuas

Our Cataracta, I suppose the Cornish Gannet, the same as the Skua of Hoier, described by Clusius. The skin of this stuffed was sent us by our worthy friend Dr Walter Needham, who found it hung up in a certain Gentlemans Hall. Hapning to read over the description of Hoier's Skua I find it exactly to agree with ours ... The Cornish Gannet, espying the Pilchard, casts himself down from on high upon it.

Ray (1678)

IDENTIFICATION AND CLASSIFICATION OF SKUAS IN 17TH AND 18TH CENTURIES

Unfortunately, the classification of most seabirds was a confused subject before the 19th century. Classification of skuas was particularly haphazard since few ornithologists saw more than one or two skua specimens, generally shot and sent to them by their field contacts, and they had great difficulty in matching such specimens with the existing printed descriptions. The fact that skuas occur in a number of age-related plumages and show distinct colour phases in the small species, no doubt made the job of classifying this group particularly difficult. A good example of the problem is the list of species given by Ray (1678), who attempted to catalogue and describe 'all the species of birds known to man'. He lists skuas and large gulls in the following way: Section 6 Gulls; (a) The greater gulls; (ii) great brown and grey types; 1. Cataracta; 2. The Catarracta of Aldrovandus; 3. The great grey gull; 4. The Coddy-moddy; 5. *Larus major*; 6. Baltner's great grey sea mew; 7. Aldrovand's Cepphus; 8. *Larus cinereus minor*; 9. Marggraves Brasilian Gull. None of these are immediately identifiable from their names, and many are impossible to identify with any confidence from their description!

The names and descriptions in the literature supposed to relate to the Great Skua are numerous. Several can be attributed to specimens of other species mistakenly referred to as skuas, while many others refer to descriptions in early works on natural history that later authors incorrectly identified as descriptions of skuas. The first true published description of a Great Skua was given by Clusius (1605) from a specimen sent to him in 1604: 'The bird sent me by Hoier (from the Faeroe Islands) was of the bigness of a great Gull, ... bill smooth, black and crooked almost like those of rapacious birds, ... toes all ending in sharp, crooked claws, and joyned together by a black membrane, ... the feathers inserting the body were of a colour between black and cinereous. Hoier writes that it preys not only on fish, but on all kinds of small birds' (Clusius 1605).

Aldrovandus (1637) gave the second published description of the species, but he mistakenly equated his bird with the description of the 'Catarracta' of Aristotle who described this large brown seabird as follows: 'The catarrhactes lives near the sea; when it makes a dive, it will keep under the water for as long as it takes a man to walk a furlong; it is less than the common hawk. The duck, the goose, the gull, the catarrhactes and the great bustard have the oesophagus wide and roomy from one end to the other' (Aristotle 342 BC).

The third account of the species was given by Debes (1673), who also obtained a specimen from the Faeroe Islands. Willughby, whose work was published by John Ray (1678), also gave an accurate description of a Great Skua, the fourth in the literature, calling it Catarracta after the name given by Aristotle and used by Aldrovandus. Ray and Willughby thought that the Catarracta and their Great Skua were the same bird as the 'Cornish Gannet' which had been described to Willughby by fishermen. The Cornish Gannet was a large, brown, seabird which used to be caught by local fishermen by fixing a pilchard onto a block of wood which was weighted below and left floating just below the surface of the sea. The birds dived at the pilchard and 'dashed their brains out by impaling themselves on the block of wood'.

It is now clear to us that the Cornish Gannets of Willughby must have been juvenile Gannets on their southward migration after fledging, and obviously not Great Skuas. Their only common feature is that both are large brown (or grey-brown) seabirds. Similarly, the Catarrhactes of Aristotle must also have been a juvenile Gannet and not a Great Skua. Great Skuas and Gannets both have a wide oesophagus, but Great Skuas do not dive underwater. It is rather ironic that Aristotle's name for a Gannet should have become the scientific generic name for large skuas as a result of the misinterpretations of early 17th century ornithologists! However, if this seems bad, things get much worse and almost inextricably confusing. Both Aldrovandus and Willughby described a bird to which they gave the name Cepphus because they considered it to be the same as the Cepphus described by Aristotle. The detailed descriptions and drawings given by Aldrovandus and Willughby make it clear that their birds were specimens of one of the *Stercorarius* skuas in juvenile or first winter plumage. However, Aristotle (342 BC) gave a description of his Cepphus as a small black and white seabird that flits lightly over the surface of the sea and dips to the water for food; clearly Aristotle's

Cepphus was one of the storm petrels! Perhaps fortunately, Cepphus did not stick as a name for any of the small skuas. The matter was even further confused when a later misinterpretation of Aristotle's writings resulted in Cepphus being passed on to the Black Guillemot, another small black and white seabird, though one that would not be seen flitting over the waves like a petrel! Hence *Cepphus grylle* as the scientific name for the Black Guillemot and *Cepphus columba* for the closely related Pigeon Guillemot. Nevertheless, several later authors read the descriptions of the Cepphus of Aldrovandus and Ray (i.e. of a small skua) and considered that these birds must also be Great Skuas. The fact that there were actually several species of skua was not appreciated at the time; and when it became clear that this was the case, several extra species were described because the colour phases and age classes differ so much that there was no reason for an ornithologist who knew skuas only from shot skins to consider them to be conspecific.

We may feel slightly superior to these fumbling ornithologists of the 17th and 18th century, but do remember that, even though we now have our numerous detailed and accurate field guides, and know that there are three species of *Stercorarius* and (arguably) three or four of *Catharacta*, we still make mistakes with them. When I visited Cambridge University Zoology Museum a few years ago I found an adult Arctic Skua still labelled *Stercorarius longicaudus*. The magazine British Birds recently contained a lively dispute over the identity of a photographed juvenile *Stercorarius* skua. Copenhagen Museum contains a South Polar Skua skin that, until it was carefully reexamined in 1975, was labelled as a juvenile Great Skua because it had never been considered that a South Polar Skua might have been collected from Greenland. In 1984 I examined the *Catharacta* skins in the British Museum (Natural History) in Tring, to discover to my surprise that a juvenile skua had been catalogued as originating from Scalloway, South Shetland Islands. One might well wonder which species this was!

Aristotle's *Natural History* (342 BC) is undoubtedly a work of great significance. It contains a wealth of excellent observation of the behaviour and structure of animals, as well as descriptions of an enormous number of species, although it lacks the illustrations that would have helped 17th and 18th century ornithologists to avoid some of their mistakes. However, many of the illustrations that were made during the 17th and 18th century do not help much either. It is blatantly obvious that most birds were known only from dead, often rather mutilated, specimens. The first illustration of a Great Skua, that of Clusius, redrawn by Ray (1678) is a case in point (Fig. 5). The bird looks little like a skua and more like a well-used teddy bear.

Albin (1738–40) described a juvenile skua, probably an Arctic Skua, to which he gave the name *Larus fuscus*, or 'Brown Gull'. The identity of this specimen is in little doubt since Albin gave detailed body measurements as well as a good illustration. Unfortunately, the name *Larus fuscus* was also used by Brisson (1760) to label a specimen which was clearly, from his description, a Great Skua. Thus, *Larus fuscus* has been the scientific name of the juvenile (Arctic) Skua, then the Great Skua, and of course now refers to the Lesser Black-backed Gull! Brisson, in the same work named a new genus, *Stercoraire*, into which he placed two 'species', *Le Stercoraire raye*, and *Stercoraire a longue queue* (longicaudus). The identity of these birds is not certain, but probably *Le Stercoraire raye* was a juvenile Pomarine, or possibly Arctic, Skua, and *Stercoraire a longue queue* was an adult light phase Stercorarius species.

Brünnich (1764) described three 'species' of small skua: *Catharacta cepphus*, a

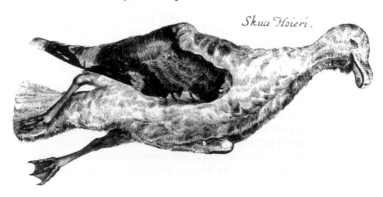

*Fig. 5   Engraving of the Great Skua sent by Hoier to Clusius; from Plate
LXVII in 'The Ornithology of Francis Willughby' (Ray 1678). This is the first
published drawing of a Great Skua, which was clearly long dead when drawn!*

specimen shot in Germany, which Brünnich considered to be the same species as
the Cepphus of Aldrovandus and, from the description, appears to have been a
juvenile of a *Stercorarius* species; *Catharacta parasitica*, a species Brünnich states
could be found in Norway, the Faeroe Islands and Greenland, and was the pale
phase of adult Arctic or Long-tailed Skuas; and *Catharacta coprotheres*, a dark
phase adult Arctic Skua.

The confusion is particularly well shown by a quote from one of the most
reliable and careful ornithologists of the late 19th century, Howard Saunders:

'Dr Coues considers that the *Larus crepidatus* of Gmelin is in all probability based
upon the young of the Pomatorhine Skua, to which Brisson gave the name of
Stercorarius striatus. It is true that Gmelin (who translated from Latham) identifies
S. striatus of Brisson with his *L. crepidatus*; but although *S. striatus* is certainly a
young Pomatorhine, it was by no means easily recognisable by the naturalists of that
day; and, moreover, Gmelin correctly cites in the first place *Catharacta cepphus*,
Brünn., which is certainly this species, and in the third line refers to 'Le Labbe ou
Stercoraire' of Buffon, whose figure ('Planche Enluminees', No. 991) is an excellent
one, besides giving an accurate description of the tail-feathers ('rectricibus duabus
intermediis longoribus'); he also refers it to the 'Black-toed Gull' of the 'Brit. Zool.,'
which is clearly this species. This would be quite sufficient to impose Gmelin's name
of *L. crepidatus* upon 'Richardson's Skua;' but the name did not actually originate
with Gmelin. On referring to Hawkesworth's 'Voyages' (1773), vol. ii. p. 15 (not vol.
i. p. 15, as erroneously cited by Latham, and of course duly copied by Gmelin, without
reference), we find in the narrative of Lieut. Cook's voyage in the *Endeavour* that 'on
the 8th October 1768 (when a little to the south of the Cape-Verd Islands) Mr Banks
[afterwards Sir Joseph Banks] shot the Black-toed Gull not yet described according
to Linnaeus's system; he gave it the name of *Larus crepidatus*.'

The Black-toed Gull is described in Pennant's 'British Zoology' vol. ii. p. 419
(1768); and plate 2 is an excellent representation of a 'Richardson's Skua' of the
year (Saunders 1876).

The problem of sorting out the taxonomic relationships between the different
plumage types of the small skuas from a knowledge of only the skins, is one with
which we can sympathise. However, as soon as ornithologists started to make visits

to the breeding grounds of skuas the problems began to resolve themselves. This is well demonstrated by the following quote from a visit to a Shetland Arctic Skua colony by Drosier: 'The north-eastern side of the island is principally occupied by the arctic gulls (Lestris parasiticus) which breed there very plentifully upon the low and mossy levels, by the edge of a small lake or pond. As the young were already hatched, I had an opportunity of observing them, several of which I had discovered concealed in the long grass; and, although many of them were covered with nothing but down, still the blue legs and black toes were very distinct, which corroborated, beyond all doubt, the surmises that the arctic gull and black-toed gull (Lestris crepidatus) are the same' (Drosier 1830).

The classification of Great Skuas by early ornithologists is given in Table 1, together with an assessment of the actual identity of some of the incorrectly identified specimens, and a similar account of the early names given to small skuas is presented in Table 2. Although the scientific binomial nomenclature was introduced by Linnaeus (1764), most authors writing before the time of Linnaeus wrote in Latin, and gave each type of bird a latin name. Often this was only two or three words long, so could be closely similar to a Linnaean name, but often it would comprise a longer description of the bird.

COLONISATION OF THE NORTH ATLANTIC BY THE GREAT SKUA

Do early descriptions tell us anything about the status of skuas? For the Great Skua they do give a fascinating and tantalising view of the early breeding status of the species in the North Atlantic. Sibbald (1684), the father of Scottish Ornithology, described a Great Skua, naming it *Cataractes noster*. This specimen was obviously watched on passage along the Scottish coast as its rapacious habit was also described, but it was clearly a species that was not well known to Sibbald, and he gave a particularly detailed description of his record as if he considered it of unusual importance. Brünnich (1764) gave the first detailed account of the Great Skua, giving a thorough and accurate description, synonymy and summary of its habits and status. He described it as breeding in the Faeroes and Iceland, but did not mention it as breeding in north Scotland. When this omission is coupled with the fact that the Great Skua was not recorded by most 17th and 18th century British naturalists, we begin to wonder whether the species bred at all in north Scotland in that period. The Great Skua was not included in the list of British birds given by Merrett (1666), and was not recorded by Brand (1701) during his tour of Orkney and Shetland, though this author gave an excellent description of the Arctic Skua. Sibbald did not find it during his visits to the Northern Isles (Sibbald 1711, 1739), and the British ornithologists Ray (1678) and Albin (1738–40), like Sibbald, knew the species only from specimens watched or shot during passage.

There is strong evidence from other sources to add to the impression that there were no breeding Great Skuas in Scotland before the mid 18th century. Seabirds were important in the diets of the human inhabitants of Orkney, Shetland and other coastal regions of Scotland for many thousands of years. At Jarlshof, in south Shetland, bones of many kinds of seabirds have been identified, including those of several species that probably did not breed there, but no Great Skua bones occurred at this site. Nor have Great Skua bones been found at any other middens. From 18 sites in Scotland examined by archaeologists and reported in the

Proceedings of the Society of Antiquaries of Scotland from 1900 to 1976, Cormorant bones were found at 15, Gannet at 14, Great Auk at nine, Guillemot, Puffin and Shag at eight each, Razorbill, Little Auk and Great Black-backed Gull at six each, Herring Gull at four, Red-throated Diver and Eider at two, and Great Northern Diver, Arctic Skua, Storm Petrel, Black-headed Gull, Kittiwake and Common Gull at one each. Three bones, tentatively assigned to Great Skua were later reassigned to Herring Gull (Dr A. S. Clarke in litt.). Apart from the obvious lack of Fulmar bones and the high incidence of Great Auk bones, the lack of Great Skua bones is remarkable. In Iceland and the Faeroe Islands, Great Skuas have long been exploited as food. Chicks would be tethered to a small peg by a length of string, and left to grow to fledging age, when they were then harvested as fully feathered chicks. This had two advantages. Firstly, tethering the chicks allowed the harvesting to be done a few days after the oldest chicks should have left the colony, and secondly, by harvesting at this age it was possible to obtain chicks with plenty of muscle but most of the juvenile fat reabsorbed. This tethering practice continued, illegally after 1900, on some of the more remote Faeroe Islands until very recently. I saw it myself during a visit in 1978. One of the older inhabitants of the island, whose command of English ran to very few words beyond 'Hull', 'Grimsby', and 'football' indicated by signs that Great Skua chicks were good eating, and I was surprised when invited into his house to shelter from the rain, to find that he had several live, well-grown Great Skua young in a cardboard box in his kitchen. Great Skua chicks were also harvested as food in Shetland during the latter part of the 19th and the first half of the 20th century, and older inhabitants on Foula when I first visited the island also knew that they were excellent eating. Since Great Skuas nest on open moorland, and are easy to reach at their present-day sites in Shetland, it seems most unlikely that they would not have been exploited if they had nested in Shetland during the Bronze Age to Viking periods for which midden bone collections have been analysed.

So the evidence suggests that Great Skuas did not breed in northern Scotland in these early periods, and the first record of their breeding in Shetland adds further support to this idea. In 1774, George Low visited Shetland and reported that there were two colonies of Great Skuas; three pairs at Saxavord, Unst, and six or seven pairs on Foula. These small numbers were despite the fact that the Great Skuas were then held in the highest esteem, carefully protected from human interference, and even provided with food to encourage their numbers to increase. It is difficult to see why the species should have been so scarce and confined to these two sites alone, unless it had either been subject to intense persecution in earlier times, for which there is absolutely no evidence, or had only recently colonised Shetland from elsewhere. I find the latter explanation more plausible, and very interesting since it implies that the Great Skua is not a long-standing member of the Orkney and Shetland seabird communities, but a new colonist that may or may not fit in with the other seabird species. The enormous increase in Great Skua numbers in Orkney and Shetland during this century (Chapter 3) is an ecological novelty rather than a return to the 'natural' situation before human persecution, since there is no evidence for human persecution or exploitation of Great Skuas from prehistoric times, and some evidence to indicate that there was none.

Etymology also supports the hypothesis that Great Skuas colonised Shetland recently and had not previously occurred as a breeding species elsewhere in Scotland. The local name for the species, 'Bonxie', was originally spelt 'Buncie', and was used only in Shetland. It is supposed to have been derived from the Norse 'bunksi', meaning a heap, or an untidy dumpy woman (Jakobsen 1921), which aptly describes the species on its breeding territory, though not in flight. No local name for the Great Skua then existed in Orkney or elsewhere in Scotland, which further supports the idea that the bird was confined to Shetland and may have arrived there shortly before Low's visit in 1774. Earlier British ornithologists did not know of this local name, or else the name did not exist before this period.

Where might these, 'Bonxies', have come from? The only areas in which there is good evidence for long-standing breeding by Great Skuas are Iceland and the Faeroe Islands. In the Faeroes the earliest records of the status of the Great Skua are confused. It was clearly breeding in 1604 when Hoier collected the first described specimen (Clusius 1605), as Hoier wrote of it 'it produces young carelessly on open ground from olive eggs, bigger than but similar to those of ducks, which are marked by thin black spots. It feeds on fish but also takes food from every kind of bird indiscriminately'. Debes (1673) who visited the Faeroes in 1672 also records the Great Skua as a breeding species 'in defending its eggs and chicks, in flying over it flies at their (intruders) heads and beats these with its wings; hence the native inhabitants, to whom the ferocity of this bird is well known, hold a knife with the sharp edge uppermost above their head, on which the bird is frequently transfixed'. The Faeroese ballad 'Fuglakvaedi', written in the 15th century, names 38 species of bird, including 'skuvur', which may well refer to the Great Skua. However, Svabo (1783, reprinted 1959) implied that Great Skuas were breeding in enormous numbers on the island of Skuvoy, a conclusion which is impossible to accept (Chapter 3). In the Faeroes predatory birds were controlled in order to protect the harvested seabirds. A bill tax was levied, requiring every man from his fifteenth to his fiftieth year to deliver a Raven's bill, or two Hooded Crow, Great Black-backed Gull, Herring Gull or Lesser Black-backed Gull bills each year. Delivery of a Sea Eagle bill exempted the bearer from the tax for the rest of his life! Somewhat surprisingly, the Great Skua was not included in the list of bill tax vermin until 1800, when one Great Skua bill became equivalent to one gull or crow bill. This rate of taxation was enforced until 1881 (Salomonsen 1935). According to Svabo, the Great Skua in the Faeroes was reduced in numbers before 1800 by collection of the young for food, yet it became official vermin only after this reduction in numbers. It is difficult to see why it was considered to be vermin when scarce, but not vermin when more numerous, and it is difficult to believe that cropping of the chicks without persecution of the adults would lead to a drastic population reduction. Great Skuas are long-lived and not all chicks would be found, so enough would surely survive to replace the few deaths of adults. Anyone who has ringed Great Skua chicks will realise that although Great Skua chicks are not very cryptic, it is impossible to find every chick! More recent instances of skua population declines caused by man all involve persecution of adults rather than harvesting of eggs or chicks (Chapter 16). It would be most interesting to explore the bill tax records collected in the Faeroes over the centuries and the information on seabird harvests and populations, but this would be a major project requiring linguistic as well as ornithological expertise. My impression from the rather fragmentary and confusing accounts I have been able to examine is that the Great Skua may not have been a common bird in the Faeroes before 1800, and its inclusion in the list of vermin after 1800 may have been a response to an increase in its numbers that was successfully checked by the resulting persecution in the 19th century (Chapter 3).

Documentation of the early status of the Great Skua in Iceland is, for obvious reasons, even more fragmentary. It was known as a breeding species in the early 17th century, being reported by Jon Gudmundsson, who lived between 1574 and 1650 (Timmermann 1949). However, the Snorra Edda, one of the classic Icelandic Sagas which was compiled in the 12th century, contains an appendix which lists 117 names of bird species then known to the Icelanders. This list contains only one name attributable to a skua 'skufr'. This name was used to describe the Arctic Skua (Zoega 1942), and is literally translated as 'tassel' or 'headscarf' (de Vries 1961). In the Faeroes the name is also used, in a slightly different form 'skuvur' or 'skuir', and was the origin of the word 'skua', adapted from the Faeroese by Hoier (Clusius 1605), and referred to the Great Skua. In Shetland the Arctic Skua was given a local name 'skooi', which is similar to the Icelandic 'skufr', but is supposed to be derived from the quite different root 'skoot' meaning excrement, upon which Arctic Skuas were considered to feed by scaring other seabirds! It is not clear whether 'skufr' was used in Iceland as a name for Great Skuas and Arctic Skuas, or whether only one species of skua occurred in Iceland in the 12th century. The present-day name for the Arctic Skua in Iceland is 'kjoi', also given as 'kjogvi' or 'tjegvi', meaning 'thief', and was used indiscriminantly for Long-tailed and Pomarine Skuas as well as Arctic Skuas (Slater 1901). The possibility that only small skuas (i.e. Arctic Skuas) bred in Iceland in the 12th century and that Great Skuas were not then found in north Scotland, the Faeroes or Iceland, is intriguing, but it may be that the Great Skua did not colonise the North Atlantic until some time shortly before the 16th century, then spread from Iceland or the Faeroes, reaching Shetland in the middle of the 18th century and spreading and becoming numerous in Scotland only after 1900. This suggestion is highly speculative, and may well be proved wrong, but I think it is worth suggesting as an idea to test.

The idea that a species from the far south of the South Atlantic should suddenly colonise the northern North Atlantic may seem remarkable, but the Black-browed Albatross has been trying to follow the Great Skua's example for some time now. Like Great Skuas, Black-browed Albatrosses have a large breeding population on the Falkland Islands as well as on numerous sub-Antarctic islands. An individual spent several summers with the Gannets on the Bass Rock and, almost certainly the same bird, then moved to the Gannet colony at Hermaness, where it has now built a nest each year while hoping for a partner to turn up. This individual has been visiting British Gannet colonies for a period of some 25 years, but another spent 34 successive seasons at Myggenaesholm, in the Faeroes, with the local Gannets, before it was unceremoniously shot there in 1894. If only two Black-brows of differing sex would get lost in the North Atlantic at the same time and meet each other!

Such recent colonisation of the North Atlantic by the Great Skua would imply that the Great Skua would be very similar in morphology and behaviour to its southern ancestor, and this could also account for the lack of cryptic colouration in the Great Skua's chicks and the apparent reduction in the aggressiveness of Great Skuas between the 18th century and the present time (Chapters 6 and 12).

EVOLUTIONARY RELATIONSHIPS AMONG SKUAS

There is no doubt that gulls are the closest relatives of the skuas, but skuas have a number of consistent features that separate them from the gulls. Their caeca are much longer; their central tail feathers project beyond the ends of the rest of the tail feathers; females are larger in size than males; plumage is predominantly brown (though some gull species are predominantly dark grey); the toes have strong hooked claws; the rhamphotheca, the nail on the distal part of the upper mandible, is complex and prominent, with four separate plates. The combination of hooked claws and webbing on the feet, and the complex rhamphotheca, are both characteristics unique to skuas, and so are diagnostic of the skua family Stercorariidae, distinct from the gull family Laridae, within the order Charadriiformes. Some systematists prefer a slightly different grouping, with the skuas placed in a subfamily, Stercorariinae, within the gull and skua family Laridae, but most authors now consider the skuas to be sufficiently distinct from the gulls to warrant a separate family of their own.

More dispute arises when we consider whether all skuas should be grouped into one genus, or should be divided into two separate genera. The argument in favour of separation is, in my opinion, very strong. The Arctic, Long-tailed and Pomarine Skuas are closely similar in adult plumage and rather different from the large skuas, they are much smaller than the large skuas, they have an arctic breeding distribution whereas the large skuas are basically a southern hemisphere genus with an outlier in the North Atlantic. These are the main criteria that led Peters (1934), Wynne-Edwards (1935) and Bannerman (1963) to divide skuas into two genera.

A contrary opinion, based largely on behaviour (Chapter 6), has been presented by Andersson (1973), following Hartert (1912) and Moynihan (1959), who preferred to classify all of the skuas in a single genus. Andersson argued that the Long Call displays of the Arctic and Long-tailed Skuas are closely similar, but rather different from that of the Pomarine Skua, which shows closer agreement with the display of the Great Skua and other large skuas. Similarly, Pomarine Skuas, like all of the large skuas, show Wing Raising posture during Long Call displays, which Arctic and Long-tailed Skuas do not. Andersson concluded that the Pomarine Skua shows closer similarity to the Great Skua than either of them do to the Arctic and Long-tailed Skua, and suggested that 'the Pomarine Skua and large skuas diverged from each other at a time when the predecessor of the two smaller skua species had already branched from the common skua ancestor'. Study of the skeletal structure of gulls and skuas (Schnell 1970) put the Pomarine Skua as intermediate between the Great Skua and the two small species, and also indicated that the Pomarine Skua could be considered closer to the Great Skua than to the smaller skuas. These arguments would suggest that all skuas should be placed in a single genus, since no clear discontinuity would exist to split them into two genera. Few systematists would wish to classify large skuas and the Pomarine Skua in one genus but the Arctic and Long-tailed in another!

Brooke (1978) pointed out a strong argument for separation of the two genera. Juvenile Pomarine, Arctic and Long-tailed Skuas are extensively barred below, whereas there is no barring in the juvenile of any large skua. Since juvenile barring is not found in any species in the family Laridae, it must be a derived character state defining *Stercorarius*. That is, it evolved in *Stercorarius* after that genus separated from *Catharacta* but before the Long-tailed, Pomarine and Arctic Skua species had separated from each other.

Since barring of the juvenile plumage in Pomarine Skuas is clearly homologous with barring in juvenile Arctic and Long-tailed Skuas, Brooke's argument seems to me to win the day. The Pomarine Skua must have branched from a common ancestor with the Arctic and Long-tailed Skuas which had evolved barred juvenile plumage after branching from the common ancestor with the large skuas. The separate genera *Catharacta* and *Stercorarius* are thus justified according to this picture of the evolutionary history of skuas. Why then, do Pomarine Skuas show such differences in behaviour from the Arctic and Long-tailed Skuas? Perhaps the answer can be found by considering the ways in which their behaviour is influenced by their body size and territory size. Great Skuas and other large skuas make little use of aerial displays. They do sometimes use a 'V-gliding cum long call' flight display over the territory, but this is not common, and most advertisement is done from the ground. This makes sense as their territories are often rather small, so that flight displays would tend to infringe the air space of neighbours and lead to serious conflicts. Being heavy birds, they are much less agile in aerial display than the smaller skuas. Because *Catharacta* skua nests may be only 10–200 m apart, ground based displays are perfectly satisfactory for large skuas to advertise and defend their territory since neighbours are well within each others' view. Long-tailed and Arctic Skuas defend territories that are usually large. Neighbouring pairs may be a kilometre or two apart on the tundra (dense Arctic Skua colonies in areas such as Shetland are rather atypical for the species). On the tundra, ground displays would be rather inappropriate for advertisement or to indicate territorial occupation to neighbours, and aerial advertisement flights make more sense. Pomarine Skuas, in years when they do breed, tend to breed at much higher densities than Arctic or Long-tailed Skuas on the tundra (Chapter 10). Pomarine Skuas also weigh considerably more than Arctic and Long-tailed Skuas. Both factors will promote ground rather than aerial displaying in Pomarine Skuas. However, ground displays by dark coloured birds would not be very conspicuous. Wing Raising, showing off the white flash at the base of the primaries, enhances the effect of the ground-based Long Call display, and so is particularly appropriate for large skuas and Pomarine Skuas. Ground-based Wing Raising displays by Arctic Skuas or Long-tailed Skuas one or two kilometres away from the nearest neighbour would not be very effective! These differences in behaviour between skuas may tell us little about their evolutionary relationships but may rather be a reflection of the size of the territory that each species normally holds, coupled with constraints on aerial agility imposed by body size.

Classification within the genus *Stercorarius* is straightforward. Linnaeus named the Arctic Skua *Larus parasiticus* in 1758, and this specific name has remained although the generic name has been changed to *Stercorarius*. No subspecies of the Arctic Skua have been described although body size and proportions of colour morphs vary with latitude. The Pomarine Skua was the second to receive a lasting scientific name. Temminck described it as *Lestris pomarinus* in 1815; again, the specific name has remained to this day, but *Lestris* has been dropped and replaced with *Stercorarius*. Finally, the Long-tailed Skua was named *Stercorarius longicaudus* by Vieillot in 1819, and was divided into two subspecies in 1932 by Loppenthin, who recognised that birds from Greenland to Siberia and east Asia had white underparts (*Stercorarius longicaudus pallescens*), and so differed from the Type specimen named by Vieillot, which originated from Scandinavia and is typical of birds from Scandinavia to the Lena Delta in Asia, which have greyish underparts (*Stercorarius longicaudus longicaudus*).

Fisher and Lockley (1954) considered that a form of skua colonised the southern hemisphere from the ancestral skua stock in the north, and then separated into distinct taxa in the south. One of these only recently, on a geological timescale, recolonised the North Atlantic to give rise to the Great Skua. This immediately leads us to consider which of the southern taxa gave rise to the North Atlantic Great Skua. Fisher and Lockley suggested that the most likely contender would have been the Tristan Skua, since it is by far the closest breeding population to the North Atlantic, but they also suggested that the Falkland Skua could be a candidate. We now know that the story is more complicated, since the Tristan and Falkland Skuas do not migrate far from their breeding grounds, but the South Polar Skua is a long distance migrant, and is a regular visitor to the North Atlantic (Chapter 4). South Polar Skuas could reach Iceland or the Faeroes as a result of their normal migrations, but Tristan or Falkland Skuas would have to be carried there by freak events. Fisher and Lockley postulated that storms might have carried birds from their South Atlantic breeding area up into the North Atlantic and so led to the colonisation.

From the appearance and measurements of the Great Skua we can probably rule out the South Polar Skua as its progenitor. South Polar Skuas have a very different plumage, even in the dark phase, and are rather smaller, with a distinctly smaller tarsus and mean body weight (Tables 3–8). Swales (1965) suggested that the Chilean Skua was the most similar southern form to the Great Skua, particularly in its rufous colouration. However, apart from the fact that Chilean Skuas have never been seen in the North Atlantic or even in the South Atlantic north of Brazil, the plumages of the two species are really rather different. Great Skuas do possess variable, but often large, amounts of rufous in the plumage, but this is in the form of highlights on individual feathers, giving a multicoloured appearance, particularly on the back. Great Skuas do not possess the uniform bright cinnamon underwing coverts characteristic of the Chilean Skua, and do not share the Chilean Skua's reputation for lacking aggressive behaviour towards intruders onto its breeding grounds, or its habit of nesting in dense colonies more characteristic of gulls (Chapter 10). According to Hagen (1952) the Tristan Skua is almost identical in appearance to the Great Skua, but when I visited Gough Island in 1983 and 1985 I found the Tristan Skua to be strikingly different from the Great Skua in a number of respects. Tristan Skuas tend to be very uniform in colour; brown and rather dark, with few or no golden hackles on the nape and auricular area. They show little or no yellow or rufous colour on the feathers. In these respects, they differ from Great Skuas and from Falkland and Brown Skuas. On the basis of plumage alone, Great Skuas most closely resemble Falkland Skuas, and differ little from Brown Skuas (Photos 3, 4, 5 and 19).

Differences in measurements provide a valuable method of identifying distinct taxa of great skuas, but do measurements tell us anything about their evolutionary history? Several authors have pointed to similarities or differences in measurements of different taxa as if these do indicate likely evolutionary relationships. This might be so if there was little selection for size of body characters. Then we could expect the most closely related taxa to show least difference in measurements. On the basis of size comparisons, Great Skuas have the longest wings, while Falkland Skuas have the shortest wings of all of the large skuas (Fig. 6). This might lead us to think that the Falkland Skua is unlikely to be the recent ancestor of the Great Skua. While tail lengths of great skuas differ little between taxa (Table 7), there are large differences in tarsus length that do not correlate closely with differences in wing length. In other words, tarsus length and wing length do not simply reflect differences in body size between *Catharacta* taxa. South Polar Skuas are long-winged but short-legged, while Tristan Skuas are long-legged but not

3. *A Great Skua showing the strong golden lanceolate 'hackles' on the neck and side of the head.* Photo: R. W. Furness.

particularly long-winged. Tarsus lengths of Great Skuas and Falkland Skuas are very similar, but their wing lengths differ remarkably (Fig. 6).

According to measurements of body weight (Table 3), Brown Skuas are larger than Great Skuas but Great Skuas have the longer wings. Devillers (1978) points out that, although Falkland Skuas have the shortest wings of all great skuas and have a shorter tarsus and bill than all but the South Polar Skua, these linear measurements are misleading. The Falkland Skua is a very massive bird, heavier, more sturdy and larger-looking than the Chilean Skua. Although there are no published weights for Falkland Skuas, I have estimated from egg size that female Falkland Skuas weigh about 1540 g (Chapter 11). This figure confirms Devillers' assertion, since female Chilean Skuas weigh about 1480 g and female Great Skuas about 1500 g (Table 3), so the Falkland Skua is heavier than either of these longer-winged and longer-tarsus taxa!

It seems likely that these differences in size and shape are due to selective pressures that have masked any evolutionary relationships between the taxa. In fact, I think we can identify two important selective pressures by considering the different sizes of the taxa.

Flight performance is greatly affected by wing loading; the mass of the bird divided by its wing area. In general, birds with lower wing loadings can fly more economically. For birds that do not migrate and do not use flight during foraging, large wings are of little value, and may indeed be a disadvantage. Replacing feathers at moult is energetically costly, and long wings may be cumbersome for locomotion on the ground. This is presumably why so many rails that colonised

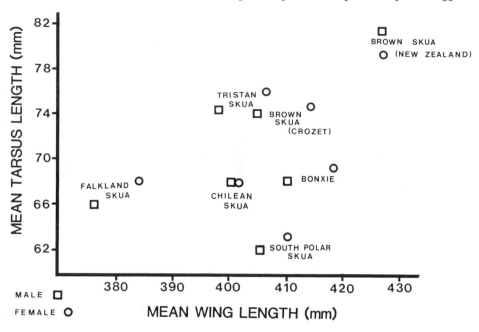

Fig. 6 *Mean wing lengths of skua taxa plotted against mean tarsus length, showing the striking differences between taxa, and the lack of correlation between wing length and tarsus length.*

4. *The Falkland Skua, which closely resembles the Great Skua in plumage, but generally has less prominent golden hackles on the neck.* Photo: M. P. Harris.

5. The Tristan Skua, at Gough Island, showing the normal very uniform brown-coloured head and neck, with few golden lanceolate feathers and with little yellow or rufous colouration on the body. Photo: R. W. Furness.

remote islands free of ground predators became flightless endemic species with vestigial wings. Among large skuas there is a clear dichotomy in foraging behaviour. South Polar Skuas, Great Skuas and Chilean Skuas obtain most of their food at sea, and certainly feed away from their small breeding territories (Chapter 7). Foraging involves long flights, and considerable aerial agility. By contrast, most Brown Skuas, Tristan Skuas and Falkland Skuas do not feed at sea during the breeding season, but prey upon seabirds breeding within their large territory. Many seabirds are attacked at night on the ground, when flight is not used at all in foraging. Outside of the breeding season, feeding behaviour may be less different between skuas, but South Polar Skuas are the only species of large skua that is a regular transequatorial migrant, reaching high latitudes in the northern hemisphere during the southern winter. Great Skuas also undertake an extensive migration after breeding, but travel only a fraction of the distance covered by South Polar Skuas. Other large skuas do not show pronounced migrations. Brown Skuas from New Zealand colonies may remain in local waters all year round, and many Tristan Skuas remain on Gough Island throughout the year (Chapter 4). Within each population, males fly more than females during the breeding season, taking a much larger share of the foraging and of aerial display and advertisement of the territory. These facts would suggest that wing loading should be less in the marine feeders that migrate, and less in males than in females. We can predict that wing loading should be least in male South Polar Skuas, and greatest in female Brown, Falkland and Tristan Skuas. In fact, this is exactly so (Fig. 7). The observed pattern of wing loading index shows that wing length is a character that is adapted to the ecological needs of each large skua taxon.

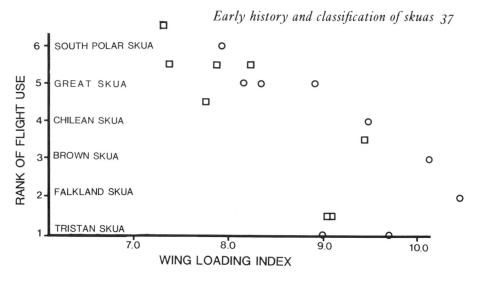

Fig. 7 *Wing loading index (defined as mean body weight in the middle of the breeding season divided by the square of the mean wing length) for males and females of each* Catharacta *taxon, plotted according to the ranked amount of flying done by the birds during the breeding season and during migration. Wing loading is defined as body weight divided by wing area, but since wing areas have not been calculated for most taxa, the square of wing length has been used as this should be closely related to wing area. Males are indicated by squares and females by circles.*

6. *Pale phase South Polar Skuas nesting at a typical site near to a penguin colony on the Antarctic Continent. Note the lack of vegetation around the nest and the open nature of the habitat.* Photo: M. P. Harris.

Tarsus length in skuas is less obviously of selective importance than is wing length. Nevertheless, the pattern of the different tarsus lengths in large skuas is probably not fortuitous. South Polar Skuas have very short tarsi, Great Skuas, Falkland and Chilean Skuas have intermediate length tarsi, Brown Skuas from Atlantic and Indian Ocean sub-Antarctic islands and Tristan Skuas have long tarsi, and Brown Skuas from New Zealand islands have particularly long tarsi. Tarsus length is clearly correlated with the typical ground vegetation length in these different areas. South Polar Skuas hold territories on barren Antarctic landscapes, where the ground is often covered with ice if not barren, or has a thin layer of lichens and mosses. Great Skuas, Falkland and Chilean Skuas hold territories on grass or heath covered nutrient-poor peaty soils, where grazing herbivores and lack of nutrients in the soil prevent tall growth of plants. Often, as on the fluvio-glacial plains of SE Iceland or in Tierra del Fuego, patches of grassy mat are broken up by patches of barren ground or gravel, and skuas tend to select the patches of grass on which to nest. Brown and Tristan Skuas breed on islands in areas of high humidity with lush growth of ground vegetation, such as tussock grass, bracken and tree ferns. The nocturnal burrow-nesting petrels (on which these skuas feed) inhabit these highly vegetated areas over which the skuas walk at night hunting for prey. Thus, tarsus length increases with increasing ground vegetation height in skua breeding habitats (see also Photos 6–8):

Skua population	Mean tarsus length (mm)	Vegetation type
South Polar Skua	61	thin layer of lichens and mosses
Falkland Skua	67	patchy short grasses and herbs
Chilean Skua	68	patchy short grasses and herbs
Great Skua	69	short tussocky grasses and heathers
Brown Skua (S. Alantic/Indian Ocean)	73	longer grasses and tussocks
Tristan Skua	74	bracken, longer grasses, tree ferns
Brown Skua (New Zealand)	80	bracken, tall grasses, tree ferns

Tarsus length shows no consistent difference between the sexes in skuas, but the trend with vegetation height does seem to be real, and so presumably has been determined by natural selection. Perhaps long tarsi are disadvantageous in open habitat where birds with long tarsi will be likely to be unstable in strong buffeting winds, while short tarsi would result in skuas in tall vegetation being unable to see far and would lead to the body rubbing on wet grass as the bird walked through the territory searching for prey.

In conclusion, the large differences in wing length between Falkland Skuas and Great Skuas should not lead us to reject the suggestion that Great Skuas most probably arose from lost Falkland Skuas that reached the North Atlantic. Body measurements are likely to evolve far more rapidly than adult plumage colouration or patterning, for which adaptive values are far less evident. It is even possible, of course, that the Great Skua has been derived from a hybrid mating between one lost Falkland Skua and one lost Brown Skua, in which case chance effects of sampling and influences of hybridisation between subspecies would be extremely difficult to predict! The true origins of the Great Skua will probably never

7. Falkland Skuas nesting in a typical site with fairly dense but short vegetation.
Photo: M. P. Harris.

be discovered from gross morphological comparisons. Biochemical or molecular genetic studies would be needed to determine their affinities, but plumage similarities lead me to put my money on the Falkland Skua as the Great Skua's closest cousin.

MODERN CLASSIFICATION

From all of the earlier considerations, an illustration of the likely evolutionary relationships of the skuas would look something like Figure 8. Details may require to be amended as we learn more about skuas in the future, but I doubt if this figure is far wrong. The South Polar Skua and Chilean Skua are undoubtedly distinct from the other large skuas at the species level because both have breeding ranges that overlap with those of *Catharacta skua* populations and yet show little hybridisation, and signs that any hybrids are of reduced fitness.

Devillers (1978) showed that Falkland Skuas breed at sites between Punta Tombo and Puerto Deseado on the coast of Patagonia, while Chilean Skuas breed along the same coast from Puerto Deseado southwards, and also occur occasionally on the Falkland Islands where they may possibly breed sporadically. Falkland Skuas from sites in Patagonia showed no significant differences in measurements or plumage from those in the Falklands, except that the proportion of darker coloured birds was higher on the South American continent. Nevertheless, the birds could all be matched by individuals from the Falklands. However, Devillers found a few birds in this region of overlap between Falkland and Chilean Skuas

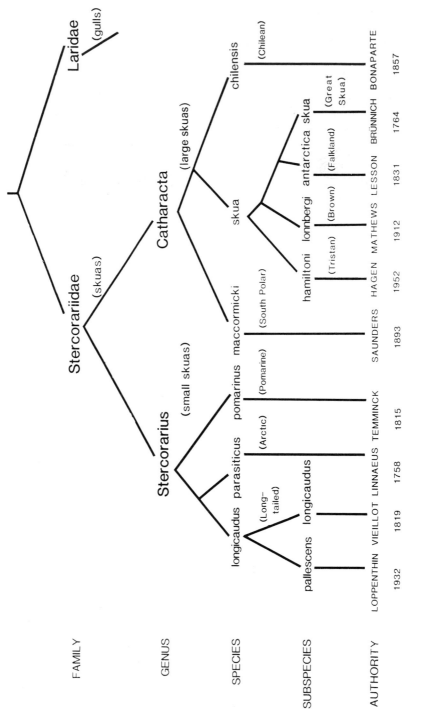

Fig. 8   *Suggested evolutionary pattern of divergence of skuas from their common ancestors. See text for explanation of the details of this arrangement.*

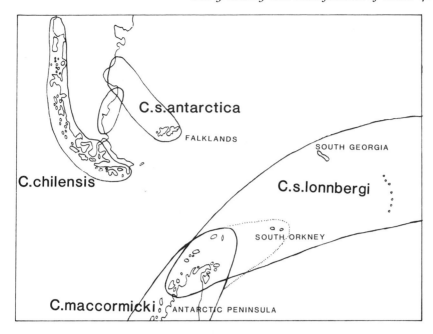

Fig. 9 Breeding ranges of Catharacta *skuas in the South American quadrant,*
showing areas of range overlap between taxa. From Devillers (1978).

at Puerto Deseado (Fig. 9) which showed characteristics of both species. One was
like a Falkland Skua in every respect except for the presence of cinnamon-
tinged areas on the throat, lower cheeks and belly. Another had too much brown
underneath to be a normal Chilean Skua and reduced red under the wing.
Altogether, Devillers considered that of ten birds examined in detail, two were
typical *chilensis*, one was a typical *antarcticus*, five were *chilensis* with signs of
possible *antarcticus* influence, one was a slightly aberrant *antarcticus*, and one was
intermediate between the two taxa. Nearby, on a small island where about ten
pairs of skuas were breeding, most birds seemed to look and behave like *chilensis*,
but two pairs consisted of typical *antarcticus*. Clearly some hybridisation is taking
place in this small area of overlap, but most pairs consist of birds of the same type
and hybrids are relatively few. In areas away from this region of overlap, Devillers
found no sign of any *chilensis* characteristics in any of the Falkland Skuas, and no
sign of any *antarcticus* characteristics in any of the Chilean Skuas, even though
some hybridisation in the zone of contact has occurred at least since 1915 (Devillers
1978). The lack of extensive hybridisation when the two forms occur together, the
lack of evidence for gene-flow between the main stocks of each form, and the clear
differences in plumage and behaviour, suggest that the two forms should be treated
as distinct species, as done by Saunders (1876) and Mathews (1913).

Overlap in the breeding ranges of South Polar and Brown Skuas on the Antarctic
Peninsula has been known for some time (Gain 1914), although there is evidence
that the overlap has increased, with South Polar Skuas spreading northwards in
the South Shetlands (Chapter 3). Hybridisation between the two forms is rather

8. Tristan Skuas at a nest site on Gough Island, in typical habitat consisting of dense and tall tussocks of grass. Often, tree ferns and bracken are also abundant within territories. Photo: R. W. Furness.

limited and apparently occurs only when birds are unable to obtain a mate of their own form (Chapter 10). Few hybrid birds are to be found and there is no evidence for extensive genetic introgression. Brown Skuas in the region are apparently not incorporating South Polar Skua genes in their gene pool to any great extent, and the converse is also true. Thus hybridisation is limited and apparently of little consequence to the gene-pools of the two forms. Of course, this situation could change if the overlap of their breeding ranges increases. More extensive hybridisation could, in theory, lead to the amalgamation of the two forms (Chapter 16). However, the present situation argues in favour of treating *maccormicki* and *lönnbergi* as distinct species – the South Polar Skua and the Brown Skua.

Whether Great Skuas, Tristan, Brown and Falkland Skuas should be considered as subspecies within *Catharacta skua*, or split into a northern and a southern species, is really a matter of taste. Brooke (1978) argued that the Great Skua should be considered a monotypic species separate from the Tristan, Brown and Falkland Skuas, since it is possible that later research will show that the Great Skua is more closely related to the South Polar Skua or Chilean Skua, in which case it would be a nonsense to place it in the same species as more distant relatives. I think this possibility is so remote that we can safely discount it and place the Great Skua where it seems to belong, with the Tristan, Brown and Falkland Skuas.

The final problem raised in this systematic story is that of nomenclature. Since Linnaeus introduced his system of nomenclature, complicated rules have been established concerning the way in which names should apply. According to the Law of Priority, if the same species (or subspecies) is independently named by different taxonomists, then the first given name should be accepted and the second suppressed. The first described specimen becomes the Type for the species or subspecies. However, steps can be taken through the International Commission on Zoological Nomenclature to conserve a later name and suppress an earlier one that should receive priority according to the rules, if the later name has gained wide acceptance and the earlier name has been overlooked or dropped from use.

In fact, the account of skua forms given by Bonaparte (1857) was overlooked by most later authors, and has caused some confusion. Bonaparte described two species of great skua; '*catarractes*' (= *skua* of Brünnich – the Great Skua), and '*antarcticus*', the southern hemisphere species. Within the latter species Bonaparte described two varieties: '*chilensis*' from the South American subcontinent, and '*madagascariensis*' from Madagascar. Bonaparte's form *antarcticus chilensis* we now know as *Catharacta chilensis*, the Chilean Skua, a distinct species. Bonaparte's *madagascariensis* has proved something of a problem.

Madagascar is far from the normal range of any skua, perhaps most likely to be visited by migrant young South Polar Skuas although few have been recorded from the tropics of the Indian Ocean. Alternatively, stray Brown Skuas from the Prince Edward Islands, the Crozet Islands or Kerguelen might occur there. The description given by Bonaparte applies to a single stray bird collected at Madagascar. Since it was named *madagascariensis* in 1857, it is an earlier scientific name than *maccormicki* given to the South Polar Skua by Saunders in 1893, or *lönnbergi* given to the Brown Skua subspecies from New Zealand by Mathews in 1912. Therefore, if *madagascariensis* was a South Polar Skua we should, according to the Law of Priority, drop *maccormicki* and establish *Catharacta madagascariensis* as the South Polar Skua. If *madagascariensis* was a Brown Skua, then we should drop the name *lönnbergi* and establish *Catharacta skua madagascariensis* as the scientific name for the Brown Skua subspecies. There are several good reasons not to do this. Firstly, *lönnbergi* and *maccormicki* are well established names in common use throughout this century, and to change either one would be unnecessarily confusing. Secondly, *madagascariensis* is singularly inappropriate as a scientific name for a skua, since Madagascar is one of the few places in the world where a birdwatcher is most unlikely ever to see a skua! Thirdly, the identity of Bonaparte's specimen is still in some doubt. It is located in the Museum d'Histoire Naturelle, Paris, and its measurements were published by Hartlaub in *Die Vogel Madagascars* (1877) as: bill length 53 mm, wing length 376 mm, tarsus length 67 mm, middle toe 40 mm. These measurements suggest that the specimen is a South Polar Skua, since the tarsus length falls well within the range for that species, and well outside the range for adult Brown Skuas. Bill length does not agree well with values for South Polar Skuas, but may have been measured to the skull rather than to the feathering. Wing length is less than would be expected for adults of either species (Table 4), suggesting that this is a juvenile specimen. We do know that wing length increases between fledging and full adult age in skuas (Table 4). The tarsus measurement is certainly not compatible with those of adult Brown Skuas but could it be a juvenile Brown Skua? I could find no statistically significant differences between tarsus lengths of adult and immature skuas of any species (Table 5). Furthermore, Barre (1976) gave the mean tarsus length of fledgling Brown Skuas at Crozet as 82 mm, and Williams (1980a, b, c) gave the tarsus length of samples of Brown Skua chicks at Marion Island as 80.5 mm at 40 days (n = 15, s.d. = 2.0), 79.3 mm at 50 days (n = 22, s.d. = 2.0) and 80.2 mm at 55 days (n = 14, s.d. = 2.0). These values are considerably greater than the measured tarsus lengths of breeding adult Brown Skuas from the Crozet Isles (males 74.2 mm, females 74.4 mm; Table 5). The implication here is that the tarsus of chicks is fully grown at fledging and indeed measures longer than in adults due to its fleshy nature. Skua legs are considerably fatter and softer in chicks than in adults, and must harden and contract after fledging. Similarly, South Polar Skua fledglings have longer tarsi than do adults. According to Reid (1967) chicks fledge with a tarsus length of about 64–65 mm, while Hemmings (1984) gives a mean fledging tarsus length of about 67 mm (read from his published graph). Adult South Polar Skuas have tarsus lengths averaging 60–62 mm in males, 61–65 mm in females (Table 5). These data do not suggest that *madagascariensis* could be a juvenile Brown Skua, although the bill length given by Hartlaub, if measured from the feathering, would rule out South Polar Skua!

Brooke (1978) suggested that the *madagascariensis* Type specimen is likely to be a South Polar Skua, but that re-measurement by a modern worker would be desirable to check this conclusion. At Brooke's request, the Type was examined by Dr J.-L. Mougin and Drs J.-F. and C. Voisin. According to Brooke (1981) their examination and drawing of the bill indicated the bird to be a small juvenile male Brown Skua rather than a South Polar Skua, but Brooke gave no new measurements to support this claim, so we are left with the problem that the specimen appears to be smaller than any juvenile Brown Skua should be.

Taxonomists may consider that it is important to adhere to the rules of nomenclature and reinstate the name *madagascariensis*. To me this seems an unnecessary confusion to add to an already complex situation. It would surely be much better to return *madagascariensis* to the scientific obscurity it has enjoyed for the last 100 years.

CHAPTER 3

Distributions and populations

At our housewarming the doctor raised his glass and proposed that the first political act of the new government of Adelie Land should be a declaration of war against skuas.... The proposal was adopted with acclaim and ... hostilities were opened by placing a home-made bomb where the skuas were accustomed to assemble. The fuse was lighted from our hut and while we waited for the explosion we drank confusion to all skuas and sang our national anthem.
  Mario Marret, member of the French Expedition in Antarctica, 1948–1953

There is little doubt that the gulls originated and evolved in the northern hemisphere. Since skuas evolved from the same stock as gulls, skuas probably also originated in the north. This supposition is supported by the northern distribution of the small skuas and by fossil remains of birds, identified as skua ancestors, found in Oregon, USA. Although these latter have been described as somewhat larger than the small skuas, they show that a form of skua, *Stercorarius shufeldti*, was present during the Pleistocene period, 50,000 years ago. This does not tell us much about the past geographical distributions of early skuas or their evolution, but it is clear that at some stage a skua ancestor must have colonised the far reaches of the southern hemisphere, subsequently to recolonise the north in the form of the Great Skua.

Fig. 10   Breeding range of the Arctic Skua.

SMALL SKUA DISTRIBUTIONS

The three small skuas now each have circumpolar Arctic breeding distributions, penetrating variable distances into the subArctic. Of the three, the Arctic Skua has the widest breeding distribution (Fig. 10) extending slightly further south and showing a more coastal tendency than the Long-tailed Skua (Fig. 11). The Pomarine Skua has a more restricted breeding distribution. It also has a gap in its circumpolar range. Unlike the other two it does not normally breed in any area between eastern Greenland and the Kola Peninsula in northwest USSR (Fig. 12). This general absence from Europe as a breeding species can be tied in with its dependence for breeding on the availability of abundant small mammals,

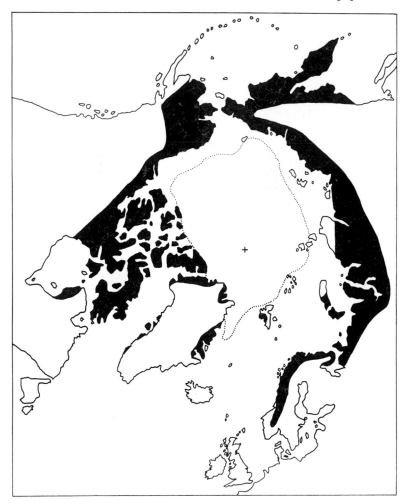

Fig. 11   Breeding range of the Long-tailed Skua.

predominantly lemmings, of the tundra ecosystems, which provide the Pomarine Skua with most of its food during the summer.

ARCTIC SKUA POPULATIONS

The Arctic Skua is frequently found breeding in association with other seabirds, from which it steals food. In Europe this habit predominates: in the Baltic and Norway the Arctic Skua breeds in small numbers generally near to tern colonies, while in north Scotland and the Faeroes it often breeds in larger colonies associated with populations of Puffins or Kittiwakes, as well as with terns. However, in

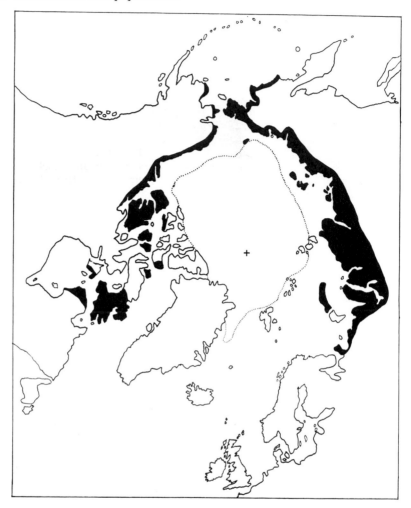

Fig. 12   Breeding range of the Pomarine Skua.

Iceland, Arctic Skuas are also found throughout the interior of the country in tundra-like habitat. In much of its range in Canada, Alaska and northern USSR it inhabits tundra far from the sea as well as associating with coastal seabird colonies.

Population sizes have shown marked changes in certain areas over this century, particularly in Britain and the Faeroes, although only these countries have been reasonably well censused more than once, so that detecting changes in population sizes elsewhere would be difficult. The greatest densities of Arctic Skuas occur in Britain and the Faeroes where they can exist by stealing fish from the huge numbers of other seabirds also present.

Qualitative records of the breeding distribution of the Arctic Skua in Britain can be found as far back as the 18th Century. The earliest indications of numbers are in the late 19th and early 20th Century. Since the earliest documented records the main breeding areas of the Arctic Skua in Britain have been in Orkney and Shetland, but they also breed in Caithness and Sutherland in the east, areas of the west coast as far south as Jura, and in parts of the Outer Hebrides.

Mainland Scotland and the Hebrides (Historical accounts)
   Osborn, in 1868 (in Harvie-Brown & Buckley 1887) wrote that the Arctic Skua in Caithness was a 'well known and abundant species, breeding in considerable numbers'. Later, Harvie-Brown and Buckley (1887) and Reid (1886) voiced fears that this population would be broken up and destroyed as the land had been bought by an Englishman who shot 'no fewer than 80 skuas'. No further information is available on the birds of this area until 1930, when there were thought to be around 9 pairs, and as few as 4 pairs in 1931 (Winnal & Yeats in Pennie, 1953). Pennie (1953) recorded 21 pairs in 4 Caithness localities. In 1974 and 1975 there were 28 pairs recorded in Caithness (Everett 1982). In 1887 Harvie-Brown and Buckley recorded the Arctic Skua as common along the east coast of Sutherland, where it still breeds in small numbers.
   Pennant (1789) found Arctic Skuas nesting on Jura in 1772, but by 1867 they were absent (Baxter and Rintoul 1953). There is no other information until 1976 (Sharrock 1976) when they were recorded breeding. Arctic Skuas may have bred on Islay, but have not been recorded since 1852 (Baxter and Rintoul 1953, Sharrock 1976). One pair of Arctic Skuas bred on Tiree in 1891, and they bred on Coll before 1898. Between 1937 and 1939 there were 15 pairs present on Coll, declining to 12 pairs in 1945 and 4 in 1949. In 1955 there were 30 to 40 pairs in early June and they increased in 1956 (Morton-Boyd 1958). More recent status on Coll is similar (Sharrock 1976).
   In 1888 (Harvie-Brown and Buckley 1888) Arctic Skuas bred in a few places in the Outer Hebrides. Although in Fleming's 'British Animals' (in Harvie-Brown and Buckley 1888) the Arctic Skua is marked as 'common' in the Outer Hebrides, Harvie-Brown and Buckley considered that, at the time of writing, the species was rare enough for the authors to think that it should not be shot (Harvie-Brown and Buckley 1888). The present total in the Outer Hebrides is around 37 pairs (Everett 1982). Arctic Skuas have bred in Argyll since at least 1931 (Baxter and Rintoul 1953) and there are about 26 pairs breeding there now (Everett 1982). The two most recent surveys of Arctic Skuas, by Operation Seafarer in 1969 (Cramp, Bourne and Saunders 1974), and the RSPB in 1974, show that mainland Scotland and the Hebrides now have less than 10% of the total British population.

Orkney (Historical accounts)
   Dunn (1837) reported that the main breeding place of the Arctic Skua in Orkney was on the Holm of Eddy (Eday). Buckley and Harvie-Brown (1891) observed that Arctic Skuas no longer bred on Eday possibly because the island was no longer heather moor, but had been cultivated. Buckley and Harvie-Brown (1891) recorded that Orkney Arctic Skuas bred only on Hoy, and even there they were restricted to one area of the island. They give no information on the numbers breeding, although they speak of them as being 'so common' that a Mr Heddle informed them that he had 'killed 60 in one season, and that next year could see no decline in their numbers'. Dunn (1837) does not mention Arctic Skuas breeding on Hoy, although Salmon (in Buckley and Harvie-Brown 1891) says that he took

a nest of this species there in 1831. In 1933, Serle (in Baxter and Rintoul 1953) counted 25 pairs on Hoy. Law (in Buckley and Harvie-Brown 1891) thought that Arctic Skuas did not breed on mainland Orkney, but Sheppard (Buckley and Harvie-Brown 1891) said that the species was common around Stromness and in 1840 he had shot many there. In 1881 Dr J. F. M'conaghy wrote (Buckley and Harvie-Brown 1891) that a specimen was shot in Sanday. He added that David Lennie, 'bird stuffer', said that Arctic Skuas used to breed at the south end of the island, but that, with the present exception, he had not seen one for years. Lack (1942, 1943) wrote that Arctic Skuas bred only on Hoy, Westray and Papa Westray. In 1943 there were at least 60 pairs on Hoy, one pair on Westray and 14 to 18 pairs at the north end of Papa Westray. This is the first record of Arctic Skuas breeding on Westray and Papa Westray. Miss Baxter saw them on Papa Westray in 1928 and was told that they had colonised the island three or four years earlier (Lack 1943). Arctic Skuas now breed over most of the Orkney islands, the largest population being on Hoy.

Shetland (*Historical accounts*)

Edmonston (1809) wrote that 'great numbers (of Arctic Skuas) breed in Zetland, most numerous on Hascosay'. Tudor (1883) found Arctic Skuas breeding in 'considerable numbers' on Noss. He also recorded them on Foula, Fetlar and Hermaness. Raeburn (1888) found several colonies in Shetland, the largest on Hermaness. In 1885 there were 30 pairs here, but at that time Raeburn believed that the colony was decreasing rapidly because of persecution by egg collectors. However, once this pressure was lifted the colony increased again and in 1887 there were 60 to 100 pairs (Raeburn (1888). Besides this colony at Hermaness, Raeburn found 50 pairs on Noss, and 30 pairs on Foula. He also found scattered pairs on many other islands. In 1891 Raeburn did not find any Arctic Skuas on Papa Stour. They are believed to have colonised this island in 1920, and in 1951 there were 10 to 12 pairs present (Venables 1951). Evans and Buckley (1899) found Arctic Skuas over most of Shetland, and reported that Hermaness and Noss were the largest colonies.

Fetlar and Yell currently have the largest breeding populations of Arctic Skuas in Shetland, followed by Foula, Fair Isle and Unst. There are population estimates available from Foula, Noss, Hermaness and Fair Isle dating from the 19th century in the first three colonies and from the time of colonisation in 1905 on Fair Isle. The numbers of Arctic Skuas on Noss have fluctuated irregularly. There were two main periods of decrease between 1934 and 1939, and again between 1947 and 1952, since when the numbers have increased between 1964 and 1968 and now seem to have stabilised (Fig. 13). At Hermaness the colony has declined. Fair Isle showed a steady rate of increase up to the last few years when there has been a decline (Fig. 14). The rate of increase of the Foula colony has not been constant. A rapid increase occurred between 1968 and 1976, until the last five years when numbers have declined (Fig. 15).

Quantitative changes in Scottish populations

Arctic Skuas nest in diffuse groups over wide areas of moorland in mainland north Scotland and the isles, and so are rather difficult to census. Large colonies on small islands (e.g. Fair Isle, Foula, Noss, Papa Westray) are more easily counted and numbers in these areas are much better known. Estimates of the total populations including pairs scattered over wide areas (Table 9) indicate that,

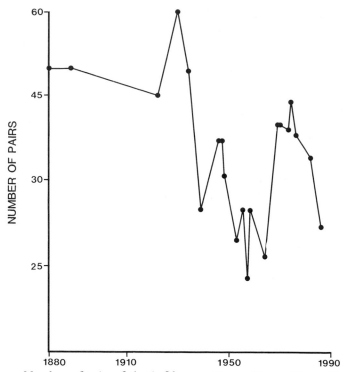

Fig. 13   Numbers of pairs of Arctic Skuas nesting on Noss, 1880–1986.

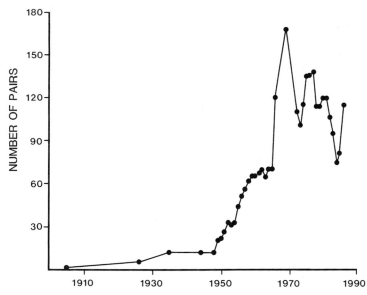

Fig. 14   Numbers of pairs of Arctic Skuas nesting on Fair Isle, 1905–1986.

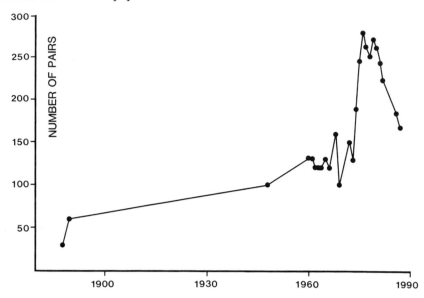

Fig. 15   Numbers of pairs of Arctic Skuas nesting on Foula, 1888–1987.

despite declines at some sites, the numbers of Arctic Skuas breeding in Scotland have increased considerably over the last 100 years, possibly particularly over the last 20 years. Increases appear to be occurring in each region occupied (Table 9). Some of this apparent increase may be due to improvements in coverage, but consideration of numbers at particular colonies confirms an upward trend in Arctic Skua numbers. However it is very clear that trends differ considerably between colonies. Some show very pronounced, but generally temporary, declines. About 60% of the breeding Arctic Skuas are in Shetland, with a further 30% in Orkney and most of the remaining 10% in the Hebrides.

Populations elsewhere
Recent estimates of Arctic Skua population sizes indicate that numbers in Scotland represent only a tiny fraction of the world population of the species (Table 10). Unfortunately, no census data exist for the three principal breeding areas, USSR, Alaska and Canada, but there are figures for typical breeding densities on these tundra habitats which suggest that there must be tens or possibly hundreds of thousands of pairs of Arctic Skuas in those areas. It seems probable that the Arctic Skua is by far the most numerous of the skua species, with perhaps in the region of 0.5 to 1 million pairs altogether, though this should be treated as little more than a guess!

It is known that Arctic Skua numbers in the Faeroes have fluctuated, at least in part as a consequence of human persecution at some colonies, but it is not clear if the population has declined as has been suggested by some authors. In 1961 there were thought to be about 1,000 pairs in the Faeroes (Joensen 1966), but Bourne stated (in Cramp & Simmons 1983) that this total had fallen to 250 pairs by 1969. However, in 1977 Erik Mortensen carried out a thorough survey and located 1,300 pairs, but Mortensen felt that there had probably been some 2,000 to 3,000 pairs of Arctic Skuas in the Faeroes in 1960 rather than the 1,000 pairs estimated by Joensen, so all authors appear to agree that numbers have declined. Nothing is known of any changes in numbers that might have taken place throughout most of the breeding range of the species, but there is no reason to think that there have been any major changes in status elsewhere.

LONG-TAILED SKUA

The Long-tailed Skua clearly has its larger populations in the USSR, Alaska and Canada, where it generally nests at a similar or slightly higher density than the Arctic Skua, but in a narrower range of habitats and over a smaller area. In Norway and Greenland there are thought to be some 1,000 to 10,000 pairs, while the Swedish population has been estimated at 10,000 pairs (Table 11). Long-tailed Skuas have attempted to breed in Scotland a few times. In 1974 a ringed adult Long-tailed Skua held territory on a central Grampian mountaintop and fed on insects and eggs of ground-nesting birds, including those of Dotterels! An adult was found dead near Grantown on Spey in June 1975. In 1980 an adult was seen between the 2nd June and 6th August, and had what was apparently a young bird with it from 16th July; it showed behaviour suggesting that the species nested in the highlands of Scotland that year. There have been numerous records of Long-tailed Skuas visiting the northern and western islands of Scotland during the breeding season, particularly in June and July. Islanders on Foula remember a pair of Long-tailed Skuas holding territory within the Arctic Skua colony one summer, but most records are of lone birds that spend only a day or two at a site, often associating with Arctic Skuas. Since 1968 there have been over 60 such records, 13 of these at Fair Isle, with four each on Hoy and Fetlar, and three each on North Ronaldsay and Harris.

POMARINE SKUA

Pomarine Skuas nest over a slightly smaller area of the USSR, Alaska and Canada than that occupied by Arctic Skuas, and do not breed in Europe, but their numbers are impossible even to guess at with any confidence. Their habit of moving in a nomadic fashion until they find sites with local lemming population 'highs' (Chapter 10) and their habit of breeding only in years when lemmings are abundant, means that their breeding population density at any one site can vary from zero to as many as ten pairs per km² in successive years. Maher found a 150-fold variation in Pomarine Skua breeding density in Northern Alaska over a period of a few years. Although Pomarine Skuas can breed at a much higher density than Arctic Skuas in good lemming years, these years are infrequent and are synchronous only over small geographical regions, so that the total population of Pomarine Skuas is almost certainly much less than that of the Arctic Skua.

GREAT SKUA DISTRIBUTION AND POPULATIONS

The genus *Catharacta* has a very restricted breeding range in the northern

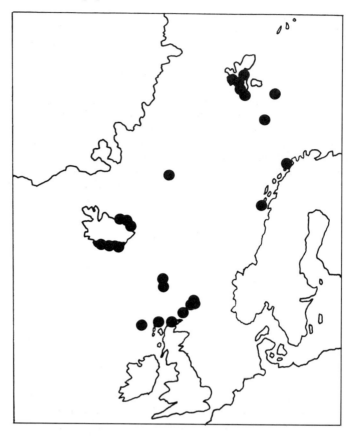

*Fig. 16   Breeding range of the Great Skua. Breeding sites in 1986 are rep-
resented by dots irrespective of colony sizes.*

hemisphere. Until recently it bred only in Iceland, the Faeroes and north Scotland,
but recently it has also colonised Spitzbergen, Bear Island, Hopen, and north
Norway (Fig. 16). Estimated population sizes (Table 12) suggest that there are
about 12,500 breeding pairs of Great Skuas in all these areas combined, and
allowing for immature nonbreeders in addition to this we can estimate that there
are some 35,000 individuals of *C. s. skua*, so that the Great Skua has a relatively
small and isolated population by comparison with most other seabirds. However,
it is much more numerous now than it was in the past.

Shetland
In Britain in 1774 the Great Skua bred at only two sites in Shetland, with three
pairs at Saxavord on Unst, and six or seven pairs on the remote island of Foula,
30 km west of Shetland mainland. We can be confident of these data, because
detailed observations of these birds were made by the Rev. George Low, whose
thorough account of his tour through Orkney and Shetland in 1774 and the wildlife

he saw was published over one hundred years later, in 1879. In his notes he specifically mentions that Shetlanders confirmed that Great Skuas did not nest at any sites in Shetland other than where he had seen them himself. He also gives a description of the encounter that he had with this rare and interesting species.

'Never man had better reason to observe or to remember the natural history of Bonxie than I at this time. I no sooner approached his quarters but he attacked me and my company with so great fury that every one of us was forced to do him obeysance for every stroke. He beat my Water Spaniel quite out of the pit, insomuch that he fled to our feet for shelter, and could not be forced out again, though a bold dog and used to otters or what else might be lamed by a gun. I defended myself the best way I could with my gun'.

He also took pains to point out the high regard in which these rare birds were then held by the natives. Because the 'Bonxie' was highly valued as a bird that chased off Sea Eagles, Ravens and other potential predators of lambs it was strictly protected and the islanders took pains to try to stop visitors from shooting specimens for their collections. In spite of the protection afforded the Great Skua, the tiny colony at Saxavord became extinct before 1861, but that on Foula grew to about 30 pairs by 1804 (Saxby 1874). Great Skuas may have colonised Fair Isle around 1800, as they were said to be breeding there in 1804 (Neill 1806), but Neill does not appear to have been a very reliable authority, and no one else gives Fair Isle as a breeding site for this species at any time during the 19th century, so if it was colonised this must have been shortlived.

Shortly after 1800, Great Skuas began to be persecuted by taxidermists from England who made trips to Shetland in order to shoot specimens to stuff and sell to gentlemen to decorate their mansions. This may be why the Saxavord colony became extinct, since Unst was then much more readily accessible than Foula. Some of the visiting collectors were discouraged from shooting; others found Shetlanders who were willing to assist them in return for cash rewards which were quite substantial in their terms. Drosier, who visited Shetland in the 1820s, was one of the first of these visiting taxidermists, and he published several accounts of his experiences. Drosier visited Foula in 1828, with the particular objective of collecting Great Skuas. His account paints a vivid picture of life on the remote island:

'I had some difficulty in obtaining a passage over, but at last procured a boat, a fair wind and a few hours brought me to the general landing place of the island. The accommodations here are miserably bad: and, as for food, milk and oat-cake of the coarsest kind can only be obtained, together with a few eggs. The skua gull, called by the natives Bunxie, is held and cherished by them with the greatest veneration and kindness; and nothing hurts their feelings more than to see the death of their favourite bird. I was particularly requested, upon my arrival, by two or three elderly natives, to spare this bird; as to the skua were almost entirely trusted the care and protection of their lambs, during the summer months, that are always allowed to wander unrestrained over the island.'

Later he describes the 'Bunxie' in great detail:
'... the roots of the primaries white, extending along the inner webs; extremities nearly black; bastard wing dark, each feather sharply pencilled with dull white. Tail consisting of twelve feathers, dark ashy brown. Bill and claws hooked, the inner claw more so than the rest.'   Drosier 1830

From the latter quote we can see that the pleas of the islanders were not altogether successful! More extensive killing by rather less sensitive individuals than Drosier followed. By 1821 the Great Skua population on Foula had not increased beyond 30 pairs, but the island was still partially protected by its isolation.

In 1828 one or two pairs of Great Skuas started to nest at Ronas Hill, an isolated spot on north Shetland mainland, and in 1831 three pairs were found nesting at Hermaness on Unst (Evans & Buckley 1899). These may have deserted Foula because of the disturbance occurring there, but this is guesswork. The Ronas Hill colony did not last long. It increased to five pairs in 1832, but then in 1836 it was totally exterminated by a Robert Dunn from Hull, who described his shooting activities in a book (Dunn 1837). The new colony at Hermaness was protected from shooting by the landowner, Dr L. Edmonston, and increased to 30 pairs by 1850. Meanwhile the Foula colony was being shot and was reduced to six pairs in 1850 and three in 1860. Shooting at Hermaness then increased, presumably because so few Bonxies were now left at Foula, and the Hermaness colony was reduced to six pairs in 1861 and five in 1871 (Saxby 1874). Foula was protected over the next two decades, and Great Skua numbers increased to 15 pairs in 1883 (Tudor 1883). Tudor may have slightly underestimated their numbers when he visited Foula, as Evans, who was an eminent ornithologist of the day (Tudor was primarily a historian), estimated that there were 60 pairs present in 1887. In 1881 one pair of Great Skuas bred at Ronas Hill, reestablishing that colony.

In the years from 1887 to 1899 a number of distinguished Victorian bird collectors visited Foula and other parts of Shetland. Conservation minded naturalists also visited the islands. A bitter controversy sprang up, with claims and counter-claims as to the numbers of Great Skuas shot each year. The collectors published inflated estimates of the numbers of breeding pairs to reduce the conservationists' claims that they were killing unreasonable numbers. There is no doubt that the intense persecution, discussed bitterly in *The Zoologist* (Barrington 1890, Harvie-Brown 1890, Raeburn 1890, 1891, Traill 1890, Clarke 1892) resulted in a big decrease in Great Skua numbers on Foula from a peak in 1890 of some 40 breeding pairs (counted by Eagle Clarke who was a well respected naturalist as well as a collector and sportsman) to only 17 pairs in 1899. The influence of this shooting was made worse by the development of a lucrative market for Great Skua eggs. Foula natives collected all the first clutches and most of the second clutches each year and sold them to egg dealers; a small number of third clutches were laid and these were allowed to hatch, not so much to conserve the population but because these eggs tended to be deficient in pigmentation and so of little commercial value to the collectors (Holbourn 1938). We do not know how many pairs managed to fledge chicks in spite of the shooting and egg collecting, but it is reasonable to assume that few would have succeeded since the egg collecting would mean that their breeding season would be seriously delayed, and chicks probably would not have fledged in time to depart south in autumn.

While Great Skuas on Foula were suffering this severe persecution, similar destruction occurred at Ronas Hill, reducing numbers there to three pairs in 1900. In 1890 a new, fourth, colony was established, with one pair breeding on Yell. This again appears to have been founded by a pair which deserted its natal area as a result of persecution and disturbance, for Clarke (1894) mentioned that the breeding grounds on Foula were shifting from one part of the hills to another each year because the birds evidently 'felt disturbed' by the persecution. At the same time, numbers at Hermaness increased, with occasional setbacks, as that colony

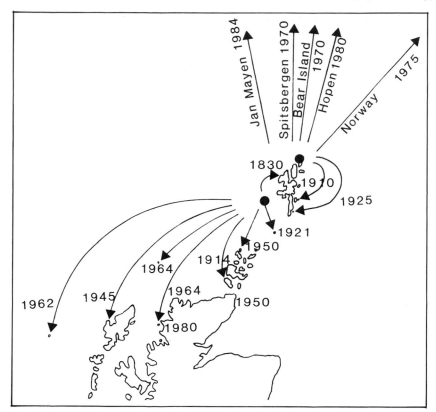

Fig. 17 Spread of the Great Skua to new breeding sites from the original colonies on Foula and Unst (marked by dots). Year of first breeding at each major new site is shown. Lines indicating colonisation movements point to the sites to which birds moved, and do not imply from which established sites within Scotland the colonists originated. However, observations of colour ringed birds at new sites show that every new colony marked on the map has recruits that were raised on Foula.

was under the watch of a full time warden from 1891 onwards. Indeed, this problem of the near-extermination of the Great Skua, and the success story of its protection, particularly at Hermaness, but also for periods at Foula, played an important role in promoting the formation of a protection of birds society and in the development of protection of birds legislation which followed at the end of the century.

After 1900, egg and skin collecting in Shetland decreased abruptly, although Great Skua eggs later became a regular food item on Foula. These were collected shortly after laying had begun, generally in the latter half of May, and this practice continued illegally but on a small scale until the mid 1970s. Relaxation of persecution allowed the Great Skua colony on Foula to grow at an almost constant rate of 7% per annum from 1900 to 1975, by which time it had reached 3,000 pairs and these nested over most of the island apart from the inhabited areas and active peat cuttings. The Great Skua population on Foula then declined in numbers after 1975, and part of this decline can be attributed to illegal shooting. The Hermaness colony also increased after 1900 but at a slower rate than at Foula, and a considerable number of new colonies became established in other parts of Shetland, in Orkney, north Scotland and the Western Isles (Table 13). The year of first recorded breeding by Great Skuas at each colony is shown in Figure 17, and this indicates the general spread southwards in Scotland during the 1920s to 1970s, to be followed by a colonisation of remoter northern areas in the 1960s to 1980s. We know that many of the colonists were Great Skuas bred on Foula because many thousands of chicks were colour-ringed at Foula, in south-east Iceland and in the Faeroes, with a colour coding for each of these localities and another one or two colour-rings coding for the year of ringing. At least one bird colour-ringed at Foula, and usually several, have been seen at each of the other British colonies, and also at sites in Spitzbergen, north Norway and Hopen. In contrast, not a single chick colour-ringed in Iceland has been found breeding at any colony outside Iceland and none of the rather few colour-ringed in the Faeroes has been found breeding in Iceland or Britain or at any of the newly formed Arctic colonies. We shall return to consider the importance of emigration in Great Skua population dynamics and some results of the colour ringing programme in Chapter 13.

The Great Skua's spread and increase is summarised in Tables 13, 14 and 15. Since their reduction to low numbers, around 1900, by skin collectors, they have increased in numbers and spread to many new sites. Not all new colonies have thrived; some have been abandoned or shot out. The southward spread of colonisation appears to have slowed in the 1960s, with little sign of further movement southwards. It is not at all clear why this should be since conditions favourable for Great Skuas appear to exist in areas such as the Small Isles and Argyll. Since 1960 most new colonies in Scotland have been a consolidation of the distribution in Orkney or extreme north-west of Scotland, while there has also been a clear movement into Arctic areas north-east of Scotland. The decadal percentage increase (Table 15) for the total Scottish Great Skua population since 1900 has generally been around 100% – i.e. the number of pairs has roughly doubled each decade. However, several other patterns are evident. As the number of pairs nesting in Shetland has increased, the rate of increase has dropped. As Orkney, the Hebrides and mainland Scotland were colonised the rate of increase of these new sites increased, drawing away young birds from Shetland (as colour ringed chicks from Shetland have confirmed). As a result, the proportion of Scottish Great Skuas that nest in Shetland has fallen from 100% up to the 1910s to only about 68% in 1985.

The Faeroes

As might be expected, we have rather less information about the changes in numbers of Great Skuas in the Faeroes than we have for British colonies, although the history in those islands was a similar one of protection and persecution as the dominant influences in the bird's fortunes. The first reference to numbers of Great Skuas in the Faeroes is the account of Svabo (1783) who stated that he was told by the Faeroese islanders that 6,000 Great Skua chicks were harvested annually on the island of Skuvoy in the years around 1700. This statistic is impossible to accept. Skuvoy is a small island, with only 1.5 km² of rough moorland, 4 km² of pasture and 1.3 km^2 of cultivated land at the present time. At present Great Skuas and Arctic Skuas both breed on Skuvoy, and together occupy 3 km^2 of the island. The remainder is not suitable habitat for them. Even if land use was rather different in 1700 (and this is unlikely since the population in those times probably made similar use of the fertile areas for agriculture and pasture), Great Skuas are unlikely to have occupied more than 5 km^2 of the island, and had they nested at the highest density presently recorded for the species (600 nests per km^2 in the Flick area of Foula) they would have had to raise more than two chicks per pair to produce the crop reputedly harvested. This would be impossible since Great Skuas only lay one or two eggs. Either 6,000 is a huge exaggeration, or Svabo confused the crop of another seabird species harvested at Skuvoy. This island has huge colonies of Puffins and Guillemots and was an important island for fowling by the Faeroese (Williamson 1948). We are unlikely ever to know how this mistake came about. Svabo's statement has been cited as an indication that Great Skuas were abundant at that time in the Faeroes, but I think this view is mistaken. Certainly, when Svabo visited Skuvoy in 1782, he found only a total of ten pairs of Great Skuas breeding there, and no more than 45 pairs have been recorded in this colony at any subsequent time (Bayes *et al* 1964). In 1828 Graba (1830) found 50 pairs breeding at Sand on Sandoy, but he did not visit any other Great Skua colonies in the Faeroes. A complete census was not undertaken until 1872, when about 36 pairs were found scattered over eight colonies on seven islands (Fielden 1872). In 1897 these had been reduced by persecution, principally by skin collectors who could not obtain enough from the Shetland colonies, to only four pairs, and each pair nested at a different island in the Faeroes (Salomonsen 1935). As a result of the near extinction of Great Skuas in the Faeroes an Act of Parliament was passed in December 1897 which protected them from any form of persecution. This act was successfully implemented, and their numbers increased to about 71 breeding pairs in 1930 (Salomonsen 1931) occupying the same four colonies as the individual pairs which survived through 1897.

After 1930 the increase of the Faeroese Great Skua population continued, although the use of chicks and eggs as food resumed, and subsequently several colonies were subject to illegal shooting of breeding adults to reduce their numbers because the Faeroese crofters disliked the Bonxies' habits of chasing sheep and lambs, attacking dying lambs, killing other seabirds and hitting people who walked into their nesting territories. The increase in numbers of Great Skuas in the Faeroes has been far less spectacular than that which occurred over the same period in Shetland. Their numbers in the Faeroes have never risen above a few hundred pairs (Table 16), and this can be explained in a number of ways, related to both human persecution and to the availability of food supplies for the expanding populations. These influences will be considered further in Chapters 15 and 16, after we have seen something of the food habits and breeding biology of these populations.

Iceland

Whereas Great Skua colonies in Britain and the Faeroes are almost all on islands, and most of these are small in area, the Great Skua in Iceland principally inhabits the fluvio-glacial outwash plains which cover vast areas along the south coasts of the country. It also nests at a far lower density in Iceland and, as a result, is extremely difficult to census. In fact it would be honest to say that no proper census of Great Skuas in Iceland had ever been carried out before 1984. The only

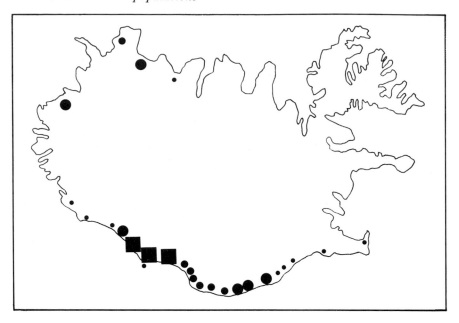

*Fig. 18   Distribution of breeding Great Skuas in Iceland. Smallest dot = 1–15
pairs;   medium   dot = 20–75   pairs;   large   dot = 100–220   pairs;   large
squares = 1000–1500 pairs. From Hansen & Lange 1985.*

figure for the population was Finnur Gudmundsson's estimate, made in 1950, of
about 6,000 pairs, which was really a guess based on his wide experience of Iceland
and its birds. Gudmundsson felt that the Great Skua population in Iceland in the
1950s was stable in numbers, but annual visits to one of the main breeding areas
in south-east Iceland by Brathay Exploration Group expeditions each year, during
which they ringed and colour-ringed about 1,000 Great Skua chicks annually,
led Dickens (1968) to suggest that numbers on the Breidamerkursandur and
Skeidarursandur had greatly declined between the 1950s and 1960s. These two
areas hold most of Iceland's breeding Great Skuas (Fig. 18), but one problem is
that they are huge areas, and their topography is not constant. Braided glacial
streams, which can be torrents during the main melt in spring, constantly divide,
rejoin and change their courses; Great Skuas are unevenly distributed over these
areas, preferring to nest in localities where short grass or moss carpets have
developed. The instability of the substratum has led to changes in colony distribution over the years. Annual visits in recent years by Brathay expeditions have
shown continuing movements of the Great Skua population, though now a road
has been constructed round the south coast of Iceland and this has involved
construction of bridges, chanelling of streams and the seeding of large areas of the
Breidamerkursandur with grass. These changes, and increased tourist traffic and
access for Icelanders, have created further shifts of Great Skua distribution, and
led Collier & Stott (1976) to suggest that its numbers in Iceland were increasing.
The ease with which Brathay groups have ringed 1,000 chicks each year certainly

indicates that there is a large Great Skua population in this area, but it would be difficult from this observation to try to reach any conclusions of the actual population size or trends. Having visited Iceland in 1978, my own limited experience of the main Icelandic colonies led me to suggest that the Icelandic population was about 5,000 pairs. I suspected that numbers had not changed greatly since the 1950s, and my feeling was that Gudmundsson's guess of 6,000 pairs may well have been about right. Fortunately, we now know that this must have been the case. In 1984 and 1985, two Danish ornithologists, Lars Hansen and Peter Lange, visited almost all of the Great Skua's breeding areas in Iceland, and censused them by searching for nests, counting pairs on territories, and by aerial survey of the enormous sandur on the south coast. Their detailed survey located an estimated 4,909 to 5,846 pairs, which confirms the earlier estimates by myself and by Finnur Gudmundsson.

There is no reason to think that Great Skua numbers in Iceland were reduced at the end of last century as they were in Shetland and the Faeroes, so that the relative numbers in each country have changed considerably. Around 1900, over 95% of Great Skuas nested in Iceland, with the Faeroes and Shetland populations reduced close to extinction. Today, the numbers in Britain are somewhat greater than in Iceland, and numbers in the Faeroes are much smaller. In addition, new colonies in Arctic areas provide the potential for a further expansion of range and numbers in the future (Table 12).

TRISTAN SKUA

The Tristan Skua *C. skua hamiltoni* has the closest breeding distribution to the North Atlantic Great Skuas, though it is thousands of miles to the south. James Fisher suggested that the Tristan Skua was the most likely ancestor of the Great Skua because one could easily imagine a group of Tristan Skuas being caught up in a storm and carried along the Atlantic storm track, which could well take them to the vicinity of Iceland, where climatic and biotic conditions are not too different from those around Gough Island and Tristan da Cunha, except that summer occurs six months later in the year, and the penguins and petrels of the subAntarctic South Atlantic are replaced by the auks and gulls of the subArctic North Atlantic. Tristan Skuas breed on each of the islands of Tristan da Cunha and on Gough Island. Richardson (1984) recorded that only 5–10 pairs were present on Tristan itself in 1972–74, because adults, eggs and chicks were destroyed by the islanders whenever possible, in order to protect their lambs and chickens. On the remoter islands, 'seahens', as they are known locally, are less subject to persecution, and there were several hundred pairs on Nightingale Island, where vast numbers of Great Shearwaters and other seabirds also breed. However, the stronghold of the Tristan Skua is Gough Island. In 1956 there were thought to be some 2,000–3,000 pairs on Gough (Swales 1965), while I guessed that there were around 2,000 occupied territories on the island in 1983 and 1985, though many pairs holding territory did not breed and there were also large flocks of nonbreeders, perhaps numbering another 2,000–4,000 individuals. I do not think my slightly lower estimate than Swales' means that numbers have decreased, since neither of us attempted a proper census. However, the Tristan Skua clearly has decreased in numbers on the Tristan archipelago and it is one of the least numerous distinct subspecies or species of skua, with a total of only about 2,500 pairs (Table 17).

FALKLAND SKUA

Devillers (1978) estimated that the total population of *C. s. antarctica* is around 3,000–5,000 pairs. It breeds throughout the Falkland Islands and on the South American continent at Punta Tombo, Camarones, Bahia Bustamante, and Puerto Deseado. The numbers at colonies on the continent are generally small. According to Devillers, there are probably several hundred pairs of Falkland Skuas in Patagonia, where their distribution partly overlaps that of the Chilean Skua. Rather little seems to be known about the effects of man on Falkland Skua numbers. Certainly we could guess that the availability of sheep carrion will be beneficial to the skuas, but nothing seems to have been published about the attitude of Falkland sheep farmers to the skuas, apart from a suggestion that they consider the geese to be more of a pest than the skuas (Chapter 16).

CHILEAN SKUA

There is very little published information about the Chilean Skua. Its behavioural postures were studied in detail by Moynihan (1962), who recorded that some 1,000 pairs nested in a colony on the shores of Lee Bay, on the north coast of Tierra del Fuego. After a visit in December 1932, Reynolds (1935) said that 'the apex of South America at the islands about Cape Horn would seem to form the nucleus of the greatest breeding ground of this skua . . . nests containing either eggs or small young were found singly or several together on the headlands and islets all along the coast . . . two large colonies were gull-like in the number and close grouping of the nests. The whole of Otaries Island was occupied by one of these big colonies and, although laying had only just commenced, there were two or three hundred skuas at the time of our visit.'

Its systematics have been considered by Devillers (1978) who found 200 or so pairs nesting on Magdalena Island, Strait of Magellan, and also described the breeding distribution of the species. Apparently, Chilean Skuas breed at numerous sites along the western coast of Chile, as well as in smaller numbers on the coast of Santa Cruz, on the eastern side of the continent. Devillers also suggests that a small number may breed on the Falkland Islands, where possibly the species hybridises with the Falkland Skua, and it certainly does so in an area of overlap on the mainland.

Devillers and Moynihan also point out that Chilean Skuas may often breed in large dense colonies with nests placed close together in the manner of gulls, as well as in loose colonies more typical of the other large skuas. In this respect, the Chilean Skua is unique among skuas. It would be interesting to find out more about Chilean Skuas, but their breeding areas are in one of the most sparsely populated and inaccessible regions of South America, where few ornithologists have ventured. The accounts that we do have suggest that Chilean Skuas are remarkably abundant, and also that they differ from other skuas in a number of ways. They do not defend their nests against human intruders and may feed extensively on sea urchins! It is possible that their apparently more gull-like behaviour has allowed them to fill a gull niche in southern South America and so resulted in their becoming rather more numerous than is usual for a skua.

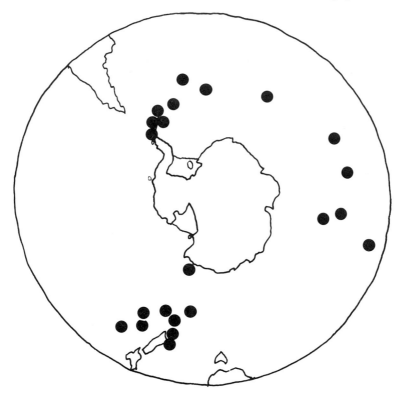

Fig. 19   Breeding range of Brown Skuas.

BROWN SKUA

Brown Skuas nest on most of the subAntarctic Islands, the northern parts of the Antarctic Peninsula where they overlap in distribution with the South Polar Skua, and on the islands south of New Zealand, which are cool temperate rather than subAntarctic (Fig. 19). Most Brown Skua populations are fairly small. Largest numbers tend to be on the larger islands that also hold particularly big populations of other seabirds on which Brown Skuas prey and scavenge. The total population of this taxon appears to be less than 10,000 pairs (Table 18). The numbers of Brown Skuas at some sites have been affected by man. On Macquarie Island the introduction of rabbits led to an increase in the Brown Skua population and subsequent rabbit control led to a fall in skua numbers. Brown Skua numbers can also show local increases close to human settlements on subAntarctic islands where scavenging at refuse can provide skuas with additional food.

SOUTH POLAR SKUA

The most southerly breeding site for any animals appears to be in the Theron

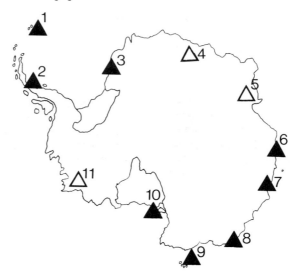

Fig. 20   *Breeding range of South Polar Skuas. Solid triangles mark sites where breeding is confirmed, open triangles refer to areas where breeding is probable but not well documented.* 1 = S. *Orkney Is.* (10 *pairs*); 2 = *Antarctic Peninsula and associated islands* (660 *pairs*); 3 = *Coats Land* (10 *pairs*); 4 = *Queen Maud Land*; 5 = *Mackenzie Bay coasts*; 6 = *Queen Mary Land* (23 *pairs*); 7 = *Wilkes Land* (830 *pairs*); 8 = *Terre Adelie* (75 *pairs*); 9 = *Balleny Is.*; 10 = *Ross Island and Ross Sea coasts* (6000 *pairs*); 11 = *Byrd Land.*

Mountains (79°S 28°W), 250 km inland from the Weddell Sea. There may be populations of Antarctic Petrels or Snow Petrels at other inland Antarctic sites further south, but these have not yet been documented. However, at Mount Faraway in the Theron Mountains some six pairs of South Polar Skuas were found breeding in association with colonies of Antarctic and Snow Petrels in January 1967. This record gives the South Polar Skua a claim to be one of the most polar of all animals. In addition to this extreme example of high latitude breeding, South Polar Skuas are likely to be seen in ones and twos anywhere in the interior of the Antarctic Continent, having been recorded not only at the South Pole itself, but also at the Soviet Union's Vostock Station which is situated close to the pole but at a height of 3,488 m (11,500 feet) above sea level. This site holds the world record for cold, with a recorded temperature of −88.3°C in winter. Even at the height of summer the mean temperature here rises only to −32.7°C, so the South Polar Skua is clearly not too concerned about living in cold climates. This species also holds the world record for the longest migration of an individual bird recorded by ringing (see Chapter 4) and, outside of its breeding season, it occurs regularly as far north as the Arctic Circle. Considered over the whole year, it is perhaps arguable that the South Polar Skua has one of the widest distributions of any bird species in the world. However, South Polar Skua breeding distribution is fairly limited and the numbers of birds at most colonies are small.

   The main breeding concentrations appear to occur around the fringe of the

Ross Sea, on the coast of Wilkes Land, and on the Antarctic Peninsula (Table 19). Clearly there are at least several thousand breeding pairs of South Polar Skuas altogether, and perhaps as many as ten thousand pairs, but there is little information for areas away from Antarctic research bases.

The breeding range of the South Polar Skua appears to have spread north into the range of the Brown Skua (Fig. 20), and this may be a relatively recent event. South Polar Skuas outnumber Brown Skuas at colonies on the Antarctic Peninsula, but some ten pairs of South Polar Skuas breed on the South Orkney Islands alongside 300 pairs of Brown Skuas, while ten pairs of South Polar Skuas share the South Shetland Islands with about 420 pairs of Brown Skuas. Some hybridisation does take place at each of these sites, but the amount is small and the scarcity of apparently intermediate birds has been taken by Devillers to indicate that these two taxa are distinctly different species rather than taxa related at a closer level.

CHAPTER 4

Migration patterns

'Movements. Migratory, but details inadequately known due to pelagic nature, absence of ringing recoveries, and difficulties of identifying juvenile and non-breeding birds at sea. Passages detected by shore-based observers certainly unrepresentative [refers to Pomarine Skuas, but similar accounts are given for Long-tailed Skua and Arctic Skua].
Cramp & Simmons (1983)

Information on the migration patterns and wintering areas of skuas comes from a variety of sources. Ringing of chicks at colonies has provided some important insights into migrations of Great Skuas, Arctic Skuas and South Polar Skuas, but only Shetland Great Skuas have been ringed with durable rings in large enough numbers so that a detailed analysis of recoveries can be made. Since only some 5–10% of ringed birds are eventually recovered and reported, the fate of most ringed birds is not known. With seabirds, those that are recovered may present a very biased picture. For example, in recent years, Arctic Skua chicks ringed at Foula have been recovered in Syria, the Sudan and Zaire, locations where Arctic Skuas are exceedingly rare! Do these recoveries indicate regular migration over the African continent or are they examples of aberrant individuals, recovered because of their abnormal behaviour?

Many birdwatchers observe skuas during the migration periods passing coastal headlands, or island observatories, such as Cape Clear, Balranald or Heligoland. Seawatching has been a popular activity for many years, but the numbers of skuas seen on passage depend very precisely on the prevailing weather conditions. It is a characteristic of all skuas that they tend to avoid the coast while on migration. This habit makes observations by seawatching from the coast particularly prone to bias, since large numbers of skuas may be passing a few kilometres beyond the range of sight of seawatchers. Particular wind directions or weather systems may bring huge numbers of skuas within sight from land, whereas, normally, these birds would pass by unrecorded. Because weather conditions have such dramatic influences on the records obtained from coastal sites it is extremely difficult to generalise about skua migrations on the basis of seawatching observations alone.

Some species are more assiduous in avoiding coasts than others. Arctic Skuas will frequently fly over headlands to take short-cuts, and will often migrate overland, but Long-tailed Skuas remain well away from coasts except when unable to fly against storms. Because of the more pelagic nature of the Long-tailed Skua, most birdwatchers have never seen this species, and yet a short trip offshore during autumn shows that Long-tailed Skuas can be as numerous as Arctic Skuas on the open Atlantic. These differences partly reflect differences in feeding ecology of the species; Arctic Skuas often stop at coastal aggregations of terns or Kittiwakes to harass these birds and steal food. Long-tailed Skuas migrate more rapidly and without feeding extensively, and rarely attack other seabirds during their migration. Great Skuas also tend to avoid land, although they will feed at fishing boats or attack birds during migration. Their avoidance of land also influences their migration routes. Very few Great Skuas pass south through the English Channel, but prefer to leave the North Sea through the more open waters round the north coast of Scotland.

More valuable data can be obtained from observations at sea. Unfortunately, it is almost impossible to obtain a complete picture from at-sea recording because seabirds are very patchily distributed and they are also highly mobile, changing their distributions over short periods of time as oceanographic patterns change. In order to obtain a reliable picture of skua distributions at sea it would be necessary to survey areas many times each month to average out the effects of patchiness, but usually at-sea records are made from small numbers of trips on vessels that are at sea for purposes other than the study of seabird distributions. As a result, conclusions drawn by one observer crossing an ocean one spring may differ radically from those of another observer crossing by the same route a year later. In addition to this, the problems of correctly identifying skuas at sea can lead to erroneous conclusions or failure to observe particular features. For example, South Polar Skuas had never been identified by ornithologists at sea in the North Atlantic before a ringed one was shot in Greenland. Now that the species is known to migrate into the North Atlantic, records of it at sea, particularly on the Grand Banks, have become quite numerous!

In this chapter I have tried to provide an outline of current knowledge of the routes and timing of skua migrations and of their major wintering areas. In several instances these remain a matter of some speculation, but perhaps reasoned speculation may lead to their being located in the near future. Much of our knowledge of skua migrations and wintering areas has been accumulated as a result of general observations of seabirds at sea and passing coasts, and the following papers, although not necessarily quoted again, are particularly important sources for the whole of this chapter: Austin & Kuroda (1953), Bailey (1966), Baker (1947), Biermann & Voous (1950), Brooks (1939), Dean *et al* (1976), Dementiev & Gladkov (1951), Dixon (1933), Jehl (1973), Jespersen (1930, 1933), Kuroda (1955, 1960),

Murphy (1936), Rankin & Duffey (1948), Wynne-Edwards (1935) and all issues of *Sea Swallow*, particularly papers by Bourne and by Tuck.

STERCORARIUS SPECIES

All three small skuas must migrate out of their main breeding areas since the Arctic tundra could not support them through the dark, cold winter. In fact, all three species are transequatorial migrants. Any immature birds that visit the breeding areas in summer migrate south first, to be followed by failed breeders and then by fledglings and successful breeders. Birds that breed in the high Arctic complete the breeding season later than those further south because the start of breeding is held up in the north until the snow and ice melt. Thus the autumn migration of the more northern skua populations starts later and proceeds rapidly. Pomarine Skuas take longer to hatch their eggs and to fledge their chicks, and so the autumn migration of this species lags behind that of the Arctic and Long-tailed Skuas.

Long-tailed Skua

When lemmings are scarce, some Long-tailed Skuas fail to breed and migrate south early. Birds may then be seen between Britain and Canada by late July, although the main autumn migration occurs in late August and the first three weeks of September. This migration is fairly rapid since Long-tailed Skuas cross many areas where conditions are apparently not suitable for them to feed during their migration. As a result, most birds have passed out of the North Atlantic by late October (Table 20). The migration route through the Atlantic is highly pelagic, so that Long-tailed Skuas are rarely seen in coastal waters. In the New World, Long-tailed Skuas also pass rapidly south to the wintering areas of the southern South Pacific. Again, they tend to remain in pelagic waters, although Brooks (1939) and Dean *et al* (1976) record that they regularly migrate overland from the northern interior of Canada and Alaska to the Pacific Ocean.

It has long been established that this species has a major wintering area in the oceanic regions around southern South America (Murphy 1936), south of about 35°S. Concentrations in winter can be high. Wetmore (1926) saw about 1,200 Long-tailed Skuas pass Cape St Antonio, Argentina, during stormy weather in early November 1920. However, the precise locations of the species' wintering area off southern South America remained a mystery until Veit (1985) reported more than 500 Long-tailed Skuas in the oceanic waters between 39° and 45°S, about 250–400 km east of Argentina, which he saw during research cruises in several successive winters (Fig. 21). About 80% of the birds Veit saw were recorded as immatures, and most were in active moult during the winter.

Another important wintering area was found by Lambert (1980) who saw thousands of Long-tailed Skuas off the coast of Namibia. There he recorded up to several hundred birds per day of observation, mainly located within the upwelling of the highly productive cold Benguela Current between 17° and 32°S, and some 50–100 km from the coast (Fig. 22). Lambert found that the birds began to arrive off Namibia in late September, reaching peak winter numbers in November. This implies that they take about four to eight weeks to get from the breeding areas to this wintering area, in which case they must feed at several suitable locations during their southward migration, even though they deliberately avoid

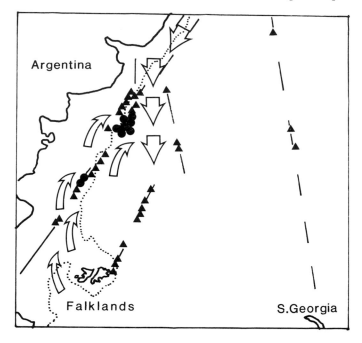

Fig. 21   Distribution of Long-tailed Skuas recorded by Veit (1985) during transects in December–March off the coasts of Argentina and Uruguay. The warm southward flowing Brazil Current is shown by broad arrows, the northward flowing cold Falkland Current by curved arrows. The 100 fathom submarine contour is marked by a dotted line. Transects during which watches for skuas were made are shown by solid lines where no Long-tailed Skuas were seen; by triangles where 1–10 birds were seen per ten mile segment; and by dots where 11–100+ were seen per ten mile segment.

coastal and shelf waters, at least in the North Atlantic. After moult during the winter months, northward migration begins about April, with the last birds departing from Namibian waters in early May. Long-tailed Skuas are seen migrating north in spring past south and west Ireland and west Scotland predominantly in the latter half of May (Davenport 1982), and arrive in breeding areas in late May and early June (de Korte 1984).

Most of the birds Lambert observed closely appeared to be immatures, but none remained off Namibia through the northern summer months. Perhaps all the birds visit the breeding areas in their first year, but this is not certain. They may remain, unnoticed, in the central region of the North Atlantic.

There are few records of Long-tailed Skuas from other areas in winter. They are not usually seen by Antarctic ornithologists, so presumably do not travel into the Southern Ocean. A wreck of perhaps a few dozen Long-tailed Skuas occurred on the beaches of North Island, New Zealand, in January 1983, which was unprecedented and may have been related to the effects of the exceptionally severe El Niño of 1982/83 (Melville 1985). Although Long-tailed Skuas have very rarely

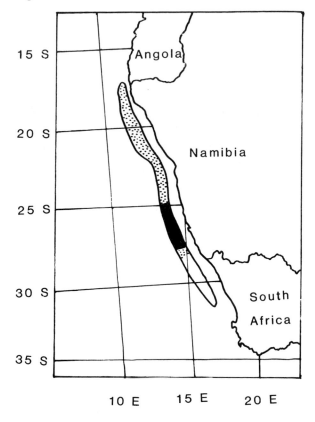

Fig. 22 Distribution of Long-tailed Skuas off southern Africa from October–
April recorded by Lambert (1980). Solid area represents 100 to more than 200
birds seen per day; shaded area represents 10–100 per day; clear area within
the boundary line represents single birds.

been recorded around Australia and New Zealand, it seems likely that birds from
Siberian, Alaskan and northwest Canadian breeding areas must winter far out to
sea over the South Pacific Ocean between 40 and 50°S, where water masses have
similar characteristics to the upwelling regions off South America and Namibia
where concentrations have been located in winter. Few ornithologists traverse the
seas between 40 and 50°S and so the wintering grounds of this species, tentatively
indicated in Fig. 23, may remain uncertain for some time.

Since Lambert and Veit each reported wintering aggregations predominantly
composed of immature birds, it seems probable that these upwelling areas are not
the preferred wintering area of the species but a suboptimal habitat. Veit suggested
that concentrations of adult Long-tailed Skuas might be found wintering in the
interface between the warm Brazil current and the cold Falkland current, where
the temperature gradient is particularly steep (Fig. 21).

Lambert recorded that Long-tailed Skuas wintering off Namibia regularly

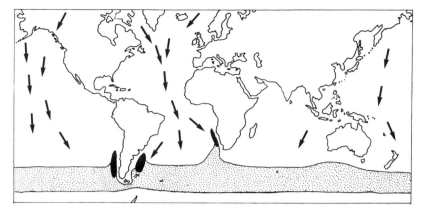

Fig. 23   Probable major migration routes and wintering areas of the Long-tailed Skua. Confirmed wintering areas used mainly by juveniles are marked black. Probable, but unconfirmed wintering area of adults is shaded.

kleptoparasitised fish from Arctic and Common Terns and Sabine's Gulls, and occasionally even robbed Cape Gannets and Yellow-nosed Albatrosses scavenging fish offal, but suggested that this was an unusual behaviour resulting from opportunities provided by fishing boat activities in the area. He considered that Long-tailed Skuas normally feed for themselves on small free-living organisms at the sea surface, a view shared by Veit. Nevertheless, the reasons for the association between Long-tailed Skuas and cold upwelling regions in winter will remain unknown until the bird's winter diet has been examined.

Although Long-tailed Skuas tend to be solitary in winter, they may migrate in large or even enormous flocks. Wynne-Edwards (1935) recorded a flock of many hundreds, and probably several thousands, of Long-tailed Skuas in the middle of the North Atlantic during spring passage in late May, and large migrating flocks have also been described by Davenport (1982) and others.

Arctic Skua

The timings of Arctic Skua migrations are closely similar to those of the Long-tailed Skua. Southward movements of failed breeders and immatures start early, in July, but successful breeders leave southern colonies such as Shetland between early August and late September. Birds from higher latitudes set off south a week or two later than the southern birds, because they started breeding later, but the peak of migration past Britain and Ireland is in September. In total contrast to the Long-tailed Skuas moving south at the same time in pelagic waters, Arctic Skuas mostly move along the continental coasts and inshore waters. Arctic Skuas tend to move more slowly south, too, often stopping for a few days at coastal sites where terns or small gulls are abundant. Estuaries and bays such as the Ythan, Firths of Forth and Tees on the east coast of Britain gather groups of tens, sometimes hundreds, of Arctic Skuas that rob local terns and gulls in autumn.

Some ornithologists have recorded large numbers of Arctic Skuas, as well as Long-tailed Skuas, migrating south in autumn down the central region of the Atlantic (e.g. Wynne-Edwards 1935), although most found very few Arctic Skuas far away from coastal waters. Nevertheless it is clear that some birds cross the Atlantic since Arctic Skuas ringed in Scotland and in the Baltic have been recovered in South America as well as in Africa.

Once Arctic Skuas have moved slowly down to the south of Europe, they seem to progress more rapidly through equatorial waters to the coastal region of South Africa. Few Arctic Skuas have been seen in the tropical coastal waters of West Africa. Since several Arctic Skua chicks ringed in Shetland have been recovered in north, east and central Africa during autumn migration it may be that this rapid southward migration from European coastal waters where there are good feeding opportunities is accompanied by a change in the habitat preference of the migrating birds. Possibly the remainder of the movement to South African waters takes place without regard to the type of substrate covered – land or sea. Another explanation for these inland ringing recoveries would be that birds were carried over the coast by bad weather and lost, but the large number of inland recoveries in Africa makes this seem improbable.

In the Pacific, migrations of the Arctic Skua are less well known, although the species is a common visitor to the west coast of the USA throughout September. Apparently very few Arctic Skuas migrate over the Central Pacific. Although Arctic Skuas arrive in Australian waters in large numbers in late September, their migration route is not known. Probably they pass rapidly down the continental coast of the west Pacific.

Arctic Skuas certainly undertake extensive overland migrations. Birds from north USSR arrive in the Persian Gulf and coasts of Arabia (Bailey 1966) and probably continue from there to winter off Australia or South Africa (Fig. 24). A bird ringed in Finland was recovered in Egypt, suggesting that it moved overland through Europe rather than migrating along the coast (Hilden 1971). It seems probable that some Canadian birds will also migrate overland from their breeding areas although this is less well known.

Most Arctic Skuas winter along the southern continental coasts of South Africa, southern South America and southern (temperate) Australasia (Fig. 24). Few Arctic Skuas are to be seen at distances of more than 50 km from coasts, and during winter they feed extensively by kleptoparasitism; robbing wintering terns and Sabine's Gulls that have also moved down from the Northern Hemisphere, and, in addition, robbing native breeding terns and small gulls.

Arctic Skuas reach these wintering areas in large numbers in September or October and remain until April. Some immature birds stay in the wintering areas all year round. During winter, Arctic Skuas may establish small home ranges in which they stay associated with locally resident gulls and terns. Barton (1982) believed that Arctic Skua numbers in local sedentary groups were limited in a territorial sort of way, since when he removed a locally resident Arctic Skua from a group of six wintering in a particular bay, its place was quickly taken by a new bird so that the local sedentary population remained at six.

Certainly, many Arctic Skuas are nomadic during the winter, following flocks of wintering terns. At one site in Cape Town, from November through to January the numbers of Arctic Skuas robbing terns, Hartlaub's and Sabine's Gulls fluctuated on a day-to-day basis between one and six individuals, with the numbers of skuas present correlating closely with the numbers of terns present. As terns moved by, the skuas followed them (B. L. Furness 1983).

Spring migration back to the breeding areas occurs in March, April and May. By April large numbers of Arctic Skuas are arriving in North Atlantic coastal

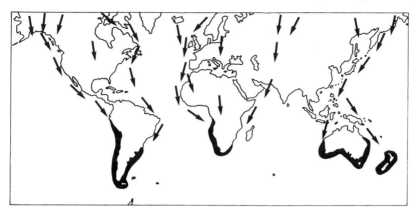

Fig. 24   Probable major migration routes and wintering areas of the Arctic Skua.

waters around Britain and off Canada. Early birds arrive at breeding grounds in Finland in mid April, but most reach them in late May (Hilden 1971, Kapanen 1977). Breeding adults begin to arrive in Shetland waters in early April, usually landing at colonies on about the 10–15 April. However, there are a few very early records; between 1968 and 1985 some 20 Arctic Skua sightings in Scottish coastal waters have been reported in March, with three in February and ten in January (Annual Scottish Bird Reports). The larger number in January than in February and the fact that most January records were in the early part of that month, suggest that the January birds are late to migrate south rather than early to return north. The only period when no Arctic Skua has been reported in Scottish coastal waters between 1968 and 1985 is from mid-February to early March (Table 20). Whether birds that remain in northern hemisphere waters through winter until January then move south in February, or whether they die because they try to stay in the north throughout the winter, we do not know. The very few records of Arctic Skuas in the northern hemisphere in February suggest that southward migration may continue until the end of February, when the first northward bound Arctic Skuas start to return.

Although some young immature Arctic Skuas may remain in Southern Hemisphere wintering areas throughout the breeding season, many migrate north to breeding areas, although they tend to move north behind the breeding adults and then migrate southwards again before the end of the breeding season. While in the north, these immature birds may visit their natal breeding colony and establish themselves at club sites, or they may wander extensively through northern waters, visiting other Arctic Skua colonies and also areas where the species does not breed, presumably prospecting for possible breeding areas to colonise. For example, several Arctic Skua chicks ringed in Shetland have been recovered as immatures in summer on the coasts of Greenland.

Pomarine Skua

Although immatures and birds that failed to breed migrate south in July and August, most adults and young pass latitudes 40–60°N in September and October, with the largest numbers recorded in October on the east coast of the USA (Wynne-Edwards 1935, Rankin & Duffey 1948) at Cape Clear, Ireland, and at Cape Griz Nez, France (Sharrock 1967, Oliver & Davenport 1970). This is about three weeks later than the main autumn migration of Long-tailed and Arctic Skuas. Pomarine Skuas apparently migrate predominantly over the waters of the continental shelf, generally but not completely avoiding pelagic regions and avoiding coasts. However, migration overland seems to be common, perhaps even over such long distances as from their Canadian Arctic breeding areas overland to the Gulf of Mexico (Williams 1965). Southward migration through coastal waters tends to be fairly leisurely. Birds feed by killing small seabirds, by scavenging at fishing boats, and by catching marine invertebrates and fish for themselves; and a few remain in the temperate northern latitudes through into midwinter at least. The Annual Scottish Bird Reports for the period 1968–83 give totals of 114 Pomarine Skuas recorded in Scottish waters in November, 22 in December, 13 in January, seven in February, but only one individual in March. However, by April the first northward bound birds are returning, and 15 were recorded in Scottish waters. In May the bulk of the northward migration passes by, though largely too far from the coast to be seen by birdwatchers. Nevertheless, 2,050 Pomarine Skuas have been reported from Scottish coasts in May 1968–83.

Very little is known about Pomarine Skua migration through the Pacific, but it is probably similar to that through the North Atlantic. There is, almost certainly, also an overland migration of Pomarine Skuas from northern USSR to the Arabian Sea where there is a significant wintering population (Bailey 1966). Some Pomarine Skuas may winter in Indonesian waters, but wintering in Australian waters is well established (Serventy *et al* 1971, Barton 1982). Pomarine Skuas arrive in the western Tasman Sea in mid October at about the same time as huge numbers of Wedge-tailed Shearwaters arrive. The Pomarine Skua numbers build up to a peak in February, undergo moult, feed on offal at fishing boats and occasionally make half-hearted attempts to rob other seabirds (Barton 1982). About 40% of the Pomarine Skuas in the Tasman Sea were dark phase, and about 35% were juveniles or immatures. The high proportion of dark phase birds suggests that the frequency of the dark morph must be rather higher than is generally thought in some breeding areas from which these wintering birds are derived. Barton and many other authors record that Pomarine Skuas are often to be found in small groups whereas the other skuas tend to be less social in winter.

Smaller numbers winter around the warm northern parts of New Zealand (Falla *et al* 1967), while King (1967) reports that Pomarine Skuas are common in the seas around the Hawaiian Islands in winter. Rather few Pomarine Skuas are to be found wintering off southern South America or South Africa, areas frequented by large numbers of Arctic (inshore) and Long-tailed Skuas (offshore). However, there is a large wintering population of Pomarine Skuas in the warmer upwelling waters off West Africa, where flocks of dozens of birds may follow ships to scavenge, and large numbers associate with and prey on other seabirds in that upwelling region, particularly phalaropes (Lambert 1971).

Pomarine Skuas also winter further north off South America than Long-tailed and Arctic Skuas and in southernmost coastal areas of North America. Murphy (1936) reported Pomarine Skuas wintering near the Galapagos Islands, while many have also been seen in winter in Panama Bay, the Gulf of Mexico and the Florida Channel. Probable migration routes and major wintering areas are outlined in Figure 25.

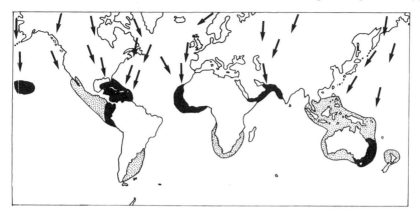

Fig. 25   Probable major migration routes and wintering areas of the Pomarine Skua. Major confirmed wintering areas in black, minor or uncertain wintering areas shaded.

Most Pomarine Skuas reach the breeding grounds in early June (Maher 1974), but small numbers of immatures remain in the winter area throughout the year while some others proceed north late, and remain at sea in the northern North Pacific or North Atlantic all summer, rather than moving onto the breeding grounds, so that the movement patterns are slightly confused by the different behaviour of adults and groups of immatures.

GREAT SKUA MIGRATIONS

Great Skua migrations are particularly well known because observations at sea and from land are supplemented by some 1,500 recoveries of birds ringed as chicks in the northern isles of Scotland and small numbers of recoveries of chicks ringed in Iceland. Unfortunately, most ringing in Iceland has been with soft aluminium rings that wear and corrode so fast that they fall off within 2–5 years. As a result, the movements of only the immature Icelandic Great Skuas can be examined. In Britain, Great Skuas have been ringed with hard alloy rings since about 1962, so that there are some 20–25 year old birds nesting in Shetland that were ringed as chicks and their rings are still completely legible. The Great Skua is Britain's most thoroughly ringed seabird, since about one third to one half of all Great Skua chicks fledged in Shetland have been ringed each year since 1962 and, as a consequence of this effort, nearly one third of those breeding on Foula are ringed and of known age. Most of this ringing effort has been due to the long-term programme of seabird ringing established by The Brathay Trust, and has been possible only because of the large numbers of volunteers who have assisted each year with searching for chicks. This sustained effort has already paid dividends by providing information on the movements of different age groups of Great Skuas and the age of return and first breeding plus annual survival rates (Furness 1978), but it has also indicated that their migration routes have changed slightly over the years, and recovery rates have fluctuated year to year. It also provides a unique, and as yet largely unexploited, opportunity to study a large colony of breeding adults of known ages from three to nearly thirty years old.

Ringing recoveries show that the migrations of Great Skuas differ between Icelandic and Scottish populations, and differ in timing and extent between age-classes up to breeding age. Biases in the recovery data make it very difficult to give quantitative statements about their migrations. For example, virtually every Great Skua recovered in Greenland has been shot or trapped in midsummer, whereas most recovered in England have been found dead during autumn migration. Although there are almost as many recoveries from Greenland as there are from England, it would be wrong to conclude that Great Skuas are common in Greenland. Probably a high proportion of those that do get there are shot and so are likely to be reported. Recoveries of ringed birds can be very interesting, and illuminating if considered carefully, but can be misleading if listed uncritically. The following are computer printouts of some selected Great Skua ring recovery details for birds ringed as chicks at Foula, Shetland. All were ringed in late June or early July, although ringing dates are not listed below:

Ring no.	Finding date	Finding location	Finding details
HW79576	23 June 1984	Fair Isle, Scotland	Found shot
HW29763	30 Oct 1984	Sidmouth, England	Oiled
HW44716	1 Feb 1977	Oran, Algeria	Exhausted on beach
HW46013	16 Aug 1983	Al Hoceina, Morocco	Exhausted on boat
HW46324	25 Sept 1980	Valletta, Malta	Caught in fishing net
HW44929	27 Oct 1980	Yamal-Menets, USSR	Shot
HW99819	17 Sept 1983	Zurich, Switzerland	Dead in lake
HW92279	21 Dec 1983	Oviedo, Spain	Caught on fish hook
HW60074	14 Dec 1977	Santo da Serra, Madeira	Killed by car
HW60719	16 Feb 1978	Demerara, Guyana	Caught by hand
HW62922	20 Aug 1977	Newfoundland, Canada	Found dead
HW80246	16 Jan 1983	Ile D'Oleron, France	Dead, nylon round foot
HW60871	1 Jul 1983	Scoresbysund, Greenland	Shot
HW69106	15 Jul 1979	Julianehab, Greenland	Shot
HW62614	16 Sept 1976	Whitby, England	Hit overhead wires
HW69527	18 Oct 1977	Achnasheen, Scotland	Killed by Peregrine
HW61816	12 June 1982	Greenland Sea 80N10W	Shot over Arctic icecap

It is clear from ringing recoveries that very few British Great Skuas visit North American coasts. Out of 1,500 recoveries, only three are from North America, and one of these was shot by a team of American research biologists collecting seabird specimens on the Grand Banks. By contrast, nearly half of the recoveries of Great Skuas ringed as chicks in Iceland and recovered away from Iceland were reported from North America, while about half of the Icelandic recoveries were from western Europe. It seems that Icelandic Great Skuas migrate either southwest to the North American coast or southeast to the European coast, while virtually all British Great Skuas migrate south down the coast of Europe. Wynne-Edwards (1935) found Great Skuas much more common over the continental shelf waters of west Europe than off the coasts of North America, and found relatively few of them far out from land. Others have confirmed this pattern, so it seems that Great Skuas' migrations, like those of Pomarine Skuas, tend to be concentrated in the zone from one or two to twenty or thirty kilometres from the coast.

Southward movement of Great Skuas from breeding areas starts as early as

July, with immature birds departing first. They are followed in August by failed breeders and the first fledglings. Most chicks and adults have left by the end of September, although a few chicks hatched from late replacement clutches may grow very slowly and not fledge until October.

The movement to winter areas is generally slow, with birds feeding at suitable coastal or offshore sites on the way. Great Skuas will often scavenge at fishing boats a few kilometres from the coast in autumn. One fisherman based in Sunderland sent me dozens of colour slides of colour ringed Great Skuas he had photographed from his boat, drawing them close in by throwing offal when they appeared, yet seawatchers on the coast of Northumberland and Durham recorded only a fraction of the number of Great Skuas he saw, and never to my knowledge got close enough views to read colour ring combinations, because of the bird's aversion to coasts during migration.

Ringing recoveries show that some chicks must pass rapidly south. A few have been recovered over 3,000 km from Foula by the end of August in the year in which they hatched, but others may be recovered in Shetland as late as December. Most recoveries of juveniles occur in September or October, and in some years 'wrecks' occur, when large numbers are driven over the coast of Europe by bad weather and may be recovered far into central Europe. One particularly poignant recovery I received was of a young Great Skua that was rescued, exhausted and emaciated, from the central reservation of a motorway in West Germany in October of its first year, kept in captivity and fed for about two weeks until it had regained its strength and then released again, only to be found dead on the shore of Lake Constance two weeks later. Probably these birds have little chance of obtaining food once they have strayed far inland, and rapidly weaken as they deplete their body reserves and tissues, as suggested by another inland recovery of a young Great Skua reported as 'shot while attacking chickens' in the yard of a farmhouse in West Germany.

About a quarter of all of the recoveries of ringed juvenile Great Skuas are reported as birds 'found exhausted', whereas rather less than 10% of adults fall into this finding category. Similarly, adults and immatures more than one year old are very rarely recovered far inland. The inexperienced juveniles are very much more susceptible to being 'wrecked' in autumn (Furness 1978). Juveniles are also more susceptible to being shot than are adults in the same region, but the tendency for birds of different ages to visit different areas can obscure this trend. In Britain, most recoveries are reported as 'found dead', partly because shooting Great Skuas without a license is illegal so that shot birds are unlikely to be reported as such, but shooting is very common in Greenland, where almost all recoveries are of birds between two and five years old. In Scandinavia, Belgium, France and Iberia, Great Skuas are often reported as caught or shot, and this is particularly true of juveniles. In Britain, however, juveniles are very rarely recovered caught in nets or on fishing lines, although this occasionally happens to adults. In general, juvenile seabirds are more likely to tangle in nets than are adults, because they lack experience in avoiding such dangers. In Shags, for example, only juveniles drown in lobster pots in large numbers (Galbraith, Russell & Furness 1981). The lack of juvenile Great Skuas becoming tangled in nets in Britain in autumn can only mean that they do not feed much on their way south, whereas adults linger in British waters for much longer and so are exposed to hazards presented by nets.

Southward movement by juvenile Great Skuas seems to continue throughout the winter, with the greatest proportion of southerly recoveries of ringed birds occurring as late as March. By this time young birds have spread over the Atlantic coast of Europe and northern Africa from 50°N to the equator, with many remaining in these wintering latitudes through the first summer until the next winter (Fig. 26a). A small proportion of first-year birds moves northwards towards the end of their first year of life, in April to August, and may be recovered in the North Sea or west of Britain. However, the bulk of recoveries of birds aged 12–15 months old occurs south of latitude 50°N. Most of the recoveries of birds 16 to 19 months old (mainly 'second-winter' birds) are from Iberian Atlantic waters, but a few occur further afield, from Malta to the USA, from the North Sea to Morocco, Brazil and Guyana. This seems to be the age at which Shetland Great Skuas are most widely dispersed. During their second summer, a few recoveries occur in the waters around Britain, but others in higher latitudes, particularly around Greenland, Iceland and the Faeroes but also in Norway, Spitsbergen and north USSR (Fig. 26b). Winter recoveries show that Great Skuas aged two to two and a half years old return to Iberian waters and regions nearby, but in their third summer most again move back to breeding areas in northern Britain or to higher latitudes. However, some two-year-olds stay in the wintering areas all summer while others move far north. Winter recoveries of three year olds show that only part of the population at this age moves down to Iberia and neighbouring regions,

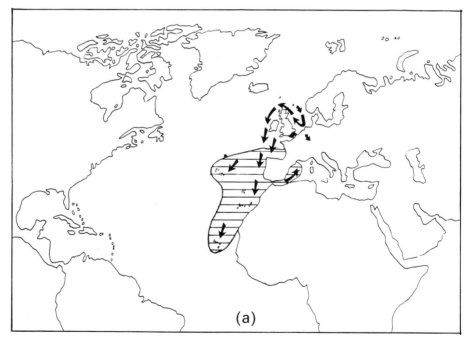

(a)

Fig. 26   Major migration routes and distributions of Great Skuas. (a) Shetland fledglings to first winter (6 months); winter range of first year birds hatched. (b) Shetland second winter (18 months) (horizontal hatching) to second summer (24 months) (vertical hatching). (c) Iceland and Shetland adults; major winter areas in black, solid arrows represent main migration route of Icelandic birds, open arrows Shetland birds.

while some remain considerably closer to the breeding areas, wintering off southern Britain and France. Four year olds show much the same patterns of movement as three year olds, but older age classes are less far-ranging. As they reach breeding

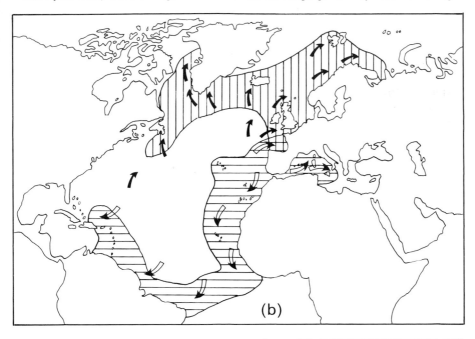

(b)

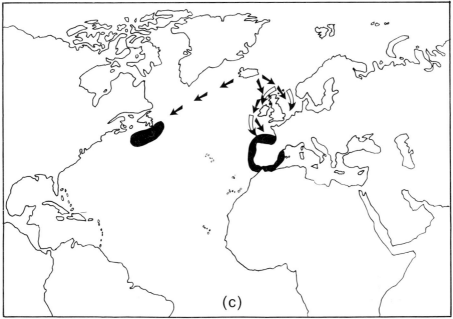

(c)

age their wanderings become much restricted. Older Great Skuas no longer visit high latitudes in summer, and generally winter between British and Iberian coastal waters (Fig. 26c). Thus, almost all of those that remain in British waters in winter are adults, but some adults move as far as western Mediterranean waters to spend the winter. Great Skuas arrive in western Mediterranean waters in October and stay until March or early April, during which period they feed mainly at fishing boats, particularly off the Catalan coast (Martinez-Vilalta *et al* 1984), and careful observations of the species from a small boat suggest that most of the birds that winter in the Mediterranean are in adult rather than juvenile plumage (Carboneras in litt.), although the identification of Great Skua age classes by plumage is rather difficult.

SOUTHERN LARGE SKUAS

Up until 1977 it was thought that Chilean Skuas, Falkland Skuas and Brown Skuas could be found as rare migrants as far north as the coast of Washington and British Columbia, and that South Polar Skuas wintered in the pack ice of the Southern Ocean (e.g. Murphy 1936, Eklund 1961). However, a careful and thorough examination of specimens in museums collected from northern wintering areas and on passage showed that this was completely erroneous (Devillers 1977). It has become necessary to delete Chilean, Falkland and Brown Skua from the list of birds recorded in North America, and to add South Polar Skua to that list instead. Details of the migration routes and wintering areas of all southern great skuas still remain unclear, but Devillers' excellent research and an astonishing ringing recovery from Greenland led to a considerable interest among seabird enthusiasts in documenting the wintering distribution of South Polar Skuas in northern waters.

South Polar Skua
We now know that the South Polar Skua is a long-distance transequatorial migrant, occasionally reaching as far north as Greenland in the North Atlantic, and regularly wintering from off Japan to British Columbia in the North Pacific. Devillers (1977) examined skuas in the Copenhagen University Zoological Museum. One specimen, which had been shot in Greenland at Disko Bay in mid July 1902, was recorded in the museum records as a juvenile Great Skua, but Devillers recognised this to be a light phase South Polar Skua, the first ever recorded in the North Atlantic. This record was included in passing in Devillers' paper on skuas of the Pacific coast of North America, and might well have been overlooked, or passed off as a freak record, but for the added impetus given by a recovery of a ringed South Polar Skua. This bird had been ringed as a chick in January 1975 near Anvers Island, Antarctic Peninsula, and was shot by an Eskimo in Godhabsfjord, Greenland, on 31 July 1975, providing the longest journey of any bird ever recorded by ringing. Added publicity about South Polar Skuas visiting the North Atlantic, created by reports of this recovery (Fullager 1976, Salomonsen 1976), led to further field expeditions to seek South Polar Skuas in the North Atlantic in winter.

Veit (1978) visited Georges Bank off Newfoundland on a research vessel for 12 days in June and 14 days in July 1977 to search for South Polar Skuas. He saw some 25 large skuas during the June trip and five in July, feeding around east

European trawlers catching Hake, and identified 8–10 of these as light phase South Polar Skuas. The other 17–20 birds were described by Veit as 'uniformly blackish individuals' with 'a pale wash barely visible on the nape'. Veit considered that these birds, which also appeared to have small bills, were probably dark phase South Polar Skuas rather than Great Skuas. However, on 13 July 1978, in a follow-up trip to Georges Bank, a skua was shot to allow identification in the hand and this turned out to be a Great Skua that I had ringed as a chick on Foula in 1977! Clearly a few one year old Great Skuas remain on the Grand Banks over the northern summer and must mix with 'wintering' South Polar Skuas. Albert Nickerson, the biologist who collected this individual described it as 'quite uniformly dark at a distance'. It would be quite reasonable to expect that most of the South Polar Skuas that migrate into the North Atlantic during the southern winter originate from the relatively small population that breeds on the Antarctic Peninsula and adjacent island groups. Almost all of these birds are dark phase, while pale phase South Polar Skuas breed predominantly in the Ross Sea area, so that Veit's observation of 8–10 pale South Polar Skuas would imply that larger numbers of dark phase South Polar Skuas should also be present. Thus the 15–17 dark birds Veit saw could well have been dark South Polar Skuas. The one year old Great Skua shot on Georges Bank is one of only three from Shetland recovered on the west side of the Atlantic, so perhaps this was rather an exceptional record. Nevertheless, some young Icelandic Great Skuas probably spend the summer there. To find out how many of the birds are Great Skuas and how many are dark South Polar Skuas it will almost certainly be necessary to catch or shoot further specimens from the Grand Banks in June–July.

Because the bulk of the South Polar Skua population breeds in the Ross Sea area, it is logical to expect the species to migrate from there into the Pacific Ocean in larger numbers than occur in the Atlantic. Certainly, the movements of South Polar Skuas in the Pacific are much better known. Birds appear in waters off Japan from May to late July, and can be found off British Columbia and Washington, where they are regularly recorded, in July to October. Off California, they are seen mainly in October. The timings of these records strongly suggest that South Polar Skuas make a clockwise loop migration around the Pacific Ocean (Devillers 1977). In the Antarctic, breeding South Polar Skuas feed mainly on small fish which they catch for themselves (Chapter 7), but Wahl (1977) observed South Polar Skuas off the Washington coast attacking flocks of California Gulls and Sooty Shearwaters and robbing them of food. These birds fed on Pacific Saury, a small shoaling surface-feeding (planktivorous) fish which itself migrates around the Pacific and may be the reason for the apparent loop migration of South Polar Skuas. Most South Polar Skuas recorded in the Pacific are pale phase birds, and this fits in with the fact that the dark phase is common only in the areas of the Antarctic south of the Atlantic Ocean.

Many of the birds collected in waters off Japan or Washington were immatures (Kuroda 1962, Devillers 1977), and it is not clear whether this is due to the greater susceptibility of young birds to mortality factors and to being shot, or whether it implies that adults migrate less far north. It is quite possible that adults tend to winter in more southerly latitudes but, if so, their winter range remains to be confirmed. Perhaps they do indeed winter in the pack ice of the Southern Ocean, as suggested by Eklund (1961) and others. Small numbers occur in the Tasman Sea, where they also chase other seabirds and rob them of food, but the one specimen collected there was also an immature bird (Barton 1982). Very few South

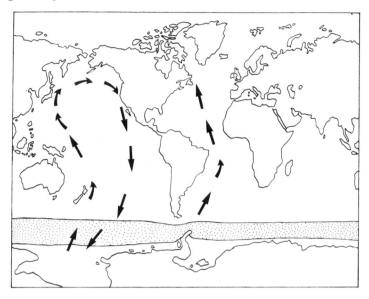

*Fig. 27   Probable migration routes and wintering areas of South Polar Skuas.
Likely wintering area of adults in the subantarctic pack-ice is shown shaded,
although confirmation is required (see text).*

Polar Skuas have been seen off New Zealand, but several have been reported near
the Hawaiian Islands.

South Polar Skuas also migrate into the Indian Ocean, and there are sight
records, collected specimens and ringing recoveries from as far north as India, Sri
Lanka and the Arabian Sea. The migration routes and wintering areas can be
tentatively indicated as in Figure 27.

Chilean Skua

Although several skuas collected off California, Washington and British Columbia have been identified as Chilean Skuas in earlier publications, Devillers
(1977) showed convincingly that these were all South Polar Skuas, and that there
were no acceptable records of Chilean Skuas in North America. The wintering
range of Chilean Skuas is probably around the breeding areas and over the cold
upwelling current off Chile and Peru (Fig. 28).

Tristan, Falkland and Brown Skuas

The wintering range of Tristan Skuas is quite unknown. Certainly, some
individuals remain in the breeding area throughout the year, but some disperse.
They probably remain within the South Atlantic between 35° and 55°S, but would
be almost impossible to identify at sea by plumage characters. Again, the winter
distribution of Falkland Skuas is unknown, but they probably do not migrate
extensively.

In many of their breeding areas, Brown Skuas may also be present throughout
the year. Murphy (1936) reported Brown Skuas present at Kerguelen in all months,

and birds from New Zealand colonies are present in local waters all year round. Brown Skuas from colonies on the Antarctic Peninsula and nearby islands certainly do depart for lower latitudes in winter.

Catharacta skuas are regularly recorded in association with fishing trawlers in offshore waters of South Africa, and occur occasionally as far north as Angola (Lambert 1971). Which of the *Catharacta skua* subspecies these are is uncertain; they are probably most likely to be Tristan Skuas or Brown Skuas.

There is only one record that stands critical scrutiny of any of these three subspecies in the northern hemisphere. A skua collected in Kerala, India, in September 1933 had a tarsus length of 76 mm, and was clearly a Brown Skua (Ali & Ripley 1969). Hudson (1968) reported the recovery, in May 1967, of a skua in the Caribbean that had been ringed as an adult, probably breeding, on Deception Island, South Shetlands, in January 1960, and recaptured and released in March 1961 on the Antarctic Peninsula at a locality where, apparently, only South Polar Skuas breed regularly. This bird was identified as a Brown Skua when ringed by British Antarctic Survey, but since South Polar and Brown Skuas breed in the South Shetlands and this was not fully understood in 1960, an error in identification is quite possible. Since few Brown Skuas ever visit the Antarctic Peninsula but over 1,000 South Polar Skuas breed there, this bird may well have been a dark phase South Polar Skua rather than a Brown Skua. South Polar Skuas are known to migrate into the North Atlantic, and so could easily be recovered in the Caribbean. Of course, odd individuals of any subspecies may get lost and wander

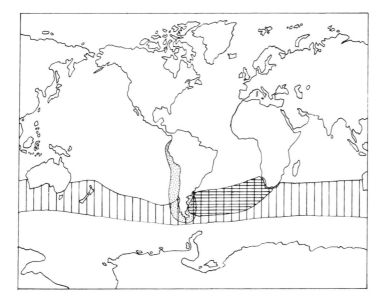

Fig. 28   Probable major wintering areas of Chilean Skuas (dotted), Tristan Skuas and Falkland Skuas (horizontal bars) and Brown Skuas (vertical bars). Note that there are small numbers of records outside these main ranges. One Brown Skua has been obtained in India, a few skuas of uncertain race occur off Namibia.

north, and indeed presumably must have done so to give rise to the Great Skua (Chapter 2).

Brown Skuas are regular winter visitors to the coastal waters of Australia, and are particularly numerous at Fremantle where up to 50 at a time can be seen (Serventy *et al* 1971). Barton (1982) noted that Brown Skuas arrived in the Tasman Sea with an uncanny regularity at the time when Pomarine Skuas left. He saw Brown Skuas from early May through to November, normally sighting them singly, about once every four hours of daylight observation. They regularly scavenged on offal and sometimes plunge-dived for food scraps.

The likely migrations and wintering ranges of Tristan, Falkland and Brown Skuas are indicated in Figure 28.

TIMING OF MIGRATION, MOULT AND BREEDING

Breeding, migration and moult are three of the most energy expensive activities of birds, and they are usually separated in time in order to avoid excessive energy loss. Most birds that are long-distance migrants avoid moulting during the migration period since a moulting migrant would pay a penalty in terms of increased energy needs to sustain both activities at once, and might also suffer inefficiencies in terms of flight capability if feathers were being replaced during migration. Many large seabirds that spend several months in breeding spread part of their moult over the latter part of incubation, when energy costs of breeding are relatively low, and then complete moult after chick rearing has finished. Herring Gulls, for example, moult two or three small inner primaries during incubation but complete the bulk of the moult after they have fledged their young.

Small skuas do not moult while they are breeding, presumably because the short Arctic summer requires them to get through their breeding as rapidly as possible. After breeding, they migrate south, and then undergo moult in the wintering area. The moult is spread through the winter, so that renewal of flight feathers is completed shortly before the northward migration back to the breeding areas.

Among large skuas, South Polar and Great Skuas show the most extensive migrations. Both start to moult only after they have moved to their wintering areas. As a result of confining moult to the wintering period, South Polar Skuas grow flight feathers much faster than most gulls or other large skuas do. Salomonsen (1976) noted that South Polar Skuas may grow three primaries at once, resulting in a noticeable gap in the extended wing, whereas Great Skuas do not normally grow more than two primaries at a time. Veit (1978) also reported that the South Polar Skuas he saw on Georges Bank were experiencing heavy moult of flight feathers and coverts.

Moult patterns of Brown, Falkland and Tristan Skuas are not well known, but Swales (1965) reported that Tristan Skuas begin primary moult when their chicks are about to fledge, which they presumably can do only because they do not undergo a rapid long-distance migration such as that of the South Polar Skua.

CHAPTER 5

Reversed sexual size dimorphism

Normal sexual size dimorphism in higher vertebrates is commonly explained as a result of sexual selection favouring larger males in contests over mates (Darwin 1871). Reversed sexual size dimorphism, i.e. with the female being the larger sex, has for a long time attracted the interest of evolutionary ecologists. Over the years, a large number of hypotheses have been put forward to explain the reversed sexual size dimorphism in birds of prey. A widely accepted hypothesis applicable to these birds has not yet been found.

Widen (1984)

Skuas, like frigatebirds and almost all terrestrial birds of prey, show reversed sexual size dimorphism. Females are larger than males in most measurements and in weight. In order to understand why this might be, it may help to consider the normal situation in other kinds of birds and how it arises and is maintained. We can then consider the particular characteristics of skuas, frigatebirds and birds of prey that result in their showing the opposite of the normal pattern.

EVOLUTION THROUGH SELECTION FOR BODY SIZE

Evolutionary Biology tells us that Natural Selection will favour the size of bird best adapted to its local environment. Larger and smaller individuals will, on average, pass on fewer copies of their genes than those of the optimal size. This is known as 'Stabilizing Selection' because it results in the elimination of size extremes from the population and keeps the average size of members of the population the same from generation to generation.

Indeed, most adults in a bird population within a small geographical area are very similar in size to all the others of the same sex, and this suggests that Stabilising Selection does occur with respect to body size in birds. However, in most species of birds, males are slightly larger than females, and this may arise for one of two reasons. Males may differ from females of the same species in the niches that they occupy. This difference could reduce competition between the sexes for food, so resulting in the optimal size of males and females differing and allowing them to exploit distinct and separate feeding niches. This in itself would not inevitably lead to males being larger than females. If separation of the ecological niches of the sexes was the sole reason for sexual dimorphism in body size then it would be equally likely that males would be smaller than females to achieve the same result. We might expect that half the world's birds would have males larger than the females and half have males smaller than their females. Of course, since species that are closely related are derived from a common ancestor, we would expect the difference to be consistent between the sexes of related bird species. All skuas could have females larger than the males because the ancestral stock from which they all evolved was like this. The problem here is that the skuas' closest relatives, the gulls, show the opposite pattern. In virtually all gull species the males are larger than the females. The same is true of more distantly related groups within the suborder *Lari*: the terns and skimmers, and of the closest related suborders, the auks and waders. Only in a few particular cases, such as the phalaropes, are females larger than males. This suggests that as skuas separated from gulls the difference in size between males and females must have been reversed by selective pressures arising from the way of life of the skua. Clearly reversed sexual size dimorphism has arisen independently in frigatebirds, in skuas, in owls, and in the different families of birds of prey. This indicates that some other force is acting, which is related to the particular way of life of these birds.

Charles Darwin (1871) argued that male birds (and other animals) are normally larger than their females due to a process he first described, and termed 'Sexual Selection'. Darwin argued that males compete for females and if so, larger males are likely to win when in competition with smaller males. Sexual Selection may favour the largest males, although Natural Selection would favour males of the same size as the average female. Then we could think of Sexual Selection as a force causing male birds to be larger than the ideal size for the species in terms of survival. Larger males would gain in relative fitness through greater access to females and hence have a higher reproductive output. They may, for example, be better able than smaller males to establish and defend a territory. This increased reproductive opportunity will, however, be at the cost of a reduction in survival through being larger than the ideal size for aspects of their biology not related to reproduction.

Thus, Sexual Selection may lead to the general tendency for males to be larger than females. Once a size difference has arisen due to Sexual Selection, it may be checked from further increasing by Natural Selection. The greater the discrepancy between the actual size of males and the optimal size for survival, the stronger Sexual Selection will need to be to maintain the size differential between the sexes.

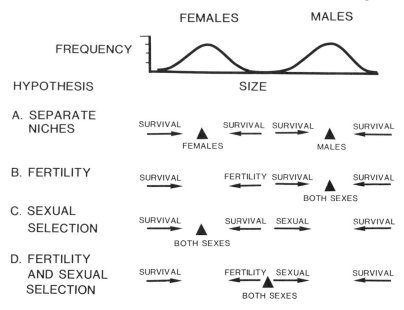

Fig. 29   Different hypotheses for the evolution of sexual size dimorphism (from Price 1984). The optimal body sizes for survival are shown by the vertical arrows. Horizontal arrows indicate the direction of selection pressures (see text).

However, there are other arguments for size differences that are completely different from this. In several species, smaller females breed earlier in the season than larger females, and as a consequence of a seasonal decline in breeding success, smaller females tend to raise more offspring. If the sexes differ in their feeding niches, as suggested earlier, then the optimal size of the sexes may differ. Niche separation between the sexes could occur in winter if food is short then, or throughout the year. Alternatively, the sexes may shift their feeding niches during the breeding season only, in order to exploit a wider prey spectrum and so provide more food for the young. In his thorough and detailed study of seabirds in arctic USSR, Belopolskii (1961) raised yet another argument, that size dimorphism tends to be correlated with the degree of differentiation of the breeding roles between the sexes. Auks, where both sexes contribute similarly to the breeding effort, show minimal size dimorphism. Gulls, where the sexes show a small degree of role specialisation, show a small amount of sexual size-dimorphism. The greatest difference in sex roles in the arctic seabird community is found in the Eider, which also shows the greatest sexual size-dimorphism. These different theories can be illustrated graphically as in Figure 29.

So much for theories. Can we test between them? Are male birds in fact generally bigger than they ought to be for survival because of strong Sexual Selection? Do males occupy a different niche, for which larger body size is adaptive? Are females smaller than they ought to be for survival because of strong selection for increased breeding success of small females? To answer these questions we would need to know how survival rates of male and female birds vary with body size and how the reproductive success of each sex is affected by body size. Such data are not easily obtained.

By studying Darwin's Medium Ground Finch in the Galapagos, Price (1984) showed that males of this species averaged 5% larger in body weight and 3 to 4% larger in several linear measurements, but showed no detectable differences of importance in their diets or feeding behaviour. However, small females bred at a younger age than large females, creating strong selection for small body size, while small males were less likely to obtain mates than were large males, creating sexual selection for large male size.

By analysing ring recovery data for Herring Gulls which were measured at ringing, it has been possible to show that annual mortality rates of the smallest and largest males and females are higher than mortality rates of average sized members of each sex (Monaghan & Metcalfe 1986). Thus, although male Herring Gulls are about 18% larger than females in mean body weight, stabilising selection is acting with respect to body size (as indicated by head and bill length) within each sex. Optimal body size for survival appears to differ between the sexes. Unfortunately, we do not know whether body size influences reproductive success in Herring Gulls. Nor is it clear what the disadvantages of unusually small or large size are that cause the size-related mortality differences. During feeding on refuse tips, larger Herring Gulls achieve a greater feeding success than smaller ones, so the high mortality of the largest males is rather unexpected. Monaghan & Metcalfe (1986) suggest that it might be due to the fact that the largest birds also need the most food, or to the poorer manoeuvrability of the largest birds.

SIZE DIMORPHISM IN SKUAS

In every skua species, females average heavier than males during the breeding season, which is the only time of year for which data are available. Female Great Skuas weigh, on average, 11% more than males. The weight difference in favour of females is also 11% for Tristan Skuas and South Polar Skuas, 12% for Long-tailed Skuas, 14% for Pomarine Skuas and 16.5% for Arctic Skuas (Table 3). Only two male and two female Chilean Skua weights have been published and both females weighed more than both males, but the degree of the dimorphism cannot be estimated from such a small sample. Similarly, female Brown Skuas are heavier than males, but small sample numbers for this species preclude more detailed analysis. The percentage weight difference between the sexes seems to be quite similar in all the skua taxa, perhaps being most pronounced in the Arctic Skua. When compared with the differences in weight between the sexes of gulls (Fig. 30) it is clear that the extent of the sexual dimorphism is very similar, although in opposite directions between gulls and skuas.

Differences in body weight between the sexes could be due to differences in the amounts of fat and protein reserves carried, although it seems unlikely that such a large difference in reserves would occur. However, it can be confirmed that the dimorphism is more to do with size differences than with amounts of energy reserves carried. Females of all skua taxa are larger than males in several linear body measurements. In terms of wing length, females exceed males on average by 0.2% in Chilean Skuas, 1.4% in South Polar Skuas, 1.3% in Long-tailed Skuas, 1.8% in Arctic Skuas, 2.2% in Falkland Skuas, 2.9% in Brown Skuas, 2.7% in Great Skuas, 2.7% in Tristan Skuas and 3.0% in Pomarine Skuas (Table 4).

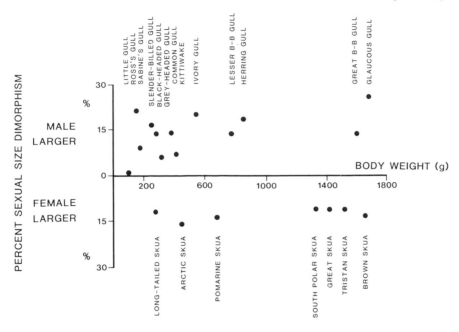

Fig. 30   Sex dimorphism in the weights of gulls and skuas (difference in mean weight of the two sexes as a percentage of the mean for the two sexes) plotted against body weight (mean for the two sexes).

These percentage differences are much less than the differences in weight, but this is to be expected since weight is proportional to the cube of linear dimensions. A weight difference of 11–17% should correspond to linear differences of about 2.2–2.4%, values closely in agreement with the recorded sex-differences in wing length. As with weight, the degree of sexual dimorphism of wing length is virtually the same in gulls and skuas, although in opposite directions (Fig. 31).

Tarsus length is also generally greater in female skuas (Table 5) although the percentage difference is small in most species. Bill length is greater in females in the Arctic, Pomarine and South Polar Skua, but the sex difference is negligible in Great Skuas and Brown Skuas, while bill length is greater on average, in male than in female Long-tailed Skuas and Tristan Skuas, although the difference is so small that it could not be used with any confidence to assess the sex of individual birds (Table 6).

Tail length in skuas shows very little difference between the sexes, perhaps with a slight tendency for males to have longer tails than females in most species (Table 7). In adults of the three species of *Stercorarius* skuas, the length of the elongated central tail feather tips projecting beyond the other tail feathers is longer in males than in females (Table 8). Although none of these differences in tail length is statistically significant in isolation, the consistent trend demonstrates that this is indeed a real difference, but one that is so slight and overwhelmed by individual variation that it is probably of no biological importance. In the Long-tailed Skua

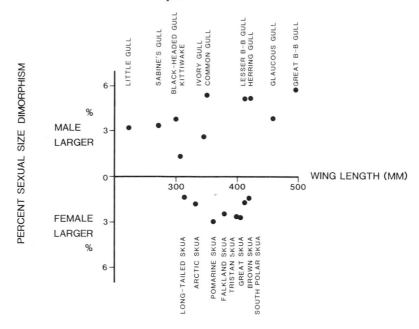

Fig. 31   Sex dimorphism in the wing lengths of gulls and skuas (difference in mean wing lengths of the two sexes as a percentage of the mean for the two sexes) plotted against wing length (mean for the two sexes).

the male tail-tips average 3–4 mm longer than in females, a difference of 2% of tail-tip length. In the Pomarine Skua the male's tail-tips average 3 mm longer (3%) and in the Arctic Skua male tail-tips are 4.5 mm longer (5.6%) than those of the females. While females are generally larger than males, their tail and tail tips are shorter, and so the ratio between lengths of body parts may differ between the sexes. Thus the shapes of males and females differ.

EXPLANATIONS FOR REVERSED SEXUAL SIZE DIMORPHISM

There is a plethora of hypotheses to explain why females are larger than males in birds of prey, and some of these could apply to the skuas and frigatebirds too. These ideas are discussed below. Since most of the ideas have been derived from observed sexual dimorphisms in birds of prey, and it is therefore inappropriate to test the ideas with the same data from which they were derived, I have tried to examine how the patterns of sexual dimorphism in skuas fit with the predictions of the different hypotheses.

Dimorphism in relation to prey type

The fact that the female is larger than the male is apparently connected with a raptorial lifestyle, since it occurs in owls, birds of prey of four quite different families, frigatebirds and skuas, having arisen independently in each of these

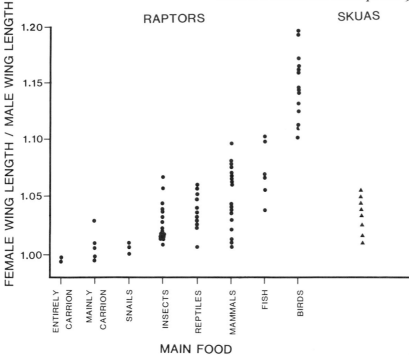

Fig. 32 Sexual size-dimorphism in birds of prey and skuas in relation to diet. Each data point for birds of prey represents one species which feeds almost exclusively on one prey type. Data from Newton (1979). Each data point for skuas represents one species, taking the weighted mean difference in wing lengths from Table 4. The skuas are, in order of increasing sexual dimorphism, South Polar, Long-tailed, Brown, Arctic, Falkland, Great, Pomarine and Tristan.

groups by parallel evolution. Furthermore, the degree of size difference between the sexes is clearly related to the prey taken. Raptors that feed on birds show the greatest sex-dimorphism in body size, while carrion-feeders show virtually no dimorphism in size. This relationship with prey has been discussed in some detail (Newton 1979, 1986) and is not disputed, although the reason for the relationship is not clear.

If we put skuas onto the same graph as constructed by Ian Newton for birds of prey specialising on particular diets, we can see that skuas show less size dimorphism (as indicated by wing lengths) than bird-eating raptors, and slightly less size dimorphism than many of the mammal-eating raptors (Fig. 32). Since skuas feed to a large extent on small mammals and birds, and by kleptoparasitism, the degree of sexual size dimorphism is, perhaps, rather less than we might have expected from the trends seen in raptors.

Sexual selection for aerial agility in territorial defence
The males of many birds of prey advertise territorial ownership and attract females by aerial displays. Smaller birds are more agile in flight than larger birds.

They can accelerate faster, climb faster, roll faster and turn through a smaller radius. These advantages for smaller males could lead to sexual selection by female choice for more agile partners, with the ability to display-flight more impressively; or they could enable smaller males to win territories in aerial combat with larger, and therefore less agile, males. Rather than sexual selection favouring big strong males that can win combats on the ground, it favours small and agile males that can out-manoeuvre and out-climb their opponent in aerial combat (Widen 1984). This hypothesis would imply that sexual selection is the main reason for differences in body size between the sexes, whether males are larger or smaller than females, according to the way in which they defend the territory and display for mates.

Could reversed sexual size dimorphism in skuas also be explained by sexual selection for small, agile, males? In the *Stercorarius* skuas, aerial displays and territorial conflicts are very common, and appear to be more important than displays that are ground based (Chapter 6). In the *Catharacta* skuas there are far fewer aerial displays and most territorial and sexual interactions take place on the ground. Nevertheless, large skuas do show a stiff-wing display flight, and in defending the territory, males will divebomb an intruding conspecific that has landed on the ground and will chase the intruder in the air (Chapter 6). Although both sexes will participate in defending the territory, males play the major part in this, and so selection pressures for aerial agility will be stronger for males. This is likely to be particularly so for the *Stercorarius* species. Thus we might expect the small skuas to show a greater degree of dimorphism. The data are consistent with this. The percentage difference in weight between the sexes is greatest in the Arctic Skua (16.5%), Pomarine Skua (14%), and Long-tailed Skua (13%), and least in the Great Skua, Tristan Skua and South Polar Skua (11%). Statistically, the dimorphism is more pronounced in *Stercorarius* than it is in *Catharacta*, and this fits the argument given above rather well. However, sexual dimorphism in skuas is much less in terms of wing lengths than it is in body weight, and the two parameters are not closely correlated with each other. According to the theory of flight, aerial agility would be favoured by short, rounded and broad wings, yet male *Stercorarius* skuas have wings that appear to be very similar in shape and size to those of females. Nevertheless, aerial agility would also be favoured by a reduced wing loading in males. The wing loading is the weight of the bird divided by the area of the wings, and the lower body weight of male skuas taken together with their wing size being only slightly less than that of females, means that male skuas should indeed have a lower wing loading, and so a greater power of acceleration and manoeuvrability.

Sexual selection for small males where the male advertises and defends the territory by aerial display also fits the observed dimorphisms in birds of prey very well (Widen 1984). In general, species that feed on birds and mammals are most strongly territorial and have extensive aerial displays, and so it is difficult to tell whether dimorphism increases as a consequence of prey type or as a consequence of territoriality and display, which is a function of prey type. Widen argued that if food differentiation between the sexes were a major factor in the evolution of reversed sexual size dimorphism then the feet of birds of prey should show a particularly high degree of sexual dimorphism. In fact, tarsus length is less dimorphic in 38 out of 49 species of North American birds of prey than are other variables. Furthermore, Widen argued, several studies have shown very little difference in the prey of male and female hawks (although other studies have!). An interesting species in this situation is Eleonora's Falcon, which feeds on birds migrating south over the Mediterranean during its autumn breeding season. Unlike other birds of prey that specialise on bird prey it is only slightly size-dimorphic, but it is also exceptional as a predator of birds in that it breeds in colonies rather than territorially. Thus it fits the territorial defence hypothesis well. One problem with this hypothesis is that, although it can account for the observed degree of reverse sexual size dimorphism in birds of prey and skuas, it does not predict the significant reversed sexual size dimorphism that occurs in owls, which do not seem to use aerial combat for territorial defence.

Some other hypotheses

Several reasons for the link between dimorphism and diet have been put forward, that could provide alternatives to the aerial territorial defence hypothesis outlined above. The most convincing alternative has to do with competition and the breadth of feeding niches (Newton 1979). Few predators exploit birds or mammals as prey, while many species feed on insects or carrion. With less interspecific competition among predators on birds or mammals, there is more scope for males and females to partition food between them according to size. While this explanation accounts for the size dimorphism, it does not explain why males should be the smaller sex.

In birds of prey, the male does the hunting for the pair and chicks while the female remains close to the nest and does most of the guarding. It has been argued that small size allows the male to prey on smaller species, which are more abundant than larger species. Another suggestion is that it is advantageous for the male to be small to reduce energy expenditure by the pair, since he is more active than the female during the breeding season. Another proposed explanation is that larger female size promotes successful pair formation, allowing the female to hold her own against the aggressive, but smaller, male. Presumably the argument here is that male hormones lead to male birds being more aggressive than females, and that birds of prey are particularly aggressive because of their mode of feeding, so that larger female size is particularly important in birds of prey. This argument appears to have little of substance to support it. Another suggestion is that larger female size increases the likelihood that the female will be able to defend the young against nest predators while the male is absent, foraging (Storer 1966).

Andersson & Norberg (1981) produced a detailed and careful review of many of these arguments, and argued that the larger size of the female, allowing her better prospects of defending the young, had probably been the initial selective force for reversed size dimorphism in predatory birds, and that this was brought about because the female has to rely on the male to supply her with food while she forms eggs. While carrying eggs she would risk their damage if she hunted for herself, and their weight would reduce her hunting efficiency anyway. Once the female has taken the role of defender of the nest and left the male to provision the family, then further specialisation of the sexes into distinct breeding roles seems inevitable.

Do skuas fit with or refute these various arguments? To decide, we need to consider the extent to which the sexes differ in diets and in breeding roles.

SEX DIMORPHISM IN DIETS OF SKUAS

The only extensive comparison of the diets of male and female skuas was performed by Belopolskii (1961), who shot very large numbers of Arctic Skuas and examined their stomach contents. This procedure suffers from several difficulties and biases, one of the most serious of which is that skuas frequently regurgitate food to the mate and feed together on this regurgitate. Stomach contents of one bird may be a mixture of food it has obtained itself and food it has been given by its mate. This behaviour will tend to reduce the apparent differences in diet between the sexes.

Belopolskii found that males contained a higher proportion of fish in their stomachs, and females contained more invertebrates, berries, birds and mammals (Table 21). He found that this trend in diet was consistent from place to place, and was most obvious over short periods of time, since both sexes changed diet as seasonal abundance of foods altered. Female Arctic Skuas, for example, were much more likely than males to take bird eggs from nests within their territory. The differences observed by Belopolskii imply that, during the breeding season, female Arctic Skuas spend more time feeding within the territory, while males mostly feed at sea. Nevertheless, the differences in stomach contents between the sexes that Belopolskii demonstrated were small, and, even allowing for the fact that males give food to females, it would be difficult to argue that the two sexes occupy significantly different feeding niches during the breeding season.

In Long-tailed Skuas breeding in North East Greenland, the males took more marine foods than the females and less insects, but the differences in diet were slight, with both sexes feeding predominantly on lemmings, berries and insects within their territory (de Korte 1986). Two other studies of Long-tailed Skua breeding ecology (Andersson 1971, Taylor 1974) described more pronounced dimorphism in feeding. Males predominantly fed on rodents and females took insects. However, these statements were based largely on direct field observations rather than on quantitative study of stomach contents.

I was unable to see any clear differences in feeding habits of male and female Great Skuas on Foula, as both sexes fed almost exclusively on Sandeels and discarded fish from trawlers, and both sexes would scavenge on a wide variety of animal carcasses and occasionally prey on seabirds and other animals. Certainly, diets of the sexes differed much less on Foula than Great Skua diets differed between colonies, and even over a period of years on Foula!

Differences in diets and feeding habits of the sexes in these studies were negligible or slight, and probably result more from differences in the breeding time allocation of the sexes than from differences in their feeding capabilities due to size differences. Whether skuas show differences in diet between the sexes outside of the breeding season is quite unknown, but in view of the close similarity in diet while breeding, it seems most unlikely that sexual size dimorphism in skuas has a noticeable influence on their diets or feeding behaviour at any time of year. This conclusion should lead us to dismiss the idea, at least for skuas, that size dimorphism allows the sexes to exploit different feeding niches.

SEX DIMORPHISM IN BREEDING ROLES OF SKUAS

Although there is little evidence for differences in feeding niches between the sexes of skuas, there are very pronounced and dramatic differences in the roles of the sexes during breeding. As one might expect, the patterns vary to some extent between studies, but the general pattern is one of the female skua remaining close to the nest and defending the eggs and chicks throughout most of the breeding season, and being provisioned by the male.

Incubation

In every skua population that has been studied, males and females take turns at incubation. According to Maher (1974) all three species of small skuas in Alaska 'share incubation duties equally', but Maher did not present any data to support this assertion. In all other studies in which incubation by birds of known sex has been watched, the sexes do not share the work equally. According to Andersson (1973), female Pomarine Skuas took about 75% of incubation duties. On Foula, female Arctic Skuas undertook 54% of the incubation (B. L. Furness 1980). Among pairs of Long-tailed Skuas where the sexes were known, females were seen on the eggs for 63% of 156 random observations, and in one pair watched continuously for 26 hours, the female incubated for 61% of the time that the eggs were covered (de Korte 1985). Malte Andersson (1971) recorded that the female Long-tailed Skua does most of the incubation, brooding of young chicks and preparation of food items to present to the young, while Kampp (1982) states that female Long-tailed Skuas incubate 75% of the time.

I found that female Great Skuas were on the nest at 65% of 200 spot observations that I made throughout incubation by marked birds at ten nests on Foula. According to Barre (1976), Brown Skuas share incubation approximately equally, but he studied only one nest and did not present any quantitative data. On Gough Island, where I established a useful study group of individually colour-ringed and measured breeding adults, I found that the presumed female (assuming that the female was the larger bird in each case) was on the nest on 59% of my visits to the territories. Eklund (1961) found that a female South Polar Skua incubated for 7 hours 33 minutes while the male incubated for 2 hours 9 minutes during a continuous observation at one nest. However, by watching five or six marked pairs of South Polar Skuas, Young (1963) showed that the share of incubation duties varied between pairs. In most instances the female did more of the incubation than the male, but in one or two cases this was reversed. Young also found that the situation changed slightly as incubation proceeded. Early in incubation females took a total of 58 out of 110 hours of the nest duties (53%), while towards hatching the females incubated for 51.5 hours out of 84, or 61% of the time. This pattern was confirmed by Spellerberg's (1971) study of South Polar Skuas, although he found an even more pronounced tendency for females to take most of the incubation duties. In his study, females did about 60% of incubation during the first half of the incubation period, and about 75% during the latter half of the incubation period.

The small size of the Sparrowhawk male means that he probably could not cover the eggs effectively, and so the female does all incubation (Newton 1986). Although size and shape differences between the largest female skua and the smallest male skua in each species probably place no constraints on their abilities to incubate satisfactorily, the greater share of incubation duties by the female allows the male more time for other activities. This can be seen as a strategy to allow the male to spend more time foraging in order to provision the female, perhaps because the male is a better hunter, or to allow the female to remain by the nest because she is better able to defend it against predation.

Foraging

In gulls and terns, males courtship-feed their mates before egg-laying, and there is evidence to show that courtship-feeding has important consequences not only for pair-bonding, but also in a direct way for breeding success. Females that obtain more food from their mate produce larger eggs and have a higher breeding success (Hunt 1980). In all skua species, males courtship-feed their mates, and thus help the female to produce eggs. Since skuas lay only two eggs rather than the three produced by most gulls, and carry large fat and protein reserves early in the breeding season that can influence their ability to breed (Chapter 11), courtship-feeding may not be so important for skuas as it is for terns and gulls. Nevertheless, in many skua populations the males feed the females not only before egg-laying, but, unlike gulls and terns, throughout incubation, and in some populations during chick-rearing as well. Thus skuas show a division of labour between the sexes that is more like that found in birds of prey than like that of their nearest relatives, the gulls.

The extent of this division of labour varies. Great Skuas in Shetland during the 1970s showed one extreme: in some pairs that I watched on Foula the female may not have left the territory for weeks at a time, or may have travelled no further than the local bathing site for a wash and preen, while her mate brought all the food she needed to the territory. In general, before laying and during incubation, males did most of the foraging and females rarely left the territory. After the eggs had hatched, the females continued to depend on the mate to provide food for themselves and the chicks. As the chicks grew, and their food requirements increased, females began to forage to help the male to provision the family. The progressive increase in foraging by the female presumably reflected the difficulty in obtaining enough food as chick demands increased, and perhaps also as the availability of food declined through the season. An example of the seasonal changes in foraging by one pair of Great Skuas on Foula is shown in Figure 33. Spellerberg (1971) found the same in the South Polar Skua. The females remained in the territory continously throughout incubation while the male left it to forage for both birds if the territory contained no penguins (Fig. 34). Where penguins were present, both sexes would forage in the rookery within their territory. Shortly after the chicks had hatched the females began to leave the territory to assist the male in foraging for the chicks. Spellerberg noted that up until chick hatching the female of a breeding pair would not accept food offered by man, whereas the male would. However, the female would happily accept the same food if the male picked

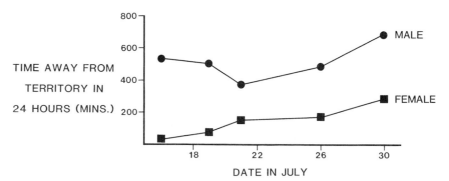

Fig. 33   Time spent away from the territory by the male and female of a pair of Great Skuas at Foula in 1974.

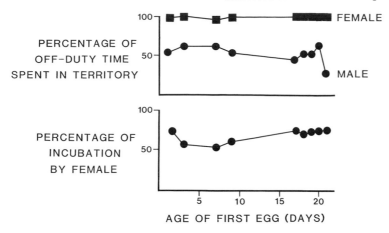

Fig. 34 Time allocation by male and female South Polar Skuas (from Spellerberg 1971).

it up and offered it to her! This suggests that the female South Polar Skuas during the incubation period somehow switch off the motivation to feed for themselves, in order to concentrate on their role as defender of the nest.

Young's (1963) observations of the chick feeding behaviour and foraging trips by South Polar Skuas on Ross Island showed that both sexes made similar numbers of foraging flights; usually three or four per adult per day. However, Young also found that female South Polar Skuas remained in the territory throughout pairing and the incubation period, relying on the male for food.

Male Brown Skuas on Signy Island made more foraging trips than the females, although females accepted much of the food from the male and then later fed it to the chicks (Burton 1968). In the Pomarine Skua, observed during incubation in NE Alaska by Andersson (1973), males did almost all of the hunting for lemmings, and carried food or regurgitated it to the female and then shared the tearing apart of the lemmings, achieved most easily by the two adults pulling in opposite directions since they do not use their feet to hold prey down.

In the Long-tailed Skua, males hunted about six times as much as females during the chick-rearing period (Andersson 1971), while Kampp (1982) found that the male did all of the foraging for the pair during the incubation period. During the early chick-rearing period, de Korte (1986) found that the female foraged less than the male, with the male providing 71% of chick feeds. The female hunted only within a few hundred metres from the young, while the male foraged in the outer parts of the territory. Later in chick-rearing, the male still foraged more than the female, but the discrepancy became smaller.

On Foula, the Arctic Skua shows a slight division of labour, but a much less pronounced one than that found in the Great Skua. During the incubation period the female leaves the territory about twice per day, for a total of 120 minutes. During this time she is presumably foraging, although she may also visit freshwater communal bathing sites. The male makes about five trips per day, totalling 150 minutes. He may occasionally feed the female, but this is less common than in

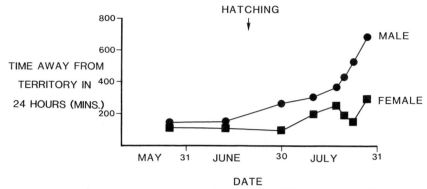

Fig. 35   Time allocation by male and female Arctic Skuas at Foula, Shetland.

most other skua populations that have been studied. During the early part of chick-rearing, the male spends about twice as long away from the territory as the female. Later, as the chicks become larger, the time each sex spends foraging increases, especially in the female, so that the differential between the sexes becomes smaller (Table 22, Fig. 35).

Thus the pattern is similar in all skuas; males forage more than females and feed their mate as well as the chicks, but the female takes an increasing share of foraging as the chicks grow, reducing the division of labour until foraging effort is fairly similar between the sexes when the chicks fledge. Probably the situation is flexible, and responds to factors such as food availability; for skua populations living in situations where food is scarce and the chicks risk starvation, females will take a larger share of foraging and put less effort into the protection of the young. Why save the chicks from risks of predation if they are going to starve as a result!

Defence of eggs and chicks

Female Brown Skuas spend much more time than males in brooding small chicks, and tend to stay closer to the chicks and help them to feed (Burton 1968). The same is true of Long-tailed Skuas (Andersson 1971) and probably of other species too.

Skuas may feed almost exclusively within their territory, as with Pomarine and Long-tailed Skuas in the high Arctic, Tristan Skuas on Gough Island and Brown Skuas which have penguins or nocturnal burrow-nesting petrels in their territory. At the opposite extreme, they may feed almost entirely outwith and distant from the territory, like Great Skuas and Arctic Skuas in Shetland, and South Polar Skuas away from penguins in the Antarctic. In the latter group, the female is left for extended periods to guard the eggs and chicks unassisted. In these populations it seems inevitable that the ability of the female to deter nest or chick predators will be important. In the skuas where foraging occurs predominantly within the territory, the large size of the territory may also mean that, effectively, only the female is close enough to the nest much of the time to defend her chicks against predation while the male is on the fringes of the territory searching for food.

It has been a common finding of most studies of skua breeding success that egg and chick predation are the predominant causes of breeding failure (Chapters 11 and 12), so that there is bound to be a strong selection pressure favouring characteristics that reduce the risks of such predation. One characteristic is appropriate behaviour. Chicks are usually guarded by at least one parent, and an adult leaves to forage only when the mate has returned unless conditions for feeding are extremely bad (Chapter 12). Another attribute that could plausibly be important is large size in the female, since it is reasonable to think that larger females will be more successful in deterring predators. In my PhD study of Great Skuas on Foula in the mid 1970s, I found that chicks were virtually always protected by at least one adult. Disappearance of eggs or chicks from study territories, which could be attributed to predation by conspecifics, tended to occur synchronously in time, and occurred on days when few territories contained two adults, suggesting that absence of the second adult greatly increased the risk of losses. Unfortunately, I did not have information on the size of the female in each territory so I could not compare the performance of different sized females in protecting their young, but such a study would be relatively straightforward to perform and the results would be particularly interesting in helping to determine whether reversed sexual size dimorphism in skuas is largely attributable to the role of the female as guardian of the young, as seems highly likely.

Richard Perry (1948) recorded of the Arctic Skua on Noss 'one bird of a pair – invariably I think, the female – was much more severe in its mobbing than its mate, and while both birds of a pair would display, the female was again invariably the most persistent and extravagant in her antics'. This strongly supports the argument that the larger size of the female is related to her leading role in defence of the eggs and young.

Territorial defence
South Polar Skuas showed no significant differences in the territorial defence activities of males and females (Trillmich 1978). Indeed, it is clear that both sexes of all species of skua will defend the territory against other skuas, regardless of whether their mate is present or absent. The male undoubtedly establishes the territory and is probably the more vigorous in its defence, but females will drive away unknown birds of either sex that attempt to land within the territory while the male is absent, and will defend the territory against neighbouring breeding males. There seems to be no reason for reversed size dimorphism as far as the defence of the established territory is concerned, though the possibility that smaller size and consequently greater aerial agility may enable smaller males to establish territory cannot easily be discounted.

CHANGES IN SIZE WITH AGE

Tail-tip length in small skuas increases with age (Table 8) but this is probably a sexual display character of little importance for survival. Indeed, the particularly elongated central tail feathers of Long-tailed Skuas and Pomarine Skuas may represent a handicap for adults by increasing aerodynamic drag during flight (Chapter 6).

Most of the few published weights of skuas after fledging but before returning to breed are of birds of uncertain status, shot opportunistically at different dates during the summer on the arctic tundra, or of young birds found starving and exhausted during autumn migration. It would be inappropriate to compare these data with measurements of breeding adults. By using a cannon net at club sites on Foula I was able to catch nonbreeding Great Skuas, many of which had been ringed as chicks and so were of known age. These birds, three to seven years old, averaged 1,307 g in late June, compared to average weights of breeding adults of 1,350 g in males and 1,480 g in females. The immatures were of unknown sex, though there were probably approximately equal numbers of males and females. They clearly weighed much less than breeding adults (Fig. 36). It is interesting that immatures, although several years old, are clearly lighter in weight than breeding adults. It seems probable that this is principally due to their carrying less fat and protein reserves than adults. Might it be partly due to immatures being incompletely developed? While immature Great Skuas at Foula were not statistically different from adults in terms of tarsus length, head length, bill length or depth, the wing length of the immatures averaged 410 mm compared with an average in adults on Foula of 418 mm. The mean for immatures is smaller even than that for male adults (414.5 mm) (Table 23). However, only wing length seems to be incompletely developed. The same is generally true for other skua species (see Tables 4 to 7). All other measures of body size are the same as for breeding adults, apart from Pomarine Skua bill lengths, and Great Skua tail lengths measured on museum specimens (I did not take this measurement from live birds on Foula because it is dangerous to poke a ruler up the tail of a live Great Skua). There are several possible explanations for the short wings of immatures. Feathers may be costly to produce because they require large amounts of sulphur amino acids for the synthesis of keratin. Immature birds may make do with smaller than optimal length primaries (and tail feathers in Great Skuas) to reduce the costs of feather growth. At present this idea cannot be discussed much further since the costs of feather growth in skuas are unknown. Energy costs of moult have been measured in Chaffinches and House Sparrows, and are high in these species. The costs can be estimated for penguins, which fast during feather growth so their weight loss gives a measurement of the energy costs of moult and existence. These data also suggest that feather synthesis is expensive, but whether or not this presents a problem for immature skuas is unclear. Certainly, skuas have particularly large amounts of plumage, presumably as an adaptation to life in cold environments (Chapter 3). Since immatures do not have the costs of breeding that adults have, it seems difficult to imagine that they could have difficulty in meeting the costs of moult as well as adults do, even if the immatures are generally less experienced and less competent than adults.

Smaller wing length in immatures may be adaptive rather than imposed upon them. In small passerines, juveniles suffer very much higher rates of predation than do adults, because they are less experienced and perhaps because they spend more time in feeding. Juvenile passerines also tend to have shorter wings than adults, and it has been suggested that shorter wings increase the ability of juveniles to escape from predators such as Sparrowhawks because they allow greater manoeuvrability in flight! This argument does not fit too well with the fact that many juvenile passerines (and immature Great Skuas) also have shorter tails than adults. The tail is very important for control of flight manoeuvres, and it would make more sense, if aerial agility was of particular importance, for juveniles to have longer tails than adults. Nor is it likely than an ability to avoid aerial predators is important for immature skuas, so this argument would not explain their smaller wing lengths.

If immatures weigh less than breeders, then to achieve the same (optimal) wing loading as in adults, immatures would need to have a smaller wing area than breeders. This would be most easily achieved by having shorter flight feathers.

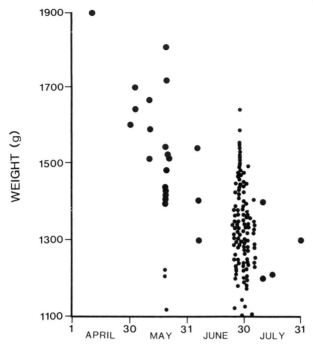

Fig. 36   Seasonal weights of immature and adult Great Skuas on Foula. Adults are marked by large dots and immatures by small dots.

Thus, the age-related differences in wing lengths of skuas do not necessarily imply that immatures are structurally smaller than the optimal size for survival, although the lighter weight of immatures (at least in Great Skuas but probably in all species) requires explanation. This is discussed further when I consider the age of first breeding and reasons for deferred maturity in skuas (Chapter 13).

CONCLUSIONS

All skua species show reversed sexual size dimorphism, females weighing 11–17% more than males. There is little or no evidence for differences in the feeding niches of the sexes; slight differences in diet can be attributed to differences in the activity patterns of males and females. Female skuas spend far more time close to the nest site than do males, and take the leading role in care and protection of the eggs and chicks. The male feeds the female, providing her with almost all her food requirements during pairing and incubation, but she takes an increasing share of foraging as chicks grow, though never equalling the male's contribution.

The clear division of labour between the sexes, suggests that the task of the female to defend the young against predation has been the principal reason for the evolution of larger size in female skuas. This interpretation suggests that Andersson and Norberg's (1981) arguments concerning the mechanism of evolution of reversed sexual size dimorphism in birds of prey apply equally well for skuas.

CHAPTER 6
Behaviour

Our arrival in Foula, to carry on there the operations of the Trigonometrical Survey, excited the wonder of the Foulaese very much; when they understood our intention of carrying our baggage to the summit of the Snuke, and living among the Bonxies, they considered the attempt would be fruitless and rash. A respectable old woman, who seemed to pay great respect to the Hill Trows, gave us her blessing at parting, assured, that if we were really going to live among the Bonxies, we should never return safe again.
Capt. Vetch of the Corps of Royal Engineers, M.W.S., M.G.S. etc (1822)

Skuas as a group have rather few display postures compared with gulls, and their displays are generally aggressive in intent, with no equivalents to the appeasing postures used by gulls to inhibit fighting. Indeed, skuas fight rather often, and their behaviour seems simple and primitive by comparison with the subtleties of gull communications. Skuas on club sites or in their territory appear particularly stupid as a result of their limited repertoire of behaviour, but this anthropomorphic interpretation is not really valid. Skua displays serve their purpose. Presumably the fact that, by and large, skuas nest well spaced apart in large territories, often only defending the core of the territory against intruders, means that there has been less need for complex displays, unlike gulls, which often nest in dense colonies, with the consequent need to avoid overt conflicts (Burton 1970).

AGGRESSIVE POSTURES

Skuas possess three principal groups of aggressive postures, 'Upright', 'Oblique' and 'Bend' (Fig. 37). Often the Oblique and Bend are accompanied by 'Wing Raising' and 'Long Call' to produce the 'Long Call Complex' which is involved both in territorial advertisement and in agonistic encounters and shows differences in form between different skua taxa (discussed below).

The Upright, Oblique and Bend may all be seen in any species of skua, particularly during conflicts between territorial males, early interactions between the sexes and at club sites.

Fig. 37   Aggressive postures adopted by skuas.

The Upright
This posture is exactly analogous to the Upright of gulls. The Upright is the most common aggressive posture of skuas, and is closely associated with the tendency to attack or escape. Some authors have subdivided the Upright into Aggressive, Anxiety and Intimidated categories (Fig. 38), although postures adopted in the field may be intermediate between these and may change from one to another during an interaction. Andersson (1976) showed that it was possible to predict that a bird giving the Aggressive Upright would be likely to attack the bird with which it was interacting within a minute of adapting the posture, whereas birds that adopted the Intimidated Upright were likely to flee shortly afterwards. These observations suggest that the postures have stereotyped signal values that allow birds to communicate their intentions and so reduce the amount of physical fighting. This idea that postures communicate intentions has been challenged by another school of thought, which suggests that birds in conflict with each other do not communicate what they are going to do next. Rather, they are 'poker-faced'

Fig. 38   Forms of the Upright posture.

and do not allow their opponent to know whether he will win or lose the conflict before the interactions have reached their outcome. Certainly, most postures used by interacting skuas are aggressive in intent; only the Intimidated Upright seems to be a signal of fear and submission as well as aggression, and this display is seen particularly in the female when the pair-bond is not fully formed and her mate adopts the Aggressive Upright towards her. In this situation it may pay the female to signal her deference to her mate in order to avoid escalation of an interaction into fighting.

The Anxiety Upright is generally used by one partner to communicate to its mate concern about, for example, a strange skua flying overhead, and is often followed by an alarm call or by the Long Call Complex.

The Bend

Also termed Bent Neck by some authors, this posture is adopted very slowly and deliberately, and is often followed by the Long Call Complex. The bird points its head and bill downwards, often with the bill buried in the breast feathers, and raises the feathers of the nape, and sometimes lifts the tail (Fig. 39). It is commonly seen when an intruder approaches a confident bird, and Andersson (1976) showed that it is frequently followed by attack.

The Oblique

The Oblique is a posture that is also found in gulls. In large skuas and the Pomarine Skua it is frequently accompanied by Wing Raising and the Long Call to form the Long Call Complex, but Arctic and Long-tailed Skuas do not show Wing Raising although they will give the Oblique with the Long Call from a high point on the ground within their territory, a posture that, in pale phase birds, exposes their white breast and belly to maximum effect.

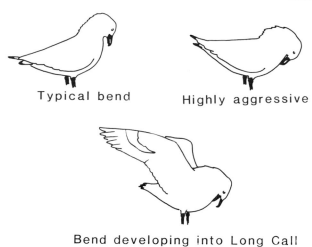

Typical bend   Highly aggressive

Bend developing into Long Call

Fig. 39   Forms of the Bend posture.

THE LONG CALL COMPLEX

The Long Call Complex is by far the most conspicuous display of skuas, and is used to advertise territorial ownership, as a threat to other males and to attract a female, and as a greeting to the mate. The display consists of the Oblique or Bend posture if the bird is on the ground, combined with Wing Raising and the Long Call, and the performance shows variations from bird to bird so that, in all probability, it serves to provide individual recognition of territory owners. The Long Call Complex is given by all skuas, but only large skuas and the Pomarine Skua perform it on the ground (Photo 9). Arctic and Long-tailed Skuas have an aerial equivalent in which they adopt a gliding flight with wings held in a species-characteristic position and give the Long Call at the same time. Pomarine Skuas and Great Skuas have both the ground version and an aerial version of this display, and in the aerial versions these species also differ from each other and from the two smaller species in wing posture. In the Long-tailed Skua the wings are held with the tips bent well below the horizontal, while in the Arctic Skua the wings are held only very slightly below the horizontal. When the Pomarine Skua gives the display in flight it holds its wings slightly above the horizontal. Although Great Skuas, Chilean Skuas and other large skuas give the same aerial display rather less often, when they do they hold the wings in a steep V, well above the horizontal and close to $45°$ from the vertical (Fig. 40). Thus the aerial Long Call Complex has species-specific differences in wing posture that may be important signals when well-spaced territories are being advertised by aerial flight.

Reasons for the more aerial display of the two smallest skuas are discussed in Chapter 5; in essence, the aerial and ground-based Long Calls are equivalent, suiting the flight capabilities and territory sizes of the different species.

The most detailed study of the Long Call Complex has been made by Pietz

9. *A Tristan Skua on Gough Island giving the Long Call display with Wing Raising.* Photo: R. W. Furness.

(1985), who compared the behaviour of South Polar and Brown Skuas breeding at Palmer Station on the Antarctic Peninsula. She found no difference in the behavioural repertoires of the two species, but showed that there were consistent slight interspecific differences in the performance of the Long Call Complex. Although nearly a quarter of the Long Call postures adopted by the two species were indistinguishable, Brown Skuas tended to hold the neck bent forward while South Polar Skuas tended to hold the head further back (Fig. 41). The head postures of the Falkland, Tristan, Chilean and Great Skua are indistinguishable from those of the Brown Skua, so that the South Polar Skua is the odd one out in this set. Again, this difference may serve as a species recognition signal when sympatric Brown and South Polar Skuas are establishing territories in the same area.

Pietz (1985) points out that the long calls of Brown and South Polar Skuas both show a great deal of consistent individual variation, but the pitch of Brown Skua calls tends to be slightly higher than that of South Polar Skua calls. The pattern of the call, however, is very similar between the two species, and similar to those of the Great Skua and the Pomarine Skua. By contrast, the Long Calls of Arctic and Long-tailed Skuas are rather different, though similar to each other (Fig. 42).

The function of the white wing flash in skuas is obviously to emphasise the Wing Raising display and act as a signal to the opponent or potential mate. Spellerberg (1971) investigated this in the South Polar Skua by painting out the wing flashes on two females and a male in three different breeding territories during the pre-laying period. The two females so treated were subjected to persistent swooping attacks by other, unpaired, females, and were eventually displaced from their territories. The displaced females both failed to find a new male and did not breed. The painted male managed to breed as normal, with no apparent effect to his ability to maintain the territory. With a sample size of only two females and one male it would be foolish to read too much into this experiment, but it does suggest that the white flash plays an important role in display and so influences the ability of birds to hold territorial status. It is worth noting that the two most aerial skuas, the Arctic and Long-tailed, have the least pronounced wing

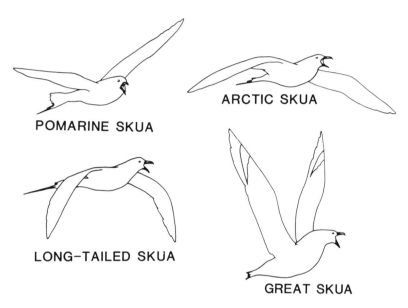

Fig. 40   Wing positions maintained during aerial Long Call displays by skuas.

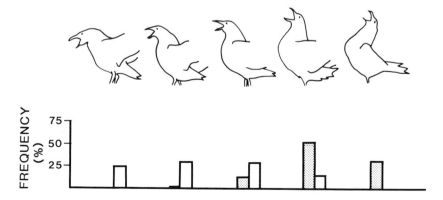

Fig. 41   Neck positions held by South Polar (dotted histograms) and Brown Skuas (open histograms) during the Long Call Complex. From Pietz (1985).

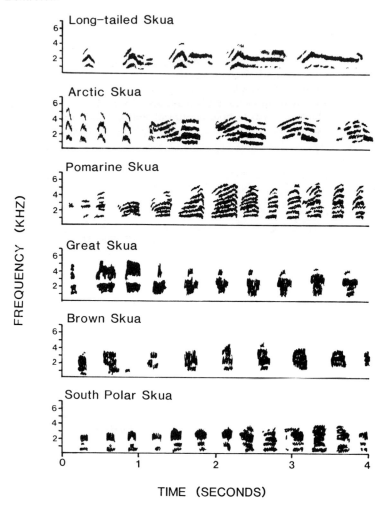

Fig. 42 Sonagrams of the Long Calls of skuas.

flashes, being particularly restricted in the Long-tailed Skua. This would be compatible with their having lost the ground-based Long Call Complex with Wing Raising from their display repertoires.

PAIR FORMATION

In most skuas, established breeders retain the same mate from year to year, and when they return to their breeding territory in the spring, the pair has to be reformed. The exception to this is the Pomarine Skua, which does not retain the same mate or territory, but behaves nomadically and breeds opportunistically, only when lemming abundance allows. Male skuas generally arrive on territory before females, but if the male is one of the first to arrive, his mate, too, will probably be one of the first females. How this synchrony is determined is not known, but it is probably by photoperiodic control. Almost certainly the birds do not remain together outside the breeding season, and do not meet until they return to the territory. Probably their synchrony is due to the fact that individuals tend to return at the same time every season and so are most likely to pair up in their first breeding season with a bird that arrives at the same time. Synchrony in subsequent seasons is due to this temporally assortative pairing in their first season together, and not due to some mysterious process of communication between mates before they get back to the colony.

When the female joins her mate on the territory, the initial behaviour between the birds is hostile. The male challenges the newly returned female and she responds by behaving submissively, or by retreating. Only after the two have been together for a few days do they begin to act as a pair, mutually displaying at intruders and showing signs of breeding behaviour. Quite often, strange females will arrive at the territory before the mate of the previous season returns, and the male may tolerate a succession of strange females which are serially displaced by others, until the established mate returns and claims her rightful place by driving out the new female (Stonehouse 1956, Furness 1977). Presumably, if the established female fails to return, then one of these unattached females will become the new mate of the territory owner.

When males that do not own a territory arrive in the spring they establish a claim to a high point of ground between the territories of other males. Neighbours often succeed in driving these interlopers away, but in time a bird will change from retreating when attacked to holding its ground and slowly enlarging its area of ownership, frequently giving Long Call displays to indicate its territorial rights to neighbours and, equally importantly at this stage, to attract a mate.

Although some immature birds gain breeding territories or become mated to territorial males at the start of a season, much of the establishment of pairs and of new territories occurs later in the season, at a time when it is too late to consider breeding in that year. Part of the pairing and territorial behaviour of skuas that breed in colonies occurs in the club sites of the immatures, and part occurs when the most dominant club birds move to fringe areas of the colony and establish themselves towards the end of the season. It is not known whether this practice behaviour by immature birds may establish long-lasting pair bonds and territorial ownership, or whether these birds are the ones that arrive early in the next season and look for mates and territories then. The role of clubs and the patterns of territorial establishment in colonial skuas are discussed from the ecological point of view in Chapter 10, but it is worth noting here that the club site is one of intense behavioural interaction between immature birds of both sexes, and one where much of the behavioural repertoire and the functional significance of skua postures has been analysed (Perdeck 1960, Andersson 1976).

One of the important displays between prospective mates occurs on the ground within the territory, when the birds approach each other and display their tails. In this Tail Raising posture, the bird bows forward slightly and lifts the tail high over the back. This gives the partner a clear view of the central tail feathers, which are diagnostic in the small skuas not only of species, but also of age, in that the immature birds have much shorter central tail feathers than do full adults. The clear differences in the shape and lengths of central tail feathers in the small skuas must be largely a result of selection for species recognition. In fact, the central tail feathers of Pomarine Skuas are probably something of a handicap to them, since it is common for adults to deliberately bite off the elongated parts of these feathers as soon as they have formed a pair and begun to breed.

SCOOP MAKING

In established pairs, scoop making, or scraping behaviour, may begin only a couple of days after the pair has reformed, providing ground conditions allow it. The male usually takes the initiative in this, moving about the territory giving the Soft Call and Scraping at likely nest sites. In Scraping the bird lowers its breast and makes alternating scratching movements with the feet. At intervals it rotates in the scoop to continue from a different angle. The female follows the male around, and may take over Scraping when he leaves the scoop he is making. Pairs may make several incipient scoops each day until the female begins to favour one particular site. Then she will go directly to that site and start Scraping or Sideways Nest Building. This latter behaviour is the same as one of the nesting behaviours of gulls, in which the bird in the scoop picks up small objects or pulls at dead grass, with a sideways movement of the head, and drops them onto the nest rim.

Once the pair have settled on a particular scrape, they may show a Squeaking Ceremony, in which both birds stand at the scoop in a crouched position with heads down and tails raised, giving high pitched squeaks, and this Squeaking Ceremony usually signifies that the eggs will be laid in that scoop.

The amount of nest material deposited on the rim is dependent on the extent of Sideways Nest Building behaviour by the female. No nesting material is carried to the nest and the rim is fashioned from material within reach when the female is in the scrape. Most skua nests are no more than a bare depression surrounded by a rim of dead grasses or pebbles. Many Arctic Skua nests are very difficult to spot because of the lack of nesting material, but Great Skuas may produce extravagant and untidy circles of dead grass around the scrape that can be seen as light brown halos contrasting with the dark green vegetation.

Completion of scoops and the squeaking scoop selection ceremony then leads on to the start of mating behaviour.

MATING BEHAVIOUR

As soon as the pair have formed, the female becomes reliant upon her mate for food. She obtains this by adopting a hunched begging posture and moving in front of the male, while making a soft purring call, and tossing the head. She may tap at the base of the male's bill if he does not regurgitate at once. All skuas show the same begging behaviour, and in all species this behaviour by the female may lead

to copulation sequences rather than feeding. When about to mount the female, the male may give a copulation call, consisting of a series of short soft notes. He then stretches his wings and hops about, or 'Dances', and then if the female behaves appropriately, he flaps up from beside the female onto her back. The female raises her tail and lifts her wings out of the supporting feathers to help her to balance. During the procedure, the male balances by flapping his wings and calls continuously until cloacal contact is achieved. Then he rests his wingtips on the ground, a posture which is not performed by gulls, falls silent and waggles his tail.

Perdeck (1960) quantified the behavioural sequences between inexperienced male and female Great Skuas on clubs at Noss. Out of 76 occasions when the female started to beg, the male responded by regurgitating food on 31. Only two of these instances of regurgitation (6.5%) led on, after further dancing by the male and begging by the female, to copulation. By comparison, on the 21 occasions when the male responded to the begging female by giving the copulation call and dancing, this was followed by copulation nine times (43%). According to Spellerberg (1971) and Perdeck (1960), male skuas were more likely to regurgitate than to courtship dance if the female was aggressive or begged particularly vigorously. The male skua needs to provide his mate with enough food to quieten her down before he can consummate their relationship. The female makes certain by this behaviour that she is given enough food to form the two eggs as well as maintain herself.

INCUBATION

Incubation behaviour seems to be remarkably uniform throughout the skua family. Once the female has laid the first egg she remains on it and incubates, so that the second egg, laid two to four days later, is behind the first in development. As a result, eggs hatch in the order in which they were laid, though usually the interval between hatching is shorter than that of laying, presumably because incubation is less effective during the first couple of days after the laying of the first egg. According to Spellerberg (1971) female South Polar Skuas take all of the incubation between the laying of the first and second egg, leaving the nest to be fed by the male, but not allowing the male to incubate until the clutch is complete. Stonehouse (1956) also reports that only the female Brown Skua undertakes incubation between the laying of the first and second eggs, and that the two sexes share incubation duties thereafter. This may also be true of other skuas, but does not seem to have been reported. The female undertakes more than half of the incubation duties in all skuas, and data suggest that the share of incubation by the female increases as incubation progresses (Chapter 5). Incubation bouts generally last for about two or three hours at a time, although change-overs may occur sooner if the incubating bird is disturbed from the nest by an intruder to the territory.

Nest relief usually occurs when the off-duty bird indicates readiness to incubate by approaching the nest and standing beside the incubating bird. Sometimes one partner, usually the female, will be unwilling to leave the eggs and the relieving bird may then attempt to push its mate gently off the nest! Occasionally a bird that is incubating will leave the nest before its mate has signalled readiness to incubate, but eggs are rarely left uncovered for long. Perdeck (1963) describes a 'squeaking ceremony' in Great Skuas that may take place during nest relief, when the approaching bird utters a soft call, to which its mate replies, and these then develop into a squeaking duet. This is apparently the same display as occurs when the nest site is first selected.

Retrieval of eggs

One aspect of skua incubation behaviour came as a particular surprise to me. It is well known that gulls have a form of stereotyped egg retrieval behaviour. If an egg rolls onto the lip or out of the nest, a gull will roll it back into the nest cup by placing its bill, held vertically, over the far side of the egg and pulling back towards the nest. Skuas on Foula do not do this. If a Great Skua egg rolls out of the nest it will be ignored. This can happen quite often if the birds nest in a colony where sudden disturbance can be frequent. When an incubating skua rises quickly off its nest it may lift one of the eggs in the feathers around its brood patch and so deposit the egg out of the nest cup. Occasionally, both eggs may be lost from the nest cup, particularly if the nest is on sloping ground (skuas prefer to avoid nesting on a slope but some pairs apparently cannot find better sites on Foula). When both eggs roll out, then the bird that settles to incubate will settle on either one, pulling vegetation around it to form a new nest, but will ignore the other egg. At change-over the mate may well settle onto the ignored cold egg, and as a result neither develops to hatch! This seems remarkably wasteful, and I can only suppose that egg-rolling behaviour in gulls evolved after they had branched from the skuas, and that most skuas rarely encounter eggs displaced from the nest. I have only seen the displacement of eggs as a common phenomenon among Great Skuas on Foula, where many pairs nest on sloping ground, the colony is unusually dense, and the birds are often disturbed from the nest by other skuas, sheep, ponies or people.

One feature of incubation by skuas that may increase the risk of eggs being lifted out of the nest is the practice of incubating the eggs with one egg resting on each foot, which has been documented for the South Polar Skua (Spellerberg 1971) and Long-tailed Skua (Andersson 1976), and so is probably normal practice in other skuas. This behaviour may be important to reduce heat loss from the eggs through the base of the nest, and may explain why skuas do not provide insulating lining as most birds do.

Reactions to foreign eggs and chicks

Because skua nests are well spaced and territories are vigorously defended, the chances of a foreign egg getting into a skua's nest are small. I have only twice found a skua clutch on Foula containing three eggs in some thousands of Great Skua and hundreds of Arctic Skua nests examined. Both were Great Skua nests, at one of which three birds were present and the eggs were probably laid by two females. At the other, all three eggs appeared similar in colour and pattern and were probably laid by one female. However, South Polar Skuas, like several other skuas, are predators of the eggs of other birds. Crawford (1974) reported a South Polar Skua near Cape Hallett which had an Adelie Penguin's egg in its nest which it was incubating, and it seems that the skua must have stolen this to eat, but carried it to its nest and then accidentally begun to treat it as if one of its own eggs. This observation led Yasuomi Tamiya and Masahiro Aoyanagi (1982) to try an experiment to see whether a South Polar Skua could incubate an Adelie Penguin egg successfully and raise the chick. They placed a penguin egg that had been carried by a skua from the penguin rookery but left, undamaged, on the ground, into the nest of a pair of South Polar Skuas that had lost one of their two eggs to a neighbouring skua. The skuas incubated their own and the penguin egg for 20 days until the penguin egg hatched. The skuas then guarded and brooded the penguin chick while continuing to incubate their own egg. That the skuas accepted the penguin egg is really quite remarkable, since it is pure white and so dramatically different in appearance from the skuas' own egg, though similar in size. Again, from an anthropomorphic viewpoint, this suggests that skuas are rather stupid, but presumably skuas have not experienced any significant nest parasitism that would lead to their evolving an ability to discriminate between their own and foreign eggs in the way that most cuckoo hosts do.

During one of my first seasons on Foula, and long before I read Tamiya and Aoyanagi's paper, one of the residents, Jim Gear, suggested to me that I should try an experiment to see if it might be possible to cross-foster Great Skuas with gulls. His idea was that the Great Skua was a vulnerable species and so we should take active steps to try to introduce them into localities further south in Scotland where they do not breed but where it might be possible to rear their chicks by putting eggs under gulls. His hope was that such a programme would provide security for the future of the species, but perhaps also a better excuse for a reduction of 'Bonxie' numbers on Foula! The experiment seemed worth trying out of curiosity, so I took a clutch of two fresh Great Skua eggs and swapped them for two Great Black-backed Gull eggs that had been incubated for three or four days. These I took from a solitary gull pair on the clifftop near to where I was living on Foula so that I could easily keep an eye on their progress. The foster parents hatched both gull eggs, and the Great Black-backed Gulls hatched both skua eggs, so neither seemed concerned about the switch of the eggs or the slight difference in size and patterning of those they were given.

RELATIONSHIPS BETWEEN ADULTS AND YOUNG

Eggshell removal
After hatching, the parents usually remove the egg shells from the nest, often before the chick has even begun to dry. This practice is also found in gulls and is presumably adaptive. It has been explained as a way of reducing the conspicuousness of the nest to predators since the white inside of the eggshell is quite eye-catching. However, there is another important reason for the behaviour. In Great Skuas, the removal of the eggshell sometimes does not happen during the interval between the hatching of the first and second eggs, and on several occasions I have come across nests where the hatching second egg has become trapped inside the halved first eggshell in such a way that the second chick was unable to push open its shell and chick died as a result.

Chick care
Once hatched, the skua chicks remain under the parent and are brooded almost continuously at first and then, as the chicks develop the ability to control their own body temperature, brooding becomes less frequent. Adult skuas allow the chicks to come out from under the cover of their brood patches or from the hollow between wing and body, and explore around the nest, but will call them back if danger is perceived. The male presents food to the female, who takes charge of

Fig. 43   Method of tearing large prey such as lemmings.

giving it to the small chicks. Where skuas are feeding on small fish, presentation of fragments of fish is relatively straightforward. Skuas feeding on seabirds or on lemmings have more difficulty in preparing food that is suitably small for young chicks to swallow. In order to tear up a lemming into suitable pieces, both members of a pair must cooperate by pulling with their bills in opposite directions (Fig. 43). Maher (1970) found that when the female in a pair of Pomarine Skuas died, the male continued to bring the lemmings to the young, but did not feed them; they did not eat the food for themselves, so cooperation between the adults may be essential for success, at least when they are small. Older chicks will cooperate with the female in tearing the meat to pieces (Andersson 1971).

During the first day or two after hatching, skua chicks do not usually beg for food, but the female will offer tiny fragments to them. Curiously, a few pairs of Great Skuas breeding for the first time do not manage to get their act together, and are unable to make the necessary transition from incubating/brooding behaviour to offering food to the young. On several occasions I have seen first time breeders fail to offer to feed the chicks that they have hatched. Then the chicks become restless and appear from under the brooding bird and beg in a very weak fashion. In at least two instances, this did not lead to the adults feeding their chicks, and the chicks died of starvation. Presumably the skills of successful parenthood involve some learning as well as instinctive behaviour.

By the time chicks are 3–4 days old they begin to take the initiative for feeding. They beg for food by giving a long, high-pitched, whistling trill note, while jumping up and down in front of the adult, holding the wings out horizontally or flapping them (or the wing buds in tiny chicks), and pecking from below at the adult's throat or breast. This pattern of behaviour seems to be identical in all skuas, from Long-tailed Skua (Andersson 1971) to Great Skua (Furness 1977) and South Polar Skua (Spellerberg 1971).

The male regurgitates food onto the ground, and large chicks feed for themselves from this pile, whereas small chicks are carefully fed by the female. Any food not taken by the chicks is then eaten by the female, and she may later regurgitate this to the chicks. Once the chicks are large, they may persistently follow the female around the territory, begging for food. If the male does not return with food the female may eventually be harassed into leaving the young unattended in order to satisfy their demands, and to escape from their attentions.

In normal cases, within a few days chicks have begun to wander over the territory, whether hungry or not. In the Long-tailed Skuas that Malte Andersson studied in northern Scandinavia, where nests were spaced about 600–1,300 m apart, the two chicks would wander as much as 300 m from the nest, though generally remaining within 50–100 m of each other. On Foula, where Great Skuas nest some 20–100 m apart, chicks also range from the nest, but do not normally encroach into neighbour's territories. Chicks seem to learn where the territorial boundaries are, presumably from the vocalisations of their parents who will call them back if they stray too far. As Spellerberg also noted for the South Polar Skua, adults always seem to be aware of the location of their chicks, even when danger threatens and the chicks are hiding; and they will call at the chicks to crouch if they start to move before the threat has passed. Long-tailed Skuas, and other skuas, possess different vocalisations for different kinds of threat. Long-tails mob ground predators with a repetitive call 'kreck' containing high and low pitched components, making the position of the adult easy to locate. For aerial predators such as falcons, they use a high-pitched pure tone 'kliu' which is very difficult to localise (Andersson 1971). These calls presumably warn the chicks not only of impending danger, but also of the type of predator that is approaching.

Reactions to foreign chicks

In the experiment of Tamiya and Aoyanagi, the penguin nestling that hatched under the South Polar Skua looked completely different from a skua nestling, being covered with entirely white down and sitting upright. However, the skuas happily accepted this strange chick. The parent skuas and the penguin chick greeted each other with their normal displays (Photo 7). Unfortunately, they proved unable to feed it, and as a result it starved and died when less than five days old. Adelie Penguins feed their chicks by regurgitation of partly digested krill which the chick takes from the parent's throat, and the South Polar Skuas gave up trying to give food to the penguin chick after a few unsuccessful attempts (Tamiya & Aoyanagi 1982).

My experiment with cross-fostered Great Skua and Great Black-backed Gull chicks also had an unsuccessful outcome, which with hindsight I should, perhaps, have predicted. The gull foster parents brooded their skua chicks assiduously, and occasionally bent down to touch them with their bill, but never fed them. Similarly, the Great Skua foster parents showed every bit as much care and attention to the gull chicks, but failed to feed them. The tiny gull chicks pecked at the tip of the Great Skua's bill but elicited no response other than startled withdrawal of the adult. The skua chicks jumped up and down flapping their wing buds and giving their thin trilling cry in front of the gull foster parents, and the gulls looked at them in surprise but did not recognise this as food begging. After 48 hours, during which the gull and the skua foster parents had not attempted to feed their foster chicks, I had to abandon the experiment and return the chicks to their natural parents.

10. The South Polar Skua with its foster Adelie Penguin chick. Neither bird recognised the behavioural communication of the other species. Photo: Y. Tamiya.

The large gulls have a red spot at the tip of the yellow bill, which Tinbergen showed was a signal that released the food begging behaviour of gull chicks; the chicks are programmed to peck at a red spot on a light coloured background and will give the pecking response even to a cardboard model or a pencil providing the colour pattern is correct. The uniform black bill of the Great Skua does not provide the correct stimulus for the gull chick, and being tapped on the bill tip is not the best way to stimulate the adult skua to regurgitate. The jumping crying chick is the special releaser that initiates regurgitation by adult Great Skuas. Cross-fostering between skuas and gulls is impossible because the signals between adults and chicks of one species cannot be understood by the other.

Since South Polar Skuas are quite willing to accept a penguin chick in place of one of their own, and Great Skuas will accept gull chicks, it is hardly surprising to find that skuas will accept foreign skua chicks. However, accepting the creature that emerges from an egg does not mean that skuas will also accept chicks that come into their territory after their own eggs have hatched. According to Spellerberg (1971), South Polar Skuas 'will also adopt a strange chick that has been placed or has wandered into their territory even if they already have a chick', and he describes how one pair that held a territory including the Base Hut tried to adopt two captive chicks that he kept in an enclosure, giving alarm calls and regurgitating food in front of the chicks. However, on Foula, I found that Great Skuas were generally hostile towards the chicks of neighbours and were more likely to eat them than to adopt them!

DEFENCE AGAINST PREDATORS

Chicks of all skuas show cryptic behaviour when a predator is present. As soon as adults show alarm by calling or by attacking an intruder the chick will run to the nearest suitable hiding place and crouch motionless until danger has passed and its parents have settled. First-time visitors to skua colonies helping me to find chicks to ring and measure often have considerable difficulty in finding skua chicks, especially Arctic Skua chicks, because of their cryptic behaviour. Once you get to know where to look for them they become quite easy to find; behind tussocks of grass, under banks of peat, in hollows, between rocks or cut peat turfs, but undoubtedly their behaviour will reduce the risk of their being located by predators.

Adults defend their eggs and chicks in a way that has made skuas notorious. When a ground predator approaches their nest or young the skuas fly up to some 3–10 m above the intruder, and then swoop down at it, sometimes striking with their feet. This behaviour varies between species and according to the stage of breeding, nest density, and the character of individual birds. In my experience, the Arctic Skua shows the behaviour in its most impressive and effective form. Arctic Skuas generally swoop down from the side or rear, rarely attacking from in front except when attempting to move sheep away from the nest. Their swoops are distinctly more cautious if the intruder watches them dive down, but usually result in physical contact if the intruder is not looking directly at them when they do so. Their swoops are usually accompanied by a 'tik-a-tik' call, occasionally interspersed with an angry-sounding 'churr'. Their agility allows them to direct a rapid but not very heavy blow to the head of the intruder, whether human, dog or sheep, though with dogs the Arctic Skua generally aims for the rump of the animal to avoid the risk of being caught in the dog's jaws. Certainly, the diving attacks of skuas are not without risk to the birds. On two occasions on Foula I have seen sheepdogs succeed in jumping up at attacking Arctic Skuas and catching them in their jaws, while I once watched a day visitor to Foula, who was irritated by Arctic Skuas diving at him as he walked along the road, succeed in killing an adult by throwing a stone at it as it stooped at him.

Many dogs prefer to run for cover when attacked by skuas, but a few experienced ones clearly enjoy the game of snapping at skuas and I watched John and Isobel Holbourn's dogs on Foula deliberately running out to tease the pairs of Arctic Skuas that nest on the croft for many minutes. The dogs would crouch low on the ground as the skua swooped and then leap up at the bird with its jaws wide and tail wagging. I could not help feeling that these skuas were also enjoying the performance. They obviously recognised the dogs and realised that they were not a threat to their young, yet persistently dived at them considerable distances away from the danger area around their chicks. When the dogs walked to heel with Isobel the skuas gave up their attacks because the dogs would not respond, and while they dived at strange people each time they walked past, they had learnt to recognise Isobel and did not attack her. By contrast, the same skuas made concerted efforts to drive a visitor's dog away from their nest area but stopped attacking it as soon as it had fled from the immediate vicinity.

Arctic Skuas are generally noisy in their attack of ground predators, and the pair work together as a team with coordination of their behaviour. As soon as one bird has stooped down from one side, the other will start to dive from behind. As it passes the intruder its mate will be turning, to make the next swoop from a different angle, but never getting into its mate's flightpath. As the birds are highly agile and can turn quickly between dives, one bird passes the intruder's head every three seconds or so. With intruders such as dogs or Arctic Foxes that respond by snapping at the adults as they dive, the dives tend to be from a greater height and

so less frequent. When victims ignore the skuas, as many sheep do, or attempt to duck or crouch (as many people do!), the skuas tend to make more vertical but shorter dives, turning more quickly and so making more attacks per unit of time. If the victim of their attacks flees then their dives become particularly fierce and contact more forceful. It is undoubtedly a mistake to run away from a diving skua! Ultimately, with sheep that refuse to move away, the skuas may hover over the animal's head, directing pecks at it, or even land on its back or head and pull at its wool to try to make it move away from the nest area.

The attacking behaviour of Great Skuas is rather different. To start with, they seem to lack the ability of Arctic Skuas to coordinate their swoops. Often one Great Skua will be half way in its dive at an intruding human, sheep or dog in its territory when it realises that its mate is simultaneously swooping down on a collision course, so that the two birds have to abort their attacks in order to avoid flying into each other. This is yet another aspect of Great Skua behaviour that leads the anthropomorphic observer to think of them as being exceptionally stupid birds! Perhaps this drastic lack of coordination is partly due to the fact that, by contrast to the very noisy attacking of the Arctic Skua, Great Skuas are usually silent as they attack. This lack of vocalisations undoubtedly makes their swoops more frightening to people, particularly as the Great Skua produces a sudden loud swoosh as it passes the intruder's head at full speed. A very small proportion of Great Skuas 'scream' as they are attacking – a hoarse high-pitched call that is similar in quality to the voice of southern hemisphere large skuas but is quite unlike the normal more mellow sounds made by Great Skuas. This charge call detracts from the surprise element of its attack, at least for humans, since it allows the intruder to be aware of the bird's position and activity overhead, even while concentrating on searching for the eggs or chicks. I can speak from considerable experience here; ringing and measuring the chicks requires both hands, and so leaves the head totally unprotected against the blows of a 1.5 Kg bird travelling at upwards of 10 metres per second (Photos 11–13).

Whereas, when attacking people, Arctic Skuas on Foula dive to hit, Great Skuas dive to miss by a narrow margin. The difference in strategy seems to be due to the latter's inferior aerial agility, although both species will dive to hit sheep, being aware that sheep cannot retaliate in the same way as people or dogs. However, some pairs are much more aggressive than others. The Great Skuas that scream while attacking tend also to be most likely to make deliberate physical contact

11. A Great Skua swooping at an intruder (the photographer) near its nest.
Photo: R. W. Furness.

12. A Great Skua with legs down, having just struck an intruder on the head with the back of its feet. Photo: R. W. Furness.

13. An Arctic Skua making an almost vertical attack on an intruder lingering for a long time close to its chick. Photo: R. W. Furness.

rather than an occasional error of judgement. On Foula, there are a few skuas that never attack a human intruder at all, but most are moderately aggressive. Where Great or Arctic Skuas nest at much lower densities in some other parts of Shetland, such as Yell or Shetland mainland, they tend also to be much less aggressive. Either the more aggressive individuals are the ones most likely to succeed in establishing a territory within a dense colony, and less aggressive ones are forced to move to areas where competition is less, or dive-bombing behaviour requires some social stimulation from neighbouring birds before it can develop fully.

Attacks on ground predators certainly intensify as the incubation of the clutch proceeds, and reach a peak shortly after hatching (Fig. 44), before waning as the chicks age. On my first visit to Gough Island in October 1983, I was surprised to find that the Tristan Skuas there did not dive at me in the manner of Great Skuas. They tended to be quite fearless of man, yet they did not attack even when I handled their eggs to measure them. As I approached them on their recently-laid eggs they would stand up and give the wing-raising display, but generally remained on the ground with the off-duty bird standing between me and its partner on the nest. However, when I visited Gough Island in November 1985 during the period when eggs were hatching I found that the same skuas behaved quite differently. They were still quite fearless, but attacked me the way Great Skuas in Shetland would attack a sheep; they would dive-bomb and hit hard, and if that failed to drive me away, most disconcertingly, they would land on my head and start pecking vigorously if I failed to fend them off. Clearly the tendency to attack a ground predator is just as strong in the Tristan Skua on its predator-free breeding grounds as it is in the Great Skua, but, unlike the latter, the Tristan Skua on Gough is not scared of man. However, it does seem to require some period of incubation before its aggressive behaviour towards intruding humans develops.

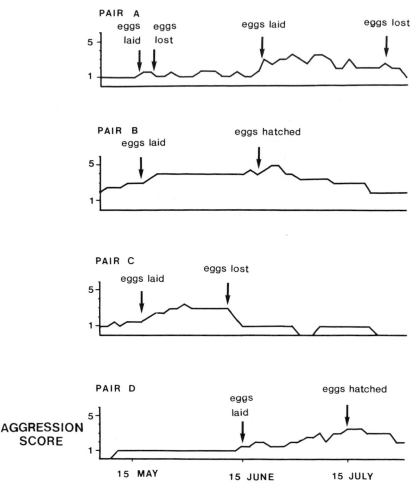

Fig. 44   Increase in the intensity of swoop attacking behaviour of skuas as incubation proceeds, and decrease as chicks grow, or after eggs are lost. Data for Great Skuas at Foula.

Although they breed in regions where there are no ground predators other than species recently and unfortunately introduced by man, Brown Skuas and South Polar Skuas are also well known for their aggressive swooping behaviour, and are also fearless of man, so that catching skuas in the Antarctic by means of a long-handled net, 'butterfly-style', became one of the sports of the Antarctic (Eklund 1961). By contrast, Chilean Skuas rarely attack intruders by swooping as the other skuas do, and the scarce performance of such a characteristic skua behaviour is odd. Perhaps the fact that Chilean Skuas tend to nest in dense gull-like colonies makes the defensive swooping behaviour inappropriate, but several species of large gulls do show a similar swooping behaviour to that of skuas, so this explanation seems rather weak.

Presumably the swooping attacks by Brown and South Polar Skuas must have evolved before skuas colonised the southern hemisphere, since the swoop behaviour is the same in the Arctic species as in the southern species, and there are no natural predators of southern skuas to have elicited such behaviour. It is particularly interesting that the behaviour has been maintained in the Brown, Tristan, Falkland and South Polar Skuas, and apparently became rather less common only in the Chilean Skua. Wilson (1907) reported the highly aggressive swooping attacks on Antarctic explorers by skuas when man first started to visit the Antarctic, so clearly the reaction to human intruders has not been learnt since man first explored the far south. However, Spellerberg observed that unattached female South Polar Skuas frequently swoop at the established female within territories early in the breeding season, and often succeed in taking over from the established female by doing so. Thus the swooping behaviour of skuas at ground predators may simply represent a redirection of this intraspecific behaviour to another function. Since many Chilean Skuas nest in dense colonies with little space for birds to swoop down at the female of each pair, this swooping behaviour may not be of much use to Chilean Skuas attempting to displace established nest owners, though Moynihan (1962) says that Chilean Skuas he watched were often seen to chase each other in aerial contests, and occasionally swooped down at a bird on the ground.

The evidence suggests that the famous swooping attacks of skuas have evolved partly as a behaviour used to take over the territory of established birds, and that this role has led to the maintenance of the behaviour pattern in skua populations that breed in regions where there are no ground predators to drive off.

DISTRACTION BEHAVIOUR

Many species of waders show elaborate distraction-lure displays, which involve highly stereotyped species-characteristic movements and postures that serve to attract the attention of a ground predator and to lead it away from the vicinity of the bird's eggs or chicks. Such behaviour is not found among most other Charadriiforms. Gulls, terns and auks do not perform distraction-lure displays, although gulls and terns will vigorously mob a ground predator near to their nest. Skuas dive at ground predators, as discussed earlier, but only the Arctic Skua also possesses a full distraction-lure display that can be used to decoy ground predators from the nest if outright attack fails (Photos 14, 15).

14. A light phase Arctic Skua in low intensity distraction display. Photo: R. W. Furness.

Wilson (1907) relates that the Falkland Skua will feign injury to distract from its nest, but nobody else has ever reported distraction displaying by any of the large skuas. Great, Brown, Tristan and South Polar Skuas certainly do not perform distraction-lure behaviour and I suspect that Wilson was wrong to think that such behaviour is part of the Falkland Skuas' normal repertoire.

According to Cramp and Simmons (1983) Pomarine and Long-tailed Skuas also use a distraction-lure display like that of the Arctic Skua, although less commonly. However, most accounts of these species either do not mention such displays or state that they are both rare and incomplete. It is rather strange that the Arctic Skua should have an elaborate distraction display and yet Pomarine and Long-tailed Skuas hardly ever show such behaviour. According to Maher (1974) 'The Parasitic Jaeger frequently performs an elaborate distraction display. It is characterised by plaintive calling and by a leading or luring movement away from the nest or young while the wings are extended and beaten spasmodically. Neither of the other jaegers performs this display, although elements of it are present in their behaviour under the same circumstances. Both the Pomarine and Long-tailed Jaegers will occasionally land near an intruder and run or walk from the nest or young, sometimes calling and holding their wings up in an incipient flight position. Only once in approximately two thousand visits to Pomarine Jaeger nests, did I see an adult make a complete distraction display like that of the Parasitic Jaeger, and I have seen one or two distraction displays by Long-tailed Jaegers. The behaviour is extremely rare, although incipiently present, in these two species, in contrast to the Parasitic Jaeger'.

The principal ground predator of the eggs and chicks of small skuas in the Arctic is the Arctic Fox, and this animal is harassed relentlessly by all three species when it comes close to their nest. Maher says that Pomarine Skuas are particularly effective in driving off a fox by dive-bombing attacks, presumably because of their greater size, and he suggests that the virtual absence of a distraction display in the Pomarine and Long-tailed Skuas implies that this is not as effective a strategy as overt aggression. Indeed, according to observers who witnessed Arctic Foxes searching for Arctic Skua nests in northern Alaska, the foxes ignore the distraction

15. A light phase Arctic Skua distracting from its nest by running and crying past the intruder. Photo: R. W. Furness.

displays of adults and go on searching until they find the nest. Maher (1974) considered that the existence of the distraction-lure display in the Arctic Skua could only be attributed to its being of selective advantage in more southerly maritime populations, and so maintained in the Arctic populations as a result of gene flow. He suggested that Arctic Foxes were sufficiently intelligent predators to learn that a displaying adult meant that a nest or brood was to be found. Although ground predators of Arctic Skuas in more southerly maritime breeding areas may be no less intelligent, Maher suggested that the closer nest spacing by Arctic Skuas in these regions will lead to groups of skuas from neighbouring territories all giving the distraction display at short distances all round the predator, thus leading to confusion. Certainly, Williamson (1949) described this sort of communal distraction display by Arctic Skuas in colonies on the Faeroe Islands, and so the distraction-lure display may be much more effective in these lower latitudes. In the Arctic, skua nests are so much further apart that distraction displays would only be made by one pair of skuas at a time, which may aid the fox in focussing its searching in appropriate areas on the tundra. Diving attacks may be much more appropriate in this situation.

Williamson (1949) has published the only detailed account of the distraction-·lure behaviour of the breeding Arctic Skua, which he considered to change in form as the stage of the breeding season progressed. He said of the behaviour early in incubation that the bird leapt into the air, rising several feet vertically and then flopping down onto the ground, crouching and spreading its wings and flapping them up and down. Often this would alternate with swooping attacking flights. Generally these displays were silent, but occasionally a bird would give a plaintive cry that sounded like the call of a young bird soliciting food. Later on, when the eggs were well incubated or the chicks newly hatched, the display was somewhat different. The birds would run along with the body held upright and the wings trailing, often with one wing held fully extended and the other half-closed, or would remain stationary with the wings thrashing the ground and the tail fanned and depressed. The display would be accompanied by crying, and would often alternate with the bird flying around the predator or diving at it. Rarely, birds would adopt a false-brooding posture although they would not be sitting on eggs or young. I must admit that I am not completely convinced by Williamson's idea that the form of distraction display changes with the time in the breeding season. My experience is that different birds show different forms of the distraction display, and that the form of the display differs depending on how intensely motivated the bird is. If it is alone in the territory and the chicks are large, then the bird is likely to give only a half-hearted performance, whereas if both birds are present and have made a determined but unsuccessful attempt to drive the intruder away, then they are likely to give a much more noisy and extravagant display with much thrashing of the ground with their wings. However, Williamson makes the interesting point that the light phase birds are much more conspicuous than dark phase birds when making the distraction display, and therefore the display should be more effective in colonies of predominantly light phase birds.

Although skuas clearly do lose a lot of eggs and chicks to ground predators in the Arctic, the efficacy of the distraction-lure display is quite unknown, and the evidence suggests that aggression against ground predators is more effective than distraction, at least in the Pomarine and Long-tailed Skuas, and the Arctic Skuas nesting at low density in the Arctic. Perhaps the display is only effective where skuas nest in close proximity, as in the Arctic Skuas of maritime lower latitudes, but this is exactly where the proportion of light phase birds is least! Perhaps it represents a secondary strategy if open attack fails. There is clearly a need for a careful investigation of the functional significance of this display in the Arctic Skua.

CHAPTER 7

Food and feeding

Brown Skuas are catholic in their tastes and inclined towards experiment. As their gullets seem to operate with equal facility in either direction, the swallowing of indigestible material along with more orthodox foods causes them no inconvenience; more than one bar of soap, a quantity of material impregnated with formalin, corks, and alcohol-soaked cotton-wool were missed from the work table by the hut, to be recovered later in pellet form not far from the Yellow-Green nest. It was necessary to extinguish cigarette-ends before dropping them in the presence of a skua; any small object found on the ground would be picked up immediately and usually swallowed forthwith.

Stonehouse (1956)

FEEDING METHODS EMPLOYED BY SKUAS

Skuas are best known to most birdwatchers as pirates and predators, but in fact they display a remarkable diversity of feeding methods, from traditional kleptoparasitism (stealing food from other seabirds), to predation on seabird adults, eggs or chicks, passerines, waders and game birds of the tundra, hawking for insects, preying on lemmings, rabbits and other mammals, catching shoaling fish and krill at the sea surface, scavenging on dead mammals or birds, intertidal or marine invertebrates or on refuse tips. While the predominant feeding methods during the breeding season are fairly well documented, foods and feeding methods at other times are poorly known:

Breeding season:
Skua	Locality	Main feeding methods (ranked)
Pomarine	Arctic tundra	predation of microtine rodents

Long-tailed	Arctic tundra	predation of microtine rodents, insects, birds
Arctic	Arctic tundra	birds, eggs, berries
Arctic	coasts	kleptoparasitism
Great	Iceland, Faeroes	predation of seabirds, scavenging, piracy
Great	Shetland, Orkney	discards, fishing for Sandeels
Tristan	Tristan, Gough	nocturnal predation of petrels on land
Falkland	Falklands	highly varied, including petrels, fish, penguins
Chilean	S. America	intertidal invertebrates, scavenging, predation
Brown	Macquarie Is.	rabbits, nocturnal predation of petrels
Brown	Marion Is. etc.	nocturnal predation of petrels, predation and scavenging on penguins
South Polar	Ross Sea	fishing for krill, fish, scavenging on penguins
South Polar	Pointe Geologie	scavenging on refuse, predation on penguins

Nonbreeding season:

Skua	*Main feeding methods*
Pomarine	predation of small seabirds, scavenging, kleptoparasitism
Arctic	kleptoparasitism
Long-tailed	picking small items off the sea surface, kleptoparasitism
Great	scavenging, discards, predation, kleptoparasitism
Tristan	nocturnal predation of petrels, scavenging
Falkland	not known
Chilean	not known
Brown	not known
South Polar	not known, but probably mainly fish caught for itself

Kleptoparasitism is one very specialised feeding method that is particularly associated with skuas, and that habit is the subject of Chapter 8. In this chapter I shall deal with each of the other major feeding methods in turn rather than considering the feeding ecology of each species, since most skua species use most of these feeding methods when they live in the appropriate habitats.

EXPLOITATION OF TUNDRA ECOSYSTEMS

Arctic, Long-tailed and Pomarine Skuas may all live throughout the short Arctic summer on tundra habitats far from the sea, where they can breed without having to make any use of marine food resources. Although the several different species of lemmings and other microtine rodents are the main prey of skuas and Snowy Owls in tundra habitats, there are differences in the feeding niches and predatory behaviour of the three small skua species that reduce competition between them and allow them to share breeding ranges to some extent. Also, in some tundra habitats, there are no lemmings at all; for example, in central Iceland, in Greenland and Spitzbergen, where Long-tailed Skuas and Arctic Skuas can breed regularly and in fairly large numbers by exploiting other foods (Kampp 1982).

By studying all three small skuas breeding in northern Alaska, Maher (1974) was able to show that the food habits of breeding skuas differed between species in three areas within this region (Figs. 45 to 47). Breeding Pomarine Skuas fed almost exclusively on Brown Lemmings, with less than 3% of the diet consisting of birds, eggs, fish and insects. Breeding Long-tailed Skuas also depended mainly on microtine rodents, but of a variety of species as well as Brown Lemmings (Fig. 48), and also took a wider variety of non-mammalian prey, including large numbers

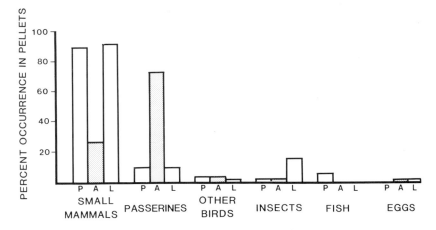

Fig. 45   Diets of breeding Pomarine (open histograms), Arctic (hatched histograms) and Long-tailed Skuas (open histograms) at Cape Sabine in north Alaska, as indicated by the percentage occurrence of prey types in pellets. From Maher (1974).

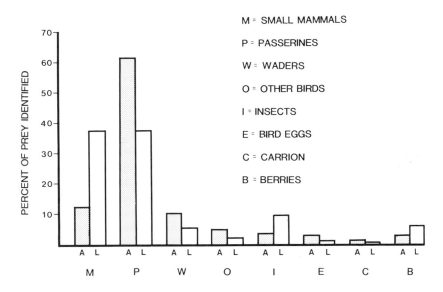

Fig. 46   Diets of breeding Arctic (hatched histograms) and Long-tailed Skuas (open histograms) at Kaolak River in north Alaska, as indicated by percentage occurrence of prey types in pellets. From Maher (1974).

of birds, insects, berries and some bird's eggs. Breeding Arctic Skuas fed predominantly on small birds, which represented from 65% to 94% of the diet, taking fewer microtine rodents but some insects, berries, fish and carrion. Transient, nonbreeding, skuas showed similar differences in diet to those of breeding birds

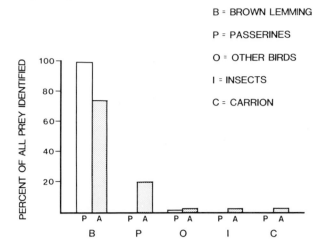

Fig. 47   Diets of breeding Pomarine (open histograms) and Arctic Skuas (hatched histograms) at Barrow in north Alaska as indicated by percentage occurrence of prey types in pellets. From Maher (1974).

of each species, but the nonbreeders all tended to exploit a wider variety of prey than the breeding adults (Fig. 49).

Maher's data show clearly that Arctic Skuas breeding on tundra habitats make little use of microtines as food, even during years of high lemming abundance. Arctic Skuas on the tundra are primarily predators of small birds, whereas Pomarine and Long-tailed Skuas are primarily predators of microtine rodents. However, during the breeding season the Pomarine Skua is an obligate microtine rodent predator, feeding almost exclusively on the Brown Lemming as it is unable to exploit alternative prey of the tundra ecosystems to a significant degree. As a result, Pomarine Skuas are unable to breed where microtine rodents are not available in large numbers. Further, they require a habitat with little vegetation cover so that the rodents are unable to hide, and so can only breed in years of rodent population highs on open tundra. Long-tailed Skuas are less dependent on lemmings. They can exploit microtine population highs, but they can also turn to birds, and particularly to insect prey, where or when rodents are not available. Maher found that insects represented more than half of the stomach contents of a shot sample of nonbreeding Long-tailed Skuas, but occurred in significant numbers in only 9% of Arctic Skua stomachs, and in none of the nonbreeding Pomarine Skuas sampled (Figs. 45–47).

Among the bird prey taken by Arctic Skuas in northern Alaska, 96% were passerines, and two-thirds of the waders they took were chicks. Long-tailed Skuas took a similarly high proportion of passerines, and virtually all of the waders they predated were chicks. Most of the passerines taken by both species were Shorelarks, the most abundant passerine of the area, so that these two skuas showed a high degree of dietary overlap in terms of the bird prey taken. To some extent, high numbers of lemmings make passerines and waders more vulnerable to predation because of physical disturbance of their nests by lemmings, so that any competition between these skuas for bird prey would be most likely during years when lemmings were scarce. Arctic and Long-tailed Skuas hold mutually exclusive territories in which the breeding birds feed, so that competition for food would probably only occur between nonbreeders which tend to gather into roaming flocks composed of all three small skua species. Pomarine Skuas took relatively few birds as prey, and most were waders or goslings, so that there is little overlap with the avian prey of the Arctic and Long-tailed Skuas (Fig. 48).

These dietary differences come about partly as a result of the size differences between the skua species. Long-tailed Skuas, the smallest by far, are adept at catching insects in midair or from the ground, and catch lemmings by dropping down onto them from the air. Pomarine Skuas, being much sturdier, would be less able to catch insects or passerines, but are capable of digging lemmings out

A. BIRDS

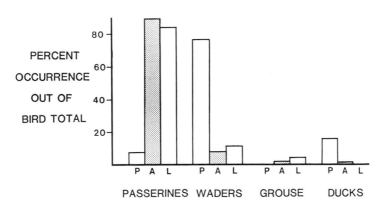

B. MAMMALS

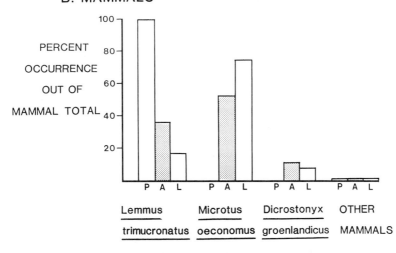

Fig. 48   Birds and mammals in the diets of breeding Pomarine (open), Arctic (hatched) and Long-tailed Skuas (open) in north Alaska. From Maher (1974).

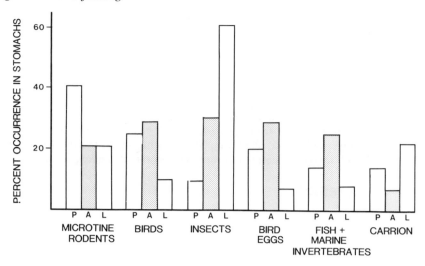

Fig. 49 Diets of nonbreeding (transient) Pomarine (open), Arctic (hatched) and Long-tailed Skuas (open) in north Alaska as indicated by percentage occurrence in stomachs of shot samples of 56 Pomarine, 32 Arctic and 40 Long-tailed Skuas. From Maher (1974).

of the vegetation or ground as well as jumping on them in the open.

Arctic Skuas have such a wide prey spectrum that they can breed every year in the same territory, and so can gain benefits from retaining the same mate in successive years, which enhances breeding performance (Chapter 10), whereas Long-tailed Skuas may fail to breed in years when microtine rodent abundance is very low. However, like the Arctic Skua they hold a large feeding territory on the tundra to which they return each year, giving them the advantage of getting to know their territory well and being able to retain the same mate from year to year. Pomarine Skuas only attempt to breed when and where rodents are abundant. Lemmings show a population cycle of about 3–4 years duration, with huge fluctuations in numbers from trough to peak, although this so-called cycle is not totally regular, and is not in phase over wide areas. As a result, Pomarine Skuas that arrive on the tundra in spring will wander around looking for a suitable area where lemming densities would allow them to breed, since they cannot turn to any alternative prey as Long-tailed Skuas do. This behaviour, which is clearly caused by their inflexible feeding requirement, has important consequences for their breeding biology in general, since it means that birds are unable to retain the same mate from year to year and tend to set up their territory in a different area each year. Pomarine Skuas pay the penalty of their narrow feeding specialisation by having to forgo the advantages of a stable breeding pair bond and territory, and instead are nomadic, exploiting any suitable rodent concentration they can find. If none is found then they simply do not breed that summer.

Because of the important differences in the diets and feeding behaviour of the three small skua species there is little evidence of interspecific competition for food, although each species defends its territory against all skuas irrespective of species.

Pomarine and Long-tailed Skuas hunt over the tundra as individuals. One member of the pair stays by the nest to incubate or to defend the chicks while the other bird patrols the territory looking for lemmings. By contrast, Arctic Skuas are reported by Maher frequently to hunt in pairs with the chicks left unguarded. The members of the pair cooperate in capturing small birds, and presumably do so because this substantially improves their hunting success. To me, Maher's observations are particularly interesting because my experience of Arctic Skuas breeding in Shetland is that one adult always remains with the chicks to defend them and the territory unless feeding conditions are so bad that the chicks are in danger of starvation. The pair hunting behaviour of Arctic Skuas in northern Alaska is something that I would never have expected. It must surely increase the losses of chicks to predators such as other skuas, Snowy Owls, Arctic Foxes, or mustelids, and so suggests to me that Maher's Arctic Skuas had little choice but to resort to such feeding tactics. Perhaps the choice was to guard the chicks and see them starve, or to risk the chicks being taken by predators while they hunted together.

Arctic Skuas are, nevertheless, highly competent predators in the Arctic tundra ecosystem. They can be particularly efficient at raiding eggs from exposed nests. Magnus Enquist found that about half of all of the diver eggs laid in part of western Iceland were apparently taken by Arctic Skuas, so he carried out a series of experiments, using artificial Red-throated Diver nests, model Red-throated Divers and gull eggs painted to resemble diver eggs, in order to discover how Arctic Skuas managed to locate and predate diver nests. He showed (Enquist 1983) that skuas tended to search places where there were likely to be diver nests, because dummy nests placed on the banks of ponds were more often predated by Arctic Skuas than identical nests placed on the open tundra. Also, by placing a dummy Red-throated Diver at half of the model nests at the water edge for 24 hours before leaving the eggs exposed, he was able to show that Arctic Skuas used the adult divers as a cue for locations to check for eggs. Nests where he had previously placed dummy adults were raided more quickly by skuas than were those that had not been advertised by the presence of an apparently incubating bird the previous day (Fig. 50). Arctic Skuas not only know what sort of sites to search for diver eggs but also remember where divers have been seen incubating. Arctic Skuas cannot steal eggs from nests where a diver is present, so they must hope to chance upon those that the bird has left, as for example when disturbed by humans. Since

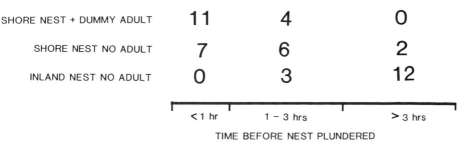

Fig. 50   Time taken for Arctic Skuas to plunder artificial Red-throated Diver nests, set up with or without a dummy diver, and adjacent to water or inland. From Enquist (1983).

nests are rarely left unattended, Arctic Skuas must be efficient in searching, and
in the use of remembered cues, to be able to predate such a high proportion of
nests. Enquist also noted that the presence of humans on the tundra attracted
Arctic Skuas, suggesting that they are aware of the possibility of incubating birds
being disturbed from their nests by people. Martin and Barry (1978) studied the
feeding behaviour of Arctic Skuas in northern Canada and observed that skuas
were quickly attracted by any disturbance within goose colonies, and used these
to attempt to predate nests temporarily uncovered.

PREDATION OF SEABIRDS AND LAGOMORPHS

Several populations of skuas feed predominantly by predation of seabirds.
During the breeding season, the Tristan Skua on Inaccessible Island, Tristan da
Cunha, took only one non-avian prey, goose-barnacles, and these represented only
2% of the pellets of indigestible material regurgitated by the skuas (Fraser 1984).
White-bellied Storm Petrels, Broad-billed Prions, White-faced Storm Petrels and
Common Diving Petrels made up almost 90% of the total prey recorded (Fig. 51),
with very small numbers of six other seabirds and three landbirds making up the
rest of the diet. On Gough Island, this same skua species feeds virtually entirely
on seabirds. It preys particularly on Broad-billed Prions, Soft-plumaged Petrels
and Atlantic Petrels, but also on Kerguelen Petrels, White-faced and White-bellied
Storm Petrels, Common Diving Petrels, Great and Little Shearwaters, and on
Rockhopper Penguins, their eggs and chicks. Goose-barnacles also occurred rarely
in pellets on Gough Island, but most skuas fed almost entirely on the island (Fig.
52).

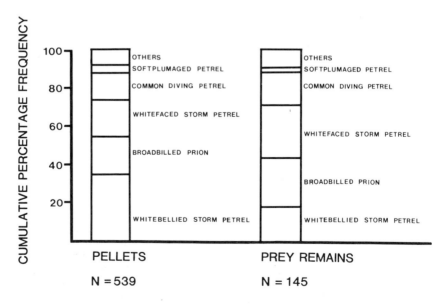

Fig. 51   *Diet of Tristan Skuas on Inaccessible Island, Tristan da Cunha, as
assessed by examination of pellets and prey remains. From Fraser (1984).*

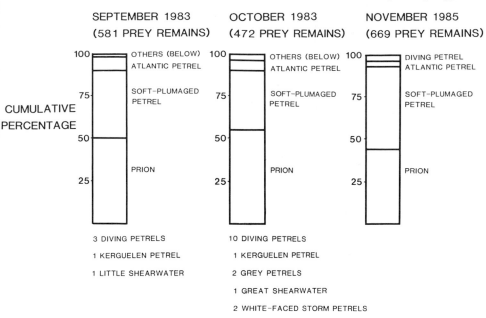

Fig. 52   Diet of Tristan Skuas on Gough Island as assessed by examination of prey remains, September and October 1983, and November 1985.

I had visited Foula for twelve years in succession and got to know Great Skuas and their way of life, and, having seen populations of Great Skuas at other North Atlantic colonies, I concluded that the bird is unusually lazy. Great Skuas, whatever their feeding method, spend much of their day on the territory apparently doing nothing. They usually cease feeding well before darkness, and in the morning are one of the last of the seabirds to take wing and to feed. It is most unusual to see them attempting to feed at night, and the nonbreeders at colonies roost on their club sites from early evening until sunrise or later, although they may fly around at night if disturbed, so they are not totally impeded by darkness. When I visited Gough Island I was taken aback to discover that the closely related Tristan Skua behaves in a quite different way, feeding almost exclusively at night, although it does share the Great Skua's tendency to do very little for most of the time. Throughout the day the Tristan Skuas just sit around and show little interest in anything. At night they walk about their territory, listening for movements of petrels on the ground. When they locate a bird on the surface they jump on it and attack it with their beak. Like all other skuas they do not use their feet to hold down the prey, which makes it far more difficult to subdue and kill the petrels as a result. Watching skuas on Gough attacking petrels I saw the victim escape on several occasions and bolt down the nearest available burrow to safety. But of course the skua's webbed feet cannot be used like the talons of birds of prey. The webbing and foot structure do not allow skuas to take a grip, and so they must do the best they can with the bill alone. Each territory holding pair of Tristan Skuas on Gough manages to kill one or two petrels nightly despite their anatomical

16. A Tristan Skua on Gough Island attempting to tear open a dead Rockhopper Penguin on the beach. Photo: R. W. Furness.

limitations, and this seems to allow them to spend most of the night and all day doing little or nothing. In fact, they often eat only the choicer parts of their kill and leave the rest to rot, or to be eaten later.

Tristan Skuas patrol the areas of their territory where the ground cover is relatively sparse and where there are plenty of petrel burrows, and when they succeed in making a kill they generally carry the body to one specific site within the territory which they use as a larder. The larder soon becomes more of a midden, since the uneaten leftovers accumulate in layers, allowing the ornithologist to study their past diet in the manner of an archaeologist digging through the food remains and refuse of an ancient human settlement. It seems more likely that in carrying their prey onto this spot they are using it as a store rather than attempting to keep their territory tidy, so I have coined the term 'larder' for the feature. The larder may contain remains of as many as a hundred carcasses of petrels in an area of about 5m^2, and skuas often visit their larder during the day to pick at some of the recent partly-eaten corpses. This is particularly the case when small chicks are present, as they can be fed at the larder. In general, there is only one larder on each territory, and it is usually close to the nest site and to the sitting mound where the birds rest when off-duty (Fig. 53). Although larders are present in almost all Tristan Skua territories, other skuas do not seem to gather their prey remains in this way, unless the fact has gone unreported in the literature. Certainly, Great Skuas leave the corpses of auks and Kittiwakes scattered all about their territories. The Flightless Moorhen on Gough Island and the introduced mice will pick meat scraps from skua kills, but they steal very little and cannot be the reason for the skuas gathering kills into larders. There are no other animals on Gough likely to take skua kills, so the behaviour cannot be a response to other predators or scavengers. Immature and nonbreeding skuas are chased away from territories if they attempt to land, and are displayed at when they fly over, so there is little or no chance for nonbreeders to rob territory holding birds of prey remains. Tristan Skuas nesting on the barren summits of Gough, where the vegetation is a thin carpet of mosses and short grass, are less tidy, and it may be that the larders are made mainly because they allow skuas to find the prey remains which, if left where they were killed during the hours of darkness, might be difficult to relocate in the prevailing thick bracken, tree ferns and tussock grass of the lower parts of Gough Island, where most of the skuas and burrow nesting petrels occur.

Tristan Skuas can also get at petrels by digging through the soft peaty ground to open up burrows if they can hear a petrel. I was surprised to discover that a hunting skua would often ignore my torch beam and allow me to watch as it walked from burrow entrance to burrow entrance, putting its head into each in

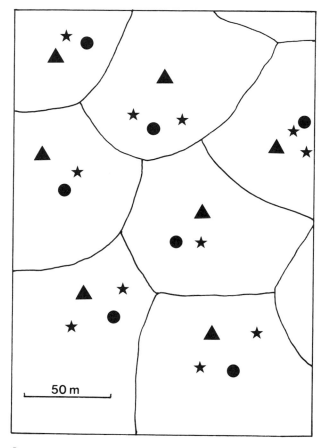

Fig. 53   Location of larders (stars) and sitting mounds (triangles) in relation to nests (dots) and territorial boundaries (continuous lines) in Tristan Skuas on Gough Island.

turn, until it found one where it could hear a petrel moving around inside. It would then start to pull the burrow open with its bill, twisting and turning and tugging at the old plant roots until it could pluck the petrel from the burrow. This performance took quite a long time, and I doubt whether it is common, as few burrows showed signs of having been attacked. During the periods that I visited Gough, spanning the start of egg laying to the latter part of chick rearing by the skuas, petrels on the surface at night were so numerous that skuas could find all the prey they wanted, just by jumping on petrels they found.

Since Tristan Skuas kill petrels at the breeding colonies while they are in the open, not in the burrows, the question of the status of such petrels obviously needs to be considered. Breeding petrels that own a burrow generally land at the burrow entrance and disappear rapidly underground. Immature petrels that are looking for a mate and a breeding site, an unoccupied burrow that they can take over, tend to alight and then to sit around in the open or visit a number of burrow entrances to see if they are tenanted or not. This would suggest that skuas would be much more likely to chance upon these nonbreeders rather than established

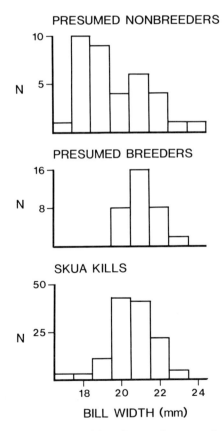

Fig. 54 Bill widths of presumed breeding and presumed nonbreeding Broad-billed Prions on Gough Island compared with bill widths of prions eaten by Tristan Skuas.

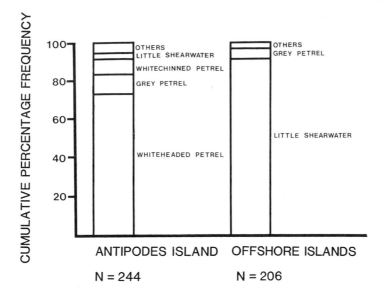

Fig. 55   Diet of Brown Skuas on Antipodes Island, and on Bollons and Archway Islands, New Zealand. From Moors (1980).

breeding birds. The plumage pattern of immature petrels is indistinguishable from that of breeding adults, but in some seabird species there is a tendency for the biometrics of immatures to differ from those of older adults. For example, wing lengths of nonbreeding, predominantly immature, Storm Petrels are, on average, shorter than those of breeders (Furness & Baillie 1981), while the bill depth of Herring Gulls is a character that increases up to at least nine years of age, several years after the onset of breeding of most Herring Gulls (Coulson *et al.* 1981). The main prey species taken by the skuas on Gough Island, the Broad-billed Prion, shows a wide range of bill widths from bird to bird. Fledgling prions have narrow bills and it seems likely that bill width is a character that increases over the years of immaturity. I used bill widths of prions eaten by skuas to see if I could discover which age classes were particularly susceptible to predation. I was unable to find many prions incubating in burrows, so I also classified as breeders birds which I caught at night that had bare, vascularised brood patches, or which regurgitated large boluses of food. Individuals with feathered brood patches when breeding birds were hatching eggs were classified as nonbreeders, and most were probably immature birds. Measurements (Fig. 54) showed that breeding adults had bill widths of at least 20 mm, whereas many nonbreeders had narrower bills. The bill widths of prions killed were often smaller than those of most breeders and, clearly, skuas were killing some nonbreeders. Because we caught many birds by dazzling them in flight with a powerful spotlight, we probably sampled young nonbreeders that would not normally land in the colony to explore for burrow sites. This likely bias in the sampling means that it is not possible to deduce precisely what proportion of the prey were breeders rather than nonbreeders. However, I think it is probable that burrow-seeking nonbreeders form the majority of birds killed.

Skuas at many other colonies feed mainly on nocturnal burrow-nesting petrels.

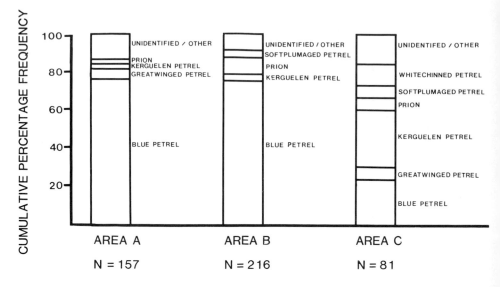

Fig. 56   Diet of Brown Skuas at three different sites on Prince Edward Island, showing the tendency for skuas to prey on whichever birds are locally available. From Adams (1982).

In some areas of the Falkland Islands, Falkland Skua territories are littered with carcasses of prions. On many of the islands off New Zealand the Brown Skuas predate White-headed Petrels, prions, White-faced Storm Petrels, Little Shearwaters, and even White-chinned Petrels (Fig. 55). On Prince Edward Island, in the southern Indian Ocean, Brown Skuas feed mainly on Blue Petrels, Kerguelen petrels and prions (Fig. 56). On Macquarie island the Brown Skuas predate rabbits and Black Rats, but also take White-headed Petrels, prions, and scavenge on penguins and seals (Jones & Skira 1979). To a large extent, the differences in diet reflect the availability of prey species at these locations.

Great Skuas in Iceland, the Faeroe Islands, and on St Kilda take many seabirds but predation is much less extensive at most Scottish colonies. Also, Great Skuas prey almost entirely on seabirds that are active during the day rather than on burrow-nesting petrels, and where Storm Petrels are an important part of the avian diet, they are probably caught at sea rather than at night at colonies. To some extent, differences in species predated by Great Skuas reflect prey availability. For example, ducks and geese form a substantial part of the avian prey of Great Skuas in Iceland, but few are available in Shetland and so are rare in the diet there (Tables 24, 25). However, it is clear that certain feeding techniques have developed in some areas but not in others, and have presumably spread within colonies by imitative learning. Thus, for example, Great Skuas on Foula kill large numbers of fledgling Kittiwakes but never take eggs or chicks from Kittiwake nests (B. L. Furness 1979), whereas at Hermaness they take Kittiwake eggs and nestlings, but rarely kill fledglings (Andersson 1976). On Noss, they took few Kittiwake eggs or nestlings before 1984 when Kittiwakes had a catastrophic breeding season and many nests were deserted. A few pairs of Great Skuas took advantage of this and fed on the abandoned eggs. In 1985 much larger numbers of Kittiwake eggs were predated on Noss, indicating that this habit had begun to spread within the colony. Imitative learning assumes a certain degree of specialisation of individual feeding habits. Bayes *et al.* (1964) found that some individual Great Skuas at a colony in the Faeroes fed almost entirely on Kittiwake eggs while these were available. Other pairs specialised in cannibalism, two pairs took Oystercatcher eggs but no Kittiwake eggs, two pairs took Fulmar eggs, and one pair took Whimbrel eggs but no Kittiwake eggs. On Foula, one particular pair fed almost exclusively on adult Black Guillemots which they caught by standing on boulders above occupied nests and pouncing on adults as they emerged. The same pair used this unique feeding technique in four successive seasons.

The spread of a particular feeding technique has been noted by Finnur Gudmundsson at an Icelandic colony. Before 1940 he had never recorded Great Skuas in Iceland killing adult Fulmars, but this practice has since spread slowly from one site in south Iceland. It now occurs in several localised areas, but is still confined to a small number of individuals. Further diversity of feeding is produced by the various techniques employed by other Great Skuas to prey on the same species of bird. Some predate Puffins by catching them in flight over the sea, and this may be considered to be the extension of the kleptoparasitic habit; rather than threatening to attack Puffins, the skuas actually do so. Others may stand over the entrance of Puffin burrows and pounce on emerging birds, some may try to reach down into burrows that Puffins have just entered, others may harass them on the sea surface, hovering over them as they resurface after diving to escape, until the

Puffin tires and can be lifted out of the water. Feeding specialisation will presumably increase the foraging efficiency of individual skuas, although this would be difficult to demonstrate quantitatively, but in addition, the diversity of feeding specialisations allows the population as a whole to exploit a wider range of foods, and thus reduce the extent of intraspecific competition. In addition, the generalised and opportunistic nature of the Great Skua allows unexpected or transient food sources, such as flocks of disoriented migrant passerines, or lost racing pigeons, to be exploited, and allows imitative learning of novel and successful feeding techniques among birds in neighbouring territories. However, this very flexibility combined with individual specialisations means that the diet of skuas does not necessarily reflect the availability of prey, and prey remains should be used with caution as an index of populations of seabirds close to skua territories.

FISHING

Outside of the breeding season, there is little to suggest that skuas of any species feed to a great extent by catching fish for themselves at sea, although rather little is known about the habits of skuas in winter, and winter distributions of South Polar Skuas and Long-tailed Skuas suggest that they probably take small fish. During the breeding season, many populations of South Polar Skuas feed predominantly by catching krill or fish for themselves, and Great Skuas in Orkney

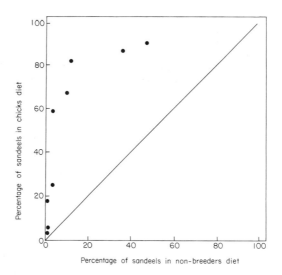

Fig. 57   Proportion of diet comprising Sandeels in the diets of Great Skua chicks and nonbreeders at weekly intervals between June and August 1975 at Foula. The solid line shows the expected relationship if chicks and nonbreeders both took Sandeels equally. From Furness & Hislop (1981).

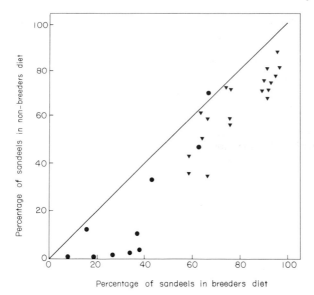

Fig. 58   Proportion of diet comprising Sandeels in the diets of Great Skua breeders and nonbreeders in 1975 (●) and 1976 (▼), showing that breeders took more Sandeels than nonbreeders. The solid line shows the expected relationship if breeders and nonbreeders took Sandeels equally. From Furness & Hislop (1981).

and Shetland also feed by fishing. For the short period during early summer when Sandeels frequently rise in tight shoals to the surface, Great Skuas quickly congregate over Sandeel shoals and splash onto the sea surface, sometimes submerging as much as half a metre, plucking out beaksful of Sandeels. In this situation they compete with Fulmars, large gulls and Gannets which all fight for position over the shoals, although Great Skuas spend little time attempting to rob the other species. It seems they can do better by taking Sandeels directly from the shoal. The period during which they form the bulk of the Great Skua's diet varies from year to year, and also between categories within the population. Sandeels represent a much greater proportion of the diet of chicks than of nonbreeding adults (Fig. 57), and a greater proportion of the diet of breeders than that of nonbreeders (Fig. 58). Adults feed their chicks preferentially on Sandeels, presumably because Sandeels are nutritionally better than alternative foods. They have a higher calorific value than whitefish such as Haddock or Whiting discards, and contain little indigestible material. One of the more gruesome experiences whilst handling thousands of chicks was when one half-grown Great Skua regurgitated an entire Arctic Skua chick weighing about 150 g! Much of this meal would have been digestible only with great difficulty, and of little benefit to the youngster, even if it did completely fill its stomach.

The ease with which Great Skuas are able to get their daily food requirements can be assessed to some extent by the amount of time that they spend away from the territory, since most of it goes into foraging. In 1976, the higher the proportion of Sandeels in the diet, the less time Great Skuas spent away from the territory (Furness & Hislop 1981); which suggests that Sandeels could be caught more quickly than other food, as well as providing chicks with a higher quality diet. The fact that nonbreeding birds took discards to a greater extent than did breeding birds, suggests that competition for Sandeels may have forced the nonbreeders to make more use of discards as a more easily obtainable food though one of lower quality.

Although Sandeels appear to be the preferred food of Great Skuas in Orkney and Shetland, they are only briefly available in early summer. Sandeels were of no commercial importance until recently, and a significant fishery for Sandeels around Shetland only started in 1974, and it is only since then that Shetland Sandeel stocks have received attention from fishery biologists. As a result, relatively little is known about the stock sizes, age composition or behaviour of these fish, although a general tendency has been demonstrated on both sides of the North Atlantic for Sandeel stocks to have increased as a consequence of the over-exploitation of stocks of other fish, particularly Herring and Mackerel in the 1960s. Great Skuas and other surface-feeding seabirds do not search for individual Sandeels, but for shoals of millions of fish. It is believed that these shoals form when Sandeels feeding in the upper plankton-rich layers of the sea are attacked by predatory fish such as Cod or Whiting. The Sandeels attempt to minimise the chances of their being eaten by trying to get to the middle of the shoal, where they will be protected by the mass of other Sandeels; as a result, the shoal becomes an almost solid ball of wriggling fish, with those at the bottom of the shoal trying hardest to get to the middle. The ball tends to rise to the surface, and if it is large it may break the surface as the Sandeels at the bottom push their way up. Any passing seabird is likely to notice such a Sandeel ball, and nearby seabirds quickly home in on the first bird to start diving onto the fish. Within a matter of a minute or two several hundred seabirds may have gathered overhead. At first any seabird can exploit the fish, but as numbers build up, terns and Kittiwakes are pushed aside by the larger species. As the feeding flock develops it takes up a characteristic structure, with Gannets, Fulmars and Great Skuas dominating the centre immediately above the Sandeel ball, and large numbers of Great Black-backed Gulls, Great Skuas and Herring Gulls in a surrounding ring, and some Kittiwakes in a sparser outer zone. Birds plunge to the sea surface or onto the ball itself and rise with their beaks full of fish. A few plunges are probably enough to give a bird a full stomach, and satiated birds are immediately replaced by newcomers drawn in from some considerable distance. These feeding flocks may continue for a few minutes or as long as half an hour, during which time the ball may drift quite a distance in the surface currents, while, presumably, predatory fish are making unseen inroads into the bottom of the ball (Fig. 59). Eventually the shoal either breaks up or sinks, or is almost totally consumed, and large numbers of heavily laden seabirds heading off towards the colony provide the only visible clue to the event. The day to day availability of these balls of Sandeels is unpredictable, as is their spatial distribution. Sometimes no surface feeding flocks of birds are to be seen at all. On other days there may be dozens, sometimes in all directions, sometimes clustered in one area in a particular direction from the colony. Great Skuas have only to patrol the sea around their colony, keeping a sharp lookout for Sandeel balls and, even more importantly, for any signs that other seabirds have found a ball.

The seasonal pattern of Sandeel availability is reflected in their importance in

Fig. 59   A feeding flock at a ball of Sandeels.

Great Skua diets (Fig. 60). Furthermore, their importance in the diet has clearly changed over the years and this may well reflect the changing fortunes of the Shetland Sandeel stocks. There are two types of dietary information that we have collected each year on Foula. Firstly, the proportion of skua chick regurgitates of each prey type during the first two weeks of July, and secondly, the proportion of regurgitated pellets at club sites that include each prey type during the same period. These data sets are complementary in that chicks are fed almost exclusively on Sandeels, and so a decrease in the proportion of Sandeels in chick regurgitates reflects a major shortage of that food, whereas nonbreeders have a more varied diet, taking discard fish as an easy way to achieve their food requirements without competing for places over Sandeel balls.

Over the years, the proportion of chick regurgitates of Sandeels has declined slightly, whereas the proportion of Sandeels in the diet of nonbreeders has decreased dramatically, almost to zero (Fig. 61). This decrease probably relates to changes in Sandeel biology because there has, up to 1986, been little change in the availability of alternative foods. However, industrial catches of Sandeels around Shetland increased to a peak in 1982, and then declined. This recent decline may be due to the effects of over-fishing for Sandeels; the depleted stock losing its

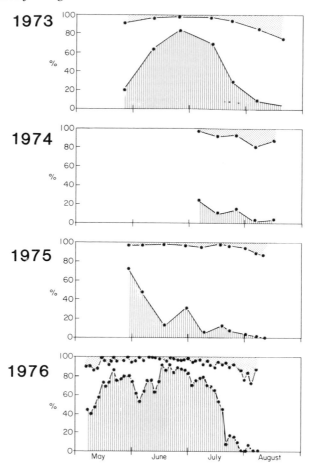

Fig. 60   Percentage composition of the diet of nonbreeding Great Skuas at Foula through parts of the breeding seasons in 1973 to 1976. Sandeels are represented by vertical hatching, whitefish discards by lack of shading, and other items (birds, mammals, invertebrates, berries and eggs) by stippling. From Furness & Hislop (1981).

ability to produce abundant new generations. Alternatively, a change in some important oceanographic condition may have caused poor recruitments of Sandeels. There is no evidence to confirm or refute either hypothesis; we need to know much more about the biology of the Sandeel, but we do know that its larval production has been poor in recent years and this must have important implications for Great Skuas and for other Shetland seabirds (Chapter 16).

The fishing behaviour of South Polar Skuas is similar to that of Great Skuas. It has been overlooked by many Antarctic ornithologists because it is rarely seen, whereas interactions between skuas and penguins are easily observed and are striking. Professor Euan Young gave a good description of fishing South Polar

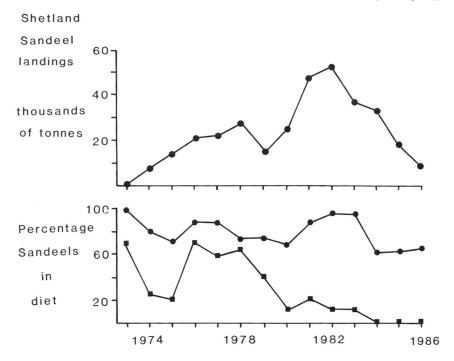

Shetland
Sandeel
landings

thousands
of tonnes

Percentage
Sandeels
in
diet

Fig. 61   Sandeels as a proportion of the diet of Great Skua chicks (dots) and nonbreeding Great Skuas (squares) on Foula in the first half of July each year from 1973 to 1986 (lower graph), compared with the changes in the Industrial catch of Sandeels around Shetland (upper graph).

Skuas (Young 1963): 'Until late December the ice extended in an unbroken sheet to the north of the Cape with clear water along the northern horizon. A continuous stream of birds flew to and from there ... Fishing was observed on two occasions but only once from reasonably close at hand. There were 20 or 30 birds when first noticed but the number soon increased to 80 to 100. From time to time one of the birds when flying within a few feet of the sea, plunged down immersing the head and breast. The wings were extended well back and avoided much of the initial splashing. This drop was so contrived that the birds faced in to the wind on the water surface, allowing them to lift easily into the air again with a single wing beat. The tail of the fish often projected from the beak for a time after regaining flight. No calling was heard and it seems likely that the irregular flight of fishing birds attracts others when a shoal is discovered'. The birds studied by Young were feeding mainly on the common Antarctic fish *Pleurogramma antarcticum*, but Eklund (1961) also records that South Polar Skuas will fish for krill in much the same way.

Many authors have been at pains to point out that skuas often do not make any attempt to catch fish for themselves: Arctic Skuas in north USSR were never seen fishing at sea by Belopolskii (1961). Arctic Skuas in Shetland certainly do not fish for themselves (Furness 1978).

The skuas' senses of smell and taste

During their ill-fated expedition to the South Pole, Scott and his party observed South Polar Skuas several times far inland in Antarctica, as far south as latitude 80° 20'S over the polar icecap. They believed that these skuas had been attracted there from the coast by wind-borne odours from the slain sledge dogs (Gain 1914). Wilson (1907) had also seen South Polar Skuas far from the sea, including one at a camp he established 170 miles inland from the Antarctic coast, and he also believed that South Polar Skuas were able to scavenge by means of a phenomenally acute sense of smell. These views run contrary to the general opinion of later ornithologists, that birds of all species have a very poorly developed sense of smell. Tinbergen (1953) found no evidence whatsoever to suggest that Herring Gulls could detect smells and be guided by them to find food. General reviews of olfaction in birds concluded that their sense of smell is feeble and plays a very small role in sensory perception (Romer 1955). Do skuas make use of an exceptional ability to smell carrion over great distances as suggested by the observations of polar explorers? Eklund (1961) performed experiments in the Antarctic to test this idea in view of the later finding that birds do not, in general, make use of olfactory cues. He had observed that skuas would quickly find lumps of meat put out on the ice surface at Wilkes Station (where South Polar Skuas were common and bred close by). Skuas would hover over the meat and drop down onto it. On five occasions he placed meat in sealed transparent polythene bags from which he considered that no smells could emanate, and placed these on the ground. Each time a skua ripped the plastic open within a minute of seeing the meat, demonstrating that the birds could locate meat easily by sight alone. On six occasions he placed similar chunks of fresh meat under a thin layer of powdered snow, and not one of these was located by a skua even though the thin layer of snow would have provided no barrier to smell. Then he experimented with a captive South Polar Skua to confirm this result. He buried fresh chicken livers in an outdoor bottomless box in which the skua was confined, with the livers covered by a layer of light snow. The bird paid no attention to the cache and even sat down on it, but when he presented chicken livers to the bird it ate them immediately. These tests do strongly suggest that skuas have little, if any, sense of smell, and so they tend to agree with the general opinion that birds do not find food by olfaction. However, recent research has changed this view for some kinds of birds. Some South American vultures find carcasses in the dense rain forests primarily, and very efficiently, by using their highly developed sense of smell. Petrels foraging at sea can also locate food from its odours. Experiments by Hutchinson *et al.* (1982) showed that petrels would approach a float with a wick dipped in a solvent containing extract of fish significantly more often than they approached a float with a wick dipped in the solvent alone, and were very much more likely to land beside the float giving off a food odour. An anatomical examination of petrels shows that they have particularly large olfactory lobes, and that those from high latitudes have the largest olfactory lobes of all petrels, which might be expected since volatile odours will be less easily released in the cold of high latitudes. Eklund's experiments suggest that skuas do not use smell, and they do not appear to have the large olfactory lobes that would be required for an effective sense of smell at high latitudes. From this it would appear that the observations of South Polar Skuas far inland from the Antarctic coast simply indicate that these birds range the whole continent in search of food, and possibly were attracted to early polar explorers by their tracks over the snow or by other visual cues.

While skuas may not have much of a sense of smell, they scavenge on a remarkably wide variety of items, including many that demonstrate their highly opportunistic behaviour and lack of caution towards novel objects, and also suggest a very limited sense of taste! Stonehouse's (1956) description that heads this chapter records that the Brown Skuas he studied attempted to eat such items as a formalin-soaked rag, and even lighted cigarette ends! On Gough Island, the meteorologists used to feed the local Tristan Skuas on food scraps, and occasionally delighted in presenting them with such items as rump steak laced with tabasco or chilli powder. To the surprise and delight of the meteorologists the skuas would happily swallow the meat, and only discover the hot taste some seconds later. They would then regurgitate the lump, which would immediately be swallowed by another skua. This might be repeated a few times, with much wing raising display and long calling, until eventually the food stayed down.

My attempts to catch Great and Arctic Skuas using a narcotic also led me to believe that skuas, particularly the large skuas, have a limited sense of taste. I laced some hens eggs with Avertin, which is a bitter-tasting liquid narcotic, and placed these on a Great Skua club site. The first surprise was to see that many of the immature birds did not recognise eggs as food at all. Some rolled them around with mild interest, but others were as fascinated by the cardboard egg box I had left lying nearby. Soon I had a dozen skuas tearing the egg box to shreads, swallowing little bits and fighting for the rest! When this was over, some individuals returned to look at the eggs, and eventually a bird arrived that knew how to deal with them. It stabbed vertically down at an egg with its bill and broke the shell. Within seconds all the nearby birds were fighting to drink the spilled contents, narcotic and all. None of them seemed to notice the bitter taste although I had been told that most birds will refuse Avertin except in gelatin capsules. Unfortunately, none received a large enough dose to pass out and so I had to give this up as a method of catching nonbreeders, but I used it quite successfully to catch breeding birds on territory. By contrast, Arctic Skuas clearly did find the narcotic distasteful. When I tried the same technique in Arctic Skua territories the birds would drink part of the egg, then stop and wipe the bill in the grass or shake the head, as if they could detect a bad aftertaste. Nevertheless, they would often take the egg contents eventually, between bill wipings and shaking of the head, as if the taste was not quite bad enough to put them off their meal. Presumably, since the large skuas may scavenge to quite a considerable extent on rotting remains of marine mammals, seabirds and fish, a limited sense of taste may be useful!

Scavenging at sea

During the early breeding season, Great Skuas in Shetland spend much of their time simply holding territory and displaying at intruders. At this time they live partly on their considerable fat reserves. Sandeels are not readily available and there are few seabirds carrying food to be robbed. When skuas fly out to sea to feed they may spend quite a long time roaming around and are likely to chance upon dead birds floating on the sea, or driftwood covered with goose-barnacles. Goose-barnacles form a regular, but infrequent, item in their diet, mainly during the first few weeks at colonies in spring, or at the end of the breeding season when food again appears to become scarce and they begin the move south for winter.

Goose-barnacles contain large amounts of rather indigestible material and have little nutritional value, so their presence in pellets is indicative of poor feeding conditions. During the middle of the breeding season Great Skuas probably spend less time searching for food at sea, but even so the normally complete absence of goose barnacles regurgitated in pellets in May, June or early July probably indicates that they choose not to eat this poor-quality food when they can readily feed on Sandeels, whitefish discards or seabirds.

When a dead seabird or similar food item is found at sea a Great Skua will attempt to defend it from other birds. A feeding skua usually attracts the attention of others, and often large gulls and Fulmars as well, and the finder of the food will use wing-raising displays and long calls to deter the others from coming too close. Sometimes a second Great Skua will be tolerated and they may then cooperate in tearing the corpse open. Skuas often dispute with Fulmars over the ownership of corpses at sea, and the outcome can be unpredictable. Sometimes a Fulmar will be deterred by the gestures of the skua; sometimes it will rush the skua, pattering over the sea with wings outstretched, neck feathers ruffled, and bill wide open, producing a cackling noise, and this often succeeds in dispossessing the skua. Great Skuas can usually displace gulls from prey, and it is rarely possible for any gull to displace a Great Skua once it has taken possession of a corpse, although a hungry Great Black-backed Gull can sometimes drive off a skua that has already taken an ample meal off the corpse.

Exploitation of penguin and seal colonies

Describing the feeding behaviour of Brown Skuas on South Georgia, Stonehouse (1956) stated that 'stillborn and crushed seal pups, carcasses of penguins and seals, and Gentoo and King Penguin eggs and chicks formed the bulk of the diet in the vicinity of the base hut; there were no signs of predation on other species of birds and the mobbing of other birds, forcing them to drop or disgorge food, was seen on very few occasions'. These Brown Skuas held large territories, in which they nested, but, more importantly, the territories included areas of penguin rookeries or stretches of beach. Those territories which included a length of beach gave the owners sole access to seal carcasses, placentae or penguin corpses washed up on the tide-line. Territories that included a section of penguin rookery allowed the owners sole access to abandoned eggs and chick corpses, or they could predate Gentoo Penguins of their eggs and small chicks. This situation is typical of many Brown Skua populations throughout the sub-Antarctic. The association between skuas and penguins has been a well-known feature, studied in particular detail by Professor Euan Young (1963a, b, 1972, 1977).

By defending an area of penguin rookery against other skuas, territory holders may actually reduce the amount of predation the penguins suffer, since non-breeding skuas and pairs that do not have penguins within their territory will be unable to exploit this food supply. Just how the size of the skuas' territory is determined and the effect that this has on the dynamics of the skua-penguin interaction are discussed further in Chapter 10. However, one consequence of this territorial system is that nonbreeding skuas are denied the best feeding areas, which are held by territorial pairs, and must scavenge elsewhere.

On occasions, the presence of a particularly attractive and large item of food within a breeding skua's territory can tempt nonbreeders to transgress the territorial boundary to feed. Stonehouse (1956) describes this situation on South Georgia, where sealers would regularly leave up to half a dozen flensed seal carcasses in a pile on the beach. The skua owning the territory was unable to drive away all the nonbreeders that were attracted, and was obliged to join the interlopers around the food. Once the seals had been reduced to a pile of bones, the breeding skuas managed to drive the last few nonbreeders away and re-establish their territory.

I witnessed a similar transgression during my visits to Gough Island, although in this case the nonbreeding skuas invaded the territory of a breeding pair in order to feast on a pile of steak and pork chops put out for the birds on the roof of the weather station.

Scavenging at fishing boats

Although small skuas make little or no use of waste from fishing boats, Great Skuas, particularly in Shetland, obtain much of their food during the breeding season from this source. They may also follow fishing boats to a considerable extent in winter. This is particularly common in the Mediterranean, where they are normally seen attending fishing boats and rarely feed by other methods. At some stages during the breeding season in Shetland discarded whitefish from fishing boats form most of their diet (Furness & Hislop 1981). Association between Great Skuas and fishing boats also occurs around Iceland, but to a much smaller extent. Off Iceland and the Faeroes, fishing boats use a much larger net mesh than that used by boats in British waters, and as a result discard far less small fish.

Furness & Hislop (1981) concluded that almost all whitefish eaten by Great Skuas around Shetland had been thrown back by fishermen because they were too small or were species of little or no commercial value. Information on the amounts of fish discarded suggested that Great Skuas could sometimes take a high proportion of all such fish and that this seemed to be a very important part of their diet. Between 1983 and 1985, Anne Hudson was employed on a grant from the Natural Environment Research Council to study the extent of discarding by fishing boats around Shetland and the ways in which seabirds exploited such fish. Anne spent many days on the boats, recording discard fish species and sizes and the behaviour of birds as each measured fish was discarded. The dense flocks around the boats, and the often rough Shetland seas, made this work particularly difficult, but much of the detailed analysis could be done from video recordings in the comfort of a laboratory with replay and slow motion facilities.

Anne found that boats fishing for Sandeels, Herring or Mackerel provided few feeding opportunities for seabirds, but that those catching whitefish (predominantly Haddock and Whiting) discarded large quantities of small and unmarketable fish, and also cleaned fish and threw or washed the offal overboard between hauls and on the way back to harbour. Offal (fish livers and intestines) represents about 12.5% of the weight of whitefish landed (excluding flatfish where there is less offal). It is possible to estimate the amount of offal made available by using the data for fish landings from each fishery area around Shetland. Similarly, the total of fish discarded can be estimated, knowing that the quantity discarded in 1983–85 represented, on average, about 27% of the total catch brought on board (Hudson 1986). Amounts of fish discarded varied greatly from catch to catch. Sometimes almost the entire catch consisted of small fish or of species such as Gurnards and Saithe, for which there is no market in Shetland, and over three-quarters of such a catch could be thrown back. Sometimes as little as 5–10% might be discarded. Only by making numerous trips over each season can a reasonably accurate picture be got of the extent of discarding. Furthermore, discarding varies regionally, seasonally, and between years. Whitefish tend to produce very large year classes every few years, and when such classes grow to become catchable there will be particularly high discarding rates as these numerous small fish are caught. The problem was that, up to 1986, the net mesh size used caught fish that were below the legal minimum landing size. Small fish are less valuable than large fish, kilo for kilo, and so if fishermen are restricted to a quota, it pays them to throw back small but marketable fish until their catch is composed of as high a proportion of large fish as possible.

This management system is a biological nonsense. If discards survived to grow to a larger size and were then caught again it would make some sense, but discards are dead or moribund when discarded. They float on the surface for quite some time, because their swim bladder has usually ruptured and their stomach been everted by the reduction in pressure as they are hauled up from the bottom, and most of them end up in the stomach of some seabird. Anne Hudson estimated that seabirds swallowed 75% of all discards, and almost all of the offal, from Shetland boats each summer during her study.

Thus discarding is an inefficient way of regulating whitefish catches and it would make biological sense to increase the size of the mesh used until small, unwanted, fish can pass through and survive to grow to a larger size. Fishing efficiency in the North Sea is so high that most fish are caught, so any small fish left to grow is likely to be caught later. Unfortunately, some fishing boats in some regions depend for their livelihood largely on small-sized fish just above the legal limit for landings.

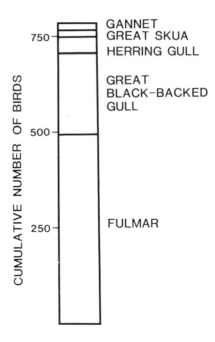

Fig. 62   *Mean numbers of scavenging seabirds associated with fishing boats catching whitefish around Shetland in summer 1983–85 (April to July inclusive). Total of 72 observations from trawlers. From Hudson (1986).*

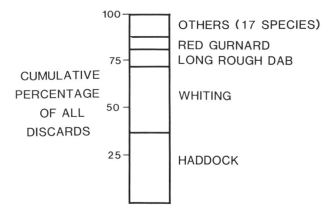

Fig. 63   Numbers of each species of fish discarded in a total of 7,605 discards randomly sampled on trawlers around Shetland in summer 1983–85. From Hudson (1986).

Net meshes are rather imperfect when discriminating between fish just below and just above the wanted size. Some slightly larger fish may wriggle through while some smaller ones may in fact be caught. An increase in mesh size allows undersized fish to escape through the net, and although it reduces catches of small but still marketable fish in the short term, it has a beneficial long term effect. In January 1987 the legal minimum net mesh size for whitefish boats in the North Sea was increased by 5 mm, as a fish stock conservation measure. This is too little to solve the problem of excessive discarding, and further mesh increases are likely over the next few years, but a slow improvement is intended to minimise the hardship to some fishermen caused by short term reductions in catches.

These changes will undoubtedly have profound effects on scavenging seabirds in the North Sea (which includes Orkney and Shetland waters according to the definition used by fisheries biologists). The impact on Great Skuas could be particularly severe, which is why I am devoting so much space to this topic here.

Over the ten years up to 1986, fishing boats around Shetland threw overboard enough offal and discard fish to support in the region of 200,000 scavenging seabirds (Hudson 1986). Because offal has a far higher calorific value (7–13 kJ per gram, wet weight) than discard whitefish (3.5–5.5 kJ per gram wet weight), it can provide much of the energy needs of seabirds. Anne found that Fulmars succeed, by their aggressive behaviour, in obtaining virtually all of the offal and exclude Great Skuas, gulls and Gannets, although in the rare instances when Fulmars are absent, Great Skuas may take the offal and fight off the gulls and Gannets. However, Fulmars generally ignore discarded whole fish because they are too large for them to swallow. Nevertheless, Fulmars represent considerably more than half of the scavenging seabirds supported by fishery waste, and about two-thirds of all seabirds at trawlers around Shetland in summer (Fig. 62). Of those feeding on discards, Great Black-backed Gulls are the most common, outnumbering Gannets and Great Skuas by about 20 to one (Fig. 62).

In the period summers 1983–85, the discard fish made available by trawlers were mainly Haddock and Whiting (Fig. 63), in length generally 25–33 cm (Whiting) and

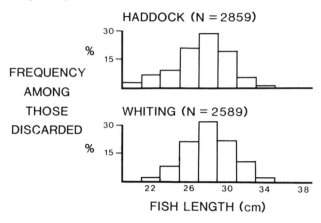

Fig. 64 *Lengths of Haddock and Whiting discarded from whitefish boats around Shetland in summer 1983–85. From Hudson (1986).*

23–32 cm (Haddock) (Fig. 64).

Scavenging seabirds at trawlers, including Great Skuas, compete for discarded fish on the sea surface and show some preferences for particular species and sizes of discards. Most flatfish, and fish with bony surfaces such as Gurnards, tend to be rejected when Haddock and Whiting are available. There is some kleptoparasitism too. Anne looked at the complex interactions around trawlers and produced a detailed PhD thesis describing the results and implications (Hudson, 1986), and I can only summarise, here, some of the important points as far as Great Skuas are concerned. Firstly, it came as a surprise to me to learn that they lost out as a result of kleptoparasitism around fishing boats! Although they stole and succeeded in swallowing a higher proportion of the fish than any other scavenging seabirds, they had 1.3 fish stolen from them for every fish that they were able to keep. Given their reputation as kleptoparasites, this result needs further explanation! It comes about because Great Skuas have difficulty in swallowing the larger-sized discards, whereas Gannets and Great Black-backed Gulls can manage them more easily, and it seems that the likelihood of having your fish stolen depends partly on how long you take to swallow it. As fish length increases, so does the time taken to lift the fish out the water and swallow it, but it increases faster for Great Skuas than for Gannets or Great Black-backed Gulls (Fig. 65). Because Great Black-backed Gulls greatly outnumbered Great Skuas, they stole more fish from them than the skuas managed to rob for themselves even though the gulls showed less inclination to robbery. Great Skuas clearly are disposed to this method of getting food, even around boats where the odds are against them.

Anne recorded a total of 3,776 whitefish that she had measured and experimentally discarded during normal fishing operations, which were taken and swallowed by seabirds. Great Skuas obtained only 9% of these, whereas Great Black-backed Gulls took 73%, Gannets 12%, Herring Gulls 3%, Fulmars 2% and Lesser Black-backed Gulls 1%. Since Great Black-backed Gulls outnumbered the skuas by about 20 to one at boats, but obtained only eight times as many fish, the skuas seem to have been doing rather better than the gulls. This is partly what one might expect because the Great Skuas do tend to be more aggressive and to displace Great Black-backed Gulls from the prime sites just behind the boat. However, the skuas dropped far more fish per feeding attempt than did Great Black-backed Gulls or Gannets. Of all fish that were dropped, 21% were dropped by Great Skuas and most were of above average length (Fig. 66).

The outcome of the dominance of Great Skuas in terms of getting to the prime feeding position (except against Fulmars, but these make little attempt to get discards), together with their inability to deal efficiently with larger discards, is that the fish they swallow tend to be shorter than the average discards, whereas those swallowed by Great Black-backed Gulls and Gannets are equal to or larger than average (Fig. 67).

From the above, the implications of the increase in net mesh size become apparent. Although Great Skuas can bully their way to the discarded fish, if net mesh size is increased there will be fewer discards small enough for Great Skuas to swallow. Additionally, the total of discards should, in theory, be much reduced, and so the competition for those that there are will increase. Great Skuas are likely to find that Great Black-backed Gulls rob them of the fish they fail to swallow quickly enough.

I suspect that if the proposed increases in net mesh size go ahead as planned

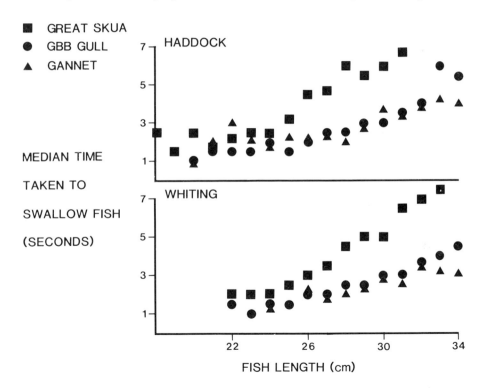

Fig. 65 Time taken to swallow (a) Haddock, and (b) Whiting, in relation to fish length, for Great Skuas (squares), adult Great Black-backed Gulls (dots) and adult Gannets (triangles). From Hudson (1986).

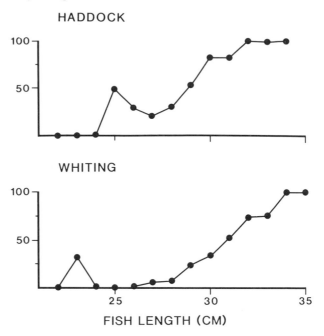

Fig. 66   Percentage of fish dropped by, or stolen from, Great Skuas in relation to fish length for (a) Haddock, and (b) Whiting. From Hudson (1986).

(as they should for the long term benefit of the fishing industry), then one outcome will be that Great Skuas will have to turn increasingly to other methods of getting food; presumably predation and kleptoparasitism of auks and Kittiwakes. If so, the impact on these birds could be severe (Chapter 16).

Scavenging on refuse tips

Chilean Skuas gather in large numbers, with Southern Black-backed Gulls (also called Kelp Gulls or Dominican Gulls), on the refuse tips of southern Argentina and Chile. The feeding behaviour of these species on refuse tips has not been studied, but Devillers (1978) has photographs of Chilean Skuas and Southern Black-backed Gulls standing and sitting together, waiting for fresh refuse to be brought onto the tip, and other authors have commented on the tendency for Chilean Skuas to exploit refuse. This contrasts with the situation in the North Atlantic. Great Skuas seldom visit refuse tips, although Herring Gulls, Lesser Black-backed Gulls, Great Black-backed Gulls, Ravens, Hooded Crows and Starlings occur in large numbers on tips in Orkney and Shetland in areas close to big colonies of breeding Great Skuas.

In May 1980 we visited Shetland with cannon nets to catch Herring Gulls at Sullom Voe refuse tip, which gave us a chance to watch a few Great Skuas foraging with thousands of gulls, and we could form some ideas as to why the skuas make so little use of this food source so beloved by gulls. It was obvious that the few skuas behaved quite differently from the gulls. Herring Gulls loaf around the tip

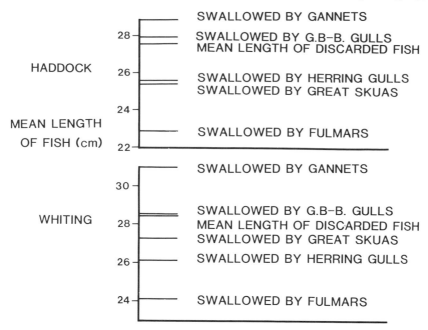

SWALLOWED BY GANNETS

28 ——— SWALLOWED BY G.B–B. GULLS
MEAN LENGTH OF DISCARDED FISH

HADDOCK   26 ——— SWALLOWED BY HERRING GULLS
SWALLOWED BY GREAT SKUAS

24

MEAN LENGTH
OF FISH (cm)   22 ——— SWALLOWED BY FULMARS

SWALLOWED BY GANNETS

30

SWALLOWED BY G.B–B. GULLS
WHITING   28 ——— MEAN LENGTH OF DISCARDED FISH
SWALLOWED BY GREAT SKUAS
SWALLOWED BY HERRING GULLS

26

24 ——— SWALLOWED BY FULMARS

Fig. 67   Mean lengths of (a) Haddock, and (b) Whiting, swallowed by different scavenging seabirds in relation to the mean length discarded. From Hudson (1986).

until fresh food is dumped or turned over by the bulldozer. Then they fly over and circle above the food until a large flock has gathered. They give feeding calls, the level of excitement seems to increase, and the flock slowly drops lower towards the food, with individual gulls dropping lower still and then lifting again as if scared to be the first to land. Eventually one or two birds, usually immatures, do touch the ground, snatch up food morsels and fly off. Suddenly, the rest of the birds begin to land and gobble the food, and the last birds often find little left. Herring Gulls show this characteristic behaviour on tips in summer and winter, and Lesser Black-backed Gulls behave in much the same way. In winter, occasional Glaucous and Iceland Gulls on tips tend to patrol areas away from dense flocks of Herring Gulls. We often noticed that an Iceland or Glaucous Gull would find food in front of our cannon net and start feeding, only to quit the catching area as soon as the Herring Gulls began to land in numbers all around. I have yet to ring an Iceland or a Glaucous Gull as a result! Great Black-backed Gulls also tend to feed in a more solitary way than Herring Gulls, often temporarily defending a small area of the tip, and frequently robbing other birds of food they are digging from the refuse. Great Skuas, like Iceland and Glaucous Gulls, tend to move around the tip individually, avoiding flocks of Herring Gulls. Rather surprisingly, they showed no interest in the Herring Gulls and did not try to rob them of their food. One striking feature of Great Skua behaviour on the tip was their lack of caution, particularly in view of the reluctance of Herring Gulls to land on food unless other birds had done so. Herring Gulls avoid novel things on the tip, but

Great Skuas explore them, although this brash behaviour does not mean that they get the best pickings, since the Herring Gulls used skuas as their 'food-tasters'. Once a skua had located a good new patch of food the mob of Herring Gulls would quickly move in and, surprisingly, the skuas would give way, not attempting to stand their ground. In view of the dominant and aggressive nature of Great Skuas in other situations I found it quite disconcerting to see them frightened off by the hordes of Herring Gulls.

We examined the way in which Great Skuas and Herring Gulls exploited food at Sullom refuse tip, and on a waste dump outside Scalloway fish factory, by putting out piles of food on seven occasions. Spreading the food usually attracted large numbers of gulls, which circled overhead but did not land. Although only a small number of Great Skuas was present, on five of the seven occasions the first bird to land and feed was a skua. On each of these occasions it landed directly on the food, and immediately selected and swallowed a large morsel. Within seconds the loafing gulls flew to the area and landed in large numbers. The skua then picked up a second food item and flew off, leaving the gulls to fight over the rest. Several gulls, particularly immatures, attempted to steal food from other gulls leaving the feeding area, but none of the skuas were seen to attempt klepto-parasitism. On the remaining two occasions no skuas were present, and it took considerably longer for the first gull to land and begin feeding (Furness *et al.* 1981). Since Great Skuas regularly flock with gulls behind fishing boats it is surprising that they behaved in such a solitary manner on the tip. The contrast between the typical hesitancy of the gulls and the apparently fearless and direct approach of the skuas was particularly striking, as was the facilitating effect that the skuas had for the gulls. Refuse tips are a highly competitive feeding situation, and if Great Skuas are displaced by incoming Herring Gulls then it is an obvious advantage to arrive first, but the reason why the skuas give way to the gulls so readily is obscure, other than that a large flock of Herring Gulls seems able to intimidate them. The success of Great Skuas on refuse tips in the southern hemisphere may be due largely to the absence of an equivalent of the socially feeding Herring Gull. The only common gull of that region is the Southern Black-backed Gull or Kelp Gull, which is neither particularly social nor aggressive when feeding, and so the Chilean Skuas and Falkland Skuas seem able to hold their own in a way that Great Skuas cannot on tips in Shetland, even though they clearly dominate Herring Gulls around fishing boats or over shoals of Sandeels, klep-toparasitise, and even prey on adult Herring Gulls at sea and at colonies.

In the Antarctic, establishment of research bases has influenced the numbers of penguins and skuas in the immediate vicinity of several of these. One of the clearest examples has been the effect of a refuse tip close to the French base at Pointe Geologie, Adelie Land. South Polar Skuas at this colony have increased, from 80 or 90 in 1965, to 320 in 1977. This increase has been attributed to extra food for the skuas, which had previously fed by predation and scavenging on Adelie Penguin eggs, chicks and carcasses, but quickly took to feeding almost exclusively on garbage when the tip was opened (Jouventin & Guillotin 1979). In addition to this local increase the number of breeding pairs in the area went up from 29 to 40. As breeding numbers increased, so did breeding success, with most pairs fledging both chicks, but this was short-lived and as the numbers levelled off, the breeding success fell back to about the level of the years before refuse became available. Finally, the switch to feeding on refuse seems to have led to a reduction in synchrony of breeding among the skuas. Whereas they had previously laid in close synchrony with the breeding of the Adelie Penguins, after changing to a diet of refuse the spread of laying by skuas widened from 14 days in 1964–65 to 58 days in 1976–77. The changes suggest that the South Polar Skua numbers had been limited by food availability, and that refuse allowed the breeding success and population to rise, until the excess food had been fully utilised by 1976–77, causing breeding success to fall and numbers to level off. Since South Polar Skuas do not normally breed until about six years old, and young birds only return to the breeding area when three or four years old, increased breeding success cannot have been the direct cause of the population increase, since both occurred simultaneously. The indications are that adult and immature survival, or more probably recruitment of immature skuas from elsewhere, caused the growth in the population.

FEEDING AT SEA OUTSIDE OF THE BREEDING SEASON

The migrations and wintering areas of skuas are poorly known, but their feeding activities in winter are almost completely unrecorded. Arctic Skuas are known to feed to a large extent by kleptoparasitism during migration and in winter; their use of the coastal zone makes it possible for ornithologists to observe their feeding at these times of year. Great Skuas clearly do scavenge at fishing boats a great deal in winter. Many ring recoveries from the wintering areas in the Bay of Biscay and off Portugal come from birds caught in fishing nets or on baited lines. Ornithologists also see Great Skuas coming to fishing boats in winter. In the western Mediterranean, Carlos Carboneras recorded that this was, apparently, the only important source of food exploited by Great Skuas, although they would occasionally make desultory attempts to kill or to rob smaller seabirds.

The migration route of the South Polar Skua (at least of the immatures) in the Pacific suggests that this species follows the Pacific Saury movements and, by implication, presumably catches these small fish as its winter food.

Pomarine Skuas which winter in the warm, but rich upwelling areas, off West Africa, are thought to feed largely by predation of small seabirds such as phalaropes, and by scavenging; while the activities of Long-tailed Skuas are hardly known at all, since their main wintering areas are uncertain, and the immatures that winter off Namibia and off Argentina have rarely been seen feeding.

Presumably the Brown, Tristan, and Falkland Skuas scavenge at sea on dead fish, seabirds and marine mammals, goose-barnacles and other surface organisms, and occasionally by robbing or killing seabirds. This is largely supposition, although supported by a few at-sea observations.

CHAPTER 8

Kleptoparasitism

There is a fowl called Scutiallan, of a black colour and as big as a Wild Duck, which doth live upon the Vomit and Excrements of other Fowls, whome they pursue and having apprehended them, they cause them to vomit up what they have lately taken, not yet digested: the Lord's Works both of Nature and of Grace are wonderful, all speaking forth His Glorious Goodness, Wisdom and Power.

Rev. John Brand (1701)

THE DEFINITION OF KLEPTOPARASITISM

Kleptoparasitism, also called piracy, robbing, or food parasitism, is the deliberate stealing by one animal of food which has already been captured by another. It can occur between conspecifics or between species, and is quite widespread throughout vertebrate animals, but is best known in birds, and is particularly characteristic of many skuas. The behaviour has been reviewed by Brockman and Barnard (1979) who showed that kleptoparasitism occurs much more frequently in particular families of birds than in others. Most recorded instances of kleptoparasitic interactions are trivial and of no evolutionary consequence, an example being the stealing of food from a Golden Eagle by three Magpies reported by Dixon (1933). The Magpies must just have happened to be in the right place at the right time, but probably never attempted to do the same thing again throughout their lives. By contrast, some species may use kleptoparasitism as an important feeding technique. This is true of some of the skuas, which have often been considered to be highly evolved as specialist kleptoparasites.

THE EVOLUTION OF SPECIALIST KLEPTOPARASITES

Brockman and Barnard suggested that kleptoparasitism is most likely to evolve as a feeding strategy where there are large concentrations of potential hosts, large quantities of food being carried, and the food which is carried should be large, discrete masses, available in a predictable manner and visible to the kleptoparasite. Also, the kleptoparasite should itself be short of food in order that robbing would be more profitable than capturing food directly, otherwise it would be a waste of time and energy to steal food when it could be obtained more easily by conventional means! Duffy (1980) suggested that seabirds would tend to rob victims that had access to prey at greater depths in the sea than they could exploit for themselves, while Kushlan (1978) showed that, in herons, larger species tended to rob smaller ones.

Since seabirds generally nest in large colonies, carry food to their young from a wide area of surrounding sea, and mainly feed on large and discrete prey such as fish, they fulfil most of the requirements listed by these authors, and it is not surprising that kleptoparasitism is most widespread among seabirds. Many species of gulls and terns resort to stealing food on an opportunistic basis. Frigatebirds, skuas and sheathbills are often considered to be specialist kleptoparasites, regularly able to make a living predominantly or entirely by kleptoparasitism. Sheathbills have a peculiar method of stealing food from penguins. As penguin adults regurgitate boluses of krill to their chicks sheathbills will hurl themselves bodily into the penguin's head or back and cause the adult to spill its food onto the ground. The sheathbill then grabs some of the food from beside the startled penguins and runs away.

Frigatebirds and skuas employ aerial chases of their hosts and scare them into dropping food in order to avoid the apparent threat of being beaten up or killed. These birds are generally thought of as having evolved their characteristic body structure in order to be efficient in this technique. Frigatebirds are well known for their tiny unwebbed feet and particularly light skeleton which weighs considerably less than their feathers! Also, frigatebirds have only a vestigial preen gland so cannot waterproof their plumage. This may seem improbable for a seabird since it means that they cannot land on the sea or dive for fish, but must remain clear of the water when away from land. The tiny feet and long wings also make it extremely difficult for them to take off from the ground so that they must nest on treetops. The traditional evolutionary explanation for these features has been that the frigatebird has lost its preen gland and reduced its skeleton and feet in order to minimize its body weight. Together with its exceptionally large wings, this results in frigatebirds having a uniquely low wing loading (body weight per unit wing area), supposedly to enhance their ability to chase and pirate other seabirds. This idea is quoted by Brockman and Barnard and by numerous earlier authors. Skuas do possess a preen gland, and have a general shape and structure far less extreme than that of frigatebirds, but they do appear to differ from their close relatives the gulls in certain respects. Can these differences also be attributed to evolution for kleptoparasitic ability? One of my research students, Richard Caldow, has recently been considering this question. By examining theories of the aerodynamics of flight he predicted a number of adaptations that would improve the ability of skuas to rob other seabirds. For example, they should be capable of faster flight, more rapid acceleration and greater manoeuvrability than gulls in order to rob their victims, and particular muscle structures and wing shapes would provide these attributes. Richard is comparing the anatomy and muscle physiology of skuas with that of gulls to see if his predictions are supported. Although his work is still in its early stages, it would appear that they are. Skuas have more powerful flight muscles than gulls, and stronger flight feathers, so that they can generate greater thrust and overtake their victims. It seems that skuas have evolved from their common ancestor with the gulls in a direction adapting them to a life of robbery with violence! Perhaps this seems rather an obvious conclusion, but the apparently obvious is not always correct, even if it has been held to be so for generations.

Professor Colin Pennycuick, an expert on bird flight, has recently studied frigatebird flight and concluded that frigatebirds are not evolved as kleptoparasites after all, but have their highly adapted structure in order to allow them to soar and glide over the tropical seas with great efficiency and low energy expenditure. A study of frigatebird flight muscles by Kuroda (1961) found that frigatebirds are apparently unique in possessing a special layer of muscle within the pectoralis major, and this layer has the job of holding the wing in the gliding position. This devolution of particular roles to layers within the muscle is an energy saving device since it allows most of the muscle to relax while the bird is gliding and soaring. Pennycuick's studies of frigatebirds show that they feed mainly by snatching flying fish in mid air, a practice which requires great flight agility. Most of the time frigatebirds soar and glide over the sea, waiting for an encounter with a flying fish. Their ability to kleptoparasitise boobies and other tropical seabirds seems to be a consequence of their adaptation to feed on flying fish and, in fact, many colonies of frigatebirds exist in areas where there are few potential victims to rob. Frigatebirds seem to make use of robbery much less than is commonly believed, and the conspicuous nature of the act has led to its being overemphasised as a feeding strategy. This shows how easily evolutionary 'just so stories' can become accepted fact until someone actually looks critically at the situation. Frigatebirds may well have evolved certain adaptations to enhance their ability to rob seabirds, but it seems probable that their unusual morphology is largely attributable to their need to soar at low cost and to be able to snatch flying fish out of the air, while kleptoparasitism is only of secondary importance.

Nevertheless, skuas and frigatebirds may have adapted to kleptoparasitism to a greater extent than opportunists such as gulls and terns. Are skuas and frigatebirds better kleptoparasites than the opportunists as a result? Considering evolutionary theory we could predict that there might be an evolutionary 'arms race' in which the species that were victims of kleptoparasitism would develop ever more elaborate mechanisms of defence in order to avoid being exploited by the kleptoparasites, which would become increasingly adapted to the piratical way of life. Although there have been few quantitative studies of frigatebirds chasing other seabirds, detailed studies of kleptoparasitic feeding by skuas have been numerous because this is a behaviour of particular interest to ethologists and ecologists. There are also many studies of kleptoparasitism by gulls and terns, so that it is possible to make a comparison between specialists and opportunists to see if there are differences in the ways that specialists rob their victims (Furness 1986).

The first surprising finding is that the so called specialists, frigatebirds, Arctic, Great and South Polar Skuas, are apparently no more successful at robbing their victims than are gulls or terns, which we have classified as 'opportunist' kleptoparasites, with no obvious adaptations to this way of life. The percentage of chases that were successful in causing the victim to drop food averaged 23% for

frigatebirds and Arctic Skuas, 19% for Great Skuas and South Polar Skuas, but 26% for gulls and terns (Furness 1986). These averages are not statistically different and certainly do not suggest that skuas are particularly successful at robbing seabirds. When the outcome of chases by skuas, gulls or terns, of one particular species of host is compared there is still no evidence of any superiority of skuas, so it is not simply the case that opportunists only chase species that are easy to rob. Furthermore, it may seem surprising that only some 20% or so of chases are successful and that victims usually escape with their food. However, this is similar to the situation with birds of prey, where only a small percentage of attacks results in prey capture (Curio 1976).

One short study provides something of an exception to the situation described above. Kent Forssgren (1981) observed the interactions between Caspian Terns nesting on islands outside Stockholm, in the Baltic Sea, and the Arctic Skuas and Lesser Black-backed Gulls that robbed them of their fish. He found that Arctic Skuas were successful in 68% of chases and gulls only in 38% of their chases, which suggests that in this study, where the performance of gulls and skuas chasing the same host species under identical environmental conditions could be directly compared, skuas performed better than the opportunists. Forssgren's study is the only one I know of that compares specialists and opportunists side by side against identical odds.

Perhaps the low average success rate of chases by skuas is a misleading statistic. Where kleptoparasitism is not a profitable feeding strategy it presumably will not be attempted often enough to allow the success rate to be measured by ornithologists. A success rate of 10–20% may be enough to make kleptoparasitism worthwhile, in which case we might expect that the success rate will generally be of this order. Indeed, adaptations to reduce the energy costs of kleptoparasitism in specialists, if they exist, might even mean that skuas could make a profit from kleptoparasitism in a situation where the success rate was so low that it would not be profitable for gulls or terns, so we may be wrong to consider the success rate as a measure of kleptoparasitic efficiency at all.

Are there then any clear differences between the chases of skuas and of gulls and terns that would suggest a degree of evolutionary adaptation of skuas for this way of life? One feature of specialist kleptoparasites is that they rarely attempt to rob conspecifics, whereas opportunists such as gulls and terns very often do steal from conspecifics. There does seem to be one other clear difference that might not be immediately self-evident. Since the energy cost of an unsuccessful chase may be considerable, it is reasonable to expect kleptoparasites to be highly discriminating between potential hosts with and without food to surrender. This would suggest that species which carry food in the bill rather than swallowing it would be selected for attack, and Brockman & Barnard (1979) stated categorically that 'only individuals with visible food in the bill are attacked or pursued by a kleptoparasite'. Ten of the 76 interactions listed by Furness (1986) involved hosts which swallow food for their chicks and never carry it in the bill. These hosts were Gannet, Red-footed Booby, Kittiwake, and Blue-eyed Shag, respectively chased by Great Skuas, frigatebirds, both Arctic Skuas and Great Skuas, and South Polar Skuas. In addition, Great Skuas chase Herring Gulls, Great Black-backed Gulls and Arctic Skuas at Foula (Furness, 1978), species which all regurgitate food to their young but are much less abundant at this colony than auks, so that fewer than 10 chases of each of these species were recorded in that study. In fact, the proportions of available Gannets, *Larus* gulls and Arctic Skuas chased by Great Skuas are rather high, suggesting that these species are nevertheless favoured victims.

Guillemots carry fish to their chick inside the bill and throat, and thus hidden from view unless the fish is large enough for the tail to protrude, whereas Puffins, Razorbills and Black Guillemots all carry fish dangling across the bill and clearly visible to kleptoparasites. One might expect that Guillemots would be chased less often or less successfully than the other auks if visibility of food was an important factor in determining kleptoparasitic behaviour, but the proportions of incoming Puffins, Razorbills and Guillemots chased by Arctic or Great Skuas at Foula were very similar, while Black Guillemots were rarely, if ever, chased. Proportions of chases by Great Skuas which were successful, suggest that Puffins are most easily robbed (38% of chases observed at Foula in 1975 and 1976 were successful), but Great Skuas had a higher success against Guillemots (29%) than against Razorbills (18%) and not lower as predicted if fish visibility was critically important.

The success rate of Arctic Skuas at Heddlicliff, Foula, in robbing Kittiwakes was consistently higher than that against Puffins, Guillemots or Razorbills, and yet Kittiwakes regurgitate to their chicks, and many of the adults close to the colony which might be chased by an indiscriminating skua would be nonbreeders or off-duty adults with no food in their crops.

Taking the specific case of Great Skua chases at Foula reported by Furness (1978) we find that 93 chases were of hosts which swallowed food and 30% of these were successful, 113 chases were of hosts which carry food inside the bill and 29% of these were successful, and 261 were of hosts which carry fish across the bill and fully visible, and 35% of these chases were successful. We would expect the last class to be the largest, since most seabirds at Foula behave this

way. Success rates differ little between groups, suggesting that Great Skuas find it almost as easy to discriminate between hosts with and without food whether that food is swallowed or held visible in the bill.

Perhaps it is unreasonable to expect that kleptoparasites should be unable to discriminate from a distance between hosts with or without food in their stomach, since this is likely to influence characteristics of the host's flight and behaviour, but this ability, which 'specialist' kleptoparasites clearly do have, may not be shared by 'opportunist' kleptoparasites such as gulls and terns. Only one of the interactions reported in the literature involves a gull or tern pirating from birds which have swallowed food. Hulsman (1976) recorded kleptoparasitism among Silver Gulls, Crested, Lesser-crested, Roseate, Black-naped and Bridled Terns, and remarked on the fact that, in marked contrast to the other species, the Bridled Tern was rarely harassed and only once robbed of food, because, unlike the other terns, it fed its mate and chicks by regurgitation.

It would appear then that skuas are more efficient kleptoparasites than are opportunists such as gulls or terns, but how they detect which individual hosts are carrying food and so worth chasing is not known. Thus, although comparisons of chase success rates do not show any clear difference between 'specialist' and 'opportunist' kleptoparasites, this distinction may still be valuable. Skuas and frigatebirds appear to differ from gulls and terns in being able to assess whether or not birds which regurgitate to feed chicks are carrying food, and do not often chase conspecifics for food, which suggests a more highly evolved form of kleptoparasitism.

THE SELECTION OF HOSTS

Arctic Skuas in Shetland do not attempt to splash-dive onto surface shoals of Sandeels but steal the same fish from gulls, terns, and auks. This has led some ornithologists to consider the Arctic Skua to be stereotyped into kleptoparasitic behaviour, but it seems more likely that it cannot compete for positions in dense seabird flocks above fish shoals and employs kleptoparasitism instead. Great Skuas do fish for themselves because they are large and powerful enough to compete with Gannets, Great Black-backed Gulls and Fulmars, whereas Arctic Skuas avoid these dense flocks and the risk of serious injury if they did try to participate.

The hosts robbed by skuas in Shetland all lost large, discrete, food items to their kleptoparasites, with one possible exception. Kittiwakes robbed by Arctic or Great Skuas at Foula often regurgitated a well-digested mush of Sandeel or zooplankton which it was impossible for the kleptoparasite to handle. Whether the reward was complete fish, or a useless liquid, presumably depended on how long after food-capture the Kittiwake arrived back at the colony. In spite of the high success rate of chases of Kittiwakes, only a very small proportion of returning birds is usually chased, suggesting that skuas avoid wasting energy where the rewards may be worthless.

Kleptoparasites might do best to chase those species that can be robbed which carry the largest food items. Guillemots carry much larger fish than do Puffins. Great Skua chase success rates are similar for these two species of victim, so Guillemots should be preferred to Puffins as victims. In fact, this does appear to be the case, although only a very small proportion of the incoming adults of either species is attacked. Arctic Skuas chase Guillemots less often than Puffins, and have a lower success rate, so that the potential advantage of selecting species carrying larger prey is lost.

There is a suggestion that Arctic Skuas' interactions with their hosts are sufficiently highly evolved that they can persist without damage to the host, but are at a level to sustain the parasite. Only two of the interactions recorded in the literature deprive the hosts of as much as 1% of their food or involves the attack of more than 2% of the potential victims (Furness 1986). The two exceptions are particularly interesting. One is the case of Arctic Skuas robbing Puffins in south Iceland. There, in 1973, 6% of incoming Puffins were chased and 4% were robbed of food, but the Arctic Skuas had an abnormally low breeding success that year, when Arctic Terns unusually did not breed in the area (Arnason & Grant, 1978). In most years these skuas also chase Arctic Terns and their impact on Puffins might well be less than that observed in 1973. The other exception involves Caspian Terns nesting in colonies in the Baltic (Forssgren 1981) where they are robbed by Arctic Skuas and gulls. Bergman (1982) found that the feeding behaviour of gulls in the Finnish archipelago changed over the years as their numbers increased. They moved from being solitary nesters defending a feeding territory around the breeding site, to colonial nesters that fed socially. With increased social feeding, and apparent food shortage, kleptoparasitism became more common as a feeding strategy. Forssgren (1981) recorded that about one quarter of all of the Caspian Terns carrying fish to their chicks at colonies in the Baltic near Stockholm were robbed by gulls or skuas, with gulls taking about 60% of the stolen fish despite having a lower chase success rate than the Arctic Skuas. However, Forssgren recorded that Caspian Terns breeding solitarily were not chased, and had a higher breeding success than in the colonies where many chicks died of starvation because gulls and skuas had stolen so many fish. Forssgren found that colonial terns tried to reduce their losses to gulls and skuas by returning to the colony in groups, and so swamping the kleptoparasites, and also in many cases the mate guarding the chick would fly out to join the incoming bird with the fish and accompany it back to the nest, and this behaviour also reduced the success of the kleptoparasites. Nevertheless, he suggested that colonies of Caspian Terns were declining and solitary nesting increasing as this provided the best way for the terns to avoid being robbed. The high impact of the skuas on the terns in this study may therefore have come about as a consequence of the reduction in the numbers of tern colonies available for robbing, and this situation itself may be ascribed to the increase in numbers of gulls and their increased use of kleptoparasitism as a feeding strategy. The opportunist kleptoparasites may be to blame in this case and the Arctic Skuas may have suffered the consequences of the overexploitation of the terns by the gulls.

In contrast to the consistently small impact of the 'specialist' kleptoparasites on their hosts, some 'opportunist' kleptoparasites chase and rob high proportions of hosts and seem likely to cause host population instability. Hulsman (1976) found that Silver Gulls rob Lesser-crested Terns of about one quarter of the fish they catch and attempt to bring back to chicks. At Walney Island, Herring Gulls lost one third of their food to Lesser Black-backed Gulls (Verbeek, 1977); and Puffins at Great Island, Newfoundland, lost about 10% of the fish they brought for chicks to kleptoparasitic Herring Gulls (Nettleship, 1972). These high rates of parasitism may not be stable over evolutionary time since they are likely to have a harmful impact on the host population.

ATTACK STRATEGIES

Most kleptoparasitism by skuas involves aerial interceptions or chases. In some relationships the kleptoparasite can fly faster than its victim (e.g. Great Skuas robbing Gannets, Arctic Skuas robbing Kittiwakes). In these interactions the victim is usually harried for a period of several seconds or even minutes, until it gives up food or the skua gives up the chase. Such chases may result in physical attack and in convoluted aerobatic manoeuvres, and may lead to several other kleptoparasites joining in (Andersson, 1976; Hatch, 1970, 1975). In other cases, the victim is capable of flying as fast, or faster than the kleptoparasite in continuous horizontal flight, so the attack involves either head-on confrontation causing the victim to brake (e.g. some attacks on Puffins by Arctic Skuas (Grant, 1971)) or the kleptoparasite stoops onto the victim from above. Most chases of auks by skuas are of the latter type. If the victim notices the stooping skua in time it can accelerate to maximum speed and avoid being caught. If it is slow to react then the skua is able to catch up with it before it has time to take evasive action and in this situation it is more likely to drop its food (Furness, 1978).

Arctic Skuas rely mainly on their aerodynamic agility to outmanoeuvre their victims, and 50% of chases recorded at Foula were initiated from a similar height to their victim. Chases were usually begun from behind the victim, but in 25% of cases an Arctic Skua intercepted the path of the victim, so reducing its flight speed. Great Skuas almost invariably initiated a chase by circling above potential victims, then, when an individual had been selected, stooping at it from behind at great speed. They appear to rely on surprise to effect a successful robbing, except when chasing Gannets which they can easily outfly. Then the game is to grab the Gannet's wingtip and tilt it into the sea. As soon as the Gannet takes off again the Great Skua repeats this and lands on the water nearby. This can continue several times until, usually, the Gannet gives up and regurgitates, after which the skua allows it to take off again and fly on unmolested. Victims of chases show two main methods of evading skuas. Some, mainly the auks, dive into the sea, and then the skua usually gives up the attack unless the impact with the water caused the victim to lose its fish. Other victims may try to outfly the skua. Auks attempt to do this by accelerating to their maximum speed in straight and level flight, which is apparently faster than either a Great or Arctic Skua can manage. Others, particularly terns and Kittiwakes, twist and turn in the air in an attempt to shake off the skua that is reminiscent of a First World War dogfight. Only Gannets show any concerted attempt to fight back, and this seems to bring them little reward.

FACTORS AFFECTING THE OUTCOME OF CHASES

One of the main determinants of the outcome of attacks is how quickly the host responds to the approaching kleptoparasite (Furness, 1978). Auks can fly faster than skuas in level flight, but chases are initiated by the skua stooping from above so the auk has to accelerate fast before the skua reaches it if it is to keep its fish. It can only do so if it sees the skua in time. This is influenced by physical conditions such as visibility (Furness, 1978). Kleptoparasites increase their success rate by chasing more in conditions of poor visibility (Andersson, 1976). Chase success may be increased by kleptoparasites adopting a plumage which hosts find difficult to detect. Andersson (1976) suggests that the dark plumage of Arctic Skuas which feed by kleptoparasitism may be a form of aggressive camouflage. Certainly, in areas where the light phase predominates the species is generally a terrestrial predator rather than a kleptoparasite. Dark plumage of frigatebirds and Great Skuas may also be cryptic since most other seabirds are light in colour, but this interpretation is disputed (Nelson, 1980).

Hosts may be able to improve their detection of kleptoparasites by forming a search image (a mental picture of a skua), and Arnason (1978) has suggested that the polymorphic plumage of the Arctic Skua results from 'apostatic selection'. In simple terms, the victim will be looking out for dark phase skuas and will avoid these, but may not recognise the pale phase bird as a threat. Thus the unrecognised rare morph will have a higher chase success than the recognised common morph. Furness & Furness (1980) presented data showing no significant differences in chase success rates in relation to plumage colour of Arctic Skuas, but Rohwer (1983) points out that this result is compatible with the theory and that the theory has not yet been tested critically.

Grant (1971) found that Puffins turned away from the colony more often when the rate of attacks by skuas was high, implying that they were able to assess the risk of attack and respond accordingly. Furness (1978) found that Puffins and Kittiwakes were more likely to avoid attack when large numbers of Arctic Skuas were present. Presumably birds are more vigilant if they realise that skuas are in the vicinity. The victims can further reduce the likelihood of losing food by returning to the colony in groups, thus swamping the kleptoparasite (Grant, 1971).

Puffins are more vulnerable to kleptoparasites when nesting on flat ground rather than on slopes (Nettleship, 1972), when nesting at inland colonies where diving into the sea to avoid chases is impossible (Arnason & Grant, 1978; Furness, 1978), and when nesting at height above sea level (Furness, 1978). Skuas selectively attack hosts in the more vulnerable situations, which increases their success rate but reduces the relative breeding performance of hosts in poor habitat (e.g. Nettleship, 1972).

Kleptoparasites can improve their rate of food gain by learning to detect individuals with food in the stomach. At a mixed-species colony this will not only identify hosts which may provide higher food rewards (such as Gannets chased by Great Skuas), but will also reduce the patrolling time required before another victim is located (B. L. Furness, 1980). Compared to the duration of chases, patrolling times are very long and may strongly influence the profitability of this feeding method.

Probability of success may be increased if several kleptoparasites chase a single victim, but reward per kleptoparasite usually decreases (Hatch, 1970, 1975; Andersson, 1976; Furness, 1978; Arnason & Grant, 1978) indicating that kleptoparasites join chases to reduce patrolling time rather than to increase yield per chase to themselves.

Kleptoparasites may be able to increase the likelihood of success by chasing birds at particular distances from the colony (Arnason & Grant, 1978), and by chasing birds flying towards rather than away from the colony (Maxson & Bernstein, 1982, but see also Arnason & Grant, 1978). Most attacks by skuas, frigate-birds and terns occur close to the host's colony, where the density of victims is likely to be highest, so patrol times shortest, but kleptoparasites sometimes choose to fly out to host's feeding areas (Hulsman, 1976; pers. obs.), where they may have a higher rate of successful chasing (Hulsman, 1976).

Hosts may reduce the chances of being attacked by selecting prey species which are less conspicuous or less profitable (Fuchs, 1977), or by selecting smaller sized prey than they would in the absence of kleptoparasites (Thompson, 1983). Kleptoparasites often selectively attack hosts with large prey but exceptions have been reported. Roseate Terns stole fish which were similar in size to those they caught for themselves but smaller than the average carried by the hosts (Dunn, 1973) and Black-headed Gulls selected Sandwich Terns with large Sandeels but neglected birds with gadoids which, although shorter, were heavier (Fuchs, 1977). In this case the gulls appeared to select for fish length or visibility rather than mass.

Few chases result in physical contact with the host, but very rarely a chase by a skua may lead to the victim being caught and killed, and this or physical removal of food from the host's bill must be the main threat which may cause hosts to release food. Maxson & Bernstein (1982) found that physical contact, particularly if directed at the underparts, increased the chance of Blue-eyed Shags giving up food to South Polar Skuas. There is slight evidence to suggest that the 'willingness' of the host to give up food may vary. Hulsman (1976) found that chases of Lesser-crested Terns by Silver Gulls were twice as likely to be successful at the feeding area at sea than at the colony. Significantly more chases of Arctic Terns returning to the colony by Arctic Skuas at Foula were successful in 1975 and 1976 than in 1978, 1979 or 1980. Chase success rate appears to correlate both with the number of tern chicks fledged and with the breeding success of the colony (Furness, 1983). This may imply that in years when food was abundantly available close to the colony and breeding numbers and success were high, terns were more willing to lose fish than in years when food was scarce and chick survival was at risk. In the latter case terns may have been trading off greater risk of physical attack for increased chances of keeping their chicks alive.

THE IMPORTANCE OF KLEPTOPARASITISM TO SKUA POPULATIONS

Arctic Skuas arrive in spring at breeding sites in Shetland and Iceland after all other seabirds except terns, which return shortly after the skuas. The Arctic Skua appears to feed mainly by kleptoparasitism even at this early stage although there have been no studies of the details of their feeding behaviour early in the breeding season. According to Grant (1971), Kittiwakes are the main source of food in spring in Iceland and Puffins are only chased when their chicks have hatched. Arctic Skua hatching appears to be synchronised with Puffin hatching (Arnason & Grant, 1978), and Arctic Skuas in this area of Iceland and in Shetland have such small nesting territories that, unlike their conspecifics in Alaska or elsewhere in the arctic interior (Maher, 1974), they would be unable to obtain sufficient food within the territory to allow breeding, or perhaps even survival (B. L. Furness, 1980). They therefore depend upon kleptoparasitism from local colonial seabirds. Unlike any other kleptoparasitic species, Arctic Skuas may subsist by kleptoparasitism both during winter and during the breeding season, since they are known to rob food from terns and gulls in the southern hemisphere during the northern winter (B. L. Furness, 1983). However, it is not clear whether they also need to use other feeding methods at this time or during migration.

No species of bird is an obligate kleptoparasite, and only the Arctic Skua may possibly contain some individuals which subsist throughout the year from kleptoparasitism. Most kleptoparasitic species obtain only a small proportion of their energy requirements in this way, and only for part of the annual cycle. Furthermore, even those for which kleptoparasitism may be very important usually have alternative feeding methods which are employed by part of the population while others are kleptoparasitic.

Plumage polymorphism

Arctic Skua. A very curious anomaly prevails with regard to the colouring of the plumage. Birds are found indiscriminately breeding together, of a uniform blackish brown colour, quite resembling in this respect, Larus Cataractes [the Great Skua]; and others having the underparts, throat and cheeks yellowish white. This difference in colour is apparent when the young birds are in the nest; and the parents may be both black, or both of the other kind, or one of the black and one of the white-bellied variety, and the young will be either two black, two white-bellied, or one of each indiscriminately. I have seen two black young birds in the nest of two white-bellied. I have shot, dissected, and domesticated many individuals, without obtaining any clew to this singular anomaly; the two varieties being precisely similar in every particular but that of colour.

Edmonston (1843)

The form of the Arctic Skua with white underparts is quite as common in Shetland as the sooty race. The two forms mate indiscriminately, though pairs which match in colour are perhaps the most common.

Evans & Buckley (1899)

ADAPTIVE VARIATIONS IN PLUMAGE WITHIN BIRD SPECIES

Most bird species have a variety of plumages. In many species there are differences in plumage between the sexes, varying from very slight differences (as in the Gannet, where the male usually has a slightly yellower nape and crown than the female) to the extreme sexual dimorphism of most ducks or peacocks. Some species show seasonal changes in plumage pattern (for example the white winter Ptarmigan and the brown summer plumage). Young birds often differ in appearance from adults. Only in a few species are there plumage polymorphisms that are not due to age, season or sex, in which birds may exhibit one of two or more plumages or 'phenotypes'. One of the best known of these is that of the Arctic Skua, which has been described as the most striking plumage polymorphism in a European bird. Pomarine Skuas share the same polymorphism, and it could be argued that Long-tailed Skuas do, too, although the dark phase is exceedingly rare in this last species. Great Skuas are generally thought of as being monomorphic in plumage although they exhibit a high degree of individual variation of a continuous nature. However, the South Polar Skua also has dark and light colour phases. These do not seem to correspond directly to the dark and light phases of the smaller skuas, and may have arisen independently, but there are some intriguing similarities in the polymorphisms of Arctic Skuas and South Polar Skuas.

Skuas show little consistent plumage difference between the sexes, but in the case of the South Polar Skua detailed study has shown that the sexes can be identified though with difficulty, on the basis of colour. The plumages of birds are considered generally to reflect adaptations to particular life-styles. Polygamous birds are usually sexually dimorphic, with males being more brightly coloured in polygynous species (ones in which males mate with several females and leave the female to do most, or all, of the incubation and chick-rearing, as in most ducks or in Black Grouse or the Ruff). Females are more brightly coloured than the males in polyandrous species (ones in which females may mate with several males, as in phalaropes or the Dotterel). This is because sexual selection favours more brightly coloured individuals in the sex which is competing more strongly for mates (males in ducks, females in phalaropes). Drab, or cryptic colouring is generally favoured for the sex which incubates the eggs.

Plumage polymorphism, independent of age and sex, in birds has been the subject of a number of reviews. Huxley (1955) recorded plumage polymorphism in about 22 of 134 bird families, but considered it frequent only in seven of these, particularly in petrels, herons, hawks, falcons, owls and skuas. The frequent occurrence of plumage polymorphism in birds of prey (which could be considered to include skuas) led Paulson (1973) to suggest that there was a common selective pressure resulting in the frequent independent evolution of several colour phases in predatory birds to enhance their success in catching intelligent prey such as birds and mammals. Numerous other theories have been put forward to explain the existence of plumage polymorphism in skuas, ranging from its relationship with feeding success, through to effects on the timing of breeding or the rates of heat loss from the different coloured plumages, and these are each considered later in this chapter.

PATTERNS OF PLUMAGE POLYMORPHISM IN THE SOUTH POLAR SKUA

Colour patterns

Ainley *et al.* (1985) defined the colour phases in adult South Polar Skuas as follows:

Dark phase – birds were brownish olive and virtually uniform with the sepia of the wing coverts, scapulars and spinal tracts. The hackles on the head and neck of many of these dark skuas had orange-yellow to buffy brown tips which exhibited a glossy sheen.

Light phase – the dark back contrasted sharply with the buffy yellow to orange-yellow head and neck, and buffy yellow to pale or smoke-grey body plumage. The hackles on most of these individuals exhibited a bright sheen covering a much larger area of each feather than in dark phase birds.

Intermediate phase – varied in colour between the darkest light phase, from which no clear boundary could be discerned, to almost the colour of the lightest dark phase, though a discontinuity existed between dark phase and intermediate phase. Intermediates also had a sheen of intermediate intensity on the hackles, and tended to be speckled light and dark on the neck and body (Photos 17, 18).

Clinal variation

On the Antarctic Continent the light phase of the South Polar Skua predominates. At Cape Crozier, Ross Island, Spear examined 115 breeding adults (Ainley *et al.* 1985) and found that 19% were dark phase, 23% intermediate, and 58% light phase. On the opposite side of Ross Island, at Cape Royds, Spellerberg (1970) found 14% dark, 66% intermediate, and 20% light phase birds. The differences in proportions of intermediate and light phases in these two samples were attributed to difficulties in defining the intermediate-light boundary.

On the Antarctic Peninsula, the dark phase is most common, with very few light birds present (Watson 1975, Pietz in litt.). Thus, as in the Arctic Skua, the dark phase tends to be more frequent at the warmer end of the species' breeding range.

Clearly the classification of light and intermediate phases is somewhat arbitrary since no discontinuity exists between them, but dark birds apparently can be distinguished satisfactorily from intermediates. One complicating factor is that the colour of the plumage does vary according to the age of the bird and time after

17. A light phase South Polar Skua on its nest at Cape Bird, Ross Island, Antarctica, showing the strong colour contrast between the uniformly pale head and body and the dark wings and back. Photo: Y. Tamiya.

18. A dark intermediate phase, or possibly a pale dark phase, South Polar Skua at Admiralty Bay, Antarctica. Photo: M. P. Harris.

moult. Exposure to sunlight results in fading and old worn feathers tend to be lighter in colour than freshly grown ones. Presence of nonbreeders in samples will lead to a higher estimate of the proportion of intermediate rather than light phase birds, because immature skuas tend to have fewer old, worn and faded body feathers. Hence birds classified as intermediates in the spring may fade to become pales by late summer!

PATTERNS OF PLUMAGE POLYMORPHISM IN THE ARCTIC SKUA

Colour patterns

Adult Arctic Skuas may be identified as dark phase, light phase, or intermediate. Dark phase, or melanic, individuals are a dark brown all over. Intermediates may have some white neck feathers and slightly lighter brown belly feathers, or may differ from darks only in having a few pale straw-coloured or yellowish feathers on the sides of the neck and ear coverts, giving them a dark capped appearance. Pale phase, or light phase, birds have a white belly, breast and neck, some having a darker band across the breast.

However, these phases are not clearcut. There are all grades between intermediate and dark, and the dividing line between these phases is arbitrary. The distinction between dark and intermediate phases is made by workers on Fair Isle, but most other ornithologists have classified adult Arctic Skuas into only two categories; pale and dark. The pale phase is sharply marked off from the intermediates. In the chicks, distinctions are less evident than in the adults, but a pale morph can be defined in well grown chicks as having white or brownish-white belly feathers, and broad rufous tips to the back feathers and wing coverts. Intermediate phase chicks are defined as having darker back feathers with narrow rufous tips, and dark tips to the belly feathers, while dark phase chicks have completely dark feathers on the back and wing coverts, and belly feathers are also dark, both at the tip and proximally. Although chicks on Fair Isle have routinely been allocated to these three colour phases, there is continuous variation in chick colour and the three morphs are arbitrary divisions. Of 38 birds on Fair Isle, ringed and classified as chicks and subsequently recaptured as adults, eleven were classified as a different colour phase as adults, although all eight pale chicks that returned were classified as pale adults (O'Donald 1983). Thus the chick colour phases correspond to some extent to those of the adult plumage, but either the correspondence is poor, or errors are often made when classifying chicks.

The genetic basis of plumage polymorphism
O'Donald & Davis (1959) suggested that the colour phases of the Arctic Skua may be determined by a simple genetic mechanism, with two alleles at a single genetic locus determining colour. Pale birds would be homozygotes for the recessive allele, intermediates would be heterozygotes, and dark birds homozygotes for the dominant allele. Because the distinction between dark and intermediate phases is arbitrary, we could expect some misclassification of homozygous dark and heterozygous birds. Nevertheless, some of the Fair Isle breeding data fitted this simple model. Pale × pale pairs produced only pale chicks, while dark × dark pairs produced mainly dark chicks. Pale × dark matings should produce only intermediate chicks, which most did, although clearly some misclassification was occurring since some pale and some dark chicks were found from these last pairings (Table 26). O'Donald (1983) considered that some chicks were incorrectly classified and some homozygote dark adults were phenotypically indistinguishable from some heterozygotes. However, O'Donald & Davis (1959) found that the ratios of chick phases produced by various adult combinations deviated seriously from expectation. Far more intermediate chicks were produced than a two–allele, single-locus, model would predict. This suggested either that more than one genetic locus was involved in determining colour phase, or that strong selection took place against pales and darks between hatching and fledging. The deviation would require nearly half of the dark and pale chicks to die even if survival of intermediate chicks was 100%. If any intermediate chicks died then losses of pales and darks would need to be even greater. This is quite an impossible proposition, since we know that chick survival on Fair Isle is very much higher than this difference would allow (Berry & Davis 1970). On Foula, most Arctic Skua chick deaths are due to accidents or predation rather than to low chick viability, and the same is probably true on Fair Isle. Berry & Davis (1970) showed that there was no greater deficit of homozygotes in broods of one chick (where one chick had died) than in broods of two chicks, which rules out the selective death hypothesis. However, O'Donald (1983) concluded that, even allowing for hypothetical differences in viability of chicks, he could not explain the different phase discrepancies. This, together with the errors in classification of chicks and the lack of distinction between dark and intermediate phases of adults, made O'Donald (1983) decide that 'the original assumptions of O'Donald & Davis' model are clearly false' and 'we must conclude that the classification of chicks is too uncertain, subjective and inconsistent for genetic analysis'.

Having been unable to determine the mode of inheritance by examining colour phases of chicks produced by particular combinations of adults, O'Donald (1983) examined the proportions of each phenotype of 105 offspring that later returned to Fair Isle as adults, in relation to the phases of their parents. This gets round the problem of misclassification of chicks. However, some problems arise here too, since errors in the classification of dark and intermediate phenotypes clearly occur if these are determined by the hypothesised dark and light alleles. The data do not fit a simple model in which pales and darks are homozygotes and intermediates are heterozygotes. If dark 'Intermediates' are classified as intermediates then the Fair Isle breeding data show a significant deficit of dark phase offspring produced by intermediate × intermediate matings. If dark 'Intermediates' are classified as dark phase in order to get round this discrepancy, then pale × intermediate matings produce some dark offspring, which is quite incompatible with pale and dark being homozygous for alternative alleles at a single locus. O'Donald (1983) concluded that this simple genetic model is acceptable despite the failure of the data to support it, since he attributed the discrepancies to errors in classification rather than to the model being incorrect. However, the story may not be so simple, since colour phase appears to be influenced by the sex of the bird (see later in this chapter), a factor that has been consistently disregarded by all previous research on Arctic Skua plumage polymorphism.

Clinal variation

The proportion of pale phase Arctic Skuas increases from south to north. The frequency of the pale phase is lowest in Finland, at about 4%. In Spitsbergen and Bear Island about 99% are pale, while in arctic Canada and north USSR east of Novaya Zemlya dark phase birds (throughout this section dark = dark plus intermediate) are virtually unknown. The approximate geographical distribution of the phase frequencies is shown in Fig. 68, which is based on data in Southern (1943) and O'Donald (1983). It can be seen that a high frequency of dark phase birds extends particularly far north in northern Scandinavia, and the frequency of pale birds increases very rapidly over a short distance to the north and east of north Norway. Whatever factors cause this clinal variation, apparently they are particularly pronounced over a small range in this area.

It is perhaps worth noting in passing that, at least in the North Atlantic where detailed studies have been made, the clinal variation in plumage polymorphisms in the Fulmar and the Guillemot show similar geographical patterns to that in the Arctic Skua. The frequency of dark phase Fulmars and bridled Guillemots increases from south to north in the North Atlantic. Dark Fulmars, bridled Guillemots and pale Arctic Skuas all occur at higher frequencies on the west side of the Atlantic than they do at the same latitude on the east side. The frequency of bridling in Guillemots correlates closely with minimum air temperatures during the breeding season, and to some extent with sea surface temperature at the breeding site (Birkhead 1984). Possibly the same factors affect the frequency of the dark allele in Fulmars and the pale allele in Arctic Skuas.

Clinal variation in the frequency of the colour phases could be the result of a number of different processes. It could result from the spreading out of the gene for melanism from its place of origin, although this seems implausible, since the same mutation for melanism would have to have occurred at several places along the southern edge of the Arctic Skua's breeding range, which is most unlikely. In addition, this argument would also mean that the melanic forms of the Pomarine Skua, Long-tailed Skua and South Polar Skua would have to be the result of

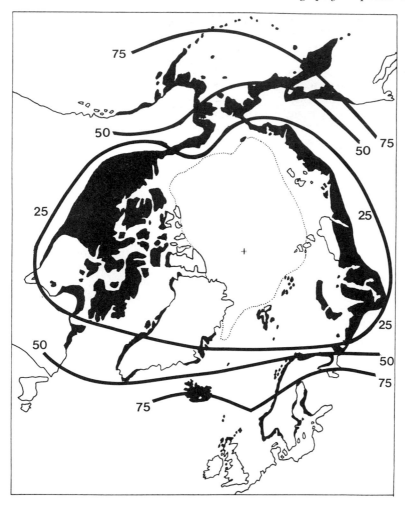

Fig. 68 Geographical distribution of colour phase frequencies in the breeding range of the Arctic Skua. Lines mark the locations where the dark phase represents 25%, 50% and 75% of the population. Note that the frequency of the dark phase does not reach 50% on the tundra areas of north USSR or inland Canada, but is particularly high in southern oceanic regions and in the Baltic.

independent mutations rather than a polymorphism derived from their common ancestor. Alternatively, the cline could result if dark birds had a selective advantage at the south of the species' range and pale birds had an advantage in the north. Then gene flow would establish a cline with the most rapid change in the phase ratios at the point midway between the regions where each phenotype was superior. At these in between points neither morph would have a selective advantage. In the Arctic Skua about 50% of the birds are dark in north Norway, south Greenland

and much of Alaska (Fig. 68). A third potential explanation for the cline and for differences in phase proportions between neighbouring colonies could be that the frequencies of the phases represent a balance between opposing selection pressures that differ between colonies and with latitude. These alternative ideas and their implications are discussed in detail by O'Donald (1983).

Some possible selection pressures affecting colour morph frequencies are considered later in this chapter, but first it is worth examining historical and recent data to see if there is any evidence to suggest that the frequencies of the phases have been changing in a systematic way over the years. O'Donald (1983) showed that the dark phase had increased in Iceland between 1940 and 1970 (Table 27). There has been a significant increase in the dark phase in the Varanger area of NE Norway, from 45% darks in 1937–52 to 67% darks in a sample in 1972 and 58% darks in 1976–78 (Table 28). O'Donald (1983) argued that the dark phase had not changed in frequency on Fair Isle over the period 1948–76, but the data suggest that darks have increased here too (Table 28), from 75% of the population between 1943 and 1959 to 80% between 1973 and 1979 (Fig. 69). The frequency of darks was also significantly higher in Orkney in 1982 (76%) than in 1943 (62%), although this result (Table 29) should be treated with caution since the 1943 sample was based on only 81 birds at just two colonies, at a time when Arctic Skua numbers on Orkney were much less than they are now.

On Foula, the percentage of darks is higher now (76.6%) than it was in 1948 (70%) or in the mid-1970s (70–73%), but very similar to the percentage estimated in 1890, so there is no evidence of any consistent longterm increase in darks here (Table 29), though the dark allele may have been increasing in frequency over the last 40 years (Fig. 69). On Noss, the percentage of darks again appears to have increased, from 78.5% in the 1930s and 74.4% in the 1940s, to 85.2% in 1974 and 88.6% in 1986 (Fig. 69). The increase in the frequency of dark phase between the 1930s–40s and the 1970s–80s is statistically significant (Table 29, $\chi^2 = 4.58$, $p < 0.05$).

These data suggest that the dark morph has been increasing over the last 40 years or so in some areas, particularly where it occurs in about half of the population. Unfortunately, such a pattern of increase would be compatible with each of the explanations for the existence of the cline, and all we can deduce is that recent conditions may be favouring the dark allele.

The frequency of dark phase birds also shows some interesting local heterogeneity that is not directly related to the general south-north cline. The cline should result in the pale allele decreasing in frequency from Foula and Noss (which lie at exactly the same latitude on opposite sides of Shetland), south to Fair Isle, and decreasing again from Fair Isle south to Orkney. The data (Fig. 69) show that the frequency of the pale phase has usually been higher on Orkney than on Fair Isle, and lowest on Noss, suggesting that local factors have an important influence.

PLUMAGE POLYMORPHISM IN POMARINE AND LONG-TAILED SKUAS

Pomarine Skuas have a light phase and a dark phase plumage exactly equivalent to the morphs of the Arctic Skua, and this polymorphism can be seen in immatures as well as in adults. However, the dark phase is relatively rare, forming between 5–20% of populations in all parts of the range, and showing no systematic variation

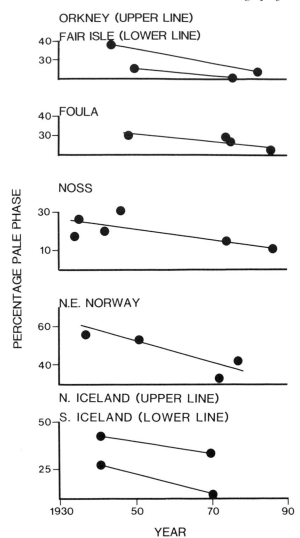

Fig. 69   Changes with time in the frequency of the pale colour phase in different Arctic Skua populations.

in frequency such as the cline found in the Arctic Skua. Percentages of dark phase Pomarine Skuas are 5% in west Greenland, 10% in Franz Josef Land, 15% on Baffin Island, 20% on the Yamal peninsula (Southern 1944), 5% in northern Alaska (Maher 1974), 3.5% on Banks Island, Canada (Manning *et al.* 1956) and 7.6% in Alaska (Frame 1973).

Similarly, the Long-tailed Skua has a pale and a dark phase, but the dark form of the adult is exceptionally rare, and is apparently known only from populations in Greenland. Among juveniles, two colour morphs occur; a light morph and a barred morph. The genetic basis of these, and their adaptive values, if any, are completely unknown. No dark phase juvenile plumage appears to be known.

PATTERNS OF PLUMAGE IN RELATION TO SEX

In most skuas the plumage pattern of the two sexes is considered to be indistinguishable, but females are slightly larger than males in total body size and in most, although not all measurements. When birds form pairs they apparently choose their mates to some extent on the basis of size. Large females tend to pair with large males, and so it is almost invariably the case that the larger bird in a pair is the female. Ainley, Spear and Wood (1985) studied a population of South Polar Skuas with which they themselves were not familiar but where the individuals in 43 colour ringed pairs were of known sex because they had been observed mating and courtship feeding over a number of previous years. They found that in 38 of the 43 pairs a size difference between the members of the pair was visible in the field, and in every case the bird they identified as the larger of the pair was the female. In ten pairs that were captured the female was from 30–290 g heavier than the male. While making these observations they also noticed that the colour of birds tended to differ in a consistent way between the members of pairs. In most cases, females were paler in colour, and it was possible to identify correctly the sex of the members of 31 of the 43 pairs on colour difference alone. Thus difference in colour was a less valuable guide to sex than difference in size, but clearly did tend to exist between the sexes.

The situation in the South Polar Skua is somewhat complicated by the fact that the population can be divided into three colour phases, light, dark and intermediate, as described in a previous section of this chapter. Ainley, Spear and Wood compared colour of birds without subdividing them into phases, and it is not established whether males tended to be darker than females of the same colour phase or whether there were simply far more dark phase males and more light phase females in their sample. Ainley, Spear and Wood classified 26% of male South Polar Skuas at Cape Crozier as dark phase but only 2% of females as dark phase, so it seems that a major part of the sex difference in colour that they describe was due to differences in the proportions of colour phases within the two sexes. At Cape Crozier, light phase South Polar Skuas predominate, but on the Antarctic Peninsula most birds are of the dark phase. W. Z. and S. G. Trivelpiece and N. J. Volkman examined twelve pairs of South Polar Skuas at King George Island in the Antarctic Peninsula region, and found that the male was smaller and darker in colour in ten of these pairs, was smaller but of the same colour in one, and was the same size but darker in the last. The difference in colour between males and females in South Polar Skuas seems to hold both in regions where light birds predominate and in regions where dark birds predominate. This suggests that there is a general tendency for male South Polar Skuas to exhibit a higher proportion of dark phase individuals than do females in the same population. This leads on to the idea that the determination of colour phase, which is presumably under genetic control, may be influenced by sex-linked genes or by the hormonal background of the individual bird. Whether this sex difference in colour has any significance for South Polar Skuas is not clear. No detailed studies of South Polar Skua biology in relation to colour phase have been made. However, the genetics and implications of colour phase have been studied in detail in the Arctic Skua so it is to that species that we should now turn our attention.

It is generally believed that colour phase in the Arctic Skua is independent of sex. Even the authors of the quotes that head this chapter knew that the dark, intermediate and light colour phases of the Arctic Skua included both male and female birds; they shot plenty to check this very point! However, it does seem to be the case that colour phase in the Arctic Skua is influenced by the sex of the individual. Of 24 Arctic Skua skins from Iceland examined, three quarters of the dark phase birds were males and three quarters of the light phase birds were females (Cramp & Simmons 1983). According to Berry (1977), in 60% of Arctic Skua pairs on Fair Isle the male was darker than the female. This is remarkably reminiscent of the situation in the South Polar Skua! In his book on the colour phases of the Arctic Skua, O'Donald (1980) never discusses that the proportions of the different colour phases differ between the sexes, and calculates the expected frequencies of matings between the phases on the assumption that the phases are equally frequent in the two sexes. However, O'Donald gives a table of the colour phases of Arctic Skuas studied on Fair Isle where the observations over a series of years recorded 46 dark females, 106 dark males, 224 intermediate females, 183 intermediate males, 89 light females and 49 light males. Thus 13% of the females were dark and 25% light, while 31% of the males were dark and only 14% were light. There is less than a one in one thousand probability that such a difference in the proportions of the colour phases between the sexes would occur by chance. Richard Perry found exactly the same trend among the Arctic Skuas on Noss in 1946. Of the dark phase birds on Noss, 69% were males and 31% females; while among the light phase birds (Perry 1948) the proportions were approximately reversed, with females predominating. In view of these data, I decided to examine the Arctic Skuas on Foula to see if the same discrepancy occurred there. In May 1987 I watched birds mating and recorded which bird was the male on the assumption that males mounted females during copulation and not vice versa. These observations showed the same trend as before (Table 30). Thus we can conclude that there is a strong tendency for the frequency of dark phase Arctic Skuas to be higher among males than among females, on Noss, on Fair Isle, on Foula and in Iceland. It is interesting that the sex difference in the Arctic Skua is in the same direction as that in the South Polar Skua. In both species there are more dark phase males and more light phase females than would be expected if the colour phase were independent of sex. Whether this implies that the plumage polymorphism is determined by the same genetic mechanism in these two species is another matter. If this was the case then the gene for the plumage polymorphism would exist in all skua taxa since it must predate the separation of the large skuas from the small skuas. However, the pattern of the light phase plumage is quite different between South Polar Skuas and small skuas, and it may be that they evolved independently and happen by chance to show similar differences between the sexes, though such a striking coincidence seems improbable.

Curiously enough, there may even be sex-related colour variation in the Great Skua. Although I had never noticed a tendency for sexes to differ in colouration, and had not paid any particular attention to this point, after discovering this sex-related variation in Arctic and South Polar Skuas I discovered a passage in Perry (1948) that I had previously overlooked: 'as I got to know individuals of some pairs it appeared to me that the majority of the females were paler plumaged than their mates'. In May 1987, Richard Caldow and I recorded that male Great Skuas

on Foula were darker than their mate in 18 pairs, no different in ten pairs and
paler in only one pair, confirming Perry's observation.

TIMING OF BREEDING HYPOTHESIS

While acknowledging the theoretical interest to population geneticists of the
consequences of the plumage polymorphism in the Arctic Skua, Professor Sam
Berry, who has also worked on the Fair Isle Arctic Skuas, put forward a simple
explanation for the existence of the colour phases and the cline in frequency of
the pale phase with latitude. 'In Arctic Skuas, mating behaviour is initiated by
the female approaching the male, who reacts angrily against her. This approach-
rejection cycle goes on for some time until the male weakens and finally accepts
the female. Mating then takes place. The significant point is that dark birds are
less aggressive than light ones: a dark male does not react as vigorously as a pale
against an importunate female, and matings involving a dark male are set up earlier
than those with a pale one.' In fact, Davis (1976) showed that dark phase males
breed ten days earlier than pale phase birds at their first breeding attempt, but in
subsequent seasons there are no significant differences in timing of breeding
between the phases. Nevertheless, earlier breeding during the first attempt
increases breeding success since it tends to decrease with later dates of laying.
According to Berry & Johnston 'The higher the proportion of pales in a colony,
the later will be the breeding season. In the north of its range, Arctic Skuas feed
largely on lemmings and voles which become common late in the summer; further
south it has to adjust its time of breeding to that of the Gulls and Terns on which
it preys, and they in turn will breed at a time when food and climate are best for
raising their own broods. The dark/light segregation is really a mechanism for
varying the time of peak breeding which happens to produce a colour difference
of no apparent importance to the birds themselves.'

Unfortunately the data do not support exactly this argument. Firstly, the mean
laying date of Arctic Skuas in northern Alaska, where they feed on terrestrial prey
on the tundra, is earlier than the mean laying date of Arctic Skuas on Spitsbergen
and Bear Island, where most food is obtained by kleptoparasitism (Table 31). On
the tundra the Arctic Skua feeds only to a small extent on lemmings, and relies
more on small birds, eggs, berries and insects (Chapter 7) and so it probably times
its breeding to suit the availability of these prey. On Spitsbergen the Arctic Skuas
obtain most food by robbing Kittiwakes, but they do not synchronise their breeding
with the Kittiwakes because they are unable to lay until the snow cover has melted.
Cliff-nesting seabirds are able to start breeding without this constraint so that the
Arctic Skuas lay much later relative to Kittiwakes on Spitsbergen than is the case
in Shetland. Timing of breeding of Arctic Skuas in Spitsbergen also varies greatly
year to year, whereas Kittiwakes have a fairly regular laying date; snow melt at
skua nesting sites is, again, the explanation.

Differences in the timing of breeding of light and dark birds are insufficient to
produce the different breeding dates of southern and northern skua populations.
Let us take a hypothetical extreme to show this. If colony A contained 100% dark
phase birds and colony B 100% pale phase birds, and if every male bred only once
and was replaced by a new male each season, then the mean laying date at colony
B would be ten days later than the mean at colony A. In fact this is clearly

unrealistic, since we know that the southernmost Arctic Skua colonies contain about 25% pale phase birds, and less than half of the males change mates or die between seasons (O'Donald 1983). If we are less extreme we could compare a model colony similar to Fair Isle, where about 80% of the males are dark, with a high latitude colony, where 100% are light, and allow a maximum of 50% of the birds to be inexperienced breeders at each site. Then the high latitude colony would have a mean laying data no more than four days later than Fair Isle. In fact, Arctic Skuas on Spitsbergen (mean laying date 1 July), where 99% are pale, lay about 33 days later than Arctic Skuas on Fair Isle (mean laying date 28 May). This is more than three times the greatest possible difference in breeding time between colour morphs, and more than ten times that to be expected from a more realistic calculation.

Lovenskiold (1964) states that the timing of breeding is determined by the date of snow melt on Spitsbergen, which varies greatly from year to year. Arctic Skua territories are not occupied until the melt occurs, and then the pair has to come into breeding condition, mate and produce eggs, so that the laying date is dependent on the date of territory occupation. One could argue that the selective advantage would be strongly in favour of birds that could form the pair quickly in this situation and so lay as soon after the snow melt as possible. If the dark phase males are indeed less aggressive and form pairs more easily than light ones, then this might favour dark males more in Spitsbergen than it would in Shetland, where birds begin to arrive back at the colony as early as 16 April, a whole month before the first eggs are laid. At Spitsbergen, laying may start some two weeks after first return, while in northern Alaska, Maher reported that most pairs laid only two to eight days after occupying the territory, and he suggested that these birds may actually have arrived as pairs, having met up earlier elsewhere.

In northern Alaska about 50% of Arctic Skuas are light, but the timing of breeding varies extensively between sites according to the return date. At Cape Sabine, which skuas pass on migration early in the season, Arctic Skuas laid around 4 June. The next site to be occupied was the Kaolak River, where laying occurred around 3 June. At Lake Peters the first Arctic Skuas arrived on 27 May and laying occurred around 9 June. Finally, Barrow was occupied on 4 June and laying occurred around 17 June. Thus differences in the timing of breeding related to arrival dates in the breeding area and did not correlate with colour phase differences (Maher 1974).

Individual Arctic Skuas at Fair Isle laid on almost the same date each year. The mean laying date of the population hardly varied at all, and the first egg was laid between 16 and 20 May each year. Furthermore, the first bird to return almost always arrives between 14–17 April. The regularity implies strong photoperiodic control of the timing of breeding. Further north, snow melt becomes important and skuas have to wait until conditions allow them to breed.

Arctic Skuas on Spitsbergen feed largely by kleptoparasitism, as do those in Shetland and east Murman. Arctic Skuas at the sites Maher studied fed on tundra birds, insects and small mammals. However, the tundra breeding skuas laid much earlier than those on Spitsbergen, and at about the same time as those in east Murman. Thus Berry & Johnston were wrong to suggest that light phase birds delay breeding to synchronise with the small mammals of the tundra. It would also be wrong to suggest that the allele causing light phase plumage made the timing of Arctic Skua breeding later at higher latitudes where the allele is more frequent. We have seen that the difference in timing is not enough to adjust to the much later laying dates required at some high latitude sites. However, the dark allele does result in an increased breeding success for inexperienced dark males compared with inexperienced pale males at Fair Isle, so natural selection favours the dark allele through earlier breeding. At higher latitudes this advantage might not exist, and this could result in the clinal variation observed, with the dark allele most frequent at low latitudes. In this case, the function of the polymorphism would be slightly different from that proposed by Berry & Johnston. Rather than adjusting the timing of breeding to prey availability at different latitudes, the dark allele would confer a benefit to birds at low latitudes, but a different advantage would be required to explain the light allele's predominance at high latitudes. One such advantage has been described by O'Donald (1983). Pale phase birds tend to start breeding at an earlier age, and as a result have a greater lifetime reproductive success.

ASSORTATIVE MATING AND SEXUAL SELECTION IN THE ARCTIC SKUA

The first warden of Fair Isle Bird Observatory, Ken Williamson, started making detailed records of the colour phases and breeding statistics of the Arctic Skuas nesting on Fair Isle in 1948, when only 15 pairs bred. Peter Davis, the second warden, continued this study until he left in 1962, when the population had increased to 71 pairs. Between 1973 and 1979, O'Donald and co-workers revived the study, gathering a large body of information on the breeding ecology in relation to colour phase. These data were used by O'Donald in a series of papers concerning assortative mating, sexual selection and demography, and these are critically reviewed in O'Donald (1983).

Assortative mating

As long ago as 1899, Evans & Buckley suggested that Arctic Skuas tend to mate with a partner of the same colour phase; positive assortative mating takes place. This conclusion was scientifically tested by Southern (1943) in his seminal review of the colour phases of the Arctic Skua. At Smolen and at Gamvik, in Scandinavia, and in a sample at Noss, Shetland, counted in 1935, the numbers of dark × dark, pale × pale and dark × pale combinations showed no significant difference from the frequencies that would be predicted if colour phases were equal between the sexes and birds paired at random with respect to colour. However, in a sample at Noss counted in 1942, there were significantly more like pairs. Out of 22 pairs, only one consisted of a pale mated to a dark bird, and this result would have occurred by chance less than one time in a hundred. Positive assortative mating was again found on Noss in 1946, when Perry counted the phase combinations present. However, data collected in the 1940s and 1950s from Fair Isle, Foula, Unst, Yell and Fetlar combined, and Caithness showed little evidence for assortative mating at those sites (O'Donald 1959). Examining the numbers of matings within and between morphs at colonies in Iceland in 1971, Bengtson & Owen (1973) found significant negative assortative, or 'disassortative', mating. More of the pairs than would be predicted by chance were pale × dark. No deviation from random mating was found in a population in Finland (Hilden 1971), while Davis & O'Donald (1976) found significant positive assortative mating on Foula in 1975. Data from NE Norway gave no evidence for deviations from random mating between colour phases (Gotmark *et al* 1981). Counts for all Orkney colonies, in which 858 pairs were classified, showed that dark × dark, pale × pale and dark-× pale pairings occurred as would be expected from random mating (Meek *et al* 1985).

When all of the data are considered (Table 32), it appears that positive assortative mating does occur in some instances, but this is by no means universal. In the majority of colonies in most years matings are as would be expected if they formed by chance with respect to colour phase.

The situation on Noss is particularly odd. In 1935 the Noss birds showed no evidence of assortative mating. In 1942 and 1946 there was a very marked deficit of dark × pale pairings. Matings were highly assortative. However, by 1963 the matings were again compatible with random pairing, as they were in 1986.

The situation becomes even more complex if we take sex into account. The sex ratio within the dark and pale morphs is biased. There are more dark males than dark females and more pale females than pale males, at least in colonies in the northern isles of Scotland and in Iceland. Thus the expectation should be that random mating between the sexes would lead to an excess of dark × pale pairings. This certainly does not generally occur. In Table 32, only one study out of 22 found a trend for disassortative mating. Thus the data show a greater tendency towards assortative mating than comparison against a null hypothesis of random assortment of colour morphs would suggest. True 'expected' frequencies would differ from random assortment according to the extent of the difference in phase ratios between the sexes.

On Fair Isle and Foula, O'Donald (1983) and Berry & Davis (1970) classified birds into three, rather than two phases; dark, intermediate and pale, allowing a more detailed investigation of assortative mating. Berry & Davis also examined the situation on Fair Isle with regard to the known sex of the birds, and showed that there was a marked and statistically significant excess of inter-mediate × intermediate matings (Table 33). Some 60% of matings involved a male darker than his mate, as would be expected, since dark phase birds are mostly males and pales mostly females. Berry & Davis suggested that females prefer dark males, but if this were true then pale males would have difficulty in recruiting into the breeding colony. In fact, pale males tend to recruit at a younger age than dark males, and there is little reason to suggest that any territorial male is unable to obtain a mate, so any preference for dark males among females cannot have any material effect on the likelihood of pale males attracting a mate.

In 1974, counts of Arctic Skuas on Foula showed a significant excess of pale × pale matings which led O'Donald, Davis and Broad (1974) to suggest that Arctic Skuas on Foula differ in the pattern of assortative mating from those on Fair Isle. On Fair Isle, intermediates mate assortatively, whereas on Foula the data indicated that pales mate assortatively. These patterns could differ between the colonies as a consequence of separate evolution and lack of gene flow. However, we know that many birds do move between Fair Isle and Foula. Furthermore, in 1975, a more thorough study on Foula showed that this difference no longer existed. In 1975 the patterns of assortative matings on Foula and on Fair Isle were statistically indistinguishable (O'Donald 1983).

Evidence for assortative mating in the Arctic Skua is confusing and the situation is complicated by uncertain influences of previously neglected sex differences in phase proportions, and by changes in the pattern with time and between colonies. There appears to be a slight tendency for birds of like colour morphs to pair more often than would be expected by chance, but there is no evidence to suggest that any birds are unable to obtain a mate as a result of these colour preferences.

Sexual selection

Charles Darwin suggested the idea of sexual selection. He thought that polygamous males would gain a selective advantage if they had characters that improved their chances of mating. In monogamous species he suggested that sexual selection would occur if early breeding resulted in a greater production of young, and better males tended to pair with early-breeding females. In the Arctic Skua, breeding success declines with laying date. The last pairs to breed produce only about a half as many offspring as the earliest breeders. Sexual selection would favour females that chose early-breeding males and, likewise, early-breeding males, by conferring a higher reproductive output. Attempts to demonstrate this in the Arctic Skua have not been entirely successful, but are discussed in detail by O'Donald (1983).

DEMOGRAPHIC CORRELATES OF COLOUR PHASE IN ARCTIC SKUAS

Before considering the different hypotheses put forward to explain the plumage variation, it is useful to review some of the advantages and disadvantages that might be associated with the alternative colour morphs; colour could correlate with survival rate, age at first breeding, or breeding success.

Adult survival rate

O'Donald (1983) showed that there was no difference on Fair Isle in the average survival rates of breeding dark, intermediate and pale birds, or between the sexes, over the period 1948–1962 (Table 34). Nor did survival rates of each colour morph differ significantly between 1973 and 1975 or between 1976 and 1978, although the average survival rate in this last period was much less than usual due to illegal shooting of birds.

Age at maturity

Arctic Skuas ringed as chicks at Fair Isle provided information on the age of first breeding of each colour morph. Pale birds tended to start breeding at a younger age than intermediates or darks. About one-third of the pale birds first bred when three years old. Hardly any intermediates or darks bred before they were four years old, and half when five years old or older (Table 35). Clearly, pales should have a strong selective advantage due to their earlier recruitment into the breeding population. However, this advantage is offset by influences on breeding success, as outlined below.

Breeding success

O'Donald (1983) presented a detailed analysis of the breeding success of Arctic Skuas on Fair Isle. This showed that, not surprisingly, the breeding success of birds nesting for the first time is lower than that achieved in subsequent years. When the number of chicks fledged per breeding attempt is compared, it becomes clear that pale birds have a lower breeding success than that of intermediates or darks, both in their first breeding season and subsequently. The difference is particularly marked for the first breeding attempt (Table 36). Inexperienced pale males fledged an average of 0.63 chicks per pair while dark males fledged 0.91 chicks per pair. In later years pale males fledged 1.27 chicks per pair compared to the 1.43 chicks per pair of dark males. The variation in the reproductive rates of Arctic Skuas on Fair Isle appears to be determined by two factors. By breeding at a younger age pale males suffer a lower breeding success than dark birds in their first breeding season. Secondly, most, but not all, females of each colour generally prefer to mate with dark males and so the early pair formation with dark males increases their breeding success.

Demographic consequences

Comparison of the allele frequencies (assuming a two-allele, single-gene determination of colour phase) between breeding adults and their offspring on Fair Isle shows no evidence of a marked difference in fitness between pale and dark birds. The frequency of the pale allele among chicks is almost exactly the same as among male and female adults (Table 37). On Fair Isle, dark males benefit from sexual selection, while pale females gain a selective advantage due to their earlier age of first breeding. O'Donald & Davis (1975) concluded that 'the component of selection in favour of pale birds is considerably greater than the component of selection in favour of dark males'. However, differences in fitness between phases are very slight, and small changes in the data base can change the conclusion reached. With more extensive data O'Donald (1983) calculated that, according to the demographic data for each sex and colour phase, selection should eventually eliminate the pale allele on Fair Isle. It would be reduced to one per cent in about 1,000 years time, unless migration from further north boosted the level of pales. This calculation is based on the assumption, perhaps open to doubt, that colour phase is determined by two alleles at a single locus and not affected by sex.

It would be wrong to expect the Arctic Skua at high latitudes to show the same demographic values as the population on Fair Isle. At high latitudes pales may be favoured for unknown reasons, but their tendency to start breeding at a younger age than darks may be important. According to Belopolskii (1961) some Arctic Skuas in north USSR breed when only one or two years old. He demonstrated this by ringing chicks and by shooting large numbers of breeding adults in subsequent seasons. This very young age of first breeding was possibly a consequence of the depletion, earlier, of the breeding stock by shooting. Culling of Herring Gulls on the Isle of May resulted in immature birds starting to breed two or three years earlier than they would otherwise have done (Coulson *et al.* 1982). If Arctic Skuas tend to breed at a younger age in most of the Arctic than they do on Fair Isle then this will select strongly for the pale morph, since it is able to attain breeding status earlier than darks.

These characteristics which seem to correlate with colour must be weighed against other specific environmental pressures.

HEAT-LOSS HYPOTHESIS

Although I am not aware of any published account of the significance of colour phase in Arctic Skuas in terms of conservation of heat, it has often been considered to be a possible explanation for the cline in the frequency of light and dark phases. It is commonly held that light phase birds are better adapted to conserve heat in the cold high latitudes in which the light morph predominates. In fact, this is totally incorrect.

Dark materials absorb more radiant energy from the sun than do light materials, and so dark plumage will aid a bird to take up radiant solar energy. Of course both colour phases of the Arctic Skua have dark wings, backs, tails and crowns, so all of the exposed upper surfaces are virtually identical in the two morphs. It is the colour of the underparts that differs. When birds radiate heat into their surroundings this is lost in the infra-red waveband. Although white and dark-brown plumages differ in their abilities to absorb solar radiation (which does not include a significant component in the infra-red part of the spectrum), they are identical in their properties of radiating energy in the infra-red. Thus heat loss by radiation from the plumage of Arctic Skuas will be identical irrespective of plumage colour. This simple fact of physics means that we need to look elsewhere for a functional explanation for the plumage morphs and the existence of the frequency cline.

AGGRESSIVE CAMOUFLAGE HYPOTHESIS

Having spent a summer observing the robbing behaviour of Great Skuas and Arctic Skuas at Hermaness, Andersson (1976) pointed out that the dark plumage of Great Skuas and most Arctic Skuas at Shetland made them particularly difficult to see against the background of Shetland cliffs or against the sea. He suggested that, in view of their feeding ecology, 'it appears probable that dark colouration is adaptive in allowing skuas to approach prey closely before being discovered, i.e. a form of "aggressive camouflage" '. In fact, dark skuas are probably less conspicuous against most backgrounds.

The hypothesis is that the dark phase of the Arctic Skua has a greater success than the light, in certain habitats, in robbing other seabirds of their food and so is at an advantage in areas where this is the main feeding method during the breeding season (and presumably during winter as well). Presumably, then, the pale phase must have some advantage in tundra regions that at least equals that of being dark, so that the polymorphism is maintained by opposing selection pressures at opposite ends of the cline, with gene flow along the cline causing the fairly smooth gradient in colour frequencies. We can consider this argument along three lines. Is dark plumage likely to be advantageous for a kleptoparasite? This raises the question why are so many gulls and other surface-feeding seabirds generally white or white and black. Secondly, does the distribution of the dark morph actually fit the hypothesis that populations dependent on kleptoparasitic feeding should consist predominantly of dark phase birds? Thirdly, is there any evidence to suggest that dark phase birds actually achieve a greater success rate than that achieved by pale phase birds?

What are the benefits of white or dark plumages for seabirds?

Most gulls, terns and boobies have extensive white plumage, or contrasting black and white patterning. Skuas, frigatebirds, and certain gulls that are solitary feeders or are regularly kleptoparasitic, have predominantly dark plumage, as have many immature gulls. Is white plumage beneficial for social surface-feeding seabirds and dark plumage beneficial for other feeding styles? Some very recent work sheds light on this long-standing controversy. Although there has been some dispute concerning whether white seabirds are more or less conspicuous than dark

seabirds foraging out at sea, there is a general concensus that the black and white contrasting plumage of most adult gulls, Gannets and others is indeed more conspicuous, particularly when the birds are flapping rather than gliding, as occurs when they have located a surface shoal of fish and are preparing to dive onto it. In this case, it would seem that many gulls and other seabirds actively signal their activity to potential competitors searching for food nearby. At first sight this seems to be foolish or altruistic. If a gull finds a shoal of fish at the surface why should it inform other birds? Even if the presence of a large shoal meant that the gull could obtain as much food as it could carry, it could not, as a result of natural selection, evolve conspicuous plumage to advertise its feeding success to competitors. Doing good for others requires 'Group Selectionist' arguments, or complicated stories based on reciprocal altruism or kin selection. Since foraging seabirds are unlikely to be in the immediate vicinity of numerous relatives, or birds that they know that might reciprocate their help in the future, these mechanisms can be discarded in this instance. It would only pay a bird to advertise the location of a fish shoal if, by attracting other birds, it would increase its own chances of obtaining food. This may seem an improbable result, but in fact it can occur among flock-feeding seabirds. It would be extremely difficult to demonstrate in the field, but some field data provide indications of how flocks interact with the prey on which they are feeding. Kittiwakes in flocks off Alaska were shown to have a higher plunge success rate and a higher rate of prey capture than Kittiwakes feeding solitarily, but flocks were short-lived because feeding activities of the Kittiwakes drove the prey below the Kittiwakes' plunging depth. As a result, the flock nucleus had a higher prey capture rate than did birds that later joined the flock (Bayer 1983). How seabirds may achieve a higher prey capture rate by feeding in a flock has been elegantly demonstrated by a laboratory experiment using flocks of Black-headed Gulls trained to dive into a large tank for fish (Gotmark *et al.* 1986). Each gull in flocks of six had higher prey capture rates than gulls in flocks of three, although the latter did better than any bird individually. This was because the diving birds altered the vulnerability of the prey fish. Video filming showed that the fish shoal was split into smaller and looser groups by a flock of diving gulls than it was when attacked by a solitary gull. By forcing the fish into a more dispersed shoal, flocks of gulls increased the vulnerability of all the fish to predation, whereas the primary function of shoaling is to reduce it. Furthermore, when hunting in flocks the gulls caught more of the fish from a head-on or sideways direction. When gulls were hunting alone most of the fish they did catch were caught from behind. This occurred because fish that were fleeing from one gull would be driven towards another when the gulls were feeding as a flock, whereas solitary gulls had only fleeing fish for capture. In this laboratory study the authors were able to show that frontal and side attacks by gulls were more successful than those from the rear, even when the flock size was as small as six. Thus the total catch per gull rose with flock size because attacks were more frequent and success rate was higher.

Gotmark, Winkler and Andersson argue that seabirds in the wild often encounter hunting conditions similar to those set up in their experiment, when schools of fish are driven to the surface by predatory fish or marine mammals. In such situations, a flock of seabirds can feed on the shoal for some considerable time in some instances. Certainly I have watched flocks of seabirds diving onto surface shoals of Sandeels for up to 20 minutes or more before the fish cease to be available. In such situations it seems reasonable to infer that the white plumage of most flocking surface-feeding seabirds provides a means, favoured by natural selection, of attracting other birds to form a feeding flock, and hence to improve the prey capture rate of the first birds to find the shoal.

If conspicuous white plumage helps socially feeding birds such as adult gulls, terns and Gannets, then why are skuas, frigatebirds and immature gulls generally brown? Presumably the costs of attracting attention outweigh benefits to be gained from flocking, and this might make sense for young gulls. While adults may gain by attracting others to disturb fish shoal structure, young gulls tend to be displaced by dominant adults from feeding sites, and brown plumage may help them to avoid losing the chance to exploit whatever food source they can find. Frigatebirds do not splash-dive for food since their plumage is wettable. Their preen gland has atrophied to minimise body mass and to improve their aerial agility. They feed largely by snatching flying fish in midair, and to a small extent by picking food items off the sea or by kleptoparasitism. None of these techniques would be enhanced if they had a conspicuous signal plumage to attract other foraging seabirds.

From study of the outcome of chases by skuas I found that the chances of a skua successfully robbing its victim often increased considerably if the victim was slow to react to the approaching threat, and so presumably it had been slow to detect the skua. This was particularly true of chases of auks (Furness 1978) where auks that reacted quickly to an approaching skua could effect an escape either by diving into the sea, or by accelerating to top speed flight. If dark plumage makes skuas less conspicuous then this should greatly increase their success in robbing auks and, perhaps, to some extent also when robbing other seabirds. Thus Andersson's suggestion that the dark plumage of skuas is a form of aggressive camouflage seems highly plausible; consistent with what we know about the functions of plumage colour in terms of flock versus solitary foraging methods, and consistent with the importance of surprise in effecting successful kleptoparasitic attacks.

O'Donald (1983) argued that a difference in chase success rate between dark and light phase birds would not necessarily mean that the phases would differ in fitness. Fitness (their genetic contribution to future generations) would be affected only if a higher chase success rate by dark birds increased their breeding success, the quality of the chicks they produce, or their survival. O'Donald suggested that their fitness was probably not affected by their chase success. He argued that, since Arctic Skuas spend relatively little time foraging each day, they could easily increase their foraging effort to make up for a lower chase success rate. If this were true, then influences on foraging success could not explain the evolution of the plumage polymorphism. I think O'Donald's dismissal of an ecological explanation relating to foraging is premature. He is certainly correct to point out that chase success rate will only matter if it does contribute to differences in fitness. However, there are good reasons to think that it does, at least some of the time. Drent & Daan (1980) showed that animals can only sustain work over periods of many days up to a metabolic ceiling of about four times BMR (Basal Metabolic Rate). It is known that the energy cost of horizontal flapping flight at maximum range speed (a relatively slow speed that minimises energy expenditure per unit distance travelled, a sort of 'cruising speed') is in the region of 10BMR (Ellis 1984). Of course, birds can exceed the 4BMR threshold for a day or two, but only by using stored fat reserves. Arctic Skuas, when chasing victims, fly at or close to their top flight speed, and often have to twist and turn in flight, so that the energy cost of their chasing is probably very high indeed. An Arctic Skua could probably not spend more than eight hours a day in foraging without exceeding a daily average of 4BMR. Thus Arctic Skuas standing around on territory may appear to be idle and to have plenty of opportunity to increase their work rate, but this may not be so. The 4BMR ceiling appears to correspond to the top physiological rate at which animals can process food and generate energy. Just how it operates is not really understood, but field studies have shown that it applies to a wide range of warm-blooded animals, so it probably will restrict the foraging endurance of skuas. If so, then any increase in chase success rate would be highly advantageous.

Field studies of Arctic Skuas also suggest that chase success rate can be of crucial importance to breeding success. On Foula, between 1971 and 1980, most pairs of Arctic Skuas succeeded in raising two chicks without there being any sign of chicks going short of food. However, since 1980 the Arctic Skuas on Foula have had poor breeding success, and part of this seems to be due to the reduction in numbers of Arctic Terns on the island, the reduced breeding success and numbers of Kittiwakes, and possibly auks as well. Arctic Skuas have had more difficulty in obtaining food and their chick survival has been poor.

In Iceland, Arnason & Grant (1978) studied a population of Arctic Skuas that normally robbed Arctic Terns and Puffins, but in one year the Arctic Terns failed to return and, with only Puffins to rob, the skuas had too little food for successful breeding. Only 0.27 chicks were raised per pair, much less than normal for Arctic Skuas. Many chicks disappeared in the first few days after hatching. In the first week of chasing Puffins, skuas were at a negative energy balance and were apparently unable to meet the needs of their chicks (Arnason & Grant 1978). In such a situation, an increased chase success rate due to plumage type could, in theory, make all the difference between failure and successful breeding.

Does the distribution of the dark morph fit the aggressive camouflage hypothesis?
If the dark phase of the Arctic Skua exists to enhance the success of kleptoparasitic foraging, then we would expect birds in all populations that are extensively kleptoparasitic during the breeding season to be predominantly dark phase and those that forage by other methods to be predominantly pale. To some extent, this pattern is found. Arctic Skuas in most of the high Arctic populations feed predominantly on small terrestrial birds, insects and small mammals of the tundra,

and these skua populations consist almost exclusively of pale phase birds. Arctic Skuas breeding in Scotland, the Faeroes, Iceland and Scandinavia are predominantly dark and are largely kleptoparasitic. However, some areas do not fit the hypothesis that feeding method and colour phase are linked. In eastern Murman, on the north-west coast of the USSR, Belopolskii (1961) found that fish comprised about half of the diet of Arctic Skuas, and most of this was obtained by kleptoparasitism. Belopolskii does not report the phase ratios in his study population, but data presented by Southern (1943) indicate that the Murman coast is an area where the proportion of dark phase birds is declining rapidly from west to east, with about 70% of the birds in east Murman being light phase. If dark phase birds were favoured by having higher chase success, then this high proportion of pale birds is unexpected, though it could result from gene-flow from nearby populations where the birds are all pale and feed on tundra habitats.

In Spitsbergen, 99% of the Arctic Skuas are pale, but Lovenskiold (1964) clearly states 'The Arctic Skua seems to be more or less dependent on other birds for food, never fishing or in any other way trying to get their food directly. They attack other birds and strike them until they disgorge their food. The bird mostly preyed upon is the Kittiwake, but Black Guillemots and Little Auks are also sometimes pursued.' Other authors add Arctic Terns to the list of species robbed in Spitsbergen, and also state that Arctic Skuas may feed on the eggs of terrestrial birds in the area. However, kleptoparasitism is clearly very important in this population of pale phase birds. This is not a new development, since the first published description of kleptoparasitism by skuas was made in Spitsbergen, from a visit in 1604 by the explorer Jonas Poole.

Unfortunately, rather little is known about the feeding habits of many other populations of Arctic Skuas, such as those in parts of eastern Asia which are predominantly of dark phase birds. Do these feed mainly by kleptoparasitism? In addition to the contrary behaviour of pale phase birds in Spitsbergen, there is a lack of support for the hypothesis from data for the region of the Great Slave Lake and Upper Mackenzie River in northwest Canada, an inland area where skuas feed on terrestrial prey since there are no seabirds to rob. Peble (1908) recorded that most Arctic Skuas in that area were dark phase birds. If the dark phase predominates at inland localities at the south of the species' breeding range in North America (Fig. 68), the dark-light cline here clearly cannot be due to changes in the adaptiveness of plumage morphs for kleptoparasitism. In conclusion, the geographical pattern of distribution of the colour morphs does not fit well with that predicted if dark plumage enhanced kleptoparasitic success.

Does dark plumage increase chase success?

Malte Andersson did not present any data to support his argument that the dark phase of the Arctic Skua uses aggressive camouflage to enhance its success in robbing other seabirds. However, Arnason (1978) argued that the rarer (light phase) morph was more successful at robbing Puffins at an Icelandic colony, although O'Donald (1983) showed that the differences claimed by Arnason were not statistically significant. In Iceland and at several Shetland colonies, Furness & Furness (1980) found no significant differences in success of light and dark phase Arctic Skuas when chasing Arctic Terns, Guillemots or Puffins. Nor did the speed of reaction of victims differ in relation to the colour phase of the attacking skua. These data suggest that dark phase birds have no advantage over the pale phase birds when robbing seabirds, but the argument becomes more complicated when the possible consequences of the benefits of rarity are also considered, in the next section of this chapter.

APOSTATIC PREDATOR POLYMORPHISM HYPOTHESIS

In apostatic selection, a given morph is favoured in direct proportion to its rarity, through frequency-dependent predation. Higher animals tend to form a mental image, or 'search image', of a common food item on which they concentrate their search, overlooking rarer though acceptable items as a result. For example, thrushes tend to take snails of the common shell pattern and largely to ignore the few that have different shell patterns. Similar results can be obtained if birds in the garden are offered a mixture of different coloured pastry squares. The birds tend to feed on the most common colour of pastry and it is believed that they have formed a search image which increases their proficiency at finding it. Of course, humans use search images too, so the idea is easy to understand. Following on from this, the idea that predators use search images of common prey types suggests that rare morphs of prey should have a selective advantage over the common morph. This idea of apostatic selection has been used to explain many poly-morphisms in prey animals. Payne (1967) and Paulson (1973) then turned the idea on its head and suggested that the frequent occurrence of plumage polymorphisms in predatory birds could be explained as a result of apostatic selection too. Paulson argued that 'the rarer of two morphs of a predator should be less familiar to a potential prey individual and thus have a greater chance for successful capture of that individual. This slight advantage of the rarer morph should lead to balanced polymorphism in the population.' He predicted that polymorphism in predators should be correlated with the intelligence and visual acuity of the prey; clearly snails can do little to support the prediction, but small passerines are caught by an attacking predator on only a small proportion of attacks (Curio 1976), which suggests that they react quickly and early to the common morph of a hawk, whereas they might be slower to recognise the threat presented by a rare colour morph of the same species. Secondly, Paulson predicted that the plumage polymorphism, to be effective should be expressed ventrally, as it is that that the victims see in the approaching predator. Paulson showed that diurnal birds of prey have an unusually high frequency of polymorphic species, that their plumage poly-morphisms are predominantly expressed ventrally, and that species that prey on birds and mammals are most often polymorphic. Thus the data for birds of prey strongly support the hypothesis that apostatic selection has led to plumage polymorphism in many birds of prey that feed on 'intelligent' prey, and Paulson extended his argument to suggest that the plumage polymorphism in Arctic and Pomarine Skuas evolved and is maintained by the same mechanism.

Data to support this idea were provided by Einar Arnason (1978). He recorded chase success at a Puffin colony in south Iceland, where about 75–85% of the Arctic Skuas nesting locally were dark phase. During chases involving a single skua the pale phase birds induced Puffins to drop their fish in 81% of the chases, and 63% for the dark phase birds. Where chases were by two skuas, a pale and a dark bird pair was more successful than a pair of dark birds (Table 38). When larger numbers were chasing there was also a trend to a higher success rate if a pale bird was involved. Arnason (1978) made one-tailed tests of the equality of percentages to decide whether or not these differences were statistically significant.

He concluded that for single skuas, and for chases by two birds, pale phase birds had a significantly higher success, and he argued that this finding was in accord with the prediction of the apostatic selection hypothesis. Pale birds are rarer than darks and so will be less familiar to Puffins. Arnason calculated that each Puffin at the colony he studied would probably be chased twice a week by a skua, and nine out of ten chases he observed involved only dark phase birds, so that Puffins would be likely to learn a dark 'kleptoparasite image'.

O'Donald (1983) reanalysed Arnason's data by χ^2 tests and showed that the differences in chase success between phases were not statistically significant when tested by this more appropriate method, casting some doubt on the conclusions reached by Arnason. Further data on the success rate of chases by dark and pale morphs (Table 39) showed no evidence for a consistently higher success rate in the rarer morph. Nor did victims show any difference in their speed of reaction to approaching dark or pale skuas (Furness & Furness 1980). In Northeast Norway, where the two colour morphs are almost equal in frequency, dark phase Arctic Skuas spent slightly longer away from their territory than did pale birds. On average the foraging trips of dark birds lasted for 74 minutes compared with 64 minutes for pale birds, but the sample sizes were small and so the difference was not statistically significant. As a result, Gotmark *et al* (1981) interpreted this to mean that the phases did not differ in chase success rate. If the difference of about 15% between these means is a true difference then it could be biologically important, but one complication here is the possibility that the dark birds were predominantly males and the pales females. We know that males do more of the foraging to feed the chicks (Chapter 5), so the difference may be due to differences in the roles of the sexes rather than to colour phase.

None of the data gathered so far clearly demonstrate that the rare colour morph enjoys a greater chase success rate due to its rarity. However, Rohwer (1983) pointed out that the apostatic selection hypothesis does not predict that the rare morph will inevitably have a higher success rate. If it did then the frequency of that morph should increase until the success rate of the two morphs was identical. This result would occur when the two colour phases were equally common if, and only if, the alleles for colour phase had no effects on fitness other than through their influence on chase success rate, *and* the two colour morphs were equally easy for prey to perceive. If, as Malte Andersson suggested, dark phase Arctic Skuas employ aggressive camouflage, then the rare pale phase birds in Shetland and Iceland colonies may, as a result of apostatic selection, gain an advantage to cancel this out. If the chase success rate of pale and dark birds is equal in Shetland this may not disprove the aggressive camouflage and apostatic selection hypotheses, but may indicate that the two processes are in equilibrium! In order to test this idea it would be necessary to examine the chase success rate of dark skuas where the dark morph is rare, as for example in northwest USSR or around 70°N in Greenland. Dark birds in these areas should have the additive benefits of aggressive camouflage and apostatic selection. Their chase success rate should be higher than that of pale birds. If so, then the high frequency of pales at these localities must be due to some other, greater, selective advantage of the pale morph for reasons not related to foraging efficiency.

Two critical tests of the apostatic selection hypothesis have been suggested by Rohwer (1983). In Shetland, southern Scandinavia and Iceland, the common, and probably more cryptic, dark phase should gain the benefits of aggressive camouflage and so have a higher success than pale phase skuas in chases of naive prey. This discrepancy should disappear or be reversed, for chases of experienced prey. The most convincing test of the hypothesis would be to compare the chase success of individuals of different colour morphs before and after their relative frequencies had been altered by removals or by dye-marking pale birds dark. It would be predicted that after a substantial proportion of pale birds had been removed or painted dark, the remaining pale birds should enjoy a gradual increase in their foraging success relative to that of the darks. This intriguing experiment waits to be done!

CONCLUSIONS

Despite the long-term studies on Fair Isle, we cannot claim to know how the plumage polymorphism in the Arctic Skua is maintained, or even to understand the genetic mechanism by which colour phase is inherited. In view of the evidence for a sex difference in colour, and failure of breeding data to fit, the simple model of a single gene with two alleles seems to be refuted. It seems quite likely that the polymorphism in the South Polar Skua is determined by the same genetic mechanism as that in the Arctic Skua, Pomarine Skua and Long-tailed Skua, because the South Polar Skua and the Arctic Skua both show a tendency for males to be darker than females, and for the pale morph to increase in frequency with breeding latitude.

The dark morph may occur at a high frequency at low latitudes because it promotes seasonally early breeding and so is favoured in areas where early breeding is possible as well as advantageous. The colour phases are not a mechanism to control the mean laying dates at each latitude, because some populations in the far north breed much later than could be accounted for as a consequence of colour. Probably pale Arctic Skuas have an advantage in the north, so that the cline is caused by opposing selection pressures at each end of the species' breeding range and is smoothed by gene flow between neighbouring areas.

There appears to be assortative mating in some colonies; pairs of the same colour are more frequent than would be expected if males are in excess among darks and females in excess among pales. There is also evidence from Fair Isle of sexual selection by female preference for melanic males. Because the dark, intermediate and pale birds on Fair Isle do not differ in their survival rates as chicks or as adults, seasonally earlier breeding by dark males and their greater reproductive output must be the main selective advantage of the dark allele in Shetland. Calculations suggest that the dark allele should be increasing in Shetland. Counts of colour phases in Scotland, Iceland and NE Norway suggest that the dark phase has indeed been increasing in these areas since the 1930s.

In the far north, Arctic Skua longevity may be less than in the more benign environments where dark birds predominate. If so, the earlier age of recruitment into the breeding population in north USSR may be common to high latitude Arctic Skua populations. This would mean that pale birds would have a strong selective advantage due to their earlier sexual maturation, and could explain the lack of melanics in high latitude populations. However, this is highly speculative, as survival rates of Arctic Skuas breeding in the Arctic are unknown, and age of first breeding is known only for the area in north USSR where Belopolskii shot a large part of the population for studies of the biometrics, fat reserves and anatomy of skuas.

The dark phase of the Arctic Skua may benefit from aggressive camouflage, allowing it to rob other seabirds more successfully because it is less conspicuous than the pale phase, but field studies have yet to provide a convincing test of this hypothesis. The fact that the annual survival rates of pale and dark birds from Fair Isle are identical does not support this idea, since Arctic Skuas feed to a large extent by kleptoparasitism during the winter, and it might be expected that a higher chase success rate for the dark birds would enhance overwinter survival if some of the mortality is due to food shortage. Also, the lack of dark skuas in the largely kleptoparasitic populations on Spitsbergen and Bear Island conflicts with the idea that darks occur in areas where kleptoparasitic feeding is important.

The apostatic selection hypothesis is also difficult to sustain, since the advantage to the rare pale morph may nullify the advantage to the common, but more cryptic, dark morph. No data on chase success rates are yet available from regions where the dark morph is the rarer type. Overall, it seems unlikely that the plumage phases evolved and are maintained primarily as a consequence of their influences on feeding success. The genes' effects on age at recruitment and on the timing of breeding appear to be the most important ones. Perhaps colour phase is but a secondary consequence of the genes' actions, and of rather little ecological importance in itself. Doubtless further research will eventually shed light on this complex and confusing issue.

CHAPTER 10

Breeding systems and social organisation

The Shooi is very far more numerous than its illustrious congener, and is the very sauciest bird in all the sky, not even excepting the Merlins and the Piccatarries. It is not every bird that can enjoy a joke, and the Shooi really does seem to appreciate one thoroughly. It is as good as a comedy to witness his outbreak of high spirits, as he suddenly sweeps up high into the air, with a taunting cry, half peacock, half tom-cat, and leaves far behind him the bewildered stranger whom he has befooled hopelessly of the track of the nests by his admirable simulation of broken leg, broken wing, and broken prospects in general.

Saxby (1874)

NOMADISM IN POMARINE SKUAS

Like almost all other seabirds, all the skuas except the Pomarine Skua show mate and site fidelity from year to year. Advantages of mate and site fidelity are well understood, thanks to detailed studies of individually marked seabirds within small colonies, such as the long-term study of Kittiwakes on a North Shields warehouse (Coulson & Thomas 1985). By returning each year to the same nest site where the mates of the previous year can meet, pairs can re-establish themselves quickly in the spring, allowing them to breed earlier and more successfully. The benefits in terms of reproductive success are so great in long-lived birds that it requires most peculiar circumstances to make seabirds adopt a different reproductive strategy. In the Pomarine Skua, the cyclic changes in lemming abundance do just that. The Pomarine Skua is such a specialist predator of lemmings during the breeding season that it is unable to breed unless lemming numbers are sufficient. Arctic and Long-tailed Skuas breeding on the tundra do not suffer this problem so markedly as they can, to some extent, switch between prey types; birds, insects and berries are alternative foods to small mammals, and the Arctic Skua normally feeds on these even when lemmings are abundant. Long-tailed Skua breeding success is closely related to lemming numbers, and in particularly poor lemmings years the birds do not breed at all, but the species returns to the same territory each year and obtains the benefits of mate and site fidelity in most years when breeding is possible (Andersson 1981). Since Pomarine Skuas would be unable to breed at all when lemming numbers were even moderately low, there would be no benefit to be gained from retaining the same territory and mate. Since fluctuations in lemming abundance are never totally synchronous from place to place, Pomarine Skuas can often find localities where lemmings are still plentiful and where breeding is possible despite the larger general area of low lemming availability. Such pockets may be in different places from year to year, and so the Pomarine Skua adopts a nomadic habit which is unique among skuas. In spring it returns to the tundra, and searches for a suitable area in which it can breed. Once such a site is located it establishes a territory and attracts a mate. If no space is available because the area is already fully occupied by Pomarine Skuas, it will move on to seek some other suitable site. In bad years it will not breed at all; in a good year it will accept the first mate it can obtain in a suitable breeding site. It is this complete dependence of the Pomarine Skua on high densities of lemmings, and the fluctuations in lemming abundance and their unpredictable spatial patchiness, that make it impossible for Pomarine Skuas to practise mate fidelity. Without a fixed territory in which to meet, it is impracticable to retain the same mate from year to year.

TRIOS: POLYGYNY AND POLYANDRY

Compared with other groups of birds, seabirds have remarkably straightforward and simple breeding relationships. All seabirds are predominantly monogamous, and most pair for life. Seabirds do not, for example, indulge in the promiscuous mating of lekking species or in the serial mating of many arctic waders. There are no cases of seabirds having 'helpers at the nest' in the manner of babblers, bee-eaters and many other birds (Campbell & Lack 1985).

Among seabirds, a few species are unable to practice life-time site and mate fidelity. These include the Pomarine Skua, which is nomadic and takes a new mate each time that it breeds because it does not have a fixed territory where it can reform the partnership with a previous mate. Some other seabirds also take a new mate at each breeding attempt, as in many frigatebirds where the sexes differ in the time they require between breeding attempts. However, these species remain essentially monogamous. One well-documented deviation from the normal breeding relationship in seabirds is found in a small proportion of individuals in some species of gulls, where female-female pairs have been recorded (Hunt 1980). This phenomenon is relatively infrequent and is clearly unlikely to prove an evolutionary success! It may have arisen due to an imbalance in the sex ratio so that some

19. A Brown Skua trio of a male and two females sharing a nest on South Georgia. Photo: W. N. Bonner.

females are unable to obtain male partners (Hunt 1980), or it may be due to effects of organochlorine pollutants, which can cause feminisation as a result of their chemical similarity to sex hormones of the oestrogen group.

Among skuas, monogamy is also the general rule, and all species except the Pomarine Skua are usually mate- and site-faithful from year to year. However, in some large skuas a minority of birds breed as trios rather than as pairs. On Foula I recorded two clutches of three eggs out of about 2,000 clutches examined. One of these was probably due to a single female laying three eggs, but the other was the product of two females that shared a nest scrape and a single male. This trio probably did not last for long as I was unable to relocate it the next season. Despite the fact that skuas are anatomically incapable of incubating three eggs properly and the fact that three birds were competing to share incubation duties at this nest, two of the three eggs did actually hatch out, although the third failed to develop fully. A trio consisting of a male and two females sharing the nest (Photo 19) was also found among the Brown Skuas of South Georgia (Bonner 1964). This trio also had a clutch of three eggs, which Bonner opened and found to contain embryos of unusually differing sizes. This probably resulted from the difficulty of incubating three eggs when skuas have only two brood patches and can only take two eggs onto their feet (Andersson 1976).

Normally, female skuas are highly aggressive towards another female that attempts to come into their territory, and it is difficult to see how these trios come about. However, the two trios containing two females as described above, and a similar trio found among the Brown Skuas of Signy Island, South Orkneys by Burton (1968), are the only recorded instances of polygyny in skuas. Although it is interesting to record that they exist, these rare cases cannot be considered to be of any real evolutionary or ecological importance. However, they may indicate an excess of females in the population unable to obtain a mate with a territory.

In contrast, trios consisting of two males and one female have been reported in several large skua populations and may represent an important proportion of the population in a few sites. Richdale reported to Bonner that about two-thirds of the Brown Skua nests on the islands off New Zealand were attended by three adults, apparently always two males and one female, with a clutch of two eggs, which all three birds would defend. Young (1978) found trios comprising two males and one female at five of eleven nests on Rangatira island in the Chathams, New Zealand. This polyandrous breeding by skuas is most unusual among birds. Most of the few species of bird in which polyandry occurs are species where polyandry is serial. That is, the male is left by the female to do all of the incubation of the first clutch while she takes a second mate and lays another clutch, as in several ratites, game birds and waders (Campbell & Lack 1985). Simultaneous polyandry is known in a very few species, such as the Galapagos Hawk, Harris's Hawk, a jacana, the Tasmanian Waterhen, and the Noisy Miner, an Australian honeyeater. In the last species the females are promiscuous within a communal group. In the others each female may take two or more males to help her to rear the young. The common ecological factor promoting this behaviour is food scarcity, such that pairs have great difficulty in rearing young but larger groups have a greater success because several males can forage for the family (Campbell & Lack 1985). In the Brown Skua, because the male forages for the female and chicks, having two males doubles the amount of food to be shared by the family. Young (1978) found that the Brown Skuas on Rangatira Island had an exceptionally high breeding success, with 1.55 chicks fledged per territory which is better than achieved by any other skua colony that has been studied (Chapter 11), although his observations of only eleven territories do not allow a meaningful statistical comparison between the performance of pairs and trios.

Polyandrous trios occurred at more than half of the Brown Skua nests around Stewart Island and at three of 27 territories on the Snares Islands (Young 1978). On Marion Island Williams (1980) found polyandrous trios at three nests out of an unspecified total and stated that almost certainly more trios were present among the 400 or so occupied Brown Skua territories on the island. Trios were also recorded among Brown Skuas at the Crozet Islands (Barre 1976, Derenne *et al* 1976). There was one polyandrous trio among Tristan Skuas on Gough Island out of a total of 31 territories where I individually colour ringed adults. No detailed studies of Falkland Skua breeding biology have been made, but Devillers (1978) did not report any trios in that taxon. Trios do not seem to occur among South Polar Skuas, nor have they been reported in Chilean Skuas. Among Great Skuas, Young (1978) quotes a correspondent who, having found trios at each of the four nests on Mousa, shot the birds and ascertained that they comprised a female and two males at each nest. I find this record astonishing. Apart from the fact that Great Skuas are legally protected birds and so cannot be shot in Shetland, I have never seen a polyandrous trio in any skua colony in the North Atlantic! Certainly there were none on Foula at any of the thousands of territories I examined, and I think I would have noticed a trio had one been present during the brief visits I have made to almost all of the Great Skua colonies in Scotland, Iceland, the

Islands and Norway.

Williams (1980) showed that chicks attended by trios on Marion Island grew faster (Chapter 12) and probably fledged with greater fat reserves than chicks attended by pairs, although hatching success and chick survival did not differ between pairs and trios. The improved chick growth is most likely to be due to more food being provided by two males than by one, and may well affect post-fledging survival. If so, food shortage may promote the formation of polyandrous trios. That this is not the whole story is clear from the fact that polyandry is so rare among other species of birds, and does not occur in the South Polar Skua. The South Polar Skua has a much lower chick survival rate than the Brown Skua, and most second-hatched chicks fail to survive because of food shortage which leads to the older chick killing its younger sibling. Thus, polyandrous trios would seem to be particularly appropriate for the South Polar Skua and yet they do not occur. This may be because evolution has not chanced upon that solution in the South Polar Skua. It would be wrong to assume that evolution will always find the best answer. However, polyandrous trios may not occur because they would not be appropriate for the South Polar Skua. The apparent scarcity of trios in the large skuas that feed at sea (Great, South Polar and Chilean Skuas) and the presence of trios in large skuas that feed on noctural burrow-nesting petrels (Brown Skuas, Tristan Skuas) may be of taxonomic significance, or may be related to differences in territorial behaviour as a result of diet. Skuas predatory on seabirds are continuously within their moderately large territory, and this may facilitate the maintenance of trios in some way. It would be interesting to examine the Falkland Skua in this regard, since this idea would suggest that they should also commonly have trios. It is perhaps surprising that Pomarine Skuas, apparently, have not evolved a system by which polyandrous trios could breed in years when moderate lemming numbers were still too few to enable pairs to breed. This may occur and have been overlooked.

Burton (1968) found two trios on Signy Island among Brown Skuas. One lasted for only one season and the sexes of the birds were unknown. The other was in existence in 1958 when records started and continued at least until 1965, although two birds disappeared (presumed dead) and were immediately replaced during that period. This trio comprised two females since in one year four eggs were found in the nest. These failed to hatch, as the birds were unable to incubate them all at once.

A trio of Tristan Skuas was found on Gough in 1984, in a territory where no birds bred in 1983. All three birds were individually colour ringed in 1984. They had only a single egg that season, which hatched successfully. In 1985 there was still a trio in this territory, but one of the ringed birds had been replaced by an unringed individual. Measurements of this new bird and of the original three indicated that the trio consisted of one female and two males, and it was the female that had left and been replaced. We found the missing female in an adjacent territory, paired in 1985 with the male that had bred in that territory in the previous two seasons but whose previous mate did not return in 1985. In 1985 the trio produced a clutch of two eggs, both of which hatched successfully at about the same date as most other clutches were hatching. The territory occupied by the trio was on the edge of the colony, rather small and close to a club site, but it is difficult to see why the female from the trio chose to move into the neighbour's territory if having two male partners enhances the growth rate of her chicks. One noticeable feature of the two males in the trio was that they were decidedly less aggressive than most Tristan Skuas. This may have facilitated their forming a trio in the first place, but may mean that the two males together were unable to hold a large or high quality territory.

TERRITORY SIZE

Defending a territory against conspecifics, and in some skuas also against skuas of other species, can be costly in terms of time and energy. Several studies of other kinds of birds have shown that territory size is a compromise between the benefits of large size and the costs of maintaining it. In skuas, similar restraints on territory size also apply. Of course, the optimal size will depend on several factors, particularly on whether or not the birds maintain the territory as an exclusive feeding area, and on the effects, if any, that territory size has on the likelihood of a male obtaining a mate and on the chances of eggs or chicks being taken by predators (including neighbouring conspecifics). The sizes of territories vary considerably even within one colony of skuas. Some of this variation may be adaptive; certain areas may be better in quality in some respect, allowing a skua to maintain a smaller territory but still hold as much of that resource as required. It is easy to see that a skua feeding exclusively within a small territory in an area of high density burrow-nesting petrels could find as much food as could be obtained from a much larger territory where the petrel density was low.

However, Great Skuas on Foula do not feed to any important extent within their breeding territory. The territory size is largely concerned with breeding; small territories lead to a risk that neighbours may intrude and steal the eggs, or that chicks will wander out of the defended area and may be killed by neighbours. It might be expected then, that Great Skuas' territories on Foula would all be similar in size, providing sufficient protection for the eggs and chicks for minimum cost in terms of territorial defence. In fact, territory size varies considerably, and it soon seemed to me that this was strongly influenced by the aggressiveness of the territory owners, which itself varied greatly.

Relationships between individual aggressiveness and territory size in Great Skuas

I decided to try to quantify aggression of Great Skuas on Foula in two seasons of fieldwork for my Ph.D. degree. I gave points on the following scale according to the response of the more aggressive member of each pair of birds to my intrusion onto their territory:

Score	Actions by the Great Skuas in the territory
1	Both adults left the territory when I walked towards the nest
2	Circled above me but did not dive-bomb me
3	Swooped at me but rarely or never hit me
4	Swooped frequently but hit only occasionally
5	Swooped frequently and hit me on most swoops

Clearly the above categories are only points on a continuous scale, but in general it was fairly easy to assign each pair into one of these categories. I assumed these to indicate increasing degrees of aggression, not only towards a human, but also towards other intruders to the territory, such as dogs, sheep, and other Bonxies. This appeared to be valid, since I often saw birds that had been particularly aggressive towards me also vigorously attacking other Great Skuas, but some birds

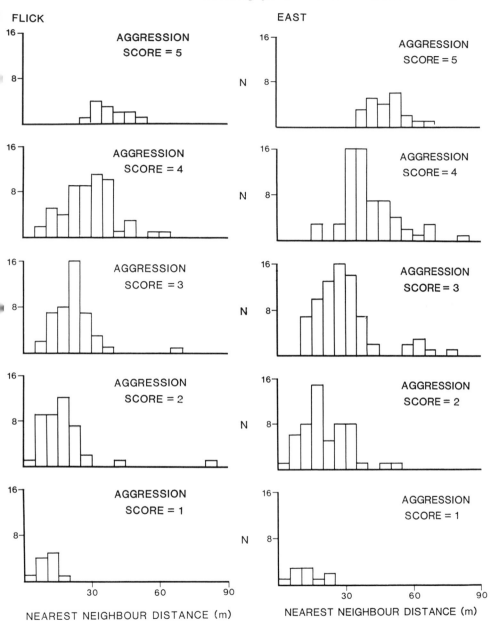

Fig. 70 (left) Nearest-neighbour nest distances in relation to the aggression score of pairs of Great Skuas in the Flick area of Foula in 1975.

Fig. 71 (right)   Nearest-neighbour nest distances in relation to the aggression score of pairs of Great Skuas in the East area of Foula in 1975.

may react differently to different types of territorial threat.

When one Great Skua was away from the territory the single bird remaining was noticeably less aggressive than when its mate was present, even if the absent bird was the more timid of the pair. Clearly they feel safer when their mate is there to help attack intruders. In order to obtain results that were not affected by such factors I only gave aggression scores when both adults were present and the birds were about half way through incubation. In each case I scored only the aggression of the more aggressive bird. For a sample of 881 pairs examined I found that only 6% of pairs included one member that fell into the most aggressive category. The majority of pairs never actually hit people, and 6% of pairs simply flew away from the territory! I also found that the aggression scores differed slightly between different parts of the colony (Table 40). Pairs nesting on the periphery of the colony or around club sites tended to be less aggressive than pairs in well established areas in the centre of the colony, and this actually had an effect on territory size and breeding performance. The more aggressive pairs tended to hold larger territories (Fig. 70 and 71), although the average territory size (as measured by nearest neighbouring inter-nest distances) for Great Skuas with an aggression score of five was greater in the East area than in the Flick area. In Flick, where overall nesting density was particularly high, the mean nearest neighbour distance for pairs with an aggression score of five was 39 m (s.d. = 7.2, n = 13), compared to a mean of 50 m (s.d. = 7.8, n = 22) for equivalent pairs on the East area, where overall nesting density was lower. Aggressiveness of individuals clearly has an important effect on the territory size they obtain, but territory size also seems to depend on the siting of the territory within the colony.

The aggressiveness seems to be a characteristic that a bird retains from year to year, and is probably largely determined genetically, although I got the impression that certain cohorts tended to be particularly aggressive or quiet. Birds colour-ringed yellow + white (1968 chicks) almost always seemed to be particularly aggressive and I learned to look out for breeders with that colour combination! Perhaps the birds' experiences as chicks or immediately after fledging may influence their future 'quality'. In 1968 there were unusually few ringed chicks recovered in their first autumn and winter. By contrast, there was a wreck of first-autumn birds in 1969, and the few colour-ringed survivors of the 1969 cohort that returned to breed were noticeably unaggressive individuals. To demonstrate a physical basis for this anecdotal observation would probably be quite a task, but I suspect that there is some physical basis to this story.

Whatever the reason for the differences in aggressiveness between birds, these have clear effects on the territory size that the pair maintains, and also, directly or indirectly, on hatching and fledging success (Chapters 11 and 12).

Changes in territory size as colony size changes
Information on the area of breeding territory occupied by a number of pairs over many years exists for the Arctic Skuas on Foula, Noss and Fair Isle. On all three islands, Arctic Skuas feed almost exclusively outside their breeding territories, so that the principal function of the territory appears to be to allow males to attract a mate and to give protection to the eggs and chicks against attack by other skuas. On all three islands, space for nesting is limited, since the islands are small and contain some areas unsuitable for skuas. As a result, the nesting density of the Arctic Skua has increased as numbers breeding increased and as Great Skua colony limits encroached into Arctic Skua areas. For example, on Noss, the Arctic

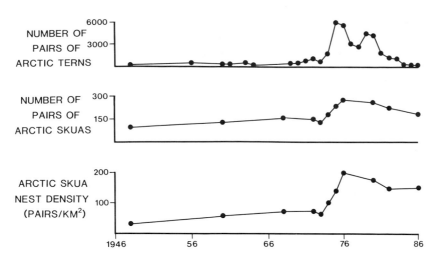

Fig. 72   Average nesting densities of Arctic Skuas on Foula over recent years in relation to the numbers of pairs of Arctic Skuas and Arctic Terns present.

Skua colony increased from 37 pairs in 1946, nesting at a density of 62 pairs per km² with a nearest neighbour nest distance averaging about 70 m, to 44 pairs in 1974 restricted to a smaller nesting area by the expansion of the Great Skua colony. Nesting was at a density of 147 pairs per km² and a nearest neighbour nest distance averaging about 45 m. By 1982, Arctic Skua numbers on Noss had declined to 34 pairs, possibly because of the pressure for space imposed by Great Skuas; nesting density had increased to 170 pairs per km² which seems to be about as high as Arctic Skuas can tolerate. On Foula, nesting density of Arctic Skuas increased from 33 pairs per km² to a peak of 200 pairs per km² in 1976, but then fell, reaching 149 pairs per km² in 1982 and rather less by 1986 (Fig. 72). The competition for space between Arctic and Great Skuas is discussed in Chapter 16. There is some evidence presented there to indicate that the Arctic Skua suffered a reduction in breeding success at the very high nesting densities it reached on Noss and Foula, but it also seems possible that high density nesting may have some benefits. It may well enhance the ability of Arctic Skuas to repel site-seeking Great Skuas more effectively by promoting communal mobbing by several closely nesting pairs.

Differences in territory size between skua populations
    Arctic Skuas show an extraordinary range of nesting densities and territory sizes between populations. In Shetland, they reach remarkably high densities of 20–200 pairs per km², with nearest neighbour nest distances of 5–200 m, whereas in northern Alaska they nest at densities of around 0.02–0.2 pairs per km², only one-thousandth of the density in Shetland colonies! Nearest neighbour nest distances in Alaska are much larger, usually about 400–1000 m (Table 41). In Alaska, the Arctic Skua feeds predominantly within its territory, so that the function of a territory is important in determining its size. In northern Scandinavia this can be seen quite clearly. Andersson & Gotmark (1980) found that pairs of Arctic Skuas,

nesting at Syltefjord and Holmfjellet, fed largely by kleptoparasitism away from the territory, and nested at densities of about 10–25 pairs per km²; whereas at Falkgarden, the Arctic Skuas were thinly spread at an average density of about 0.5 pairs per km², and these birds obtained significantly more of their diet, though apparently still less than half their intake, from within their territory.

Differences in territory size between years

In the Pomarine and Long-tailed Skuas (Photo 20), which depend to an important degree on small mammal prey during breeding, territory size varies between years according to prey availability (Fig. 73). Pomarine Skuas, particularly, may breed at a wide range of densities, from 0.1 to 13.7 pairs per km² depending on lemming abundance, while Long-tailed Skuas tend to maintain larger territories, varying between 0.1 and 1.7 pairs per km² (Table 41). Clearly, the skuas must assess prey availability as they set up the territory, and defend an area large enough to include sufficient prey to support their breeding attempt.

Differences between skua taxa

Given the broad range of territory sizes found within particular skua species, comparisons between species can be confused, but, in general, skuas that feed within their territory have far larger territories than those that feed at sea (Fig. 74). Thus, South Polar Skuas tend to maintain much smaller territories than do

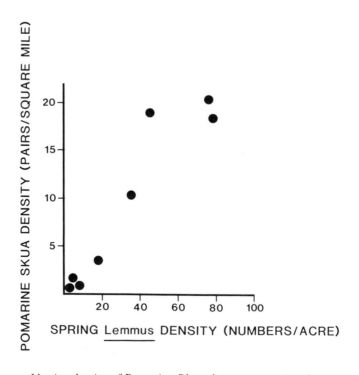

*Fig. 73   Nesting density of Pomarine Skuas between years in relation to small
mammal abundance. From Maher 1974.*

20. *A pair of Long-tailed Skuas on a territorial mound. Skuas commonly tend to establish a preferred sitting area on a high vantage within their territory.*
Photo: J. de Korte.

Brown Skuas. However, Trillmich (1978) found that some South Polar Skuas at Cape Hallett defended territories that included parts of the Adelie Penguin rookery, while others had no penguins within their territory. Pairs with penguins to exploit had a significantly higher breeding success, whereas pairs without penguins in their territory fed exclusively at sea.

The Tristan Skuas on the lower parts of Gough Island have very small territories for a skua that feeds almost entirely within the territory, but they have one to three petrel burrows per square metre within their territories which is an extraordinarily high density of potential prey.

Territory maintenance
Little work has been done on the effort that skuas put into maintaining their territory. On Foula, continuous observations of three pairs of Arctic Skuas over 24 hours showed that pairs spent 100, 101 and 234 minutes in flight associated with 44, 58 and 74 instances of territorial defence. Most instances were to chase away Arctic or Great Skuas (Table 46). By comparison, Andersson (1973) recorded that a pair of Pomarine Skuas in Alaska chased only 30 intruders in 24 hours. However, Maher (1974) found that Pomarine Skuas, also in Alaska, made about four territorial defence chases per hour, which must work out at more than 50 chases per 24 hour period. Trillmich (1978) found that South Polar Skuas took

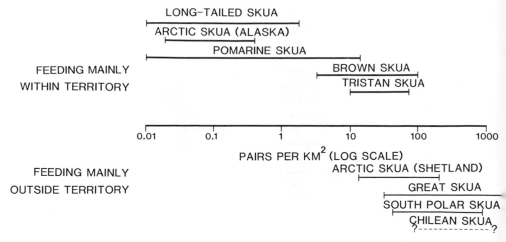

Fig. 74 Nesting densities of skuas in relation to whether they feed predominantly within the territory or outwith the territory.

off about four times per hour to chase away intruders; thus the rate of territorial defence seems to be fairly similar in all these populations despite enormous differences in territory size, from c 500 m² in the Foula Arctic Skuas watched to c 200,000 m² in Alaskan Pomarine Skuas.

Although intruders usually give way to territory owners without resistance, sometimes intruder pressure can overwhelm the ability of an established bird or pair. It seems to be common, but little studied, for unmated female skuas to attempt to take over from an established female by swoop attacking her in her territory. This behaviour has been mentioned by a number of authors and its effects have been seen in cases where the established female, although still living, has been displaced from her mate (Chapter 6). Pairs of skuas usually work together to defend their territory against intruders, and so unattached females probably find it difficult to dispossess established females and most skuas remain together from year to year in the same territory. However, skua pairs can be overwhelmed by sheer numbers of intruding nonbreeders on occasions. At the weather station on Gough Island, two pairs of Tristan Skuas hold territories which have their common boundary running across the roof of the building. The pair at the front of the building are treated as pets by the meteorologists, being regularly given scraps of food from the window of the dining room. The pair at the rear have the kitchen in their territory, and often walk in to scavenge if the door has been left open. The two pairs know each other well and show little aggression towards each other; the roof of the building is clearly understood to be a limit not to be transgressed, although either pair may fly up onto the roof to see what is happening in the others' territory when they can hear their neighbour giving frequent Long Calls. On several occasions while I was staying on Gough Island the cooks for the day would take more meat out of the freezer than was required, and the excess was often given to these skuas. However, the meteorologists did not appreciate that putting gifts of steak and pork chops on the roof caused their pets more aggravation than benefit. The meat would attract overflying nonbreeding skuas that would start to circle above the building, much to the annoyance of the territory owners who would respond with Long Call displays. More nonbreeders would be attracted by the circling flock until there were soon so many that they began to pluck up enough courage to try to land beside the food. When this happened the first to land would be furiously attacked by both the territory owners, who would ignore the fact that they transgressed into each other's territory as a consequence of all the fighting. The nonbreeder would fly off in panic, having made little attempt to hold his ground, but while the territorial skuas were flying after him, other nonbreeders would drop down to snatch at the food. The territorial birds would fly back to chase these off, and perhaps land beside to food to Long Call, but the sheer numbers of nonbreeders attempting to get onto the food overwhelmed the territorial birds, and eventually they gave up attacking and either stood aside until all the food had gone and the nonbreeders began to leave, or they would sometimes join in the fight for the food, with perhaps marginally more success than the majority of the nonbreeders. Clearly territories are only defendable until intruder pressure becomes excessive. Large food rewards can make territory ownership ineffectual in the face of hordes of hungry nonbreeders.

TERRITORY ESTABLISHMENT

The way in which skuas establish themselves as the owner of a territory from which the previous owner has been removed has been described by Young (1972). He caught three South Polar Skuas on adjacent territories, which resulted in the fourth bird deserting. He then found that a new pair took up residence within the vacated area less than 20 hours after the owners had been removed. This new pair then expanded the limits of their held area until after another 24 hours it corresponded to most of the original two territories combined. Neighbouring pairs took over small parts of the boundary zone, but allowed the newcomers to take the vacant area without much conflict. As a result of the fact that established pairs know the territorial boundaries and accept them, and the fact that new birds are quick to move into an available territory, the territory pattern within a colony probably remains for many years; often territories will exist for far longer than the lifespan of breeding adults that occupy them, and will pass from owner to owner. Because skuas are longlived birds it will be rare for both members of a pair to die between breeding seasons, and so one of the pair will return to the territory and take a new mate, though females that lose their mate may move to a new territory to join a lone male.

On Gough Island, I caught adult Tristan Skuas at night by dazzling them with a torch. For ten consecutive nights I managed to remove one adult each night from one particular territory not far from the weather station. Every time, a new bird took the place of the one I had removed within six hours of sunrise the next morning, irrespective of the sex of the bird I caught. During the period the boundaries of that particular territory showed no detectable changes although a total of twelve different skuas had held it! Clearly, established breeders show an understanding of their territorial boundaries that reduces conflict with neighbours to a minimum; most conflict occurs with nonbreeding skuas that often fly over territories seeking to adopt a vacant site. It was also clear from my experiment on Gough that there was a large pool of nonbreeders seeking territories, and these birds were very quick to take the opportunities I presented to them.

Among small skuas on the Arctic tundra the situation is rather different. There the nesting distribution of skuas changes from year to year according to the availability of small mammal prey, and so territorial boundaries must be redefined each season. However, it seems to be a common feature of most skua populations that there is a considerable body of nonbreeding birds capable of taking a territory and breeding there if one becomes available as the result of the death or disappearance of the owner. This begs the question, why is there only a limited number of territories, such that part of the population capable of breeding cannot do so? In the Pomarine and Long-tailed Skuas it is clear that the numbers that breed in any one year are determined by small mammal abundance. In the Great Skua and Tristan Skua, and in the Arctic Skua in Shetland where I have experience of studying the birds, the situation is far from clear. It is tempting to say that the number of territories is determined by the social behaviour of the birds in the colony, such that they do not exceed the numbers that can be supported by local food resources, but such an explanation brings forward ideas of Prudential Restraint and Group Selection, concepts that are considered untenable by most biologists. With Pomarine and Long-tailed Skuas the birds seem to defend a territory large enough to allow them to breed successfully, and in years when small mammals are scarce the territory clearly needs to be larger, which reduces the density at which the skuas can breed. If breeding habitat is limited, then there will be a surplus of birds capable of reproducing but unable to gain a satisfactory territory because of the intense competition. For skuas that feed outside the territory the same mechanism cannot apply, since there is no reason to defend a larger territory in years when food is scarce, given that territorial defence will undoubtedly carry a cost, and it might even make better sense to defend a smaller territory in years when food is hard to obtain. However, all of the evidence indicates that Great and Arctic Skuas in Shetland maintain territories that are stable in size and location from year to year, regardless of changes in food availability. Changes in territory size seem to come about slowly as a consequence of increases or decreases in numbers of pairs breeding at a colony, as described earlier in this chapter. This leaves a dilemma; why do some skuas fail to create a new territory but move into a territory if one becomes available? Rather than arguing that the number of territories to be allowed has been decided by some social convention within the colony, it seems more likely that some skuas have reached a stage of physiological maturity which is sufficient to allow them to reproduce but is inadequate to allow them to set up a new territory between established birds. Perhaps the chances of a skua breeding successfully in a territory that it established on the edge of the colony or away from the colony would be less than the chances of its eventually getting a place within the existing colony on the disappearance of an established bird and then breeding there successfully. The processes of maturation, from being a young nonbreeding bird to becoming an established member of the breeding population, are ones that are critical to the understanding of bird population dynamics. We do not understand these processes in any species, but skuas would provide an excellent group in which they could be investigated.

CLUB SITES

At small established colonies of skuas there are no club sites, but these form a

21. A Great Skua club site beside Rossies Loch on Foula. Note the erosion of peat caused by the trampling of nonbreeding skuas and, in particular, the tendency for sheep to graze on clubs where the skua defecation enriches the peat and encourages rapid growth of sweet grasses. In the photograph there are three brown and one white sheep grazing on the club site, where 21 Great Skuas and one Great Black-backed Gull are present. Photo: R. W. Furness.

prominent feature of large colonies. Club sites are small areas, usually about 50–100 m in diameter, where immature nonbreeding skuas gather in a flock to rest together or to display and begin to practice agonistic and reproductive behaviour (Photo 21). The presence and size of clubs depends on the health of the skua colony. Where a colony is declining there will be no club at all. Where a colony is large and densely occupied there may be many clubs, fairly evenly spaced through, and around the fringes of the colony, as on Foula (Fig. 75). Small colonies that have recently been founded may have a large club if many birds are colonising the area from elsewhere. Thus the small Great Skua colony on St Kilda has, associated with it, a large club of immatures, many of which carry colour rings indicating that they were themselves reared on Foula but have emigrated to the small but rapidly expanding St Kilda population.

Where a colony is apparently near to saturation and birds seem unable or unwilling to establish new territories on the edge of the colony, they may establish territories on the fringe of club sites. These tend to be tiny; in Great Skuas often less than 5 m in diameter, and usually the birds fail to hatch their eggs because nonbreeders from the club disturb them and the eggs are broken. Attempting to breed on the edge of a club seems to be an act of desperation on the part of skuas unable to find a vacancy in an established territory. Their chances of fledging a chick must be little better than zero. As Great Skua numbers on Foula have fallen since 1977, the numbers of birds in clubs have decreased considerably (Table 43), as has the amount of nesting on club fringes. These changes imply a density-dependence in breeding success. As numbers reach a maximum, an increased

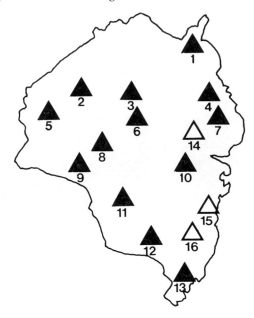

Fig. 75   Locations of club sites and bathing sites on Foula used by Great Skuas and Arctic Skuas. See Fig. 98 for maps of the areas occupied by skua colonies on Foula. Great Skua sites (solid triangles): 1 = Strem Ness club, 2 = Flick club and bathing site, 3 = Netherfandal club, 4 = Bottle club, 5 = Kame club, 6 = Overfandal bathing site, 7 = Rossies club and bathing site, 8 = Liorafield club, 9 = Hamnafield club, 10 = Mill Loch bathing site, 11 = Daal club, 12 = Noup club, 13 = South Ness club. Arctic Skua sites (open triangles); 14 = Peatbanks club, 15 = Manse bathing site, 16 = Airstrip club.

proportion of birds of breeding age will fail to establish themselves on traditional territories and either will not breed, or will breed unsuccessfully on club fringes, or they must emigrate. In fact, age of first breeding seems to vary according to ecological circumstances (Chapter 13), and is partly a consequence of the relative difficulty in obtaining a territorial place within the colony.

BATHING SITES

Skuas are very fond of bathing in fresh water, though they will bathe communally in seawater where freshwater sites do not exist. On Foula during the breeding season there is a constant stream of Great Skuas gliding down from the hills to Mill Loch where they gather in a flock of 20–150 birds to bathe in a tight group at the upwind end of the loch. Other groups bathe on Overfandal Loch, on the Fleck Lochs and, in recent years, on Rossies Loch and in the Daal (Fig. 75). These bathing sites are quite distinct from the club sites, for although they do contain nonbreeders, they are largely composed of off-duty breeding birds. Individuals visit the bathing sites for periods of a few minutes to upwards of an hour, with the long stays presumably by nonbreeders. On arrival, birds usually land directly in the water and begin a thorough routine of wing splashing, head ducking, and rolling onto their backs. Many of the actions look somewhat exaggerated, as if for display rather than function, and the bathing birds certainly seem to stay in close groups and become excited by the communal activity. During bathing, birds often squabble vociferously, or give the Long Call with wing raising, but there is nothing to indicate any particular communicative role in bathing behaviour itself. After a bout of bathing, individuals will move to an area of well worn grass beside the loch or pool where they preen themselves thoroughly before flying back to the territory. During bathing, when numbers in the water have built up to a high level, it is not uncommon for the whole flock suddenly to take off in total silence and rise up, much in the way that terns may do in their 'dreads' or panic flights. Then some birds fly off to sea in a group, and others drop back down onto the water to continue bathing with a resumption of noisy squabbling, calling and display, intermingled with splashing, ducking and rolling in the water. These 'dreads' during bathing seem to occur at random and for no reason, then, as noted, birds may leave the bathing site in groups (although birds arrive to bathe solitarily). Early in my observations of Great Skuas I speculated that this behaviour might provide some birds with an opportunity to depart to sea to forage in the company of birds that knew where food was available, an information centre hypothesis. I doubt now if this is likely, because Tristan Skuas also bathe communally on Gough Island yet they feed almost always solitarily on land at night, and so could not use an information centre in this way. Also, the 'dreads' seem to occur only when numbers in the water exceed a certain level; no 'dreads' occur at the small bathing sites on Rossies Loch and in the Daal. If the 'dreads' had a useful function then birds would do better to bathe as one group rather than founding new sites as the colony grew. Finally, shoals of Sandeels rise to the surface in a highly unpredictable way, and even over a short period of time birds would be unlikely to be able to return to previous feeding areas and still find Sandeels some hours later. Most Great Skuas seem to feed well within sight of Foula and so they can probably see and fly out to feeding areas without the need for an information centre at the colony. Presumably, bathing sites are only used to clean and maintain the plumage, and 'dreads' are a manifestation of alarm induced in the birds by one or two individuals in such a way that a wave of fright passes through the entire flock. Skua 'dreads' while bathing seem to have no positive function.

Numbers of skuas using bathing sites show a clear diurnal rhythm. Few birds bathe in the early morning, but numbers build up to a mid afternoon peak, before dwindling to nothing in the evening.

INTERSPECIFIC HYBRIDISATION

Interspecific hybridisation occurs between the marine-feeding South Polar Skua and the terrestrial-feeding Brown Skua, and between the marine-feeding Chilean Skua and the terrestrial-feeding Falkland Skua. It is interesting that the two overlapping distributions involve one marine-feeding and one terrestrial-feeding skua, so that the taxa are unlikely to come into competition for food.

Why does hybridisation occur at all, and are there barriers to prevent it from increasing? Rather little is known about hybridisation between Falkland and Chilean Skuas, except that it is rare and probably only occurs in a small area of

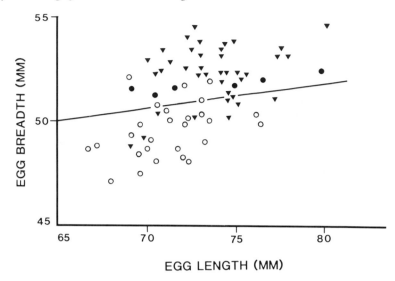

Fig. 76   Measurements of skua eggs at Signy Island, showing the close similarity in size between those laid by females in pairs of Brown Skuas (triangles) and those laid by females in interspecies hybrid pairs (dots). Open circles represent eggs laid by females in pairs of South Polar Skuas. From Hemmings (1984).

South America where the breeding ranges of the two overlap (Devillers 1978). Hybridisation between Brown and South Polar Skuas has been the subject of more detailed study near the United States base at Palmer Station on the Antarctic Peninsula and at Signy Island, the British base in the South Orkney Islands, where South Polar Skuas are spreading north as the availability of their preferred food, the fish *Pleuragramma*, has apparently increased.

In the case of overlap between Chilean and Falkland Skuas very few hybrid pairs were seen, indicating that each species tended to mate by preference with a conspecific rather than taking a mate at random from all available skuas. Assortative mating of this kind will tend to keep hybridisation at a low level. At Signy Island, three hybrid pairs of South Polar/Brown Skua were present in the 1981–82 season. One of these remained mated in the next season. In one pair the South Polar Skua died and the Brown Skua paired with another Brown Skua. In the third, both the South Polar Skua and the Brown Skua returned in the 1982–83 season, but the Brown Skua paired with a conspecific rather than with its South Polar Skua mate of the previous season. In all three pairs the Brown Skua was believed to be the female of the pair, both on the basis of relative body size and of egg size produced, which was closely similar to the norm for that species (Fig. 76). This is also true of hybrid pairs at Anvers Island (Neilson 1983), and the explanation for this seems to lie with the timing of breeding in the two species. Brown Skuas return to the area before South Polar Skuas, and so a female Brown Skua that has been unable to obtain a mate of her own species can still pair with an early-returned South Polar Skua male that has just established his territory. This mechanism is supported by the observation (Table 44) that the South Polar Skuas in hybrid pairs were among the earliest of their species to return to the colony (Hemmings 1984). It would appear that the male South Polar Skuas are taken advantage of by the very much larger female Brown Skuas that are left after all Brown Skua males that hold territories have obtained mates. Nevertheless, the breeding success of hybrid pairs seems to be the same as that of normal pairs of Brown Skuas or South Polar Skuas (Hemmings 1984). Whether the hybrid offspring are as viable as normal young is not yet known, and so the future development of hybridisation is unclear. If, as it seems, it is only due to surplus female Brown Skuas hybridising rather than failing to breed at all, the practice might be more damaging to South Polar Skuas than to Brown Skuas, but its ultimate effects will depend on the fate of the hybrid offspring produced.

CHAPTER 11

Breeding: laying to hatching

During the South Georgia expedition of 1912–13 I became extremely well acquainted with the Brown Skua, which has left, I believe, a more vivid impression in my memory than any other bird I have met. The skuas look and act like miniature eagles. They fear nothing, never seek to avoid being conspicuous, and, by every token of their behaviour, they are Lords of the far south.

Murphy (1936)

There are numerous published accounts of the breeding biology of skuas, allowing comparisons to be made between populations and between species. In this chapter, I shall outline the aspects relating to laying, incubation and hatching success.

TIMING OF LAYING

Bird Observatory staff usually try to record the date of laying of the first Arctic Skua egg on Fair Isle each year, and over the period 1967–80 the annual reports record dates of 16–20 May. The range of first egg dates of only five days is really quite remarkably small. Clearly the birds breed at a time determined by some predictable environmental cue, almost certainly daylength. Although it is relatively easy to record the date on which the first egg is laid each year, it requires a rather more intensive study to record the mean laying date of pairs in a colony. On Foula, we have obtained such data not by examining every nest each day during the laying period, but indirectly and much more easily, by measuring Great Skua chicks. We have measured a large proportion, usually more than half, of all the

216

chicks hatched each season since 1975, and it is possible to estimate the hatching date of each measured chick with an average accuracy of about plus or minus one day. From a sample of chicks we can then estimate the mean, most frequent, median, earliest and latest hatching dates, making the assumption that the eggs that fail to hatch are a random sample, unbiased in terms of their laying dates. In fact, few eggs fail to hatch, but there is a slight tendency for eggs laid late to fail, so the estimate of the mean laying date will be slightly biased. Nevertheless, a comparison on Foula between laying dates estimated by my detailed study of nests as part of my Ph.D. in 1975 and 1976, and laying dates estimated from chick measurements indicated that the two methods give closely similar results.

From 1975–84, the first hatching date of Great Skuas on Foula varied between 29 May and 5 June, a range of eight days. The most frequent hatching date varied from 11–20 June (range 10 days), the mean hatching date was 13–24 June (range 12 days), and the latest successful hatching date 27 June–22 July, a range of 26 days. The range of variation of these parameters increases with the date. The implication of this is that the correct timing of breeding is most critical early in the season, and is probably controlled more by internal factors such as a biological clock or sensitivity to daylength, whereas events later in the season may be more susceptible to environmental factors. Certainly, I was unable to find any statistically significant correlations between the date of first laying or mean laying date each season and weather data, plankton abundance and timing or fish stock data. However, there has been a tendency for Great Skua breeding to start and, particularly, to stop earlier in the season since 1981, and it is possible that this is linked to the fact that Great Skua breeding numbers on Foula have fallen in this period, whereas they had been increasing continuously from 1900 to 1977 or 1978. The recruitment of Sandeels around Shetland has been poor since 1983, and the industrial fishery for Sandeels in the 1980s has tended to catch earlier in the season than it did in the 1970s. This may suggest that Sandeels have become available earlier, but we know too little about Sandeel biology to make anything of these observations at present. It seems to me that a long series of data on the distribution of laying dates of seabirds and their diets and breeding success would be very valuable if it could be examined in conjunction with data on Sandeel stocks, reproduction and availability.

Great Skuas on Foula laid over a period of 25–50 days in the seasons 1975–84. As with most other birds, the breeding success of Great Skuas (and other skuas that have been studied) declines with laying date. Great Skuas that lay in the last quarter of the laying period have only about a 25% chance of producing a fledgling that early breeders have. Most pairs lay within a few days of the date the first egg is laid, and there is a tail of birds that lay late. Some of the tail is due to young, inexperienced, pairs (Table 45) that take longer to begin breeding; some is pairs laying replacement clutches for eggs lost, early, during incubation. The Great Skua can lay two replacement clutches if it loses its eggs immediately after each clutch is completed. However, pairs tend to replace only up to a certain date, and after that they will simply remain holding their territory until birds start to disperse away from the colony in late summer.

Although there is quite a spread of laying dates within colonies, there are more striking differences between populations. Arctic Skuas that breed in Shetland, around 60°N, begin laying in mid May; earliest egg dates on Fair Isle average 16 May, on Foula the earliest egg date was 15 May. Mean laying dates are at the end of May; 26 May at Foula, 28 May at Fair Isle and 30 May at Noss (Table 46).

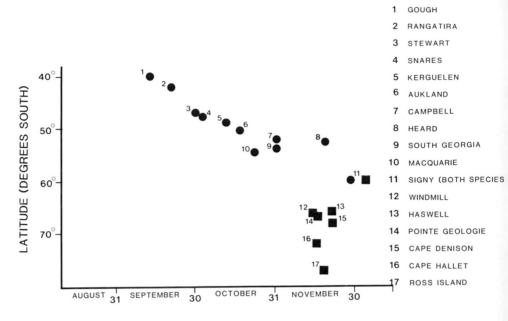

Fig. 77   First egg dates of Brown Skuas (dots) and South Polar Skuas (squares)
in relation to the latitude of the breeding colony. From Young (1977).

Further north, laying is later. At 68°N in eastern Murman, USSR, Arctic Skuas
start to lay on 2 June and the mean laying date is 13 June. In northern Alaska
(71°N), first eggs are usually in the first ten days of June, and mean laying date
from 5–20 June. On Bear Island and Spitsbergen (75°N and 78°N), first egg dates
may be between 7 June and 6 July depending on the date of snow melt, and mean
laying date is in July (Table 46). An interesting point here is that the Arctic Skua
is unable to breed in synchrony with its food source. On Bear Island and Spitsbergen the cliff-nesting seabirds that Arctic Skuas rob, such as Kittiwakes and
guillemots, breed only a few days later than they do in Shetland, whereas the
Arctic Skua is considerably delayed because it cannot lay before the flat tops of
these islands become relatively snow free. No work has been done on the effects,
if any, that the relative difference in date of breeding has on the skuas. One likely
effect is that the skuas in Spitsbergen and Bear Island will have a more pronounced
seasonal decline in food availability than do the Shetland birds, since many auks
and Kittiwakes will have dispersed from their colonies before the Arctic Skuas
have fledged their young.

Young (1977) pointed out that the southern large skuas also show a variation in
date of laying that relates to breeding latitude. Tristan and Brown Skuas have first
egg dates that vary from mid September at Gough Island to late November at
Signy Island. South Polar Skuas start to lay rather later than Brown Skuas, and
their first egg dates show little or no relationship with latitude (Fig. 77). Young
suggested that the slight deviations of certain points from the regression line for
Brown and Tristan Skuas could be explained by variations in climate. Where

conditions are unusually cold for the latitude skuas seem to breed later than latitude alone predicted. This suggests that the skuas time their breeding to fit into seasonal production cycles the timing of which is largely determined by temperature.

Although skuas seem to time their breeding with seasonal patterns that relate to latitude and climate, and so presumably to the time of peak availability of food, it is clear that in some localities, such as Spitsbergen, they are forced by ground conditions to breed later than they would otherwise do. One factor affecting the date of laying is the amount of time required for the formation of the pair bond and courtship activities, and this is considered next.

DURATION OF THE PRE-LAYING PERIOD

In Shetland, the first Arctic Skuas arrive at colonies on the 16–18 April each year. First arrival dates at more northern latitudes are rather later; late May in northern Alaska, and as late as mid June in Spitsbergen in some years (Table 46). In fact, the difference in dates of first arrival with latitude is greater than the difference in first egg dates. As a result, Arctic Skuas have a shorter prelaying period at the colony at higher latitudes. In Shetland, the average period between first arrival and first laying is 30 days, but it is only some 8–14 days in Spitsbergen. According to Maher (1974), Arctic Skuas in northern Alaska lay about 7–12 days

22. *The appearance of the breeding habitat of Long-tailed Skuas in East Greenland on 23 May 1974, the day on which the first individuals were seen returning to the area.* Photo: J. de Korte.

*23. A Long-tailed Skua above its nest (foreground) on an area of wet tundra
in East Greenland in mid-June. Photo: J. de Korte.*

after first arrival, which is even quicker than in Spitsbergen. Since Arctic Skuas
apparently can lay only seven or eight days after their return to the territory, the
consistent period of 30 days between return and laying in Shetland requires some
explanation. Probably the most likely reason for this is that breeding is not
constrained by the time required to pair, but that birds reoccupy their territories
as soon in spring as conditions allow. The seasonal improvement in food availability
is certainly much more rapid at high latitudes, and so the time required for
conditions to permit breeding, rather than just territory occupation, will be shorter

24. The summer marine environment of Cape Hallett, Antarctica, where there has been a colony of 100–200 pairs of South Polar Skuas over the last 20 years. Photo: J. G. Pascoe.

at higher latitudes. If there is competition for territories, as there seems to be in skuas, then it would pay a bird to return to the colony as early as the available food will allow. Skuas usually return to their territories carrying large fat reserves, and this may enable them to reoccupy the territory at a time when they could not maintain themselves from the food then available and must draw on their reserves. Belopolskii (1961) showed that Arctic Skuas in eastern Murman lost about 10% of their body weight between arrival in spring and hatching, while my own data show that Great Skuas return to the colony on Foula weighing about 25% more than they do by the time their eggs hatch (Furness 1977). By contrast, Tristan Skuas on Gough Island showed no detectable differences in weight between the period immediately before egglaying and hatching. Their lack of a weight change fits in with the fact that many Tristan Skuas remain at Gough throughout the year, and there is no shortage of food in the period before laying as there is for the Great Skua and Arctic Skua. If we accept the idea that the availability of food for Great Skuas increases in the spring, then the idea that birds reoccupy their territory when a certain threshold is reached and begin to breed when another threshold is reached, can also explain why some birds breed later than others and why nonbreeders arrive at the colony after breeders. Individuals will have different threshold food requirements due to differences in their foraging skills or stored food reserves. In general, we can expect that nonbreeders will have lower feeding efficiencies and less food reserves, and so could not return to the colony so early in the season. Such environmental influences must also interact with inherent differences in timing due to genetically programmed sensitivities of individuals to daylength or hormone levels, since it is well known that certain birds always arrive relatively early or relatively late each year (O'Donald 1983).

*25. The author examining hatching eggs under a Tristan Skua on Gough Island.
The lack of fear of man in these birds is striking.* Photo: S. Anderson.

CLUTCH SIZE

Skuas almost always lay two eggs. Only about 10–20% of pairs lay a single egg,
and clutches of three or four eggs are extremely rare, and usually the result of two
females laying in one nest. Out of some 2,000 clutches I examined on Foula, I
found only one clutch of three Great Skua eggs that appeared, from their shapes
and colourations, to have been produced by a single female. O'Donald (1983)
described how one female Arctic Skua on Fair Isle consistently laid clutches of
three eggs each year. That this is aberrant is clear from the fact that these clutches
generally failed to hatch. Brooding skuas can only keep two eggs warm at a time,
since they have only two brood patches and can incubate only a single egg on the
web of each foot. Andersson (1976) showed by experiment that the Long-tailed
Skua, also, could not incubate clutches of three eggs properly. He added a third
egg to each of four normal clutches of two and found that most of the clutches
then failed to hatch. Two pairs succeeded in hatching one egg each, but both
chicks died shortly after hatching. By comparison, ten control pairs with clutches
of two eggs hatched 19 of their 20 eggs. The Great Skuas that I found with a
clutch of three eggs had slightly better success. Some eggs hatched and produced
chicks that survived. In this case I can only assume that the birds managed to
keep embryos alive by ensuring that each egg was against a brood patch often
enough and long enough to keep it developing. However, it is clear that skuas,

with only two brood patches and the habit of placing eggs on their feet, are effectively restricted to brooding clutches of only two eggs. Since their closest relatives, the gulls, generally have three eggs and three brood patches, the two egg clutch in skuas has almost certainly evolved from a three egg clutch of an ancestor. In some skuas, there are times when food supplies would allow a brood of more than two chicks to be raised. For example, Andersson (1976) showed that in a good lemming year, Long-tailed Skuas could raise three chicks to fledging if given an extra chick around hatching. I showed that Great Skuas on Foula in the mid 1970s were also capable of raising extra chicks (Furness & Hislop 1981), and argued that this was due to the favourable conditions then provided by increased stocks of Sandeels and large amounts of discarded fish. Andersson (1976) suggested that the two egg clutch of skuas and their use of the feet on which to incubate the eggs could be attributed to the need for skuas to avoid nest predation. Gull nests, thickly lined with grasses, are rather obvious structures that can only be protected from ground predators by communal mobbing and by nesting at sites where such predators cannot gain access; for example gull colonies often situated on small islets in lakes or on stacks off the coast. Skuas, particularly on the Arctic tundra, are less able to site nests where predators cannot get at them, and so the lack of nest material may be strongly advantageous. Andersson (1976) tested this hypothesis by placing Common Gull eggs, which look similar to Long-tailed Skua eggs, in pairs, with dummy gull nests around half of the pairs of eggs. Three days later, all of the eggs in the dummy nests had been taken by predators, whereas seven others remained, a significant difference showing that nest material increased the risk of predation.

If food were the only factor of importance, then skuas would probably have a more flexible clutch size, as owls do, but the need for nests to be unlined to avoid predation and hence the requirement to use the feet to insulate eggs from the ground, probably induces skuas to lay only two eggs.

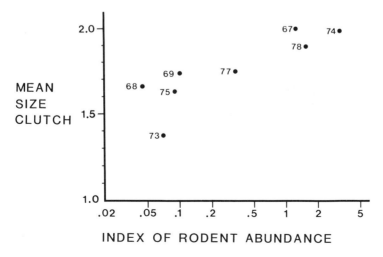

Fig. 78   *Mean clutch size of Long-tailed Skuas in N. Sweden in different years in relation to rodent abundance. From Andersson (1981).*

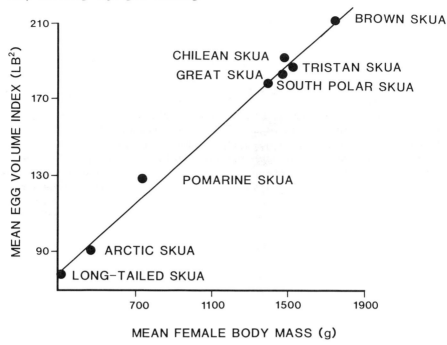

Fig. 79 Relationship between the mean volume index of eggs and mean female body weight in skuas.

Some *Catharacta* skuas, such as Brown Skuas, Tristan Skuas and Great Skuas, make fairly substantial scrapes and use some grass to line these. *Catharacta* skuas are much less at risk of nest predation than are Arctic breeding small skuas, and it may be that their restriction to a clutch of two eggs is due to their evolutionary origins and would no longer be advantageous. However, the lack of birds genetically programmed to lay three eggs, and the lack of a third brood patch, may inhibit the large skuas from evolving a clutch of three again.

Clutches of one egg are often laid by young skuas with no previous breeding experience. Nevertheless, some skuas regularly lay only one egg each year, suggesting that this is an inherent characteristic of a small proportion of the population. Andersson (1981) showed that the mean clutch size of Long-tailed Skuas in N. Sweden varied between years depending on rodent abundance; in years when voles and lemmings were abundant the clutch size was 1.9–2.0, whereas in years when many pairs of skuas failed to breed at all because rodent abundance was low, clutch size averaged as little as 1.4–1.7 (Fig. 78), so it is also clear that the clutch size depends on environmental factors as well as on the age and genetic constitution of the bird.

EGG SIZE

Egg size can be estimated most easily by measuring egg length and breadth, and computing the volume index, Length × Breadth^2. The mean of this index of egg size shows a close relationship with mean body weight of females of the species during incubation (Fig. 79). Since egg measurements are available for all species of skuas (Table 47), it is possible to estimate from Fig. 79 that the female Falkland Skua, which has a mean egg volume index of 192, should have an average weight during incubation of about 1540 g. No published data for Falkland Skua weights exist, so this estimate remains to be confirmed! However, the close fit between body weight and egg volume index suggests that egg size is largely constrained by female anatomy.

Within a population, egg size and shape varies. Second laid eggs tend to be rather shorter but often slightly broader than first laid eggs, and usually are slightly smaller in volume than the first egg (Furness 1977). I used this difference quite successfully to predict which egg in each clutch should start to hatch first. Eggs of different females also differ in volume and shape. Volume in particular can correlate with hatching success. To some extent it is possible that poor quality birds may produce small eggs and have low hatching success, so it is dangerous to infer that small size causes low hatching success. The two are certainly correlated in Brown Skuas (Williams 1980) and in Great Skuas (Furness 1983), but it would be necessary to perform swapping experiments between nests in order to tease apart the influences of egg size and of female quality. Nevertheless, Williams (1980) showed that larger eggs result in chicks with larger food reserves at hatching, which can be important for early survival of chicks (Chapter 12).

HATCHING SUCCESS AND EGG LOSSES

Hatching success varies considerably between different skua populations studied, but is generally high. In most cases, 60–70% of skua eggs hatch, although high predation rates, inclement weather or food shortages can have drastic effects on hatching success. When considered over all studies of each taxonomic group, hatching success of Great Skuas (73%), Brown Skuas (71%) and South Polar Skuas (66%) does not differ much between groups, and without doubt the range of hatching success found between colonies is much the same in each group (Table 48). South Polar Skuas suffer slightly lower average hatching success because in some years at some sites hatching success can be severely reduced by storms. For example, Ensor (1979) recorded a hatching success of only about 24% at Cape Bird in 1977–78, which he attributed to snowdrifts up to one metre deep on the nesting area during the early part of incubation, when in most years snow had already melted and gone.

Factors causing egg losses

Among Great Skuas on Foula in the mid 1970s, egg predation by conspecifics accounted for 10.6% of all eggs laid, and 'addled' eggs (including infertile eggs and eggs in which the embryo died during development) accounted for 17% of all eggs that survived 27 days in the nest. Less important causes of loss were eggs rolling out of the nest (2.5% of eggs laid) while 2.8% of fertile eggs that survived to hatching suffered embryo death during hatching (Table 49). Predation of eggs was very much higher for pairs with low aggression indices. Pairs with an aggression score of four or five, the two highest categories, lost only five out of 289 clutches, whereas pairs with an aggression score of one (and so generally with tiny territories too) lost 26 out of 47 clutches to predation by neighbours or by nonbreeding Great Skuas. Predation risk was clearly determined, directly or indirectly, by adult aggressiveness.

While the first-laid and second-laid eggs in clutches of two showed no statistically significant differences in rates of predation, addling, rolling out of the nest, or dying during hatching, clutches of one egg were significantly more likely to be eaten by conspecifics or addled, the frequency being about twice as high as in clutches of two (Furness 1984).

Young birds tended to have lower aggression scores, lay later in the season, probably produced smaller clutches, and certainly had a lower hatching success, so that the interrelationships between factors can be complex, making it difficult to determine which are the causal factors. Some addling of Great Skua eggs on Foula may be caused by occasional flooding of nests during heavy rain, but the numbers of addled eggs appear to be unusually high in the Great Skua, and this might possibly be linked to effects of pollutants, although this has yet to be confirmed (Chapter 14).

Although many other studies of skua breeding estimated hatching and fledging success, few were detailed enough to give reliable information on the causes of losses. Maher (1974) believed that most egg losses among Arctic Skuas in northern Alaska were due to predation or interference by Pomarine Skuas or by Glaucous Gulls. He also attributed some egg losses in Long-tailed and Pomarine Skuas to predation, largely by foxes, and to infertility or to trampling by migrating caribou. In addition, in many years when rodent densities were low, skuas would desert clutches for no obvious proximate reason. Overall, predation of nests by foxes seems to have been the largest single cause of egg losses in his studies. Andersson (1976) found that predators took 8 of 11 eggs that failed to hatch from a sample of 55 Long-tailed Skua eggs he studied in N. Sweden, and de Korte (1986), studying Long-tailed Skuas in E. Greenland, found that predation by Arctic Foxes accounted for 22 eggs, six were addled, two were deserted, and only 14 hatched. Clearly, predation of skua nests on the Arctic tundra is an important factor in determining hatching success, and Arctic Foxes seem to be the main nest predator. On Foula, Arctic Skuas are not subject to ground predators to any significant extent; introduced hedgehogs do take one or two eggs, but most egg losses are attributable to nest robbing by other skuas, to flooding or to addling, and hatching success is much higher than found among skuas on the Arctic tundra. Among Brown Skuas, hatching success is also generally high; the few egg losses are generally due to predation by other skuas or to eggs being rolled from the nest or addled (Burton 1968, Williams 1980). South Polar Skuas also lose a few eggs in these ways, but suffer an additional loss due to bad weather. Young (1963) reported a study at Cape Royds when in one season 16 out of 94 eggs were lost; six were addled, two were taken by other skuas, and eight were deserted. By comparison, in the year when snow covered the breeding areas at Cape Bird, Ensor (1979) reported that 75.2% of eggs were lost, some flooded and addled or washed out of the nest as a result, but most taken by other skuas during and after the storms. Spellerberg (1971) reported that South Polar Skua hatching success varied from year to year because of the vagaries of the weather, from a low of 58% in the poor summer of 1964–65 to a high of 74% in the benign summer of 1963–64.

In conclusion, small skuas on the Arctic tundra suffer most egg loss as a result of predation by Arctic Foxes, egg losses in South Polar Skuas can be high in years of stormy weather and losses are directly attributable to effects of the weather. Brown Skuas and Great Skuas often have hatching success of 70–80%, with the few losses attributable to addled eggs or predation by conspecifics.

CHAPTER 12

Breeding: hatching to fledging

The degree of hunger experienced by the first chick regulates the intensity of its aggressive behaviour, which in turn affects the second chick's survival. Aggressive behaviour restricts the second chick's access to the nest area and deprives it of parental attention, increasing its susceptibility to starvation, exposure and predation.

Procter (1975)

Skua chicks hatch out at an advanced stage of development. After they have dried out under the parent they can leave the nest and run around in the vegetation, hiding if the parents signal alarm, and soliciting brooding and feeding as required. The skuas show a number of adaptations to aid the survival of chicks; chick down colour and cryptic behaviour may camouflage it from predators; asynchronous hatching may improve the chances of at least one chick surviving to fledge. In this chapter I compare the chick rearing strategies of the different skuas and the degree of success that they achieve.

CHICK DOWN COLOUR

All of the small skuas hatch chicks with a dense dark brown to grey down. The down of the Arctic Skua chick is darker and browner than that of Pomarine Skua chicks; and Long-tailed Skua chicks have down a still lighter grey-brown. Nevertheless, the downy chicks of all three small skuas are highly cryptic when they crouch motionless against the sparse vegetation, earth and stones of the tundra or dry heather moor on which they tend to occur. By comparison, Great Skuas have very conspicuous downy chicks. These are a light pinkish grey or sandy colour, very different from their normal background of dark peat or grasses in Shetland and the Faeroe Islands, black volcanic ash or grass in Iceland. This

26. A Brown Skua on South Georgia brooding its two or three day old chick under its wing. Photo: W. N. Bonner.

contrast between Great Skua and Arctic Skua downy young (Photos 27, 28) was one of the most vivid memories of my first visit to Foula, and anyone who has attempted to find skua chicks to ring will be aware how much easier it is to find Great Skua chicks than those of their smaller relative.

The down colour of Great Skua chicks is apparently much the same as that of the chicks of most other *Catharacta* taxa. Recently hatched chicks of Tristan Skuas on Gough Island looked to me almost exactly like Great Skua chicks, though possibly slightly less pink in colour. Murphy (1936) says that the downy chick of the Chilean Skua closely resembles that of the Great Skua. The chick of the Brown Skua has sandy to dark brownish grey down (Watson 1975). The one species that differs from these is the South Polar Skua, and here the ideas concerning down colour are a little confusing. According to Murphy (1936) South Polar Skuas have grey-blue down at hatching, but this changes colour to brownish as a result of absorption of oil from the subcutaneous tissues. Eklund (1961) states that all South Polar Skua downy young he saw at a number of different colonies were slaty blue-grey, and none were buff or brown, and he considered that the down colour was quite different from that of Brown Skua chicks. Watson (1975) describes newly hatched South Polar Skua chicks in the far south of the Antarctic Continent as 'pale sandy gray with a bluish cast', but says that chicks of the same species at colonies on the Antarctic Peninsula were quite different, with two colour morphs, either 'sandy in colour', or 'dark brownish grey with a tendency toward a bluish tone'. He also mentions that both colour forms may occur in the same brood, and suggests that some of the chicks of South Polar Skuas on the Antarctic Peninsula may be indistinguishable, on the basis of colour alone, from those of Brown Skuas.

The different South Polar Skua chick colours at Antarctic Peninsula colonies might be related in some way to the existence of colour phases in the adults of this species, but no work has yet been done on this. Alternatively, the different colour of chicks might be a result of genetic introgression. Hybridisation with Brown Skuas, which may have been occurring for some time on the Antarctic Peninsula, may have resulted in the genes for down colour from Brown Skuas being

27. A Great Skua chick about ten days old, showing the lack of cryptic colouration of the pale pinkish-brown down against a background of dark green grasses on Foula. Photo: R. W. Furness.

28. An Arctic Skua chick crouching in grass and lesser pennywort on Foula, showing a closer match with the background than would be the case with a Great Skua chick. Photo: R. W. Furness.

incorporated into the South Polar Skua population there. Again, this possibility is pure speculation. To resolve it would require detailed genetic studies of the different skua populations in areas of overlap and away from overlap. Such studies would be most interesting and rewarding, and might shed light on many questions concerning the evolutionary history of *Catharacta* taxa.

Despite some uncertainty about the exact colour of the down of South Polar Skua chicks, it is clear that most *Catharacta* chicks tend to be light sandy to pinkish brown or pinkish grey in down colour, rather than the dark brown to grey of the small skuas. Does this mean that *Catharacta* chicks do not need to be cryptic? Clearly the chicks of the small skuas will be exposed to predation by a wide variety of animals, such as other skuas, Snowy Owls, falcons, gulls and crows, Arctic and Red Fox, mink, and even Polar Bears! By contrast, *Catharacta* chicks in the southern hemisphere have few, if any, predators other than conspecifics. Nevertheless, a rather crude experiment has shown that South Polar Skua down colour may aid in protecting chicks against predation. Twelve downy chicks were dyed red or purple by injecting a vital stain into one of the two eggs in twelve clutches a few days before hatching. Six of these twelve chicks disappeared during early growth, presumed to have been taken by predators. Only four out of 32 natural coloured chicks disappeared (Eklund 1961). The results suggest that the brightly coloured chicks were more easily found by predatory neighbours or nonbreeders, although the experiment could be criticised for the small sample size used and for the lack of a proper control. It could be argued that the injection procedure itself might have affected the chicks adversely, and the control sample should have been injected with a colourless material to give them as near equal treatment as possible.

If *Catharacta* chicks are somewhat cryptically coloured in their Antarctic environment, they most certainly are not at North Atlantic colonies, at least to human eyes. Nevertheless, Great Skua chicks do suffer predation, so it could be expected that cryptic chicks would have a selective advantage. This potential advantage is probably quite substantial. On Foula in 1975 and 1976 a detailed study of 881 nests showed that a total of 37 out of 1168 chicks disappeared from their territories, apparently due to predation. This represented half of all chick mortality although the only predators ever detected were neighbouring adult Great Skuas (Furness 1984). In 1983 and 1984 on Noss, Anne Hudson found that predation of Great Skua chicks was very much greater than I had found on Foula, apparently because Noss Great Skuas in 1983 and 1984 had less favourable feeding opportunities than the birds I had studied. Whether the Noss or the Foula results are more representative is not really important. In both situations, predation of chicks was the main proximate cause of losses between hatching and fledging, so one would expect that selection for crypsis would be strong. The fact that Great Skua chick down is the 'wrong' colour for the background at North Atlantic colonies adds to my conviction that Great Skuas have colonised the North Atlantic from the south, and have not yet had time to evolve a more appropriate down colour and shade.

ASYNCHRONOUS HATCHING AND BROOD REDUCTION

All skuas species usually lay two eggs, with an interval of two or three days between them. However, unlike most birds, skuas start to incubate as soon as the first egg is laid, and so the second egg is later in its development by two or three days. The second egg is usually smaller, and because the nest temperature gradually increases during the first couple of days of incubation of the first egg, the second egg derives an immediate benefit. As a result, the hatching interval is less than the laying interval. Nevertheless, the difference in weight and stage of development of the two chicks is such that the larger chick can quite easily, and in some situations does, kill its smaller sibling. Asynchronous hatching and brood reduction through fratricide can be found in all skuas, and in many raptors and owls, some corvids, boobies, gulls, cormorants and herons. It is considered to be an adaptive response, resulting in the early death of the second chick when food is in short supply. This then allows the first chick to have all of the food the adults provide. Brood reduction may allow one chick to survive, without it both chicks may starve.

If the Great or Arctic Skuas in Shetland in the 1970s were the only skuas whose chick growth had been studied, asynchronous hatching in skuas would seem to be of no adaptive value. Most skuas in Shetland in the 1970s fledged both chicks if both eggs hatched, and the growth rates of A and B chicks were virtually identical. Indeed, they grew better than chicks in broods of one, probably because the begging of two chicks resulted in each being fed more than the begging of one chick alone elicited (Furness 1983).

In contrast, at many colonies of South Polar Skuas the second hatched chick rarely survives, and the laying of the second egg seems almost wasteful (Wilson 1907). Young (1963) showed that the smaller chick died as a result of the aggression of the older sibling, which he suggested was caused by hunger. Spellerberg (1971) showed that the second chick had a better chance of surviving the briefer the interval between hatching of the two eggs. By swapping chicks of different ages between broods and by removing chicks temporarily and depriving them of food, Procter (1975) examined the roles of age difference and hunger status in a more rigorous experimental way. He showed that hunger released the aggressive behaviour of South Polar Skua chicks, irrespective of whether they were first or second hatched individuals, but the greater size and strength of the older chick allowed it to dominate its sibling. The greater the size difference the more easily dominance was achieved, but weight and size difference themselves did not cause aggressive behaviour in well fed chicks.

The consequence of the aggressive behaviour of hungry first chicks towards the smaller sibling was that the younger chick was deprived of parental attention and brooding, and so made more susceptible to starvation or death due to predation or exposure. The first chick generally began to attack its sibling if it fell below about 80% of the normal weight for its age. Reanalysing Spellerberg's data, Procter (1975) showed that the few broods in which both chicks survived to fledging were ones in which the chicks were particularly heavy for their age. It seems likely that the lack of sibling aggression and brood reduction in Great Skuas in Shetland is due to their well fed condition. In the last few seasons the chicks of Great Skuas have been less well fed, and spend more time begging for food. In a few cases I have seen sibling aggression between chicks, suggesting that Shetland Great Skuas may now be finding feeding sufficiently difficult that brood reduction may begin to develop. In the 1970s, Great Skua chicks in Shetland rarely, if ever, fell to less than 80% of the normal weight, and so their inherent sibling aggression was not triggered, and pairs of chicks could often be found side by side in the territory.

PATTERNS OF CHICK DEVELOPMENT

Stercorarius and *Catharacta* differ dramatically in the way in which their chicks develop. Small skuas have chicks that sprout feathers early in their growth, and they do not put on much fat. The emphasis is on rapid maturation. *Catharacta* chicks remain down-covered until they are well on their way to peak weight, and much of that weight is fat. Then towards the end of their development they rapidly grow their feathers, lose much of their fat store, and often fledge at a slightly lower weight than the peak they had reached if well fed. The accumulation of large reserves of fat and late development of plumage is a growth characteristic found in most petrels and shearwaters, and is associated with a high probability of adults being unable to provide their young with food for extensive periods of time. Survival of unfed chicks will be better if they have fat reserves to draw on rather than developed feathers, which cannot be used as an emergency energy supply. *Catharacta* skuas may adopt this chick growth strategy in order for them to be able to survive through periods of severe Antarctic storms, or periods of bad weather that preclude efficient foraging at sea. Small skuas on the Arctic tundra can usually expect good summer weather once the thaw has arrived, and so should be able to feed their chicks daily without periods of interruption. Further, if their chicks grew more slowly and stored fat reserves, they might pay a greater penalty in the autumn by being unable to complete their development in time to migrate south before the short Arctic summer ended. Thus, the radically different chick growth strategies of *Stercorarius* and *Catharacta* can probably be attributed to these environmental differences between their major breeding areas.

Williams (1980) examined the growth of Brown Skua chicks at Marion Island in relation to the size of the eggs from which they hatched. He analysed egg composition and showed that larger eggs contained proportionately more water and albumin. Chicks hatching from larger eggs tended to be heavier but little larger in body measurements. As growth proceeded, disparity in weight and measurements persisted, and Williams suggested that larger eggs allowed chicks to start on their growth pattern more quickly after hatching. In his study, survival of chicks was not affected by egg size, but the larger reserves of chicks from larger eggs probably reduce the risk of starvation immediately after hatching.

Weight increase in skua chicks can often be described by a logistic growth equation. For the Great Skua at Foula in the 1970s all chicks except those few hatched after 20 June followed the growth equation:

$$\text{Weight (g)} = \frac{1167.075}{1 + 16.955e^{-0.176\,t}}$$

where t is the chick age in days after hatching (Furness 1983).

The fit between observed chick weights and this mathematical function is quite remarkably close (Fig. 80). There is no logical necessity for chick growth to follow this particular type of mathematical equation; in some birds logistic equations give a poor fit to actual growth patterns. However, the fact that a logistic equation provides a better fit than alternatives such as the Gompertz or Von Bertalanffy equations may indicate that chick growth is not constrained by food shortage. Where food is short, chicks increase in weight by a decreasing amount as they grow, because they need to devote more energy to tissue maintenance. In skuas,

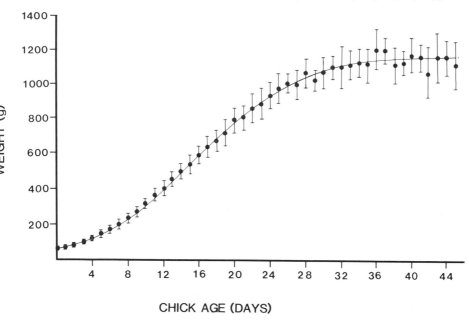

Fig. 80   Weights of Great Skua chicks in relation to age, for chicks hatched on Foula in the mid 1970s before 20 June. Dots represent means for each day of age. Vertical lines indicate one standard deviation. The solid curve shows the best fit logistic growth equation. From Furness (1977).

the logistic growth curve often fits well, and the daily weight gain by chicks is close to a constant value, from a few days after hatching to about two-thirds of full size. This implies that parents are able to give chicks increasing amounts of food as the chicks grow, to provide for their larger maintenance requirement and to continue their constant rate of weight gain. For Great Skua chicks at Foula, shown in Fig. 80, the mean daily weight gain from 8–25 days was 43 g. This is very similar to the maximum measured rates of growth of Brown and South Polar Skuas, although some populations of the latter species show much lower growth rates indicative of less favourable feeding conditions. Daily weight gain for South Polar Skua chicks averaged 46 g at Cape Hallett (Reid 1966), but only 37 g for A chicks and 33 g for B chicks at Signy Island (Hemmings 1984), and 35 g for all chicks combined (predominantly broods of one) at Cape Royds (Young 1963). For Brown Skua chicks, daily weight gain averaged 49 g for single chicks, 45 g for A chicks and 39 g for B chicks at Marion Island (some of these fed by two males at the nest) (Williams 1980), 45 g for single chicks, 47 g for A chicks and 44 g at South Georgia (Osbourne 1985), but only 32 g for chicks at Antipodes Island, New Zealand (Moors 1980). Given that Brown Skuas are rather larger and heavier than Great Skuas or South Polar Skuas, their chick daily weight gains ought to be larger, but the difference in weight gain suggest that chick growth may be of value as an indicator of food availability during the breeding season.

Weights, weight gain and measurement of Long-tailed Skua chicks of known

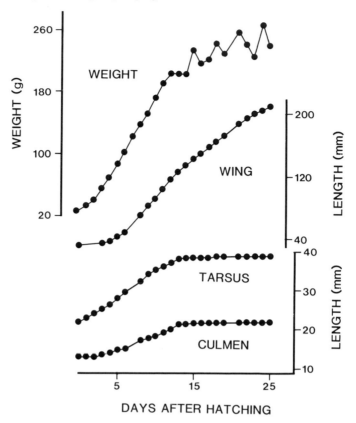

Fig. 81   Growth curves for Long-tailed Skua chicks, showing the differences in timing of growth of the tarsus, bill, wing and weight. From de Korte (1986).

ages were given by de Korte (1986). He found that a logistic equation fitted the pattern of weight gain of chicks in East Greenland well. However, Maher (1974) found that weight gain in the chicks of Arctic, Long-tailed and Pomarine Skuas in northern Alaska was extremely variable between years and sites, depending on food availability. In years when food was scarce, chicks grew more slowly, particularly towards the end of their development. The growth pattern is better described by a Gompertz equation in these seasons.

In all skuas, tarsus and bill develop rapidly during the first half of chick growth, whereas wing growth starts slowly and then accelerates. This can be seen in the Long-tailed Skua chicks (Fig. 81) measured by de Korte (1986) and in South Polar Skua chicks (Fig. 82) measured by Hemmings (1984), as well as in Great and Arctic Skuas (Furness 1977).

FLEDGING SUCCESS

Fledging success, the proportion of chicks hatched that survives to fledge, tends to be very high (80–95%) in Great, Tristan, and Brown Skuas, and among Arctic Skuas at low latitude colonies, but very variable between sites and between years in South Polar Skuas and small skuas in the Arctic (Table 48). The fledging success of South Polar Skuas decreases with increasing latitude, but is as high as that of the Brown Skua at Signy Island, one of its northernmost breeding localities (Hemmings 1984).

Causes of chick losses

In my study population of Great Skuas on Foula in the mid 1970s, the birds successfully raised to fledging 93.3% of 1168 chicks hatched. Only 3% of chicks

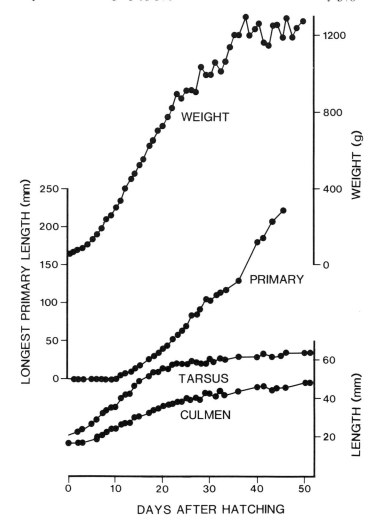

Fig. 82   Growth curves for South Polar Skua chicks, showing the differences in timing of growth of the tarsus, bill, wing and weight. From Reid (1967).

died of starvation and 3% were taken by predators, the only predator detected being adult conspecifics. Clutches of one egg suffered relatively more chick starvation than clutches of two (Table 50), and there was also a significantly higher number of chicks starved from B eggs than from A eggs in clutches of two (Table 51). The higher rate of chick starvation from clutches of one egg can only be due to inexperience or poor quality of birds with single-egg clutches, but starvation of B chicks in broods of two may be due to rare instances of sibling aggression in Great Skuas leading to brood reduction.

In the South Polar Skua, the reduction in fledging success is largely attributable to losses of B chicks as a consequence of sibling aggression, although the proximate causes of death may be exposure, starvation or predation by conspecifics (Hemmings 1984). Chick losses can be particularly high if there are severe storms during the chick rearing period or if sea ice fails to break up to allow adults to feed at sea close to their breeding area.

By contrast, low fledging success in small skuas in the Arctic can usually be attributed to high predation rates by Arctic Foxes, Snowy Owls or other predators rather than to predation by conspecifics, or to starvation of chicks due to food shortage. Studies of the Snowy Owl pair that nested for a number of years on Fetlar in the 1970s showed that Arctic Skua chicks represented nearly a quarter of all the prey taken by the owls to feed their own chicks! The selection pressure must be strong for small skua chicks to be highly cryptic and to grow as rapidly as possible in order to avoid being located by a predator, while minimising the food demands placed on their parents if food is scarce. Among chicks of *Catharacta* skuas, protection by a parent against attacks from conspecifics must be a high priority, while the ability to store fat reserves will help chicks to survive through periods of bad weather.

CHAPTER 13

Population dynamics

Of all the ocean birds that I have had to do with the skua has the greatest hold on life. It has the cat's nine lives and a few extra for good measure. Whenever we desired to keep one of the various birds we caught for either scientific or commercial purposes, a sharp blow on the head usually finished it instantly. Not so the skua. One calm day we were out in a boat trying to capture a white-headed petrel, when a wandering skua was tempted by the bait. As I had never had one to dissect, I thought we might capture this one. It was easily hooked and drawn into the boat, given a sharp rap on the head that we thought was sufficient to kill it, but this only annoyed it, so it was given a regular knockout blow as we certainly had no desire to see it suffer. It fell into the bottom of the boat apparently dead, but soon revived. Then the second mate, who was pulling stroke oar, grabbed it and gave it a blow sufficient to kill a good healthy ox and wrung its neck. Now it did seem finished, and we devoted our energies to the capture of the white-headed petrel aforesaid. A few moments later the second mate gave a yelp – the skua had given him a nasty jab in the leg and was scrambling over the gunwale of the boat. We did not try to detain it, for it surely had earned its freedom.

Murphy (1936)

The rate of increase or decline of a skua population depends on the adult survival rate, juvenile survival rate, age at first breeding, breeding success of the population, and the rates of emigration and immigration. Obtaining data to allow these parameters to be estimated requires a long and detailed study, and none has provided measurements of all of these for any one skua population. However, enough data exists to allow a comparison between skua taxa and to provide some insights into the most important influences on skua population dynamics.

ADULT SURVIVAL RATES

Skuas are long-lived seabirds. Andersson (1981) found that 90% of a small sample of marked Long-tailed Skuas in N. Sweden returned to their territories the next year, and de Korte (1986) estimated adult annual survival rate of this species in East Greenland at 89%. On Fair Isle, breeding Arctic Skuas had survival rates that varied between different time periods. From 1973–75, average annual survival rate was 88.6%. During these years the colony was the subject of an extensive study and there was probably no shooting of skuas by crofters. However, from 1948–62 the average adult survival rate was 80.1% and from 1976–78 it was 74.7% (O'Donald 1983), and it is known that shooting of breeding adults occurred then because several bodies were found with shot wounds. The estimate of 88.6% for 1973–75 is therefore the most likely to reflect the true annual survival rate of Arctic Skuas on Fair Isle when not subjected to human persecution.

Survival rates of large skuas seem to be slightly higher; 91% in the Brown Skua at Signy Island (Burton 1968), 92.5% in the Tristan Skua on Gough Island (three individuals disappeared between one breeding season and the next from 40 marked), 93% in the Great Skua in Shetland (Furness 1978), and 94% in the South Polar Skua on Ross Island (Wood 1971). The estimate for Great Skuas was derived from an analysis of ring recovery data, and it is typical of ring recovery data that survival rates are underestimated by comparison with results from studies of individually marked breeding birds. Nevertheless, all these estimates for *Catharacta* skuas are very similar. Since I analysed Great Skua ring recovery data up to 1974, there has undoubtedly been an increase in the illegal shooting of adult Great Skuas in Shetland, but it is difficult to make use of ring recovery data to examine whether this has had a detectable effect on adult survival rates since shot ringed birds are far more likely to be reported that birds that die for other reasons, and shot birds are often reported as 'found dead' because shooting is known to be illegal.

IMMATURE SURVIVAL RATES

Catharacta skuas do not normally return to their breeding areas at one year of age, except in the case of Tristan Skuas, where some young birds do not migrate away from the colony at all, and some one year old small skuas remain in wintering areas, so that it is impossible to estimate the survival rates of birds in their first year from observations of marked individuals at colonies.

O'Donald (1983) suggested that the survival rate of Arctic Skuas through their first year of life might be 70%, but this was only a guess to allow further calculations about population dynamics to be made. The only estimate of first year survival rate in skuas that is based on data is that for Shetland Great Skuas, which I derived from ring recovery data. This gave an estimated first year survival rate of 80% for Great Skuas (Furness 1978). These recovery data also suggested that survival rates of immatures through their second year of life were virtually the same as those of breeding adults.

AGE AT FIRST BREEDING

The age at which skuas start to breed varies between species and between colonies, but also varies a great deal between individuals, complicating comparisons between colonies or species. Most studies in which age at first breeding has been determined make use of ringing of chicks to provide birds of known age. With birds where age can be estimated with accuracy from the plumage, an alternative procedure is to examine breeders for evidence of immature plumage. This can be done with *Stercorarius* skuas but not with any confidence with *Catharacta* skuas.

Plumage changes with age in small skuas

Skua leg colour changes with age. In the Great Skua, chicks that are just emerging from the egg have pinkish legs, but once the chick has dried off and the legs have lost the curvature imposed by the eggshell they become a blue-grey colour. Only a matter of days later the legs begin to darken and become a very dusky brownish grey, and then almost black in large chicks. At this stage the legs often have small bluish or pink blotches and are soft-skinned and rather fat. By comparison, in adults, the legs are completely black, and heavily armoured with thick black scales. This last transition occurs after the young fledge, but before the birds are one year old, since all of the one and two year old Great Skuas I have examined have legs identical to those of breeding adults.

In the small skuas, leg colour develops more slowly. As a result, it can give a crude indication of the age of a bird up to about five years old. In all three small skuas the downy chicks have pale blue-grey legs and feet with a pinkish tinge, and as the chick grows the tip of the foot turns black. At fledging, the bird has pale blue legs and upper regions of the toes, pinkish-blue webs between the upper parts of the toes, and black on the distal half of the toes and webbing. The black on the legs spreads gradually down from the tibia and up from the toes, until eventually the entire leg and foot is black. According to Cramp & Simmons (1983) this progressive darkening takes up to five years, and proceeds faster in the Arctic Skua than in the Pomarine or Long-tailed Skuas.

Age (years)	Proportion of surface of tarsus that is black:		
	Arctic Skua	Pomarine Skua	Long-tailed Skua
0 (fledging)	0–10	0	0
1	30–90	0–20	0–20
2	50–100	0–50	0–20
3	80–100	10–90	5–80
4	90–100	80–100	—
5+	100	100	100

In addition to the progressive darkening of the legs during the first few years of life in small skuas, the length of the central tail feathers increases with age up to about the fifth year (Table 52). These details, together with the presence of barring on the underparts on some immatures, allows the age of young small skuas to be estimated. Such estimates must be made with caution, as aberrant individuals may also occur. One breeding Arctic Skua on Foula with heavily barred underparts was present for at least five years with no visible loss of the barring as it aged.

Age at first breeding in small skuas

By examining the plumage of breeding Pomarine Skuas in northern Alaska, Maher (1974) estimated that some Pomarine Skuas started to breed when only two years old, and that most started to breed before their fifth year. According to de Korte (1985), Long-tailed Skuas in Greenland usually start to breed when three years old. Belopolskii (1961) showed, by ringing Arctic Skua chicks in eastern

Murman, that some took up territories when only one year old, but such an early age of recruitment is unknown in Shetland. A ringing study at Fair Isle showed that Arctic Skuas there bred for the first time at three to seven years old. The average age of first breeding at Fair Isle was 4.2 years, both for females and for males (Davis 1976). The difference in age at first breeding between these two populations probably reflects the difficulty that Arctic Skuas have at low latitude colonies in establishing themselves as owners of a territory. However, the fact that Belopolskii shot a large number of Arctic Skuas in his study area, to obtain stomach contents samples, may have encouraged immatures to move into vacated territories at a particularly early age.

Maturity is deferred for longer in the South Polar Skua. Spellerberg (1971) found that most began to breed when five or six years old. Wood (1970) found that 0.8% of four year olds bred, increasing to 58% of eight year olds. His study population did not include ringed birds more than eight years old, so the maximum age of first breeding was not determined, but the mean age of first breeding was obviously greater than seven years.

Great Skuas similarly show a long period of immaturity, with a wide spread of age at first breeding. I was able to record the age of first breeding for some Great Skuas at Foula by observing cohort colour ringed birds taking up places in the colony. This allows accurate records of the ages of young first time breeders, but it becomes increasingly difficult to be confident that older colour ringed birds moving into a territory are first time breeders and have not already bred elsewhere. Some idea of the oldest ages at which Great Skuas first start to breed can be gained from the ages of birds on the nonbreeder club sites, but the problems of finding all first time breeders in a big colony make it impossible to give an accurate estimate of the mean age of first breeding. During my detailed work at Foula in the mid 1970s, when nesting numbers and density were very high, Great Skuas were never found breeding at three or four years old. Out of 60 individuals known to be nesting for the first time, only three were five years old, 19 were six, 27 were seven and 11 were eight years old. Observations at club sites showed that there were extremely few two year olds that returned to the colony, with most club birds being three, four or five years old. However, the clubs also had small numbers of six to ten year old birds present, indicating that some had probably not taken up territory until at least ten years old, and since Great Skuas often occupy a territory for a season before breeding, the oldest age of first breeding may be eleven years or more. Probably, a very small number of birds fail ever to establish themselves in a territory and remain attending the clubs throughout their life. It might be a reasonable guess to suggest that the mean age of first breeding of Great Skuas at Foula was about seven or eight years in the mid 1970s.

The mean age of first breeding of Great Skuas is not known for other colonies, but the earliest ages of breeding have been recorded at several sites. At Fair Isle, a large part of the Great Skua breeding population consists of birds ringed as chicks at Foula, and so of known age. There, three individuals were found breeding for the first time when four years old, and another four at five years old. At St Kilda I found three Great Skuas, colour ringed as chicks on Foula, nesting when four, five and six years old. I do not know if they had bred previously, but even if they had not, they were clearly starting to breed at a younger age than they do at Foula. Similarly, a colour ringed bird nested at the new colony on the Shiants when only four years old. No three year old Great Skua has yet been found to breed, but birds may breed when four years old at small and rapidly increasing colonies, whereas at the large dense colony on Foula, no four year olds, and few five year olds, managed to breed in the mid 1970s. Clearly age of first breeding is flexible, depending on the amount of competition for territories or perhaps for other resources.

BREEDING SUCCESS AND POPULATION STABILITY

Considering Arctic Skuas in Shetland, reasonable guesses of population factors would seem to be: annual adult survival 85%, annual juvenile survival 60%, mean age at first breeding 4.2 years, breeding success 1.0 chicks fledged per pair per year. These values taken together would result in a population increase of 2.3% per year, similar to the sorts of rates of increase observed in much of Shetland over recent decades. On the Arctic tundra, small skuas have a breeding productivity that averages only about one-quarter that of Arctic Skuas in Shetland. For their populations to remain in balance, as they obviously do overall, skuas on the tundra would need to have either a higher survival rate or earlier age of first breeding, or both, to compensate for their lower breeding success. Juvenile survival of skuas from the tundra is unlikely to be higher than that of Arctic Skuas from Shetland, since the birds fledged in the Arctic are not better fed than those in Shetland, have a longer migration to undertake to wintering areas, and migrate later because their breeding season is delayed in the far north, so they are more likely to meet harsh autumn weather. Belopolskii's and Maher's observations suggest that breeding may well start at an earlier age in the Arctic.

The difference in the earliest age of first breeding among Great Skuas at different colonies (though all fledged at Foula) indicates that recruitment is responsive to density-dependent influences, presumably involving competition for territories. As a consequence, skua populations may be partly buffered against changes in environmental conditions; breeding production may increase when population density is reduced, and this has important implications for the conservation and management of skuas (Chapter 16).

CHAPTER 14

Pollutants

Skuas may occasionally become oiled or snared by artefacts, but the most serious problem is presented by toxic chemical pollution. The members of the Great Skua superspecies appear to be among the most consistently contaminated seabirds, with average levels of 7 ppm DDE and 17 ppm PCBs in Scotland ... 2.5 DDE and 3.5 PCBs at Tristan da Cunha ... and at least one part per million of one or the other of these compounds in the Antarctic.

Bourne 1976

Many chemical pollutants in the environment are taken up by wildlife and become concentrated in animal tissues. Predators feeding on contaminated prey may then accumulate even higher levels of pollutants, and so top predators can often provide the most sensitive monitor of pollutants, and may be particularly vulnerable to their harmful effects. Thus, birds of prey provided one of the clearest indications of the harmful environmental effects of DDT because the high levels accumulated by birds such as Peregrines and Sparrowhawks caused eggshell thinning, reduced breeding success and caused declines in their populations. The story of organochlorine pollution and its effects on birds of prey is now well known, and has been particularly well described by Newton (1979) and Ratcliffe (1980).

Similarly, the use of alkyl-mercury seed dressings in Scandinavia caused a considerable increase in the levels of mercury in the terrestrial, freshwater and adjacent marine ecosystems. Mercury is particularly prone to accumulate in fish, and this was quickly apparent because birds of prey such as Sea Eagles and Ospreys were seriously affected by mercury accumulated from their food (Berg *et al* 1966, Helander *et al* 1982).

In both these cases, harmful effects to top predators alerted conservationists to a serious pollution problem and steps were quickly taken to reduce the use of DDT throughout Europe, and mercury seed dressings in Scandinavia. These examples demonstrate the value of top predators as 'Environmental Canaries', indicators of ecosystem health. Skuas are top predators in the marine ecosystem, and as a consequence they are obvious species to use as a monitor of pollutant levels in the seas and oceans. The *Stercorarius* skuas are much less useful in this respect since they feed at a lower trophic level than *Catharacta* skuas, and during the breeding season to a much larger extent in terrestrial food chains. As a result, this chapter deals almost exclusively with the *Catharacta* skuas, and particularly with the Great Skua since it is reasonable to assume that southern hemisphere skuas are exposed to lower levels of pollution than those found in the North Atlantic.

ORGANOCHLORINES

When I started visiting Shetland to study Great Skuas in 1971, I was aware that levels of organochlorines would be of interest in these birds, so I began sending samples of livers, muscle and body fat from Great Skuas that I found freshly dead as a result of accidents or shooting, to the Institute of Terrestrial Ecology research laboratory at Monks Wood, Huntingdon, or to Dr Jim Bogan at Veterinary Pharmacology in Glasgow University who was analysing samples for Bill Bourne. These samples went down by post, sealed in margarine tubs. As the Foula mailboat only sailed once a week in those days, and often did not sail at all if the weather was bad, my Great Skua tissues could often stay in the Foula Post Office for five or six days, and sometimes two weeks, before going to the mainland. In 1971 there were no deep freezers on Foula in which I could store the samples, so Harry Gear, the postmaster, would tie a string around the parcel and hang it from the ceiling of the tiny island Post Office so that the abundant house mice found it more difficult to get at the source of the exciting smells that leaked out of it. Harry considered this solution preferable to trapping the mice, and never once suggested that the packages really should not be left to smell out the Post Office. I believe that all the samples did actually get through the postal system, but I can imagine that the people receiving them may have been less than enthusiastic about opening the margarine tubs!

Some problems with organochlorine analysis

The organochlorines generally found in seabirds are the insecticides DDT (Dichloro-diphenyl-trichloro-ethane) and its metabolites DDD and DDE, dieldrin (1, 2, 3, 4, 10, 10-hexachloro–6, 7, epoxy-1, 4, 4a, 5, 6, 7, 8, 8a, octahydro-1, 4-endo-exo-5, 8-dimethanonaphthalene), and the industrial compounds PCBs (polychlorinated biphenyls). DDT is quickly converted in animal tissues into DDE, which is a much more stable compound, so that residues of this pesticide are usually measured as DDE, and high levels of DDT itself are often taken to indicate contamination of samples. Organochlorines in general are lipophilic, and so dissolve in the fat of animals. Dieldrin, DDT, DDD and DDE each produce unique and readily distinguishable peaks on a trace recorded from a gas-liquid chromatograph, and the height of each peak can be measured to give the amount of the compound in the tissue sample analysed. PCBs are also lipid soluble, and can also be measured by analysis of the peaks obtained by gas-liquid chromatography.

Organochlorine levels in seabirds are normally determined in lipid extracted from eggs, or from samples of liver, muscle or body fat taken from adults. Many analyses have been performed on birds found dead or that have died in convulsions. Not surprisingly, concentrations in the liver of starved birds tend to be extremely high, since body fat reserves will have been used up. However, the total body burden may be quite small, since mobilisation of fat reserves removes the main store of organochlorines and causes the high liver levels. Nearly half of the determinations of organochlorines in 250 seabirds listed in Bourne (1976) were samples from individuals found dead from unknown causes, and in many cases the organochlorine levels tabulated include mixtures of healthy and starved birds, with no indication of total body burdens. Such analyses tell us rather little about organochlorine pollution of the environment, and can give a misleading impression of the variation in levels of contamination within a population. For example, one of the highest levels of PCBs ever recorded in a wild bird was 1079 ppm (parts per million, equivalent to mg per kg), found in the liver of a Great Skua that was picked up dying in west Wales, but no healthy Great Skua collected at breeding colonies has had more than 99 ppm of PCBs in the liver. The bird found in Wales probably died of PCB poisoning, but this would have occurred because the bird had starved and redistributed the organochlorines that had been held, inert, in its body fat and muscle lipids.

The distribution of organochlorines between organs varies greatly from bird to bird and it may be that this information could be of use in the assessment of the pollution condition of the bird, but at present we do not know enough about the reasons for the observed tissue distribution patterns, except that healthy seabirds have most of the residues in fat reserves, whereas high levels in the liver and other organs tend to imply poor condition.

One technical problem that PCBs present is that they exist as many different isomers, or molecular forms, each of which produces a series of peaks when analysed on a gas-liquid chromatograph. Thus PCB residues give a complex series of peaks on a sheet of paper that has somehow to be converted to a single value for the amount of PCB present. Since the proportions of the different isomers vary according both to the origins and natures of the PCBs originally in the environment, and also as a result of degradation of PCBs within the animal – and some isomers are more readily broken down than others – it is impossible to give an exact and accurate value for the quantity of PCB present in a bird tissue sample. This is usually best estimated with reference to a particular PCB standard, such as Aroclor 1262, or to a single particular peak, and so two different analytical laboratories may quote slightly different values for the PCB level measured off the same trace. In addition, because PCB analysis is fairly complex, results can also differ between laboratories because of slight differences in procedures. For critical comparisons it is preferable to compare results obtained from a single analyst, or to intercalibrate between laboratories.

Robinson *et al* (1967) showed that young seabirds reach a dynamic equilibrium of organochlorine levels within a short period of exposure; within the first year of life in Shags and Kittiwakes in east Britain. One of their main foods, Sandeels, showed a pronounced seasonal cycle in organochlorine levels, suggesting that the residence time of organochlorines in animal tissues is relatively short. That study, and that of Tanabe *et al* (1984) showed that organochlorine levels were higher at higher trophic levels, and the latter study showed that the more lipophilic and less metabolisable organochlorines tended to represent a higher proportion of the total in animals at higher trophic levels. This indicates that much of the organochlorine burden is broken down and lost, but that this is a selective process. Seabirds therefore provide a slightly different measure of organochlorine pollutants than would samples of seawater or plankton, but they have the advantage of con-centrating the pollutants into more easily measurable amounts and they average out short-term and small-scale geographic variation. They therefore provide a better general measure of pollution levels for an area of sea or ocean.

Since seabirds may show pronounced annual cycles in body weight due to regulated changes in fat reserves, levels of organochlorines, as assessed in terms of their concentration in tissues, may give quite misleading impressions. A study of Herring Gulls from Lake Michigan showed that maximum body burdens of organochlorines were found in midwinter, when the birds had their largest fat stores, but that the highest tissue concentrations occurred in midsummer, when the gulls reached their leanest stage (Anderson and Hickey 1976). Great Skuas show a particularly large decrease in stored lipid over the summer, and so it is probable that the total amount of organochlorines in the body will fall over the period of fat mobilisation, but that the concentration of organochlorines in body tissues will increase, particularly in the liver. Fortunately, almost all of the adult skuas sampled for organochlorine analyses have been collected as healthy breeding adults during the incubation period, early during the period of weight loss. It would be risky to compare organochlorine concentrations in tissues from birds collected at different times of the year, and the difficulties of calculating total body burdens have prevented people from expressing organochlorines in that way, even though it would be the best method for comparisons.

Seabird eggs provide a more straightforward index of organochlorine levels and also avoid the need to kill healthy birds. Levels in eggs usually, but not always, correlate with levels in the birds laying them. However, Mineau (1982) found that organochlorine levels increased with laying sequence in Herring Gulls. This is probably due to an increased use of fat reserves by the female as successive eggs are formed. Body fat will contain more organochlorine residues than lipid derived directly from food. It may be a common phenomenon in seabird clutches, but the difference between first-, second- and third-laid eggs reported by Mineau was small compared to differences found between birds or between populations, so should not seriously affect the value of eggs as indicators of organochlorine levels in seabird populations, and hence in marine ecosystems.

Levels of organochlorines in different skua populations

As expected, the Arctic Skuas that have been analysed for organochlorines had much lower levels than those found in Great Skuas (Table 54). Three Arctic Skuas from north Scotland, collected between 1971 and 1975, had very similar levels of DDE and PCBs to a sample of ten collected in Iceland in 1973, and these were about an order of magnitude lower than levels in Great Skuas. Although PCB levels were very closely similar between Scottish and Icelandic skuas, DDE levels tended to be slightly higher in the Icelandic samples, so that Arctic Skuas and Great Skuas in Iceland both tended to have lower ratios of PCB to DDE than did conspecifics in Scotland. This suggests that levels of DDE were higher in the western North Atlantic, and that the ratio of PCB to DDE may increase across the North Atlantic from west to east. Similar patterns have been found in other species of seabirds, and, in addition, it has been found that the ratio of PCBs to DDE varies between species. Kittiwakes tend to have particularly high ratios, skuas much lower ones, but the significance of this is not clear.

I have not found any data on the levels of organochlorines in Long-tailed Skuas, Pomarine Skuas, or Arctic Skuas from high latitude breeding areas, but these would almost certainly be low, even by comparison with the relatively low levels in Icelandic and Scottish Arctic Skuas.

When compared with the levels found in Great Skuas, other *Catharacta* skuas also show much less organochlorine contamination. The discovery of detectable amounts of DDE in skuas, penguins and other seabirds in the Antarctic (Tatton and Ruzicka 1967) demonstrated in a very striking manner that wildlife throughout the world has been exposed to DDE contamination, because DDE is transported not only in wildlife, but also in the atmosphere, and eventually is deposited and taken up by plants and animals in remote regions. Skuas in the Antarctic have higher concentrations of DDE than do any other Antarctic seabirds because they stand at the apex of the Southern Ocean food chain. The measured DDE levels in South Polar Skuas, which may accumulate DDE during their winter migrations into the northern hemisphere, and in Brown Skuas, which apparently remain in fairly lightly contaminated southern latitudes, are usually less than the DDE levels generally found in Great Skuas. However, a single Tristan Skua contained levels of DDE similar to the highest found in Great Skuas (Table 54). The southern hemisphere skuas seem to have very much less PCB than is found in Great Skuas, and the ratio of PCBs to DDE in the southern hemisphere skuas is particularly low by comparison with the ratio in Great or Arctic Skuas, indicating that PCBs have not been carried into southern hemisphere marine ecosystems to any great extent.

Changes in organochlorine levels over the years

DDT was first developed as an insecticide in the 1940s and its use rapidly increased until its harmful effects on wildlife were discovered in the late 1960s. Thereafter, its use in Europe and North America declined dramatically, until, by the late 1970s, it had been largely replaced by less persistent pesticides. However, the use of DDT has continued to increase worldwide, predominantly now in third world countries where no other pesticides are as cheap and effective against many major pests and vectors of diseases. Dieldrin came into use in the mid 1950s, but its harmful effects on predators were also realised in the late 1960s, and its use was quickly restricted. By contrast, PCBs are not insecticides, but are industrial organochlorines that have a wide variety of uses, particularly as insulating com-

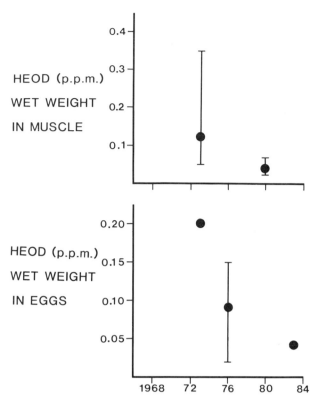

Fig. 83   Levels of HEOD (dieldrin) in Great Skua tissues and eggs collected in Shetland. Dots show geometric means, and vertical bars show ranges.

pounds, plasticisers and lubricants. These chemicals have been manufactured and in use since about 1930, and their tendency to accumulate in the fat of wildlife at the top of food chains was not appreciated until it was noticed that analyses of DDE levels produced numerous unexpected peaks near to, but quite distinct from, peaks produced by DDT, DDD and DDE in gas-liquid chromatographs. These unidentified peaks were initially ignored when they were small relative to the levels of organochlorine pesticide peaks, but in some samples of tissues from birds of prey the unidentified peaks were too large to ignore. Eventually they were identified as being due to PCBs, and these were found to have some similar toxic effects to organochlorine pesticides. Monsanto, the principal manufacturer of PCBs, introduced some voluntary restrictions in the uses of PCBs in processes where environmental contamination seemed likely, such as their incorporation into paints. However, production of PCBs worldwide has not been reduced, and the restrictions in PCB usages in North America and Europe appear to have had little or no effect in reducing PCB levels in wildlife. One reason for this may be that PCBs are even more resistant to biodegradation than are the organochlorine pesticides, and so there is bound to be a long time-lag between reduced emission of PCBs into ecosystems and a fall in their levels in animals high in the food chain.

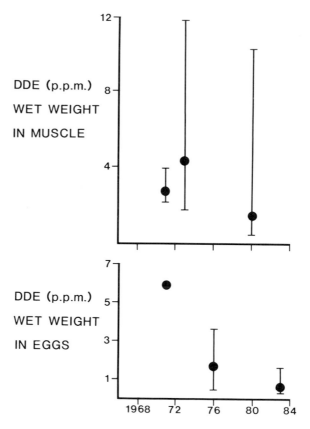

Fig. 84   Changes in levels of DDE in Great Skuas. Dots show geometric means, and vertical bars show ranges.

Levels of dieldrin and DDE in Great Skua tissues and in eggs have clearly declined during the 1970s (Figures 83 and 84). No other skua species has been analysed over a period of years, so we cannot say how levels in Arctic, Antarctic or sub-Antarctic skuas have changed, but it is quite likely that there have not been any decreases in DDE levels in these more remote areas, although, of course, these populations generally have had much lower DDE levels than those found in Great Skuas.

PCB levels in Great Skuas show a less consistent trend than those of DDE or dieldrin. In muscle samples, there is little evidence to suggest that PCB levels have changed over the period, except that the highest individual values recorded have increased from 32 ppm in 1971 to 47 ppm in 1974, and 72 ppm in 1980 (Figure 85). Liver samples suggest that PCB levels increased between 1971 and 1980, with maximum individual values increasing from 18 to 99 ppm. Egg samples seem to show a different pattern. PCB levels in eggs appear to have fallen since reaching a peak in 1974 (Figure 85). Why these results for eggs disagree with those

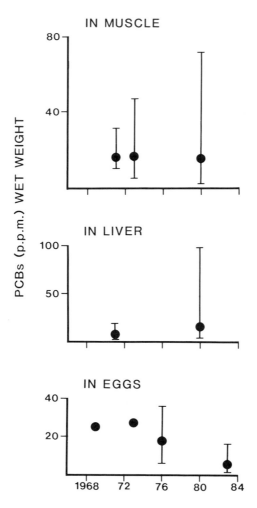

Fig. 85   Changes in levels of PCBs in Great Skuas. Dots show geometric means, and vertical bars show ranges.

for tissues is not clear. As is usually the case with organochlorine analyses, the sample sizes analysed were rather small, and this makes the comparisons less reliable. The feeding conditions for adults during egg laying may have quite a large effect on organochlorine levels in the eggs they produce, depending on the extent to which yolk lipids are derived from body fat rather than from ingested food. For this reason, the levels measured in eggs may be less reliable as indicators of general environmental contamination than those obtained from body tissue samples, where tissues have been collected by shooting healthy birds.

The evidence suggests that PCB levels in tissues have probably increased in Great Skuas since 1970 rather than decreased. This conclusion would agree with results of PCB analyses in Golden Eagles from Rhum (which feed largely on seabirds), so that the evidence points to a widespread, but possibly slight, increase in PCB contamination of the North Atlantic marine ecosystem.

Influences of age and sex

Since nearly half of all the adult Great Skuas on Foula have been ringed as chicks, and so are of known age, the Foula Great Skuas present an exceptional opportunity to examine the relationship between organochlorine levels and the age of the bird. Sandra Muirhead analysed tissues from 20 ringed adult Great Skuas between four and 15 years old that had been shot to protect lambs, and found that there was no correlation at all between the levels of DDE or PCBs in body fat or in muscle and the age of the bird, but that DDE and PCB levels in the liver appeared to show a tendency to increase with age (Figures 86 and 87). However, there was a very high degree of individual variation and the rank correlations between levels and age are weak (0.40 and 0.36) and not statistically significant, so we should conclude from this that organochlorine levels in adult Great Skuas are not related to age for birds more than four years old. Levels in fledglings are very low, and hardly any higher than in eggs, so the organochlorine burdens must increase with age at first, but clearly they reach a dynamic equilibrium while Great Skuas are still fairly young. On average, birds more than four years old presumably lose organochlorines at the same rate as they take them in.

One of the routes by which organochlorines can be lost is via egg production, since the egg yolk is rich in lipid, and organochlorines are transferred into eggs from the female body stores as well as from food. Bogan and Newton (1977) found that a female Sparrowhawk killed after laying had put more than half her total body load of DDE into her six eggs. We might expect males to carry higher organochlorine burdens than females, since males do not have this route of elimination open to them. In the Great Skua the evidence for this is very slight. In the sample of 20 adults analysed, there were no statistically significant differences between the sexes in levels of DDE in liver, muscle or adipose tissue, or in levels of PCBs in muscle or adipose tissue, although the females had a significantly lower mean level of PCBs in the liver than did males. Perhaps the general lack of clear differences in organochlorine levels between the sexes in Great Skuas is due to the small clutch size of this species. Laying only one or two eggs gives the female little opportunity to reduce her organochlorine burden relative to that of males. Also, the great individual variation in organochlorine levels regardless of age or sex, which presumably relates to such factors as individual feeding specialisations and differences in wintering ranges, means that any relationships with age or sex are rather difficult to detect without having enormous sample sizes. In general, it seems that, at least above four years of age, the age and sex of a Great Skua has little or no importance in determining tissue organochlorine levels, and in addition individual variation is enormous.

Effects of organochlorines on skuas

There is no clear evidence that any skua population has been adversely affected by the levels of organochlorine pollutants it carries. Great Skuas in Iceland in 1973 had the highest levels of organochlorine pesticides recorded in skuas, but little is known of their breeding biology or changes in numbers. Compared to these Icelandic birds, Great Skuas on Foula in the mid 1970s had slightly lower levels of dieldrin and DDE, but almost exactly the same levels of PCBs. Great Skua numbers breeding in northern Britain have been increasing, and the fledgling

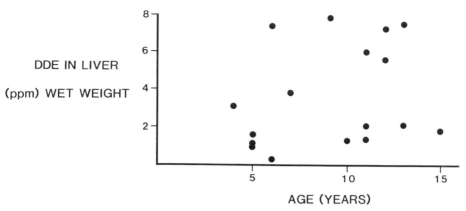

Fig. 86 Relationship between DDE levels in the liver and the age of Great
Skuas. From Muirhead (1986).

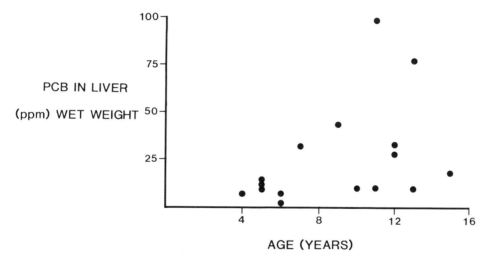

Fig. 87 Relationship between PCB levels in the liver and the age of Great
Skuas. From Muirhead (1986).

production of Shetland Great Skuas is higher than that of most other skua
populations, so any harmful effect of organochlorines could only be slight and
inconsequential in terms of population dynamics. Nevertheless, it is possible
that adult survival or breeding success might be less than it could be without
organochlorine contaminants. It would be useful to know whether the recorded
levels of organochlorines have detectable effects on Great Skuas.

The fact that dieldrin, DDE and PCBs tend to occur together, and that levels
of each pollutant in different individuals within populations are often correlated,
makes it difficult to relate harmful effects to any one organochlorine alone. Fur-

thermore, different species of seabird show widely different sensitivities to toxic effects of organochlorines. Levels that would be highly toxic to pelecaniforms such as Gannets or Brown Pelicans appear to have no detectable effect on gulls. Owing to the habits that skuas share with their relatives the gulls, of opportunistic feeding and scavenging, skuas may also be much less sensitive to pollutants than birds such as pelecaniforms that are less likely to be exposed to the wide ranges of natural toxins that scavenging seabirds would normally experience.

All chlorinated hydrocarbon compounds (organochlorines) appear to be capable of damage to the nervous system and liver of vertebrate animals. However, these substances are lipid-soluble, and so are held mainly in body fat, where they are relatively inert and harmless. Organochlorine toxicity becomes a serious problem only as body fat is mobilised when the bird is either unable to meet daily energy requirements from its food, or is reducing its fat stores in order to follow a regulated seasonal cycle of body weight change. Great Skuas show an unusually large fluctuation in fat stores through the year, and their enormous mobilisation of fat in the breeding season could make them particularly prone to developing increased levels of organochlorines in the liver during the summer months.

One of the best known effects of organochlorine pollution is eggshell thinning. This has been a major factor in the population declines of some predatory birds. Laboratory studies have shown that DDE, the stable metabolite of DDT, is the major cause of eggshell thinning, through its effects on calcium metabolism. Dieldrin may also cause thinning to a small extent, but seems to be far less effective than DDE in this regard. PCBs may not cause shell thinning at all.

Shells of freshly laid eggs can be up to 15% thinner than normal without any noticeable reduction in their chance of hatching successfully, but a reduction in shell thickness of more than 15% leads to an increase in egg breakage and lowered hatching success (Blus *et al* 1974). Shell thickness indices for Great Skua eggs in the British Museum collection in Tring averaged 1.78 for 30 eggs collected in Iceland before 1940, 1.66 for 58 eggs collected in the Faeroe Islands before 1940, and 1.74 for 59 eggs collected in Shetland before 1940. None of these eggs could have been affected by DDE or dieldrin and so provide a control against which to compare contaminated egg shell thicknesses. Statistically, the pre-1940 Faeroese sample had a significantly thinner shell than the Icelandic or Shetland samples, but the reason for this is not known. However, the thickness index for 12 Icelandic eggs collected in 1973 was 1.76, and an identical value was found for 95 eggs measured at Foula in 1976. Neither of these values is significantly different from the pre-1940 indices for the same populations, showing that DDE levels in Great Skuas are too low to have any effect on shell thickness, and so are almost certainly too low to affect Great Skua breeding success.

Gannets containing about twice the concentrations of DDE found in Icelandic Great Skuas laid eggs with shells 20% thinner than normal and it has been shown that hatching success of Gannet eggs at Canadian colonies has been inversely correlated with levels of DDE. Over recent years the decline in DDE levels has been associated with an increase in hatching success. However, Herring Gulls in Wisconsin with DDE levels about ten times higher than in Icelandic Great Skuas showed only a 10% reduction in eggshell thickness and no reduction in breeding success. Since Great Skuas probably have much closer physiological similarities to Herring Gulls than to Gannets, it seems likely that DDE levels in Great Skuas have never reached the levels that would have influenced their reproduction, and now that DDE levels in Great Skuas are clearly declining it is most unlikely that this pollutant will ever threaten Great Skua breeding performance.

More concern may need to be directed towards PCBs, because levels of these compounds appear to be increasing in marine environments and in Great Skuas. Curiously enough, despite the numerous studies of the effects of PCBs on breeding success of laboratory and wild birds, we do not really know whether or not PCBs affect seabirds. Hens fed PCBs have been shown to produce normal numbers of eggs of normal size and normal shell thickness, but with reduced hatchability. Embryo death during hatching is particularly common with high levels of PCBs in hens' eggs (Scott *et al* 1975). Gross deformities of embryos may also occur (Tumasonis *et al* 1973). Other laboratory studies have shown that PCBs are toxic to a wide range of birds, and that the degree of toxicity varies between PCB isomers, depending on the details of molecular structure. Field studies have produced rather less clear results. A detailed study of Herring Gull populations on the Great Lakes with differing levels of PCBs, showed that hatching success was least at the colonies where PCB levels were highest, and that much of the reduction in hatching success was due to embryo death. Eggs taken from these colonies and hatched in incubators showed exactly the same pattern as found in the field, with eggs from colonies where PCB levels were highest having the lowest hatching success. This implies that the levels of PCBs in the eggs affected egg hatchability and not just the incubation behaviour of the parents (Gilman *et al* 1977). Gilman then tried to demonstrate the toxic effects of PCBs by injecting doses into relatively uncontaminated eggs in the field and monitoring their hatching success in comparison with control eggs injected with the solvent alone. Although the controls had a much reduced hatching success than normal because the solvent proved to be toxic, the eggs given high doses of PCBs in the solvent showed no greater reduction in hatching success than that caused by the solvent alone! Gilman and his co-workers suggested that PCBs may not be embryotoxic but might affect the laying female in such a way that the eggs she produced were of poorer quality (Gilman *et al* 1978).

Harris and Osborn (1981) performed a careful field experiment in which they implanted PCBs into Puffins and monitored their behaviour and breeding performance. Although dosed Puffins took up the PCBs to peak levels of 2 to 48 ppm wet weight in the liver, levels which are similar to those found in Great Skuas since the early 1970s, the dosed birds showed no differences whatsoever in breeding success or behaviour compared to controls. This unexpected result suggests that PCBs may be much less toxic to seabirds than had been thought. However, some other explanations are possible. PCBs might only be toxic in conjunction with DDE, or Puffins may happen to be particularly insensitive to PCB toxicity. Possibly of crucial importance, Puffins on the Isle of May, where this experiment was carried out, have been increasing in numbers at an unusually high rate. These birds carry large fat reserves that provide a relatively inert store for the PCBs and so may mean that the physiological effects of PCB toxicity would not be manifest unless the birds were stressed and had to deplete their fat stores. It is possible that rather different results might have been obtained at a colony where Puffins had a less easy life. In most studies where levels of PCBs in eggs and adults have been examined, the levels in eggs correlate closely with levels in the laying female, indicating that lipids in the egg are partly derived from the body stores. Harris and Osborn found no such correlation in the dosed Puffins and their eggs, which suggests that they were able to produce the egg directly from ingested food, which also indicates the unusually favourable conditions then prevailing at that colony.

These somewhat confusing results make it difficult to assess whether present PCB levels in Great Skuas should cause concern. Certainly the trend for PCB levels to increase in marine ecosystems and top predators should be considered carefully, but do PCB levels present a threat to Great Skuas? We might expect that they could reduce egg hatchability, but I have not been able to study hatching success in relation to PCB levels within clutches in the way that has been done for some other species, partly because I have not had an opportunity to perform large-scale analyses of PCB levels, and partly because removal of one egg from a Great Skua nest will almost certainly reduce the incubation drive of adults left with only a single egg. In effect you could end up studying the effect on hatching success of your study of hatching success! What can be done more easily is to compare the hatching success, rates of embryo death and chick death at hatching between Great Skua populations contaminated with PCBs and populations of other skuas that have much lower PCB levels, or populations of gulls, terns and other seabirds in which PCB levels are thought to be low. Such populations of uncontaminated seabirds are taken to provide a base line showing the amount of egg failure that might be expected. When this kind of comparison is made it is difficult to be sure that it is a fair test. Breeding performance of Great Skua populations with high levels of PCBs should ideally be compared with breeding performance of Great Skua populations with low levels of PCBs, or with the breeding performance of the same populations from earlier times when no PCBs were present in the environment. Unfortunately, no suitable historical data exist, and all present Great Skua populations are contaminated with PCBs to a similar high level. Great Skuas might have a high proportion of addled eggs because of the way in which they incubate, or because the nest sites they select often allow flooding and the eggs to be chilled, rather than as a result of the effects of PCBs.

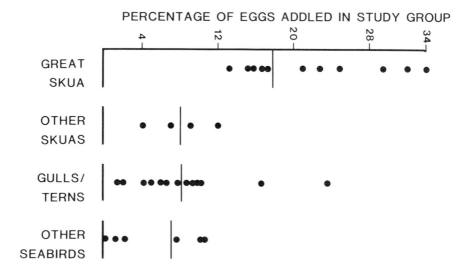

Fig. 88 Proportion of addled eggs produced by Great Skuas compared with proportions produced by other seabirds. Horizontal lines represent sample means and dots indicate values from each separate study.

PERCENTAGE DYING DURING HATCHING

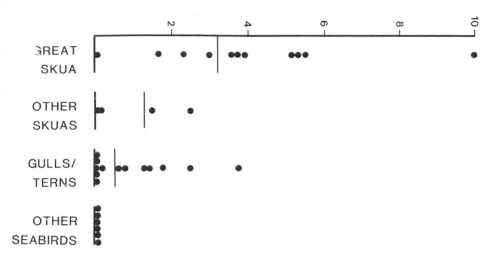

Fig. 89 *Proportions of Great Skua chicks dying during hatching compared with proportions for other seabirds. Horizontal lines represent sample means and dots indicate values from each separate study.*

The comparison between Great Skuas and other skuas seems likely to provide the most satisfactory of these comparisons, which must be treated with some caution because of the numerous ecological factors that might have effects on the results obtained.

On Foula and Fair Isle, studies of Great Skua nesting in the mid 1970s showed that an average of 17.7% of eggs which survived through the incubation period failed to hatch. Further, 3.2% of all the chicks that began to hatch died before emerging from the eggshell, and six out of 1,437 chicks which hatched were grossly deformed, most often with incompletely developed eyes or twisted bills. Are these unusually high values? Comparison with studies of other seabirds suggests that they are indeed high (Figs. 88, 89), and statistical tests confirm this (Furness and Hutton 1980). Great Skuas appear to produce twice as many addled eggs as normal and two to eight times as many chicks die while emerging from the egg as would be expected from the results of the other studies. However, it is not certain that these differences are due to PCB effects. Addled eggs result both from embryo death and from some eggs being infertile when laid. Of 122 addled Great Skua eggs examined on Foula in 1976, 70% showed no embryonic development while 30% had dead embryos at various stages of development. These values imply that 12% of Great Skua eggs on Foula are infertile when laid, while 6% of viable eggs suffer embryo death. Since PCBs are not thought to affect egg fertility, the high level of infertile eggs probably cannot be attributed to PCB effects, but embryo death, and particularly death of chicks during hatching, are consistent with PCB poisoning, as are the chick deformities recorded at Foula.

Furness and Hutton (1980) suggested that these signs of increased egg infertility and embryo death might be the result of PCB or heavy metal pollution, but that this could not be determined with any certainty without further research. Since then we have learnt a great deal more about heavy metal levels in pelagic seabirds (some of this is discussed later in this chapter) but we still lack any firm evidence to show that PCBs are responsible for any of the high level of embryo mortality in Great Skuas. If they are, then their effect is small in its influence on overall breeding success, but the fact that PCB levels are presently on the increase in Great Skuas means that this possibility should be investigated.

Influences of seasonal changes in weight

The organochlorines in adult Great Skuas would be most likely to have toxic effects on birds when they reach minimum body weight in late summer as a result of drawing on their fat stores. Knowing how much weight Great Skuas lose we can estimate approximately what the peak concentrations of organochlorines might be at this potentially sensitive time.

On average, Great Skuas lose about 500 g body weight over the spring and summer, and this is probably largely fat reserves in adipose tissue. If this tissue contains, on average, 200 ppm of PCBs (Muirhead 1986), then one-tenth of a gram of PCB will be mobilised. Clearly, some of this will be broken down, and some will be redistributed via the blood into all organs of the body that contain lipid. Since the liver contains about 20% of the lipid of a Great Skua that has used up its adipose tissue stores, then the PCB level in the liver of an average bird might increase to as much as 400 ppm at the time of chick fledging, when adults reach their lowest weight. Of course, some Great Skuas have considerably more than the average load of PCB, and in these individuals the concentrations of PCB reached in the late summer may be close to the levels that could cause death. While these calculations are highly speculative, they do suggest that some attention should be paid to the PCB levels attained in Great Skuas at their time of minimum lipid store in order to see whether the concentrations reach toxic levels.

HEAVY METALS

In contrast to the considerable body of research that has been done on the occurrence and effects of organochlorines in seabirds, rather little was known until very recently either about the effects, or even the levels, of heavy metals in seabirds. Many heavy metals are known to be highly toxic, and are liberated into the atmosphere or discharged into the sea by man's activities. However, they also occur in the environment as a result of natural processes such as the weathering of rocks and volcanic activity, and so they must have been a factor to which seabirds have always been exposed to some extent. The principal questions that need to be answered are – have heavy metal levels in skuas increased as a consequence of pollution? – do heavy metals have harmful effects on skuas?

My interest in heavy metals developed by a curious and totally unexpected event. One summer, after a long field season during my PhD research, working on the Great Skuas of Foula, I decided to visit Fetlar on the way home to see the Snowy Owls. While wandering around the island I met another birdwatcher who seemed to be searching for the owls. He asked if I had come across any Snowy Owl feathers, which I assumed he wanted for a field notebook as a souvenir of his visit to Fetlar. We chatted for a while, and I discovered that he actually wanted the feathers to analyse them for heavy metals. I had met Malcolm Hutton, then a research student mainly studying lead levels in London pigeons, but with an infectious interest in heavy metals and their possible importance as pollutants. Clearly we had to take advantage of our complementary interests, since the levels of heavy metals in Great Skuas were completely unknown, and since the Great Skua is the top predator in its marine ecosystem, the opportunity to investigate the levels of these potential pollutants seemed too good an opportunity to miss. I promised to send Malcolm some Great Skua tissues and feather samples from Foula next season. This was particularly worthwhile in his view because I was able to collect samples from birds ringed as chicks and so he could look at the metal levels in relation to the ages of the birds concerned. This provided the first opportunity to investigate the relationship between adult age and metal levels in birds, although it had already been shown that many heavy metals accumulate with age in large predatory fish and in marine mammals. The next summer I sent yet another series of margarine tubs through the post, hoping the weather would not be too hot in London! Harry Gear viewed the new address on the smelly packets with some concern. 'Is this another person wanting these bits of "Bonxies" now!' It must have been almost too much for him to believe that I could be finding a growing market for my samples.

Metal levels in different skuas

Malcolm Hutton analysed kidney, liver and feather samples from twelve Great Skuas of known age that I had posted to him from Foula, and discovered that the oldest bird contained 336 ppm of cadmium in the kidney (dry weight). This was, as far as we knew, the highest concentration of cadmium that had then been found in any seabird. Mercury levels were also rather high and suggested that heavy metals in Great Skuas would repay further study. After Malcolm Hutton and I discovered that Great Skuas carried these remarkably high levels, and that there was a possibility that they might be high enough to be having harmful effects on breeding success, a study of other pelagic seabirds, at St Kilda, showed that Fulmars and Manx Shearwaters, which had metal levels similar to those in Great Skuas, appeared to be suffering kidney damage as a consequence. Several kinds of damage to the cells could be seen by electron microscopy which were to all intents and purposes identical to kidney lesions induced in captive Starlings given mercury or cadmium in their diet (Nicholson and Osborn 1983, 1984). This result was somewhat surprising, since the seabirds collected at St Kilda had been apparently healthy breeding adults. Osborn and his co-workers had previously taken the view that mercury and cadmium levels were high in pelagic marine ecosystems for natural reasons that had nothing to do with pollution, since heavy metal pollution would be expected to be most evident in coastal regions rather than far out in the oceans, while coastal species of seabirds generally have less mercury or cadmium in their tissues than do the pelagic seabirds, such as Fulmars, storm petrels, Manx Shearwaters and Great Skuas.

Discovery of kidney damage seemed incompatible with this idea. If mercury and cadmium have always been accumulated to high levels by pelagic seabirds, then it is difficult to believe that they have evolved no better way of coping with the toxic metals than to suffer breakdown of their kidney tissues. The only explanation suggested was that perhaps the damage to the kidneys, although very obvious in electron microscope examination, may not actually cost the birds much in terms of kidney efficiency or replacement of damaged cells, in which case there would be little or no selection pressure to evolve greater tolerance to heavy metals. My initial reaction to this was that it seemed far more likely that the damage indicated that environmental exposure to the heavy metals had increased, and that this must surely be due to pollution. The most obvious way to start to test this hypothesis seemed to be to look at mercury and cadmium levels in skuas from what I assumed would be an unpolluted 'control' site in the South Atlantic, against which the levels of mercury and cadmium in Great Skuas from the apparently polluted North Atlantic could be compared.

I was able to make this comparison when I was offered the chance to visit Gough Island in 1983. This seemed particularly appropriate as a control sample since Gough lies in an area of remote ocean over 1,000 miles from any industrial sites, and has a population of several thousand Tristan Skuas, the population that James Fisher and Ronald Lockley suggested most likely to have given rise to the North Atlantic Great Skua.

Surprisingly, and totally contrary to my expectations, mercury and cadmium levels in Tristan Skuas turned out to be higher than those in Great Skuas (Figure 90). Tristan Skuas had, on average, 26 ppm of cadmium in the kidney (wet weight) while Great Skuas had, on average, 12 ppm. Tristan Skuas had mean levels of 7.4 ppm mercury in the liver, compared to a mean of 4.2 ppm in Great Skuas. On examining levels of mercury and cadmium in a wide variety of other seabirds on Gough Island we found that Tristan Skuas actually had lower levels than some of the larger procellariiforms. In fact, Wandering and Sooty Albatrosses had the highest levels of all, with ten times the concentrations of mercury found in Tristan Skuas, and three to five times as much cadmium! Evidently there are processes of accumulation of these metals in pelagic marine ecosystems, that we are not yet aware of, that cause these extraordinary metal levels in large albatrosses. While mercury and cadmium levels may well be elevated in some regions as a consequence of pollution, there can be very high accumulations by apparently natural processes. The high levels in seabirds at Gough do not appear to be having harmful effects on the birds, although kidney samples from Gough seabirds do show the same evidence of damage found in Fulmars and shearwaters from St Kilda. These unexpected findings have not resolved many questions as yet, but they have indicated that there are some interesting processes yet to be elucidated, and that high concentrations of heavy metals in skuas and other pelagic seabirds do not necessarily mean that pollution is responsible. Nevertheless, skuas can provide some further insights into the little known subject of metal accumulation, as discussed in the remainder of this chapter.

Relationships with age and sex
Levels of heavy metals in eggs and chicks are much less than those found in adults, so it follows that the levels must increase with the age of birds, up to a certain stage. Organochlorines seem to reach a dynamic equilibrium by the time birds are only a year or two old. By contrast to this, in marine mammals and in fish, it appears that some heavy metals, particularly mercury, may gradually increase in concentration throughout life. In these cases, it would seem that the metals, which are not only toxic in large amounts but are also non-essential even in trace quantities, are bound up by particular proteins called metallotheionines, some of which are designed specifically for detoxification of heavy metals. What happens in seabirds is rather less clear.

Sandra Muirhead found a significantly lower level of cadmium in female Tristan skuas than in males, but no statistically significant difference in levels between the sexes in Great Skuas. She also found no clear difference in mercury levels between

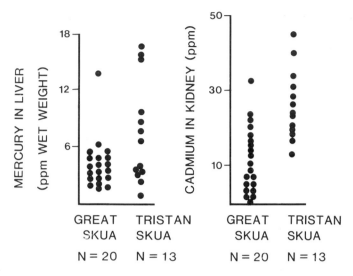

Fig. 90   Mercury and cadmium levels in Tristan Skuas at Gough Island and Great Skuas at Foula. Values are in parts per million (p.p.m.), i.e. mg kg⁻¹, wet weight of tissue.

the sexes, though again, most females tended to have lower levels. These trends might be expected, since females can lose metals into eggs. Our analyses showed that the amounts of cadmium passing into Great Skua eggs were very small, averaging only 0.011 ppm, while mercury levels were much higher, averaging 0.474 ppm. The fact that a sexual difference is more pronounced in the case of cadmium may simply reflect that the total amount of cadmium in the Great Skua is very much less than the total amount of mercury, since cadmium is almost all found in the kidney and liver, particularly the former, whereas mercury is found in those tissues but also throughout the muscles, where cadmium levels are extremely low.

From our sample of thirteen Great Skuas of known age, Malcolm Hutton and I found that mercury and cadmium levels increased with the age of the bird, although the correlations for mercury in relation to age were rather weak. Sandra Muirhead analysed another 27 birds of known age for cadmium and 20 for mercury, and she also found positive correlations between metal levels and the age of the bird, but again these were weak (Table 55), and only that for cadmium in muscle was statistically significant. The correlation coefficients, generally around 0.2 to 0.4, indicate that age explains only about 5–15% of the variation in metal levels from bird to bird. Since females tend to have lower levels than males, the sex of the bird will also determine some of the remaining variation, but most of the variability can only be attributed to individual differences, presumably in such things as dietary specialisations and migration patterns. During the breeding season, adult Great Skuas at Foula feed mainly on Sandeels and discarded Haddock and Whiting from fishing boats, so that their intake of mercury will be determined by levels in these foods. However, some individuals specialise on killing seabirds, from which they may obtain higher levels of mercury.

The implication of these results is that there is a dynamic equilibrium in tissue metal levels. Uptake from the bird's food must nearly balance the rate of loss of these metals from the body, with little build-up in the tissues over the years. In this respect, skuas appear to be better able to cope with heavy metals than are fish and marine mammals, which rely on binding and detoxification because they apparently do not have comparable mechanisms to eliminate heavy metals from the body. As discussed later, the ability of skuas to lose metals via their feathers may reduce their need to detoxify heavy metals by permanent storage, as found particularly in fish, although our work on known-age Great Skuas has been the only such study, so it is risky to assume that all birds will show similar patterns.

Relationships between metals and tissues

Different elements show varying affinities for particular tissues, and may interact in informative ways. In Great and Tristan Skuas, and in most other seabirds that have been examined, cadmium levels are highest in the kidney, but vary greatly between individuals. Levels of zinc and copper, both of which are essential for various metabolic processes, show much less variation between individuals, and follow 'normal distribution' patterns. This indicates that the concentrations of these essential metals are regulated around a species norm. There is no known physiological requirement for cadmium, so there is no reason to expect cadmium levels to be similarly regulated. However, cadmium concentrations in Great and Tristan Skuas also follow normal distribution patterns (Fig. 91), which suggests that the amounts of this element stored in the tissues may also be regulated. While the levels of zinc and copper in Great and Tristan Skuas are very similar, cadmium levels differ, with Tristan Skuas having higher levels, which appear to reflect a higher level in the food chain. This difference between the closely related species suggests that cadmium levels may not be regulated very strictly, but may largely be dependent on the prevailing environmental exposure.

Levels of mercury, which tend to be highest in the liver, show a distribution pattern that is clearly not the same as a normal distribution. There are a few individuals with very much higher levels of mercury than general; the distribution is skewed (Fig. 92). This suggests that mercury levels are not metabolically regulated, but depend on the dynamic balance between passive intake and elimination processes.

In the Great Skua kidney, the concentrations of copper and zinc tend to correlate to some extent with that of cadmium (Figs 93 and 94). It can be interpreted from this that cadmium may interfere with the metabolic regulation of zinc and copper.

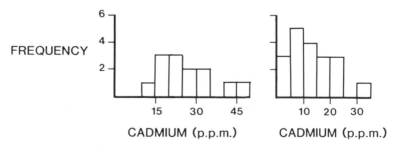

Fig. 91 *Distribution of cadmium concentrations in the kidneys of Great Skuas and Tristan Skuas. From Muirhead (1986).*

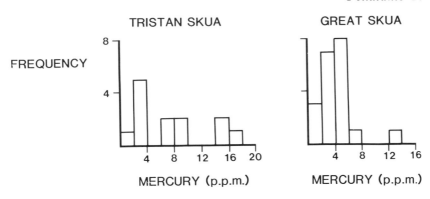

Fig. 92 Distribution of mercury concentrations in the livers of Great Skuas and Tristan Skuas. From Muirhead (1986).

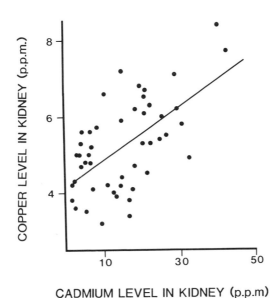

Fig. 93 Relationship between cadmium and copper levels in kidneys of Great Skuas. From Muirhead (1986).

It is believed that this occurs because high levels of cadmium switch on the DNA that codes for the production of a specific protein that binds and detoxifies cadmium, but also takes up other metal ions, such as copper and zinc. This binding of essential metals probably results in greater total copper and zinc levels as the concentrations of free ions is regulated at the appropriate levels irrespective of levels bound to proteins. It is possible that high levels of cadmium could result in copper or zinc deficiency symptoms in skuas as a result of the binding of these metal ions by metallotheionines produced to bind excess cadmium. Such deficiency

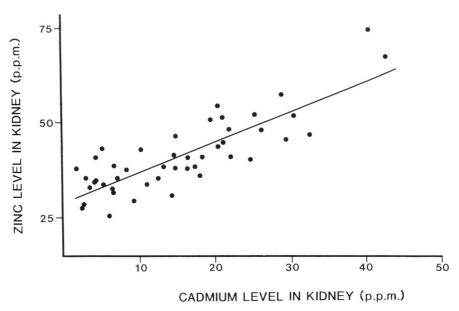

Fig. 94   Relationship between cadmium and zinc levels in kidneys of Great Skuas. From Muirhead (1986).

diseases are known in farm animals exposed to vegetation with high levels of certain toxic metals such as cadmium and selenium.

Mercury levels correlate closely with levels of selenium in the liver of Great Skuas (Fig. 95) and this is also thought to be related to processes of detoxification. Mercury will bind with selenium to form a complex such as mercury selenide. Selenium itself is toxic, though much less so than mercury, but the mercury–selenium complex is much less toxic than either element on its own. The high levels of selenium found in Great Skuas that have high levels of mercury are thought to indicate that the birds detoxify the mercury by forming mercury–selenium complexes that result in an increased retention of selenium in the body. Selenium is normally held in the body only for a period of some days, but mercury atoms remain in the body, on average, for many months. Experiments with fish have shown that radioactively labelled selenium remains in the body for about the biological half-time of mercury if high levels of mercury are present, but for only about one-tenth this time in fish that have not been administered with mercury. We performed experiments with fish because it would be very difficult to do the same work with seabirds in captivity, but I expect that skuas would show a similar result. The implication is that they are able to reduce the potentially toxic effects of mercury through complexing this with selenium.

Elimination of metals

Although many papers have been published on levels of mercury in feathers from seabirds and birds of prey, most of these studies have examined only a single primary feather from each individual. A few studies have compared mercury levels in different parts of the plumage, and indeed, it has been suggested that the time

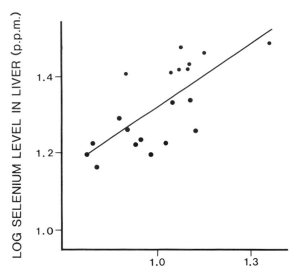

*Fig. 95   Relationship between mercury and selenium levels in Great Skua
livers. From Muirhead (1986).*

of year during which mercury intake is highest can be seen from differences in
mercury levels in different primary feathers. In other words, the mercury level in
a feather would reflect the level in the diet at the time of feather growth. Since it
is known that primaries are moulted in a fixed sequence and at a particular season,
it has been inferred that high mercury levels in the innermost primaries of an
Osprey indicated that it obtained most of its mercury in the breeding area and
much less in Africa, since the primaries grown late in moult had low levels of the
metal. On examining levels of mercury in different primaries of Great Skuas and
a Tristan Skua, we found that these too tended to show a decline in mercury
concentrations from primary 1 to primary 10 (Figure 96). Did Great and Tristan
Skuas obtain most of their mercury during the breeding season too? This seemed
most unlikely. Tristan Skuas normally remain close to or at their breeding site all
year, and feed on the same diet at all seasons too. Great Skuas move south in the
autumn and primary moult begins early in autumn, but there is no reason to
believe that they change to a diet that is low in mercury as their primary moult
progresses.

   We found that this pattern of a drop in mercury levels through the moult
sequence applies to other feather tracts too, and can even be seen within single
primary feathers, where the tip of primary 1 has a higher level of mercury than
the base, which has about the same level as the tip of primary 2. Similar results
have also been found with Kittiwakes, Fulmars, Manx Shearwaters, Atlantic
Petrels, Soft-plumaged Petrels, Kerguelen Petrels, Great Shearwaters, Peruvian
Boobies, Gannets, Sparrowhawks, Peregrines, Black Guillemots and Guillemots,
and so it seems to be a normal pattern related to moult rather than to short-term
changes in diet. Mercury levels in individual feathers apparently do not reflect the

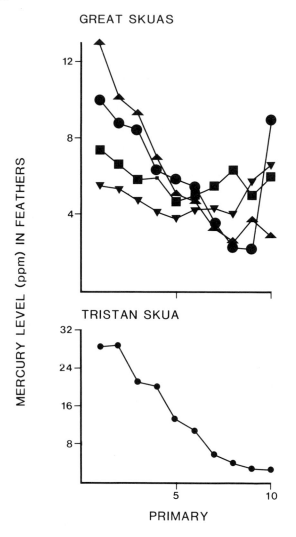

GREAT SKUAS

MERCURY LEVEL (ppm) IN FEATHERS

TRISTAN SKUA

PRIMARY

*Fig. 96   Pattern of mercury concentrations in primary feathers of Tristan Skua
and Great Skuas in relation to the sequence of moult.*

mercury content of the diet alone, but also indicate the extent to which mercury
has been stored in the bird's tissues. Feathers that are grown early in the moult
tend to have highest mercury levels while those grown late tend to have low levels
(Table 56). This suggests that there is a build-up of mercury in the body between
moults and that this is shed during moult, late-grown feathers getting less of the
burden because less remains. This discovery means that some care needs to be
taken when sampling feathers for mercury analysis since levels vary by as much
as an order of magnitude in different parts of the plumage. Whether the levels in
individual feathers can tell us much about changes in the dietary intake is less

clear. One or two of the Great Skuas we have examined show anomalies in the mercury levels. For example, two individuals had relatively low levels in primaries 1 to 7, with a slight drop in levels through this sequence, but had considerably higher mercury levels in primaries 8 to 10. This might mean that these birds moved to an area where mercury contamination was particularly high towards the end of moult; or could mean that they had to draw on their fat reserves towards the end of moult and so mobilised higher levels of mercury. Obviously some experimental work may answer these questions, but it would appear that the levels of mercury in feathers are determined in a much more complex way than by the levels in the diet.

The main ways in which heavy metals are lost from body tissues of skuas are likely to be by defecation, and by incorporation of metals into external products; eggs and feathers. The importance of these routes in birds is not clear, but we can assess this to a first approximation from data on the levels of mercury in different tissues, eggs and feathers of Great Skuas from Foula. Great Skua eggs generally contain about 0.5 ppm of mercury. Since the normal clutch size is two eggs, the contents weighing an average of 90 g each, this amounts to 0.09 mg of mercury lost into eggs each year for the average breeding female. Since this route is not available to males, there might be a tendency for mercury levels in males to be at a higher mean equilibrium level than in females if loss of mercury into eggs is an important route of elimination. Some seabirds do indeed show lower levels of mercury in females, but there is little evidence for this in Tristan Skuas or Great Skuas, possibly in part because the levels of individual variation are high and so differences between the sexes tend to be masked unless large sample sizes are available for comparison. The result is much the same with regard to expected differences in levels of organochlorines between the two sexes.

The quantity of mercury lost from the body into the plumage depends on how much of the plumage is moulted each year and on the mean levels of mercury in different feather groups. Certainly, the primaries, secondaries and tail feathers of Great Skuas are normally replaced annually. Some parts of the plumage may be renewed twice a year, because there is a small nuptial moult in the spring, mainly of feathers on the head and neck. Probably about half of the coverts and body feathers are renewed each year, but this has not been studied in any detail. From careful examination of birds it is possible to detect feathers, particularly on the back and among the scapulars, where the wear and bleaching are very pronounced. Immature Great and Tristan Skuas rarely show these, and it seems likely that moult is more complete in immature birds than in breeding adults. Possibly this is because adults may find it difficult to obtain enough energy, or sulphur amino acids, to pay the costs of replacing all of the plumage in addition to breeding each year.

On the basis of a complete replacement of all feathers once a year, an average Great Skua would lose 0.52 mg of mercury to the feathers (Table 57); if we assume that only half of the body feathers and wing coverts are replaced, then the figure would be 0.34 mg. Probably the truth lies between these two values, but certainly the plumage takes up much more mercury than the eggs. How much mercury is there in a Great Skua that cannot be accounted for by these two routes of elimination? In an average Great Skua the mercury level in muscle is around 0.8 ppm in early summer. Levels in the liver and kidney are considerably higher, but these organs represent only a small part of the body mass, so that muscle contains the largest amount of mercury. Altogether, we can estimate that a typical

Great Skua carries 0.98 mg of mercury in its body tissues in early summer. Since it will not begin moult for a few weeks, the body burden may increase slightly until autumn, but it is clear that there is more mercury in the body tissues than can be put into the plumage during moult, when perhaps about half of the accumulation is lost. (Table 57).

Since we know that adult Great Skuas do not show a strong tendency for mercury levels to increase with age, mercury must be approximately in dynamic equilibrium, and so losses from body tissues over the year must equal intake. The fact that moult takes place in a restricted part of the year means that the opportunities to reduce mercury levels in body tissues may not correspond to the times when most mercury is ingested. Mercury burdens in Great Skuas may show quite marked annual cycles, but unfortunately we have information only for birds collected early in the breeding season.

Plumage as a monitor of historical levels of mercury

Feathers are predominantly composed of the protein keratin, but many elements may be incorporated into feathers during their growth. Metals, in particular, may pass from the blood into feathers where they are usually bound firmly to sulphur amino acids that are particularly prevalent in keratin. The levels of metals in feathers have been shown to correspond to the amounts of the metal circulating in the blood at the time of feather formation, although metals can also become bound onto feather protein after growth has been completed, and even, under some circumstances, as a purely chemical process after the bird has died.

The concentrations of different elements incorporated into feathers has been used as a way of determining the geographical origins of some geese, ducks and Peregrines. The idea here is that the elemental composition of the feathers reflects the elemental composition of the bird's food which, in turn, reflects the elemental composition of the soils of the region. In this way, it is sometimes possible to tell where a bird came from. For example, Peregrines reared as chicks in West Greenland, the Yukon, Alaska and the Colville River, Alaska showed statistically significant differences in feather concentrations of manganese, vanadium, sodium, mercury and bromine in such a way that 97% of fledglings could be assigned to the correct natal areas on the basis of the measured concentrations of these and four other elements in the feathers (Parrish *et al* 1983). The success of this technique depends on there being clear differences between elemental concentrations between regions, which is not always the case, but it does suggest that feathers could also be used to monitor levels of potentially serious anthropogenic pollutants; particularly elements such as the heavy metals mercury or cadmium.

Feathers have two great advantages as monitors of metals. They can be taken from live birds without any harm to the birds since only one or two small feathers are sufficient for analysis. They also present a wonderful opportunity to examine levels of pollutants in the past. They can be taken from birds in museum skin collections in order to examine changes in metal levels over a period of many decades. Museum collections are often extensive, and contain particularly large numbers of many seabirds collected towards the end of last century as well as specimens from earlier and from more recent periods, so that effects of industrial heavy metal pollution should be evident from an analysis of feather samples from these birds, providing there has been no contamination *post mortem*.

Seabird feathers as a monitor of heavy metal pollution trends have a particular importance because other attempts to monitor changes in heavy metal levels at a global scale have been rather unsuccessful. At present it is known that industrial activity releases large quantities of mercury into the atmosphere and into water, and it is not clear whether this has resulted in an increased level of mercury in natural ecosystems except at a local scale. Certainly many small estuaries or bays have been seriously polluted by mercury (the famous Minamata Bay in Japan, where many people suffered mercury poisoning as a result of local pollution is perhaps the best known example) and the Baltic and Mediterranean are also considered to have suffered increased levels of mercury as a result of man's activities, but has mercury pollution affected levels in the world's oceans? The main thrust of studies attempting to answer this question has been the analysis of heavy metal levels in ice cores from Greenland or the Antarctic. Ice can be dated in these cores, and so levels of heavy metals present in the environment at different periods in the past can be assessed. Such cores have shown a clear increase in lead levels in Greenland and the Antarctic since industrial activity began. However, results for mercury are particularly unclear. Levels in ice are close to the detection limits of analytical instruments, mercury analysis being technically rather more difficult than the analysis of most other metals, and contamination of ice samples during transit to, or in research laboratories, has been suspected. A recent review of this subject, published in *Nature,* concluded that all attempts to measure the changes in global mercury contamination have been unable to provide a clear picture of what changes have taken place (Wolff & Peel 1985). In view of this, it is well worth exploring the possibility that seabird feathers may be able to demonstrate global changes in mercury contamination.

A study of mercury levels in the sixth primary of Guillemots and Black Guillemots showed that levels had increased considerably in birds from Baltic colonies over the last 150 years (Appelquist *et al* 1985). Encouraged by the success of this study, Sandra Muirhead and I decided to look at mercury levels in feathers of skuas from museum collections and present day samples, to see if we could show the changes that have taken place in mercury levels in the North Atlantic, South Atlantic and southern oceans.

Our initial attempt was singularly unsuccessful. At once we hit upon a problem that had also been found by some other workers looking at mercury levels in birds of prey, which does not seem to have been found by Appelquist and co-workers. The famous Carl Linnaeus, founder of modern taxonomy and systematics, had recommended that bird skins prepared for museum collections should be treated with 'sublimate' as a preservative. Sublimate is the chemical mercuric chloride, and so many of the specimens collected before the end of the 19th century had incredibly high levels of mercury in the feathers as a result of being treated in this way. The most contaminated specimens we analysed had about 1000 times as much mercury in the feather as we have found in any living bird! Unfortunately, this mercury contamination as a consequence of the preservation of the skin cannot be entirely washed off the feathers, even with the most thorough ultra-sonic bathing. Mercury on the surface of feathers, when the feathers are at all damp, will react chemically with the keratin, and may become bound into the protein in exactly the same way as the metal atoms that are incorporated during the growth of the feather. Some studies have simply discarded measurements of mercury levels in museum specimens that seem unreasonably high, assuming that these are due to contamination by sublimate. Some other studies have not mentioned this problem, and some of these apparently did not even wash the feathers before analysis. We found that some museums had much higher levels of sublimate in the specimen drawers than others, and often the levels of mercury could also be unexpectedly high in feathers of birds collected recently but placed against old and contaminated skins in the same drawer. As a result, we felt unable to use with confidence the measurements of total mercury levels in the museum feathers we examined.

The mercury accumulated in the tissues of seabirds is predominantly in the organic form, methyl-mercury. From the few analyses that have measured separately the levels of inorganic mercury and methyl-mercury in feathers, it would seem that almost all of the mercury that passes into seabird feathers during their growth is also methyl-mercury. This means that it should be possible by biochemical techniques to separate the organic mercury, derived from the bird, from the inorganic mercury, derived almost entirely from the preservatives used in museums. Then we should be able to make a reliable comparison between historical and present-day levels of mercury in skuas and other seabirds. Meanwhile, it remains unclear whether or not levels of mercury in pelagic marine ecosystems have increased as a result of anthropogenic activities.

CHAPTER 15
Skuas and agriculture

If I had my way there would only be one pair of Bonxies on Noss. And they would be stuffed!

Peter Manson, shepherd of Noss 1974, 1975, 1976 . . . .

The breeding distributions of skua species are mainly in the high latitudes; the Arctic, the Antarctic and the sub-Antarctic. These regions are the ones where man has shown little interest in agriculture, so it may seem unnecessary to devote a whole chapter to considering the relationships between skuas and agriculture. However, the conflict between skuas and local people is an excellent example of the difficulty of reconciling conservation interests with the real or imagined interests of local inhabitants who may have little influence with legislative authorities. Certainly it is true that skuas and farmers come into conflict in very few places, and the conflict directly affects only a very small number of people. Skuas breed in association with agriculture in northern Britain, the Faeroes and Iceland, northern Scandinavia, Tristan da Cunha, the Falkland Islands, and the Chatham Islands off New Zealand. These tend to be areas where the profit margins of agriculture are small, and so any harmful effect is undesirable.

Since skuas tend to occur in relatively small numbers by comparison with populations of other seabirds, they are comparatively easy to eradicate if they are perceived to be a pest. Like other seabirds, skuas tend to be long-lived as adults, with a long period of immaturity and a relatively low production of young. These characteristics mean that killing of adults can drastically reduce their numbers, but that removal of eggs or chicks has relatively little effect, particularly in the short term. At the temperate limits of their ranges, in areas where they may come into conflict with man, skua populations are rather vulnerable. Conservation interests may then conflict with the interests of agriculturalists. Such situations have arisen in northern Britain and the Faeroes in particular, but also on Tristan da Cunha. In each of these areas some skua colonies have been seriously persecuted by local people and have declined in numbers as a result. We will consider the conflicts between skuas and agriculture and the problems of resolving them.

ATTITUDES TO SKUAS IN SHETLAND

Each year when I visit Foula I try to get to Noss, the small island National Nature Reserve, for a day or two. Noss was declared a nature reserve largely because of its colonies of Great and Arctic Skuas, Gannets and other seabirds, but it is also a productive island for sheep farming. It lies conveniently accessible from Lerwick by a short ferry crossing to Bressay and a pleasant walk over this island to Noss Sound, where from the shore one has to hail the boatman on Noss to transport visitors across the narrow sound in an inflatable boat. Noss is inhabited all summer by the boatman and the warden, who look after visitors to the reserve and the interests of the wildlife. In spring it is also temporary home for the shepherds who manage the island's flock of sheep. Many of my visits have coincided with the sojourns of the shepherds, and I have always been greeted with the outstandingly open warmth typical of Shetlanders' hospitality. The initial greeting is always the same though. 'So you are back to see your "Bonxies" again. If I had my way there would only be one pair of "Bonxies" on Noss. And they would be stuffed!' We both treat it as a good joke. He knows that I am particularly fond of skuas. He finds the interest of a scientist from 'doon sooth' eccentric, but is willing to tolerate such visitors because he accepts that values are different outside Shetland. My regular return also suggests that I take my interest more seriously than many who come to study Shetland for a couple of weeks and disappear again with unknown results. While we chat I feel somewhat embarrassed to be one of the many visitors who come to Shetland in order to understand the ecology of the isles and their wildlife. Of course crofters know their local wildlife intimately. Who are we to tell them about the animals and birds they live with day in, day out? If he can spare the time we have a cup of coffee before he goes off to attend to whatever he has to do with the sheep, and I go off to do whatever it is I do with the skuas.

I have always been certain that Peter Manson, the Noss shepherd, would not really wish to see Great Skuas eradicated from the island. At the same time, his joke does reflect a deep dislike of skuas, and one that has become widespread among Shetland crofters and shepherds and more strongly felt over recent years. This culminated in 1985 in the issuing of a licence by the Department of Agriculture and Fisheries for Scotland (DAFS) under the Wildlife and Countryside Act of 1981 in order to allow the shooting of 20 Great Skuas on Noss. This was held to be necessary because the birds were causing 'serious damage to livestock, foodstuffs for livestock, crops, vegetables, growing timber or fisheries', the only conditions for which DAFS is able to license the killing of skuas which are otherwise protected by law.

At several sites elsewhere in northern Britain skuas are shot because crofters feel that they have to do so in order to protect their animals. However, the authorities have tended to deny that skuas cause 'serious damage' and so in the view of conservationists at least, this shooting is illegal. Understandably, crofters feel upset that they need to break the law in this way. They particularly resent the fact that conservationists from 'doon sooth' do not understand their problems and object to the killing of these birds as unreasonable and unnecessary as well as illegal. Everyone loses in this situation. Ill feeling towards conservation and skuas increases and eventually skuas are blamed even for things for which they are not responsible. Skuas are shot anyway, possibly more extensively than even crofters would say is necessary.

The present day antipathy towards skuas, particularly Great Skuas, is in stark contrast to the attitude of Shetland crofters in earlier times. The first description of Great Skuas in Britain was that of the Reverend George Low, who visited the islands in 1774. His observations were not published until 1879, but contain a striking passage about the high esteem in which the rare 'Bonxie' was then held: 'In Foula there is a privileged bird, no man will dare shoot it, under the penalty of 16s 8d sterling, nor destroy its eggs: when they meet it at sea, whatever fish they have in the boat Skua always gets a share, and all this out of gratitude for beating off the Eagle, who dares not venture to prey on the island during the whole of the breeding season. Skua is not so strong as the Eagle, but much more nimble: strikes out at him without mercy, with such effect that he makes the other scream aloud, and his retreat is so sudden as to avoid all danger from the Eagle'.

The eagle concerned, the Sea Eagle, became extinct in Shetland in 1918 after years of persecution and last nested on Foula in the first year or two of this century. However, other sheep scavengers or predators such as Ravens are driven away from skua colonies so that these are unable to attack ewes or lambs, and confine their activities to coastal areas or localities where there are no skuas.

In 1774 there were only half a dozen pairs of Great Skuas on Foula. Since 1900 the numbers of Great Skuas have increased dramatically throughout the Northern Isles, and it is this increase coupled with the aggressive and predatory nature of these birds that has turned the attitude of crofters against them. Certainly the aggressive nature of Great Skuas towards people and livestock has been known since the first accounts of the species were published, as shown in the two following passages: 'Nor are the very summits of the hills without their share of the winged race. Here we find that remarkable bird the Skua, called here the Bonxie, six pairs of which possess the highest ridge of Liorafield. I followed one at some distance from the rest, which made me part company, and received several very rude salutes for my impudence from three, who made at me with the utmost rage; I defended myself the best way I could with my gun, fired several times at them, but as none dropped, the report did not startle them in the least rather seeming to enrage them more. When the inhabitants are looking after their sheep in the hills the Skua often attacks them in such a manner that they are forced to defend themselves with cudgels by holding them above their heads' Low (1879).

'When, however, his nest is approached, he shews a determination to defend his possession with his life. Ravens, eagles, hawks or other birds, are soon pursued from the territory they inhabit. On approaching the nest an attack immediately commences; male and female in rapid succession descend from a considerable height, with a velocity and noise truly startling; horses, cattle, and sheep, are immediately put to flight, and receive no intermission of attack until well driven from the nest; and if man, bent on sinister purposes, continues to brave the Bonxie's fury, he will seldom accomplish his aim without carrying away marks of war' Vetch (1822).

I have already suggested that the previous quote by Captain Vetch may indicate that the behaviour of Great Skuas has changed as they have adapted to life at North Atlantic colonies. The skuas in the Southern Hemisphere colonies such as Gough Island or South Georgia are very much more aggressive than present day North Atlantic Great Skuas. At such places the birds have no long-term experience of persecution by man, and so they attack without fear people who intrude on their territories. In Shetland, or the Faeroe Islands, Great Skuas have been severely persecuted; adults shot for taxidermy, eggs robbed for collections, eggs and chicks harvested for food, adults shot because they have been considered a pest. All this has changed the 'Bonxie' into a much more wary bird than its Antarctic cousin. Presumably the most timid individuals have tended to survive better than the most aggressive ones when adults have been persecuted. Great Skuas still dive-bomb people but generally try to avoid coming too close; only a small minority will actually hit. In fact their aggression towards people increases from a very low level before eggs have been laid to a peak around hatching, and then declines again as the chicks get older and better able to hide or defend themselves. If the birds lose their eggs or chicks then they quickly become less aggressive towards people until a replacement clutch is laid. If they have infertile or addled eggs then they may incubate for considerably longer than the normal 29 to 30 days, and their aggression declines as the period after expected hatching increases.

I discussed how I quantified the aggressive response of Great Skuas, earlier; only 6% of pairs included a bird that regularly hit me when I walked up to its nest during the middle of the incubation period. In more than half of all pairs neither adult would make physical contact with me in order to defend the eggs, and at 6% of territories both birds would leave the territory rather than dive-bomb an intruding person. Thus Great Skuas are not as fiercely aggressive as many people believe. In 14 years of studying these birds, during which I have measured thousands of clutches of eggs or small chicks, and walked through an enormous number of territories, I have never received a single cut from a dive-bombing Great Skua. The birds hit with the back of the feet, and do not use the wings because this would clearly risk serious injury to the bird. Nor do they attempt to use their sharp claws. To do so would risk becoming hooked onto their victim which would be likely to do them more harm than good. Being hit by a Great Skua is very annoying, particularly since it is rather unpredictable and so comes as a surprise. I find much more annoying the loss of nerve by some birds as they swoop down, releasing a shower of foul smelling fluid onto the person below. This could be a much more effective response but fortunately Great Skuas do not have the intelligence to realise this!

Only once have I been effectively hurt by a Great Skua attack. On that occasion I was measuring the chick of a particularly aggressive pair of birds. Both adults were hitting me each time they swooped down and I was unable to wave them away because I needed both hands to hold and measure the chick. After I had been hit a dozen or so times I had got very annoyed, and having finished writing the measurements I grabbed the rule, balance, notebook and pencil and quickly stood up to get away from the parents. At exactly the same moment one of the adults was just reaching the bottom of its swoop and had the undercarriage dropped in order to hit my head. By standing up I received the full force of the bird on the back of my neck. Nearly one and a half kilograms of angry Great Skua hit me at about 80 km per hour, which knocked me to the ground and blurred my vision for a moment. As I came round I saw that the skua was equally dazed lying on the ground a few metres away. I tried to grab at it but it managed to struggle free and flapped away in a very laboured manner. I expect it also took more care in future confrontations! This accident was my fault rather than the skua's and even in this unique instance I suffered no more than a sore neck and bad temper for a few hours.

By comparison with Great Skuas, Arctic Skuas are generally much more effective in their attacks on people. Firstly they are much better at coordinating their attacks. Great Skuas will dive at a person irrespective of the activity of their mate, and remarkably often both birds have to abort a dive when they see their mate on a collision course from another angle. Arctic Skuas usually manage to fly in partnership, one bird following up the attack executed by its mate. Arctic Skuas are also very much more aerobatic, and can turn and attack from the other side in a fraction of the time that it takes a Great Skua to reach the top of its swing, turn and start down again. Because they are more agile, Arctic Skuas hit more often than Great Skuas do, although being much lighter their impact is less. Unlike Great Skuas, which are often silent in their attacks, Arctic Skuas tend to be very noisy, screaming at the intruder all the time. Although disconcerting, this at least means that you can usually keep track of where both birds are and when you are about to be hit. As I found with Great Skuas, the Arctic Skuas also vary greatly in aggressiveness from bird to bird. A study of the Arctic Skuas on Fair Isle found that 40% did not dive-bomb a person beside the nest, and only 8% dived more than ten times before giving up (Cooper 1979).

Shetland and Orkney children love to induce attacks from skuas. Toddlers at peat banks may be frightened by unexpected swooping birds, but as soon as the bairns are old enough to go out and play by themselves they tease the skuas, attempting to catch them as they swoop down. To the working crofter such attacks can be a real nuisance. Although Great Skuas generally avoid areas frequently used by man, Arctic Skuas often nest where crofters have to work, at peat cutting, hay fields, lambing parks, roads or airstrips. Frequent attacks by Arctic Skuas lead to the occasional clutch being trodden on or sometimes adults being shot, though most crofters are fond of Arctic Skuas and would not harm them. On Foula, where expansion of the enormous Great Skua colony has pushed Arctic Skuas into nesting at very high densities, particularly in areas used by crofters, the islanders are very tolerant of Arctic Skua attacks. One or two individuals remove Arctic Skuas from around their peat banks, but most islanders take active steps to protect the Arctic Skua, which has their sympathy as the victim of the increasing and more powerful Great Skua. Only the Fair Isle community seem to think that dive-bombing by Arctic Skuas constitutes a danger to people. They applied to the Secretary of State for Scotland for permission to cull Arctic Skuas on Fair Isle, in part because children were frightened by skuas and so unable to play out of doors, and because skuas attacked people on foot or on bicycles on the road and were likely to cause accidents as a result.

Having watched children on Fair Isle and on Foula deliberately cycling backwards and forwards along a short stretch of road through Arctic Skua territories, purely for the excitement of being dived at by skuas I was not at all surprised that the Secretary of State for Scotland agreed with his Wildlife Advisory Panel that this application to cull Arctic Skuas should be rejected! In the *Shetland Times* of Friday 24 January 1986 this issue came to the fore again because articles had been published complaining about the extensive illegal shooting of Arctic Skuas on Fair Isle. Neil Thomson, one of the Fair Isle community, admitted to 'managing the skuas the same way as you manage anything else' although other islanders claimed that shooting of Arctic Skuas was not a policy of the islanders but something that might perhaps be done covertly by some people. Neil Thomson justified such activities as follows 'they are very rare birds and they're nearly all here. If you had a bird that was attacking people in Hyde Park they'd call in the pest control officer. We live very close to nature and we think we know it better than someone who's learned it all out of other people's books.'

In fact the Arctic Skua colony on Fair Isle holds only about 3 or 4% of the Scottish Arctic Skua population, but one has to sympathise with the view that birds behaving in the same way as Arctic Skuas do on Fair Isle, but in an English urban environment, would generate a public outcry that would elicit a very rapid response. This is certainly the case with Herring Gulls that have colonised urban areas. Gulls elsewhere may cause many serious problems, for example by transmitting bacterial contamination to drinking water supplies. Despite this, unless their effects are intolerable they tend to go unchecked because control measures cost money. By contrast, urban nesting gulls in many residential areas have been shot, trapped or poisoned because they annoy residents by dive-bombing to protect their rooftop nests (though far less vigorously than skuas do), and irritate people by their noisy calling and fouling of cars and washing hung out on the line. Gulls in an urban environment are considered to be a pest to be exterminated if possible. Skuas on remote islands are, in the eyes of the Urban dweller, romantic rare birds in need of protection. If skuas nested in urban environments instead of on remote islands they would no doubt have been exterminated long ago! Perhaps it is no wonder that some crofters feel that their views are not even considered when decisions about skuas are made. To quote one crofter who has considerable sympathy for nature conservation: 'It is a bad public relations situation for nature conservationists when a crofter's years of observation are ignored, but a report by a student visiting Shetland for a couple of weeks is listened to'.

At first sight the nuisance caused by Arctic Skuas dive-bombing people seems unimportant and it has probably become more of an issue than it deserves because other complaints about Arctic Skuas on Fair Isle have also fallen on deaf ears. However, the islanders on Fair Isle clearly do perceive this to be a problem, and it does little for conservation in the broad sense simply to tell them that being dive-bombed by birds, rare or otherwise, is one of the penalties of a remote rural existence. Unfortunately, as we shall soon see, dive-bombing by skuas is one of the least serious conflicts that skuas generate between crofters and conservationists.

PREDATION OF LAMBS, EWES AND OTHER LIVESTOCK

Although Great Skuas used to be credited with defending sheep from the attacks of eagles and other predators, they themselves have increasingly been accused of attacking and killing lambs and distressed ewes. Often it is unreasonably assumed that dead partly eaten lambs must have been killed by skuas, but it is clear that on rare occasions Great Skuas will kill a live lamb or ewe. More often perhaps they will scavenge on carcasses and be blamed for killing animals that died for other reasons. Great Skuas can become scapegoats for poor sheep husbandry, which is all too common in Shetland.

Crofters who have considerable experience of Great Skuas and their interactions with sheep describe the situation as follows: 'Normally a ewe eats all the "debris" of lambing, and some can be so keen to do so that they chew off their lamb's tail or ears. Uncommonly the afterbirth may be left entirely. This sometimes happens because the ewe is disturbed, which is particularly likely when sheep are lambing close together in a field rather than on the hill. "Bonxies" learn that afterbirths may be found and some wait around the sheep for these. They soon associate a lambing ewe with the appearance of an afterbirth, and will sit in attendance waiting until the ewe is busy licking and attending to the lamb. They then sneak up behind her and tug into any afterbirth hanging from the ewe. The next stage is the unpleasant one. If the ewe goes on her back, or the first of a pair of twins doesn't get to its feet before the mother starts lambing the second, then any "Bonxie" with experience of feeding on afterbirths may start to tear at the ewe or lamb. Sometimes a ewe lambing a big single lamb will go on her back with the effort of lambing the head, and is unable to get up or to complete the dropping of the lamb. The helpless animal, with blood about her tail and the protruding head of a half-born lamb is quickly attended by "Bonxies". If not found quickly by the shepherd then the "Bonxies" may well have taken out the tongue and eye of the lamb and the eye of the ewe and have picked a hole in the belly and started dragging out the intestines of the live ewe.'

According to crofters on Foula the number of ewes or lambs lost to Great Skuas is very low, and very much less than are lost for other reasons. Predation by Great Skuas occurs during the lambing period but is very rarely seen later in the year. One crofter, with just over 200 Shetland ewes, runs the sheep on the hill until late March. They are brought into the crofts for lambing mid April to mid May. Normally, Foula sheep on the hill achieve a lambing rate of 60–70% (ie 60 to 70 lambs per 100 ewes) while those brought into the crofts produce about 100% (with about 10% of ewes producing twins, but balanced by 10% failing to produce a surviving lamb). Even this is considerably below the normal 120–140% achieved by mainland sheep in, for example, southern Scotland. From the 200 or so sheep attended by this crofter, over a period of many years only some six or seven sheep have been severely attacked by Great Skuas while in trouble lambing, but these sheep and lambs were carefully attended and protected from skuas, whereas less intensive care might have allowed skuas to attack larger numbers. Nevertheless, loss of lambs to Great Skuas is trivial by comparison with other losses. The main concern of at least most crofters I have spoken to is the suffering of the few individuals lost to Great Skua attacks, and the distress caused to the crofters in finding a severely wounded ewe or lamb.

Predation of ewes and lambs may be due to a small number of individual Great Skuas. The species is extremely adaptable in its feeding behaviour but individuals tend to specialise in a few particular techniques or prey types. However, birds are quick to learn new feeding methods from each other, so that a habit of feeding on afterbirths, or of attacking distressed lambing ewes or unprotected lambs, might spread once established. It is clear from dietary studies that Great Skuas have difficulty in finding food easily, early in the breeding season. Their preferred food,

Sandeels, is not available in quantity before late May and few seabirds are carrying food to be stolen. Numbers of immature seabirds available to be predated are low early in the season. In April the first Great Skuas at the colonies feed to a large extent on such items as goose-barnacles scavenged off driftwood at sea and on adult auks and Kittiwakes. The Great Skua also makes extensive use of large fat reserves in spring and loses a great deal of weight. The possibility of feeding on afterbirths and sheep at a time of year when food is short is one which Great Skuas would find highly attractive.

Nonbreeding (immature) Great Skuas do not visit breeding colonies until long after breeding birds have taken up their territories. Presumably they arrive later in order to avoid the shortage of food at the start of the season. Clearly any predation by Great Skuas on lambs or ewes in April–May must be due to breeding birds, not nonbreeders. Because the species is highly territorial most of the predation will be by the pair owning the territory within which it occurs. However, even breeding Great Skuas will feed in groups in areas where there is no defended territory, if food is available, so that removal of all breeding territory owning birds from crofting areas where sheep are held for lambing would not *necessarily* prevent Great Skua predation. In my opinion it probably would be a successful measure since it is the close contact between Great Skuas and lambing sheep that leads to instances of scavenging of afterbirths, and eventually to predation. If areas where sheep were held for lambing were maintained free of Great Skua territories (which would not mean a loss of a very large number of pairs given the present distribution of the species) then birds from other parts of the islands would be unlikely to discover afterbirths as a food item (Photo 29).

On the Shetland hills, ewes are generally left to lamb unattended by crofters, and I have often seen ewes in dreadful condition for lack of proper shepherding. Some ewes may be left unsheared for several years in succession and fleeces become filthy and tangled. Some ewes get their hind legs caught in loose fleece and become unable to walk. Particularly when wet, ewes may fall on their backs and are unable to get up, often held down by the heavy tangled fleece. In June, July and August ewes that die like this (after many days of struggling on their back) are very rarely fed on by Great Skuas. Some have the tongue and lips picked out. Very few are torn open and may lie there for months. Other scavengers (e.g. Ravens, gulls, crows) are usually unable to attack the corpses because they are chased off by the skuas. Great Skuas seem to prefer to feed on fish at sea and appear to have no difficulty in getting enough food that way at this time of year. One year a ewe with hind legs cut to the bone by tangled wool died on one of the Great Skua club sites (although used by up to 150 immature Great Skuas, club sites have short well manured rich grass and are a favoured grazing area for sheep). The ewe remained substantially uneaten for weeks although skuas would even sit on top of the carcass while resting at the club site.

Dr Keith Houston visited Shetland in summer 1973 in order to produce a report for the Department of Agriculture and Fisheries for Scotland on the predation of sheep by Great Skuas and other birds. He dismissed the claims of some Shetland crofters that Great Skuas should be culled in order to protect sheep. He concluded that the numbers of lambs lost to bird predation were very small, while losses due to poor standards of husbandry were often very high. Many crofters own a few sheep that represent only a small part of their livelihood and often these animals are effectively left to look after themselves. Under these circumstances some predation by birds is to be expected and is probably of dying or sickly animals.

29. A Great Skua landing on an area of heavily grazed grass on Foula, where sheep are confined for lambing. Areas with short vegetation such as this are relatively unattractive to Great Skuas as breeding sites, but with population increase some pairs have established territories in such areas where they conflict more noticeably with crofting interests. Photo: R. W. Furness.

At present in Shetland predation is a rare event of little economic importance, but the threat of it requires responsible crofters to spend far more time attending their lambing ewes than would otherwise be necessary. However, if Great Skuas suddenly became short of food in summer, as could happen if Sandeel stocks decline further, or the whitefish industry ceased discarding small whitefish, then this situation could change. This conservation problem is discussed further in Chapter 16.

One skua population in the Southern Hemisphere appears to have had a more intimate association with sheep farming than we have so far experienced at North Atlantic colonies. The northernmost Brown Skua colony in the eastern sub-Antarctic is at Rangatira Island, east of New Zealand. Here, in 1937–38 some fifty or so pairs of Brown Skuas bred on the island and scavenged extensively from the sheep population there. Sheep were removed from Rangatira Island and skua numbers fell. In 1974–75 only 22 territories were occupied by Brown Skuas, which had changed to a diet of nocturnal petrels. Fleming (1939) believed that skua numbers on Rangatira Island were 'artificially' high in 1937–38 because they were able to scavenge from sheep, and Young (1978) thought that this was a reasonable

30. A Shetland ewe carrying a fleece that has not been sheared for several seasons and has partly fallen off, with a danger of tangling around the animal's legs. Poor husbandry is the reason why Great Skuas can attack these ewes when they fall and are unable to get up. Photo: R. W. Furness.

conclusion since the situation after the removal of the sheep suggested that the skuas had declined as a direct consequence. Brown Skuas appear to be able to make much greater use of sheep carrion than Great Skuas presently do in the Northern Isles of Scotland.

In the Faeroe Islands also, Great Skuas are accused of killing lambs and ewes, and large numbers of skuas have been shot. Faeroese Great Skua colonies tend to be much smaller than Scottish ones but the birds there do not have large stocks of Sandeels or discarded whitefish on which to feed. Faeroese Great Skuas are more dependent on predation as a feeding method, but as far as I am aware no scientific studies of the extent to which they attack sheep in the Faeroes have been carried out.

On Tristan da Cunha the 300 or so islanders have stocks of sheep, goats, chickens, pigs, cattle and other animals, and they also harvest large numbers of penguins, albatrosses, shearwaters and petrels and their eggs as food. The Tristan islanders have an intense dislike of the Tristan Skuas, which they consider to be vermin. Because these skuas are held to predate livestock, particularly chickens and lambs, the islanders shoot or destroy by whatever means available any adult skuas, eggs or chicks that they can get at. As a result, the Tristan Skua population on Tristan itself is now almost extinct. In 1974, only some 5–10 pairs remained (Richardson 1984) and I saw only one or two nonbreeding birds on Tristan in October 1983. There were some 100–500 pairs on the nearby Nightingale Island and 50–100 pairs on Inaccessible Island in the mid 1970s (Richardson 1984). By comparison, the undisturbed Gough Island, some 370 km away from Tristan and not exploited by Tristan islanders except for the harvesting of surrounding fish and crayfish stocks, while only about two-thirds the size of Tristan, supports about 2,000–3,000 pairs of Tristan Skuas. Clearly persecution of skuas on Tristan has all but destroyed what once must have been a sizeable skua population, and numbers on the other Tristan archipelago islands are probably held down by persecution.

Since sheep farming is an important activity on the Falkland Islands and there are some 2,000 or so pairs of Falkland Skuas there (Croxall *et al* 1984) it seems likely that skua-sheep interactions must occur there too. However, Cawkell & Hamilton (1961) stated of the Falkland Skua: 'This is an unpopular and fairly common breeding visitor. Sheep dogs will not work and take shelter under the horses when it stoops at them. It has been seen to attack a dying sheep but is not counted as an enemy of the sheep and acquires some merit in the eyes of the farmers by eating the eggs and young of the Upland Goose'. Grazing of pastures by geese seems to be a more contentious issue than attacks on stock by skuas!

CHASING SHEEP AND RESTRICTING THEIR GRAZING

On Fair Isle, crofters believe that sheep are prevented from grazing the hill vegetation by skuas. They claim that the skuas, particularly Arctic Skuas, attack sheep that enter their territory and drive them out. Once sheep have been moved out of one territory the skuas in the next chase them on until either the sheep gather in undefended areas between territories or, more usually, are driven to the cliff edges.

Most of the island of Foula is occupied by skua territories. Some 1,925 sheep (January 1985 DAFS figure) graze on the island. During the summer most of the sheep concentrate their grazing on clifftop grassland or skua club sites, where grass growth is strongest and coarser vegetation absent. A similar situation occurs on Noss.

While there are no skua territories on much of the clifftop grassland, Great Skua territory density is highest immediately around the club sites, so the sheep appear to choose to graze in areas of high Great Skua density because the grazing is good. The fact that they also congregate on clifftop grassland does not necessarily mean that they are forced to do so by skua aggression – they may prefer these areas because the grazing is better.

Fair Isle crofters applied for a license to shoot Arctic Skuas mainly because of the alleged loss of hill grazing for the sheep and consequent increased loss of sheep over the edges of cliffs. Permission was refused but illegal shooting has been extensive, and, in fact, the Arctic Skua colony was rapidly reduced to half the maximum number reached a few years earlier. No other Shetland crofting community appears to support the Fair Isle viewpoint. Foula crofters protect Arctic Skuas. John Scott and his shepherds on Bressay and Noss consider that the sheep choose to graze the coastal grass by preference and would do so in the absence of skuas in summer. This may even result in an improvement of the winter grazing! However, on Foula the islanders do believe that losses of sheep and ponies have occurred as a result of animals being startled by dive-bombing skuas. One or two ponies are believed to have been chased and to have gone over the cliff as a result. Some eight ewes were found drowned in a small steep-sided pool in the peat and this has been attributed to the aggression of Great Skuas. Of course direct proof is lacking but it is common enough to see animals being chased by skuas.

A report to the Crofters Commission by Stewart Moore in June 1983 assessed the complaints of the Fair Isle crofters about Arctic Skuas as follows: 'The lambing percentage on the hill is in the region of 100% but when the lambs are weaned off the ewes there is about a 25% loss. Of this figure some 51 (15%) are felt by the grazings committee to be related to the fact that the sheep have to graze along the cliffs and as a result the lambs are lost over the edge by falling over steep banks or grazing on very steep and almost inaccessible ledges where they can get down to but from where they cannot get back and the inevitable results. This loss of 51 lambs amounts to a loss of 3 per shareholder and a loss of about £50 of income for each household on the island which may not seem to be a large amount of cash but can be quite significant. The grazing of the scattald is very variable ranging from coastal turf to heather moor which can also be associated with peat cutting crust and bare stony ground. The grazings clerk put forward the theory that the heather may be harmed by the fact that the sheep are being kept from grazing it when the young growth is available and that it is subsequently becoming hard and woody and that the sheep are not keen to graze this older heather and as a result the growth becomes unpalatable and when it dies off it leaves large barren areas in the hill. The people feel that they have as much if not more right to let their sheep graze freely on the common grazings than the birds have to keep them off when they are nesting and some of them seem to think that there is more interest in keeping the birds on the island than the humans.'

Clearly the distribution of Arctic Skuas over most of the common grazing on Fair Isle (Figure 97) could prove a serious problem if Arctic Skuas do indeed prevent sheep from grazing. As a result of the complaints of the Fair Isle crofters a study of the Arctic Skuas in relation to sheep grazing and movements was commissioned by The National Trust for Scotland, owners of the island. This study (Cooper 1979) showed that the numbers of sheep on the area occupied by nesting Arctic Skuas was indeed lower during the peak skua breeding period than during the early or late parts of the breeding season when skua aggression was less. Also, numbers of sheep on the inland wet flushes were higher during bad weather (Table 58). Cooper suggested that these patterns were only partly due to skua activity. In addition, she pointed out that sheep are highly selective feeders, and show a seasonal pattern of use of grasses and heather, such that grazing on grasses predominates in summer while grazing on heather predominates in winter. There is also a subsidiary peak of grazing on heather in late summer when the

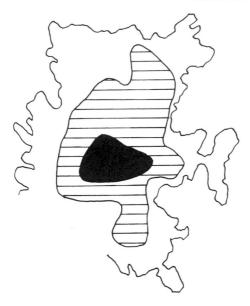

*Fig. 97   Distribution of Arctic Skua breeding territories on Fair Isle, shown for
1950 (black area) and 1980 (horizontal bars). From Fair Isle Bird Observatory
Annual Reports.*

new season's unlignified shoots are sufficiently grown to provide good grazing and
the grasses are becoming fibrous (Hunter 1962). According to Cooper: 'It is
possible that the Arctic Skuas may be preventing the sheep from grazing on the
heather from May until August but this is a time when the heather is not normally
grazed much by sheep (Hunter 1962). It is likely that the Arctic Skuas delay the
movement of the sheep onto the heather but it is not considered that this will
cause any great loss in the quality or quantity of the heather grazing, especially as
the seasons are later in Fair Isle than in South East Scotland where most experimental work on heather grazing by sheep has been done. Also the heather on Fair
Isle consists mainly of older plants so the nutritional value will not change greatly
with time.'

'The sheep in areas other than those influenced by the Arctic Skuas also showed
this seasonal preference for grasses. On the flush areas however the activities of
the Arctic Skuas may cause a loss of grazings. The sheep usually select short grass,
so once the ungrazed grass in the flush areas has become too long it is of little
interest to the sheep until the winter when the sheep eat the "hay". This may
improve the winter grazing a little but it is in spring that the ewes nutritional
requirements are highest. Underfed ewes produce poor lambs and little milk, and
so the production of lambs from the hill is reduced.'

Cooper found that sheep generally only moved a few steps forward when dived
at by Arctic Skuas, while many sheep ignored skuas and would even use skua nest
marker canes as scratching posts! Mortality of sheep also appeared to be low in
summer. Only one distinctively marked sheep of 47 individually recognisable

animals, was lost during the time that the Arctic Skuas were nesting on the hill. The number of ewes lost each year from the common grazings has been recorded since 1972 and the figure has risen over the years, from 39 ewes in 1972 to 63 in 1977. Arctic Skua numbers also increased over this period and the Fair Isle crofters believe the two to be related. However, in 1978 sheep losses suddenly increased to 109, while Arctic Skua numbers fell from 138 pairs in 1977 to 114 pairs in 1978. Statistically, there is a correlation between sheep losses and Arctic Skua breeding numbers, the correlation coefficient being about 0.4. This is a fairly low correlation, suggesting that larger numbers of Arctic Skuas do cause more sheep to be lost, but that other factors have a greater influence on the numbers of sheep losses. In 1978, for example, nearly two and a half times as many sheep were lost than was predicted from the number of nesting pairs of Arctic Skuas. Probably most sheep mortality occurs in winter or early spring and the quality of grazing and weather conditions at those times of year seem largely to be responsible.

ATTACKING SHEEPDOGS AND PREVENTING SHEEP DRIVES

Both Great and Arctic Skuas are particularly aggressive towards dogs, and will hit them repeatedly and hard. Many dogs flee for cover, for example between their owner's legs, while a few actually enjoy attempting to catch a dive-bombing skua in their jaws. A few sometimes succeed. Even well trained dogs are severely upset by skuas and it is very difficult to drive sheep in a skua colony since the dogs do not shepherd properly, and sheep are also moved by skuas in unwanted and unexpected directions.

Skuas tend to press home their attacks most vigorously on animals that are running, and sheep that are being moved to a pen through a skua territory tend to flee from the attacking skua. On Foula, many sheep pens are situated at coastal sites or adjacent to the outer wall of crofts, localities where skua territories tend to be least numerous anyway. However, it was the problem of driving sheep through skua territories on the outer part of Noss that persuaded the Department of Agriculture and Fisheries for Scotland that Great Skuas should be culled because they were causing significant damage to agriculture by disrupting sheep gathering activities there.

Skuas are most aggressive towards dogs and sheep when they have eggs or young; i.e. in Shetland from mid May to late July. Once chicks are well grown their parents become much less aggressive and, in fact, the gathering of sheep in late summer is not really affected by skuas.

SOLUTIONS TO THE PROBLEMS

Skuas do little damage to agriculture and what they do is of minor economic importance, but it constitutes a nuisance or thwarts the desire of the crofter to see every individual sheep and lamb healthy and unharmed. However, there is a problem to be solved, and that is largely one of the public image of skuas and the attitude of crofters. By refusing to accept that anything needs to be done, conservation bodies have generated ill feeling both towards skuas and to themselves. It might be valuable in the interests of conservation as a whole, in the interests of the long-term future of skua populations, and in the interests of the crofters' peace of mind, to take steps to minimise the conflict between skuas and crofters. Action could be taken that would not result in the loss of more than a trivial number of skuas from specific situations, but by so doing it would remove the incentive from crofters, who would otherwise be likely to shoot on a more indiscriminate basis. Since it has proved to be impossible to prevent illegal shooting, steps that remove the desire to shoot skuas would be beneficial.

This is a thorny conservation problem. The 1981 Wildlife and Countryside Act only allows licenses to be issued by DAFS for shooting birds where 'serious damage' can be demonstrated. Foula appears to be the only island where Great Skua predation on lambing ewes and lambs is a problem, and it is only serious in terms of animal suffering and consequent distress to crofters. However, I feel that this is a sufficient reason to consider remedial action. Crofters already take illegal action, and the bad name that the Great Skua has obtained throughout Shetland (the opposite of its earlier reputation as an unwitting but valuable defender of sheep from attacks by Sea Eagles) means that now it is illegally persecuted not only at breeding sites where it may indeed be a problem, but indiscriminately at breeding colonies and even at sea.

I quote: 'I had a firearm of my own last lambing season and shot any "Bonxies" as soon as they started sitting about. We had no animal interfered with by birds for the first year. Coincidence? I doubt it.'

'We have no license to shoot "Bonxies" but in fact we do shoot about 30–40 each spring as they take up territories in our lambing park.'

'8 sheep drowned in a loch and islanders fenced it in to stop the blind flight of ewes into it when they are chased by "Bonxies". About 100 "Bonxies" were shot there that year and it made no visible difference the year after.'

'There is quite a bit of culling of "Bonxies" at ——. This is to protect lambing sheep and the broods of ducklings and chickens many people bring out there.'

'Only on an odd occasion are "Bonxies" shot because people don't like them. People have quite a tolerance of anything if they don't harm anything else and they would never shoot an Arctic Skua for instance, despite their dive-bombing. In my opinion the "Bonxies" that are shot are all killed for practical reasons.'

'Everyone dislikes "Bonxies", as well as Fulmars, Ravens and Great Black-backed Gulls, and recently quite a number of fishermen have taken to shooting "Bonxies" when there is not much else happening on the boat. Particularly sandeel boats do this.'

'I enclose a map [of Fair Isle] on which I have marked the area to which we wish to restrict the Arctic Skuas. This would leave, on the east side or right hand side of the line approx. 40 pairs or one third of the present skua population. We would not harrass the skuas inside this area. If it would simplify the boundary, we could put a line of posts on the hill, at say 200 metres apart to the east side of which the skuas could nest. All other Arctic Skuas we propose should be removed from the hill by an organised cull during the spring/summer of 1980. I must point out that the crofters have now taken a hard line on this subject and failure to comply with our request will have disastrous effects for the entire skua population.'

Clearly it is difficult to prove damage by skuas, and in most cases no serious damage does occur, but in a few situations it does, whereas the fact that crofters are seriously upset by skuas can be considered damage to their way of life. Sheep which are left to lamb on the hill are left to cope with a multitude of problems, of which the remote possibility of predation by skuas is only one. This should be considered one of the many risks of not taking sheep in for lambing, and it would be unreasonable to argue that skuas should be controlled on the hill in order to protect sheep. Rather, sheep ought to be properly looked after within crofts during lambing.

Similarly, crofters can generally cope with gathering sheep despite skuas, except occasionally where a pair of skuas nests in a vital position in the sheep drive. Where this occurs it would seem reasonable to allow such pairs to be removed, but again indiscriminate shooting cannot be justified. I can see no justification for shooting skuas at sea or birds that dive-bomb people.

It would seem that there is no satisfactory evidence that sheep suffer a restriction of grazing as a result of being chased by skuas from territories. A more appropriate test would be to compare grazing by sheep in relation to skua numbers as the skuas arrive at the colony in spring and depart in autumn; and to compare the grazing distributions of sheep on islands where there are skuas, with those where there are few or no skuas. Perhaps this kind of study may be made soon, but it is difficult to see how the attitude of people can be changed. Now that skuas have a bad reputation they seem to be blamed for everything, however unlikely. Studies by visiting scientists from the south are unlikely to convince crofters that their ideas about the birds they live with are wrong.

After the problem of Great Skuas nesting in areas of Noss where they interfered with management of sheep, I suggested that an alternative to shooting might be to disturb settling birds regularly in order to put them off that area of the island. Great Skuas seem particularly unwilling to nest in areas regularly frequented by people. This was tried out, with considerable success, and the Noss wardens' regular walk through these areas made it unnecessary for any birds to be shot. Such a solution is clearly not practical where the skua numbers are high or where people cannot afford the time needed to deter the birds, but approaches using deterrents to the establishment of birds in the spring have not yet been given any serious consideration as an alternative to shooting.

CHAPTER 16

Skuas and conservation

The birds of prey and other vertebrate predators are, in a sense, key species in their particular ecosystems. Because they stand at the top of the pyramid of numbers and represent the terminal focus of energy in a wildlife community they are likely to be sensitive to any important changes that may occur in the whole system.

Ratcliffe (1980)

Conservation problems almost always arise because, deliberately or accidentally, man has upset the natural balance between animal species. Some animals may increase in numbers and become pests that require management to control their harmful effects. Other animals may decline in numbers and then steps need to be

285

taken to prevent their populations from being driven to extinction. Skuas can belong to either of these two categories. Under some circumstances local skua populations may be at risk, while the increases of other skua populations can threaten the well-being of some of their prey species.

Skuas can kill staggering numbers of seabird prey. Take for example the situation on Gough Island, in the South Atlantic. Some 2,500 pairs of Tristan Skuas breed on Gough Island, and by visiting a sample of territories on a semi-regular basis I found that each pair kills one or two, and occasionally three, nightbirds (mainly Broad-billed Prions and Soft-plumaged Petrels) each night. In addition, there are large flocks of nonbreeding skuas that roam around the island or gather on club sites, and these also feed mainly on nightbirds. According to the meteorologists on Gough, skuas are present throughout the year, though some individuals may go away for part of the winter. If we assume that breeding adults are present for 300 days per year, and kill two nightbirds each night, and if we ignore predation by nonbreeders, then as a very rough estimate the whole skua population kills about 2500 times 2 times 300, nightbirds per year. A staggering one and a half million nightbirds per year! Even though this figure is very crude, I am confident that the Tristan Skuas of Gough Island kill at least one million seabirds each year. They are a formidable population of predators! In this case though, their impact is much less than it might appear. There are many tens of millions of nightbirds on Gough Island. Skua predation is most unlikely to be detrimental to these populations, and may well be directed more at immature petrels rather than at the breeding adults. Nevertheless, the Great Skua population of Foula is about the same size as the population of Tristan Skuas on Gough Island and it is abundantly clear that the Foula seabirds could not withstand predation even remotely similar to the level that skuas on Gough exact. If Foula Great Skuas ever turned to killing seabirds as a major source of food then they would be a very serious threat to other seabird populations.

In order to take steps to ensure that skua populations continue to remain healthy but do not damage other parts of the wildlife community we need to draw on the knowledge of skua biology outlined in earlier chapters. In this chapter we will consider both those skua populations that might be considered vulnerable, and some of the problems that increases in other skua populations may present. Conservation problems that may arise as a result of the accumulation of pollutants by skuas have already been considered.

VULNERABLE SKUA POPULATIONS: I ARCTIC SKUAS IN THE BRITISH ISLES

Likely causes of Arctic Skua population changes are human persecution and disturbance, changes in the availability of food due to changes in numbers or breeding success of terns, Kittiwakes, Guillemots or Puffins that are robbed, changes in nesting habitats (e.g. through ploughing and seeding of hill land), competition for nesting space with Great Skuas, and predation by them and other predators. Population change is complicated by the fact that many birds reared at one colony will eventually recruit to breed at another. There are numerous recoveries of birds ringed as chicks that have moved to breed elsewhere, for example from Foula to Fair Isle or vice versa, Noss to Fair Isle or vice versa, Noss to Whalsay, and so on. Colonies within Shetland cannot be considered independently of each other; increases at one colony could be due to high breeding success at other colonies nearby.

Competition with Great Skuas

Nest site preferences of the Arctic Skua and Great Skua differ, but habitat tolerances overlap so that in some areas the two species do compete for space. This is particularly the case at Foula, Hermaness (Unst) and Noss, but in the near future may also affect the distribution of Arctic Skuas on Fair Isle if Great Skua numbers continue to increase there.

On Foula, as the number of Great Skuas grew, the Arctic Skua was pushed into increasingly poorer areas for nesting and into steadily smaller territories. With the smaller territories, Arctic Skua chicks became more vulnerable at fledging since parents found it difficult to keep their flying young within the territory. This led to high rates of predation by Great Skuas. Smaller territories also increased boundary conflicts and intrusions of Great Skuas led to an increased mortality of adult Arctic Skuas attempting to defend their territory. Since 1977, when Great Skua numbers began to fall on Foula, few Arctic Skuas (either adults or fledglings) have been killed by Great Skuas, and it should be stressed that Arctic Skua breeding numbers actually increased, despite the effects of the Great Skuas, between 1973 and 1976.

Many authors (e.g. Pennie 1948, Baxter & Rintoul 1953, Venables & Venables 1955) have claimed that the increase of the Great Skua during the 20th century has resulted in a decrease in numbers of Arctic Skuas breeding in Shetland colonies, but their view has been supported only by circumstantial evidence. Pennie (1948), after visiting Foula, stated that Arctic Skua numbers were 'diminishing owing to the ravages of the Bonxies; practically none of the young being allowed to reach maturity', but he provided only one estimate of the number of birds in the Arctic Skua population of the island. Jackson (1966) recorded that Great Skuas kill Arctic Skua chicks on Foula, and, because they return to the colony earlier in the year, they may establish territories in areas formerly occupied by Arctic Skuas, which, when they return to the island, are unable to regain their territory from the larger and more powerful species. Jackson considered that interspecific territoriality coupled with the general increase of Great Skua numbers and the similarity of the nesting requirements of the two species would have a more serious long-term influence on Arctic Skua populations than direct predation by Great Skuas.

Since Great Skuas in northern Britain feed partly by kleptoparasitism and Arctic Skuas rely almost totally on kleptoparasitism, there is also a possibility that increased numbers of Great Skuas could affect Arctic Skua feeding success.

Competition for space: as numbers of Great Skuas at Foula, Hermaness and Noss have increased, Arctic Skuas have been forced by competition for space to move into smaller areas or areas not previously occupied by either species. On Foula, Arctic Skuas have been pushed into areas of short, cliff-top grassland, marginal cultivation (fenced-in derelict fields), scalped peat (where peat has been cut down to bedrock so that now only a thin layer of lichens, grass and *Empetrum* grows between stones), or areas where there is regular human disturbance (airstrip, road and active peat cuttings). These changes are shown in Fig. 98, which give maps of the skua colony boundaries over the last 50 years or so. Increases in Great Skua numbers on Hermaness have had a similar effect (Fig. 99). Similarly, Arctic Skuas have been pushed around by the expansion of Great Skua numbers on Noss (Fig. 100). Furthermore, nesting densities of Arctic Skuas have increased,

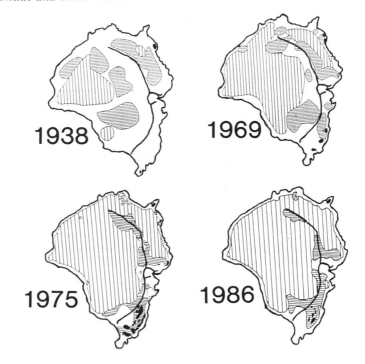

Fig. 98   Changes in the area of Foula occupied by Great Skuas (vertical bars),
Arctic Skuas (close horizontal bars), and Arctic Terns (black).

particularly at Foula and Noss where Arctic Skuas have been unable to move into
new areas (Table 59).

Data are not available to determine the extent to which this increased nesting
density reduces breeding success, but by analogy with other seabird studies it is
reasonable to infer that it will have some detrimental effect. On Noss, Perry (1948)
recorded a hatching success of 80% for Arctic Skuas nesting at a density of 61
pairs per km^2. In 1974, Kinnear (1974) recorded a density of 157 pairs per km^2
with a hatching success of 65%. However, part of the hatching failures observed
by Kinnear may have been due to the greatly increased numbers of people visiting
Noss National Nature Reserve rather than to increased Arctic Skua nesting density
per se. Davis and O'Donald (1976) showed that, on Fair Isle, Arctic Skuas with
small territories had lower breeding success than those with larger territories, but
in this case young and inexperienced birds had smaller territories so that the effect
may be due to age, experience, or individual quality rather than territory size.

Casual observations on Foula would suggest that the breeding success of Arctic
Skuas at high nesting density is reduced by intraspecific conflicts, often exacerbated
by human disturbance, but that the overall effect is rather small. High nesting
density may even assist Arctic Skuas in allowing neighbouring pairs to aid each
other in driving potential predators away. Since Arctic Skuas have clearly been
pushed into nesting areas that they would not have used in the absence of Great
Skuas it seems reasonable to infer that they will have suffered some reduction in

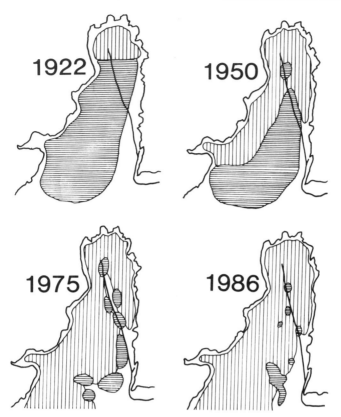

Fig. 99   *Changes in the area of Hermaness occupied by Great Skuas (vertical bars) and Arctic Skuas (close horizontal bars).*

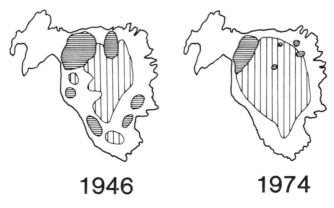

Fig. 100   *Changes in the area of Noss occupied by Great Skuas (vertical bars) and Arctic Skuas (close horizontal bars).*

breeding performance. However, even on Foula there is no sign that this has been a cause of Arctic Skua population decrease. Numbers increased as Great Skua numbers peaked but have fallen since 1979 even though Great Skua numbers have declined and the colony boundaries have slightly contracted (Table 59). On Unst, while numbers of Arctic Skuas at Hermaness have fallen, the numbers on Unst as a whole have apparently not decreased.

In fact, immature Great Skuas establish claims to a territory in July in the year before they first attempt to breed, so that the process does involve direct conflict with established nesting Arctic Skuas. Arctic Skuas are much more agile in the air and can easily drive off a Great Skua in flight, but once a Great Skua has landed it can withstand dive-bomb attacks by the smaller species which eventually gives up and concedes ground to the Great Skua. On occasions, a Great Skua may succeed in catching an attacking Arctic Skua and kill it. Conflicts of this sort lead to the death of numbers of Arctic Skuas in areas where young Great Skuas are expanding colony limits. However, the Great Skuas rarely eat the Arctic Skua adults they kill so this is clearly a territorial conflict and not predation for food. Since the expansion of the Great Skua colony on Foula ceased in 1977 very few Arctic Skua adults have been killed, but during the peak of incursion into Arctic Skua areas the death rate represented an important addition to natural mortality (Table 60). At the peak of territorial conflict between the skuas on Foula the Arctic Skuas suffered a mortality rate of about 3–5% per year in addition to the normal annual mortality of about 10–20% per annum (Table 61). O'Donald (1983) has demonstrated that, if Arctic Skua annual mortality due to other factors was the same at Foula as that measured at Fair Isle in the absence of shooting (i.e. between 10 20% per annum), and the breeding success, age of recruitment and survival to recruitment were also the same, then this additional adult mortality due to Great Skua predation should cause the Foula Arctic Skua colony to decline since gains would not match losses. This is not exactly what happened, because Arctic Skua colonies do not act as independent entities but provide a pool of recruits which move between sites according to circumstances. Also, it is likely that the Arctic Skua annual survival rate on Fair Isle has been affected by illegal shooting, and survival (in the absence of Great Skua predation) may well be higher on Foula than at Fair Isle.

In conclusion, at Foula, Hermaness, Noss, and possibly now at Fair Isle, Arctic Skuas may have suffered a reduction in breeding success due to their inability to withstand competition for territorial space with Great Skuas. The intolerance of Great Skuas for human disturbance or dislike of short vegetation around the nest means that Arctic Skuas may not be completely ousted from these areas, and the data clearly show that Arctic Skuas have been able to tolerate the losses of ground suffered without a significant effect on their numbers. However, conflict with Great Skuas may mean that these Arctic Skua colonies are a drain on the production of others and they may be dependent on immigration from elsewhere to sustain them, and this may not be possible in the long term.

Predation: at some colonies (e.g. Noss) there are apparently few records of Great Skuas killing Arctic Skua chicks or fledglings. On Foula this does happen. Jackson (1966) recorded that between 1956 and 1965 very variable numbers of Arctic Skua fledglings were killed by Great Skuas. In 1960 he estimated that 20% were killed while in 1961 the figure was only about 2–5%. From 1969 to 1976 the figure was between 10% and 43% (Table 62). Since 1977 no records have been kept, but rather fewer Arctic Skua fledglings have been killed. The great variation between years appears to be due to variations in the availability of other food sources to Great Skuas and the relative timing of the breeding seasons of the two species. When Arctic Skua nesting is early, the chicks may fledge before Great Skua chicks are at peak food demand. It is clear, however, that the extent of predation on Arctic Skua fledglings increased between the late 1950s and the 1970s and has fallen in the 1980s. Thus the peak predation coincided with the time when many Great Skua territories abutted and reduced the size of Arctic Skua territories. Consequently, Arctic Skua chicks were unable to make their initial practice flights without danger of straying over Great Skua territories. Similar predation has been noted at Hermaness (Albon *et al* 1976).

As with the effect of Great Skuas on Arctic Skua breeding success and adult survival, predation on fledglings will make colonies adjacent to Great Skuas less likely to be self-sustaining and more dependent on recruitment of immigrants from other Shetland sites.

Competition for food: the species chased by the two skuas in northern Britain are often different, and so there will be less conflict in this area. However, at some colonies both species chase Puffins and Guillemots extensively, and Great Skuas occasionally join in and take over a chase initiated by an Arctic Skua. Also, Furness (1978) showed that the chances of chases being successful decreased as the number of skuas in the area increased. This can be attributed to a greater vigilance or awareness on the part of potential victims when many skuas are patrolling for victims. It is therefore possible that the presence of hunting Great Skuas may reduce the chase success of Arctic Skuas, particularly since both species usually patrol for victims within two kilometres of the cliffs, where incoming seabird densities are highest.

Whether the reduced success rate of chases of auks by Arctic Skuas, due to the presence of large numbers of Great Skuas, would affect Arctic Skua breeding success is another matter. It is clear that Arctic Skuas spend only a very small part of the time available actually hunting, so that a slight reduction in foraging success might only mean that breeding adults would have to devote more time to foraging and less to sitting about in the territory. Since auks provide only a small part of their food, it is more likely that the availability of their preferred hosts, Arctic Terns and Kittiwakes, are of greater consequence than subtle influences of Great Skuas on auk susceptibility to robbing.

Influences of food availability
In a study of Arctic Skuas in SE Iceland, Arnason & Grant (1978) found that heavy chick mortality occurred during the first week after hatching. At this time they calculated that the Arctic Skuas, which were feeding by stealing fish from Puffins, had a negative energy balance. They pointed out that, normally, a large colony of Arctic Terns nested nearby and provided a food source for Arctic Skuas. In this season the terns had deserted and they attributed the high mortality of skua chicks to the lack of terns to rob.

There are, however, Arctic Skua colonies that can thrive in the absence of terns (e.g. Fair Isle), so clearly Arctic Skuas can get enough food from Kittiwakes and auks in certain situations. Arctic Skuas at the north end of Foula rarely see terns since the main tern colony is 5 km away at the south end of the island. However, most Arctic Skuas nest on the southern part of Foula and do chase terns extensively.

Over the past 10 years we have measured Arctic Skua wing lengths and weights at Foula and related weight to wing length (the latter as an index of chick age).

The relationship shows remarkably little variation from year to year, implying that chick growth is much the same every year. This suggests that Foula's Arctic Skuas have always been able to provide chicks with adequate food. This is in spite of large changes in numbers and breeding success of terns on Foula and changes in numbers of Arctic Skuas.

Observations of Arctic Skua time budgets on Foula showed that breeding adults spend considerably less than the total time available actually foraging. Under conditions generally prevailing at Foula, Arctic Skuas can increase foraging effort in order to make up for any reduction in food availability that has occurred in recent years. B. L. Furness (1980) found that, in 1979, Arctic Skuas on Foula spent less than one third of the available time foraging early in July (assuming that one adult must always be present in order to protect the chicks), but up to 60% of the available time late in July when food availability appeared to be declining. On Foula it is most unusual to find an Arctic Skua chick that is apparently hungry, and no territory is left unguarded by at least one adult. The same is true on Fair Isle, where O'Donald (1983) states that adults have little difficulty in feeding chicks.

While food shortage rarely seems to hit Arctic Skuas in Shetland, there is some evidence to suggest that breeding numbers may change in response to the availability of victims to rob during the summer. At Foula, Arctic Skua numbers increased when Arctic Tern numbers increased, and have declined since tern numbers fell. At Papa Stour numbers of Arctic Skuas and Arctic Terns increased in parallel up to 1977, but although tern numbers have generally been high in subsequent years, they have often failed to fledge any young and Arctic Skua numbers have fallen. It is not possible to state that skua numbers are controlled by tern numbers and success, but the two may well be related.

In the last few years in Shetland, Arctic Terns and Kittiwakes have suffered food shortages, possibly due to declines in Sandeel stocks, and it may be that Arctic Skuas will be affected in turn. While it is clear that at present Arctic Skuas have a considerable amount of slack time that could buffer them against food shortage, parasites generally suffer more than their hosts when the host's food supply is reduced, and it is impossible to make any firm prediction as to what will happen in this area in the future. It should be stressed that this is an area where monitoring of the situation is strongly to be recommended.

Human persecution and disturbance

Arctic Skua colonies tend to be small by comparison with those of other seabird species and the adults normally have a high annual survival rate. Hence they are susceptible to being reduced in numbers through killing of breeding adults. For a long-lived seabird the destruction of eggs has much less effect on population size. Similarly, reduced breeding success caused by disturbance of nesting skuas is less likely to be a problem than is direct persecution of adults.

In most crofting areas Arctic Skuas are popular birds, and shooting is confined to the few pairs that nest close to active peat cutting areas where dive-bombing skuas annoy crofters working at the peats. Small numbers have been shot (illegally) on Foula. On Fair Isle the attitude to Arctic Skuas is rather unusual, and shooting has been more extensive but irregular. It is documented that shooting was particularly evident between 1969 and 1973, 1976 to 1978 and since 1981 (Fair Isle Bird Observatory Reports, O'Donald 1983, 1986). During the period 1973 to 1975 there were detailed studies of Arctic Skuas on Fair Isle and adults were individually known (colour ringed). As a result shooting was probably very restricted or even absent. Estimates of the average annual mortality rates for these periods show that shooting has contributed significantly to the adult mortality (Table 61). We cannot say exactly what the normal mortality rate is since it is not certain that the estimate for the years 1973–75 is typical of other years. Variation from year to year is to be expected as a result of weather conditions, food availability and so on. Here we only need to point out that the Arctic Skua numbers on Fair Isle have increased during periods when shooting was infrequent or absent, and have decreased when shooting was extensive. As far as I am aware, Fair Isle has the only Arctic Skua colony in Scotland the size of which is a direct result of the level of illegal human persecution.

Habitat destruction

Arctic Skuas generally nest on moorland, derelict crofting land or rough grassland. All of these habitats are liable to change: in Caithness afforestation of moorland may threaten Arctic Skuas, while in Orkney and Shetland apportionment of common land, ploughing and reseeding may remove some nesting areas. However, most changes to habitat seem likely to result in the movement of Arctic Skuas into adjacent areas rather than in a reduction in breeding numbers. The only areas where Arctic Skua colony sizes are likely to be particularly sensitive to habitat alterations may be small islands where they already nest at high density on limited areas – for example Foula. Meek *et al* (1985) suggest that agricultural improvement to moorland habitat on Sanday and Stronsay, Orkney, may be extensive enough to affect Arctic Skua numbers on those islands and indeed Sanday is one of the very few sites where numbers have fallen between the 1974 and 1982 censuses. Agricultural changes may have local effects on Arctic Skuas, but it seems improbable that development of marginal land will be so extensive as to reduce overall population size significantly.

VULNERABLE SKUA POPULATIONS: 2 SKUAS PERSECUTED BY MAN

Scottish Great Skuas

Few Great Skua colonies have decreased in size during this century. Only eight established breeding sites in Shetland have become extinct. At these, the largest number of breeding pairs in any year was one (Tronda, Gluss and Eynhallow), two (Cava and Urie Lingey), five (Vaila and Flotta) and nine (Papa Stour). In other words, no colony that has reached double figures has failed to thrive. No doubt some other sites have been colonised for a short time by one or two pairs that have then either given up or been shot before being recorded by ornithologists. Certainly, some of the documented extinctions were attributed to direct persecution, and adults were shot specifically to stop a colony from developing. Four other colonies have a history of periodic drops in breeding numbers which suggest shooting of breeding adults (Fair Isle, Hascosay, Mousa, and Papa Westray). At the first two of these shooting has actually been documented, and undoubtedly there would be very many more pairs of Great Skuas nesting on Fair Isle but for shooting. Between the periods of shooting, the rate of increase of Great Skua numbers has been similar to that at other, undisturbed, colonies.

Whether shooting has affected numbers breeding at other colonies is less clear; numbers peaked on Foula in 1977 at 2,980 pairs and fell to 2,670 pairs in 1980.

Probably there were about 2,500 pairs in 1985 and the Nature Conservancy Council counted 2,495 in 1986. Although Great Skuas have been shot on Foula in the past, the rate of increase was around 7% per annum from 1900 up to 1977, which was almost identical to the rate of increase for the whole British population. In order to stop the increase in 1977 by shooting alone it would be necessary to kill an extra 400 to 500 Great Skuas each year over and above the average number shot in earlier years. I believe that some 50 to 300 birds have been shot each season in recent years on Foula, but I do not believe that the decline in numbers since 1977 can be accounted for by shooting alone, since the decrease in numbers has been greater than would be accounted for by the numbers shot. Furthermore, apparently there has also been a decrease at Hermaness National Nature Reserve, where the species is fully protected. Thus it would appear that a natural check on Great Skua numbers is beginning to act in Shetland (excluding Fair Isle where numbers have been held artificially low by shooting).

Faeroe Island skua populations

The Great Skua in the Faeroes was subject to human exploitation and persecution during the 18th and 19th Centuries and its numbers declined as a result. By 1872 the population had been reduced to about 36 pairs, and most of the blame for this has been put on skin collectors from Britain and elsewhere in Europe. Collection of adults continued after 1872, and the population of Great Skuas was reduced in 1897 to only one pair remaining at each of four separate sites. In December 1897, an Act of Parliament was passed in the Faeroes that gave protection to the Great Skua. It had the desired effect, and numbers recovered, increasing to about 71 breeding pairs in 1930, occupying the same four colonies as the four pairs in 1897.

This history shows two important things. Firstly, Great Skuas are easily reduced in numbers by shooting and their populations are vulnerable to such persecution. Secondly, numbers can recover even if only single pairs remain. Of course it is possible that some immature Great Skuas were present in 1897 that could have started to breed soon after, and numbers might also have increased as a consequence of immigration of birds from Iceland, though there is no evidence to suggest that such an influx took place and some to suggest that it did not. While skuas may be very vulnerable to human persecution, they appear to be able to breed quite happily as individual pairs and do not, like some seabirds such as Gannets, Kittiwakes and many terns, seem to need a number of conspecifics breeding nearby.

The fact that skuas breed on a large number of islands and mainland sites throughout the Antarctic, subAntarctic, and areas of the North Atlantic, and have become divided into several species and subspecies, suggests that skuas are good colonists but do not normally settle far from their natal area to breed. If they regularly dispersed to other breeding areas then the high level of genetic differentiation between local populations would be destroyed by gene flow.

The history of the Great Skua in the Faeroe Islands, like that of the small colonies in Shetland, suggests that Great Skuas are surprisingly capable of surviving and increasing from very low numbers, despite the devastation that can be caused by shooting.

VULNERABLE SKUA POPULATIONS: 3 HYBRIDISATION IN THE ANTARCTIC

South Polar Skuas and Brown Skuas may hybridise at colonies on the Antarctic Peninsula, and Falkland Skuas occasionally hybridise with Chilean Skuas. It is not clear, however, whether this hybridisation is the consequence of recent range expansions and new contacts, or whether it has been going on for a long time. If it is the result of recent range expansions that have been brought about partly by man's activities (providing more food and so allowing populations to increase and spread), then it is possible that some populations might become so interbred between species that their taxonomic distinctions would be lost. This possibility would depend on the extent to which pairs tend to form preferentially between members of the same species rather than between two birds of different species, and on the viability and fertility of the hybrids produced. Hybrids certainly are produced as a result of pairings between species, and it would appear that these are viable. At the moment, not enough is known about the amount of gene flow between skua species in these hybrid zones or the extent to which hybridisation is an increasing phenomenon, but it appears to be occurring at a number of colonies to a small extent.

PROBLEMS CAUSED BY INCREASES IN SKUA NUMBERS

Catharacta skuas are such generalist and opportunistic feeders that they have been able to adapt to new feeding opportunities presented by man. As a result, their populations have in some instances been able to increase and this can cause problems for conservationists. Where Great Skua numbers have grown in response to extra food, there is the potential problem that these birds will need to return to more traditional feeding methods, to killing other seabirds, while presumably their own breeding success would suffer and their numbers would fall back towards earlier population levels. It is impossible to say how much damage such a change would cause, but modern concepts of ecosystem interactions suggests that changes are not necessarily always reversible. It would be unreasonable to suggest that increased predation by skuas resulting from the loss of supplementary food supplied by man would be likely to cause irreversible reductions in numbers of the traditional prey seabirds, or of skuas themselves. It would be true to say that we do not know just what the consequences would be. This is disturbing since numbers of *Catharacta* skuas at several sites in the Antarctic and subAntarctic have increased due to man and could pose conservation problems. Most striking of all such problems may be the increase in numbers of Great Skuas in northern Britain, which have undoubtedly become high due to the increased availability of Sandeels and discard whitefish from fishing, and could not be supported by kleptoparasitism and predation alone.

Skuas in the Antarctic and subAntarctic
Chilean Skuas and Falkland Skuas are commonly found scavenging on refuse tips in the Falklands and southern south America (Devillers 1978), but the importance of this food source is unknown, nor is it known whether populations have increased in these areas over recent years. However, numbers of South Polar Skuas at the colony of Pointe Geologie in Adelie Land, Antarctica, have been greatly influenced by a refuse tip, close to the buildings of the French Antarctic

base. The South Polar Skuas which had previously fed at sea and opportunistically on Adelie Penguin eggs, chicks and carcasses, quickly took to feeding exclusively upon garbage (Juventin & Guillotin 1979). The number of birds at the colony increased from 80–90 in 1965/66 to 320 in 1976/77, and during the rapid growth in numbers most breeding pairs managed to raise two chicks rather than one; a sure sign that food was particularly abundant, since South Polar Skuas very rarely succeed in fledging more than one of the two chicks. The skuas also seem to have altered the timing of breeding so that, instead of being synchronised with the breeding of Adelie Penguins, they became more variable in chronology. This may reduce competition for food at the garbage dump since, if pairs are not synchronised, their peak food demands will occur at different dates. As skua numbers at Pointe Geologie increased, so breeding success fell, suggesting that the super-abundance of garbage relative to skua numbers was short-lived.

Great Skuas can make some use of refuse tips. In Shetland, small numbers feed at the refuse tip within the site of Sullom Voe Oil Terminal, although these birds appear to be overwhelmed by flocks of Herring Gulls. Rather surprisingly, the Great Skuas were seen to move away whenever Herring Gull flocks landed on freshly dumped food which the Great Skuas had already found. Due to their failure to cope with dense flocks of noisy Herring Gulls, Great Skuas have not exploited tips to the same extent as the Chilean, Falkland and South Polar Skuas.

On Macquarie Island, Brown Skua distribution and breeding success are closely related to the distribution of introduced rabbits, which have become an important component of the diet, and are probably responsible for an increase in skua numbers (Jones & Skira 1979). Similarly, Brown Skua numbers on Rangatira Island, New Zealand, were maintained at a high level by availability of sheep carrion, and subsequently declined when sheep were removed. The implications of these increases in skua numbers as a consequence of supplementary food supplied by man are not altogether clear. Jouventin and Guillotin suggest that South Polar Skua predation on Adelie Penguins was reduced because all the birds took to feeding exclusively on garbage. By contrast, Jones and Skira suggest that the increased numbers of Brown Skuas supported by rabbits on Macquarie Island will have also increased predation by the skuas on burrow-nesting seabirds such as prions and gadfly petrels, since Brown Skuas feed on both rabbits and seabirds on Macquarie. They suggest that a programme to reduce rabbit numbers would benefit the seabirds since it would cause skua numbers to decline, and with it their predation on burrow-nesting birds. On the other hand, Young (1978) found that Brown Skuas on Rangatira Island, although reduced in numbers after removal of sheep, changed from diurnal feeding primarily on sheep carrion to nocturnal feeding almost exclusively on burrow-nesting seabirds. Presumably the impact of numerous hungry skuas on these seabirds will have been particularly severe immediately after removal of the sheep.

These perturbations of skua numbers by man's activities may cause some slight harmful effects on other wildlife populations, but, in general, skuas seem to exist at levels that have very little impact on their prey populations. It would only be when skua numbers have been greatly increased by man that they might have serious effects on their victims. Such a potential problem is highlighted in the next section of this chapter.

Great Skuas in northern Britain
Great Skuas nesting in Scotland obtain a small proportion of their food during

the breeding season by predation on birds and eggs of a wide variety of species. The Great Skua has been increasing at a rate of about 7% per annum, and this increase has led to claims that Great Skua predation causes declines or extinctions of nearby seabird populations (Stenhouse 1926, Pennie 1948, Baxter & Rintoul 1953, Venables & Venables 1955). Red-throated Divers, Kittiwakes, Arctic Skuas, Eiders and Arctic Terns were considered to be most severely affected. Great Skuas do prey on these species, but more recent census data show no declines in numbers of these or other species that can be attributed to skuas (Parslow 1973, Furness 1978).

We need to assess possible future effects of predation by Great Skuas on populations of their prey species, as an understanding of this impact may become important if Great Skua numbers increase further, or if changes in fish availability result in increased predatory feeding by Great Skuas.

Pellet analysis on Foula in the mid 1970s showed that bird remains represented 1–2% of all Great Skua feeds. Using a simulation model, I estimated the energy requirements of the Foula Great Skua population to be 3×10^8 kcals per breeding season (Furness 1978). If the average bird eaten by a Great Skua weighs about 500–600 g then about 400 g of digestable material will be consumed per bird. This will represent about 700 kcals per bird, so 1% of total food requirement taken as birds will mean about 4,500 birds, 2% will mean 9,000 and so on. The figures are conservative in that most birds eaten by Great Skuas will probably weigh less than 500–600 g, so that numbers of birds eaten may well be higher. Doubtless some are eaten as carrion, but the proportion is not known. However, if Great Skuas at Foula were to feed exclusively by predation the minimum number of birds needed would be 450,000! Clearly this is an impossible situation. However, the possibility that predation by Great Skuas might increase due to changes in availability of other kinds of food must be given careful consideration and it is not reasonable to infer that since current levels of predation are having no serious effect on other wildlife populations that this must continue to be so.

Numbers of corpses of birds eaten by Great Skuas on Foula were recorded for the years 1969 to 1976 (Table 63) though, of course, some birds are killed and eaten at sea, and for some prey species these may be far more than the number of corpses recorded on the island. For other prey species, however, the land totals are probably close to the actual totals. The proportions of the main species eaten on Foula and the proportions of these species in pellet collections made in 1975 and 1976 are compared in Table 64. Comparison of these two sets of data show that corpse records greatly underestimated the proportions of auks and greatly overestimated the proportion of skua young in the diet. In 1975 and 1976, 256 young skuas were eaten on Foula. As young skuas are very unlikely to be eaten at sea this is considered to be the total number eaten in those years. Pellet data show that young skuas form 2.9% of the birds eaten in those years. It follows that $256 \times 100/2.9$, or 8,830 birds were eaten, giving an average of 4,415 birds eaten during each breeding season by Foula Great Skuas in 1975 and 1976. This estimate agrees fairly well with the observation that birds formed less than 2% of the Great Skua diet during the breeding season, since bioenergetics modelling predicted that 1% of diet would be equivalent to 4,500 birds eaten.

In Table 65 the mean number of birds of each species and age category eaten by Great Skuas each year on Foula in the mid 1970s is compared with the total number present on Foula each summer. No more recent data are available but it is probable that the situation has not changed greatly since then. All species listed in Table 65 have high annual survival rates, so that the predation by Great Skuas could represent an important additional mortality factor for these populations. Possibly the impact of Great Skua predation on Storm Petrels is the least well established datum in Table 65 since the estimate of the number of Storm Petrels available to be preyed upon around Foula is rather tentative. The true Storm Petrel population size is very difficult to estimate, and is composed of uncertain proportions of wandering nonbreeders that may only spend a few days in the locality before moving on. However, it is clear that the impact of Great Skua predation on Storm Petrels, Kittiwakes, Black Guillemots, Eiders, Arctic Skuas and Oystercatchers may be sufficient to have a noticeable influence on their population dynamics.

Killing of Great Skua chicks and fledglings is much more likely to occur under conditions of food shortage because under good conditions the parents generally prevent it. There was a tendency for more Great Skua chicks to be killed in years when birds formed a higher proportion of the diet (Furness 1981), and this may be a mechanism whereby a reduction in food supplies will reduce Great Skua breeding success by inducing a large increase in cannibalism.

On Foula, the majority of eggs predated by Great Skuas were those of conspecifics. Again, this may reduce breeding success in times of food shortage. The Red-throated Diver is the only species to lose an appreciable proportion of its eggs to Great Skua predation. In 1975 and 1976, Great Skuas took 22 of 56 eggs laid on Foula by Red-throated Divers, representing 67% of egg losses in those seasons. However, most pairs laid replacement clutches and overall breeding success of Red-throated Divers on Foula is higher than at most other sites studied. Although, on average, Red-throated Divers lose nearly 40% of eggs and 14% of chicks to Great Skuas their breeding success averaged 0.7 chicks fledged per pair between 1956 and 1985, and the number of breeding pairs increased from one to thirteen. This high breeding success on Foula appears to result partly from the lack of human disturbance, and the island has the highest recorded breeding density of Red-throated Divers in relation to the area of available shallow water feeding of any area in Scotland (Merrie 1978). Predation from the huge Great Skua colony has clearly had no detrimental effect, since nonbreeding divers are frequently seen attempting to move onto lochs where established birds are nesting. There are probably now no suitable lochans that are not normally occupied, so the population of divers is doing very well indeed.

Predation on Arctic Skuas also appears to be severe, but there is little to suggest that this is having harmful effects on the Arctic Skua population, as discussed earlier in this chapter.

It is not possible to determine what proportion of birds eaten by Great Skuas were killed rather than scavenged as carrion. Since the seabird populations are large it is reasonable to expect that bird carrion will be plentiful, so the predatory impact of Great Skuas may be considerably less than it might seem. The data collected in the 1970s on Foula show that, with the exception of the Black Guillemot where one pair of Great Skuas did seriously reduce breeding numbers, no other bird population has suffered as a result of the growth of the Great Skua population. Clearly this situation may change if in response to a reduced food supply the skuas turned increasingly to predation. Presumably they would continue to predate the same species as at present, but more heavily, and one might expect populations of Storm Petrels, Arctic Skuas, Red-throated Divers, Kittiwakes, Oystercatchers, Eiders, auks, and indeed Great Skuas themselves, to be severely affected.

References

Adams, N. J. 1982. Subantarctic skua prey remains as an aid for rapidly assessing the status of burrowing petrels at Prince Edward Island. *Cormorant* 10:97–102.

Ainley, D. G., Spear, L. B. & Wood, R. C. 1985. Sexual color and size variation in the South Polar Skua. *Condor* 87:427–428.

Albin, E. 1738–40. *A Natural History of Birds.* London.

Albon, S., Brazier, H., Frost, D., Martin, A. & Mason, D. 1976. University of East Anglia Shetland Isles Expeditions 1973/4. Norwich.

Aldrovandus, U. 1637. *Ornithologiae hoc est de Avibus historiae libri.* Bononiae.

Ali, S. & Ripley, S. D. 1969. *Handbook of the birds of India and Pakistan.* Oxford University Press, Bombay.

Anderson, D. W. & Hickey, J. J. 1976. Dynamics of storage of organochlorine pollutants in Herring Gulls. *Environ. Pollut.* 10:183–200.

Andersson, M. 1971. Breeding behaviour of the Long-tailed Skua *Stercorarius longicaudus* (Vieillot). *Ornis Scand.* 2:35–54.

Andersson, M. 1973. Behaviour of the Pomarine Skua *Stercorarius pomarinus* Temm. with comparative remarks on Stercorariinae. *Ornis Scand.* 4:1–16.

Andersson, M. 1974. Temporal graphical analysis of behaviour sequences. *Behaviour* 51:38–48.

Andersson, M. 1976. Predation and kleptoparasitism by skuas in a Shetland seabird colony. *Ibis* 118:208–217.

Andersson, M. 1976. Social behaviour and communication in the great skua. *Behaviour* 58:40–77.

Andersson, M. 1976. Population ecology of the long-tailed skua (*Stercorarius longicaudus* Vieill.). *J. Anim. Ecol.* 45:537–559.

Andersson, M. 1976. Clutch size in the Long-tailed Skua *Stercorarius longicaudus*: some field experiments. *Ibis* 118:586–588.

Andersson, M. 1981. Reproductive tactics of the long-tailed skua *Stercorarius longicaudus*. *Oikos* 37:287–294.

Andersson, M. & Götmark, F. 1980. Social organization and foraging ecology in the Arctic Skua *Stercorarius parasiticus*: a test of the food defendability hypothesis. *Oikos* 35:63–71.

Andersson, M. & Norberg, R. A. 1981. Evolution of reversed sexual size dimorphism and role partitioning among predatory birds, with a size scaling of flight performance. *Biol. J. Linn. Soc.* 15:105–130.

Applequist, H., Draback, I. & Asbirk, S. 1985. Variation in mercury content of Guillemot feathers over 150 years. *Mar. Pollut. Bull.* 16:244–248.

Aristotle 342 BC. *Historia Animalium* translated into English by Thompson, D. W., 'The Works of Aristotle Vol. 4'. Published 1910, Clarendon Press, Oxford.

Arnason, E. 1978. Apostatic selection and kleptoparasitism in the parasitic Jaeger. *Auk* 95:377–381.

Arnason, E. & Grant, P. R. 1978. The significance of kleptoparasitism during the breeding season in a colony of Arctic Skuas *Stercorarius parasiticus* in Iceland. *Ibis* 120:38–54.

Austin, O. L. & Kuroda, N. 1953. The birds of Japan. *Bull. Mus. Comp. Zool.* Vol. 109.

Bailey, R. 1966. The seabirds of the southeast coast of Arabia. *Ibis* 108:224–264.

Baker, R. H. 1947. Observations of the birds of the North Atlantic. *Auk* 64:245–259.

Balfour, E. 1968. Breeding birds of Orkney. *Scott. Birds* 5:89–104.

Bannerman, D. A. 1963. *The Birds of the British Isles* Vol. XII. Oliver & Boyd, Edinburgh.

Barré, H. 1976. Le skua subantarctique *Stercorarius skua lonnbergi* (Iles Crozet). *Comt. Natl. Francais rech. Antartiques* 40:77–103.

Barrington, R. M. 1890. The Great Skua (*Lestris catarrhactes*) in Foula. *Zoologist* (1890):297–301.

Barton, D. 1982. Notes on skuas and jaegers in the Western Tasmanian Sea. *Emu* 82:56–59.

Baxter, E. V. & Rintoul, L. J. 1953. *The Birds of Scotland*. Oliver & Boyd, Edinburgh.

Bayer, R. D. 1983. Black-legged Kittiwake feeding flocks in Alaska: selfish/reciprocal altruistic flocks? *J. Field Orn.* 54:196–199.

Bayes, J. C., Dawson, M. J., Joensen, A. H. & Potts, G. R. 1964. The distribution and numbers of the Great Skua breeding in the Faeroes in 1961. *Dansk Orn. Foren. Tidsskr.* 58:36–41.

Bayes, J. C., Dawson, M. J. & Potts, G. R. 1964. The food and feeding behaviour of the Great Skua in the Faeroes. *Bird Study* 11:272–279.

Belopolskii, L. O. 1961. *Ecology of Sea Colony Birds of the Barents Sea*. Trans. Israel Programme for Scientific Translations, Jerusalem.

Bengtson, S. A. & Owen, D. F. 1973. Polymorphism in the Arctic Skua *Stercorarius parasiticus* in Iceland. *Ibis* 115:87–92.

Berg, W., Johnels, A., Sjostrand, B. & Westermark, T. 1966. Mercury content in feathers of Swedish birds from the past 100 years. *Oikos* 17:71–83.

Bergman, G. 1982. Population dynamics, colony formation and competition in *Larus argentatus, fuscus* and *marinus* in the archipelago of Findland. *Ann. Zool. Fennici.* 19:143–164.

Berry, R. J. 1977. *Inheritance and Natural History*. Collins, London.

Berry, R. J. & Davis, P. E. 1970. Polymorphism and behaviour in the Arctic Skua (*Stercorarius parasiticus* (L.)) *Proc. Roy. Soc. Lond. B.* 175:255–267.

Berry, R. J. & Johnston, J. L. 1980. *The Natural History of Shetland*. Collins, London.

Biermann, W. H. & Voous, K. H. 1950. Birds observed and collected during the whaling expeditions of the 'Willem Barendsz' in the Antarctic, 1946–1947 and 1947–1948. *Ardea* 37:suppl. 123 pp.

Birkhead, T. R. 1984. Distribution of the bridled form of the Common guillemot *Uria aalge* in the North Atlantic. *J. Zool., Lond.* 202:165–176.

Blus, L. J., Belisle, A. A. & Prouty, R. M. 1974. Relations of the brown pelican to certain environmental pollutants. *Pest. Monit. J.* 7:181–194.

Bogan, J. A. & Newton, I. 1977. Redistribution of DDE in Sparrowhawks during starvation. *Bull. Environ. Contam. Toxicol.* 18:317–321.

Bonaparte, C. L. 1857. *Conspectus Generum Avium*. Brill, Leiden.

Bonner, W. N. 1964. Polygyny and supernormal clutch size in the Brown Skua, *Catharacta skua lönnbergi* (Mathews). *Br. Antarct. Surv. Bull.* 3:41–47.

Booth, C. J. 1976. Great Skuas probably killing Mountain Hare and rabbits. *Scott. Birds* 9:125.

Bourne, W. R. P. 1976. Seabirds and pollution. pp. 403–502 in *Marine Pollution*, Johnston, R. (ed.) Academic Press, London.

Bourne, W. R. P. & Brogan, J. A. 1972. Polychlorinated biphenyls in North Atlantic seabirds. *Mar. Pollut. Bull.* 11 : 171–175.

Boyd, J. M. 1958. The birds of Tiree and Coll. *Brit. Birds* 51 : 41–56.

Brand, J. 1701. *A brief description of Orkney, Zetland, Pightland Firth and Caithness.* Edinburgh.

Brisson, M. J. 1760. *Ornithologia.* Paris.

Brockman, H. J. & Barnard, C. J. 1979. Kleptoparasitism in birds. *Anim. Behav.* 27 : 487–514.

Brodkorb, P. 1967. Catalogue of fossil birds: Part 3: Family Stercorariidae. *Bull. Florida State Museum* 11 : 211–212.

Brook, D. & Beck, J. R. 1972. Antarctic Petrels, Snow Petrels and South Polar Skuas breeding in the Theron Mountains. *Br. Antarct. Surv. Bull.* 27 : 131–137.

Brooke, R. K. 1978. The *Catharacta* skuas (Aves: Laridae) occurring in South African waters. *Durban Mus. Nov.* 11 : 295–308.

Brooke, R. K. 1981. What is *Stercorarius madagascariensis* Bonaparte? *Ardea* 69 : 144.

Brooks, A. 1939. Migrations of the skua family. *Ibis* 3 : 324–328.

Brun, E. 1979. Present status and trends in population of seabirds in Norway. pp. 289–301 In Bartonek, J. C. & Nettleship, D. N. *Conservation of Marine Birds of Northern North America.* U.S. Fish & Wildl. Serv., Wildl. Res. Rep. 11. Washington, D.C.

Brünnich, 1764. *Ornithologia borealis.*

Buckley, T. E. & Harvie-Brown, J. A. 1891. *A vertebrate Fauna of the Orkney Islands.* David Douglas, Edinburgh.

Burton, R. W. 1968. Breeding biology of the Brown Skua, *Catharacta skua lönnbergi* (Matthews), at Signy Island, South Orkney Islands. *Br. Antarct. Surv. Bull.* 15 : 9–28.

Burton, R. W. 1968. Agonistic behaviour of the Brown Skua, *Catharacta skua lönnibergi* (Matthews). *Br. Antarct. Surv. Bull.* 16 : 15–39.

Burton, R. W. 1970. Biology of the Great Skua. pp. 561–567 in *Antarctic Ecology.*

Campbell, W. D. & Denzey, F. J. 1954. Great Skua killing Heron. *Brit. Birds* 47 : 403.

Caryl, P. G. 1979. Communication by agonistic displays: what can games theory contribute to ethology? *Behaviour* 68 : 136–169.

Caughley, G. 1960. Observations on incubation and chick rearing in the Antarctic Skua. *Notornis* 8 : 194–195.

Clarke, W. E. 1892. Report on the Great Skua (*Stercorarius catarrhactes*, Linnaeus) in Shetland during the season of 1891. *Ann. Scot. Nat. Hist.* (1892) : 87–92.

Clarke, W. E. 1894. The persecution of the Great Skua *Stercorarius catarrhactes*. *Ann. Scot. Nat. Hist.* (1894) : 8–12.

Clusius, C. 1605. *Exoticorum libri decem.* Leyden.

Collier, R. V. & Stott, M. 1976. Review of ornithological studies in southeast Iceland 1973–1975. *Brathay Field Studies Report* 29 : 1–18.

Copper, S. M. 1979. Report on the interactions between the Arctic Skuas (*Stercorarius parasiticus*) and the sheep on Fair Isle, Shetland. Unpubl. report to National Trust for Scotland.

Coulson, J. C., Duncan, N., Thomas, C. S. & Monaghan, P. 1981. An age-related difference in the bill depth of Herring Gulls *Larus argentatus*. *Ibis* 123 : 499–502.

Coulson, J. C., Duncan, N. & Thomas, C. 1982. Changes in breeding biology of the herring gull (*Larus argentatus*) induced by reduction in the size and density of the colony. *J. Anim. Ecol.* 51 : 739–756.

Cramp, S., Bourne, W. R. P. & Saunders, D. 1974. *The Sea-birds of Britain and Ireland.* Collins, London.

Cramp, S. & Simmons, K. E. L. 1983. *The Birds of the Western Palearctic, Vol. 3.* Oxford University Press, Oxford.

Crawford, R. D. 1974. Incubation of an Adelie Penguin egg by a South Polar Skua. *Notornis* 21 : 262–263.

Croxall, J. P., Evans, P. G. H. & Schreiber, R. W. 1984. *Status and Conservation of the World's Seabirds.* ICBP, Cambridge.

Cunningham, W. A. J. 1959. Great Skua nesting in Outer Hebrides. *Scott. Birds* 1:124.
Curio, E. 1976. *The Ethology of Predation*. Springer-Verlag, Berlin.

Darwin, C. 1871. *The descent of man and selection in relation to sex*. Murray, London.
Davenport, D. L. 1975. The spring passage of the Pomarine Skua on British and Irish coasts. *Brit. Birds* 68:456–462.
Davenport, D. L. 1982. The spring passage of Pomarine Skuas and Long-tailed Skuas off the South and West coasts of Britain and Ireland. *Irish Birds* 2:73–79.
Davis, J. W. F. 1976. Breeding success and experience in the Arctic Skua, *Stercorarius parasiticus* (L.). *J. Anim. Ecol.*
Davis, J. W. F. & O'Donald, P. 1976. Territory size, breeding time and mating preference in the Arctic Skua. *Nature* 260:774–775.
Dean, F. C., Valkenburg, P. & Magoun, A. J. 1976. Inland migration of jaegers in Northeastern Alaska. *Condor* 78:271–273.
Debes, L. J. 1673. *Faeroae et Faeroa Reserata*. Copenhagen.
Dementiev, G. P. & Gladkov, N. A. 1951. *Birds of the USSR*. Vol. 3. Israel Prog. Sci. Trans., Jerusalem (1969).
Devillers, P. 1977. The skuas of the North American Pacific coast. *Auk* 94:417–429.
Devillers, P. 1978. Distribution and relationships of South American skuas. *Le Gerfaut* 68:374–417.
Dickens, R. F. 1968. The North Atlantic population of the Great Skua. *Brit. Birds* 57:209–210.
Dixon, C. C. 1933. Some observations on the albatrosses and other birds of the southern oceans. *Trans. Roy. Can. Inst.* 19:117–139.
Dixon, J. S. 1933. Three magpies rob a Golden Eagle. *Condor* 35:161.
Dott, H. E. M. 1967. Numbers of Great Skuas and other seabirds of Hermaness, Unst. *Scott. Birds* 4:340–350.
Downes, M. C., Ealey, E. H. M., Gwynn, A. M. & Young, P. S. 1959. Birds of Heard Island. *ANARE Repts. Ser. B.* 1:1–135.
Drent, R. H. & Daan, S. 1980. The prudent parent: energetic adjustments in avian breeding. *Ardea* 68:225–252.
Drosier, R. 1830. Account of an ornithological visit to the islands of Orkney and Shetland in the summer of 1828. *Mag. Nat. Hist* (1830):321–326.
Drury, W. H. 1960. Breeding activities of Long-tailed Jaeger, Herring Gull and Arctic Tern on Bylot Island, Northwest Territories, Canada. *Bird-Banding* 31:63–79.
Duffy, D. C. 1980. Patterns of piracy by Peruvian seabirds: a depth hypothesis. *Ibis* 122:521–525.
Dunn, E. K. 1973. Robbing behaviour of Roseate Terns. *Auk* 90:641–651.
Dunn, R. 1837. *The Ornithologist's Guide to the Islands of Orkney and Shetland*. Hull.

Edgar, A. T. 1961. Some observations on White-fronted terns and skuas. *Notornis* 9:120–121.
Edmonston, A. 1809. *A View of the Ancient and Present State of the Zetland Islands*.
Edmonston, T. 1843. A fauna of Shetland: Birds. *Zoologist* 2:459–467.
Eisenhauer, J. H. 1977. Parasitic jaegers prey on adult Ptarmigan. *Auk* 94:289–290.
Eklund, C. R. 1961. Distribution and life-history studies of the South-polar Skua. *Bird-Banding* 32:187–223.
Eklund, C. R. 1964. The Antarctic Skua. *Scientific American* 210:94–100.
Ellis, H. I. 1984. Energetics of free-ranging seabirds. pp. 203–234 In Whittow, G. C. & Rahn, H. (eds.) *Seabird Energetics*. Plenum Press, New York.
Enquist, M. 1983. How do Arctic Skuas *Stercorarius parasiticus* search for diver eggs? *Ornis Fenn.* 60:83–85.
Ensor, P. H. 1979. The effect of storms on the breeding success of South Polar Skuas at Cape Bird, Antarctica. *Notornis* 26:349–352.
Evans, A. H. & Buckley, T. E. 1899. *A Fauna of the Shetland Isles*.
Evans, P. G. H. 1984. 'The seabirds of Greenland: their status and conservation'. pp. 49–

84, and 'Status and conservation of seabirds in Northwest Europe' pp. 293–322. In Croxall, J. P., Evans, P. G. H. & Schreiber, R. W. *Status and Conservation of the World's Seabirds*. ICBP, Cambridge.

Everett, M. J. 1982. Breeding Great and Arctic Skuas in Scotland in 1974–75. *Seabird Report* 6: 50–58.

Ewins, P. J., Wynde, R. M. & Richardson, M. G. 1986. The 1986 census of Arctic and Great Skuas on Foula, Shetland, Unpubl. Report to NCC.

Ewins, P. J., Bird, D. R., Ellis, P. M. & Prior, A. 1987. The distribution and status of Arctic and Great Skuas in Shetland, 1985–86. Unpubl. Report to NCC, RSPB, Seabird Group and Shell UK Ltd.

Falla, R. A., Sibson, R. B. & Turbott, E. G. 1967. *A Field Guide to the Birds of New Zealand*. Riverside Press, Cambridge.

Ferdinand, L. 1947. Studier af fuglelivet pa Faeroerne. *Dansk orn. Foren. Tidsskr.* 41: 1–37.

Fielden, H. W. 1872. The birds of the Faeroe Islands. *Zoologist* (1872): 3245–3257; 3277–3294.

Fisher, J. & Lockley, R. M. 1954. *Sea-birds*. Collins, London.

Fleming, C. A. 1939. Birds of the Chatham Islands. *Emu* 38: 492–509.

Forssgren, K. 1981. The kleptoparasitic behaviour of the Arctic Skua *Stercorarius parasiticus* and the Lesser Black-backed Gull *Larus fuscus* with the Caspian Tern *Hydroprogne caspia*. *Mem. Soc. Fauna Flora Fenn.* 57: 5.

Fraser, M. W. 1984. Foods of Subantarctic skuas on Inaccessible Island. *Ostrich* 55: 192–195.

Friedmann, H. 1945. Birds of the U.S. Antarctic Service Expedition, 1939–41. *Proc. Amer. Philos. Soc., Phila.* 89: 305–313.

Fuchs, E. 1977. Kleptoparaitism of Sandwich Terns *Sterna sandvicensis* by Black-headed Gulls *Larus ridibundus*. *Ibis* 119: 183–190.

Fullager, P. J. 1976. McCormick's Skua, *Catharacta maccormicki*, in the North Atlantic. *Australasian Seabird Group Newsletter* 7: 18–19.

Furness, B. L. 1979. The effects of Great Skua predation on the breeding biology of the Kittiwake on Foula, Shetland. *Scott. Birds* 10: 289–296.

Furness, B. L. 1980. Territoriality and feeding behaviour in the Arctic Skua (*Stercorarius parasiticus* (L.)). Ph.D. thesis, University of Aberdeen.

Furness, B. L. 1981. Feeding strategies of the Arctic Skua *Stercorarius parasiticus* at Foula, Shetland, Scotland. pp. 89–98 in Cooper, J. (ed.) *Proc. Symp. Birds of the Sea and Shore*, 1979. Cape Town, African Seabird Group.

Furness, B. L. 1983. The feeding behaviour of Arctic Skuas *Stercorarius parasiticus* wintering off South Africa. *Ibis* 125: 245–251.

Furness, B. L. & Furness, R. W. 1980. Apostatic selections and kleptoparasitism in the Parasitic Jaeger: a comment. *Auk* 97: 832–836.

Furness, R. W. 1977. Effects of Great Skuas on Arctic Skuas in Shetland. *Brit. Birds* 70: 96–107.

Furness, R. W. 1977. Great Skuas as predators of mammals. *Scott. Birds* 9: 319–321.

Furness, R. W. 1978. Kleptoparasitism by Great Skuas (*Catharacta skua* Brünn.) and Arctic Skuas (*Stercorarius parasiticus* L.) at a Shetland seabird colony. *Anim. Behav.* 26: 1167–1177.

Furness, R. W. 1978. Movements and mortality rates of Great Skuas ringed in Scotland. *Bird Study* 25: 229–238.

Furness, R. W. 1979. Foods of Great Skuas at North Atlantic breeding localities. *Ibis* 121: 86–92.

Furness, R. W. 1981. The impact of predation by Great Skuas *Catharacta skua* on other seabird populations at a Shetland colony. *Ibis* 123: 534–539.

Furness, R. W. 1981. Seabird populations of Foula. *Scott. Birds* 11: 237–253.

Furness, R. W. 1982. Methods used to census skua colonies. *Seabird* 6: 44–47.

Furness, R. W. 1983. Variations in size and growth of Great Skua *Catharacta skua* chicks in relation to adult age, hatching date, egg volume, brood size and hatching sequence. *J. Zool., Lond.* 199:101–116.

Furness, R. W. 1984. Influences of adult age and experience, nest location, clutch size and laying sequence on the breeding success of the Great Skua *Catharacta skua. J. Zool., Lond.* 202:565–576.

Furness, R. W. 1986. The conservation of Arctic and Great Skuas and their impact on agriculture. Unpubl. report to NCC.

Furness, R. W. 1986. Kleptoparasitism in seabirds. In *Seabirds feeding ecology and role in marine ecosystems.* Croxall, J. P. (ed.) Cambridge University Press.

Furness, R. W. & Furness, B. L. 1981. A technique for estimating the hatching date of eggs of unknown laying date. *Ibis* 123:98–102.

Furness, R. W. & Baillie, S. R. 1981. Factors affecting capture rate and biometrics of Storm Petrels on St. Kilda. *Ring. & Migr.* 3:137–148.

Furness, R. W. & Birkhead, T. R. 1984. Seabird colony distributions suggest competition for food supplies during the breeding season. *Nature* 311:655–656.

Furness, R. W. & Hislop, J. R. G. 1981. Diets and feeding ecology of Great Skuas *Catharacta skua* during the breeding season in Shetland. *J. Zool., Lond.* 195:1–23.

Furness, R. W. & Hutton, M. 1979. Pollutant levels in the Great Skua. *Environ. Pollut.* 19:261–268.

Furness, R. W. & Hutton, M. 1980. Pollutants and impaired breeding success of Great Skuas *Catharacta skua* in Britain. *Ibis* 122:88–94.

Furness, R. W., Monaghan, P. & Shedden, C. B. 1981. Exploitation of a new food source by the Great Skua in Shetland. *Bird Study* 28:49–52.

Furness, R. W., Muirhead, S. J. & Woodburn, M. 1986. Using bird feathers to measure mercury in the environment: relationships between mercury content and moult. *Mar. Pollut. Bull.* 17:27–30.

Furness, R. W., Hudson, A. V. & Ensor, K. in press. Interactions between scavenging seabirds and commercial fisheries around the British Isles. In Burger (ed.). *Interspecific Interactions of Birds and other Marine Vertebrates.* Columbia University Press, Columbia.

Gain, L. 1914. Oiseaux antarctiques. *Doc. Sc. Deux. Exp. Ant. Fr.* 200 pp.

Galbraith, H., Russell, S. & Furness, R.W. 1981. Movements and mortality of Isle of May Shags as shown by ringing recoveries. *Ring. & Migr.* 3:181–189.

Gibbs, R. G. & Mawby, P. J. 1968. Ornithological observations in the Faroes, 1966. *Dansk Orn. Foren. Tidsskr.* 62:137–140.

Gilman, A. P., Fox, G. A., Peakall, D. B., Teeple, S. M., Carroll, T. R. & Haymes, G. T. 1977. Reproductive parameters and egg contaminant levels of Great Lakes Herring Gulls. *J. Wildl. Manage.* 41:458–468.

Gilman, A. P., Hallett, D. J., Fox, G. A., Allan, L. J., Learning, W. J. & Peakall, D. B. 1978. Effects of injected organochlorines on naturally incubated Herring Gull eggs. *J. Wildl. Manage.* 42:484–493.

Glegg, W. E. 1926. The Great Skua in Shetland. *The Oologists' Record* 6:2–9.

Götmark, F. & Andersson, M. 1980. Breeding association between Common Gull and Arctic Skua. *Ornis Scand.* 11:121–124.

Götmark, F., Andersson, M. & Hilden, O. 1981. Polymorphism in the Arctic Skua *Stercorarius parasiticus* in NE Norway. *Ornis Fenn.* 58:49–55.

Götmark, F., Winkler, D. W. & Andersson, M. 1986. Flock-feeding on fish schools increases individual success in gulls. *Nature* 319:589–591.

Graba, C. J. 1830. *Tagebuch gefuhrt auf einer Reise nach Faro im Jahre 1828.* Hamburg.

Grant, P. R. 1971. Interactive behaviour of Puffins (*Fratercula arctica* L.) and Skuas (*Stercorarius parasiticus* L.). *Behaviour* 40:263–281.

Gray, R. 1871. *The Birds of the West of Scotland including the Outer Hebrides.* Thomas Murray, Glasgow.

Gudmundsson, F. 1954. Islenzkir fuglar IX. Skumur (Stercorarius skua (Brünn)). *Natturufraedingurinn* 24:123–136.

Haftorn, S. 1971. *Norges Fugler*. Oslo.

Hagen, Y. 1952. The Birds of Tristan da Cunha. *Res. Norweg. Sci. Exped. Tristan da Cunha 1937–38*. 20: 1–248.

Hamilton, J E. 1934. The sub-Antarctic forms of the Great Skua (*Catharacta s.skua* (Brünn)). *Discovery Rep*. 9: 161–174.

Hansen, J. M. 1984. The population of Long-tailed Skuas *Stercorarius longicaudus* at Kaerelv, Scoresby Sund, East Greenland, 1979. *Dansk Orn. Foren. Tidsskr*. 78: 99–104.

Hansen, L. C. L. & Lange, P. 1985. Census of the Great Skua (*Stercorarius skua*) Iceland 1984–1985. Hansen & Lange, Aarhus.

Harper, P. C., Knox, G. A., Spurr, E. B., Taylor, R. H., Wilson, G. J. & Young, E. C. 1984. The status and conservation of birds in the Ross Sea sector of Antarctica. pp. 593–608 in Croxall, J. P., Evans, P. G. H. & Schreiber, R. W. (eds.) *Status and Conservation of the World's Seabirds*. ICBP, Cambridge.

Harris, M. P. & Osborn, D. 1981. Effect of a polychlorinated biphenyl on the survival and breeding of puffins. *J. Appl. Ecol*. 18: 471–479.

Hartert, E. 1912. *Die Vogel der palaarktischen Fauna*. Berlin.

Harvie-Brown, J. A. 1890. The Great Skua on Foula. *Zoologist* (1890): 434–435.

Harvie-Brown, J. A. & Buckley, T. E. 1887. *A vertebrate Fauna of Sutherland and West Cromarty*. Edinburgh.

Harvie-Brown, J. A. & Buckley, T. E. 1888. *A vertebrate Fauna of the Outer Hebrides*. Edinburgh.

Hatch, J. J. 1970. Predation and piracy by gulls at a ternery in Maine. *Auk* 87: 244–254.

Hatch, J. J. 1975. Piracy by Laughing Gulls *Larus atricilla:* an example of the selfish group. *Ibis* 117: 357–365.

Helander, B., Olsson, M. & Reutergardh, L. 1982. Residue levels of organochlorine and mercury compounds in unhatched eggs and the relationships to breeding success in White-tailed Sea Eagles *Haliaetus albicilla* in Sweden. *Holarct. Ecol*. 5: 349–366.

Hemmings, A. D. 1984. Aspects of the breeding biology of McCormick's Skua *Catharacta maccormicki* at Signy Island, South Orkney Islands. *Br. Antarct. Surv. Bull*. 65: 65–79.

Hilden, O. 1971. Occurrence, migration and colour phases of the Arctic Skua (*Stercorarius parasiticus*) in Finland. *Ann. Zool. Fenn*. 8: 223–230.

Holbourn, I. B. S. 1938. *The Isle of Foula*. Edinburgh.

Hopkins, C. D. & Wiley, R. H. 1972. Food parasitism and competition in two terns. *Auk* 89: 583–594.

Houston, W. W. K. 1973. Predation of sheep by birds in Shetland. Unpublished report to DAFS (East Craigs).

Hudson, R. 1968. The Great Skua in the Caribbean. *Bird Study* 15: 33–34.

Hulsman, K. 1976. The robbing behaviour of terns and gulls. *Emu* 76: 143–149.

Humphrey, P. S., Bridge, D., Reynolds, P. W. & Peterson, R. T. 1970. Birds of Isla Grande, (Tierra del Fuego). Smithsonian, Washington.

Hunt, G. L. 1980. Mate selection and mating systems in seabirds. pp. 113–151. In *Behavior of Marine Animals Vol. 4: Marine Birds*. Burger, J., Olla, B. L. & Winn, H. E. (eds.). Plenum, New York.

Hunter, R. F. 1962. Hill sheep and their pasture: a study of sheep-grazing in south east Scotland. *J. Ecol*. 50: 651–658.

Hutchison, L. V., Wenzel, B. M., Stager, K. E. & Tedford, B. L. 1982. Further evidence for olfactory foraging by Sooty Shearwaters and Northern Fulmars. pp. 72–77 In *Marine Birds: their Feeding Ecology and Commercial Fisheries Relationships*. Nettleship, D. N., Sanger, G. A. & Springer, P. F. (eds.) Canadian Wildlife Service, Ottawa.

Huxley, J. 1955. Morphism in birds. *Proc. XI Int. orn. Congr*. (1954): 309–328.

Ijzendoorn, E. J. van, 1981. On identification of immature Arctic Skua and Long-tailed Skua. *Dutch Birding* 3: 10–12.

Ingram, C. 1949. Great Skua's method of killing large birds. *Brit. Birds* 42: 223.

Jackson, E. E. 1966. The birds of Foula. *Scott. Birds* 4: suppl.

Jakobsen, J. 1921. *Etymologisk Ordbog over det norrone sprog pa Shetland.* Copenhagen.

Jehl, J. R. 1973. The distribution of marine birds in Chilean waters in winter. *Auk* 90: 114–135.

Jensen, J. K. 1982. Possible wintering area for Maccormick's Skua on the Newfoundland Banks at Flemmings Cape. *Dansk Orn. Foren. Tiddskr.* 76: 148.

Jespersen, P. 1930. Ornithological observations in the North Atlantic Ocean. *Danish Dana Exp. 1920–22 Rept.* 7: 1–36.

Jespersen, P. 1933. Observations on the oceanic birds of the Pacific and adjacent waters. *Vidensk Medd. fra Dansk naturh. Foren.* 94: 187–221.

Joensen, A. H. 1966. *Fuglene pa Faeroerne.* Rhodos, Copenhagen.

Johnston, B. R. 1971. Skua numbers and conservation problems at Cape Hallett, Antarctica. *Nature* 231: 468.

Johnston, G. C. 1973. Predation by Southern Skua on rabbits on Macquarie Island. *Emu* 73: 25–26.

Jones, E. & Skira, I. J. 1979. Breeding distribution of the Great Skua at Macquarie Island in relation to numbers of rabbits. *Emu* 79: 19–23.

Jouventin, P. & Guillotin, M. 1979. Socio-ecologie du skua antarctique a Pointe Geologie. *Terre Vie, Rev. Ecol.* 33: 109–127.

Jouventin, P., Stahl, J. C., Weimerskirch, H. & Mougin, J. L. 1984. The seabirds of the French Sub-Antarctic Islands and Adelie Land: their status and conservation. pp. 609–626. In Croxall, J. P., Evans, P. G. H. & Schreiber, R. W. (Eds.) *Status and Conservation of the World's Seabirds.* ICBP, Cambridge.

Kampp, K. 1982. Notes on the Long-tailed skua *Stercorarius longicaudus* in West Greenland. *Dansk Orn. Foren. Tidsskr.* 76: 129–135.

Kapanen, M. 1977. Migration of the Arctic Skua in eastern Finland. *Ornis Fenn.* 54: 123–126.

Kemp, J. B. 1984. Identification of first-winter Pomarine Skua. *Brit. Birds* 77: 27.

King, W. B. 1967. *Seabirds of the Tropical Pacific Ocean.* Smithsonian Institution, Washington, D.C.

Kinnear, P. K. 1974. Report on skua survey carried out on behalf of the Nature Conservancy Council on Noss NNR, 1974. Unpubl. report to NCC.

Korte, J. de, 1972. Birds, observed and collected by 'De Nederlandse Spitsbergen Expeditie' in West and East Spitsbergen, 1967 and 1968–'69; second part. *Beaufortia* 19: 197–232.

Korte, J. de, 1972. Birds, observed and collected by 'De Nederlandse Spitsbergen Expeditie' in West and East Spitsbergen, 1967 and 1968–'69; third and last part. *Beaufortia* 20: 23–58.

Korte, J. de, 1977. Ecology of the Long-tailed Skua (*Stercorarius longicaudus* Vieillot, 1819) at Scoresby Sund, East Greenland. Report of the Nederlandse Groenland Expedite Scoresbysund 1973, 1974 and 1975. Part one: distribution and density. *Beaufortia* 25: 201–219.

Korte, J. de, 1984. Ecology of the Long-tailed Skua (*Stercorarius longicaudus* Vieillot, 1819) at Scoresby Sund, East Greenland. Part two: arrival, site tenacity and departure. *Beaufortia* 34: 1–14.

Korte, J. de, 1985. Ecology of the Long-tailed Skua, *Stercorarius longicaudus* Vieillot, 1819, at Scoresby Sund, East Greenland. Part three: clutch size, laying date and incubation in relation to energy reserves. *Beaufortia* 35: 93–127.

Korte, J. de, 1986. Ecology of the Long-tailed Skua, *Stercorarius longicaudus* Vieillot, 1819, at Scoresby Sund, East Greenland. Part four: breeding success and growth of young. *Bijdr. Dierk.* 56: 1–23.

Korte, J. de, 1986. Aspects of breeding success in Tundra birds. Ph.D. thesis, University of Amsterdam.

Kuroda, N. 1955. Observations on pelagic birds of the Northwest Pacific. *Condor* 57: 290–300.

Kuroda, N. 1960. Analysis of seabird distribution in the northwest Pacific Ocean. *Pacific Sci.* 14: 55–67.

Kuroda, N. 1961. A note on the pectoral muscles of birds. *Auk* 78: 261–263.

Kuschert, V. H. 1981. Das vorkommen der Raubmöwen (*Stercorariidae*) auf Helgoland unter besonderer Berücksichtigung des Einfluges im Sommer 1979. *Die Vogelwelt* 102 : 121–132.

Kushlan, J. A. 1978. Non-rigorous foraging by robbing egrets. *Ecology* 59 : 649–653.

Lack, D. 1933. Nesting conditions as a factor controlling timing of breeding in birds. *Proc. Zool. Soc., Lond.* 231–237.

Lack, D. 1942. The breeding birds of Orkney. *Ibis* : 461–484.

Lack, D. 1943. The breeding birds of Orney. *Ibis* : 1–27.

Lamb, H. H. 1972. *Climate: Past, Present and Future* Vol. 1. London.

Lambert, K. 1971. Seevogelbeobachtungen auf zwei Reisen. *Beitr. Vogelkd., Leipzig* 17 : 1–32.

Lambert, K. 1980. Ein Überwinterungsgebiet der Falkenraubmöive, *Stercorarius longicauduus* Vieill. 1819, vor Südwest-mid Südafrika entdeckt. *Beitr. Vogelkd., Jena* 26 : 199–212.

Lambert, K. 1981. Hinweise zur feldornithologischen Bestimmung der Raubmöwen. *Der Falke* 28 : 42–51.

Linnaeus, C. 1764. *Systema Naturae.* Holmiae.

Lockie, J. D. 1952. The food of Great Skuas on Hermaness, Unst, Shetland. *Scott. Nat.* 64 : 158–162.

Lockwood, W. B. 1984. *The Oxford Book of British Bird Names.* Oxford University Press, Oxford.

Lovenskiold, H. L. 1964. *Avifauna Svalbardensis.* Norsk Polarinstitutt, Oslo.

Low, G. 1879. *A Tour through Orkney and Schetland in 1774.* Kirkwall.

Löfgren, L. E. unpubl. Distribution and foraging ecology of skuas (*Stercorariinae*) during the nonbreeding season.

Lukowski, A. B. 1983. DDT and its metabolites in the tissues and eggs of migrating Antarctic seabirds from the regions of the South Shetland Islands. *Pol. Polar Res.* 4 : 135–141.

Maher, W. J. 1970. The Pomarine Jaeger as a Brown Lemming predator in northern Alaska. *Wilson Bull.* 82 : 130–157.

Maher, W. J. 1974. Ecology of Pomarine, Parasitic and Long-tailed Jaegers in Northern Alaska. *Pacif. Coast Avifauna.* 37 : 1–148.

Martin, M. & Barry, T. W. 1978. Nesting behaviour and food habits of parasitic jaegers at Anderson River delta, Northern Territories. *Can. Field Nat.* 92 : 45–50.

Martinez-Vilalta, A., Ferrer, X. & Carboneras, C. 1984. Situación de los págalos (*Stercorarius* sp.) en el litoral Catalán (ne de la Peninsula Ibérica). *Misc. Zool.* 8 : 217–223.

Mathews, G. M. 1913. *The Birds of Australia.* London, Witherby.

Maxson, S. J. & Bernstein, N. P. 1982. Kleptoparasitism by South Polar Skuas on Blue-eyed Shags in Antarctica. *Wilson Bull.* 94 : 269–281.

Meek, E. R., Booth, C. J., Reynolds, P. & Ribbands, B. 1985. Breeding skuas in Orkney. *Seabird* 8 : 21–33.

Meinertzhagen, R. 1959. *Pirates and Predators.* Edinburgh.

Meininger, P. L. 1977. Pomarine Skua taking Black-headed Gulls. *Limosa* 50 : 145.

Melville, D. S. 1985. Long-tailed Skuas *Stercorarius longicaudus* in New Zealand. *Notornis* 32 : 51–73.

Merikallio, E. 1958. Finnish birds: their distribution and numbers. *Fauna och Flora Fenn.* 5 : 1–181.

Merrett, C. 1666. *Pinax rerum Naturalium.* London.

Merrie, T. D. H. 1978. Relationship between spatial distribution of breeding divers and the availability of fishing waters. *Bird Study* 25 : 119–122.

Mineau, P. 1982. Levels of major organochlorine contaminants in sequentially-laid Herring Gull eggs. *Chemosphere* 11 : 679–685.

Monaghan, P. & Metcalfe, N. B. 1986. On being the right size: natural selection and body size in the Herring Gull. *Evolution* 40 : 1096–1099.

Moors, P. J. 1980. Southern Great Skuas on Antipodes Island, New Zealand: observations on foods, breeding, and growth of chicks. *Notornis* 27:133–146.

Morvan, P. le, Mougin, J. L. & Prévost, J. 1967. Ecologie du skua antarctique (*Stercorarius skua maccormicki*) dans l'Archipel de Pointe Geologie (Terre Adelie). *L'Oiseau et R.F.O.* 37:193–220.

Moynihan, M. 1959. A revision of the family Laridae (Aves). *Amer. Mus. Novitates* 1928:1–42.

Moynihan, M. 1962. Hostile and sexual behaviour patterns of South American and Pacific Laridae. *Behaviour* 8(suppl):1–365.

Muirhead, S. J. 1986. The accumulation, storage and elimination of metals and organo-chlorines in the Great Skua *Catharacta skua skua* and metal accumulation in Atlantic Procellariiformes. Unpubl. PhD Thesis, University of Glasgow.

Muller-Schwarze, D. & Muller-Schwarze, C. 1973. Differential predation by South Polar Skuas in an Adelie Penguin rookery. *Condor* 75:127–131.

Munkebye, O. 1973. First proof of breeding of Great Skua (*Catharacta skua*) on Bjornoya. *Nor. Polarinst. Arbok 1971*:122.

Murphy, R. C. 1936. *Oceanic birds of South America*.

Neill, P. 1806. *A tour through some of the Islands of Orkney and Shetland*. Edinburgh.

Nelson, J. B. 1980. *Seabirds*. Hamlyn, London.

Nettleship, D. N. 1972. Breeding success of the Common Puffin *Fratercula arctica* L. on different habitats at Great Island, Newfoundland. *Ecol. Monogr.* 42:239–268.

Newton, I. 1979. *Population Ecology of Raptors*. Poyser, Berkhamsted.

Newton, I. 1986. *The Sparrowhawk*. Poyser, Calton.

Nicholson, J. K. & Osborn, D. 1983. Kidney lesions in pelagic seabirds with high tissue levels of cadmium and mercury. *J. Zool., Lond.* 200:99–118.

Nicholson, J. K. & Osborn, D. 1984. Kidney lesions in juvenile Starlings *Sturnus vulgarus* fed on a mercury-contaminated synthetic diet. *Environ. Pollut. A* 33:195–206.

Norderhang, M. 1983. Endringer i forekomstene av storjo og svartbak pa Svalbard. *Var Fuglefauna* 6:30–33.

Norrevang, A. 1955. Forandringer i den faeroske fugleverden i relation til klimaaendringen i det nordatlantiske omrade. *Dansk Orn. Foren. Tidsskr.* 49:206–229.

Norrevang, A. 1960. Sofuglenes udvaelgelse af ynglebiotop pa Mykines, Faeroerue. *Dansk. Orn. Foren. Tidsskr.* 54:9–35.

O'Donald, P. 1959. Possibility of assortative mating in the Arctic Skua. *Nature* 183:1210–1211.

O'Donald, P. 1960. Assortative mating in a population in which two alleles are segregating. *Heredity* 15:389–396.

O'Donald, P. 1972. Sexual selection by variation in fitness at breeding time. *Nature* 237:349–351.

O'Donald, P. 1980. *Genetic Models of Sexual Selection*. Cambridge University Press, Cambridge.

O'Donald, P. 1983. *The Arctic Skua*. Cambridge University Press, Cambridge.

O'Donald, P. 1986. Skua decline. *New Scientist* No. 1490:63.

O'Donald, P. & Davis, P. E. 1959. The genetics of the colour phases of the Arctic Skua. *Heredity* 13:481–486.

O'Donald, P. & Davis, J. W. F. 1975. Demography and selection in a population of Arctic Skuas. *Heredity* 35:75–83.

O'Donald, P. & Davis, J. W. F. 1976. A demographic analysis of the components of selection in a population of Arctic Skuas. *Heredity* 36:343–350.

O'Donald, O., Davis, J. W. F. & Broad, R. A. 1974. Variation in assortative mating in two colonies of Arctic Skuas. *Nature* 252:700–701.

O'Donald, P., Wedd, N. S. & Davis, J. W. F. 1974. Mating preferences and sexual selection in the Arctic Skua. *Heredity* 33:1–16.

Oelke, H. & Steiniger, F. 1973. Salmonella in Adelie Penguins and South Polar Skuas on Ross Island, Antarctica. *Avian Dis.* 17:568–573.

Oliver, P. J. & Davenport, D. L. 1970. Large passage of seabirds at Cap Griz Nez. *Seabird Rept.* 1970:16–24.

Olsen, K. M. & Christensen, S. 1984. Field identification of juvenile skuas. *Brit. Birds* 77:448–450.

Oreel, G. J. 1981. Bill colour of Pomarine Skua. *Dutch Birding* 3:77.

Osborne, B. C. 1985. Aspects of the breeding biology and feeding behaviour of the Brown Skua *Catharacta lönnbergi* on Bird Island, South Georgia. *Br. Antarct. Surv. Bull.* 66:57–71.

Owen, C. 1971. Long-tailed Skua feeding on inland refuse tip. *Brit. Birds.* 64:194.

Parmelee, D. F. 1985. Polar adaptations in the South Polar Skua (*Catharacta maccormicki*) and the Brown Skua (*Catharacta lönnbergi*) of Anvers Island, Antarctica. *Acta XVIII Cong. Int. Ornithol.* Vol 1:520–529. Ilyichev, V. D. & Gavrilov, V. M. (eds.). Nauka, Moscow.

Parmelee, D. F. & Neilson, D. R. 19 . Bipolar migration of South Polar Skuas.

Parrish, J. R., Rogers, D. T. Jr. & Prescott-Ward, F. 1983. Identification of natal locales of Peregrine Falcons (*Falco peregrinus*) by trace element analysis of feathers. *Auk* 100:560–567.

Parslow, J. L. F. 1973. *Breeding Birds of Britain and Ireland.* Poyser, Berkhamsted.

Pascoe, J. G. 1984. A census of the South Polar Skua at Cape Hallett, Antarctica. *Notornis* 31:312–319.

Paulson, D. R. 1973. Predator polymorphism and apostatic selection. *Evolution* 27:269–277.

Payne, R. B. 1967. Interspecific communication signals in parasitic birds. *Amer. Natur.* 101:363–375.

Pennant, T. 1789. *A tour in Scotland and voyage to the Outer Hebrides, 1771–1776.* Caledonian Zoology.

Pennie, I. D. 1948. Summer bird notes from Foula. *Scot. Nat.* 60:157–163.

Pennie, I. D. 1953. The Arctic Skua in Caithness. *Brit. Birds* 46:105–108.

Perdeck, A. C. 1960. Observations on the reproductive behaviour of the Great Skua or Benxie, *Stercorarius skua skua* (Brünn), in Shetland. *Ardea* 48:111–136.

Perdeck, A. C. 1963. The early reproductive behaviour of the Arctic Skua, *Stercorarius parasiticus* (L.) *Ardea* 51:1–15.

Perry, R. 1948. *Shetland Sanctuary.* Faber & Faber, London.

Peters, J. L. 1934. *Check-List of Birds of the World.* Harvard University Press, Cambridge, Massachusetts.

Pietz, P. J. 1985. Long call displays of sympatric South Polar and Brown Skuas. *Condor* 87:316–326.

Pitelka, F. A., Tomich, P. Q. & Treichel, G. W. 1955. Breeding behavior of jaegers and owls near Barrow, Alaska. *Condor* 57:3–18.

Pitt, F. 1922. The Great and Arctic Skuas in the Shetlands. *Brit. Birds* 16:174–181, 198–202.

Pitt, F. 1923. *Shetland Pirates.* Allen & Unwin, London.

Pollock, K. 1963. Great Skua breeding on St Kilda. *Scott. Birds* 2:427.

Poole, J. 1625. *A briefe Declaration of this my Voyage of discoverie to Greenland.* Samuel Purchas, London.

Prestt, I., Jefferies, D. J. & Moore, N. N. 1970. Polychlorinated biphenyls in wild birds in Britain and their avian toxicity. *Environ. Pollut.* 1:3–26.

Price, L. W. 1969. Nesting of the Long-tailed Jaeger in southwest Yukon territory: an extension of the known breeding grounds. *Can. Field Nat.* 83:138–141.

Price, L. W. 1973. The local ecological effect of Long-tailed Jaegers nesting in the subarctic. *Arctic* 26:253–255.

Price, T. D. 1984. The evolution of sexual size dimorphism in Darwin's finches. *Amer. Natur.* 123:500–518.

Proctor, D. L. C. 1975. The problem of chick loss in the South Polar Skua *Catharacta maccormicki. Ibis* 117:452–459.

Pryor, M. E. 1968. The avifauna of Haswell Island, Antarctica.

Rabbits, B. 1975. Pomarine Skua taking Black-headed Gulls. *Brit. Birds* 68:430–431.
Raeburn, H. 1888. Summer birds of Shetland. *Proc. Roy. Phys. Soc. Edin.* (1888): 542–562.
Raeburn, H. 1890. The Great Skua on Foula. *Zoologist* (1890):354–355.
Raeburn, H. 1891. The Great Skua (*Stercorarius catarrhactes*); its present status as a British bird. *Scot. Nat.* (1891): 18–20.
Rankin, M. N. & Duffey, E. A. G. 1948. A study of the bird life of the North Atlantic. *Brit. Birds* 41:suppl. 42 pp.
Rasmussen, E. V. 1981. Storkjovens *Stercorarius skua* forekomst i Sydskandinavien, isaer Danmark, 1970–1978. *Dansk Orn. Tidsskr.* 75:41–46.
Ratcliffe, D. A. 1980. *The Peregrine Falcon*. Poyser, Calton.
Ray, J. 1678. *The Ornithology of Francis Willughby*. John Martyn, London.
Reed, T. M., Langslow, D. R. & Symonds, F. L. 1983. Arctic Skuas in Caithness, 1979 and 1980. *Bird Study* 30:24–26.
Reid, B. E. 1967. The growth and development of the South Polar Skua (*Catharacta maccormicki*). *Notornis* 13:71–89.
Reid, W. 1886. Habits of the Arctic Skua as observed in Caithness. *Zoologist* 10:180–182.
Reynolds, P. W. 1935. Notes on the birds of Cape Horn. *Ibis* 5:65–101.
Richardson, M. E. 1984. Aspects of the ornithology of the Tristan da Cunha group and Gough Island, 1972–1974. *Cormorant* 12:123–201.
Robinson, J. A., Richardson, A., Crabtree, A. N., Coulson, J. C. & Potts, G. R. 1967. Organochlorine residues in marine organisms. *Nature* 214:1307–1311.
Rohwer, S. 1983. Formalizing the avoidance image hypothesis: critique of an earlier prediction. *Auk* 100:971–974.

Salmonsen, F. 1931. Om nogle for Faeroerne nye eller sjaeldnc Fuglearter. *Dansk orn. Foren. Tidsskr.* 29:
Salmonsen, F. 1935. Aves vol. 3, part 2. In *The Zoology of the Faeroes*. Sparck, R. & Tuxen, S. L. (eds.). Copenhagen.
Salmonsen, F. 1976. The South Polar Skua *stercorarius maccormicki* Saunders in Greenland. *Dansk Orn. Foren. Tidsskr.* 70:81–89.
Saunders, H. 1876. On the *Stercorariinae* or Skua gulls. *Proc. Zool. Soc., Lond.* (1876): 317–332.
Saunders, H. 1880. On the skuas and some other birds observed in the Shetland Islands. *Zoologist* 4:1–6.
Saxby, H. L. 1874. *The Birds of Shetland, with Observations on their Habits, Migration and Occasional Appearance*. Edinburgh.
Schnell, G. D. 1970. A phenetic study of the suborder Lari (Aves), parts I-II. *Syst. Zool.* 19:35–57, 264–302.
Scott, M. L., Zimmermann, J. R., Marinsky, S., Mullenhoff, P. A., Rumsey, G. L. & Rice, R. W. 1975. Effects of PCBs, DDT and mercury compounds upon egg production, hatchability and shell quality in chickens and Japanese Quail. *Poultry Sci.* 54:350–368.
Sellors, G. & Smith, T. G. 1984. Identification of first-winter Pomarine Skua. *Brit. Birds* 77:27.
Serventy, D. L., Serventy, V. & Warham, J. 1971. *The Handbook of Australian Seabirds* A. H. & A. W. Reed, Sydney.
Sharrock, J. T. R. 1967. The seawatching at Cape Clear Bird Observatory. *Seabird Rept.* 3:21–26.
Sharrock, J. T. R. 1976. *The Atlas of Breeding Birds in Britain and Ireland*. Poyser, Berkhamsted.
Sibbald, R. 1684. *Scotia Illustrata, sive prodromus historiae naturalis*. Edinburgh.
Sibbald, R. 1711. *Description of the isles of Orkney and Zetland*. Edinburgh.
Sibbald, R. 1739. *A collection of several treatises in folio concerning Scotland*. Edinburgh.
Skira, J. 1984. Breeding distribution of the Brown Skua on Macquarie Island. *Emu* 84: 248–249.

Slater, H. H. 1901. *Manual of the birds of Iceland*. Edinburgh.

Southern, H. N. 1943. The two phases of *Stercorarius parasiticus* (Linnaeus). *Ibis* 85: 443–485.

Southern, H. N. 1944. Dimorphism in *Stercorarius pomarinus* (Temminck). *Ibis* 86: 1–16.

Spellerberg, I. F. 1969. Capturing and immobilizing McCormick Skuas *J.A.V.M.A.* 155: 1040–1043.

Spellerberg, I. F. 1970. Body measurements and colour phases of the McCormick Skua *Catharacta maccormicki*. *Notornis* 17: 280–285.

Spellerberg, I. F. 1971. Breeding behaviour of the McCormick Skua *Catharacta maccormicki* in Antarctica. *Ardea* 59: 189–230.

Spellerberg, I. F. 1971. Aspects of McCormick Skua breeding biology. *Ibis* 113: 357–363.

Spellerberg, I. F. 1971. Mallophaga on the South Polar Skua. *Pac. Insects Monogr.* 25: 19–20.

Sproul, J. A., Bradley, R. L. & Hickey, J. J. 1975. Polychlorinated biphenyls, DDE and Dieldrin in Icelandic seabirds. Unpubl. Report to U.S. Interior.

Stenhouse, J. H. 1926. The Great Skua in Shetland. *Scot. Nat.* 162: 169–173.

Stonehouse, B. 1956. The Brown Skua *Catharacta skua lönnbergi* (Mathews) of South Georgia. *F.I.D.S. Sci. Repts.* 14: 1–25.

Storer, R. W. 1966. Sexual size dimorphism and food habits in three North American accipiters. *Auk* 83: 423–436.

Svabo, J. C. 1959. Indberetninger fra en Reise i Faeroe 1781 og 1782. Kopenhagen.

Swales, M. K. 1965. The seabirds of Gough Island. *Ibis* 107: 17–42 and 215–229.

Tamiya, Y. & Aoyanagi, M. 1982. Notes on the incubation of an Adelie penguin egg by a pair of South Polar Skuas. *Tori* 30: 163–164.

Tatton, J. O. & Ruzicka, J. H. A. 1967. Organochlorine residues in Antarctica. *Nature* 215: 346–348.

Taylor, I. R. 1979. The kleptoparasitic behaviour of the Arctic Skua *stercorarius parasiticus* with three species of tern. *Ibis* 121: 274–282.

Taylor, P. S. 1974. Summer populations and food ecology of Jaegers and Snowy Owls on Bathurst Island N.W.T. Thesis, University of Alberta.

Thomson, A. I.. 1966. An analysis of recoveries of Great Skuas ringed in Shetland. *Brit. Birds* 59: 1–15.

Thompson, D. B. A. 1983. Prey assessment by plovers (Charadriidae): net rate of energy intake and vulnerability to kleptoparasites. *Anim. Behav.* 31: 1226–1236.

Thorpe, R. I. 1981. Spring passage of skuas at Handa. *Scott. Birds* 11: 225–226.

Timmermann, G. 1949. *Die Vogel Islands*. Reykjavik.

Tinbergen, N. 1953. *The Herring Gull's World*. Collins, London.

Traill, A. L. 1890. The Great Skua on Foula. *Zoologist* (1890): 434.

Trillmich, F. 1978. Feeding territories and breeding success of South Polar Skuas. *Auk* 95: 23–33.

Tudor, J. R. 1883. *The Orkneys and Shetland, their past and present state*. London.

Tumasonis, C. F., Bush, B. & Baker, F. D. 1973. PCB levels in egg yolks associated with embryonic mortality and deformity of hatched chicks. *Arch. Environ. Contam. Toxicol.* 1: 312–324.

Ulfstrand, S. & Hogstedt, G. 1976. How many birds breed in Sweden? *Anser* 15: 1–32.

Uspenski, S. M., Beme, R. L., Priklonski, S. G. & Vekhov, V. N. 1962. *Ornitologiya* 4: 64–86.

Vader, W. 1980. The Great Skua *Stercorarius skua* in Norway and the Spitsbergen area. *Fauna norv. Ser. C., Cinclus* 3: 49–55.

Veit, R. R. 1978. Some observations of South Polar Skuas (*Catharacta maccormicki*) on Georges Bank. *Am. Birds* 32: 300–302.

Veit, R. R. 1985. Long-tailed Jaegers wintering along the Falkland Current. *Amer. Birds* 39: 873–877.

Venables, L. S. V. 1951. The birds of Papa Stour. *Scot. Field* Oct. 1951:41.

Venables, L. S. V. & Venables, U. M. 1955. *Birds and Mammals of Shetland*. Edinburgh.

Verbeek, N. A. M. 1977. Interactions between Herring and Lesser Black-backed Gulls feeding on refuse. *Auk* 94:726–735.

Vetch, Capt., 1822. Account of the island of Foula. *Mem. Wernerian Nat. Hist. Soc.* 4: 237–252.

Voison, J.-F. 1979. Observations ornithologiques aux iles Tristan da Cunha et Gough. *Alauda* 47:73–82.

Vries, J. de, 1961. *Altnordisches Etymologisches Worterbuch*. Leiden.

Wahl, T. R. 1977. Notes on behavior of California Gulls and South Polar Skuas off the Washington coast. *Murrelet* 58:47–49.

Watson, A. 1957. Notes on birds in arctic Norway. *Sterna* 2:65–99.

Watson, G. E. 1975. *Birds of the Antarctic and Sub-Antarctic*. Amer. Geophys. Union, Washington D.C.

Wetmore, A. 1926. Observations on the birds of Argentina, Paraguay, Uruguay and Chile. *U.S. Natl. Mus. Bull.* 133.

Widen, P. 1984. Reversed sexual size dimorphism in birds of prey: revival of an old hypothesis. *Oikos* 43:259–263.

Williams, A. J. 1980. The effect of attendance by three adults upon nest contents and chick growth in the Southern Great Skua. *Notornis* 27:79–85.

Williams, A. J. 1980. Aspects of the breeding biology of the Subantarctic Skua at Marion Island. *Ostrich* 51:160–167.

Williams, A. J. 1980. Variation in weight of eggs and its effect on the breeding biology of the Great Skua. *Emu* 80:198–202.

Williams, A. J. 1984. The status and conservation of seabirds on some islands in the African sector of the Southern Ocean, pp. 627–636. In J. P. Croxall, P. G. H. Evans & R. W. Schreiber (eds.), *Status and Conservation of the World's Seabirds*. ICBP, Cambridge.

Williams, L. E. 1965. Jaegers in the Gulf of Mexico. *Auk* 82:18–25.

Williamson, K. 1945. On scarce breeding species in the Faeroe Islands. *Ibis* 87:550–558.

Williamson, K. 1948. *The Atlantic Islands: the Faeroe Life and Scene*. London.

Williamson, K. 1949. The distraction behaviour of the Arctic Skua. *Ibis* 91:307–313.

Williamson, K. 1957. The Bonxies of Fair Isle. *Bird Notes News* 27:164–169.

Williamson, K. 1965. *Fair Isle and its Birds*. Oliver & Boyd, Edinburgh.

Wilson, E. O. 1907. Aves: British Natl. Antarct. Exped. 1901–1904. *Zoology* 2:1–121.

Wolff, E. W. & Peel, D. A. 1985. The record of global pollution in polar snow and ice. *Nature* 313:535–540.

Wood, R. C. 1970. A population study of South Polar Skuas (*Catharacta maccormicki*) aged one to eight years. *Proc. XV Int. orn, Congr., The Hague*, 1970:705–706.

Wood, R. C. 1971. Population dynamics of breeding South Polar Skuas of unknown age. *Auk* 88:805–814.

Wynne-Edwards, V. C. 1935. On the habits and distribution of birds on the North Atlantic. *Proc. Boston Nat. Hist. Soc.* 40:233–346.

Young, E. C. 1963. The breeding behaviour of the South Polar Skua *Catharacta maccormicki*. *Ibis* 105:203–233.

Young, E. C. 1963. Feeding habits of the South Polar Skua *Catharacta maccormicki*. *Ibis* 105:301–318.

Young, E. C. 1967. Skua studies. *Tuatara* 15:142–148.

Young, E. C. 1972. Territory establishment and stability in McCormick's Skua. *Ibis* 114:234–244.

Young, E. C. 1977. Egg-laying in relation to latitude in southern hemisphere skuas. *Ibis* 119:191–195.

Young, E. C. 1978. Behavioural ecology of *lönnbergi* skuas in relation to environment on the Chatham Islands, New Zealand. *N.Z.J. Zool.* 5:401–416.

Zoega, G. T. 1942. *Icelandic-English Dictionary*. Reykjavik.

Tables 1–65

TABLE 1: *Classification of specimens considered to be Great Skuas, with suggestions as to correct identity of those misidentified.*

Name given	Authority	Work	Actual identity
Catarrhacta	Aristotle 342 BC	Historia Animalium	juv. Gannet
Cepphus	Aristotle 342 BC	Historia Animalium	petrel sp.
Skua hoieri	Clusius 1605	Exotic Decem Libri	
Catarrhactes omnis	Aldrovand 1637	Ornithologiae III	
Cepphus	Aldrovand 1637	Ornithologiae III	juv. Arctic Skua
Skuen debes	Debes 1673	Faeroae et Faer. Res.	
Catarracta	Ray 1678	Willughby's Orn.	
Cornish Gannet	Ray 1678	Willughby's Orn.	juv. Gannet
Cateractes noster	Sibbald 1684	Scotia Illustrata	
Larus fuscus	Albin 1738–40	Nat. Hist. Birds	juv. Arctic Skua
Laurs fuscus	Brisson 1760	Ornithology	
Catharacta skua	Brunnich 1764	Orn. Borealis	
Le Stercoraire raye	Brisson 1760	Ornithologie	juv. small skua
Larus catarractes	Linnaeus 1766	Syst. Nat.	
Larus keeask	Latham 1790	Ind. Orn.	
Lestris catarractes	Illiger 1811	Prodromus	
Catarracta fusca	Leach 1816	Syst. Cat. Brit. Mus.	
catarhactes	Vieillot 1819	N. Dict. d'Hist. Nat.	
pomarinus	Vieillot 1834	Gal. Ois.	
Cataractes vulgaris	Fleming 1828	British Animals	
Lestris skua	Jardine 1845	Naturalist's Library	
Megalestris catarrhactes	Bonaparte 1856	Cat. Parzud.	
Buphagus skua	Coues 1863	Proc. Acad. Nat. Sci. Phila.	
Megalestris skua	Ridgeway 1881	Nom. N. Am. Birds	
Stercorarius skua	Hartert 1916	Die Vogel Pal. Fauna	

TABLE 2: Nomenclature for small skuas.

Name given	Identity	Authority
Larus parasiticus	Long-tailed Skua	Linnaeus 1758
Stercoraire a longue queue (= Stercorarius longicaudus)	pale ad. small skua	Brisson 1760
Le Stercoraire raye (= Stercorarius striatus)	juv. Pomarine? Skua	Brisson 1760
Catharacta cepphus	juv. Arctic? Skua	Brunnich 1764
Catharacta parasitica	pale ad. small skua	Brunnich 1764
Catharacta coprotheres	dark ad. small skua	Brunnich 1764
The Black-toed Gull	Arctic Skua	Pennant 1768
Larus crepidatus	Arctic Skua	Banks 1773
Larus keeask	Pomarine Skua	Latham 1790
Larus parasiticus	Pomarine Skua	Meyer & Wolf 1810
Catarracta parasitica camtschatica	Pomarine Skua	Pallas 1811
Lestris parasitica	Long-tailed Skua	Illiger 1811
Lestris pomarinus	Pomarine Skua	Temminck 1815
Lestris crepidatus	Arctic Skua	Temminck 1815
Lestris parasiticus	Long-tailed Skua	Temminck 1815
Stercorarius longicaudus	Long-tailed Skua	Vieillot 1819
Stercorarius pomarinus	Pomarine Skua	Vieillot 1819
Stercorarius crepidatus	Arctic Skua	Vieillot 1819
Lestris crepidata	Long-tailed Skua	Brehm 1822
Lestris buffonii; Buffon's Skua	Long-tailed Skua	Boie 1822
Lestris parasitica	Arctic Skua	Faber 1822
Stercorarius cepphus	Long-tailed Skua	Shaw 1826
Arctic Gull	Arctic Skua	Drosier 1830
Lestris richardsoni; Richardson's Skua	Arctic Skua	Swainson 1831
Lestris lessoni	Long-tailed Skua	Schinz 1840

TABLE 3: Weights of skuas; data for breeding adults during middle of breeding season except where stated. s.d. = standard deviation, n = sample size, sig = probability of difference between means arising by chance (two-tailed t-tests). Positive % difference for females larger than males, negative for males larger than females. References for data: 1 = Ainley et al 1985, 2 = Barre 1976, 3 = Belopolskii 1961, 4 = Cramp & Simmons 1983, 5 = Furness, 6 = Haftorn 1971, 7 = Hagen 1952, 8 = Hamilton 1934, 9 = Humphrey et al 1970, 10 = de Korte 1972, 11 = de Korte 1985, 12 = Maher 1974, 13 = Murphy 1936, 14 = Spellerberg 1970, 15 = Timmermann 1949, 16 = Uspenski et al 1962, 17 = Morvan et al 1967, 18 = Friedman 1945.

Ref	Locality	Males mean	s.d.	n	range	Females mean	s.d.	n	range	Difference sig.	(%)
GREAT SKUA											
15	Iceland, May	1338	62.1	9	1210–1410	1525	88.7	6	1390–1630	<0.01	14
5	Noss, May	1266	35.1	5	1230–1310	1490	94.5	7	1340–1600	<0.01	18
5	Foula 1979	1343	97.2	9	1170–1490	1444	65.2	8	1360–1550	<0.05	8
5	Foula 1980	1359	81.4	36	1180–1500	1491	68.8	26	1300–1650	<0.01	10
									weighted mean 11.1%		
TRISTAN SKUA											
7	Tristan	1359	54.2	4	1175–1420	1368	135.3	4	1175–1485	n.s.	1
5	Gough Island	1429	100.2	9	1300–1600	1649	106.8	9	1550–1800	<0.01	15
									weighted mean 10.7%		
FALKLAND SKUA											
no data available											
BROWN SKUA											
2	Iles Crozet	1536	–	8	1250–1650	1735	–	6	1560–1800	<0.05	13
CHILEAN SKUA											
9	Fuego	1209	21.9	2	1193, 1224	1482	69.3	2	1433, 1531	<0.1	–
SOUTH POLAR SKUA											
1	Ross Sea	1277	95	26	1120–1440	1421	75	23	1280–1550	<0.01	11
14	Ross Island	1228	–	21	899–1392	1366	–	24	966–1619	–	11
									weighted mean 11.0%		
LONG-TAILED SKUA											
4	Greenland, May	282	23.7	4	255–303	376	30.1	10	345–444	<0.01	28
4	Greenland, incub.	266	11.8	7	250–280	286	14.8	8	269–315	<0.05	7
4	Greenland, July	281	11.7	10	266–299	304	19.8	6	278–336	<0.05	8
4	Greenland, failed	251	20.5	5	218–272	305	38.9	4	277–362	<0.1	19
4	Greenland, nonbr.	292	30.2	12	248–352	293	26.5	9	262–333	n.s.	0
12	Alaska	280	31.1	26	236–343	313	31.4	18	258–358	<0.01	11
11	Greenland	270	21.6	38	218–320	307	39.2	48	262–444	<0.01	14
									weighted mean 12.1%		
POMARINE SKUA											
10	Spitsbergen	654	34.7	4	605–685	737	49.7	5	690–810	<0.05	13
12	Alaska	648	53.4	73	542–797	740	84.4	52	576–917	<0.01	14

TABLE 3 continued

Ref	Locality	Males mean	s.d.	n	range	Females mean	s.d.	n	range	Difference sig.	(%)
16	Yakutia, USSR	660	–	9	620–800	767	–	6	680–830	–	15
4	N Atl. nonbr., July	647	15.9	6	620–663	730	27.1	5	695–767	<0.01	12
4	N Atl. nonbr., Aug.	669	20.3	6	650–700	737	49.7	5	690–810	<0.05	10

weighted mean 13.6%

ARCTIC SKUA

Ref	Locality	Males mean	s.d.	n	range	Females mean	s.d.	n	range	Difference sig.	(%)
3	E Murman, USSR	417	–	166	306–523	483	–	152	306–604	–	16
3	W Murman, USSR	420	–	10	310–539	534	–	6	386–610	–	27
6	Norway, June–July	361	–	7	335–385	408	–	12	365–470	–	12
15	Iceland, May–June	380	27.0	10	340–425	443	31.9	7	395–470	<0.01	15
4	Iceland, Jul–Aug.	383	41.1	10	325–448	461	–	12	325–525	<0.01	19
10	Spitsbergen	493	68.0	3	436–568	579	70.3	7	467–697	n.s.	17
12	Alaska	421	51.7	20	301–540	508	80.9	11	346–644	<0.01	19
4	Spitsb. laying	556	–	2	545–568	594	–	2	586–603	–	7
4	Spits. with young	491	–	3	449–530	491	–	3	467–505	n.s.	0
4	Spits. nonbr.	422	–	2	407–436	582	32.2	5	545–616	–	32

weighted mean 16.5%

TABLE 4: Wing lengths of skuas; for details see caption of Table 3. Specimens measured in museum collections are marked M since post-mortem shrinkage results in their biometrics differing from those of fresh birds (F). Date for adults and immatures or juveniles are presented separately where the measurement varies with age.

Ref	Locality	Males mean	s.d.	n	range	Females mean	s.d.	n	range	Difference sig.	(%)
	GREAT SKUA										
15	Iceland	F 403.4	10.3	9	388–417	414.0	7.3	6	404–423	<0.1	2.6
5	Foula	F 414.5	8.3	62	393–433	423.5	7.1	55	412–440	<0.01	2.2
5	Noss	F 414	7.8	5	403–424	423	5.8	7	417–431	<0.1	2.2
4	N Atlantic, ads.	M 399	7.9	31	382–414	413	7.9	17	398–428	<0.01	3.4
4	N Atlantic, juv.	M 383	10.2	9	367–400	399	12.3	11	381–423	<0.01	4.1

weighted mean 2.7%

Ref	Locality	Males mean	s.d.	n	range	Females mean	s.d.	n	range	Difference sig.	(%)
	TRISTAN SKUA										
7	Tristan	F 387	4.7	4	384–394	390	12.2	4	378–401	n.s.	0.8
5	Gough Island	F 397.9	6.0	9	388–409	412.4	9.0	9	398–423	<0.01	3.6

weighted mean 2.7%

TABLE 4 *continued*

Ref	Locality	Males mean	s.d.	n	range	Females mean	s.d.	n	range	Difference sig. (%)

FALKLAND SKUA

Ref	Locality	mean	s.d.	n	range	mean	s.d.	n	range	sig.	(%)
13	Falklands	M 376.4	–	10	366–387	384.6	–	6	378–398	–	2.2
8	Falklands	M 375.5	9.8	13	360–390	383.6	7.7	20	368–400	<0.05	2.2

weighted mean 2.2%

BROWN SKUA

8	New Zealand	M 427.5	9.7	4	421–442	427.6	12.2	11	407–447	n.s.	0.0
2	Iles Crozet	F 404	–	23	385–424	414	–	14	393–438	<0.05	2.5
17	Sub-Antarctic	M 398	7.5	8	385–405	415	19.1	4	400–440	<0.1	4.2

weighted mean 1.6%

CHILEAN SKUA

13	South America	M 394.8	–	7	390–398	395.6	–	5	387–411	–	0.2
17	Patagonia	M 400	–	2	395, 405	–	–	–	–	–	–

SOUTH POLAR SKUA

14	Ross Island	F 410	–	21	390–420	415	–	24	400–430	–	1.2
12	Antarctica	M 385	12.2	4	375–400	392	7.6	7	385–405	n.s.	1.8
18	Palmerland	M 374	–	8	362–384	380	–	10	364–393	–	1.6

weighted mean 1.4%

LONG-TAILED SKUA

11	Greenland	F 306.8	6.9	38	293–318	311.4	7.9	49	300–334	<0.01	1.5
4	Greenland, ads.	M 306	6.5	36	292–318	309	8.1	38	294–323	n.s.	1.0
4	Netherlands, juvs.	M 293	6.2	21	280–306	298	8.1	15	285–308	<0.1	1.7

weighted mean 1.3%

POMARINE SKUA

10	Spitsbergen, imm.	F 348.4	6.9	5	341–358	359	10.8	7	341–370	<0.1	3.0
4	NW Atlantic, ads.	M 363	6.4	17	354–374	373	6.1	11	363–382	<0.01	2.8
4	NW Atl. 4th yr.	M 353	8.9	7	339–362	370	6.8	8	359–379	<0.01	4.7
4	NW Atl. 3rd yr.	M 351	4.1	5	348–358	362	7.6	5	355–373	<0.05	3.1
4	NW Atl. 2nd yr.	M 348	7.7	7	337–360	357	5.3	6	352–366	<0.05	2.6
4	Netherlands, juvs	M 346	6.0	20	334–356	355	5.6	13	349–363	<0.01	2.6

weighted mean 3.0%

ARCTIC SKUA

10	Spitsbergen	F 315.9	3.2	7	311–320	325.3	3.7	11	319–331	<0.01	3.0
3	E Murman, USSR	F 321.8	–	136	–	326.8	–	120	–	–	1.6
4	Scotland/Faeroes	M 315	5.7	14	309–328	321	5.6	13	311–320	<0.05	1.9
4	Iceland	M 319	7.3	14	307–330	323	8.6	10	310–334	n.s.	1.3
4	N Norway	M 322	8.6	9	306–331	325	6.0	6	317–333	n.s.	0.9
4	Spitzbergen	M 322	5.2	11	315–328	330	3.6	14	321–335	<0.01	2.5
4	NE Greenland	M 328	4.9	7	322–336	335	6.6	9	328–347	<0.05	2.1
4	N Siberia	M 330	2.6	4	327–333	341	9.4	5	328–353	<0.1	3.3
4	Netherlands, juvs.	M 308	8.8	19	293–320	314	7.2	14	302–323	<0.05	1.9

weighted mean 1.8%

TABLE 5: *Tarsus lengths of skuas; see captions for Tables 3 and 4.*

Ref	Locality	Males mean	s.d.	n	range	Females mean	s.d.	n	range	Difference sig.	(%)
GREAT SKUA											
15	Iceland, May	F 67.3	2.2	9	64–71	69.3	1.0	6	68–70	<0.1	3.0
4	N Atlantic	M 67.1	2.2	27	64–70	68.7	2.2	22	66–72	<0.05	2.4
5	Foula	F 69.0	2.4	36	63–73	68.8	2.2	32	63–73	n.s.	−0.3
5	Noss	F 68.4	1.1	5	67–70	70.0	0.8	7	69–71	<0.05	2.3
TRISTAN SKUA											
7	Tristan	F 72.8	2.9	2	71–75	72.8	1.7	3	71–74	n.s.	0.0
5	Gough Island	F 74.2	1.8	9	72–77	75.9	2.3	9	72–79	n.s.	2.3
FALKLAND SKUA											
13	Falklands	M 66.9	–	10	64–70	68.2	–	6	65–70	–	1.9
8	Falklands	M 65.8	2.0	13	63–69	67.7	1.9	20	64–70	<0.05	2.9
BROWN SKUA											
8	New Zealand	M 81.6	9.0	4	76–95	78.9	2.1	11	74–82	n.s.	−3.4
2	Iles Crozet	F 74.2	–	23	68–79	74.4	–	14	68–78	n.s.	0.3
17	Sub-Antarctic	M 69.2	1.9	8	65–71	70.2	1.2	4	69–72	n.s.	1.4
CHILEAN SKUA											
13	S. America	M 68.6	–	7	61–72	68.2	–	5	66–70	–	−0.6
17	Patagonia	M 66.5	–	2	66, 67	–	–	–	–	–	–
SOUTH POLAR SKUA											
14	Ross Island	F 62.4	–	21	59–68	64.8	–	24	58–76	–	3.8
17	Antarctica	M 60.4	3.0	4	58–64	61.2	1.7	7	60–64	n.s.	1.3
18	Palmerland	M 62.0	–	8	58–64	62.6	–	10	59–65	–	1.0
LONG-TAILED SKUA											
11	Greenland	F 42.1	1.53	40	38–45	42.2	1.37	49	40–45	n.s.	0.2
4	Greenland	M 42.6	1.82	75	39–46	42.5	1.60	54	39–45	n.s.	−0.2
POMARINE SKUA											
10	Spitsbergen	F 53.7	1.7	5	51–55	54.0	1.2	7	53–55	n.s.	0.6
4	NW Atlantic	M 53.7	1.70	52	50–56	55.1	1.33	36	53–58	<0.01	2.6
ARCTIC SKUA											
10	Spitsbergen	F 43.0	2.0	7	40–45	44.0	1.2	11	42–46	n.s.	2.3
4	W Palearctic	M 44.3	1.66	34	41–47	44.4	2.01	46	42–47	n.s.	0.2

TABLE 6: *Bill length of skuas; see captions for Tables 3 and 4.*

Ref	Locality	Males				Females				Difference	
		mean	s.d.	n	range	mean	s.d.	n	range	sig.	(%)
GREAT SKUA											
15	Iceland	F 51.7	1.3	9	49–53	53.7	1.2	6	52–56	<0.05	3.9
4	N Atlantic	M 50.1	1.63	26	47–52	51.2	1.46	20	49–53	<0.1	2.2
5	Foula	F 49.8	1.3	63	46–52	49.8	1.6	53	44–53	n.s.	0.0
5	Noss	F 47.8	1.0	5	47–49	47.2	0.8	7	46–48	n.s.	− 1.0
TRISTAN SKUA											
7	Tristan	F 56.8	–	1	–	54.7	0.3	3	54–55	–	− 3.7
5	Gough Island	F 54.8	1.3	9	52–56	54.4	1.3	9	53–57	n.s.	− 0.7
FALKLAND SKUA											
13	Falklands	M 48.7	–	10	46–50	48.9	–	6	47–51	–	0.4
8	Falklands	M 46.6	1.9	13	44–51	48.0	1.9	20	45–52	<0.05	3.1
BROWN SKUA											
8	New Zealand	M 53.8	2.2	4	51–56	55.4	2.7	11	48–58	n.s.	2.9
2	Iles Crozet	F 57.0	–	23	54–61	56.7	–	14	53–59	n.s.	− 0.5
17	Sub-Antarctic	M 52.3	2.1	8	48–55	51.5	3.8	4	49–57	n.s.	− 1.5
CHILEAN SKUA											
13	S. America	M 52.2	–	7	49–56	53.3	–	5	51–56	–	2.1
SOUTH POLAR SKUA											
14	Ross Island	F 49.4	–	21	48–51	50.9	–	24	47–54	–	3.0
17	Antarctica	M 47.1	1.0	4	46–48	47.6	1.9	7	45–51	n.s.	1.1
LONG-TAILED SKUA											
11	Greenland	F 28.0	1.31	40	26–30	27.8	1.46	49	24–32	n.s.	− 0.7
4	Greenland	M 28.5	1.34	75	26–31	28.4	1.32	53	26–31	n.s.	− 0.4
POMARINE SKUA											
10	Spitsbergen	F 39.0	1.7	5	37–42	40.4	0.7	7	39–41	n.s.	3.6
4	NW Atlantic	M 39.8	1.49	31	38–42	40.9	1.58	23	39–44	<0.05	2.8
4	Netherlands, juvs.	M 37.8	1.41	19	36–40	39.0	1.44	13	37–41	<0.05	3.1
ARCTIC SKUA											
10	Spitsbergen	F 31.9	1.1	6	31–34	32.8	1.0	11	31–35	n.s.	2.8
3	E Murman, USSR	F 30.2	–	127	–	31.0	–	118	–	–	2.6
4	W Palearctic	M 31.1	1.18	34	29–34	31.8	1.42	46	30–34	<0.05	2.3

TABLE 7: Tail lengths of skuas (excluding the projecting central feathers); see captions for Tables 3 and 4.

Ref	Locality	Males				Females				Difference
		mean	*s.d.*	*n*	*range*	*mean*	*s.d.*	*n*	*range*	*sig. (%)*
GREAT SKUA										
15	Iceland	F 159	6.7	8	150–162	155	4.5	6	150–160	n.s. − 2.6
4	N Atlantic, ads.	M 150	5.96	21	140–162	149	3.83	12	144–156	n.s. − 0.7
4	N Atlantic, juv.	M 143	5.0	9	136–149	144	4.9	11	138–150	n.s. 0.7
TRISTAN SKUA										
7	Tristan	F 149	8.7	4	140–161	145	9.6	4	134–155	n.s. − 2.7
5	Gough Island	F 154	2.1	9	152–158	151	2.4	9	148–154	<0.05 − 2.3
FALKLAND SKUA										
13	Falklands	M 145.8	–	10	140–154	151.7	–	6	140–157	– 4.0
BROWN SKUA										
17	Sub-Antarctic	M 145	7.1	8	135–155	151	15.2	4	134–167	n.s. 4.1
CHILEAN SKUA										
13	S. America	M 148.3	–	7	140–158	139.1	–	5	135–143	– − 6.2
17	Patagonia	M 145	–	2	137, 152	–	–	–	–	– –
SOUTH POLAR SKUA										
17	Antarctica	M 135	12.9	4	120–150	148	7.8	7	140–161	<0.1 9.1
18	Palmerland	M 152	–	8	146–159	150	–	10	140–154	– − 1.3
LONG-TAILED SKUA										
4	Greenland	M 112	5.20	73	104–121	111	4.01	55	104–121	n.s. − 0.9
POMARINE SKUA										
4	NW Atlantic	M 124	4.95	50	116–134	127	5.12	36	121–136	<0.01 2.4
ARCTIC SKUA										
4	W Palearctic	M 115	5.11	38	109–122	116	4.63	48	108–125	n.s. 0.9

TABLE 8: Tail tip projection from tail end to tip of central feathers in small skuas; see captions for Tables 3 and 4.

Ref	Locality	Males				Females				Difference	
		mean	s.d.	n	range	mean	s.d.	n	range	sig.	(%)
	LONG-TAILED SKUA										
11	Greenland	F 173	27.0	21	125–231	170	17.2	27	127–208	n.s.	−1.6
4	W Palearctic	M 178	26.6	31	151–246	174	21.6	29	135–216	n.s.	−2.2
	POMARINE SKUA										
4	Netherlands, juvs.	M 15	3.9	17	9–22	13	3.9	13	7–18	n.s.	−14.3
4	Greenl. 2nd summer	M 58	–	3	50–70	44	16.1	5	25–63	–	−27.5
4	Greenl. 3rd summer	M 70	–	3	67–72	46	8.5	4	36–54	–	−41.4
4	Greenl. 4th summer	M 78	12.7	10	57–98	72	15.5	7	53–89	n.s.	−8.0
4	Greenl. adult nonbr.	M 49	–	3	38–57	40	8.4	5	32–53	n.s.	−20.2
4	Greenl. adult breed	M 95	10.4	9	75–105	92	14.5	9	65–111	n.s.	−3.2
	ARCTIC SKUA										
4	W Palearctic	M 83.2	11.3	27	65–105	78.5	7.0	26	65–90	<0.1	−5.6

TABLE 9: Summary estimates of numbers of breeding pairs of Arctic Skuas in areas of Scotland 1871 from Gray (1871), 1941 from Lack (1943), 1961 and 1969 from Cramp et al (1974), 1975 from Everett (1982), 1980–82 from Meek et al (1985) from RSPB reserve reports and various years' data from Scottish Bird Reports and Shetland Bird Reports.

Locality				Date			
	1871	1941	1961	1969	1975	1980–82	1985
Shetland				770	1,631+	1,650	1,912
Orkney		79+	158–269	230+	716+	1,034	
Hebrides	40–50			40	37	80–94	
Sutherland				1	3	19	35
Caithness				20	28+	40+	
Argyll				25	26	36	
Total				1,086+	2,441+	2,800+	

TABLE 10: Estimates of numbers of breeding pairs of Arctic Skuas in different breeding areas.

Locality	Breeding pairs	Period	Reference
Scotland	2,790	1984	Evans 1984
Faeroes	1,300	1977	Mortensen in litt.
Iceland	4,000	1970	Bengtson & Owen 1973
Greenland	1,000–10,000	1980	Evans 1984
Norway	8,000	1970	Brun 1979
Sweden	400	1975	Cramp & Simmons 1983
Finland	250	1980	,,
Bear Island	40	1980	,,
Jan Mayen	30	1940	,,
Spitsbergen	1,000–10,000	1980	Evans 1984
Canada	10,000–100,000 ?		
USSR	50,000–500,000 ?		
Alaska	10,000–100,000 ?		

TOTAL WORLD POPULATION: several hundred thousand pairs

TABLE 11: Estimates of numbers of breeding pairs of Long-tailed Skuas in different breeding areas.

Locality	Breeding pairs	Period	Reference
Sweden	10,000	1970	Ulfstrand & Hogstedt 1976
Finland	< 1,500	1950	Merikallio 1958
	1,000–1,500	1984	Evans 1984
Greenland	1,000–10,000	1984	,,
Norway	1,000–10,000	1984	,,
Spitsbergen	1–100	1984	,,
Jan Mayen	present	1984	,,
USSR	tens of thousands?		
Alaska	tens of thousands?		
Canada	tens of thousands		

TOTAL WORLD POPULATION: tens or low hundreds of thousands of pairs?

TABLE 12: *Estimates of number of breeding pairs of Great Skuas in different areas.*

Locality	Breeding pairs	Period	Reference
Iceland	5,000	1954	Gudmundsson 1954
	4,909–5,846	1984	Hansen & Lange in litt.
Faeroes	250	1984	Evans 1984
Shetland	5,000	1984	Furness 1986
Orkney	2,000	1984	,,
N&W Scotland	150	1984	,,
Spitsbergen	30	1984	Barrett in litt.
Bear Island	30	1984	,,
N. Norway	4	1984	,,
Hopen	2	1984	,,

TOTAL WORLD POPULATION: about 12,500 pairs

TABLE 13: *Formation and extinction of Greak Skua colonies in Britain.*

Decade	Colonies in Scotland	Colonies founded abroad	Colonies founded in Scotland	Extinctions
1770–79	2		0	0
1780–89	1		0	1 Unst
1790–99	1		0	0
1800–09	1		0	0
1810–19	1		0	0
1820–29	1		0	0
1830–39	2		2 Unst, N. Roe	1 N. Roe
1840–49	2		0	0
1850–59	2		0	0
1860–69	2		0	0
1870–79	2		0	0
1880–89	3		1 N. Roe	0
1890–99	4		1 Yell	0
1900–09	5		1 Fetlar	0
1910–19	9		4 Noss, Hascosay, Bressay, Hoy	0
1920–29	12		3 Fair Isle, Mousa, S. Mainland	0
1930–39	12		0	0
1940–49	14		2 Lewis, Vaila	0

TABLE 13 continued

Decade	Colonies in Scotland	Colonies founded abroad	Colonies founded in Scotland	Extinctions
1950–59	21		8 Urie Lingey, Papa Westray, Tronda, Dunnet Head, Gluss Isle, Ronsay, Eynhallow, Westray	1 Tronda
1960–69	25	Norway (1965) Bear Is. (1969)	8 St Kilda, N. Rona, Handa, Eday, Orkney mainland Gairsay, Fara, Cava	4 Gluss, Eynhallow, Urie Lingey, Cava
1970–79	29	Spitsbergen (1976)	7 Auskerry, Eilean Roan, Flotta, Calf of Eday, Papa Stour, Shiants, Stronsay	3 Vaila, Flotta, Papa Stour
1980–85	32	Hopen (1980) Jan Mayen (1984?)	3 S. Ronaldsay, Eynhallow, Summer Isles	0

TABLE 14: Interpolated decadal Great Skua colony sizes.

Year	Foula	Unst	Noss	F. Isle	Yell	N. Roe	Fetlar	Hascosay	Bressay	Mousa
1770	5	3								
1780	12	0								
1790	19	0								
1800	26	0								
1810	30	0								
1820	30	0								
1830	25	3				4				
1840	20	15				0				
1850	6	30				0				
1860	3	6				0				
1870	6	5				0				
1880	12	5				1				
1890	60	9			1	16				
1900	18	18			1	3	1			
1910	30	40	2		1	3	2	4		
1920	70	80	10		2	3	3	20	2	
1930	150	110	40	3	45	6	5	50	8	3
1940	260	200	100	1	75	10	10	50	15	3
1950	600	300	150	6	100	20	25	70	30	3
1960	1000	400	200	20	120	30	100	50	60	15
1970	2200	600	200	8	180	80	270	50	120	16
1980	2670	1000	300	40	(200)	200	(280)	8	160	9
1985	(2500)	(1000)	(350)	(72)						

Yr	S Shetland mainland	Other small Shetland colonies	Hoy	Westray	Papa Westray	Ronsay	Other Orkney islands	Handa	Lewis	St Kilda	Other Scot. is.
1910											
1920			3								
1930	3		6								
1940	3		18								
1950	4	4	36		2				2		1
1960	8	5	70	1	5	2	1		3		1
1970	20	11	250	2	5	3	6	3	11	9	3
1980	(60)	12	1300	5	3	13	50	24	18	28	10
1985	–	–	–	–	–	–	–	52	–	–	–

TABLE 15: Interpolated numbers of pairs of Great Skuas breeding in each region.

| Year | SHETLAND | | | ORKNEY | | HEBRIDES | | TOTAL | |
	pairs	% of total	% inc. over decade	pairs	% inc. over decade	pairs	% inc. over decade	pairs	% inc. over decade
1770	8	100%						8	50%
1780	12	100%						12	58%
1790	19	100%						19	37%
1800	26	100%						26	15%
1810	30	100%						30	0%
1820	30	100%						30	7%
1830	32	100%						32	9%
1840	35	100%						35	3%
1850	36	100%						36	−69%
1860	9	100%						9	22%
1870	11	100%						11	64%
1880	18	100%						18	378%
1890	86	100%						86	−52%
1900	41	100%	100%					41	100%
1910	82	100%	132%					82	135%

TABLE 15 continued

Year	SHETLAND			ORKNEY		HEBRIDES		TOTAL	
	pairs	% of total	% inc. over decade	pairs	% inc. over decade	pairs	% inc. over decade	pairs	% inc. over decade
1920	190	98%	123%	3	100%			193	122%
1930	423	98%	72%	6	200%			429	74%
1940	727	98%	80%	18	111%			745	82%
1950	1312	97%	54%	38	108%	3	33%	1353	55%
1960	2018	96%	86%	79	237%	4	550%	2101	93%
1970	3755	93%	32%	266	415%	26	208%	4047	58%
1980	4939	77%	<10%	1371	200%	80	300%	6390	20%
1985	5000?	68%		2000?		150?		7150?	

TABLE 16: *Estimated number of breeding pairs of Great Skuas in Faeroe Islands.*

Year	Breeding pairs	Reference
1872	36	Fielden 1872
1897	4	Salomonsen 1935
1930	71	Salomonsen 1935
1946	200	Ferdinand 1947
1954	200	Bannerman 1963
1961	530	Bayes et al 1964
1977	500	Mortensen in litt.
1984	250	Evans 1984

TABLE *17*: *Estimates of number of breeding pairs of Tristan Skuas at each breeding site.*

Locality	Breeding pairs	Period	Reference
Tristan	5–10	1973	Richardson 1984
Inaccessible	50–100	1973	,,
Nightingale	100–500	1973	,,
Middle Is.	1–10	1973	,,
Stoltenhoff	1–5	1973	,,
Gough Island	2,000–3,000	1956	Swales 1965
	2,000	1985	pers. obs.

TOTAL WORLD POPULATION: about 2,500 pairs

TABLE *18*: *Estimates of numbers of breeding pairs of Brown Skuas at their breeding sites.*

Locality	Breeding pairs	Reference
New Amsterdam	< 5	Jouventin et al 1984
St Paul	0	Jouventin pers. comm.
Marion & P Edward	460	Williams 1984
Crozet	400–1,000	Jouventin et al 1984
Kerguelen	perhaps 1,000–2,000	Jouventin pers. comm.
Heard	at least hundreds	Downes et al 1959
Bouvet	tens?	B.P. Watkins pers. comm.
S Sandwich	hundreds	Croxall et al 1984
S Georgia	1,000	,,
S Orkney Is.	300	,,
S Shetland Is.	420	,,
Peninsula	150	,,
Macquarie	550	Jones & Skira 1979
Auckland	300 birds = 100 pairs	B.D. Bell in litt.
Snares	150 birds = 50 pairs	,,
Campbell	200 birds = 67 pairs	,,
Antipodes	150 birds = 50 pairs	,,
Bounty	0	,,
Chatham	105	E.C. Young in litt.
S Island NZ	2	B.D. Bell in litt.
Stewart Is;	50 birds = 17 pairs	B.D. Bell in litt.
Elephant Is.	190	Croxall et al 1984

TOTAL WORLD POPULATION: about 7,000 pairs

TABLE 19: *Estimates of numbers of breeding pairs of South Polar Skuas at their breeding sites.*

Locality	Breeding pairs	Period	Reference
Ross Sea area	2,000–2,500	1984	Harper et al 1984
Ross Sea area	6,141	1980	Ainley et al 1984
Adelie Land	70–80	1984	Jouventin et al 1984
Peninsula	650	1984	Croxall et al 1984
Continent adjacent	10	1984	”
S Shetland Is.	10	1984	”
S Orkney Is.	10	1984	”
Haswell Is. Davis Sea	23	1968	Pryor 1968
Wilkes Land	2,500 birds = 830 pairs		Eklund 1961
other coasts	< 1,000 pairs?		

TOTAL WORLD POPULATION: about 5,000 to 8,000 pairs?

TABLE 20: *Monthly numbers of skuas recorded in Scottish waters published in Annual Scottish Bird Reports 1968–85. n.r. = numbers too large to record.*

Month	Long-tailed Skua	Pomarine Skua	Arctic Skua	Great Skua
January	0	13	10	29
February	0	7	3	17
March	0	1	20	hundreds
April	1	15	hundreds	n.r.
May	581	2284	n.r.	n.r.
June	31	21	n.r.	n.r.
July	41	61	n.r.	n.r.
August	78	372	n.r.	n.r.
September	52	879	n.r.	n.r.
October	15	2202	hundreds	n.r.
November	4	717	26	hundreds
December	0	102	17	c.48

TABLE 21: Relative amounts (%) of various foods eaten by male and female Arctic Skuas of East Murman, USSR, as reflected by stomach contents over entire breeding season (from Belopolskii 1961).

Food	Males (163 stomachs)	Females (142 stomachs)
Fish	45.4%	40.7%
Berries	36.6%	37.3%
Birds	6.9%	8.3%
Mammals	0.0%	0.5%
Invertebrates	11.1%	13.2%

TABLE 22: Time allocation by male and female Arctic Skuas on Foula; data collected in years 1976–79.

Date	Status	Time foraging (mins) by Male	Female	Mean trip duration Male mins	n	Female mins	n
3 June	Incubation	141	123	28	5	61	2
1 July	Young chicks	267	98	22	12	33	3
8 July	Young chicks	302	229	30	10	46	5
15 July	Medium chicks	377	255	34	11	51	5
17 July	Medium chicks	432	193	36	12	48	4
23 July	Large chicks	531	150	38	14	21	7
24 July	Large chicks	689	299	115	6	50	6

TABLE 23: Measurements of immature and adult Great Skuas in Shetland, June–July 1977–85. Immatures aged 3 to 7 years old, cannon netted on club sites, adults caught at nests.

Measurement	Immatures (n = 31) mean	s.d.	range	Adults mean	n	s.d.	range
Weight	1307	77	1140–1480	1409	74	78	1180–1650
Wing length	410	10	395–428	419	129	13	393–440
Tarsus	69.8	2	67–74	69.0	80	3	63–73
Head and bill	110.6	2	107–114	110.6	19	1	108–113
Bill length	49.6	1.4	46.4–52.3	49.6	128	1.4	44–53
Bill depth	17.6	0.6	16.8–18.4	17.7	128	0.6	16.8–18.8

TABLE 24: *Items recorded in diet of Great Skuas at North Atlantic colinies. Frequency of each item is roughly estimated in five categories from * (very rare) to ***** (very frequent).*

Food item	Locality	Frequency in diet
PLANT MATERIAL		
Crowberry	Foula	*
MARINE INVERTEBRATES		
Annelids, species not determined	Shetland	*
Crustacea, species not determined	Shetland	**
Goose barnacle	Shetland	**
Mollusca	Shetland	**
Mussel	Foula	*
Squid	Iceland	**
TERRESTRIAL INVERTEBRATES		
Cranefly larvae	Faeroe	*
Broom Moth larvae	Faeroe	*
FISH		
Sandeel	Iceland	****
	Faeroe	****
	Shetland	*****
Norway Pout	Shetland	**
Haddock	Shetland	*****
Whiting	Shetland	*****
Redfish	Shetland	**
Blue Whiting	Shetland	*
Plaice	Shetland	*
Lesser Argentine	Shetland	*
Herring	Shetland	*
Cod	Shetland	*
Torsk	Shetland	*
Saithe	Shetland	*
Poor Cod	Shetland	*
Ling	Shetland	*
MAMMALS		
Hedgehog	Foula	*
Rabbit	Shetland	**
	Orkney	*
Blue Hare	Faeroe	**
	Orkney	*
Sheep	Faeroe	*
	Shetland	*

TABLE 24 continued.

Food item	Locality	Frequency in diet
EGGS		
Red-throated Diver	Shetland	**
Fulmar	Faeroe	**
	Shetland	**
Gannet	Hermaness	**
Shag	Foula	*
Eider	Foula	**
Oystercatcher	Faeroe	**
	Foula	*
Whimbrel	Faeroe	**
Great Skua	Foula	***
	Noss	**
Herring Gull	Hermaness	***
	Noss	*
Kittiwake	Faeroe	****
	Hermaness	***
	Noss	**
	Foula	*
Arctic Tern	Hermaness	**
Razorbill	Hermaness	*
Guillemot	Faeroe	***
	Hermaness	**
Puffin	Hermaness	*
BIRDS		
Domestic ducks, geese or chickens	Shetland	*
Red-throated Diver (chicks)	Iceland	**
	Shetland	**
Slavonian Grebe (adult)	Iceland	*
Fulmar (adult)	Iceland	***
	Faeroe	***
	Shetland	**
(chicks)	Iceland	**
	Faeroe	**
	Shetland	*
Sooty Shearwater (adult)	Shetland	*
Manx Shearwater (adult)	Foula	*
Storm Petrel (adult)	Hermaness	**
	Foula	****
	Noss	*
Gannet (adult)	Hermaness	*
	Foula	*
(chick)	Hermaness	**
	Noss	**

TABLE 24 continued.

Food item	Locality	Frequency in diet
Shag (adult)	Faeroe	**
	Foula	**
Grey Heron (adult)	Shetland	*
Grey-lag Goose (adult)	Iceland	**
(chicks)	Iceland	**
Shelduck (adult)	Orkney	*
Mallard (adult)	Iceland	**
	Foula	*
Teal (adult)	Iceland	**
	Foula	*
Wigeon (adult)	Iceland	**
Scaup (adult)	Iceland	**
Eider (adult)	Iceland	***
	Shetland	***
	Orkney	***
Common Scoter (adult)	Iceland	**
	Orkney	*
Long-tailed Duck (adult)	Iceland	**
	Orkney	*
Red-breasted Merganser (adult)	Iceland	**
Coot (adult)	Shetland	*
Oystercatcher (adult)	Iceland	***
	Shetland	**
(chicks)	Shetland	***
Ringed Plover (adult)	Foula	*
Golden Plover (chicks)	Iceland	**
Lapwing (chicks)	Foula	*
Turnstone (adult)	Foula	*
Dunlin (adult)	Hermaness	*
Curlew (adult)	Foula	*
Whimbrel (adult)	Shetland	*
Snipe (adult)	Shetland	**
Great Skua (chicks)	Iceland	**
	Faeroe	****
	Shetland	***
(fledglings)	Hermaness	**
	Foula	****
	Fair Isle	*
Arctic Skua (chicks)	Iceland	**
	Faeroe	**
	Shetland	***
Lesser Black-backed Gull (adult)	Faeroe	**
	Foula	**
Herring Gull (adult)	Shetland	***
(chicks)	Hermaness	***
	Noss	***
	Foula	*

TABLE 24 continued.

Food item	Locality	Frequency in diet
Great Black-backed Gull (adult)	Iceland	***
	Shetland	**
	Orkney	**
(chicks)	Iceland	****
	Noss	**
Common Gull (adult)	Foula	**
Kittiwake (adult)	Iceland	**
	Faeroe	****
	Shetland	***
(chicks)	Faeroe	***
	Hermaness	***
	Noss	**
(fledglings)	Iceland	***
	Faeroe	***
	Foula	****
	Hermaness	**
	Noss	**
Arctic Tern (adult)	Iceland	**
	Faeroe	**
	Hermaness	**
	Foula	*
(chicks)	Noss	*
Razorbill (adult)	Iceland	**
	Shetland	**
(fledgling)	Shetland	***
Guillemot (adult)	all areas	***
(fledglings)	all areas	****
Black Guillemot (adult)	Foula	**
Puffin (adult)	all areas	****
(fledgling)	all areas	****
Rock Dove (adult)	Foula	*
Feral Pigeon (adult)	Foula	**
Cuckoo (adult)	Shetland	*
Skylark (adult)	Foula	*
Meadow Pipit (adult)	Foula	*
Wheatear (adult)	Foula	*
Crossbill (adult)	Foula	*
Starling (adult)	Foula	**

CARRION

Offal from fishing boats	Iceland	***
	Faeroe	***
	Shetland	***
Whitefish discards (see fish list)	Shetland	*****
	Faeroe	*
	Iceland	**

TABLE 24 continued.

Food item	Locality	Frequency in diet
Grey Seal carcass	Iceland	**
Stranded marine animals on tideline	Shetland	*
Fishing bait on lines	Faeroe	**
	Shetland	*
Lambs and sheep	Faeroe	***
	Shetland	**
Seabirds	all areas	****
Domestic refuse	Shetland	**

TABLE 25: A comparison of part of prey spectrum of Great Skuas at five localities studied in greatest detail, showing differences in diet between areas. Symbols are as in Table 17. nr = not recorded.

Prey item	Foula	Noss	Hermaness	Faeroe	Iceland
Fish	*****	*****	*****	****	****
Mammals	***	**	**	**	nr
Kittiwake adults	**	***	***	***	**
fledglings	****	**	**	***	***
nestlings	nr	**	***	***	nr
eggs	nr	**	***	****	nr
Great Skua fledglings	****	nr	**	nr	nr
nestlings	**	**	***	****	**
eggs	****	**	nr	**	nr
Arctic Skua chicks	***	**	***	**	**
Arctic Tern adults	*	nr	**	**	**
chicks	*	*	nr	nr	nr
eggs	nr	nr	**	nr	nr
Black Guillemot adults	**	nr	nr	nr	nr

TABLE 26: Colour phases of Arctic Skua chicks on Fair Isle in relation to colours of parents. Data from O'Donald (1983).

Mating type	Chicks produced; 1951–58				Chicks produced; 1973–79			
	Pale	Intermediate	Dark	Total	Pale	Intermediate	Dark	Total
P × P	29	0	0	29	21	1	0	22
P × I	36	42	3	81	33	78	0	111
P × D	16	39	2	57	0	63	1	64
I × I	16	37	8	61	27	162	49	238
I × D	9	125	43	177	0	79	28	107
D × D	0	12	15	27	0	9	18	27
All matings	106	255	71	432	81	392	96	569

TABLE 27: Changes in frequency of colour phases of Arctic Skua in Iceland between 1939–43 and 1970–71. From O'Donald (1983).

Period	North Iceland		South Iceland	
	Melanics	Pales	Melanics	Pales
1939–43	33	24	124	47
1970–71	89	50	372	46

χ^2 between periods of observation: 18.7, $p < 0.001$

TABLE 28: Changes in frequency of colour phases of Arctic Skuas in Varanger area of North East Norway, 1937–52 to 1972–78.

Period	Skuas counted	Percentage pale	Reference
1937	127	56	Venables (1937)
1952	37	54	Watson (1957)
1972	51	33	Bengtson & Owen (1973)
1976–78	461	42	Gotmark et al (1981)

χ^2 between periods: 10.2, $p < 0.001$

TABLE 29: Changes in frequency of colour phases of Arctic Skua at Noss, Foula, Fair Isle, and Orkney.

Colony	Period	Birds Counted	Percentage pale	Reference
Noss	1934	98	17.3	Southern (1943)
	1935	70	25.7	Southern (1943)
	1942	73	20.5	Southern (1943)
	1946	75	30.7	Perry (1948)
	1974	88	14.8	Kinnear (1974)
	1986	44	11.4	Ewins pers. comm.

χ^2 between periods 1930–50; 1970–86: 4.58, $p < 0.05$

Colony	Period	Birds Counted	Percentage pale	Reference
Foula	1890	120	25	Barrington (1890)
	1948	36	30	Southern (1943)
	1974	330	29.7	O'Donald et al (1974)
	1975	512	29.9	Davis & O'Donald (1976)
	1975	514	26.8	Furness (1983)
	1986	235	23.4	Ewins et al (1986)
Fair Isle	1943–59	216	25.0	O'Donald (1960)
	1973–79	784	20.0	O'Donald (1983)
Orkney	1943	81	38	Lack (1943)
	1982	1871	24.3	Meek et al (1985)

χ^2 between periods: 8.0, $p < 0.001$

TABLE 30: Differences in the frequency of dark and light phases among breeding male and female Arctic Skuas on Foula in 1987. Expected numbers from Null Hypothesis that the proportions of each colour phase are independent of sex.

Combination	Number observed	Number expected	Statistics
Dark × Light pairs	26	13	
Dark male × Light female	20	13	
Light male × Dark female	6	13	$\chi^2 = 6.5$ p < 0.05

From the above data and observed proportions of Dark × Dark, Dark × Light and Light × Light pairs.

	Number	Frequency of Light
Dark males	138	
Dark females	113	
Light males	18	11.5% of males
Light females	43	27.6% of males

TABLE 31: Timing of breeding in Arctic Skua populations in relation to proportions of pales and main feeding methods employed.

Locality	Percentage pale birds	First arrival	First egg	Mean laying date	Range of laying dates (days)	Feeding habit	Reference
Fair Isle	21	16/4	16/5	28/5	41	robbing	O'Donald (1983)
Barrow	50	4/6	14/6	17/6	6	tundra	Maher (1974)
Cape Sabine	50	22/5	31/5	4/6	9	tundra	Maher (1974)
Lake Peters	50	27/5	8/6	9/6	2	tundra	Maher (1974)
Kaolak River	50	—	3/6	6/6	8	tundra	Maher (1984)
east Murman	70	5/5	2/6	13/6	35	robbing	Belopolskii (1961)
Spitsbergen	99	1/6	7/6	1/7	51	robbing	Lovenskiold (1963)
Bear Island	99	—	—	1/8	—	robbing	Lack (1933)

TABLE 32: *Numbers of matings between like and unlike colour morphs of Arctic Skua at different localities and in different periods, and chi squared tests of the significance of differences from the numbers expected if pairs formed without regard to colour phase and phases were equally distributed between the sexes.*

Location	Period	DxD	LxL	DxL	χ^2	Reference
Orkney	1982	501	58	299	2.12	Meek et al (1985)
Fair Isle	1943–59	64	10	34	1.99	O'Donald (1959)
Fair Isle	1949–63	179	14	81	1.5	Berry & Davis (1970)
Fair Isle	1973–79	254	19	119	1.07	O'Donald (1980)
Foula	1948	9	2	7	0.03	O'Donald (1959)
Foula	1975	144	26	86	5.52	Davis & O'Donald (1976)
Unst	1948	36	4	15	0.80	O'Donald (1959)
Unst	1959	43	9	19	6.7	Berry & Davis (1970)
Unst	1963	13	2	10	0.0	Berry & Davis (1970)
Yell/Fetlar	1948	36	5	25	0.01	O'Donald (1959)
Caithness	1953	9	1	11	0.27	O'Donald (1959)
Noss	1935	16	1	16	1.6	Berry & Davis (1970)
Noss	1942	18	3	1	13.9	Berry & Davis (1970)
Noss	1946	21	7	9	5.04	O'Donald (1959)
Noss	1963	16	0	6	0.5	Berry & Davis (1970)
NE Norway	1976–78	45	21	67	0.72	Gotmark et al (1981)
Smolen	1921	3	1	2	0.49	Southern (1943)
Gamvik	1921	3	3	4	0.22	Southern (1943)
NE Iceland	1971	7	1	20	6.84	Bengston & Owen (1973)

N.B. Data for Foula in 1974 have been omitted since their reliability is in doubt (Davis & O'Donald 1976)

TABLE 33: *Assortative mating of Arctic Skuas on Fair Isle, 1949–63. Data from Berry & Davis (1970).*

Phase of female		Dark	Phase of male Intermediate	Pale	Total
Dark	Observed	17	26	3	46
	Expected	15.6	26.1	8.4	50.2
Intermediate	Observed	36	81	18	135
	Expected	38.2	64.1	20.7	123.0
Pale	Observed	16	18	14	48
	Expected	17.4	29.1	9.4	55.9
Total	Observed	69	125	35	229
	Expected	71.2	119.3	38.5	229

χ^2 for homogeneity: 15.2, p = 0.005

TABLE 34: Survival rates of each colour phase of Arctic Skua on Fair Isle. Data from O'Donald (1983).

Phenotypes	Period of observation 1948–1962 Survived	Died	1973–1975 Survived	Died	1976–1978 Survived	Died
Pale	111	27	119	13	95	44
Intermediate	322	85	353	50	329	101
Dark	125	27	113	12	104	34
Total	558	139	585	75	528	179

Differences in mortality between periods: $\chi 2 = 43.7$ $p < 0.001$
Differences in mortality between phases $\chi 2 = $ 1.2 n.s.

TABLE 35: Distribution of ages of first breeding of Arctic Skuas of each colour phase at Fair Isle, 1948–1959 and 1970–76. Data from O'Donald (1983).

Phenotype	Age at first breeding (years) 3	4	5	6	7	Total	Mean age
	9	12	5	2	0	28	4.0
Pale	3	26	18	5	1	53	4.53
Intermediate	1	9	7	3	0	20	4.6
Dark							
	13	47	30	10	1	101	4.40
Total							

TABLE 36: Reproductive rates of ringed Arctic Skuas on Fair Isle in first and subsequent years of breeding, in relation to colour phase. Data from O'Donald (1983).

Phenotype	breeding experience	Males number	chicks fledged per pair	Females number	chicks fledged per pair
Pale	First year	22	0.68	29	0.59
	Later years	58	1.22	102	1.29
Intermediate	First year	71	0.82	70	0.90
	Later years	191	1.29	211	1.36
Dark	First year	32	0.88	24	0.96
	Later years	108	1.49	64	1.33

TABLE 37: Apparent gene frequencies in subsamples of Arctic Skua population of Fair Isle. Data from Berry & Davis (1970).

| Category | Number of | | | | Percent frequency |
	Darks	Intermediates	Pales	Total	of pale allele
Breeding males	52	87	28	167	0.428
Breeding females	35	86	39	160	0.513
Total adults	109	204	80	393	0.463
Young fledged	117	475	178	830	0.467
Adults found dead away from Fair Isle	7	18	8	33	0.515
Birds returned to breed on Fair Isle	13	32	17	62	0.532

TABLE 38: Percentage of successful chases made by dark and pale Arctic Skuas at Puffin colony in south Iceland in 1973. Data from Arnason (1978).

Number of skuas	Colour phases of skuas	Chases observed	Percent successful
1	Dark	704	62.6
1	Pale	31	80.7
2	Dark, Dark	247	78.5
2	Pale, Dark	32	90.6
3	all Dark	73	76.7
3	1 Pale, 2 Dark	15	80.0
4 to 6	all Dark	19	73.7
4 to 6	1 Pale, rest Dark	9	88.9

TABLE 39: The percentage of successful chases made by dark and pale Arctic Skuas at different colonies in 1978 and 1979. Data from Furness & Furness (1980).

Colony	Year	Species chased	Number of chases by darks	Percentage success	Number of chases by pales	Percentage success
Hofn, Iceland	1978	Arctic Tern	37	23.4	13	15.3
Noss, Shetland	1978	Guillemot	119	12.6	27	22.2
Fetlar, Shetland	1978	Puffin	46	26.1	16	6.3
Foula, Shetland	1978	Guillemot	14	0.0	12	16.7
Foula, Shetland	1978	Puffin	88	25.0	52	15.4
Foula, Shetland	1979	Guillemot	29	20.7	6	33.3
Foula, Shetland	1979	Puffin	163	28.2	123	20.8
Foula, Shetland	1979	Arctic Tern	218	23.4	79	19.0

TABLE 40: Aggression scores obtained at each territory where both Great Skuas were present and were about half way through the incubation period. Data were gathered on Foula in 1975 and 1976. Aggression score 1 = both adults left the territory when author walked towards nest, 2 = birds circled above him without divebombing, 3 = swooped but did not hit, 4 = swooped frequently but hit only occasionally, 5 = swooped frequently and hit frequently.

Location in colony	Number of pairs	Aggression score				
		1	*2*	*3*	*4*	*5*
Central area	817	47	160	321	234	55
	100%	5.8%	19.6%	39.9%	28.6%	6.7%
Edge areas	64	5	13	28	16	2
	100%	7.8%	20.3%	43.8%	25.0%	3.1%
All nests	881	52	173	349	250	57
	100%	6%	20%	40%	28%	6%

TABLE 41: Nesting densities and mean nearest neighbouring nest distances for skuas in different areas.

Locality	Reference	Pairs per km²	Mean NN distance (m)
ARCTIC SKUA			
northern Alaska	Maher 1974	0.02–0.15	396
Fair Isle	O'Donald 1983	98 (1974–75)	c100
Fair Isle	O'Donald 1983	82 (1977–78)	c100
Noss	Perry 1948	62 (1946)	70
Noss	Kinnear 1974	147 (1974)	45
Noss	Furness 1986	170 (1982)	
Foula	"	33 (1948)	
"	"	57 (1960)	
"	"	70 (1968)	
"	"	75 (1972)	
"	"	65 (1973)	
"	"	100 (1974)	
"	"	133 (1975)	
"	"	200 (1976)	
"	"	175 (1980)	
"	"	149 (1982)	
Syltefjord	Andersson & Gotmark 1982	21	
Holmfjellet	Andersson & Gotmark 1980	14	
Falkgarden	Andersson & Gotmark 1980	0.5	

Locality	Reference	Pairs per km^2	Mean NN distance (m)
POMARINE SKUA			
northern Alaska	Maher 1974	0.0–7.9	
northern Alaska	Pitelka et al. 1955	2.3 (1952)	762
northern Alaska	Pitelka et al. 1955	13.7 (1953)	305
northern Alaska	Andersson 1973	2.4	
LONG-TAILED SKUA			
northern Alaska	Maher 1974	0.03–0.09	457
Ellesmere Island	Maher 1970	up to 0.8	
Greenland	Manniche 1910	1.7	
Sweden	Andersson 1976, 1981	0.02–0.63	
E Greenland	Hansen 1984	0.28	1500
E Greenland	de Korte 1977	0.2–0.9	1500
GREAT SKUA			
Noss	Perry 1948		53
Noss	Perdeck 1960		40
Noss	Kinear 1974		35
Foula	Furness 1977	120–4000	c26
BROWN SKUA			
Bird Is. S. Georgia	Osborne 1985	100	
Chatham Is.	Young 1978	56	215
Macquarie Is.	Jones & Skira 1979	4–20	
Signy Is.	Burton 1968		c 200
Signy Is.	Hemmings 1984		> 50
Crozet Is.	Barre 1976		c 85
SOUTH POLAR SKUA			
Cape Hallett	Young 1963		c 15
Cape Hallett	Trillmich 1978	91	
Cape Crozier	Wood 1971		19
Cape Royds	Young 1963		c 50
Signy Is.	Hemmings 1984		25
Adelie Land	Le Morvan et al. 1967		30
Anvers Is.	Parmelee et al. 1977		20
TRISTAN SKUA			
Gough Island	Furness unpubl.	10–90	
CHILEAN SKUA			
S. America	Moynihan, Murphy and others 'often nests at high density'		
FALKLAND SKUA			
Falkland Is.	K. Thompson 'dispersed 100 m or so apart above petrels'		

TABLE 42: Numbers of times that Arctic Skuas on Foula chased intruders from their territory and amount of time spent in flight in territorial defence (not including territorial display advertisement flights) over a 24 hour period during chick rearing.

Cause of disturbance	Pair A		Pair B		Pair C	
	Frequency	Time in flight (mins)	Frequency	Time in flight (mins)	Frequency	Time in flight (mins)
Great Skua	58	136	5	7	38	54
Arctic Skua	14	30	20	35	5	8
Sheep	1	1	7	20	10	14
Arctic Tern	0	0	10	14	0	0
Fulmar	1	2	1	1	1	2
Common Gull	0	0	1	1	2	3
Herring Gull	0	0	0	0	1	1
Great Black-backed Gull	0	0	0	0	1	1

TABLE 43: Maximum numbers of Great and Arctic Skuas attending each club site and each bathing site on Foula during midafternoon peak attendances around seasonal peak of nonbreeder attendance in June–July, comparing between 1977 when colony numbers of each species were increasing and 1986 when colony numbers were falling. No site is used as a club or bathing area by both species together. Birds at bathing sites include breeders and nonbreeders, whereas birds at club sites are virtually all immature nonbreeders (see text).

Great Skua Club	Maximum number of nonbreeders present in afternoon	
	1977	*1986*
1. Hamnafield	250	60
2. Kame	130	30
3. Flick	210	30
4. Liorafield	200	110
5. Daal	160	80
6. Noup	120	15
7. Bottle	160	100
8. Strem Ness	220	50
9. Netherfandal	90	110
10. Rossies	30	20
11. South Ness	0	10
ALL CLUB SITES COMBINED	1570	615

Great Skua Club site	Maximum number of nonbreeders present in afternoon	
	1977	*1986*
Great Skua bathing sites		
A. Mill Loch	180	160
B. Overfandal	160	80
C. Flick	110	65
D. Rossies	0	20
ALL BATHING SITES COMBINED	450	325
Arctic Skua club sites		
1. Peatbanks	30	4
2. Hametoun	35	12
ALL CLUB SITES COMBINED	65	16
Arctic Skua bathing sites		
A. Heddlicliff	22	8

TABLE 44: Breeding timetables of interspecies hybrid pairs compared with those of Brown Skuas and South Polar Skuas on Signy Island. From Hemmings (1984).

Group	Hatching dates of first eggs
Hybrid pairs	5 Jan, 7 Jan, 8 Jan (3 pairs in 1981–83)
Brown Skuas	20 Dec 1981, 26 Dec 1982 (earliest pairs on island) mean hatching date for all pairs is in early January
South Polar Skuas	2 Jan 1983, 7 Jan 1982 (earliest pairs on island)
	19 Jan 1982, 17 Jan 1983 (mean first eggs of all pairs)

TABLE 45: Influences of previous breeding experience on breeding performance of Great Skuas at Foula in 1975 and 1976. From Furness (1984).

Statistic	Previous breeding experience (years)				ANOVA
	0	*1*	*2*	*>2*	*0 vs 1 +*
Sample size	20	16	6	22	
Mean clutch size	1.80	1.96	1.83	1.91	n.s.
Percent eggs hatched	69	65	64	71	n.s.
Percent chicks fledged	72	95	100	97	$p < 0.05$
Mean hatching date (June)	31.55	20.69	17.50	17.50	$p < 0.01$
Percentage eggs addled	29	33	36	18	n.s.
Percentage chicks starved	28	0	0	0	$p < 0.05$

TABLE 46: First arrival and first egg dates for Arctic Skuas at different sites. References: 1 = Fair isle Bird Observatory Annual Reports, 2 = Perry (1948), 3 = Furness (1977), 4 = Belopolskii (1961), 5 = Lovenskiold (1964), 6 = de Kroon (1986), 7 = Lack (1933), 8 = Maher (1974).

Locality	First arrival date	First egg date	Mean egg date	Duration of prelaying interval (days)	Ref
Fair Isle 59°N	16/4	16/5	28/5	30	1
Noss 60°N	–	–	30/5	–	2
Foula 60°N	18/4	18/5	26/5	30	3
east Murman 68°N	5/5	2/6	13/6	28	4
Bear Island 75°N	20/6	6/7	15/7	16	5
Spitsbergen 78°N	24/5	7/6	1/7	14	6
Spitsbergen 78°N	15/6	23/6	3/7	8	7
Barrow, Alaska 71°N	4/6	14/6	17/6	10	8
C. Sabine 71°N	22/5	31/5	4/6	9	8
L. Peters 71°N	27/5	8/6	9/6	12	8
Kaolak 71°N	27/5	3/6	6/6	7	8

TABLE 47: Egg measurements for skuas: 1 = Furness 1977; 2 = Witherby et al 1941; 3 = Barre 1976; 4 = Murphy 1936; 5 = Mathews 1913; 6 = Hagen 1952; 7 = Hemmings 1984; 8 = Moors 1980; 9 = Stonehouse 1956; 10 = Bonner 1964; 11 = Williams 1980; 12 = Rand in Williams 1980; 13 = Paulian in Williams 1980; 14 = Morvan et al 1967; 15 = Falla et al 1967; 16 = Gain 1914; 17 = Wilson 1907.

Locality	Ref	eggs measured	Length (mm) mean	s.d.	range	Breadth (mm) mean	s.d.	range	Volume Index (mean)
GREAT SKUA									
Foula	1	750	71.5	–	–	50.2	–	–	180.0
Scotland	2	100	70.6	–	–	49.4	–	–	172.3
TRISTAN SKUA									
Tristan	3	25	69.6	–	–	50.7	–	–	178.9
Gough	4	3	71.3	4.1	66.6–73.7	51.0	0.8	50.3–51.8	185.5
Tristan	5	10	70	–	–	51	–	–	182.1
FALKLAND SKUA									
Falklands	6	14	69.8	–	–	51.9	–	–	188.0
Falklands	4	10	69.9	3.1	63.7–74.9	53.0	4.1	49.1–59.1	196.3

Locality	Ref	eggs measured	Length (mm) mean	s.d.	range	Breadth (mm) mean	s.d.	range	Volume Index (mean)
BROWN SKUA									
Signy	7	39	73.8	2.4	69.1–80.1	52.3	1.4	48.8–54.6	201.9
Antipodes	8	20	74.8	2.6	–	53.0	1.6	–	210.1
S. Georgia	9	20	75.5	–	71.0–82.9	53.2	–	57.0–58.9	213.7
S. Georgia	6	9	74.1	–	–	52.4	–	–	203.5
S. Georgia	10	20	74.8	2.5	71.0–79.7	51.3	2.0	48.0–54.2	196.9
Marion	11	136	76.4	–	71.0–81.9	52.7	–	50.1–56.2	212.2
Marion	12	43	76.6	–	72.2–84.2	52.6	–	50.1–60.2	211.9
Crozet	3	20	76.5	–	72.0–85.0	52.9	–	45.0–59.0	214.4
Kerguelen	13	17	75.2	–	70.8–80.0	53.3	–	50.4–54.6	213.6
CHILEAN SKUA									
Fuego	4	5	70.2	2.7	67.0–73.7	52.3	4.3	48.0–59.5	192.0
SOUTH POLAR SKUA									
Signy	7	27	71.3	2.4	66.7–76.4	49.6	1.3	47.1–52.1	175.4
Pt Geologie	14	13	71.0	–	65.0–74.0	50.7	–	48.2–52.1	182.5
C Denison	15	12	70.6	–	55.0–78.0	51.5	–	49.6–54.7	187.2
Peninsula	16	10	71.9	–	65.5–75.0	49.0	–	41.0–52.0	172.6
McMurdo	17	11	70.9	–	66.0–76.5	49.7	–	49.0–51.0	175.1

LONG-TAILED SKUA
Mean weight of egg 41 g, length 55 mm, breadth 38 mm (Cramp & Simmons 1983)
Mean weight of egg 41.1 g, s.d. 2.79, n = 69 (de Korte 1985)

POMARINE SKUA
Mean weight of egg 66 g, length 64 mm, breadth 45 mm (Cramp & Simmons 1983)

ARCTIC SKUA
Mean weight of egg 49 g, length 57 mm, breadth 40 mm (Cramp & Simmons 1983)
Mean weight of egg 50.2 g (range 49–54, n = 15; Belopolskii 1961)

TABLE 48: *Mean clutch size, hatching success, fledging success and breeding success of skuas.*

Skua	Study	Nests marked	Mean clutch size	Hatching success (%)	Fledging success (%)	Breeding success (%)
Great	Perry (1948) Noss	113	1.95	70.3	73.7	51.8
	Williamson (1957) Fair Isle	57	1.86	73.7	86.9	64.0
	Furness (1984) Foula	881	1.90	70.0	93.2	65.3
	Hudson (1986) Noss	120	1.92	83.8	52.8	44.3
Brown	Barre (1976) Crozet	76	1.78	77.0	94.9	73.1
	Burton (1968) Signy	65	1.97	66.5	90.1	59.9
	Downes et al (1959) Heard	30	–	–	–	c62
	Jones & Skira (1979) Macquarie	238	–	–	–	c39
	Moors (1980) Antipodes Is.	11	1.82	54.9	50.0	27.5
	Carrick & Ingham (1970) Macquarie	40	–	–	–	c61
	Stonehouse (1956) S. Georgia	12	1.67	59.9	75.0	44.9
	Trivelpiece (1980) Pt Thomas	24	1.67	–	–	44.9
	Wiliams (1980) Marion Is.	29	1.97	75.1	64.9	48.7
	Young (1978) Rangatira Is.	11	1.91	–	–	81.2
South	Eklund (1961) Windmill Is.	40	1.80	61.1	77.3	47.2
Polar	Ensor (1979) Cape Bird	79	1.51	23.2	85.7	19.9
	Jouventin & Guillotin (1979) Pt Geologie	210	1.52	–	–	56.6
	Le Morvan et al (1967) Pt Geologie	38	1.55	67.7	92.4	62.6
	Pryor (1968) Haswell Is.	23	1.74	62.6	71.6	44.8
	Reid (1966) Cape Hallett	472	–	–	–	c25
	Spellerberg (1971) Cape Royds	176	1.80	71.1	46.9	33.3
	Wood (1970) Cape Crozier	879	–	–	–	c20
	Young (1963) Cape Royds	67	1.91	84.3	28.6	24.1
Arctic	Perry (1948) Noss	30	1.90	80	62	49
	Maher (1974) N Alaska	21	1.86	–	–	0–75
	O'Donald (1983) Fair Isle	836	1.87	–	–	65
	Kinnear (1974) Noss	44	1.93	65	–	–
	Furness (1980) Foula	186	1.81	70	90	63
	Arnason & Grant (1978) Iceland	–	–	–	–	c15
Pomarine	Maher (1974) N Alaska	255	1.95	25–75	0–75	0–50
Long-	Andersson (1981) N Sweden	–	1.4–2	0–83	0–80	0–70
tailed	Maher (1974) N Alaska	48	1.81	–	–	0–70
	Hansen (1984) E Greenland	8	1.88	24	0	0
	de Korte (1986) E Greenland	33	1.4–2.1	0–50	0	0

TABLE 49: *Outcome of breeding attempts by Great Skuas at Foula in mid 1970s. From Furness (1984).*

Parameter	Number	Percentage
Nests studied	881	(c/1 = 93, c/2 = 787, c/3 = 1)
Eggs laid	1670	(1.90 eggs per pair)
Eggs taken by predators	177	10.6% of eggs laid
Eggs rolled out of nest	41	2.5% of eggs laid
Eggs 'addled'	250	17.2% of eggs surviving 30 days
Eggs died at hatching	34	2.8% of fertile eggs at 30 days
Hatched	1168	69.9% of eggs laid
Chicks starved	35	3.0% of chicks hatched
Chicks taken by predators	37	3.2% of chicks hatched
Chicks grossly abnormal	6	0.5% of chicks hatched
Chicks fledged	1090	93.3% of all chicks hatched

TABLE 50: *Differences in rates of egg and chick mortality factors between clutches of one and two eggs laid by Great Skuas at 880 nests marked at Foula in 1975 or 1976. From Furness (1984).*

Mortality factor	Clutches of one egg ($n = 93$ eggs) Observed	Expected	Clutches of two eggs ($n = 1,574$ eggs) Observed	Expected	χ^2	p
Predation of eggs	21	9.9	156	167.1	14.8	<0.005
Rolled out of nest	2	2.3	39	38.7	0.1	n.s.
Addled	27	12.0	222	237.0	23.8	<0.005
Died hatching	0	1.2	34	32.8	1.3	n.s.
Chick starved	6	1.3	29	33.7	18.2	<0.005
Chick predated	0	1.4	37	35.6	1.5	n.s.
Mutant chick	0	0.2	6	5.8	0.2	n.s.

TABLE 51: Differences in rates of egg and chick mortality factors between first and second laid eggs in Great Skua clutches of two eggs laid at 787 nests marked at Foula in 1975 or 1976.

Mortality factor	Expected	Observed First egg	Observed Second egg	χ^2	p
Predation of egg	78.0	79	77	0.0	n.s.
Rolled out of nest	19.5	24	15	2.1	n.s.
Addled	110.1	107	115	0.2	n.s.
Died hatching	17.0	14	20	1.1	n.s.
Chick starved	14.5	7	22	8.0	<0.005
Predation of chick	18.5	16	21	0.7	n.s.
Mutant chick	3.0	3	3	0.0	n.s.

TABLE 52: Tarsus colour of skuas of different ages. From Cramp & Simmons (1983) and de Korte (1986).

Age (years)	Proportion of the surface of the tarsus that is black Arctic Skua	Pomarine Skua	Long-tailed Skua
0 (fledgling)	0–10	0	0
1	30–90	0–20	0–20
2	50–100	0–50	0–20
3	80–100	20–90	5–80
4	90–100	80–100	—
5 or older	100	100	100

TABLE 53: Tail tip lengths (T1–T6 length) for Stercorarius species during breeding season in relation to age. Data from Cramp & Simmons (1983) (mean s.d., n.) (mm).

Age	S. pomarinus male	S. pomarinus female	S. parasiticus	S. longicaudus
1st year	15, 3.9, 17	13, 3.9, 13	17, 3.6, 3	23, 4.6, 39
2nd year	58, —, 3	44, 16.1, 5	40, 8.5, 3	56, 21.3, 4
3rd year	70, —, 3	46, 8.5, 4	51, 12.4, 8	88, 26.3, 10
4th year	78, 12.7, 10	72, 15.5, 7	61, 15.1, 24	130, 42.3, 22
Adult	95, 10.4, 9	92, 14.5, 9	82, 9.9, 62	179, 25.5, 84
Adult winter	49, —, 3	40, 8.4, 5		

TABLE 54: Organochlorine levels in skuas. Values are in parts per million (mg per kg) wet weight. Minimum and maximum values are given in parentheses below mean values.

Skua	Locality	Year	Tissue	Sample size	dieldrin	Values (ppm) DDE	PCBs	PCB:DDE ratio
Arctic	N. Scotland (Bourne 1976)	1971	liver	3	–	0.49 (0.09,1.29)	1.77 (0.5,3.6)	3.6
			muscle	3	–	0.25 (0.17,0.37)	0.81 (0.5,1.5)	3.2
Arctic	Iceland (Sproul et al 1975)	1973	muscle	10	0.03 (0.02,0.04)	0.43 (0.18,1.50)	0.98 (0.27,4.2)	2.3
			egg	4	0.07	0.53	1.30	2.4
Great	Handa (Prestt et al 1970)	1969	egg	1	–	–	25.0	–
Great	Shetland (Bourne & Bogan 1972)	1972	liver	5	–	–	6.49 (4.1,18.3)	–
			muscle	5	–	2.7 (2.0,4.0)	15.8 (10.2,32.0)	5.9
			chick liver	1	–	0.02	0.05	3.0
Great	Iceland (Sproul et al 1975)	1973	muscle	10	0.12 (0.05,0.35)	4.4 (1.8,12.0)	16.0 (5.3,47.0)	3.6
			egg	13	0.20	5.9	27.0	4.6
Great	Foula (Furness & Hutton 1979)	1976	egg	12	0.08 (0.02,0.15)	1.7 (0.4,3.6)	17.6 (6.1,36.0)	10.4
Great	Foula (Muirhead 1986)	1980	muscle	20	0.04 (0.03,0.07)	1.5 (0.45,10.3)	14.2 (1.8,72.0)	9.5
			liver	17	–	2.6 (0.38,78.0)	14.1 (1.7,99.0)	5.4
Great	Foula (Muirhead 1986)	1983	egg	6	0.04	0.53 (0.4,1.61)	6.1 (2.8,17.0)	11.6
Brown	S. Orkneys (Tatton & Ruzicka 1967)	1966	liver	2	not detected	0.9,4.0	–	–
			fat	2	not detected	5.8,26.0	–	–
Brown	S. Shetlands (Lukowski 1983)	1978	liver	10	–	0.15 (0.06,0.21)	–	–
			muscle	10	–	0.21 (0.05,0.43)	–	–
			fat	8	–	3.4 (0.99,6.7)	–	–
Tristan	Tristan (Bourne 1976)	1974	liver	1	–	2.4	3.5	1.5
			muscle	1	–	6.1	2.9	0.5
			fat	1	–	22.0	33.0	1.5

TABLE 55: Correlations between metal levels and the ages of Great Skuas.

Element	Tissue	Sample size	Correlation coefficient	Significance
(a) Furness & Hutton (1979)				
Mercury	Primary feather	12	+0.15	n.s.
	Kidney	11	+0.28	n.s.
	Liver	12	+0.45	n.s.
Cadmium	Kidney	12	+0.70	$p < 0.01$
	Liver	12	+0.57	$p < 0.05$
Selenium	Kidney	9	+0.70	$p < 0.01$
	Liver	10	+0.44	n.s.
(b) Muirhead (1986)				
Mercury	Kidney	20	+0.21	n.s.
	Liver	20	+0.35	n.s.
	Muscle	20	+0.22	n.s.
Cadmium	Kidney	27	+0.33	n.s.
	Liver	27	−0.05	n.s.
	Muscle	27	+0.40	$p < 0.05$
Selenium	Kidney	20	−0.09	n.s.
	Liver	20	+0.18	n.s.
	Muscle	20	−0.02	n.s.

TABLE 56: Mercury levels in feathers of an individual Great Skua in relation to sequence in which plumage is thought to be moulted.

Feathers ranked according to moult sequence	Mean mercury level (ppm)
Primary 1	13.0
Primary 2	10.1
Primary 3	9.4
Primary 4	7.0
Primary 5	5.1
Tail feathers	3.9
Secondaries	2.7
Body feathers	2.7 to 3.0
Coverts	2.8 to 3.2
Primaries 7 to 10	2.6 to 3.8
Head and neck feathers (partial spring moult?)	3.8 to 4.5

TABLE 57: *Amounts of mercury in different tissues and plumage and eggs of Great Skuas (sample sizes in parentheses).*

Tissue	Mean weight (g)	Mean level of mercury (ppm)	Amount of mercury (μg)
Skin	145 (3)	0.6 (4)	87
Liver	39 (3)	4.8 (30)	187
Kidney	12 (3)	3.2 (30)	38
Muscle	680 (3)	0.8 (28)	544
Heart, lung, alimentary tract	150 (3)	0.8 (3)	120
Primary feathers	16.1 (5)	6.1 (50)	98
Secondary feathers	10.9 (5)	4.2 (40)	46
Tail feathers	4.8 (5)	5.4 (20)	26
Coverts	34.0 (2)	3.1 (10)	105
Body and head feathers	77.0 (2)	3.2 (10)	246
Egg contents (per egg)	90 (500)	0.5 (12)	45

TABLE 58: *Average numbers of sheep within an Arctic Skua breeding colony area on Fair Isle at different stages in the skuas' breeding season and under different weather conditions. Data from Cooper (1979).*

Weather	Period within the breeding season			
	Prelaying (7–22 May)	Incubation (22 May–15 June)	Chick rearing (15 June–9 July)	Fledging (9 July–3 Aug)
Wet	20.0	14.5	15.7	17.0
Dry	11.0	6.0	3.9	5.5

TABLE 59: Numbers and nesting density of Arctic Skuas in relation to numbers of Great Skuas (interpolated estimates in parentheses) at Shetland colonies.

Colony	Year	Great Skua (pairs)	Arctic Skua (pairs)	colony area (km^2)	density (pairs km^2)
Foula	1948	350	100	3.0	33
	1960	(1000)	131	2.3	57
	1968	(1800)	160	2.3	70
	1972	(2200)	150	2.0	75
	1973	2500	130	2.0	65
	1974	2500	180	1.8	100
	1975	2705	240	1.8	133
	1976	2980	280	2.4	200
	1980	2670	262	1.5	175
	1982	(2500)	224	1.5	149
	1986	2495	185	1.2	150
Hermaness	1922	60	200	6.9	29
	1950	250	75	4.4	17
	1974	700	72	1.0	72
	1985	616	19	0.3	63
Noss	1946	113	37	0.6	62
	1974	260	44	0.3	147
	1982–83	388	34	0.2	170

TABLE 60: Mortality of Arctic Skua adults at Foula killed during territorial conflicts with Great Skuas.

Year	Adult Arctic Skuas killed	percentage of breeding adults killed
1969	20	10.0
1970	3	1.2
1971	11	3.9
1972	19	6.3
1973	3	1.2
1974	21	5.5
1975	17	3.4
1976	7	1.2

TABLE 61: *Estimates of annual mortality rates of adult breeding Arctic Skuas and population trends on Fair Isle (from O'Donald 1983, 1986).*

Period	Annual percentage mortality	Population rate of increase (% per annum)	Human persecution
1948–62	19.9%	+ 11%	low level of shooting
1969–73	–	– 15%	extensive shooting
1973–75	11.4%	+ 13%	no shooting?
1976–78	25.3%	– 10%	extensive shooting
1978–79	31.0%	0%	extensive shooting
1979–81	–	+ 3%	less shooting
1981–84	–	– 18%	extensive shooting

TABLE 62: *Predation of Arctic Skua fledglings on Foula by Great Skuas.*

Year(s)	Number of fledglings killed	Percentage of all fledglings killed
1956–65	–	from 2 to 20%
1969	51	43%
1970	14	10%
1971	72	43%
1972	56	31%
1973	43	28%
1974	35	15%
1975	26	15%
1976	36	10%
1980–85	–	from 5 to 20%

TABLE 63: Numbers of each bird species eaten by Great Skuas on Foula in the breeding seasons 1969 to 1976.

Species and age	1969	1970	1971	1972	1973	1974	1975	1976
Great Skua chicks*	10	15	33	70	60	22	40	13
fledglings*	25	50	200	217	151	145	73	44
Puffin adults	60	23	59	157	194	115	71	54
fledglings	5	2	9	0	0	12	1	5
Kittiwake adults	2	1	5	3	5	0	13	4
fledglings	149	14	163	73	161	332	105	63
Arctic Skua adults*	20	3	11	19	3	21	17	7
fledglings*	51	14	72	56	43	35	26	36
Red-throated Diver chicks*	0	0	0	4	0	1	0	1
Fulmar adults	2	2	3	0	6	1	20	0
Storm Petrel adults	4	0	0	0	5	9	1	1
Shag adults	0	21	14	1	1	0	11	0
Eider adults*	0	5	9	8	9	0	7	7
Oystercatcher adults*	0	3	5	4	12	8	0	1
Larus spp. adults	3	9	17	40	31	9	10	1
Black Guillemot adults*	8	4	2	19	13	7	7	3
Arctic Tern adults	7	12	0	6	1	1	4	1
All other species	6	0	10	16	16	0	14	6
TOTAL	352	178	612	693	711	718	420	247

Note: categories marked* are considered to be fully represented (i.e. all corpses are eaten on Foula and so available to be found)

TABLE 64: Numbers of corpses of birds eaten by Great Skuas in 1975 and 1976 compared to proportions of each species represented in bird pellet material collected through 1975 and 1976 breeding seasons.

	Percentage composition in 1975		Percentage composition in 1976		Percentage composition of pellets for both yrs
	Corpses	Pellets	Corpses	Pellets	
Auks	19.8	55.5	25.9	59.3	56.4
Kittiwakes	28.1	26.2	27.1	20.4	25.0
Storm Petrels	0.2	11.0	0.4	11.1	11.0
Skua young	37.1	3.7	40.5	0.0	2.9
Shags	2.6	1.8	0.0	1.9	1.8
All other species	12.1	1.8	6.1	7.5	2.9
Sample size	420	218	247	54	272

TABLE 65: *Average numbers of birds consumed by Foula Great Skua population each breeding season in relation to numbers of these birds present at Foula each year.*

(a) species assumed to be eaten on Foula but not at sea

Species and age	Average number eaten on Foula 1969–76	Average number present on Foula 1969–76	Percentage of population eaten each year
Arctic Skua young	42	190	22
Red-throated Diver young	1	7	14
Oystercatcher adults	4	60	7
Great Skua young	146	2600	6
Arctic Skua adults	13	350	4
Eider adult females	6	160	4
Black Guillemot adults	8	300	3

(b) species eaten on Foula or at sea so numbers estimated from pellet data

Species and age	Average number eaten in 1975 and 1976	Estimate of population at Foula	Percentage of population eaten each year.
Storm Petrel adults	486	9000	5
Kittiwake adults + fledglings	1104	12000 adults 9000 fledglings	5
Auk adults + fledglings	2490	130000 adults 20000 fledglings	2
Shag adults	79	8000	1

Index

THE
SPLENDORS
OF
ITALY

RÉALITÉS

THE
SPLENDORS
OF
ITALY

PREFACE BY
GUGLIELMO DE ANGELIS D'OSSAT
Director-General of Antiquities and Fine
Arts of Italy

Translated by Geoffrey Braithwaite

G. P. PUTNAM'S SONS - NEW YORK

CONTENTS

Places and works of art indicated in bold point are reproduced in color.

S ETTING out to show the development of Italian art by employing the bold graphic technique used in this book was not merely a difficult task: it was an act of bravery in every sense of the word.

Making a selection is essentially a critical action which can at times be too restrictive or too subjective. In this volume, however, the knowledgeability of the editors led them unerringly to the correct choice of themes. Condensed as it must be, this book nevertheless makes a sensitive and thoughtful contribution to the growing demands of modern "visualization."

The editors' goal has been throughout to bring together and present in an effective sequence every aspect of Italian art through the ages, avoiding those pictorial elements which now seem too familiar. Thus, in the chapters corresponding to the different periods in art history, they have succeeded in making clear the decisive influences exerted by those geniuses who are considered the masters of Western art.

The magnificent illustrations mark all the milestones along the road taken by Italian art. A vital rhythm regulates their sequence and is emphasized by the deliberate juxtaposition of facing pages. A subtle bond is created between pictures placed side by side, a bond that continues to fascinate us as we leaf through the book. The admirable continuity in artistic creation, which is the characteristic of Italy and the sign of an uninterrupted, centuries-long spiritual vitality, can be seen in the succession of images that stress the most eloquent details, and promise us the revelation of secret beauties.

This land that was the cradle of Etruscan art, where in Roman times the eloquent grandeur and the psychological introspection of the portrait blossomed together, this peninsula where the varied ferments of the Middle Ages were blended into an artistic whole, this Italy of the Renaissance where Michelangelo and Leonardo da Vinci created enduring masterpieces, this nation where the Baroque exploded with Caravaggio and Borromini, where Magnasco and Guardi worked . . . the very spirit of Italy and all the glories of the Italian genius in sculpture, painting and architecture are invoked in this incomparable book.

More than a chest filled with wonderful jewels, more than an imaginary museum —*The Splendors of Italy* is a living reality.

GUGLIELMO DE ANGELIS D'OSSAT

Director-General of Antiquities

and Fine Arts of Italy

GREEK AND ETRUSCAN ITALY

(From the 8th to the 3rd centuries B.C.)

We must begin right at the beginning—not of art, but of history, for there was of course some prehistoric art in Italy, evidence of which experts are still gathering today. This evidence shows, among other things, the existence of very ancient links between the peninsula and the eastern basin of the Mediterranean.

As far as we know today, Italy's prehistoric period ended at the close of the 8th century B.C. Two styles of art appeared at that time and developed with an ever-increasing intensity, reaching their apogee in less than 300 years.

On the one hand there was the Hellenic art of "Magna Graecia," the name given in ancient times to the regions colonized by the Greeks in southern Italy and Sicily (sometimes referring only to southern Italy). On the other hand there was Etruscan art. Both styles lead us to consider the South of Italy, and to neglect for the moment that part of the territory north of a line drawn approximately from the estuary of the Arno to the Po delta.

Magna Graecia was to see the blossoming of an art destined to arouse throughout the world the most widespread and most lasting admiration: the art that for the Western World is "Classical Art."

Central Italy was to witness the birth of an art that remained unknown or despised for many a long century, and which has been truly appreciated only in the last few decades. Through its spontaneity, its vigor and sometimes its very strangeness, it conquered the modern public as soon as its existence was made known.

From these two arts that developed simultaneously and side by side, it is the latter, the Etruscan, that seems most in accord with the sensibilities of our times. Greek works of art, the perfection of which enchanted previous generations, have probably too much assurance and too much serenity for our troubled world, in which so many of our values have been so brutally challenged.

THE DECISIVE CENTURY. Around 730 B.C. a group of Greek settlers from the island of Euboea landed at Cumae, in Campania, and settled there. From there some of them later journeyed south to settle in Sicily.

This was the beginning of a movement that was to continue for the best part of a century, carrying new waves of settlers—originally natives of Corinth, Rhodes or Crete—some to Sicily, some to the southern shores of Italy.

When this movement abated, the Etruscan civilization suddenly made its appearance in central Italy, in present-day Tuscany. The civilization that preceded it was characterized by the custom of burning the dead and placing the ashes in clay urns shaped like the huts inhabited by the living. In the new civilization the dead or their ashes were placed in richly decorated funeral chambers, which provide us with the majority of the works of art of this period.

LIGHT ON ONE SIDE, DARKNESS ON THE OTHER. There is ample evidence of Greek civilization in Italy and Sicily.

We know that the towns of Cumae, Sybaris, Crotona and Locri Epizephyrii on the Italian coast, and Messina and Catania in Sicily, were among the earliest cities to be founded, while Selinunte and Agrigento, like Paestum, in Campania, were secondary colonies set up by Greeks already established in the region when the resources of their old cities proved insufficient.

These settlers were in no way subject to the mother country. At the outset they respected the artistic theories of their country of origin. This art was still at its most primitive stage, yet by an extraordinary phenomenon it developed in the same way throughout the whole Hellenic world. There can be no doubt, as Jean Charbonneaux said, that individual regions produced individual styles. But these were blended in an admirable harmony of which the combined chords and rhythm can be explained in a material way by the sea trading that went on, and morally by that spirit of ardent emulation that political autonomy provoked and maintained amongst cities.

Indeed, artists and works of art traveled from one end of the Mediterranean to the other in a way that today seems disconcerting. The most famous sculptor of Magna Graecia, Pythagoras of Regium, who lived at the beginning of the 5th century B.C., was an Ionian, a native of Samos. He had come to settle at Regium —present-day Reggio—at the southernmost tip of Italy, where he worked not only for neighboring cities, but also received commissions from the Pelopponesus, Thebes and even Cyrene, a Greek city on the Libyan coast. Similarly, at the end of the 4th century, Lysippus, who had been Alexander the Great's sculptor and who played an important part in the evolution from classical Greek art to the more expressionistic and lively Hellenistic art, paid several long visits to Sicily.

For us Greek art is a domain that has been widely explored. We are not, of course, acquainted with all its aspects: the greatest gap in our knowledge is painting, to which the Ancients attached very great importance, and certain works of sculpture still give rise to controversy. But we know the essence well enough, the thought of which this art is a reflection—Greek philosophy, which was the first of the great philosophies, and in the bosom of which was outlined the first philosophy of art.

Quite the opposite is the case with Etruscan art. From the very beginnings of antiquity the Etruscans intrigued their contemporaries. Their religion with its secret rites, their soothsayer priests, the freedom of their morals, all gave them a reputation for strangeness, which explains why Hesiod said of them that they were the "sons of the enchantress Circe."

With a greater regard for fact, Herodotus puts forward the accepted theory of his day that they came in all probability from Lydia, in Asia Minor. Modern scholars are still questioning the value of his thesis.

Some hold this theory for the truth, others think that the Etruscans were simply the aboriginal population of Tuscany which developed exceptionally quickly. The great Italian Etruscologist, Massimo Pallotino, who recently discovered the remains of the ancient port of Caere, has put forward an intermediary hypothesis, according to which the Etruscan nation was the result of a long and complex process of formation with contributions from many different sources, both eastern and western. The French scholar Raymond Bloch is of a like opinion, but places more emphasis on the eastern element.

The Etruscans themselves have not made the solution of this problem easy. They left behind only a very small number of texts, and these are written in a language that has baffled scholars to this day. This second factor is linked to the first. Contrary to what most people think, we know the Etruscan alphabet, and it has been possible to "read" the inscriptions discovered. But the meaning of only a few words has been deciphered, as there are not sufficient elements of comparison. So it will not be by means of any new system that we shall decipher Etruscan, as was claimed several years ago, but only by the bringing to light of longer and more abundant texts, or preferably a bilingual text—an Etruscan Rosetta Stone, in fact.

It is essentially art that provides us with the key to the Etruscan world, but this is a key that does not open all doors. Behind those that remain closed lies a mystery that explains in part the fascination this people has for us—a people haunted by death and yet who could depict life in such a gripping way.

HISTORICAL COMPARISONS. The history of the Etruscans and that of the Greeks in Italy developed along curiously parallel lines. First there was a period of regular expansion. Then came a fairly long period of decadence, due above all to divisions between the cities which weakened their resistance to outside attacks. The final stage was the integration into the Roman Empire, which owed to the peoples it absorbed the chief features of its art and civilization.

The Greeks had always been farmers and sailors. The fertility of their new territories changed them into traders who traveled to neighboring countries to sell their surplus produce.

The Etruscans seem to have been gifted in all spheres. As navigators, they are said to have invented the anchor. As farmers, they left behind bronze figurines showing them ploughing their fields with the same pairs of oxen as those used by Tuscan peasants today. As metallurgists and technicians, they excelled in bronze and ironwork, and were the most highly skilled goldsmiths of ancient times. Their methods of irrigation and drainage were remarkable: ages before Fascism made it one of its propaganda themes, they had drained and cultivated the Pontine marshes, and it is to the Etruscans that Rome owes her famous sewer—the Cloaca Maxima.

Works of art formed an important element of the trade from which the two peoples drew a major part of their wealth. The Etruscans imported a vast quantity of Greek pottery vases, which they preferred above all others, while the Greeks were great admirers of Etruscan bronzes. The Etruscans also bought from the

Orient ceramics, ivory, jewels and costly textiles, either directly or through the Phoenicians. They themselves transported their own products or imported objects far to the north. It is likely that they were the people who brought to Burgundy the amazing treasures discovered some years ago in a tomb at Vix, near Châtillon-sur-Seine, which are thought to be of Hellenic origin.

Relations between Greeks and Etruscans were not always peaceful. Their search for markets for their products and for outlying ports for their commercial fleets brought them into conflict on several occasions, so the Etruscans tried to enlist the support of Carthage, the third force in the Mediterranean. Carthage, which had replaced Tyre as the Phoenicians' capital city, was essentially a trading power, hostile to the Greeks, who had taken over Sicily from the Phoenicians and had pushed them back into a few outposts in the west of the island. The Phoenicians were untiring in their attempts to win back the lost ground.

The great period of Etruscan art extended from the 7th century B.C. to the beginning of the 5th century B.C., and the great period of Greek art in Italy and Sicily lasted from the middle of the 7th century to the end of the 5th century B.C.

In both cases, the beginning of decline coincides with the first political setbacks. For the Etruscans it was the loss of Rome—where, since 616 B.C., the Etruscan dynasty of the Tarquins had reigned, transforming the little township into a great city—followed soon after by their defeat at Cumae. For the Greeks in Sicily it was the Carthaginian invasion and the capture of Selinunte and Agrigento.

From that time on, the Etruscans suffered defeat after defeat, and lost one after another all the regions under their dominion: first Capua and the hinterland of Campania, then the Po valley, and lastly Latium. On the other hand, the Greeks made two comebacks: the first at the beginning of the 4th century B.C. with Dionysius of Syracuse, who built up a vast empire into which he integrated practically the whole of Magna Graecia; the second came about a century later with Agathocles.

This period, too much taken up with wars, was unfavorable to the development of art. It was only in the course of the 3rd century, in the Hellenistic period, that Sicily and Tuscany witnessed an artistic renaissance which was not to be affected by the Roman conquest.

In the realm of art the new provinces of Rome kept a good measure of autonomy for a long time, and in the end, culturally speaking, it was the conquerors who were themselves conquered.

TWO CONCEPTIONS OF ART MEET. Greek art and Etruscan art are at the same time closely related yet worlds apart.

In its early stages Etruscan art bore the stamp of the Orient, and took its models from the Phoenicians, the Assyrians and the Cypriots. But from the second quarter of the 6th century B.C. the influence of Greece predominated. From this time on, Greek art furnished the majority of Etruscan themes and forms. But these were interpreted in an entirely different spirit, and it is to this spirit that Etruscan art owes its originality.

The decisive discovery made by Greece (and this applies also to Magna Graecia) was, in André Malraux's opinion, that the Universe could be challenged; this was man's right by conquest, to set himself up against the gods. Greek art is the first profane art.... The sacred dance in which the Hellenic figure appears is that of man at last rid of his fate.

With the Etruscans, on the other hand, as in every primitive civilization, art remains essentially at the service of the gods and the dead. It serves to honor or conciliate a host of divinities, for the most part threatening, who watch over man's every daily act, and decide the fate of the dead in the world beyond the tomb. This is also a realistic art, for a great many of its works are merely intended to replace or perpetuate the dead, or to immortalize certain moments of their existence. But its realism does not preclude stylization: a caricature can be in every way as true to life as a portrait.

For the Greeks, a work of art had to satisfy man's sensibilities and intelligence alike. They recognized that artistic feeling has an intangible quality that an exclusively logical work cannot convey. Nevertheless, they thought that harmony responded to certain rules which they resolutely sought to discover. Like Pythagoras (who lived in southern Italy), they thought that the science of numbers could give them the secret, and that this same science would also be the secret of human beauty.

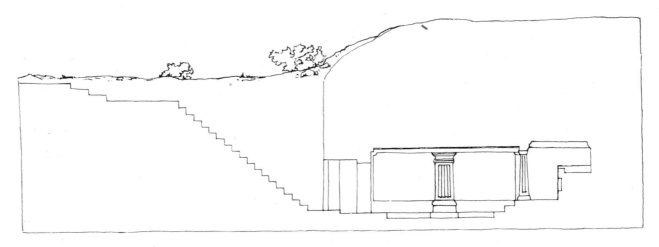

AN ETRUSCAN NECROPOLIS

In architecture this conception of art led them to build simple monuments, the better to appreciate their proportions: the ratios that link each one of their elements to the others and on which depends the impression produced by the whole work. As far as sculpture was concerned, they believed that they could "express everything —or practically everything—by the human form" but only if they were at once idealists and realists—realists in their study of and respect for anatomy, idealists in their unceasing search for perfection by improving the proportions of the body, never using old or ugly models, and by tending to create types rather than to depict easily recognizable individuals.

While unity is a dominant feature of Greek art, Etruscan art is heterogeneous and uneven. Obeying no precise esthetic doctrine, it has no scruples about borrowing extensively from its neighbors, varying from town to town and bringing forth works of high quality alongside vulgar mass-produced objects.

The evidence left behind in Italy and Sicily shows Greek and Etruscan art as curiously complementary.

Greek art survives primarily in architectural monuments—marble and stone sculpture, and, more rarely, bronzes. Etruscan art has left behind an abundance of paintings, terra-cotta sculpture, numerous bronzes and gold jewels. Save for a few ruins, brick and wooden monuments have all disappeared. Only necropolises have remained, impressive underground cities set out like the dwellings of the living.

THE MAGNIFICENT ART OF MAGNA GRAECIA. Although Greek art, in contrast to the other arts of antiquity, strove to be on a "human scale," its works were seldom conceived for the joy of man alone. Most of them had a religious purpose, and the temples and the reliefs decorating them are Magna Graecia's prime legacy to posterity.

Of those temples built of the extremely soft stone of southern Italy there remains hardly more than the magnificent and solitary column standing near the sea at Crotona. But further north, at Paestum, three superb temples still stand side by side on a deserted plain. Further north still, at Cumae, the first Greek settlement in Italy, the scanty ruins of a temple of Apollo have been found, and in 1932 a surprising discovery was made: that of the cave where the famous Sybil pronounced her oracles, one of the places most heavily steeped in mystery in ancient times. The shape of this lair, carved out of the rock itself, is strangely reminiscent of that of Creto-Mycenaean funeral monuments. Where the oldest memories of the civilizations that gave birth to Greece present in the minds of the settlers who hollowed out the cave? Or were these memories already part of the local tradition, carried to Italy by Cretan travelers more than a millennium before? This is the final enigma of the Sybil, whose oracles were always obscure.

In Sicily the ruins of some fifty temples were found. Some are virtually intact, of others nothing remains but a few stones. Most of them are sufficiently well preserved for us to be able, with a little imagination, to reconstruct their shapes and estimate their beauty.

All these temples, like those of Magna Graecia, are of the Doric order, the oldest and strictest of the three Greek orders.

At first sight all Doric temples look alike, but they do differ in a thousand and one details: in the number, spacing and entasis of the columns, the profile of the capital, the ratio between the capital and the lintel it supports, the dimensions of the entablature, and so on. To achieve greater harmony, the Greeks made much of these subtle, yet all-important, differences.

Thus in Magna Graecia an evolution took place that led from the rather heavy temples of the end of the 7th century B.C. and the beginning of the next century (like the "basilica" at Paestum, or the temple of Demeter at Agrigento) to more elegant buildings constructed in the 5th century—but before the Parthenon—like the Temple of Concord at Agrigento, or the E temple at Selinunte, with their more slender columns and lighter entablature.

To decorate its temples, Magna Graecia produced the most beautiful metopes of the Hellenic world. (Metopes are the rectangular bas-reliefs between the triglyphs in a Doric frieze.)

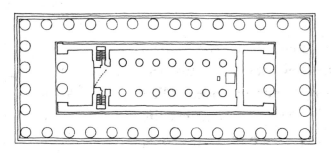

PLAN OF THE TEMPLE OF NEPTUNE AT PAESTUM

For many years some metopes in the C temple at Selinunte were held to be the finest example of this type of sculpture in the 6th century B.C. But in 1934, in the ruins of a temple near Paestum, an almost complete series of metopes was found—thirty-three out of an original thirty-six. They are crude in style but they have astonishing dramatic force.

For the classical period, the metopes of the E temple at Selinunte, which date from 460 B.C., are generally held to be the masterpiece of this form of sculpture found in Magna Graecia.

Hellenic sculpture in Sicily is perhaps less refined than that of Greece itself, but it often has a roughness and a freedom of its own that accentuate its strength and add to its charm.

As far as statuary is concerned, the riches of Italy are not limited to works produced in Magna Graecia. To these must be added those collected by the Romans and Roman copies of Greek works that have been lost, and without which the talent of certain Hellenic sculptors would have remained unknown.

Thus the panorama of Greek art that Italy offers is exceptionally wide. A country that since the dawn of its history has brought forth so many masterpieces has these vestiges of the past inevitably engraved in its memory. Well before the Renaissance, Rome was to absorb this heritage and influence the whole artistic evolution of Italy.

THE LIVING ART OF THE ETRUSCANS. Diversity and spontaneity are the chief characteristics of Etruscan art.

The frescoes that cover the walls of some Etruscan tombs are the only paintings of this period that survive. Equally striking are the splendor of the colors, the elegance of the figures, the rhythm of the designs and above all the intense impression of life that they convey. Since these paintings were executed during the period when Hellenic influence was at work on Etruria, they also reflect the great art of Greek painting that was the pride of antiquity. It is doubtless a distorted reflection, but it is infinitely valuable since no other exists.

In the primitive funeral rite of the Etruscans, the ashes of the dead were placed in an urn to which was affixed a bronze mask in the shape of a human face. This mask was later replaced by a sculptured head, which was used as a lid for the urn. This gave rise to a fascinating series of urns with human heads, called "canopuses." Later, the dead person was buried in a sarcophagus upon which he was represented either reclining as though at a banquet, or lying on his back, as was to be the custom in the Middle Ages. Thus portrait art evolved: from the simplified face on a canopus to a representation that became more and more realistic. The Romans were to perpetuate this tradition of vividly true-to-life portraits that was started by the Etruscans.

But man was not, as with the Greeks, the almost unique subject of art. The whole of Nature had its place, and one expert has even affirmed that Etruscan art was above all "an animal poem."

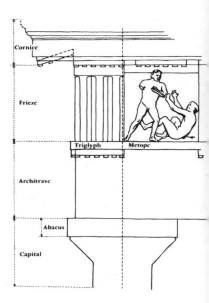

A METOPE

The "classical" art of the Greeks reveals to us the intelligence, the logical thought and the lucidity of its creators, but it shows us neither their faces nor the way they lived. On the other hand, the art of the Etruscans, which has been called "anti-classical," does tell us something of their personalities, and reconstructs life as it was lived more than twenty-two centuries ago by a people rich and vigorous, but obsessed by the fear of the magic powers they believed surrounded them.

The smiles that enliven the faces of some of the finest Etruscan statues have not the serene tenderness of Greek works of the archaic period. There is something enigmatic about them, as if they were hiding some kind of anguish. Is it not this underlying anguish that calls to mind that of the world today, and does this not explain the interest aroused by this art and amplified by its rejection of conventions and its freedom of expression?

At the foot of Mount Etna on the fertile plain of Catania (over the page), Sicily's first Greek towns were founded in the 8th century B.C. Greek settlements spread rapidly over the greater part of southern Italy and Sicily. In "Magna Graecia," as it was called, art as great and culture as brilliant as those of the mother country flourished right up to the 5th century. The monuments that have survived are among the most magnificent left to us by the Hellenic world.

MOUNT ETNA SEEN FROM THE PLAIN OF CATANIA.

Italy emerges
from prehistory

The extraordinary "nuragh" civilization began in Sardinia toward the end of the second millennium B.C. This civilization derived its name from the "nuraghs," the thousands of conical stone towers it left behind. It reached its apogee at the same time as the Etruscan civilization, between the 8th and 5th centuries B.C., and lived on with an uncanny immutability almost up to Christian times. It gave expression to its art through strange-looking bronze statuettes, the most characteristic of which represent warriors, like the one on the left. Traces of Mesopotamian, Cretan and Mycenaen art have been detected in that of the enigmatic "nuragh" civilization.

Example of an already mature art, the canopus in the form of a human head (right) is one of the first manifestations of the presence of the Etruscans in central Italy. A canopus is a rounded terra-cotta urn which was used as a receptacle for the ashes of the dead. Originally a bronze mask in the likeness of the dead person was placed over the canopus. Later, a head-shaped lid was added on which the features were represented schematically yet in an astonishingly lifelike way. From this funeral custom was born the taste for portraits which were to be one of the characteristic features of Etruscan art and, through Etruscan influence, of Roman art.

DETAIL FROM CANOPUS WITH C
HUMAN
ETR
8th TO 6th CENTURI

STATUETTE OF A WARRIOR
SARDINIAN
8th TO 5th CENTURIES B.C

The intense life of Etruscan tombs

More evocative than any document and just as accurate, this superb sarcophagus, below, shows a woman reclining as if at a banquet. By her side is her husband, affectionately caressing her shoulder. This work is evidence of the privileged place woman held in Etruscan society. Such "feminism," which is again manifest in the funerary inscriptions that often bear the name of the dead person's mother as well as his father, contrasts strongly with Greek and, later, Roman customs. Scandalized, the Greeks and Romans spread the word, with no apparent justification, that the Etruscans were a loose-living and incorrigibly sacrilegious people.

Treasure houses of ancient painting are enclosed in the tombs at Tarquinia, the religious capital of Etruria. The frescoes adorning them are all the more precious since there are today no traces of Greek painting, which certainly influenced the artists who executed them. These frescoes give a splendid account of Etruscan customs and beliefs between the 6th and 3rd centuries B.C. Festive scenes abound. Here (right) a man, larger than life size, is seen half-reclining, looking at the male and female dancers depicted on another wall. The dolphins and birds on the frieze were painted with a realism and feeling for nature that were typically Etruscan.

SARCOPHAGUS - ETRUSCAN (CERVETERI) - 6th CENTURY - VILLA GIULIA, ROME

TOMB OF LIONESSES - ETRUSCAN - ABOUT 520 B.C. - TARQUINIA.

So-called Temple of Neptune at Paestum (following page) is one of the triumphs of pre-classical Greek architecture. Dating from the first half of the 5th century B.C., it is several decades older than the Parthenon in Athens. Doric in style, like all the temples of Magna Graecia, it is, after the Theseum of Athens and the Temple of Concord at Agrigento (see page 36), one of the three best-preserved Hellenic temples. Its thick columns and its wide entablature give it the same vigor as the two ancient temples nearby, but its height and the subtlety of its proportions endow it with a more perfect harmony. Paestum, founded in the 7th century by Greek settlers from Sybaris near the Gulf of Taranto, was wrested from them three centuries later by the warriors of Lucania. ➤

Greek architecture - the expression of a philosophy

21

A mysterious Ionic smile lights up the whole of the Mediterranean

HEAD OF A WOMAN - GREEK (E TEMPLE AT SELINUNTE) - 480-460 B.C. - NATIONAL MUSEUM, PALERMO.

◄ **Vulca, the greatest Etruscan sculptor** and the only one known to us by name, almost certainly fashioned this head of Hermes (left), a fragment of one of the statues on the roof of the temple at Veii. It is made of terra cotta, the Etruscans' favorite material. Greek influence is manifest in the choice of subject, the shape of the face and the smile that makes it so appealing, yet the spirit is clearly Etruscan. Its almost disquieting tension and expressive force are diametrically opposed to the calm so beloved of the Greeks.

Parian marble was used for the faces, arms and feet of the female figures on the metopes of the E temple at Selinunte, while the rest of their bodies was carved from limestone. The head shown above, found by itself, is Greek to perfection in the harmony of its features and in the serenity of its expression. The metopes at Selinunte and the earlier ones discovered in the last few years at Paestum occupy a prominent place in pre-Phidian Hellenic sculpture.

25

HERMES - ETRUSCAN (VEII) - 5th CENTURY B.C. - VILLA GIULIA, ROME.

KOUROS - GREEK (LEONTINI) - ABOUT 410 B.C. - SYRACUSE.

This standing nude athlete, ready for the sacred games of boxing or wrestling, incarnates the Greek ideal of beauty. Less than half a century separates the figure on the right, one of the oldest found in Sicily, from the one above, which marks the progress from archaism to classicism. The body of the former is still geometrical in form, and its sculptor has not dared to carve away completely the space between the arm and the waist. The sinuous line of the back, however, was executed with consummate skill. The figure above is at the same time vigorous yet more subtle. The muscles of the stomach and chest are shown with a sureness that bears witness to a deep study of anatomy. It is clear that the Sicilian sculptors could hold their own with those of Attica or Ionia.

KOUROS - GREEK (MEGARA) - ABOUT 450 B.C. - SYRACUSE.

FIBULA WITH ORNAMENTAL PLAQUES - ETRUSCAN (CERVETERI) - FIRST HALF OF THE 7th CENTURY B.C. - THE VATICAN, ROME.

A masterpiece of ancient craftsmanship, this precious ornament is made from extremely fine gold leaf decorated with palm leaves, lions and griffins surrounded with granulations so fine that one wonders what technique the Etruscans could have used to solder the minute flecks of gold on to the jewel without melting them. Magnificent precious objects have been found in large numbers in Etruscan tombs of the 7th century B.C. They bear traces of the oriental influence prevalent at the time in Etruria, and gave rise to a considerable development in the production of luxury goods.

28

*Etruscan genius
is stamped upon
the minor arts...*

Shiny black bucchero gives a typically Etruscan finish to containers like the one on the right. ("Bucchero" was a clay from Spain imported for use in ceramics—it gave a highly polished finish.) This is one of the finest examples of the craft, decorated as it is with reliefs and made partly in animal form. Its extravagant appearance satisfied the Etruscans' thirst for the fanciful and the fantastic. Fragments of buccheros have been found all over Europe, left behind by Etruscan traders. If, as Etruscologists hope, extensive research is undertaken, it should bring to light the vast extent of the trade relations that guaranteed Etruria's prosperity in the days of its glory.

BUCCHERO - ETRUSCAN
6th-5th CENTURIES B.C.
ARCHAEOLOGICAL MUSEUM, FLORENCE.

HEAD OF A WARRIOR - ETRUSCAN (ORVIETO) - 530-520 B.C. - ARCHAEOLOGICAL MUSEUM, FLORENCE.

Beauty combines with rarity to confer exceptional interest on this warrior's head (above), for examples of Etruscan stone sculptures are by no means numerous. The Etruscans preferred to work in clay or bronze. This head, which no doubt surmounted a funeral urn and would therefore have the same characteristics as the canopus illustrated on page 19, reveals strong Ionic influence. This can be seen as much in the stylization of the sculpture as in the enigmatic smile traced on the lips of this figure.

Sinuous and elegant bronze statuettes hold a place of honor in Etruscan art. Their simplified lines, sometimes elongated out of all proportion, give them a curiously modern look, and the precision of detail provides valuable information on many aspects of the daily life of the period. The figure on the right, dating from the beginning of the 6th century B.C., shows a soldier wearing a helmet of the Cretan style, like that of the stone warrior on the opposite page ; his loincloth is also Cretan.

30

WARRIOR - ETRUSCAN (BROLIO)
ABOUT 600 B.C.
ARCHAEOLOGICAL MUSEUM, FLORENCE.

The infinite variety of Doric temples...

SYRACUSE - TEMPLE OF ATHENA
GREEK - 5th CENTURY B.C.

"The Athens of the West" was the name given to Syracuse, the home of brilliant art and culture. Syracuse owed its power to the victory of Himera, when the Carthaginians were put to flight in 480 B.C. This coincided with the completion of the temple of Athena, the colonnade of which can be seen on the left. To celebrate their victory the Syracusans added a marble roof surmounted by a statue of Athena with her golden shield, long since disappeared. It was in this temple, converted into a Christian church in the 6th century A.D., that there was introduced for the first time an architectural technique later adopted by the Greeks: the progressive reduction of the last two intercolumniations, by which the angle was shown off to its best advantage.

A taste for the colossal is strongly in evidence at Selinunte, a town set apart from the other Greek cities in Sicily, and quite near to the Phoenician settlements on the island. With the immense profits from their trade relations with the Phoenicians, the citizens of Selinunte began work, at the beginning of the 5th century B.C., on a gigantic temple of which the columns measured ten feet in diameter at their bases. One of their monolithic capitals can be seen on the right. This temple, 100 yards long and 50 yards wide, is second only—and not by very much at that—to the Olympium at Agrigento, which was built about the same time. Both were left unfinished. In 408 B.C. the over-affluent Selinunte, which had maintained a policy of cautious neutrality toward Carthage, was nonetheless sacked and burned to the ground by an invading army from Africa led by Hannibal. Two years later Agrigento met the same fate.

SELINUNTE - G TEMPLE - GREEK
520-510 B.C.

AGRIGENTO - TEMPLE OF CONCORD - GREEK - 430 B.C.

... reaches perfection

◄ **"The most beautiful of mortal cities !"** exclaimed the poet Pindar when he visited Agrigento in the 5th century B.C. And so it is still in the eyes of the modern visitor as he gazes on the sacred precincts from which rise four magnificent pillars, all that remain intact of the Temple of Castor and Pollux (previous page). It was built in about 470 B.C. with the help of the many Carthaginian prisoners taken by Agrigento at the battle of Himera and who were shared, along with a considerable haul of booty, with Syracuse, Agrigento's ally. Most of these prisoners were put to work building new monuments.

In all its classical purity, the Temple of Concord at Agrigento (above) stands out from the beautiful surrounding scenery. The walls surrounding its "cella" (opposite page), the holy chamber housing the sacred effigy, are still standing. Openings were made in the walls when the temple was converted to a church in the 6th century A.D. It was built no more than a quarter of a century later than the Temple of Neptune at Paestum, which is hardly more imposing and certainly less elegant.

Mysterious Segesta (pages 38-39) in the hills of western Sicily was not Greek. Its inhabitants were the Elymeans, seemingly the descendants of Trojan emigrants from Asia Minor in the second millennium B.C., after the destruction of the most famous of all cities. Nevertheless, Hellenic art exerted such an influence over them that they built their theater and temple in the strictest Greek tradition. The temple, silhouetted in the distance, was never completed. Remaining as it was when work was interrupted, it is an invaluable source of information on Greek building techniques. In particular its columns, still smooth, show that their fluting could only have been done last of all, so that they could be made perfectly rectilinear. This increased construction difficulties but it enabled the builders to achieve perfection in their work. The rough and naked look of the temple today only intensifies the extreme harmony and purity of its lines.

TOMB OF THE TRICLINIUM - ETRUSCAN - ABOUT 480 B.C. - TARQUINIA.

RACLES - GREEK

ETOPE IN E TEMPLE AT SELINUNTE)

OUT 460 B.C.

TIONAL MUSEUM, PALERMO.

Hurling himself at the enemy, Heracles thrusts forward in an oblique movement. This small detail (left), from one of the metopes of the E temple at Selinunte, showing the hero fighting the Amazons, makes us feel all the grandeur and dramatic impact of the scene. (A metope is the rectangular space between the triglyphs in a Doric frieze. Each one represents a dramatic scene with two or three characters carved in high relief.) It differs from Greek sculpture, where immobility is the rule, in that it is essentially full of life. Sicilian sculptors endowed it with a realism that distinguishes it from Attic sculpture, yet evokes after a fashion Olympian art. It was to Olympus that the cities of Magna Graecia sent representatives to compete in the traditional games held regularly every five years.

41

A great artist's sure brushwork on the wall of a tomb at Tarquinia has captured forever the grace of a dancer beckoning to his partner behind him. Frenzied dances enlivened the festivities of the Etruscans. They were ritual in origin, like the bloody combats of men and animals, originally organized for funeral celebrations, yet which were to develop into a somewhat cruel public sport and become in time the circus entertainments of the Romans.

... in all its movement and harmony

TOMB OF THE LIONESSES - ETRUSCAN - ABOUT 520 B.C. - TARQUINIA.

Captivating rhythm of line and color in a painting at Tarquinia, showing two dancing adolescents, evokes with consummate art the rhythm of the music to which they are cavorting. Another part of the fresco shows the accompanying musicians, one with a cithara, and the other with a double flute, the Etruscans' favorite instrument. The Etruscans used music not only for their festivities but also as an accompaniment to certain tasks, such as breadmaking, and even in hunting—to charm the animals. Following an ancient Mediterranean tradition, the dancing girl is painted in white and her partner in ochre.

One of the most splendidly harmonious bas-reliefs of Hellenic art was created, in all probability, in the extreme south of Italy at Locri Epizephyrii, a town founded by the Greeks. It comprises three panels. In the center panel Aphrodite is emerging from the waves in the arms of two companions dressed in transparent tunics. On one side a girl about to be married, all swathed in veils, is burning incense. On the other a resting nude girl (seen on the right) is playing a double flute of the kind played by the Etruscans. Each girl embodies an aspect of the cult of Aphrodite. This work, supple, subtle and of sovereign charm, dates from the first half of the 5th century B.C. It was during this period that the plastic arts of Magna Graecia reached their apogee.

DETAIL FROM THE LUDOVISI TRIPTYCH - GREEK (LOCRI EPIZEPHYRII) - 470-460 B.C. - NATIONAL ROMAN MUSEU

Hellenistic realism succeeds Etruscan violence

Pulsating life of the bronze ram at left and the extreme scarcity of Greek animal sculpture make it a doubly exceptional work. It comes from Syracuse and dates from the 3rd century B.C. While the Romans were fighting over Sicily with the Carthaginians and were gradually gaining ground, King Hiero II had, at the price of heavy concessions, kept a vestige of independence for this city, which a century earlier held sway over all of Magna Graecia. His court, a meeting place for artists, poets and scientists—including the venerable Archimedes—was the center of a brief artistic renaissance which was to be the swansong of Syracuse. The work shown here bears witness to this renaissance. Its creator, freed from the strict limitations that classicism imposed on representations of the human form, displays his genius as a sculptor of animals. Later, the Romans were to show the same genius. But here, in a spirit essentially Greek, the sculptor conferred on his subject a grandeur far transcending simple realism.

CHIMERA - ETRUSCAN (AREZZO) - 5TH CENTURY B.C. - ARCHAEOLOGICAL MUSEUM, FLORENCE.

Masterpiece of Etruscan art, this chimera (above) has a lion's head and body, and on its back two more heads—those of a hydra and an antelope. In quality of execution, this work is comparable to the famous "Lupa," the she-wolf suckling the twins Romulus and Remus, legendary founders of Rome, which became the emblem of Rome. Both have a stark power only rarely achieved, but the chimera has that additional element of the fantastic that evokes the arcane beliefs of the Etruscans. Brought to light at Arezzo in Tuscany, in 1550, it was restored, so the story goes, by the master silversmith Benvenuto Cellini. Michelangelo was so deeply impressed when he saw it that he made a drawing of it.

45

RAM - GREEK (SYRACUSE)
HELLENISTIC PERIOD
NATIONAL MUSEUM, PALERMO.

APHRODITE - GREEK (CYRENE) - HELLENISTIC PERIOD - NATIONAL ROMAN MUSEUM.

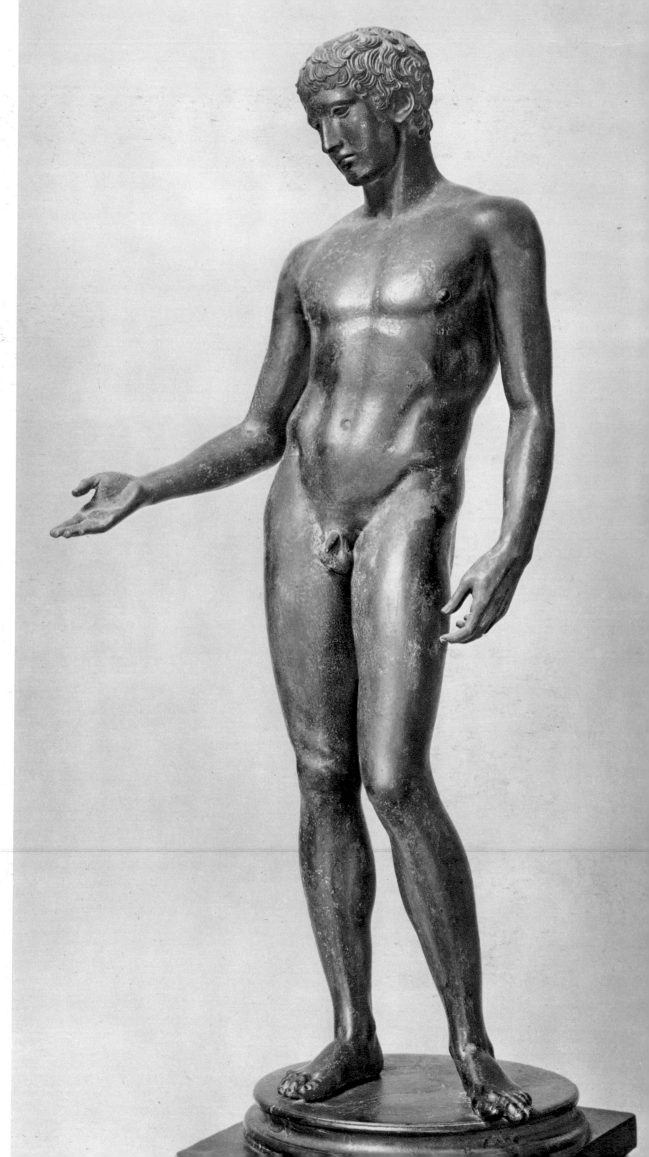

*The great canons
of classical
beauty...*

Perfect body of a woman, at left, with her soft curves, was found on the North African coast at Cyrene, which was first a Greek, then a Roman colony. The figure was executed during the Hellenistic period, as was the Venus de Milo. It bears traces of the influence of Praxiteles, for it was he who, early in this period, first dared completely unclothe his goddesses, for whom the model is thought to have been his beautiful mistress, Phryne. His work, impregnated with calm yet sensual pleasure, made for him a reputation almost as great as that of Phidias. In this statue, moreover, we can sense Greek art in the last stages of its evolution, leaning now toward grace, now toward expressiveness.

Perfect man is embodied in this "Idolino" (literally "little image"), at right, discovered in 1530 among the Roman ruins at Pesaro. It really represents a triumphant athlete about to offer a libation to the gods. It is made of bronze, the favorite material of the Greeks. But because this metal does not stand up well to the ravages of time, the number of great bronzes that have survived is very small in comparison with marble statues, which are in fact often copies of the bronzes. This is very likely the case with the Venus (Aphrodite) of Cyrene, at left. The "Idolino" has great nobility of style and is more human and less architectural than the "ephebes" (young men) discovered in Sicily, which were still archaic in conception.

IDOLINO - GREEK (PESARO) - 5th CENTURY B.C. - ARCHAEOLOGICAL MUSEUM, FLORENCE.

DYING PERSIAN - GREEK (PERGAMUM) - HELLENISTIC PERIOD - NATIONAL ROMAN MUSEUM.

... and belated expressionism...

Violent appeals to the emotions characterized Hellenistic Greek sculpture in contrast to the serenity of the classical period. This is shown in a moving way in the two heads seen here. At left, the dying Persian, eyes half-closed and lips twisted in pain, originated at Pergamum, to the north of Smyrna. It is a fragment from a colossal work executed in the 2nd century B.C. to commemorate the Greek victory over the Persians. Pergamum, after the death of Alexander the Great, had become one of the capitals of the crumbling Hellenic world, and later fell into the hands of the Romans. On the right, the woman with her hair in disorder is a sleeping Fury. Her face shows her utter exhaustion after inflicting punishments on the wretched Orestes. This figure was no doubt one of a group depicting the Eumenides. Such works abounded in the collections of the Romans, passionate admirers of Greek art. During their campaigns in Magna Graecia, Greece and the Hellenized regions of the East, they carried off statues that they either kept or had copied, and which were often executed by the multitude of Greek artists who had settled in Italy.

SLEEPING FURY - GREEK (PERGAMUM) - HELLENISTIC PERIOD - NATIONAL ROMAN MUSEUM.

... conquer Rome

Found at Herculaneum, a Roman city, two Greek bronzes today occupy an important place among the master-pieces in the museum at Naples. Here, at right, is a resting Hermes, probably an original executed in the 4th century B.C., which bears traces of the hand of Lysippus. The sculptor strove to sug-gest suspended movement: Hermes taking a short rest on Mount Ida before continuing his errand for Jupiter. The drunken faun, at left, stretching across a half-empty wineskin, appears to be playing castanets. His most realistic pose has been very boldly portrayed by the sculptor. These two bronzes, found in 1758 and 1764, still bear the green — almost black — patina so typic-al of objects found at Herculaneum, while Pompeiian bronzes are covered with verdigris, and yet the very same eruption smothered both cities.

The theater at Taormina (pages 52-53)—founded only at the beginning of the 4th century B.C., between Etna and the sea, by refugees from Naxos—was built, as was the Greek custom, looking out on a view even more beautiful than that from the theater at Syracuse. In the latter, one of the largest in the Greek world, the tragedy "The Per-sians" was performed in 470 B.C. in the presence of the author himself, Aeschylus. The theater at Taormina underwent alterations after the Roman conquest, the better to meet with the requirements of Roman spectacles. After the chorus disappeared, the "orchestra"—the circular area in which the chorus moved about—was no longer of use, so it was modified, and henceforward contained the best seats in the theater. At the back of the stage the "frons scenae" was built. Depicting the front of a palatial house, it constitutes the characteristic element of the Roman theater.

SEATED HERM
GREEK (HERCULANEU
4TH CENTURY B.C. - NAPL

50

DRUNKEN FAUN - GREEK (HERCULANEUM)
4TH CENTURY B.C. - NAPLES

CHAPTER II

FROM ROMAN ART TO CHRISTIAN ART

(From the 3rd century B.C. to the 4th century A.D.)

For more than six centuries, from the conquest of Sicily and Magna Graecia in the 3rd century B.C. to the founding of Constantinople in 330 A.D., Rome was the center of the Western World.

After taking over the entire Italian peninsula, Rome, from the time of Augustus (30 B.C. to A.D. 14), spread her dominion from the Atlantic to the Euphrates and from the Danube to the Sahara.

All over this vast empire cities were built in imitation of the "Urbs," the greatest of all cities, and were embellished by works of art inspired by those in Rome herself.

And yet posterity, which on matters of art is held infallible, has not yet passed final judgment on Roman art. It is not that Roman art has been overlooked, but opinions have varied so much in the course of time that no one knows which judgment should be taken as final.

For the men of the Renaissance, Rome, Greece's heir, held the secrets of beauty, and it was thought that they could be rediscovered by studying her ruins with deferential care and by following the rules of architecture set out in Latin treatises on the subject.

During the French Revolution, Roman art was still praised, but for politico-literary reasons rather than through any regard for esthetics.

Suddenly, in the course of the 19th century, opinion swung the other way. The more Greece was admired, the more Rome was despised. "When you pass from Hellas, so full of life, light and beauty, into the Roman world, so cold, silent and severe, the horizon begins to narrow, the sky seems darker, imagination is snuffed out and all thought stops," wrote the historian Victor Duruy at the turn of the century.

INDEPENDENT ART OR SERVILE IMITATION? Nowadays the general opinion is not so dogmatic. We do admit that Roman art is to a certain extent a "throw-back" art, as André Malraux suggests. That is to say it is "an art in which inherited forms that are empty of meaning are more in evidence than the new forms that are being developed." But it is recognized that these new forms were many, that they were often beautiful and that they played a major role in the later development of art both in Italy and in the rest of the world as well.

The Romans suffered from a curious artistic inferiority complex. Their admiration for Greek art was so great that their only thought was to collect Greek works and imitate them. Not even trusting to their own imitative skill, they brought over from Greece a throng of artists and employed them systematically in preference to their own.

True, they had been "conditioned" from the very start to Greek influence through Etruscan art, which bore the Greek stamp and of which they were the successors. This influence they were to find at every turn in their military history, first in its pure state at Syracuse and Taranto, from which they brought back magnificent artistic booty, and in Greece itself, a Roman province since 146 B.C. Then they found it superimposed on ancient Egyptian foundations at Alexandria, and finally in its ultimate form, more sensitive to the spirit of the Orient, at Pergamum, which had superseded Athens as the leader of the Hellenistic movement, and which in its turn was to be integrated into the Empire.

Although predominant, Greek influence was not the only one to affect Rome. Oriental influence also began to make itself felt as Rome made more and more conquests in Asia Minor and Arabia. While Roman cities were being built at Caesarea, Palmyra or Petra, Rome itself was adopting a whole host of oriental tastes and themes.

THE CONCRETE REVOLUTION. Like many of our contemporaries the Romans tended to prefer styles of the past so long as they were "period," and preferably Greek, to their modern equivalents. But if the old-fashioned could be easily adapted to their religious needs—their temples are copies of Greek temples, but built on plinths like Etruscan temples—it was far from easy to adapt them to the needs of everyday life.

The Romans therefore became innovators by the force of circumstance. Their architecture was primarily functional, and it was to their credit that they found clever and elegant solutions to the practical problems they faced. They were engineers first and artists second.

The population of Rome was growing at a dizzy rate, while in the provinces whole towns were springing up. Things had to be done not only quickly but also on a grand scale.

Freestone, the basic material of Greek architecture, gradually came to be used only for the most formal buildings. For the others a new material was much more maniable: concrete, which opened up as yet unknown possibilities to the builders, and led quite naturally to a change in forms.

The Etruscans had been familiar with the principles of the arch and vaulting, but they had been timid in the use of them. The Romans on the other hand proved very enterprising. Alongside an architecture of straight lines, characteristic of Greece, they introduced an architecture of curves.

Of the buildings they were able to construct, and for which there was no real Greek equivalent, the most important was the basilica, both for the role it played in the life of the citizens and by virtue of its imposing size. It was the center of activity in every city, the covered annex to the Forum, which in bad weather had few attractions. It was at the same time meeting place, money market and tribunal. It was a rectangular construction which, unless too modest in its dimensions, was divided into naves by rows of columns. Rome was to have several basilicas, each one bigger than the last.

The first Christian churches were to be directly influenced by the basilica, and even kept the original name. Thus a monument of ancient Rome is to be found at the origins of all Christian architecture.

Another of Rome's creations to enjoy a brilliant success was the triumphal arch. It made its first appearance early in the 2nd century B.C. as a result of a military and religious tradition. The general awarded the honors of a victory had, before riding at the head of the triumphal procession, to stop in front of a gateway built specially for the occasion at the sacred limits of the city, and could only pass through it after offering sacrifices to the gods. From this was born the idea of constructing monuments in the form of arched gateways to commemorate victorious campaigns.

After training themselves on civil buildings, the Romans turned to religious architecture. They applied their new knowledge to the rebuilding of the Pantheon in Rome, which had been seriously damaged by fire. Although built at the command of the Emperor Hadrian, a passionate admirer of all things Hellenic, the new temple owed very little to Greece. Round in form, it was surmounted by a superb dome of very pure design, which had no equivalent in ancient art. It probably had a symbolic meaning, representing both the celestial vault and the globe, the ideal form which holds all the secrets of numbers and of knowledge.

The Pantheon's construction marks a major date in the history of architecture. Henceforward, it was no longer enough to create a perfect interplay of lines and shadows; one had to mold the space within the monument so as to produce a feeling of exaltation or anguish. This preoccupation persisted during the centuries that followed. The problem of the arch dominated the whole evolution of the cathedral from the Byzantine period to the end of the Gothic era. And in the 16th century Bramante, working on the plans of St. Peter's in Rome, declared that he wished to "raise the vault of the Pantheon on the Basilica of Constantine."

TOWNS THAT ONLY LACK PEOPLE. The Greeks left temples, and the Etruscans tombs. But it is whole towns that still bear witness to the civilization, the art and the grandeur of Rome.

They were all built, insofar as the terrain allowed, in accordance with a plan that seems surprisingly modern, and even slightly American, with streets intersecting at right angles and a rectangular "square"—the Forum, stamping ground for politicians and arena for circus games until special amphitheaters were built at a much later date. Each city had the same series of public monuments: temples, a basilica, the "curia" (seat of the local senate), baths, a theater and eventually an amphitheater.

Two of these cities—Pompeii and Herculaneum—were preserved paradoxically enough by a natural disaster: the eruption of Vesuvius which, by covering them with a blanket of lava and ashes more than twenty feet thick, made time stop still one fateful day in August, A.D. 79.

But thanks to the progress made in archaeological techniques, other cities such as Ostia, Rome's ancient seaport, which had suffered the slow ravages of the centuries until they disappeared from the face of the earth, have been patiently exhumed in their turn. Their remains, scattered as they collapsed or crumbled, have been put back in place. Each stone, each scrap of painting or mosaic, each fragment, however small, has been religiously collected, until finally they appear again, as far as is possible, in their original state. Often only the structure or the essential lines have survived. But in many cases the interior decoration has been preserved along with countless everyday objects that, perhaps more than anything else, have the power to conjure up the people who used them in times gone by.

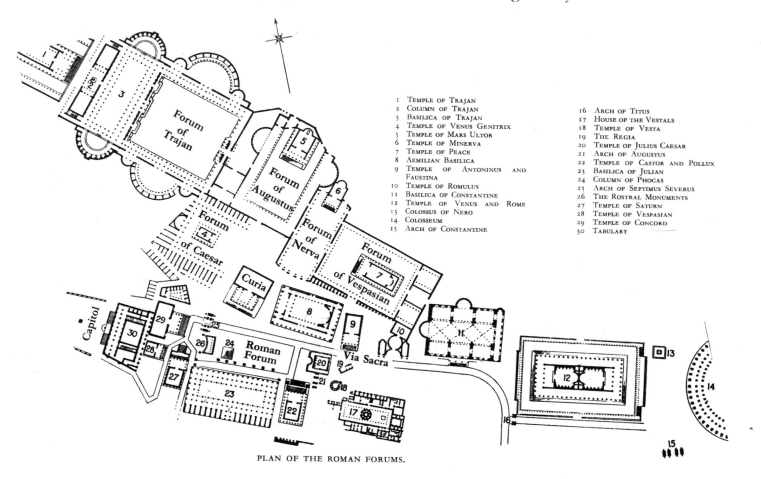

1	TEMPLE OF TRAJAN	16	ARCH OF TITUS
2	COLUMN OF TRAJAN	17	HOUSE OF THE VESTALS
3	BASILICA OF TRAJAN	18	TEMPLE OF VESTA
4	TEMPLE OF VENUS GENITRIX	19	THE REGIA
5	TEMPLE OF MARS ULTOR	20	TEMPLE OF JULIUS CAESAR
6	TEMPLE OF MINERVA	21	ARCH OF AUGUSTUS
7	TEMPLE OF PEACE	22	TEMPLE OF CASTOR AND POLLUX
8	AEMILIAN BASILICA	23	BASILICA OF JULIAN
9	TEMPLE OF ANTONINUS AND FAUSTINA	24	COLUMN OF PHOCAS
10	TEMPLE OF ROMULUS	25	ARCH OF SEPTIMUS SEVERUS
11	BASILICA OF CONSTANTINE	26	THE ROSTRAL MONUMENTS
12	TEMPLE OF VENUS AND ROME	27	TEMPLE OF SATURN
13	COLOSSUS OF NERO	28	TEMPLE OF VESPASIAN
14	COLOSSEUM	29	TEMPLE OF CONCORD
15	ARCH OF CONSTANTINE	30	TABULARY

PLAN OF THE ROMAN FORUMS.

When one strolls through the Roman Forum, there are, despite the relatively poor condition of its ruins, two moments when the past seems to spring to life in its most human, commonplace form: first, when you see on the floor of the Aemilian Basilica the traces left by a few coins which had melted in the fire that razed the basilica in A.D. 410; secondly, when you discover the jars in which the Vestal Virgins kept their wine and oil, still standing in neat rows in the cellar of the House of the Vestals.

Immediately you can imagine, in the panic caused by the fire, a frightened citizen gathering up the folds of his toga, the easier to escape the flames, and in his haste dropping his money.

You can imagine the House of the Vestals with the servants and slaves storing away the newly arrived provisions under the supervision of one of the priestesses, chosen probably from those on whom the long exercise of their high office must have conferred authority and experience. Soon, her thirty years in this house completed, she would be free to return to private life. Perhaps, as she was giving orders to her servants, she was wondering whether she would regret the honors and privileges of her position, or whether she would be really happy leading the life of an ordinary woman, when she would no longer be driven through Rome like the empress, or be accorded a place of honor at official ceremonies and spectacles.

Thus, some trivial or domestic occurrence re-creates for us life as it was nearly 2,000 years ago. As their faces and gestures are preserved in sculpture we can easily repopulate the deserted stages that Roman ruins have become with the very characters that walked there in earlier days.

A DOCUMENTARY FILM IN RELIEF. When they wanted to represent their gods or draw purely esthetic pleasure from the contemplation of a statue, the Romans invariably copied the Greeks. But the Hellenic example was inadequate when they wanted to save the memory of their civilization from oblivion through sculptured portraits and narrative bas-reliefs. Although the Romans did not create these two forms of sculpture, they did stamp them with their own personality and develop them along new lines.

From the Etruscans they inherited their taste for portrait art. Latin customs accentuated this taste. When a Roman died, his family had his bust made and placed it in the atrium (the central hall of a Roman house). To portraits of the dead were added portraits of the living, especially leading citizens of the city or the state. Instead of being reserved for the family dwelling, they were exhibited in public places and became one of the major elements of urban decoration. Finally busts were in many cases replaced by whole statues.

Busts and statues no longer represented types, but individuals full of expression and life. The question is, just how far were they true likenesses? When we see faces furrowed with wrinkles or bloated with age, we are tempted to think we are dealing with portraits realistic in a particularly cruel way. But we notice that important figures all have a majestic bearing that well befits their office, which makes us suspect that they are somewhat idealized. A lined face, if full of energy, and a stout figure, if truly dignified, were no doubt characteristic of Roman tribunes, generals and emperors. Their sculptors probably did not embellish them much, but they must have flattered them to a slight extent. With this exception, Roman portraits are of a diversity that is the best proof of their true-to-life quality.

Rome also immortalized in stone the great moments of her history and the main scenes of everyday life. The Romans did this by means of the bas-relief, a very old technique that had been widely used by the Assyrians in Mesopotamia. The Greeks had discovered it during the campaigns of Alexander the Great, and introduced it into Hellenistic art. The Romans borrowed it from them at the beginning of the Empire, and rediscovered it at its very source during their own campaigns in the East.

They gave it new life by a skillful arrangement of the scenes, by a greater delicacy in the carving, and by allotting more and more importance to nature, which had held little interest for the Greeks. Nature is featured in two ways: in the lightly sketched scenery that makes up the background of many reliefs, and the plant motifs that are brought together to form the frame or are used simply as decoration. The garlands and ornamental foliage thus carved are of such variety that it was hardly possible to invent new designs when the taste for this type of decoration was reawakened in the Gothic period.

The bas-reliefs left by the Romans, seen as a whole, make up a sort of film of their life in war and peace, though scenes of war are more common than peaceful scenes. Everything is shown with such precision that historians have discovered in these reliefs a number of details that ancient writings neglected to give about methods of fighting, the treatment of prisoners, religious rites, customs of public life, and so on.

On one of these reliefs found in the Roman Forum, we can see an emperor, probably Trajan, making a speech before an audience composed of citizens elegantly dressed in togas. They are shown where we would most like to see them now: right in the middle of the Forum, the ruins of which are today like a mere shadow of what it once was, with here and there a better preserved monument that helps us to fill in the gaps left by the others. On the reliefs, however, nothing is missing: the curia, the rostra, the portico of the Aemilian Basilica are all included and intact. The background is there in its entirety as well as the main scene.

Thus all the elements are brought together: the decor that needs only the imagination to restore it, the general scene and, in close-up, the characters, men and women, young and old, humble and mighty, unknown and famous, who all played their parts in bygone years. The game of bringing to life the dead world of ruins and museums is ever ready to begin.

THE REFINEMENT OF PRIVATE LIFE. Roman dwellings developed appreciably over the centuries. Pompeii and Herculaneum were still cities of an old type in which each middle-class or patrician family had its own house. But Ostia, on the contrary, the great trading port which reached the height of its prosperity in the 2nd and 3rd centuries A.D., had become a city almost in the modern sense of the word. It developed vertically, not horizontally. There were still some old houses, but these were dominated and stifled by new buildings three or four floors high, divided into apartments, some overlooking the street, others the inside courtyard.

In Rome this same type of house was built mainly in the plebeian districts in the center of the city, which were not so very different in appearance from what they are today.

In their houses, the Romans showed tastes that were to prevail in Italy throughout the centuries, and they proved to be highly talented decorators. Lovers of color, they covered their rooms with paintings and mosaics. Living in towns that were becoming more and more overcrowded, they created the illusion of space by decorating their walls with "trompe-l'oeil" architecture, framing familiar or mythological scenes. Or they would create the illusion that they were living in the country by decking their walls with make-believe gardens. One of the rooms in the House of Livia in Rome is like an enclosure of green, surrounded by trees among which birds are flitting about. Paintings of similar inspiration decorate one of the rooms in the House of the Orchard at Pompeii.

Mosaics, originally used for floors, were later used for the walls of houses and public buildings. They sometimes took the form of geometrical, plant or animal designs of an extraordinary wealth of invention and sometimes full of humorous

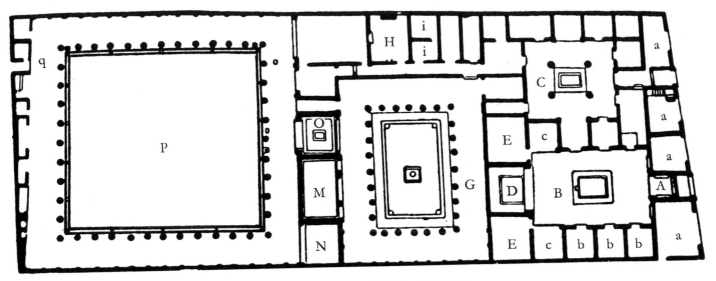

PLAN OF HOUSE OF THE FAUN, AT POMPEII

A entrance — **a.a.a.** rooms let out as shops — **b.b.b.** cubicula (sleeping chambers) — **B** atrium — **c.c.** alae (side apartments) — **D** tablinium — **E.E.** triclinium (autumn and winter dining-rooms) — **C** tetrastyle atrium — **G** peristyle (with the statue of the faun in the center) — **i.i.** baths — **H** kitchen — **M** exedra (vestibule) with a mosaic depicting Alexander the Great — **N.O.** summer dining-room — **P** great peristyle — **q** posticum (back entrance)

fantasy, as in the "Unswept Dining Room" in the Lateran Museum, where the leavings from a banquet still seem to be scattered on the floor. Sometimes, by a curious departure from their normal rôle, which calls to mind a similar trend which affected French tapestry in the 18th century, mosaics were used to reproduce paintings down to their smallest details. Thus it is that through mosaics certain color portraits have been preserved, and also a famous Greek painting of Alexander the Great's day showing the Battle of Issus, where the Persians, led by Darius, were wiped out.

Ceilings and the upper part of the walls were frequently covered with stucco, a taste for which the Romans had probably acquired in Alexandria. Lending itself to delicate and subtle effects, stucco could be said to have made the transition between bas-relief and painting. Less vigorous than the former, it had all the linear qualities of the latter.

On the whole, the interiors of Roman houses are striking for their gaiety, their brightness, and in some cases, also for their charm—all features that contrast with the solemnity of the architecture and of the "great art" of Rome. The natural exuberance of the Latins and their love of life were given free expression in this interior decoration, which bears the stamp of a people who liked to play-act and who had a weakness for the theatrical. They enjoyed living in the company of the gods and heroes who strode about their walls, or surrounded by vistas of the countryside which owed a part of their charm to their very artificiality.

Skilled craftsmen, they appreciated objects and ornaments that were precious in both senses of the word. Thus their household utensils—lamps, stoves, tripods, and so on—and their gold and silverwork are all of extremely high quality.

Such preoccupation with elegance of form was not without danger. It is only a short step from the refined to the affected, from the theatrical to the bombastic, from the brilliant to the garish. However, the limits were rarely overstepped before the very end of the Empire, when political decadence was inevitably accompanied by artistic decadence.

But art was soon to be given new life by Byzantium, and transformed by the inspiration of Christianity.

Keystone of the Western world, the Forum was the focus of Rome's political, commercial and judicial life, and the heart of an empire that from the first to the third centuries A.D. stretched from the Atlantic to the Euphrates and from the Rhine to the Sahara. The temples, shops and public buildings were built very close together on the Forum. Public meetings were held there as well as spectacles, games and fights between gladiators and animals. Triumphal processions took place there. Nowhere else in the world does every inch of ground, every stone and every pillar have so many stories to tell

ROME - THE FORUM (IN THE FOREGROUND, THE TEMPLE OF SATURN) - 5TH CENTURY B.C. TO 4TH CENTURY A.D.

Imperial Rome at times created...

ROME - (FORUM OF NERVA) RUINS OF THE TEMPLE OF MINERVA - 97 A.D.

Too small for Rome's population, which continued to grow rapidly, the Roman Forum had been inadequate since the 1st century B.C. Julius Caesar started work on a new, smaller Forum, near the old one. Augustus and several of his successors followed his example. Thus the series of Roman Fora came to be built. In the center of the Forum of Nerva was a temple dedicated to Minerva. Two Corinthian columns have survived (above), giving us some idea of the splendors of Rome, of which Augustus declared: "I came to a city of brick, and I leave one of marble."

Symbol of Roman imperialism, the triumphal arch is the result of a very ingenious use of the vault. The Romans learned the technique from the Etruscans but developed it to such an extent that it quickly became one of their major contributions to architecture. The Arch of Titus, at right, was built to commemorate the emperor's capture of Jerusalem in A.D. 70. In his triumph, the spoils from the Temple of Jerusalem and many precious objects were paraded for public view. The victory was recorded for posterity in a bas-relief of a typically Roman character decorating the arch.

ROME - TEMPLE OF VESTA - 1st CENTURY A.D.

... and often copied

The Corinthian order became the favorite architectural style of the Romans in the 1st century A.D. From this time on, the Romans were to renounce Doric architecture completely and make less and less use of the Ionic style: these two orders were proving too simple for Roman taste. In the time of Augustus, the Corinthian order was chosen for the round temple, built in Rome near the banks of the Tiber, and dedicated to Vesta, since it was of the same form as the temple of Vesta in the Forum. It is a building in that pure Greek style that the Romans thought impossible to improve upon as far as religious architecture went, and which they therefore copied faithfully.

Three elegant white marble columns surmounted by a remarkably well-proportioned entablature, at right, overlook the ruins of the Roman Forum, and are reflected here in the rain-swollen waters of the small lake of Iuturna. Here Castor and Pollux are supposed to have watered their horses on their way back to Rome to proclaim their victory over the Etruscans. These columns formed part of the temple dedicated to the two heroes. The temple was rebuilt in the early days of the Empire. The builders kept the high plinth on which the first temple, of Etruscan style, had been raised in 484 B.C. Even after adopting Greek models for her temples, Rome kept faithfully to the Etruscan custom of constructing them on a raised base.

ROME - TEMPLE OF CASTOR AND POLLUX - 484 B.C.

Sculpture immortalizes victories...

The commemorative column was of Greek inspiration, and, with the triumphal arch, was very popular with the Romans. The Emperor Trajan, uncertain which type of monument would bear the greater witness to his glory, had a triumphal arch built at Beneventum, and at Rome the column that seventeen centuries later was to be the model for the column now standing in the Place Vendôme in Paris. The bas-reliefs entwining Trajan's column (see detail at left) are among the most important works of Roman art. They form a kind of "strip cartoon in sculpture," which tells, in a way not dissimilar to that of a modern strip cartoon, the ups and downs of Trajan's campaigns against the Dacians, in the region now covered by Rumania and part of Hungary.

Strength and truth make this statue of Marcus Aurelius, at right, a masterpiece of Roman sculpture. It is also the only extant equestrian statue of ancient times. The fine, thoughtful face of Marcus Aurelius and the gentle gesture of his hand fit in well with what we know of this emperor, who, more interested in philosophy than in glory, wrote a treatise on Stoic ethics, the "Meditations." Originally the hind leg of his superb charger rested on the head of a captive Barbarian. All the equestrian statues of the Renaissance and, in particular, the Gattamelata and the Colleone (see pages 214 and 215) are directly inspired by this work. Michelangelo is said to have made the pedestal for this statue, which he set up in the Capitol Square where it still stands today.

ROME - TRAJAN'S COLUMN
ABOUT 176 A.D.

ROME - EQUESTRIAN STATUE OF MARCUS AURELIUS - 2nd CENTURY A.D.

PORTRAIT OF JULIA, DAUGHTER OF TITUS - END OF 1ST CENTURY A.D. - ROME, CAPITOL MUSEUM.

The infinite variety of Roman portraits is the best proof of their similarity. Roman portraiture derived from Etruscan art, and this bust (right), thought to be of Brutus and dating from the 3rd century B.C., marks the transition between the two periods. Its harsh realism is a characteristic of Republican-period portraiture. In imperial times sculpture became gentler and more conventional. Busts of women proliferated. That of Julia, Titus' daughter (above), late 1st century A.D., is representative of the new highly mannered trend which led the sculptor to attach as much importance to the hairstyle as to the features.

BUST OF BRUTUS - 3RD CENTURY B.C. - ROME, CAPITOL MUSEUM.

The invention of concrete permitted large-scale construction...

"How great it all is, you can imagine nothing greater," exclaimed philosopher Hippolyte Taine of the Colosseum in Rome. "Your gaze rises, falls and rises again as you take in three levels of arches; then you tell yourself that this was a circus, that these tiers of seats could hold a hundred thousand spectators, that five thousand animals were killed here, that ten thousand captives fought in its arena—and you get some idea of what life in Rome was like." The Colosseum was the biggest amphitheater of the Roman world. On the right is an outside view of the first tier of arcades, on the left an interior shot taken on the second floor, a fuller view of which can be seen through the Arch of Titus on page 65. Thanks to a liberal use of concrete blocks, the Colosseum was completed a few years after it was begun in A.D. 72. The tiers of seats were backed by four stories of galleries joined by 160 "vomitoria," approaches through which the spectators could reach their places quickly. A Roman creation, the amphitheater was not the same as the theater and was used only for games, which had in previous centuries taken place in the Forum.

ROME - VIEWS OF THE COLOSSEUM - 72-78 A.D.

... and gave added scope to civil building

Magnificent imperial palaces, worthy of their occupiers, covered the entire summit of the Palatine Hill. Indeed, vast terracing projects had to be undertaken on the hillside in order to gain more building space. After Tiberius, Caligula and Trajan, the Emperor Hadrian enlarged this site further. Its pink ruins, a view of which can be seen at right, have lost none of their singularly imposing looks. But, just as Louis XIV preferred Versailles to the Louvre, Hadrian preferred to the Palatine Hill the villa, or rather palace, he had built for himself at Tivoli. It comprised a succession of buildings set in huge gardens, doubtless planted then with olive trees and cypresses as they are today. Some, like the small baths (below) with concrete vaults and characteristic arches, were in the Roman style. They rubbed shoulders with copies of foreign monuments, such as the portico at Athens and the Temple of Serapis near Alexandria. Even the surrounding countryside had been partially created in imitation of places that Hadrian loved: there was a small-scale reconstruction of the valley of Tempe in Thessaly.

TIVOLI - HADRIAN'S VILLA, THE SMALL BATHS - 2nd CENTURY A.D.   ROME - A PART OF THE PALATINE - 2nd CENTURY A.D.

74

*Cities abounded
in immense sculptures
that were to degenerate
into extravagance*

The mystery of the quadriga in gilt bronze, at right, has long puzzled scholars. It is the only one of its kind from ancient times still in existence, and its origin is not known for certain. For many years it was thought to be Hellenistic, but now the general opinion is that it is Roman, although nobody can tell from what part of the Empire. What is certain is that no work of art has travelled so widely or been set up on sites where so many spectacles took place. Sent originally to Rome late in the 1st century A.D., these four proud steeds began by decorating a triumphal arch. Then, in the 4th century, they were transported to Constantinople, the new capital of the Empire, and put in the famous hippodrome, the scene of chariot races, plays, spectacles—and revolutions. In 1204 the Fourth Crusade, which, under pressure from Venice, had been forced to turn its attention to the destruction of the Byzantine Empire, found the horses in Constantinople, made off with them and installed them above the center portal of St. Mark's Basilica, where they can be seen today. They did, however, spend eighteen years in Paris, where Napoleon Bonaparte, who had brought them back after the fall of Venice in 1797, had them placed on his own triumphal arch at the Carrousel. More exuberant in style, but highly decorative, the marble group of the Dioscuri, at left, is a later work. Discovered in the middle of the 16th century, the figures were placed at the entrance to the Capitol, in Rome, for which they provide a magnificent frame.

The extravagance in which Roman art indulged in the last years of the Empire can be seen in the fragments of a colossal statue of Constantine (following page) which comes from the gigantic basilica he built in the Forum.

QUADRIGA - CHURCH OF ST. MARK'S, VENICE.

77

OME - GROUP OF DIOSCURI
th CENTURY A.D.

Villas equal temples in luxury

Unusual combination of Greek and Egyptian art can be seen in one of Hadrian's creations in his villa at Tivoli. First there is a copy of the Egyptian Temple of Serapis (below, in the background). Then a small-scale reconstruction of the valley of Canopus, through which runs a canal leading to the temple. In the temple Hadrian installed a great amount of Egyptian sculpture. Recently, four magnificent replicas of the Caryatids in the Erechtheum at Athens were brought up from the bottom of the canal. These were originally along the "Valley of Canopus," and used to support the portico in place of some of the columns. The rounded portico (below, in the foreground) is Hellenistic in inspiration. This influence can be seen again in the decoration of one of the rooms in the Villa of the Mysteries, at Pompeii (right). As was fashionable, it is architectural in style. By a skillful use of perspective the painter created an illusion of spaciousness and embellished the walls with iridescent colors.

TIVOLI, HADRIAN'S VILLA - CANOPUS PORTICO - 2nd CENTURY A.D.

POMPEII - VILLA OF THE MYSTERIES - PART OF THE FRESCO - 1st HALF OF THE 2nd CENTURY B.C.

The disaster at Pompeii
preserved
the framework
of everyday life...

The House of the Faun at Pompeii, so called after the charming bronze faun prancing in one of its courtyards (left), is one of the most beautiful dwellings to survive from Antiquity. It was built in the 2nd century B.C. when private houses, under Hellenistic influence, were becoming more and more vast and luxurious. Its sumptuously decorated rooms were arranged around several courtyards and colonnaded peristyles. At Pompeii, an essentially patrician city, each family had its own private dwelling in contrast to the custom in Rome and also, as recent research has revealed, in Ostia, the great trading port. There, the majority of the people lived in apartments in blocks of three or four stories, not unlike modern apartment buildings.

A perfect example of a Roman Forum, the one at Pompeii (lined with a magnificent colonnade), right, was already started when at the beginning of the 1st century B.C. Rome captured Pompeii from the Samnites, an Italian mountain people who had occupied it for several generations. In imitation of the Greek cities of Italy, a central square surrounded by a portico had been laid out. All the Romans had to do was enlarge it and surround it with the public buildings proper to Roman life: the Temple of Jupiter, Juno and Minerva—or "Capitol"—which embodied the power of Rome; the Curia, seat of the local senate; the basilica; the covered market, and several temples. The old Samnite colonnade, of which the only function was to give shade to the shops, was elongated, and a second story added for spectators when spectacles were taking place in the Forum.

POMPEII - HOUSE OF THE FAUN
2nd CENTURY B.C.

POMPEII - THE FORUM - 1st CENTURY B.C.

A ROMAN COUPLE SAID TO BE CATO AND PORTIA - 3rd CENTURY A.D. - VATICAN MUSEUM, ROME.

Almost photographic regard for truth was exercised by Roman portraitists in depicting the man in the street. The Roman couple above, called Cato and Portia, admit their humble origins in an inscription—he was a freed man, she a slave. Likewise the Pompeiian baker Paquius Proculus, who rose to be a triumvir, posed with his wife for a portrait (at right) that decorated a wall in his house. Are they thinking of their changing social status, he with a scroll, she with a stylus and writing tablets? These portraits, executed from life, are certainly not flattering. They provide a refreshing contrast to idealized official portraits. The simplicity of their poses and the modest dignity of their expressions make them perfect likenesses.

PAQUIUS THE BAKER AND HIS WIFE (FRESCO FROM POMPEII) - 1st CENTURY A.D. - NATIONAL MUSEUM, NAPLES.

This revelation of Roman painting, the Aldobrandini Fresco (following page), so called after its first owner, Cardinal Aldobrandini, was discovered in 1605, almost a century-and-a-half before Pompeii and Herculaneum. In the center part of this great fresco, representing a wedding, we can see Venus giving advice to the bridegroom, while Hymenaeus, the tutelary genius of marriage, sits at the foot of the bed waiting for their conversation to end. This remarkable work impressed many foreign artists studying in Rome by the balance of its composition, the delicate colors and the quality of its execution. One of them, Poussin, made a copy of it.

*Animal art
attains perfection...*

THE BIRDS (PART OF A FRESCO) - 1st CENTURY A.D. - NATIONAL MUSEUM, NAPLES.

Free of the rules of classical art and the conventions of official portraiture, animal subjects provided admirable scope for the talents of Roman sculptors and painters. There is an abundance of works full of vivacity and charm like the bronze deer at left, quivering, tense and lifelike. Or again, like the bird above perched delicately on the edge of a vase. This is part of a fresco on the wall of a house at Pompeii.

DEER - 2nd CENTURY TO 3rd CENTURY A.D. - NATIONAL MUSEUM, NAPLES.

... while gods and heroes are mere copies of Greek statues

HERMAPHRODITUS - 2nd CENTURY TO 3rd CENTURY A.D. - NATIONAL ROMAN MUSEUM.

Male and female beauty combine in Hermaphroditus. The son of Hermes and Aphrodite, Hermaphroditus was loved by the nymph Salmacis. Since the youth resisted her advances, she begged the gods to join their two bodies forever. The gods thought fit to grant her request, and a new being was created, half man and half woman. Such is the legend as we read it in Ovid. Late Greek sculpture favored this personage that embraced male and female beauty in one single being, the symbol of physical perfection in fact. Copies made in Rome increased in value when the original disappeared. Above is one of these very skillfully made copies. On the right, the head and shoulders; on the left, the whole statue. In the background of the left-hand photograph can be seen a Roman copy of a Greek statue of Aphrodite discovered in 1942 near the Forum.

Infinitely varied mosaics cover the floors

Past masters of the mosaic, the Romans excelled in all the minor arts. The mosaic was to remain one of the favorite media of Italian art. The floor at left, with its geometrical patterns, was made for the baths of Diocletian, now the National Roman Museum. The scene at right is part of the "Great Chase" that decorates a corridor in the Villa of Piazza Armerina, in the heart of Sicily. It shows animals from Africa being taken on board ship on their way to the Roman circuses. Here an ostrich is being manhandled up the gangway. The Villa of Piazza Armerina was built for Maximianus, one of the four emperors of the Tetrarchy featured in the red porphyry group on page 116. Its mosaics forged a link between the Roman and Byzantine styles.

Intense physical power emanates from the splendid torso (pages 94-95) of which every muscle is emphasized almost to excess. Signed by Apollonius, a Greek sculptor who in all probability lived in Rome, it is thought to be part of a statue of Hercules or Prometheus. It is less tortured in appearance than the famous Laocoon group, with which it is virtually contemporary. Like the Laocoon, it was found in the 16th century among some Roman ruins. Michelangelo was so enthusiastic about it that he referred to himself as the "pupil of the Torso." This was the first work from Antiquity to go into the papal collections which went to form the Vatican Museum. ➤

MOSAIC FLOORING - 2nd TO 3rd CENTURIES A.D. - NATIONAL ROMAN MUSEUM.

TAKING CAPTURED ANIMALS ON BOARD SHIP (FROM A LARGER MOSAIC) - 3rd CENTURY A.D.
PIAZZA ARMERINA, SICILY.

Christianity makes its appearance in a pagan setting

"Thou art Peter; and upon this rock I will build my church." To find out whether this saying is true in the literal as well as the figurative sense, Pius XII, on June 29, 1939—St. Peter's Day—ordered the most extraordinary excavations of Christian times. The body of St. Peter was in effect said to have been buried on the Vatican hill, which was later turned into a Roman cemetery, then taken over by the Christians. In 324 Constantine built the original basilica of St. Peter there, which was replaced by the present-day one during the Renaissance. Thus it was some forty-five feet under this basilica, directly under Michelangelo's famous dome, that they had to look for the tomb of the First Apostle. Over 350,000 cubic feet of earth were removed, and as much concrete poured in, so as not to undermine the basilica. Many pagan and Christian tombs were uncovered. That of Caetermius Antigone (below), with its purely Roman decorations, is one of the richest of these tombs. A Roman was also the subject of the panel on the right, found in the catacombs of St. Callistus, a meeting place and necropolis for the persecuted Christians. Forced underground, they had to adopt pagan art, but they gave it a new meaning understandable to themselves alone. Thus it is that the Shepherd carrying a lamb, at right, the Roman version of the Greek Hermes Criophoros, had become the symbol of Christ saving the soul of the faithful. This symbol has remained an integral part of Christian iconography.

ROME - EXCAVATIONS IN THE BASILICA OF ST. PETER - 2nd AND 3rd CENTURIES A.D.

THE GOOD SHEPHERD (BAS-RELIEF) - 2nd AND 3rd CENTURIES A.D. - CATACOMB OF THE CHURCH OF ST. CALLISTUS, ROME.

CHAPTER III

PRE-ROMANESQUE, BYZANTINE AND ROMANESQUE ITALY

(From the 4th century A.D. to the 13th century A.D.)

In Rome's Capitol Square, one of the world's foremost artistic and historic sites, stands a splendid equestrian statue dating from Roman times. It represents Marcus Aurelius, the philosopher-emperor and lover of peace who nevertheless had to spend the greater part of his life making war. The statue survived because of a happy mistake. Throughout the Middle Ages, when pagan works of art were being systematically destroyed, it was thought to represent Constantine, the first Christian emperor.

The reign of Constantine (307 to 337) saw the beginning of a new period in the history of Italy and of Western art. It was marked by two major events: the acknowledgment of Christianity, and the forsaking of Rome as capital of the Empire. Rome was replaced by Constantinople—a city built from nothing on the Bosphorus, between Europe and Asia. The consequences of these two events were to be incalculable.

Art, which for the Romans was first and foremost secular and social, resumed its religious character, which gave it new vigor. Italy, like her neighbor France a few years later, was to be covered by a "white mantle of churches" which, by a series of historical circumstances, were to show a greater variety of style than in any other country.

Rome was no longer even the capital of Italy: this honor was conferred alternately on Milan and Ravenna. But gradually Rome did become the capital of Christendom, though she was to remain curiously faithful to the memory of Antiquity, which was to give her monuments a mark of their own.

In Constantinople, the "New Rome," an art was born that combined the basic Hellenic features, still deeply rooted in this region which had stayed Greek in language and culture, with new elements borrowed from the nearby eastern countries, in which Persian influence had become particularly important due to the impact of the Sassanid dynasties. This Byzantine art soon spread to a large part of Italy.

It is therefore fitting that the shadow of Constantine should have presided over the birth of Christian art, which was to develop slowly and pass from a pre-Romanesque style, still quite Roman in its form, to the Byzantine style; then, integrating the most varied trends, it was to blossom forth with monuments of exceptional magnificence, which adhered serenely and closely to the Romanesque style.

But it is satisfying to the mind that this shadow should be cast by the silhouette of Marcus Aurelius. This emperor, who for all his courage could not stop the barbarians from northern Europe sweeping down toward the Danube right to the very frontiers of the Empire, takes his rightful place at the dawn of a period when

Italy was to be engulfed by an interminable wave of invasions that broke over the country for more than 600 years.

Some invaders played only a destructive part. Such is the case with the Vandals, who, in 405, advanced as far as Florence but were defeated there. So it was with the Visigoths, who five years later entered Rome and sacked the city; also the Huns, led by Attila, who ravaged the Po valley in 452; then the Hungarians, who at the beginning of the 10th century devastated Tuscany and finally reached Rome herself.

Others brought with them an already fully developed art, or themes and forms that were to influence Italy's own artistic development. These were, in particular, the Lombards, a Germanic people living in the region between the Elbe and the Oder, who crossed the Alps in 568 after infiltrating the countries of the Danube. They ruled over a large part of Italy until the creation of the Holy Roman Empire. Then there were the Arabs, who seized Sicily in the course of the 9th century, and the Normans, who succeeded them 200 years later.

CHRISTIANITY TRIUMPHANT. Christian art had already existed in Italy before Constantine's time. This was the art of the catacombs, those subterranean passages with recesses where the faithful were buried. But this clandestine art had had to be expressed in a secret language, which only the initiated could understand. It had, therefore, adopted the usual Roman motifs, but gave them at the same time new meaning. Thus a design of vine-leaves was meant to recall the words "I am the vine, and my Father is the vine-grower." While the fish, "Ichthios," meant to the initiate "Iesos Christos Theou Ios Sator"—"Jesus Christ, Son of God, our Savior." Many of these themes were retained for quite a long time after Christianity had come out into the open.

It was only after the Edict of Milan, in 313, which authorized the practice of the Christian religion, that the first churches could make their appearance in Rome. In contrast to the temples, which were used chiefly to house the statues of the gods to which they were dedicated, the churches were meeting places where the faithful came together to worship. So it was logical that they should be built on the pattern of the basilicas, buildings where the Romans used to gather.

The other Christian monuments of this period—the shrines and the baptisteries—were either round or octagonal and surmounted by a dome. The former were built over the tombs of martyred saints, and people worshipped there only on the anniversary of the saint's death. They were inspired by pagan mausoleums. The latter resembled them in some respects, but some borrowings from Roman baths can be found in their construction.

Their ground plans proved successful, as we can see from the magnificent achievement of Santa Costanza's in Rome, the mausoleum of Constantine's daughter, and they were soon used in the building of actual churches. For many years the basilica and shrine formed the basis of all Christian architecture.

The first churches, though fairly simple on the outside, were extremely rich on the inside, being decorated with a profusion of precious cloths and gold and silverwork, and their walls were covered with mosaics that were more splendid and much longer lasting than frescoes.

Their ornamentation had at first followed Roman traditions very closely, but then its spirit changed: Charles Diehl, the art historian, describes how the long friezes on the walls of the sacraria which showed scenes from the Old Testament and the Gospels became a sort of book in which the illiterate could see with their own eyes the great events of Christian history. In consequence, this type of decoration, developed more widely, lost its symbolic character and became narrative and essentially historical in subject. As was only natural, the figures took on more precise characters: the main actors in the drama tended to become stereotypes.

RAVENNA AND BYZANTINE SPLENDOR. While Christian art in Rome developed from a Latin basis, in Ravenna it took a more original form, although it also followed ancient formulas.

Can Ravenna's first monuments, dating from the middle of the 5th century, be called Byzantine? We are justified in asking this question, since Ravenna was not conquered by Justinian, an eastern emperor, till two centuries later. "To classify them as Byzantine, and then to argue that this is proof of Byzantine influence in Italy, is," said Pierre Lavedan, "to create a vicious circle. The art of Ravenna, pre-Byzantine, is in many ways the continuation of Constantinian art."

The art of Ravenna blossomed during the regency of Galla Placidia, the empress whose eventful life, stranger indeed than fiction, is the living reflection of the situation in Italy at the time of the final collapse of the Roman Empire. She was the daughter of the Emperor Theodosius, who, in 395, had divided the Empire between his two sons, giving the East to Arcadius, and the West to Honorius, who chose Ravenna as his capital. Galla Placidia was born and brought up in Constantinople. It was there that her tastes were formed. But she knew Rome as well. She was there when the Visigoths captured the town in 410. They carried her off as a prisoner when they retreated. Their new king, Ataulf, fell in love with her and married her. The wedding ceremony was celebrated with great pomp at Narbonne, where fifty young and beautiful slaves placed fifty bowls of gold and jewels at the feet of the bride. Shortly after, Ataulf was assassinated. Galla Placidia soon remarried, this time to Constantius, the commander of the armies of her brother Honorius. Her second husband fought the barbarians who had invaded Spain, was given Aquitaine in reward for his victories, and then died. His widow returned to Constantinople with her young son, Valentinian III, who, in 423, inherited the throne of the Western Empire, as his uncle Honorius had died without leaving an heir. Galla Placidia then left for Ravenna to reign in the name of her son until he came of age.

Through her, the first elements of Byzantine art reached Italy. The memorial she had built at Ravenna, perhaps for her own tomb (and which is, in fact, called the Mausoleum of Galla Placidia), was a small cruciform building, the four equal arms of which were built with barrel-vaults around a central dome. It has been compared with certain Syrian monuments of the school of Antioch, but for the West it was a pure novelty. The inside, covered with mosaics with a blue lapis-lazuli background, is one of the most dazzling wonders of Italy. The visitor, once his eyes get used to the semi-darkness, feels he is in the center of a jewel, a stone more precious and more sumptuous than all the presents given to the young Galla Placidia by her first husband, the barbarian king.

The outside is of brick, unimposing in appearance, and only a connoisseur's eye will notice the simple arrangement of blind arches, the first of its kind, and which at a later date was to become one of the characteristics of Romanesque art in its earliest stages.

Half a century later, the Western Empire went down for the last time, and an Ostrogoth king, Theodoric, reigned at Ravenna. But, captivated by the civilization and art of Rome and Byzantium, he very faithfully copied their style in the monuments he built.

Finally, in 540, Italy was reconquered by Justinian, and became unquestionably Byzantine. She became a province of the Eastern Empire, called the Exarchate, of which Ravenna was the administrative capital. Justinian stayed in this city for a short time only, and his wife, Theodora, never went there. Yet it is there that, for fifteen centuries now, the imperial couple have remained ever-present in all their glory, thanks to the mosaics that tell us what they were like. They adorn the chancel of San Vitale, which is for Ravenna what the famous church of St. Sophia is for Constantinople: the most perfect expression of Byzantine art at its apogee. These two splendid churches, built at the command of Justinian, the one ten years after the other, have different ground-plans, but both have domes and their interiors are sumptuously decorated. In them the visitor experiences that sensation of

CHURCH OF SAN VITALE, RAVENNA : GROUND-PLAN AND CROSS-SECTION

wonder, of splendor and of the infinite, that is such an essential part of all that we understand by Byzantine art.

A NEW CONCEPTION OF ART. Byzantine art gradually extended its influence to Rome, and perhaps Italian art would have evolved toward a simple fusion of Constantinian and Byzantine elements if two new factors had not radically altered the issue.

The first factor was the Lombardic invasion three years after the death of Justinian. The Lombards settled in the north, and then fought with Byzantium for the rest of the country, leaving only Ravenna, the country around Rome, part of Calabria, and narrow stretches of coast along Venezia, Liguria and Campania.

The second factor was the iconoclastic movement that started in 726 and lasted for more than a century, during which time the worship of images was forbidden and all images were ordered to be destroyed. Thus the development of Byzantine art was suddenly arrested, and the break provoked between Byzantium and Rome, where it was still maintained that painting could play a useful part in the religious education of the illiterate.

These images against which the "puritans" of Constantinople railed with so much passion were at the very center of early Christian art, whereas to the Greek, and later to the Roman way of thinking, beauty was linked to man, to the harmony of his body, to the charm of nature. Christianity distrusted this conception in its care to exalt only the spirit. Whence, as René Huyghe has observed, the contempt for formal beauty and even of its primary condition, volume, the receptacle of matter. Sculpture became suspect and the main rôle passed from form to light and thence to color, itself a kind of light. It was the triumph of painting and mosaics. But there was more to it than that. Speaking of the Ravenna mosaics, André Malraux has pointed out that their style, like that of so many other Eastern arts, was born out of the need to represent what rationally could not be represented: to represent the superhuman by the human. Golden backgrounds were used more and more because they created neither a true surface nor a true effect of distance, but another world.

It was suggested that art possessed a power of its own, independent of what it represented; art was one way of playing on man's feelings and thus of preparing him for religious emotion. The result was that perspective no longer interested the artist, and that, in depicting nature, decorative effects rather than realism were sought, whereas faces were given an intensity of expression to reflect the inner soul.

THE LOMBARDS—CREATORS OF THE FIRST ROMANESQUE ART. The Lombards enjoyed throughout Europe the reputation of being the finest masons of their day. It was they who, in the 9th and 10th centuries, created the first Romanesque art in Italy, an art characterized by the manner in which churches were built. The walls were built of stones broken with a hammer (and not cut), and comprised great arches and recesses, with under the roof a festoon of small arches (Lombardic bands) that linked the unaccentuated buttresses.

The great arches derived from those already decorating fifth-century monuments at Ravenna, while the recesses that one can see at Milan, Spoleto (the church of Santa Eufemia) and Agliate were new to Italy. Recent studies have shown that these elements have their primary origin in Mesopotamia in the second millennium B.C. Thus "emergent Romanesque art is the transformation of forms that are 4,000 years old."

Lombardic churches were most often of the basilica type, with timber roofing. What distinguished them from earlier churches was their triple vaulted apse and their columns with wide capitals, which tended to be replaced by pillars.

Like the other Germanic invaders, the Lombards introduced into Italy themes borrowed from the Scythians and the Sarmatians from the steppes of Asia: stylized animals, fantastic monsters and geometrical motifs that were later to be found decorating Romanesque churches.

THE GREAT YEAR. 1063 was a prodigious year for Italian art. In that year two of the most astounding monuments ever built in Italy were begun more or less simultaneously: St. Mark's in Venice, and the cathedral of Pisa.

These two churches, so exceptional in their dimensions, style and very magnificence, were to proclaim boldly to the world the power and fortune acquired only recently by the two great seafaring cities of the peninsula.

Pisa, mistress of Corsica, Sardinia and the Balearic Islands, held sway over the Tyrrhenian Sea, and sent its trading ships all the way to Tunisia and Tripolitania. Venice, who had imposed her sovereignty over the Dalmatian and Istrian coasts, each day increased her fruitful relations with the East. Both cities drew their inspiration from Byzantine works: the Church of Demetrius at Salonika provided the model for Pisa; and the Church of the Holy Apostles at Constantinople for Venice. Pisa allowed herself more freedom of interpretation than Venice. Nonetheless, in spite of all that has ever been said, St. Mark's remains unique in the world, for it was Venice's perpetual creation, a gigantic shrine to which every sailor felt obliged to bring some ornament. Ancient columns, marble slabs, bas-reliefs, bronzes, statues and more besides were all collected there, and placed wherever seemed best with a superb disregard for their style or their pagan origin. In this way the church "in its atmosphere of purple and gold" became a monument of inexhaustible richness, fascinating in its variety and singularity.

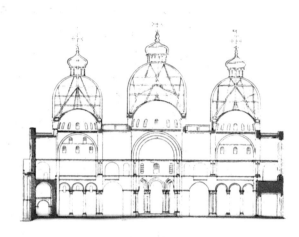

SAINT-MARK'S BASILICA, VENICE

The cathedral of Pisa is more homogeneous and more deliberately original. Its arcatures and fine marble columns exerted a strong influence on the baptistery and campanile built by its side a century after, and on the Campo Santo built yet another 100 years later.

Such preoccupation with the general effect, the kind of architectural stage-setting that Italy inherited from Rome and to which the country owes all its superb public squares, is nowhere seen to better advantage than in this group of monuments. The very ground played its part so that the Piazza del Duomo at Pisa might be like no other: it subsided under the campanile as it was being built, giving it a definite list. Unperturbed, the builders went on with their work. The "Leaning Tower," by the somewhat disquieting tension it gives, emphasizes all the more strikingly the harmony of this landscape of marble.

ROMANESQUE CLASSICISM IN THE PO VALLEY. The success and influence of the cathedral of Pisa, a specifically Italian creation, were quite considerable. There were echoes of it during the 12th century in practically the whole of the country. These are even found, though only in the façades, in the series of superb cathedrals built in the Po valley, at Parma, Modena, Piacenza and Ferrara, to name but a few which are the purest Romanesque buildings Italy has produced.

They have the balance and breadth proper to this style—which the peninsula did not adopt to the same extent as France, for example.

At the same time, in the Milan region, the Lombards maintained their age-old reputation as innovators. Though many of their churches had not as yet vaulted naves, they built in their apses some of the earliest ogival transepts, the beginnings of Gothic art.

MIRACLE OF TOLERANCE IN SICILY. But it was the south of Italy and Sicily that were the scene of Italy's most curious artistic venture in the 12th century: the strange and magnificent combination of Byzantine, Arabic and Norman styles.

When, in 1043, a young Norman, one Guillaume de Hauteville, a native of Cotentin, captured Melfi, in Apulia, Sicily was under the domination of the Arabs who had seized the island from Byzantium in the middle of the 11th century. Some fifty years later his descendants had become the masters of Sicily and of Calabria as well.

Although the Normans enjoyed the support of the pope, they showed, once they were victorious, complete tolerance toward the Arabs and Greeks of the Byzantine cult who had stayed in the island. Attracted by the Arab civilization and way of life to such a point that one of their kings, William I, even had a harem, they were fascinated also by the prestige of the East, and wanted to rival Constantinople in splendor. One of the monuments that best sums up the diversity of their tastes is the Palatine Chapel in Palermo, an "Arabian Nights treasure chest," that owes to the Arabs its wooden ceiling with stalactite-like construction, to Byzantium the mosaics on its dome, and to Rome its basilican layout with three naves.

For, while everywhere art was flourishing freely in so many different ways, Rome, preoccupied—and ruined—by the struggle between pope and emperor, remained outside the movement. When Romanesque art was about to develop into the Gothic, in Rome people were still building the old classical basilicas with timbered ceilings.

THE RESURGENCE OF SCULPTURE. The development of Romanesque art provoked a resurgence of sculpture: a sculpture subordinate to architecture, and which was little concerned with realism in its efforts to respect the limits imposed by the structure of the churches.

Throughout Western Europe sculpture was the great decorative art of the 12th century, as the mosaic had been during the Byzantine and Carolingian periods.

The date of the first sculpted portals in Italy is uncertain, and experts have wondered whether it was Italy or France that first paved the way for this new genre. Most experts today believe it to have been France. Yet there is in Rome a work that still keeps the scholars arguing; the lip of the well in the church of St. Bartholomew, on the Isola Tiberina. Was it carved, as some believe, at the end of the 10th century, in the lifetime of Otto III, who is depicted on it? If so, then it could be considered as one of the starting points of Romanesque sculpture. Or does it date only from the 12th century? In that case, it is no longer of any special interest. Evidence has yet to be found that would solve this problem.

At all events, two main trends can be seen in Italian Romanesque sculpture: the Lombardic style, barbarous and imaginative, featuring ornaments of interlacing figures and fantastic animals, an example of which is the church of San Pietro in Cielo d'Oro, at Pavia; and a milder Latin style, which can be seen especially at Modena, Parma and Verona, in which figures have the most important place and in which one can see reminders of Roman art.

The two earliest sculptors that we know are Guglielmo, who worked at the beginning of the 12th century

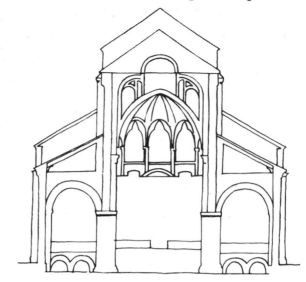

CROSS SECTION OF THE CATHEDRAL OF SAN ZENO, VERONA.

on the façade of Modena Cathedral, and Antelami, who carved the portal and the great figures that decorate the baptistery at Parma. Their art, still a little unpolished, has a remarkable rhythm and power of expression. They prepared the way for the magnificent flowering of art in the next century, when the conception of sculpture completely changed and Italy took her place in the vanguard of the plastic arts.

*The brilliance
of Byzantium
eclipses Rome...*

The Church of San Vitale, Ravenna,
was built in 530 by the Byzantine emperor
Justinian; he had just won back Italy
from the Ostrogoths who had occupied
it at the end of the 5th century. Its
construction marks the eclipse both of
Rome, replaced as capital by Ravenna,
and of Byzantine power. Like the majority of churches in the Eastern Empire,
it was built around a central point and
surmounted by a dome. The austere
brick exterior is in strict contrast to the
interior, which is ornate and full of
wonderful treasures. The delicate architecture gives it life and breadth, while
mosaics of unsurpassed splendor cover
its walls (see page 109).

RAVENNA - CHURCH OF SAN VITALE - 6TH CENTURY

... in all
forms
of art

Virtuosos without equal, Byzantine ivory and mosaic workers left an important part of their work in Italy. The ivory-workers preserved, on a small scale, the art of sculpture, at a time when sculpture tended to limit itself to pure decoration. A reflection of classical antiquity has been found in these works, which circulated freely and played an important part in the propagation of this art form from country to country. The mosaic-workers, using materials of a richness well fitted to the sumptuous tastes of the Eastern emperors, supplanted painters when important monuments had to be decorated. Both dealt generally with religious subjects, but on occasion they executed portraits, to which rarity lends an added interest. On the right we see the Empress Theodora, daughter of a circus-keeper, who started out in life as a dancer—very probably a nude dancer—and who subsequently became first the mistress, then the wife of Justinian, the conqueror of Italy. She was an exemplary empress, and when a revolt nearly overthrew Justinian (who, believing all was lost, was about to flee), it was she who gave him back his courage with the words: "I shall stay: for me, imperial purple is the finest color for a shroud." Her portrait, conventional but nonetheless lifelike, is part of a vast mosaic tableau decorating the chancel of the Church of San Vitale. She is shown wearing the imperial crown and bedecked with jewels. On the left, the Empress Irene, who reigned at Byzantium in the 8th century, re-established the worship of images after the iconoclastic period, and planned to marry Charlemagne.

THE EMPRESS IRENE - BYZANTINE IVO
8TH CENTURY - BARGELLO, FLOREN

THEODORA AND HER MAIDS-IN-WAITING - PART OF THE FRESCO FROM THE CHANCEL OF SAN VITALE, RAVENNA - ABOUT 547.

THE LAST SUPPER (MOSAIC) - 6TH CENTURY - CHURCH OF SAN APOLLINARE NUOVO, RAVENNA.

Yet the memory of Antiquity lives on...

Christendom's most enigmatic statue is also one of its most famous. The archaeological problem it presents underlines the continuity of Italian art. In effect, some consider the huge bronze St. Peter (at left) to be a Roman, others a Romanesque work. The former give the 5th century as its date; the latter, on the other hand, declare that it was cast at the end of the 14th century by Arnolfo di Cambio (the first great Florentine architect and sculptor), and intended to replace an earlier marble statue. There are few works of art over which one can make a mistake of a thousand years. The situation is explained by the frequent return to ancient sources that united Italian art for two thousand years. Each year thousands of pilgrims come to worship before this statue, and the bronze foot has been worn smooth over the centuries by their kisses.

One of the earliest representations of the Last Supper, which was to become a major subject of Christian iconography, can be found in the Church of San Apollinare Nuovo at Ravenna. This church was built in the early days of the 6th century by the Gothic king Theodoric, who ruled Italy at that time. It was dedicated to the Arian cult, a heresy subscribed to by nearly all Barbarians and many Byzantines. In this very fine mosaic panel, which is part of a series showing different scenes from the life of Jesus, Christ and His disciples are still shown reclining after the Roman fashion around a semicircular table. Christ, robed in imperial purple, is in the foregound. He was depicted, according to a very ancient custom, somewhat larger than the others. Opposite Him Judas, the only disciple shown in profile, looks horrified as he hears the Master prophesy his treachery. This work has aroused much discussion: some see on it the stamp of Rome, others that of the East. It seems to have been one of the meeting points of the two styles. Byzantium had not quite dominated Ravenna, and Roman influence still remained, though it was soon to disappear.

111

ST. PETER - 5TH CENTURY - ST. PETER'S BASILICA, ROME.

ROME - BAPTISTERY OF SAN GIOVANNI - 4TH CENTURY.

... in the two styles of sacrarium
in which Christian architecture has its roots

Rome's first churches differed little from Latin basilicas, and were, like them, rectangular buildings divided into naves by rows of columns, covered with timbered ceilings, with vaulted apses. This was particularly true of San Clemente (at left), built in the 4th century. But while in the rest of Italy these basilicas were to be transformed into Romanesque churches, vaulted, and with considerably developed apses, Rome was to remain faithful to the ancient tradition. In the 12th century a new basilica of the same type was built on the site of the old San Clemente, which had been devastated by the Normans.

The model for all Italian baptisteries, which until the 12th century were built separately from churches, the Baptistery of San Giovanni in Rome dates from the reign of Constantine, the first Christian emperor. It is octagonal and surmounted by a dome. In the middle, encircled by eight superb porphyry columns (above), is the round pool used for baptism by immersion. The round or octagonal shape, reserved at first for baptisteries and for the mausoleums of saints and martyrs, was later used for churches as well, and developed by Byzantine art.

St. Mark's Church, Venice (following page), is the crowning glory of Byzantium's second golden age. Begun in 1063 and completed in 1094, and modelled on a church in Constantinople, it is in the form of a Greek cross, crowned by five great domes. In Byzantium, as in Ancient Rome, domes seem to have had a symbolic meaning, representing the celestial vault. St. Mark's, enriched in the course of time by innumerable ornaments, many of which the Venetians brought back from the East, became one of the most sumptuous monuments in the world. ➤

113

Venice is still a vassal of Byzantium

Linking Roman and Eastern art, this group of the Tetrarchs (at left) is one of the many ornaments of foreign origin that decorate the façade of St. Mark's in Venice. It evokes an important moment in Roman history: the creation of the Tetrarchy, that is, the division of the Empire between four emperors, a move decided on by Diocletian in 293. He kept Asia Minor for himself, with Nicomedia as his capital. He gave Italy and Africa to Maximianus, whom he had made his second in command some years earlier. To the two new emperors, Constantius Chlorus and Galerius—whom he forced to divorce their wives and marry his own and Maximianus' daughters—he gave Gaul and Thrace respectively. This decision, which already marked the eclipse of Rome and the easternization of the Empire, was accompanied by the adoption at the court of Asiatic dress and ceremonial. So it is hardly surprising that the Tetrarchs, sculpted here in magnificent red porphyry, their faces and poses typical of official Roman art, should be dressed like all the warriors that can be seen later in Byzantine works.

The taste for precious materials and bright colors, characteristic of the East, is brilliantly expressed in Byzantine gold work, which was one of the chief vehicles of Byzantine art throughout Europe. The enameled plaque (at right), on which the archangel St. Michael is shown sword in hand and wings spread, is one of its most sumptuous creations. Several techniques were used in skillful conjunction. On the border, with its warriors dressed, like the Tetrarchs, in short tunics, armor and capes, polished but uncut jewels alternate with cloisonné enamel medallions, while other parts are of beaten and painted copper.

VENICE - ST. MARK'S
THE TETRARCHS - 4TH CENTURY.

ENAMELED PLAQUE - 10TH CENTU
ST. MARK'S, VENICE.

*Sicily
melting pot of
Byzantine, Arabic
and Norman art*

Remarkable tolerance was shown by the Norman lords from Cotentin, who in the 11th century took Sicily from the Arabs, who had previously wrested the island from the Byzantines. This tolerance is reflected in the art of their new kingdom. Monreale Cathedral is a perfect example: the outside decoration of its chevet (at left), with interwoven arcatures and discs, is clearly Arabic, but its architecture is Romanesque and Norman. The interior of the cathedral, wholly covered in mosaics, is a masterpiece of Byzantine art.

More Norman than Arabic, the convent of San Giovanni degli Eremiti at Palermo (right) with its simple, western style, seems to be striving to counterbalance the unusual character of the church it complements. This church, surmounted by five domes, looks more like a mosque than a Christian building. Its tower (in the background), also surmounted by a dome, and the vegetation all around, give it a highly exotic appearance.

MONREALE - CATHEDRAL - 11TH CENTURY.

PALERMO - CLOISTER OF SAN GIOVANNI DEGLI 12TH

Themes from the heart of Persia

Worthy of the Arabian Nights, the palaces of the Norman lords of Sicily were distinctly Arabic in style. Roger II, the first to bear the royal crown, built his palace at Palermo. The royal apartments and, below them, the Palatine Chapel still stand today. The chapel is a real "treasure chest" in which all the riches of Arabic and Byzantine art combine. The royal apartments are decorated with Byzantine mosaics, though certain motifs, like the lioness below, were borrowed by the Arabs from the Sassanid bestiary. The same lioness can be seen again on a splendid Moslem ewer (right), part of the collection of precious objects in St. Mark's, and which was brought back by the Venetians from Constantinople in 1204. It is made from a single block of finely engraved rock crystal.

DETAIL OF A MOSAIC - 12TH CENTURY - ROGER II'S BEDROOM IN THE NORMAN PALACE, PALERMO.

CRYSTAL EWER - 12TH CENTURY - ST. MARK'S, VENICE.

Christ,
Lord of the World,
reigns
over the basilicas

"Christ, the Lord of the World," covers the whole interior of the apse in Cefalu Cathedral (right), the mosaics of which are the oldest and most beautiful in Sicily. Its majesty evokes memories of Antiquity, but its gentle expression is a new feature of the "second Byzantine golden age" which began after the iconoclastic crisis of the 8th century. Its dimensions and its position amongst the decorations of the cathedral afford it a place of honor. Church decoration has no longer simply to depict for the illiterate events in Christian history, as it did in the "first golden age," but must also symbolize the doctrine of the Church and translate the divine hierarchy in images set out according to the order imposed by theology: Christ at the top, then the Virgin, followed by the apostles and the saints.

CEFALU - DETAIL OF THE MOSAIC IN THE CATHEDRAL CHANCEL - 1148.

Italy becomes Romanesque...

TORCELLO - ROOF OF THE CHURCH OF SANTA FOSCA - LATE 11TH CENTURY.

Reaching skywards, many campaniles were added to Roman churches in the 12th century. They are the only element of Romanesque art that the Romans accepted wholeheartedly. By the side of the sixth-century Church of San Giorgio in Velabro, at left, rises a campanile built 600 years later. It is decorated with typically Lombardic arches and columns. At the same time the church was given a portico which goes well with the Arch of Janus, one of the last Roman monuments, through which the portico and campanile can be seen.

Torcello, asylum for the Veneti fleeing from the mainland, first before Attila's Huns, then before the invading Lombards, and a haven among the islands of the lagoon, was one of the first settlements from which the Venetian Republic grew up. Nothing more remains today than a group of extraordinarily poetic buildings: the cathedral, founded in 639, the oldest Venetian monument, and the Church of Santa Fosca (above) which is connected to the cathedral by a covered gallery. It is an octagonal building of Byzantine inspiration.

... following the example of Lombardic architecture

The Benedictine Order was founded by St. Benedict on Monte Cassino in 528. It spread throughout Europe and played a leading part in the evolution of civilization and art during the Middle Ages. The reconstruction at the end of the 10th century of the monastery on Monte Cassino, which was magnificently decorated by Byzantine artists, emphasized even more this order's artistic influence in Italy. Some years later the Benedictines of Verona, encouraged by this example, sought to make of their church of San Zeno a monument that would be exceptional both in size and ornamentation. The adjoining cloister (at left) is pure and serene in style, and reflects well the peaceful spirit of their Rule.

A true illustration of the history of architecture from the 4th to the 12th century, the Basilica of San Ambrogio in Milan was built in 386 by Bishop Ambrose himself, to whom the church was eventually consecrated. It was altered in the 8th and 9th centuries, then transformed again in the 12th century, still by the Lombards, who were ever in the vanguard of Romanesque art. During the last alterations, its atrium (right) was built, through which visitors gain access to the basilica. It is majestic in its simplicity, and one can see below the roofing the typically Lombardic scalloped motifs. At the same time, the church, enlarged, was completely vaulted. Its ogival transepts are among the earliest in Europe. Yet this innovation represented here only a secondary characteristic. It was not in Italy, but in France, that its ultimate consequences were to be seen—in Gothic art itself.

VERONA - CLOISTER OF THE CHURCH OF SAN ZENO - 11TH CENTURY.

128

*Monumental
sculpture
reappears*

Guarding the door of the church, crouching lions serve to support the columns holding up the light porch that is a typical element of Italian Romanesque churches. The lion on the left, in pink marble, lies at the entrance to Modena Cathedral, the prototype of a superb series of churches built in the Po valley. From the most ancient times, the lion was a part of the Asiatic repertory, from which it passed, via Byzantine to Italy, then northward via Italy to Germany.

Man took first place once more in the sculptures at either side of the portal of the Church of San Zeno in Verona (right). He supplanted the decorative motifs of the Byzantines and the more or less mythical animals of the Lombards. These sculptures, cleverly composed in small panels, show scenes from the Old and New Testaments. They are signed by two artists: Niccolo, who executed the right-hand side, and Guglielmo, the left-hand side. Both seem to have been trained or influenced by another Guglielmo, who worked some forty years earlier. He carved the reliefs on Modena Cathedral, and played a decisive part in the history of European sculpture.

NA - LION BY THE PORTAL
HE CATHEDRAL - 12TH CENTURY.

AL OF THE CATHEDRAL OF SAN ZENO
VERONA - 11TH CENTURY.

*Pisan magic
spreads its charm
far and wide...*

The Piazza del Duomo of Pisa (previous page) where campanile, baptistery and cathedral stand side by side, splendid in their white marble, is one of Italy's most breathtaking and purely Italian wonders. "On top of the forms of ancient times," observed philosopher Hippolyte Taine, the Pisans superimposed "their own invention: a facing of little columns topped by arches, and words cannot be found to convey the originality and grace of the architecture revived in this way." During the building of the campanile, some of the stories of which can be seen on the left, the ground holding the foundations subsided. But work continued on this "Leaning" Tower, which is one of the world's great architectural curiosities.

The Pisan style triumphed over a large part of Tuscany and held full sway over the city of Lucca, whose churches were directly influenced by Pisa's cathedral. They are decorated with the same small arches, but on the façade of the Cathedral of San Martino of Lucca (right) the decor was enriched by sculptured motifs and inlaid marble in various colors, which reveal both Eastern and Lombardic influence, and which produce an effect of joyful splendor. This style spread to Sardinia, long a colony of the powerful Pisan republic, and reached southern Italy, where traces of it can be found at Troia, Benevento and even in Bari.

LUCCA - PART OF THE CATHEDRAL - 12TH CEN

*... and Florence
abounds
in marble
of many colors*

Florentine genius was expressed virtually in its entirety in the little church of San Miniato. This is one of the oldest in Florence, built in the 11th and 12th centuries on a hill overlooking the town. It is a basilica with three naves (see right) separated by two rows of columns, which are mostly surmounted by ancient classical capitals. The flooring of the central nave is covered with a marble mosaic of a rare elegance. The façade, covered with white, green and black marble, has a calm beauty that reveals the very qualities that were to distinguish Tuscan works of the Renaissance: harmony, clarity and charm. Its design, carefully blended with the structure of the church, comprises five archways, two of which correspond to the side nave (left), the three others to the central nave.

FLORENCE - THE CHURCH OF SAN MINIATO,
PART OF THE FAÇADE - 12TH CENTURY.

FLORENCE - INTERIOR OF THE CHURCH
OF SAN MINIATO - 12TH CENTURY.

134

Sculpture in marble...

VERONA - STATUE OF SAN ZENO - MID-12TH CENTURY - CATHEDRAL OF SAN ZENO.

Remarkable dynamism was given to the baptistery at Parma by the singular, many-ribbed dome that crowns it and without which this vast octagonal edifice would have looked massive and heavy. The dome rests on two tiers of loggias which emphasize the effect even more strongly. In the middle of the 13th century, some sixty years after it was finished, it was decorated with frescoes, very original in conception and heralding the next great trend in painting.

The statue of San Zeno (above) is one of the oldest single statues to have been sculptured in Italy since Roman times. The saint, a former fisherman, was consecrated bishop of Verona in 380. He is holding in his left hand his bishop's crosier from which hangs a fish on the end of a line, to remind us of his earlier occupation. This work in polychrome marble has a majestic bearing, in fine contrast to the roguish expression of the face.

*... in stone
or in bronze
undergoes
various influences...*

Abstract ornamentation and stylized figures decorate the pulpit in the little church at Gropina (left) in Tuscany. One of the oldest pulpits in central Italy, it dates from the beginning of the 11th century, which places it at the junction of pre-Romanesque art and Romanesque art proper. Its Lombardic origins can be seen in the treatment of the figures and symbols of the evangelists that stand out in the center. But the motifs on either side call to mind the very peculiar Irish art of the 7th century with its spirals and design of "interlaced men," which undoubtedly influenced the Germanic countries, where it had become known through manuscripts.

The reflection of Germanic art is in evidence here (right) in a characteristic detail of the bronze doors of the Church of San Zeno in Verona (there is a full view of the doors on page 129). Germanic art spread to Italy as a result of its magnificent upsurge at the end of the 10th century, under the impetus of the Ottonian emperors. These doors, a composite work realized no doubt by several craftsmen in the course of the 11th and 12th centuries, can be compared with those produced in the year 1000 or thereabouts at Hildesheim in Hanover. They are among the earliest made in Italy itself. Some years earlier, the doors for the churches of Amalfi and Monte Cassino had to be brought from Constantinople. They mark the beginning of a splendid series that was to include the doors of the cathedral and baptistery in Pisa, and later the fascinating doors of the baptistery in Florence (see page 201).

PULPIT OF THE CHURCH OF SAN PIETR
11TH CENTURY - GROPINA (AREZZO).

VERONA - DETAIL FROM THE DOORS OF
CATHEDRAL OF SAN ZENO - 11TH CENTU

*... from which
it will soon depart
to find
its own individuality*

The sober and noble talent of Benedetto Antelami made itself felt at Parma in the closing years of the 12th century, and great sculpture had come to stay. In Antelami's work we can see the influence of the Provençal sculptors, who were in the forefront of Romanesque art. He seems to have executed the "Descent from the Cross" (right) first, a bas-relief in the cathedral which, though still lacking in supple ease, is very moving. Later, having acquired a confidence that encouraged him to break fresh ground, he is thought to have executed the decorations for the baptistery. The latter comprises, on the outside, spandrels decorated with scenes that for the first time in Italy abide by the Romanesque rule that monumental sculpture must be strictly adapted to its setting. On the inside, a series of figures in high relief represents the months of the year. In the figure on the left, a man cutting a vine-branch, a close observation of nature is joined to a dignity of classical inspiration.

BENEDETTO ANTELAMI (DIED 1196)
THE VINE-GROWER (HIGH RELIEF) - PARMA
CATHEDRAL BAPTISTERY - 12TH CENTURY.

BENEDETTO ANTELAMI (D. 1196) - DETAIL OF TH
DESCENT FROM THE CROSS - 1178 - PARMA CATHEDRA

CHAPTER IV

FROM THE GOTHIC TO THE RENAISSANCE

(13th and 14th centuries)

Drawn by too many divergent trends, Italy was only moderately—and then fairly capriciously—Romanesque.

Her attitude to Gothic architecture was more reticent still. Adopting it very late, Italy quickly abandoned it, having failed to exploit its possibilities to the full.

But this reserve can be explained by a new factor. Since the collapse of Rome, Italy had been a crossroads of many influences, but in the 13th century she began dimly to discover her own genius, and this very quickly asserted itself in a most brilliant manner.

At the turn of the 13th century, three men—Dante, Giovanni Pisano and Giotto—expressed through their art the transformation that had taken place. Henceforth Italy was no longer Byzantine, Lombardic, Romanesque or Saracen. Despite her political divisions she found a unity of spirit at the same time as a common language. There is a definite affinity between the works of the Pisano family and Giotto and the soil that produced them. Born or transplanted elsewhere, the same artists would not have expressed themselves in the same way.

The 13th century and the beginning of the 14th saw a period of intense political, religious and intellectual activity during which the balance of power shifted, the cities changed completely in character and appearance, and an artistic revolution gave painting and sculpture their independence from architecture.

Then came a pause. The plague swept the country, and for more than twenty-five years successive epidemics emptied cities of their inhabitants. Nonetheless art continued its forward surge, and circumstances had only to become favorable again for it to bring forth the most splendid profusion of masterpieces in the whole of history: the Italian Renaissance.

VENICE TRIUMPHS OVER CONSTANTINOPLE. A significant adventure—the Fourth Crusade—marked the beginning of the 13th century. The French, Flemish, Lombardic and German crusaders, banded together at the call of Pope Innocent III, had no fleet to take them to the Holy Land. Sire de Villehardouin and a few others went to enlist the support of the only power capable of providing one: Venice. Venice agreed to put the necessary vessels at their disposal, but in return insisted on the payment of a very large sum of money. A fighting contingent, under the command of the ninety-year-old Doge Dandolo, would accompany them, and the booty would be shared equally between the Venetians and the crusaders. But despite all their efforts the crusaders could not manage to raise the sum demanded. Venice then offered to forget about the difference if the crusaders would first fight in the service of the Republic.

Thus it was that the Crusade changed its course. First they went and seized Zara, a Christian city on the Dalmatian coast that was impeding Venetian trade. Then Dandolo led the crusaders not to Jerusalem but to Constantinople, on the pretext of establishing the lawful emperor on the throne. The emperor had been deposed by a usurper, but had promised, once he was in power again, to make the Greek Church recognize the pope's authority. He was, needless to say, incapable of keeping this promise.

So it only remained for the crusaders, who had given back Constantinople to the emperor, to take possession of the city once more. They managed this on April 13, 1204, after a long siege, and took advantage of the situation to pillage the world's richest city with indescribable greed and brutality.

Venice was triumphant. The Byzantine Empire, whose vassal the city had been only a few years earlier and to which Venice owed all her wealth, was doomed. Immediately the influence of Byzantine art over Italy declined. It did continue, though, to affect painters for a time, but it was precisely because they freed themselves from Byzantium that Italian painting was born.

The day was not so far away when a Greek called Theotocopoulos was to come to Venice to study under Titian and Tintoretto before going on to settle in Toledo, where he became known as El Greco.

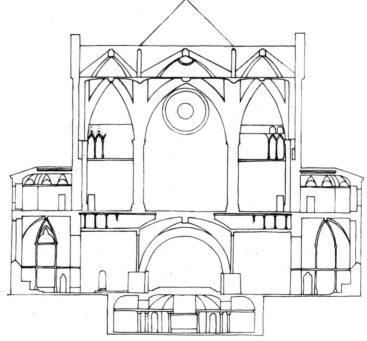

BASILICA OF SAINT FRANCIS OF ASSISI

ASSISI AND ST. FRANCIS. As this most unreligious of crusades came to an end, the son of a rich merchant of Assisi was leaving his home to renounce the world and preach self-denial and penitence. He soon gathered around him a few companions with whom he founded the first mendicant order. He loved life and every living creature, and he taught his companions to love the Lord in everything He created. After long years of traveling throughout his country, he came back to his home town and died there in 1226.

Two years later, Pope Gregory IX canonized him St. Francis of Assisi, and at the same time decided to build a basilica to house his body.

This was one of the first Gothic churches to have a truly Italian character, and by its very simplicity it is probably the noblest and most moving of them all.

The Gothic style, which had long been triumphant in France (the majority of France's great cathedrals had been finished before the end of the 12th century) had been introduced into Italy some years earlier by the French Cistercians, but their churches at Fossanova and Casamari near Rome, and at Chiaravalle near Milan, were simply copies of Cistercian churches in Burgundy. The mendicant orders

—Franciscans and Dominicans—were the first to adopt the Gothic style and give it an interpretation of their own. Then the other great monastic orders followed their example and the new architecture gradually spread throughout the country, where it had apparently been forgotten that the Lombards had been the first to create the ogival transept.

The churches of Santa Chiara in Assisi, Santa Maria Novella in Florence and San Domenico in Bologna were three of the earliest in which the Gothic style was used. But their architects had a conception of space that was very different from that shown in the French or Spanish cathedrals of the same style, stretching upwards as they do to give a feeling of exaltation. The Italians kept their taste for stability, clarity and horizontal effects, which they had inherited from classical times, and in consequence they modified the proportions of their buildings. Thus the great monastic churches of the late 13th and the 14th centuries, like Santa Croce in Florence (with its timbered ceiling), or the Frari and San Giovanni e Paolo in Venice, are spacious, light, and quite free of any aura of mystery. It often seems as though the Gothic ogives and feathered arches were employed more for their decorative than for their structural value.

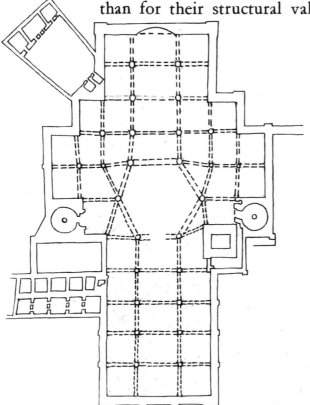

The same predilection for the horizontal can be seen in Siena Cathedral, with its spectacular black and white marble stripes, which, together with Orvieto Cathedral, is the most remarkable interpretation of Gothic architecture in Italy.

The Duomo of Florence, begun in 1300 under the direction of Arnolfo di Cambio, is as broad as it is high. Its vast dimensions, the many alterations that were made to it in the course of building, and its dome, which had been planned as its crowning glory from the very beginning (though no one had any idea as to how it would be built), all combine to make it one of those exceptional monuments that Italy has always delighted in creating. The Gothic and the non-Gothic are equally prevalent.

GROUND PLAN OF SIENA CATHEDRAL

A PRECURSOR OF THE RENAISSANCE. From the middle of the 13th century, architecture ceased to be almost exclusively religious. Everywhere civil building work, both private and public, was undertaken.

In 1240, near Bari, just below the spur of the Italian "boot," Frederick II of Hohenstaufen built for himself the Castel del Monte—"Castle on the Mountain." Half fortress, half palace, octagonal in shape, with octagonal towers at each of its corners, this building, impressive in its majesty, was as remarkable as its owner. In its structure there are elements borrowed from the Gothic, while what is left of the interior decoration bears traces of Islamic styles. Its portal, in the shape of a triumphal arch, comes straight from Constantine's Rome.

Frederick II, the son of Henry VI, Emperor of Germany, and of the Sicilian princess, Costanza, had first inherited the throne of Sicily: then, after a series of unexpected events, he had been elected Emperor of Germany, despite all precautions taken to prevent the union of the two crowns. In addition to this since the peninsula had been part of the Germanic Holy Roman Empire from the 10th century, he was also king of Italy.

But, in contrast to his predecessors, this emperor was in his tastes and culture much closer to Italy, and more especially southern Italy, than to Germany, and it was in Italy that he liked to live. He initiated an administrative reform, far in advance of his times, which would have made Sicily the first absolute monarchy of modern history. He would have liked to see Italy become the heart of his empire, which he hoped to make more Roman than Germanic.

In Frederick II Italy had produced a figure of a kind as yet unknown: a precursor of those great Renaissance lords who were soon to appear all over the country and create around themselves the most favorable climate for the blossoming of art. His was a cosmopolitan mind open to the boldest of ideas. He spoke several languages, including Greek and Arabic, had studied the sciences, was no mean poet, and brought to his court men of letters, philosophers and scientists. He was also truly pre-Renaissance in his nostalgia for the Roman Empire and his taste for classically inspired works. But he retained some characteristics of the Norman kings of Sicily from whom he was descended. Alongside Arab workmen, he employed builders trained by the Cistercian monks.

In his religious life, his freethinking shocked all Christendom, and in his private life his morals were peculiarly free: in fact, he was married three times, kept a large number of mistresses, and ran a harem.

To bring his political plans to fruition he had first to assert his authority in the north of Italy. As soon as he tried to do this the old quarrel between the papacy and the empire was stirred with greater violence than ever before, and all the Guelph cities (which in principle supported the pope, and were anyway hostile to the Ghibelline cities) rose up against him. At his death, in 1250, he controlled only the extreme south of the country. Everywhere else anarchy reigned.

By a quirk of fate, his attempts at unification had exactly the opposite result to what he intended. They only reinforced the cities' spirit of independence and the communal organization they had set up at the end of the 11th century as a reaction against the bishops and counts who had ruled them previously.

THE DEVELOPMENT OF CIVIL ARCHITECTURE. Once the power of the communes was assured, they set about embellishing their cities.

In general, the first element of urban decoration—the church or the cathedral—was already there. The second was the "palazzo pubblico," in front of which a square was laid out to provide a setting for what were regarded as the principal events in the life of the city.

This square, the city center, was rather like the stage of a theater. Thanks to the subsequent efforts of the city dignitaries, the local government and the guilds, it was to be surrounded by a harmoniously designed series of buildings which combined to give the effect of a backdrop. Among these buildings there was often a "loggia," whose function was the same as that of the ancient covered colonnades that ran along the sides of the Roman Forum. There the citizens could gather, sheltered from the rain or the sun.

So, between the middle of the 13th century and the end of the 14th century, a large number of cities were undergoing changes behind the solid ramparts that defended them from the covetousness of their neighbors. Already many of them were assuming the broad outlines of their ultimate shape.

In Florence, for example, the Palazzo Vecchio, seat of the "Signoria," the municipal council, was completed in 1314. Attributed to Arnolfo di Cambio, it was, like the Castel del Monte, a fortress, but a superbly elegant fortress of strikingly balanced proportions. The Loggia dei Lanzi dates from the last quarter of the century. At the same time, they were building the fine staircase that distinguishes the courtyard of the Palazzo Bargello, the new palace of the "podestà" (the chief magistrate of the city); Giotto's campanile was reaching completion, and the covered corn exchange was being converted to make the square church of Or San Michele.

At the same period Siena, Padua, Gubbio and many other cities were putting up public buildings and palaces in the same style as those in Florence.

Venice was familiar with most of these edifices when in 1340 it was decided to build the Doges' Palace and make it a wonder of its kind. The first masterpiece in the new style of the Most Serene Republic, it is a triumph of the unusual, a strange and captivating mixture of Gothic, Arabic and Byzantine, conceived and executed with the boldest imagination. The expanse of white and pink walls rests almost miraculously on the light framework of the double arcature. Throughout the century Venetian Gothic reigned over the lagoon and its dependent "terra firma," and its success postponed for some time the blossoming of the Renaissance in Venice.

SCULPTURE RETURNS TO THE CLASSICAL. One of the distinguishing features of Italian Gothic is that sculpture was dissociated from architecture, whereas elsewhere the two were closely linked. The façades of Siena and Orvieto Cathedrals, though decorated with magnificent carvings, are only superimposed and do not correspond to the internal logic of the building.

It was during the Gothic period that, on pulpit and tomb, great Italian sculpture was born almost at the same time as painting. This twin birth was the great artistic event of the age, and its importance was felt thousands of miles beyond the frontiers of the peninsula.

The first of the sculptors whose work sounded a new note was Niccolo Pisano, who worked in Pisa in the middle of the 13th century. He was probably a native of Apulia, and would thus have been acquainted with Frederick II's Romanizing movement. In any case, there is no doubt that he was influenced by the ancient sarcophagi that he saw in the Campo Santo in Pisa. The reliefs that decorate the pulpit of the baptistery show that he had appreciated the best qualities of the sarcophagi, but he also added a richness and vigor born of his own inspiration. From the pulpit of Siena Cathedral, which he executed with the help of his son Giovanni and his pupil Arnolfo di Cambio, we can see that he had acquired greater flexibility and developed along lines already far removed from the Ancients.

It would be interesting to know what were the respective parts played by the father and the son in this evolution. In the long run it was obvious that, of the two, Giovanni was the greater artist. His works in the cathedrals of Pistoia and Pisa are so full of movement, expression and ardor that only a talent and mastery as exceptional as his could prevent them from ending in chaos. But most surprising are his single statues that were to decorate the outside of Siena Cathedral and the baptistery of Pisa. Of the latter, some that have not got beyond the preliminary stage are mysterious in their simplicity, modest in their grandeur, and evocative of works that are either infinitely more ancient or infinitely more modern. It is by virtue of the hand of genius that wrought them that they escape the circumscribing limits of their period.

Giovanni Pisano had a great influence on the sculptors of the 14th century, including Tino Da Camaino and Andrea Pisano. But they were more sensitive to his actual forms than to his emotive powers, and their art was to evolve toward greater softness and harmony.

Arnolfo di Cambio, another of Niccolo Pisano's pupils, was an architect and sculptor like Giovanni. But with him the architect predominated, and he was the inventor of the several-storied tomb, a small-scale architectural monument that was to be in vogue in Italy up to the 18th century.

THE BIRTH OF PAINTING. In 1296 the Florentine painter Giotto came to Assisi. The decoration of the lower church, in which the best painters of the day —including Cimabue, his master—had had a share, was nearing completion. Giotto's orders were to paint, with the help of his pupils, scenes from the life of St. Francis on the walls of the upper church.

His frescoes were unlike anything seen before. Dante and Giotto were, in Henri Focillon's opinion, the descendants of the cathedral builders and great sculptors of the west. Like them they reveal that same boldness of proportion, that tenacity of purpose, cyclic power and sense of human grandeur.... Giotto defined monumental painting not only for his own century but for the ages to come.

André Malraux, who has analyzed Giotto more acutely than anyone, described his contribution to art thus: "He was the first in painting to discover the broad gesture, without making it theatrical.... His figures, against a background of new architecture or Byzantine rocks, exist in terms of one another, they look at each other. Giotto elaborated what for hundreds of years Europe was to call composition.... Only a great sculptor could have designed these frescoes, but only a great painter could have so skillfully controlled their sculptural qualities."

To a certain extent, Giotto's painting is the fruit of a spiritual meeting: that of a great artist and a saint. Nowhere better than at Assisi could one hear the echo of the "Poverello's" preaching in all its gentle sweetness and its mystical sharing in the suffering of Christ and of man. This preaching was at many points close to Gothic thought, to which Italy had been more susceptible than to Gothic architecture. Characterized by its humanism and its love for nature, this way of thinking gave more importance to "Christ made man" than to the fearful and unrelenting visions of the Apocalypse.

Malraux emphasizes that if Giotto unites Gothic love and Byzantine veneration, it is through the privilege of being a man, this privilege that was to flow beneath the surface of all Italian art like the stifled roar of an underground river.

Giotto himself carried Italian painting to a peak, but he was not the sole author of its evolution. Two painters who lived a little earlier—Cimabue in Florence, Cavallini in Rome—had cleared the way for him, from the starting point common to them all: Byzantine painting.

Cavallini's talent and the part he played would still not be fully appreciated had there not been discovered, some fifty years ago, in the Church of Santa Cecilia in Trastevere (the district of Rome situated on the other bank of the Tiber), some frescoes of his which, in the eyes of the experts, stand out from the works of his contemporaries by their movement, dignity and sense of volume. Further investigations have shown that Cavallini was pre-Renaissance in his choice of subject, for it was from ancient Roman art that he drew the elements that contribute to the originality of his style.

It was above all in his portrayal of feeling that Cimabue broke away from the Byzantine tradition, and the expressive power of his figures is doubtless the result of the Franciscan influence.

THE SCHOOL OF SIENA. While Giotto, in his frescoes, asserted his vision of the world, another innovator, the Sienese Duccio di Buoninsegna, was expressing a contemporary trend which inspired the songs of the troubadours and corresponded to the refined sensitivity of the end of the Middle Ages. This trend can be seen in a whole series of paintings and miniatures executed from the 14th century onwards throughout the greater part of western Europe. Art historians have grouped them together under the label "international Gothic style" and have picked out features common to all and which can be found in Italy as in France, in the famous collection of miniatures called "Les Très Riches Heures du Duc de Berry," for example.

Duccio was one of the initiators and the noblest representative of this movement, which contrasts with Giotto's "modernism." His art is the least monumental of all but it is wonderfully rich in fantasy. The scenes he painted are excellent in composition, they convey a feeling of touching sincerity, and yet they take place in an unreal world that has no depth. In their undulating play of lines and exquisite harmony of colors they are unequaled.

Simone Martini was the worthy successor of Duccio, and no doubt even surpassed his master, by virtue of his "divine feeling for the arabesque." At the end of his life he left Siena, the city of his birth, to go to Avignon, city of popes, where he made friends with his compatriot Petrarch, and also played an important part in the dissemination of the "international Gothic" movement.

In Italy itself, this movement spread gradually over the whole country and was carried on into the 15th century by the Lorenzetti family in Siena, Jacobello del Fiore in Venice, Altichiero in Verona and, later, Gentile da Fabriano and Benozzo Gozzoli in Florence. It became progressively weaker as Renaissance thought replaced medieval thought, but distant echoes of it can still be found in Botticelli.

Giotto's influence was less direct, but much more widespread. He was really the first painter of the Renaissance. All the other painters proceeded from him. Piero della Francesca is in some ways his spiritual heir, and Michelangelo himself, whose passionate genius seems the exact opposite of Giotto's, learned something of prime importance from him, since one of his drawings shows two figures from a fresco by Giotto.

Assisi, cradle of a spiritual revolution in the 13th century that had profound repercussions on art, can be seen on pages 150-151. We can see the basilica, formed by two superimposed churches on the side of the hill, supported by immense arches. Born of the preaching of St. Francis, the son of a rich merchant who was called the "poverello" ("little pauper"), and who was the mystic and poet of the first of the mendicant orders, this revolution turned the religious feeling of his contemporaries toward a greater humanity, and developed their love of Nature.

152

ASSISI - BASILICA OF ST. FRANCIS (FAÇADE OF THE UPPER CHURCH) - 1228-1253.

Home of St. Francis and cradle of Gothic art

SAN GIMIGNANO - 13TH CENTURY.

Dedicated to St. Francis only two years after his death and immediately after his canonization, the basilica at Assisi is one of the first creations of Gothic art which was truly Italian in character. It was built by Brother Elias, St. Francis' successor as head of the Order. He drew his inspiration from the churches built not very long before in many parts of the country by the French Cistercians, but adapted his models very freely. The façade of the upper church at left, of great simplicity and still close to the Romanesque style, is decorated with a rose window. The church itself has a single nave, as has the lower church, but it is narrower. Its walls have wide windows which flood the church with light. Thus they were especially well adapted to receive the frescoes that were painted in the last twenty years of the century and which were at the origin of all Italian painting. Assisi has changed scarcely at all since then: its houses and monuments have for the most part remained intact. The town is pervaded by a Franciscan atmosphere of peace and devotion that is perpetuated by all the faithful who come to take part in the various ceremonies held in honor of St. Francis or his disciple St. Clare, who founded the Order of St. Clare (see following page). Other Italian towns have also kept their medieval appearance, but speak another language to the imagination. This is the case, for example, with San Gimignano. In its narrow streets (right), where churches are squashed between fortress-like palaces, one thinks of the figures of Lorenzetti (see pages 174 and 175) or the warriors of Bonino da Campione (pages 158 and 159) rather than of the shadow of St. Francis of Assisi.

Public buildings multiply—a sign of expanding civil liberty

MINIATURE FROM THE "BIADAIOLO" ("CORN-CHANDLER") MANUSCRIPT - 14TH CENTURY - BIBLIOTECA LORENZIANA, FLORENCE

The desire for independence that, as early as the 12th century, set cities against the authority of the ruling bishops and the counts of the Empire frequently ended in the setting up of local governments. The latter built in the center of their cities public palaces to symbolize their power. It is for this reason that they were generally built like fortresses. One of the finest is Siena's communal palace (right), dominated by a slender tower over 300 feet high. Its elegant sweep commands the shell-shaped square, at the end of which it was built and which was bordered by dwellings and monuments in a matching style that was to impose itself on the rest of the town. In a short time, therefore, the town was wholly centered on its main square, and thus took on that typical medieval look, so well illustrated by the miniatures that embellish the account books of a Florentine corn-chandler. In the miniature reproduced above we can see the towers of Florence and Or San Michele.

Local tyrants
seize power

Princely luxury and warrior force
mingle in the three funeral monuments
to the Scaliger family in Verona. Their
style is Gothic, borrowed from Germany
and not at all usual in Italy. An accumulation of little columns, arches and statuettes is crowned on each of the tombs
by the equestrian statue of the lord
who is buried there. They belonged
to the Della Scala dynasty, but their
name is better known in its German
form — Scaliger. In the 13th century an
early Della Scala succeeded the tyrant
Ezzelino, a vassal of Frederick II, who
had Germanized the north of Italy. His
descendants gave Verona great industrial prosperity. The first two tombs are
those of Cangrande, who received Dante
at his court, and Mastino II, whose
claim to fame was the murder of his
cousin the Bishop of Verona with his
own hands. The third and finest
(right) is that of Cansignorio, their
successor. It was executed during the
lifetime of its future occupier by Bonino
da Campione, who took the earlier
tombs as his models but gave more
refinement to his work. A few years
before, in 1363, he had executed the tomb
of Bernabo Visconti in Milan, which
was surmounted by an impressive
equestrian statue, carved from a single
block of marble and originally plated
with gold and silver (left). Bernabo
had succeeded his uncle Giovanni,
archbishop and lord of Milan, while
his brother Galeazzo II set himself up
at Pavia. The alliance between Milan
and Pavia was concluded thanks to
Bernabo's marriage with Regina della
Scala. The power of these two families
lasted until the early 15th century.

NO DA CAMPIONE: TOMB OF CANSIGNORIO
IGER - 1374 - VERONA.

NO DA CAMPIONE: BERNABO VISCONTI - 1363
SFORZESCO MUSEUM, MILAN.

*Many cities
have kept
their medieval appearance*

Incomparable elegance is bestowed on Florence's Palazzo Vecchio (left) by the tower that rises boldly above it, a symbol of its prestige. It is called Arnolfo's Tower, after the great architect and sculptor Arnolfo di Cambio, who is thought to have constructed this lofty building, half-fortress and half-palace, built to house the city's magistrates and to protect them from the frequent uprisings. The equestrian statue of Cosimo I de Medici, in the foreground, is by Giovanni da Bologna.

The "Manhattan of Tuscany" could be the nickname of San Gimignano, with its thirteen towers rising above the skyline. These thirteen are all that remain of the town's original seventy-two, which proclaimed to the surrounding Tuscan countryside the considerable strength of a city that despite feudal, pontifical and imperial wars had managed to set itself up as a free commune with a democratic régime. A tower built on to a house was a sign of prosperity—to the good citizen of San Gimignano his home literally was his castle. One condition was, however, imposed: no one was allowed to build a tower higher than that on the house of the "Podestà," the chief magistrate.

FLORENCE - PALAZZO VECCHIO - 1314.

SAN GIMIGNANO - GENERAL VIEW.

*Sculpture
is revived by
a return to
Roman traditions...*

Heralding the Renaissance a century-and-a-half before its time, the vehement genius of Niccolo Pisano set Italian Gothic sculpture along the road best suited to the national temperament. By returning to ancient classical sources he regenerated the art of his time. His masterpiece is the pulpit in the baptistery at Pisa, decorated with five bas-reliefs, one of which, the "Adoration of the Magi," is shown on the right. His inspiration was provided by the Roman sarcophagi in the neighboring Campo Santo. It has even been pointed out that there are precise areas of resemblance between his Virgin and the figure of Phaedra as seen on one of these sarcophagi telling the story of Hippolytus. But this does not make Pisano a copyist. Thanks to a wholly individual vigor and freshness, combined with a remarkable knowledge of composition and perspective, he created a deeply original work that gives the modern spectator an impression of youthfulness.

NICCOLO PISANO (DIED 1278): BAPTISTERY PULPIT (DETAIL) - 1260 - PISA.

... while painting is still subject to Byzantine rules...

Cimabue, the leading painter of his day, was the creator of the first frescoes in the basilica at Assisi. If in form he still meekly followed his Byzantine masters, as his best extant painting « The Virgin Enthroned » (left) shows, in spirit he began to break away. His faces show in effect a new emotion which is no doubt the reflection of Franciscan thought. Some fifty years later, Greek conventionalism still impregnated the painting of the Madonna, in the center of Andrea Orcagna's tabernacle (right). Sculptor, architect, goldsmith, and painter—he spared none of his talents to create this sumptuous polychrome edicule in the unusual square Church of Or San Michele. The building had originally been built as Florence's corn exchange; but hardly was it completed when it was decided to turn it into a church.

CIMABUE (1240 - 1302): VIRGIN ENTHRONED - LATE 13TH CENTURY - UFFIZI, FLORENCE.

ANDREA ORCAGNA (1320 - 1368?): TABERNACLE - ABOUT 1350 - OR SAN MICHELE, FLORENCE.

... from which it broke away with Giotto...

The decisive step in Italian painting, upon which was to depend its whole future development, was taken by Giotto, who rejected the Byzantine tradition and introduced into his frescoes a truth and feeling as yet unknown. He "defined monumental painting, not only for his century but for the centuries to come." He produced his masterpiece in the Cappella dell'Arena at Padua, which he completely covered with frescoes depicting scenes from the life of the Virgin and the Gospels. In the "Meeting at the Golden Gate" (right), we are struck by the humanity of the characters and by the nobility of their gestures. Moreover, they stand out in almost sculptural relief, which is even more evident if we turn the picture and look at it upside down. Giotto's sense of the dramatic and mastery of composition are particularly evident here. The old couple, Joachim and St. Anne, bound by a gesture of deep tenderness, stand out clearly from the other figures against massive architecture that brings out the solemnity and balance of the composition. In the same Cappella dell'Arena, the Virgin and Child (left) by Giovanni Pisano, the son of Niccolo and a sculptor whose talent was even greater and more varied than that of his father, has a dignity that complements Giotto's figures, and which is manifestly classical in origin. Yet its general lines reveal the influence of French Gothic statues. But despite these influences the two artists expressed the originality of their temperament with a freedom surprising for the time.

GIOVANNI PISANO (BORN 1250): VIRGIN AND CHILD ABOUT 1300 - CAPPELLA DELL'ARENA, PADUA.

GIOTTO (1266-1336): THE MEETING AT THE GOLDE[N] GATE - 1305-1306 - CAPPELLA DELL'ARENA, PADU[A]

ANDREA PISANO (1270? - 1349): BAPTISTERY DOORS (DETAIL)-1330 - FLORENCE.

All Siena rejoiced on the day Duccio's large two-sided altar-screen, commissioned for the cathedral, was borne to its destined position. On one side the artist had painted the Virgin enthroned, while the other side was divided into some forty small panels illustrating the life of Christ. On the left, Jesus in Limbo. Founder of the School of Siena, which had a place of its own in the early days of Italian painting, Duccio followed a very different path from that chosen by his contemporary Giotto. In his paintings he sought to depict the wonderful and the unreal, and he carried illustration to a supreme degree of perfection. The rare elegance of his drawing and the exquisite harmony of his colors won him considerable fame.

The rapid evolution of art at the beginning of the 14th century is confirmed by the bronze doors, light and elegant in composition, that Andrea Pisano made for the baptistery in Florence. They are the first element of a work of which the completion was to be the great event of the Florentine Renaissance. Each of the twenty-eight panels of which it is composed, and of which we can see (above) that showing the Baptism of Christ, is enclosed within a quadrilobe—a motif common in French Gothic art. In its reliefs, we can perceive echoes of the frescoes Giotto had just painted in the Florentine Church of Santa Croce, and also of the mosaics that had for a short time adorned the dome of the baptistery, and on which Cimabue seems to have cooperated with Byzantine craftsmen. But Andrea Pisano was also inspired by the old doors of Pisa Cathedral. Thus he combined many trends to achieve a flexibility and charm that were to remain the distinctive features of the Florentine style.

169

DUCCIO (1255 - 1318): MAESTA (DETAIL) - MUSEO DELL'OPERA DEL DUOMO, SIENA.

... and painting is already producing some of its greatest masterpieces

Highlight of Sienese painting is probably Simone Martini's "Annunciation," the center part of which can be seen here, executed by the artist himself, while the angels that make up the rest of the picture were painted by Lippo Memmi, his assistant. Martini, Duccio's successor, had a style even more delicate than that of his master, and his subtle poetry lies as much in the fascinating flexibility of his lines as in the colors. Simone Martini, who had painted two magnificent frescoes for the Palazzo Pubblico in Siena, left the town of his birth on several occasions to work in Assisi, Naples, and finally in Avignon at the papal court, where he ended his days. Thus he played an important part in the expansion of Sienese art, the influence of which was felt as far away as Spain and Bohemia, and joined up with the great "international Gothic" stream to which belonged in particular the "Très Riches Heures du Duc de Berry" in France. It has recently been thought possible that there may have been some Far Eastern influence affecting the Sienese School, which could be explained by the journeys of the Franciscan missionaries to distant lands. Looking at Simone Martini's Virgin, with its sinuous design and peculiar charm, we can understand why this hypothesis was put forward.

SIMONE MARTINI (1284-1344):
THE ANNUNCIATION (DETAIL)
1333 - UFFIZI, FLORENCE.

Nature figures in painting alongside characters from everyday life

The appearance of natural scenery in Italian painting was one of the signs of its definite break with Byzantine tradition. Up to that time, the background of pictures was either of bright gold or was decorated with polychrome motifs. In the "Hermits in the Thebaid" (see detail at left) the painter, a Florentine primitive, treats the countryside with a combination of imagination and realism. On the pretext of describing the Thebaid, he shows us stylized hills that strangely resemble those that can be seen in Tuscany today (right).

Invaluable records of daily life in the 14th century, Ambrogio Lorenzetti's frescoes show us real people with all the details of their familiar dress and attitudes. Whether the painter is dealing with a religious subject, such as "St. Louis of Toulouse Taking his Vows as a Franciscan" (see detail on pages 174-175), or whether, yielding to a new trend in art, he chooses a secular subject, he shows the same realism and the same powers of observation. The refined gentlemen following St. Louis of Toulouse that he shows us here are of the same family as those he painted in the municipal palace of Siena in his "Effects of Good and Bad Government," the most extensive cycle of secular paintings of his time. These are unfortunately not at all well-preserved, but one can still see, against a background representing the principal buildings of Siena, men and women of varied classes of society performing the main tasks of city or country life. Ambrogio Lorenzetti, like his brother Pietro, an exclusively religious painter, has the grace and lyricism characteristic of Sienese painters. Both were to die in 1348 from the plague that killed with them the members of the first great School of Siena.

HERMITS IN THE THEBAID (DETAIL) - ANONYMOUS - 14TH CENTURY - UFFIZI, FLORENCE.

TUSCAN COUNTRYSIDE.

Art takes on a character of its own but remains monumental

TINO DI CAMAINO (DIED 1337): TOMB OF CARDINAL PETRONI (DETAIL) - 1318-1320 - SIENA CATHEDRAL.

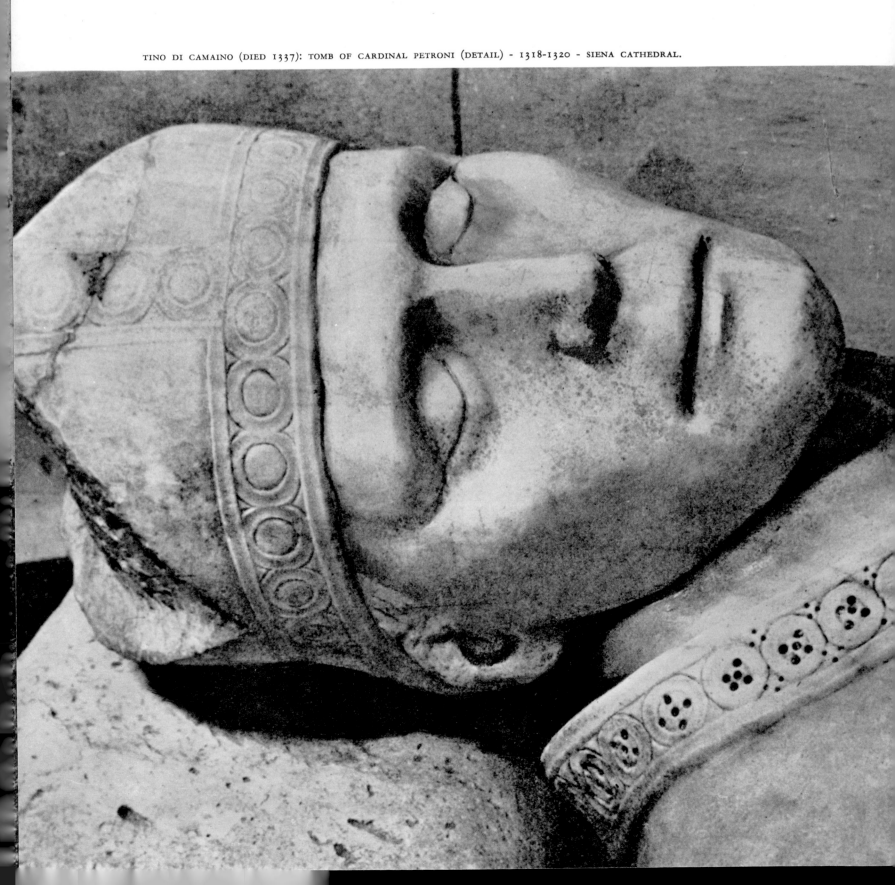

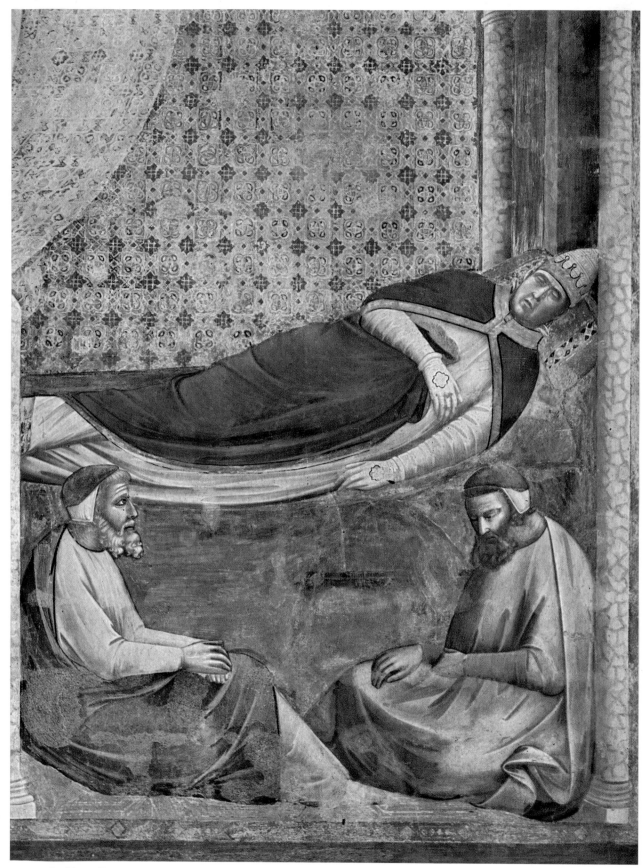

GIOTTO (1266-1336): DREAM OF INNOCENT III - ABOUT 1330 - UPPER CHURCH, ASSISI.

≪ **Most gifted of Giovanni Pisano's pupils** was the Sienese Tino di Camaino, who was first and foremost a sculptor of funeral monuments. In the tomb of Cardinal Petroni (detail at left) solid talent is combined with sober inspiration that reminds us of Giotto. And yet, at the time it was executed, the two artists did not know each other. They were to meet later in Naples, where they both worked.

Giotto's major quality is the way he renders volume and space and gives faces their full "tactile value." This can already be seen in the "Dream of Innocent III" (above) one of the painter's early works. It is part of the cycle of the "Legend of St. Francis" which he painted, with the aid of his pupils, in the upper church at Assisi. In this scene, one which shows Giotto's touch with the greatest certainty, Innocent III sees in a dream St. Francis preventing an unsteady church from collapsing. He understands that thanks to this saint, God's Church will be upheld. Its light, airy composition, the purity of its colors and its deep feeling define very well the clear, strong talent of the first great master of the Italian school, a master who has remained one of the greatest the school has ever produced.

177

*Fantasy
manifests itself
in church
architecture...*

A Gothic interpretation of the cathedral of Pisa, Siena Cathedral adopted the polychromy of its "parent," and welcomed archways and ogival transepts. But within as well as without it is covered all over with horizontal bands of black and white marble, like those on the town's coat of arms. The cathedrals of Siena and Orvieto, built at the same time, are the two most interesting Gothic cathedrals in Italy. Hardly was Siena Cathedral finished when, vast though it was, it seemed to be too small. A plan was adopted for it to be used as the transept of a new cathedral with a gigantic nave. This over-ambitious project had to be abandoned, but elements of the aisles remain.

Adorned with polychrome marble, Florence's campanile was built according to plans drawn up by Giotto, who had been put in charge of municipal works in 1334. It has three series of elegantly designed open-work windows, at right, through which can be seen in the background the tower of the Palazzo Vecchio, built twenty years previously. In the architecture of his campanile (see page 196) as in his painting Giotto shows that his sense of volume is more classical than Gothic in spirit.

ENA CATHEDRAL - 13TH AND 14TH CENTURIES.

FLORENCE - CAMPANILE BY GIOTTO - BEGUN IN 1334 - VIEW OF THE PALAZZO VECCHIO.

MILAN CATHEDRAL - BEGUN IN 1386.

... sometimes to an excessive degree...

Italy's richest and by far her largest Gothic monument, the only one to come anywhere near the great cathedrals of northern Europe, is Milan Cathedral. It took over two hundred years to build, extending over the whole of the Renaissance period. Milanese, French and German architects all played their parts in its construction, and all introduced new modifications. This prompted the great art historian Henri Focillon to say it was the "masterpiece of all false masterpieces." But, with its multitude of pinnacles, finials, scalloping and white-marble statues (above) that cover it and hide to some extent the faults of construction, it is one of the most remarkable and complete achievements of flamboyant art.

VENICE - DOGES' PALACE - SECOND HALF OF THE 14TH CENTURY.

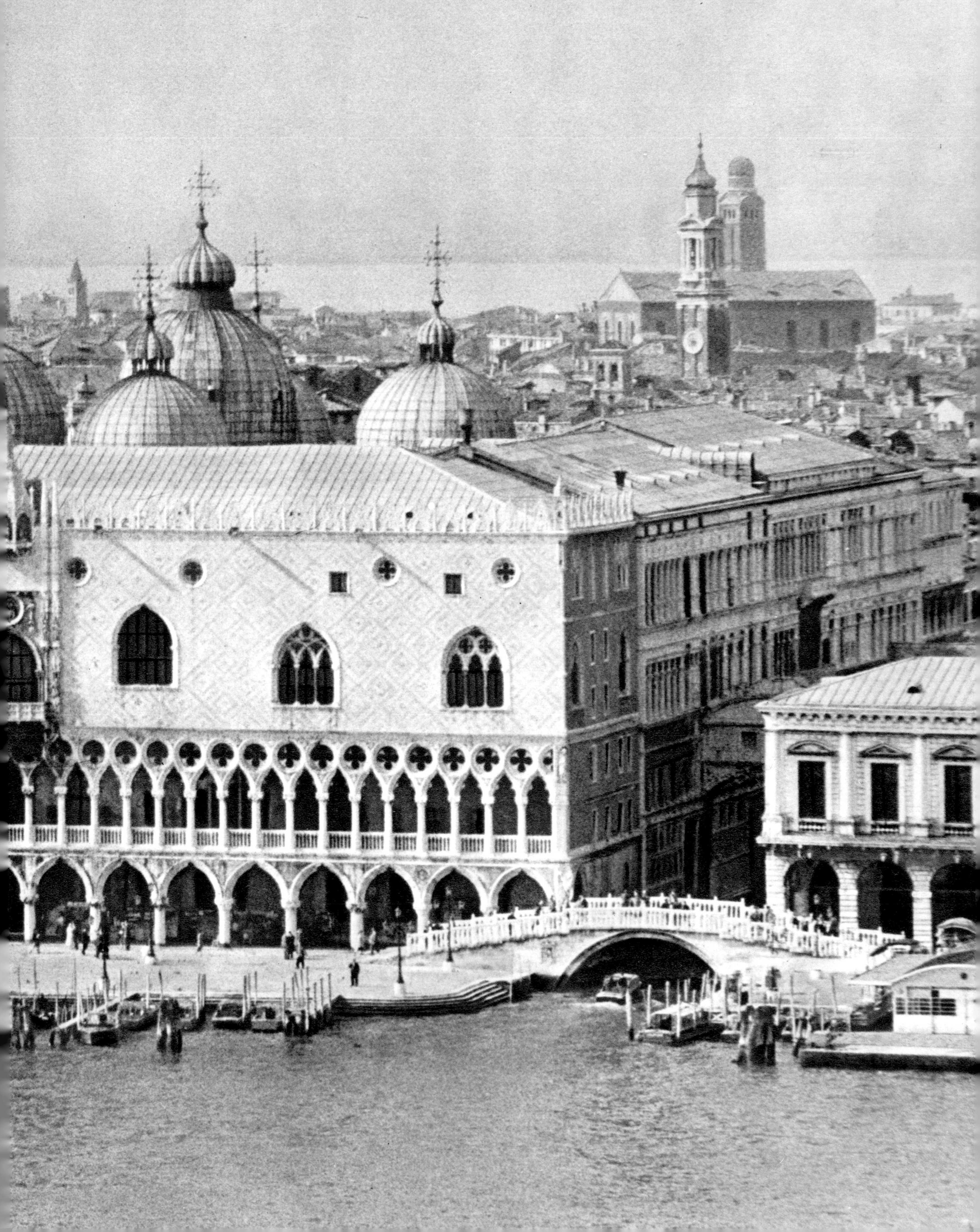

... while a new luxury characterizes civil architecture

FLORENCE - "ROOM OF THE PARROTS" (PALAZZO DAVANZATI) - 14TH CENTURY.

◄ **Dream palace on the shores of a lagoon** that its reflection tints with pink, sending back spangles of sunshine from its surface, the Doges' Palace (previous page) stands in the center of Venice, like a "solitaire diamond in its mount." It is an admirable combination of Eastern and Gothic elements. According to Byzantine custom it has at its base a portico surmounted by a loggia, both of fine open-work marble. Above this rises a smooth wall, with few openings. This bold inversion of masses—mass resting on apparent void—produces a surprising effect. The ornamentation of the center window was added at the beginning of the 15th century by the Masegne, Venice's first great sculptors. In the background can be seen the domes of St. Mark's, and on the left the campanile.

Growing luxury of living is reflected in fourteenth-century dwellings in Florence. An elegant staircase was added to the courtyard of the Palazzo Bargello (right) during this period. This palace, built between 1254 and 1346, was the house of the "Podestà," the city's chief magistrate, who lost some of his powers to the gonfalonier of justice, but kept his honorary title. The interiors of these palaces were richly decorated, adorned with painted motifs (above) that were to take on more and more importance until they became the chief element of decoration. As to the furniture — table, benches, chairs and chests — its style was soon to spread throughout Renaissance Europe.

FLORENCE - COURTYARD OF THE PALAZZO BARGELLO - 14TH CENTURY

CHAPTER V

THE RENAISSANCE

(15th century - the "Quattrocento")

In the year 1400 the plague that had ravaged Florence began to abate and finally disappeared. The following year it was decided to thank God for having rid the city of this scourge by giving the baptistery a second pair of bronze doors that would be even more beautiful than the first pair, executed sixty-five years previously by Andrea Pisano.

A competition was organized to choose the artist who would undertake the work. And so began, in this spectacular way, the century that was to be the most wonderful in Italian art and one of the greatest in the entire history of art.

The subject of the competition piece was the Sacrifice of Abraham. Two of the entries have survived: the winning entry by Ghiberti, and the runner-up by the architect Brunelleschi.

The prizewinner set to work immediately. For more than fifty years he was to devote himself almost wholly to the creation of two pairs of doors: first the pair that had been the subject of the competition, then a further pair that was commissioned from him as soon as the first was completed, and which Michelangelo was later to describe as worthy to be the doors of Paradise. During these fifty years he worked at the expense of the government of Florence, which showed no impatience, knowing full well that beautiful things cannot be created in a hurry. Ghiberti employed as his assistants some of the most promising beginners of the day. Donatello, Paolo Uccello, Luca della Robbia and Benozzo Gozzoli were among the many who passed through his studio which thus became one of the homes of Florentine art. Already one of the most remarkable features of that age can be seen: the ability of artists to pass from one medium to another, to wield now the chisel, now the brush.

Ghiberti finally produced a masterpiece that was unique of its kind. Or rather two, for many contemporary art critics prefer the first pair of doors to the more famous second pair.

Failure was to be as fruitful for Brunelleschi as success was for his rival. An exceptionally gifted artist with an inquiring mind, he began by distinguishing himself as a goldsmith, then for a time applied himself to watch-making, which he eventually gave up for sculpture.

His disappointment at the outcome of the competition was probably an important factor in his decision to try his hand at yet another genre, this time architecture. But before he did, he was one of the first to undertake the journey that for several hundred years was to be the very basis of every artist's training: he set off for Rome, accompanied by the young Donatello. Together they studied the ruins of ancient Rome, visited the earliest Christian basilicas, and returned with a rich store of teaching and ideas.

In 1420 Brunelleschi declared himself ready to take up the challenge that the architects of Santa Maria del Fiore had set, trusting in the genius of their successors. He undertook to cover the area where the nave and the transept crossed, which was still uncovered, with an immense dome that would have no apparent buttresses and would be easy to construct. This time his project was accepted and carried out, and Brunelleschi's dome, with its bold lines, became one of the greatest glories of Florence.

In contrast to his old rival Ghiberti, Brunelleschi produced more than a single work. He left in Florence monuments of exceptional diversity, all of which influenced succeeding generations. The most important are the Ospedale degli Innocenti, in which he once more used classical columns to create a portico perfect in its grace; the old sacristy of San Lorenzo in which he combined volumes to give an impression of order and purity that had not been achieved for a long time; and the church of the same name that was to be in a way the prototype of Renaissance churches.

About a hundred years after the famous competition for the baptistery doors, another competition of a more cruel character was to close the great century of Florence, that golden age that had left memories comparable to those of the century of Pericles.

Instead of bringing face to face two men both under thirty, it set an artist fifty years old against one of twenty-five: Leonardo da Vinci against Michelangelo—the man who best of all embodied the Renaissance spirit, its thirst for all that was new and its cult of beauty, against the man whose powerful personality was to leave its mark on the whole of the following century.

Leonardo da Vinci had been commissioned to decorate one of the walls of the council chamber in the Palazzo della Signoria with a fresco showing the battle of Anghiari. While he was preparing the sketch for this, Michelangelo, whose colossal statue of David had just been set up amid popular acclaim in front of that very palace, and whose hostility to Leonardo was well known, received a similar commission for the opposite wall. He took as his subject an episode from the battle of Cascina. The two sketches were exhibited together. All Florence came to look at them and compare them, and Michelangelo's work was admired as much as his rival's. But the latter, always the inventor, thought he knew the secret of success: a new formula for mixing colors that he thought superior to all others. Put into practice, this formula proved disastrous, and he had to abandon his fresco and leave it unfinished.

As for Michelangelo, too busy elsewhere, he did not even spare the time to exploit his success, but set off for Rome at the summons of Pope Julius II.

Nothing came of the meeting of these two geniuses. Even their sketches have disappeared. But this meeting did show in a dramatic way the merciless rise of the new generation, who were to put the old generation in the shade and who heralded the end of the artistic supremacy of Florence.

THE RENAISSANCE—AN ADVENTURE OF THE MIND.   The great majority of the works of the "Quattrocento," i.e. the 15th century, belong to the Renaissance, a movement which started in Italy and later spread to neighboring countries. Art historians and critics differ when it comes to defining the characteristics of Renaissance art and fixing the limits of its development in time.

Indeed, if we take "Renaissance" in its strict meaning of a return to classical sources, we must admit that Italy has had many renaissances.   Italy never really forgot the past, and we have seen that Antiquity was its inspiration in every century. Moreover, things did not change overnight, and "avant-garde" and more conservative artists were working side by side.

Rather than take sides in the arguments of the experts and try to confine the most dynamic period of Italian art within the rigid framework of a word coined after the event, we would do better to consider it, as did Fred Bérence, with the eye of an "enlightened lover" and to say with him that it was a "new awakening like that of Nature in spring."   But that particular spring was more prolific than any other because it coincided with a particularly favorable moment in the evolution of human thought.

The "Florentine miracle" was born of a change in the philosophical beliefs of the time and of a rare harmony of man with himself.

If we compare Florence at the time of the Medicis with the modern world, consumed with anguish, we realize that those sumptuous baptistery doors are really those of a paradise lost.   Today artists and intellectuals are mostly men apart, whose work expresses revolt or doubt.   Between them and the men of action, antagonism—or at best incomprehension—is the rule.   In the "Quattrocento" on the other hand, chiefs of state, "condottieri," financiers and businessmen shared the intellectual preoccupations of philosophers, artists and scientists.   They all had in common a consuming thirst for knowledge, which they quenched at the same source—that of classical thought, which had recently taken on a new lease of life. For with the decadence of Byzantium, which fell to the Turks in 1453, came an influx of Greeks who had kept alive the memory of the old Hellenic wisdom.

In this great adventure of the mind, the one big event was the rediscovery of Plato, who had taught that man is the ultimate measure of all things and that Beauty, upon which Christianity looked askance, is the ideal meeting point of the Mind and the Spirit.

There are few ideas that have changed man's outlook so much.   If we are to look for anything similar in our times, we must think for example of the revolution given to psychology by Freud or, on a larger scale, of the consequences of Marxism. But instead of setting neo-Platonism against the Christian faith, Renaissance man thought in his enthusiasm that he could reconcile the two, so he was extremely rarely led into unbelief.

In art, the adoption of Greek philosophy by the men of the Renaissance had two basic consequences.   The first, more practical, was to make them admire classical art above all things.   The second, more esthetic, was to confer upon works a value of their own, independent of their subject.   It was at this time that, in the words of André Malraux, "the artist, gradually separating creation from Christianity, led Christianity slowly to seek within itself its own raison d'être," and that the modern conception of art at last prevailed.

The "Quattrocento" was not acquainted with Greek art, save in a few of its minor productions—cameos and intaglio work. It was only from the dilapidated ruins of Roman monuments that men could get some idea of what it had been, so they had to reinvent classical art from scattered remains and fragmentary texts. It was for this reason that the Renaissance was creative and not imitative.

COSIMO DE' MEDICI, PATRON OF THE ARTS. The Renaissance can be explained by ideas, but it can only be fully understood through a knowledge of the men and particulary those chiefs of state or city leaders around whom intellectual and creative activity was focused.

The most important of these patrons are Cosimo de' Medici and his grandson Lorenzo. To know the lives of these men is also, in some measure, to know the lives of Frederico di Montefeltro, Ludovico di Gonzaga or Sigismondo Malatesta, who played similar parts in Urbino, Mantua and Rimini.

Cosimo de' Medici had already passed forty when his father, the banker Giovanni, died, leaving him his fortune and one of the biggest financial establishments in Europe. This made him the richest man in Florence. He also wanted to be the most powerful. It took him six years, a considerable amount of money and a great deal of skill to reach his goal and force upon his fellow-citizens a dictatorship admirably camouflaged under republican trappings.

The affairs of state and the administration of his bank could easily have filled his life. But he thought—and in this he was indeed a man of his times—that art and philosophy were just as important. In 1439, when the Council of the Roman and Greek Churches met in Florence, he discovered among the Greeks who were participating a scholar who had a profound knowledge not only of religious matters but also of the works of Plato. Cosimo listened to him and was inspired. Since such matters could not be dealt with in so cursory a manner he therefore decided to found in his own palace an academy for the study of Platonic philosophy, of which he became the most enthusiastic member.

His banking house had its correspondents, and his government envoys in the East. The mission of each one of these—in addition to his commercial or diplomatic work—was to unearth all the Greek and even Arabic or Hebrew manuscripts of interest that he could find, and send them back to Cosimo. Thus he hoped to discover some of the secrets of ancient wisdom, but to do the latter he needed translators and commentators, not to mention scribes. So Cosimo summoned to Florence the most cultured men in Italy, and assured them a living. Nothing is more significant than his attitude toward them, for this man, whose authority was boundless, followed their work with the application of a humble disciple and showed them the deference due to such masters of the intellect.

His relations with artists were no doubt familiar, but they were in no way condescending. They all worked for him and visited his house where they knew they would find an understanding and friendly welcome. Moreover, one of them, the architect Michelozzo, had accompanied him into exile when at the beginning of his political career his opponents had managed to have him banished from Florence for a year.

The sums of money, taken from his private fortune, that he devoted to literature and the arts are truly fantastic. Converted into present-day currency they would run into millions. At the time they were equivalent to twice the total budget of the state of Florence. He spent only a negligible part of it on his palace, country houses and his private collections. With unheard-of generosity, he even opened what was by far the most valuable of his collections, his library, to all those who wished to work there.

The rest of his expenditure went to embellish the city he ruled with an iron hand. Everywhere new buildings—churches, convents, hospitals—were built or enlarged. He entrusted the construction work to the architects Michelozzo and Brunelleschi, and the decoration to a host of painters and sculptors, including Donatello, Fra Angelico, Luca della Robbia, Filippo Lippi and several others whose talent he was in many cases one of the first to discover.

"In fifty years," he would say, "I shall only be remembered for the few buildings I have had constructed."

LORENZO THE MAGNIFICENT AND THE TRIUMPH OF FLORENCE. Cosimo had personally supervised the education of his grandson, and this was without doubt his most brilliant success. Speaking of Lorenzo the Magnificent, Marcel Brion declared that heredity and education joined forces to produce this masterpiece of the human race. His very virtue was carried to its highest degree of efficiency. None of his talents was insignificant.

In every field he continued his grandfather's work, making it more magnificent. But instead of being only the guiding spirit of the intellectual and artistic movement, he played an active part in it. He had a gift for drawing and a thorough knowledge of architecture, but above all he preferred writing poetry. His work, in which poems of philosophical inspiration mingle with lyrical pieces and some frankly libertine verses, has a far from negligible place in Italian literature. In philosophy he had been the pupil of Marsilio Ficino, whom Cosimo had placed at the head of his Platonic academy, and remained his disciple all his life. He was also drawn by the ideas of the handsome and enigmatic Pico della Mirandola, who had studied Hebrew writings and was second to none in his knowledge of the Cabala.

He gathered around himself poets, artists and philosophers, who accompanied him to his villas outside Florence to discuss freely all the great problems that occupied the men of the age. How can one reconcile the God of Plato and the God of the Christians? Have the numbers that hold the secret of harmony any magic powers? What is the importance of perspective in painting? Can astrology lead to truth? Every question, every subject, interested these fervent men, and their enthusiasm was in no way curbed—as it tends to be today—by the contradictions in their way of thinking.

Lorenzo had created a new kind of academy for artists: he opened the doors of the collection of classical works that Cosimo had started and his successors developed, and invited young artists to come and study these models. Michelangelo was one such student.

Risen to power at the age of twenty, Lorenzo devoted all the brilliance of his youth to Florence. He made her the city of gaiety, with festival after festival. Lorenzo and his friends presided over the festivities in the company of the most beautiful of Florence's young ladies. The best painters and sculptors took charge of the arrangements and saw to it that the decorations were properly executed, and the whole city took part. The works of art produced at that time, most of them for Lorenzo, reflect this joy and luxury, which, of course, were not without their excesses.

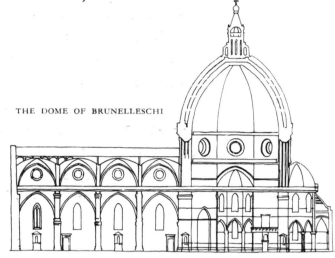

THE DOME OF BRUNELLESCHI

Soon the voice of the monk Savonarola could be heard thundering out against the depraved morals and pagan appetites of his fellow citizens. But at that time, Lorenzo was already nearing his death, which occurred in 1492, and the "Quattrocento" was nearing its end.

THE CHURCH OF SANTA MARIA DEL FIORE

THE GREAT INNOVATORS. One of the great features of the Italian Renaissance was the strength of the bonds that joined artists not only to the rest of society but also to one another. This was one reason for the abundance of talent.

Ideas and art forms circulated in a continuous current, from which each one could draw what best suited his temperament. Practically every artist contributed, by his teaching or his work, to the training of others. And if, as sometimes happened, the pupil surpassed his master, in no case did he disown him.

In the beginning, the development of art in the "Quattrocento" was determined by less than half a dozen men, who influenced almost all the others in a more or less direct way. These men were the architects Brunelleschi and Alberti, the sculptors Donatello and Ghiberti, and the painter Masaccio. Already a mutual exchange of influence was taking place.

Brunelleschi and Alberti, twenty-five years his junior, were alone responsible for the great transformation in the architecture of their century. Brunelleschi was an inventor: he knew how to use classical themes with a harmony and balance that met to perfection the as yet unconscious needs of his contemporaries. Alberti, as much a philosopher as an artist, and one of the first universal minds of the Renaissance, codified the doctrine of the new architecture, making the special point that the beauty of a building could come only from a system of proportions calculated with such an exactness that no one of its elements could be modified without destroying the harmony of the whole. But he was not content to theorize. Indeed he put his ideas into practice, notably in the Palazzo Rucellai in Florence and the Tempio Malatestiano in Rimini, the façade of which was conceived in the style of a Roman triumphal arch.

Brunelleschi's influence marked Michelozzo, Cosimo de' Medici's architect, who interpreted his borrowed themes with less boldness. Alberti's teaching was absorbed and passed on by his two pupils, Bernardo Rossellino and Luciano Laurana. The former was commissioned by Pope Pius II to change the village where he had been born into a city in keeping with the tastes of the day, to be renamed Pienza. The latter built the palace castle of Urbino for Frederico di Montefeltro, and made it the finest dwelling of the Renaissance.

During the "Quattrocento" Ghiberti enjoyed immense prestige due to the wave of admiration inspired by his baptistery doors, and no sculptor could afford to disregard him. His most direct descendants are Benedetto da Maiano and Mino da Fiesole. But in more general terms, it is to him that we must attribute that delicate and ordered grace of the majority of Florentine works during the second half of the "Quattrocento," and which appears to us today as the very mark of Tuscan art.

THE INESTIMABLE CONTRIBUTION OF DONATELLO AND MASACCIO. Donatello was the greatest sculptor of his time, and one of the greatest of all time. In his greatly varied work, he combined classical purity with the expressive intensity inherited from the Middle Ages, and added a static tension and an exacting authority that were his very own. It is hard to imagine what the art of the "Quattrocento" would have been without him, for he influenced painting just as much as sculpture.

Although he had in Desiderio da Settignano a remarkably gifted pupil, his true successors were Antonio Pollaiuolo and above all Verrocchio, both painters as well as sculptors, and both with vigorous and inventive talents.

Verrocchio's studio played an important part in the evolution of art in the second half of the 14th century. Lorenzo di Credi studied there, as did Perugino; then followed an infinitely more remarkable pupil, Leonardo da Vinci. It was, in fact, at Verrocchio's side that Leonardo spent his formative years, from the age of seventeen to twenty-five. This was the man who epitomized the aspirations and the universal curiosity of the "Quattrocento." He had no other master, and through Verrocchio he could still catch a dim echo of Donatello's voice.

Donatello's contribution passed into painting first through Masaccio, then through Mantegna. We know little of the life of Masaccio, who died at twenty-seven, and of whose work there remain only a few dilapidated frescoes in Florence. Yet there is such a similarity in bearing between his figures and the statues of Donatello, some fifteen years his senior, that most art historians recognize that they derive from one another. It is indeed the formal dignity of Masaccio's figures that recalls the work of Donatello and distinguishes Masaccio's paintings from those of Masolino, who was his master.

Toward the end of his life, Donatello stayed for some ten years in Padua, where his works produced such a vivid impression on the young Mantegna that Mantegna had no hesitation in reproducing some of their elements in the first of his great works: the altar picture in Verona's Cathedral of San Zeno. But Mantegna did not merely borrow a motif from Donatello; he owes to him the very style of his art, which exemplifies the transposition from sculpture to painting.

Through Mantegna, the connection was established between Florentine art, in which form is everything, and Venetian art, which concentrated more on color. This connection was made in the most informal way: by the marriage of Mantegna and the young Nicolosia Bellini, the daughter of Jacopo, and the sister of Gentile and Giovanni, none of whom was likley to remain intensitive to the talent of their brother-in-law.

Masaccio has often been called a "second Giotto": Giotto had introduced relief into his paintings;. Masaccio in his turn created an impression of space through the use of perspective. Moreover he showed a nobility of expression and a quiet strength that few artists have possessed. So we can understand how, as Berenson said, a few years were enough for him to show the Florentine school the path it was never to leave.

Masaccio died too young to have trained any pupils. His work spoke for him. There were two artists who fully understood it: Piero della Francesca and Filippo Lippi. But they each interpreted it in a different way. The former retained its essential significance; the latter heard only its new sonority. Between them, however, they passed on to all the painters of their century the lesson that this great master had taught.

Piero della Francesca was to Masaccio as Alberti was to Brunelleschi. He was the theoretician of pictorial perspective, and wrote a treatise on the subject. In his work, one of the highlights of the "Quattrocento," he created, in a more sensitive and less deliberate way perhaps than Raphael in later years, that ideal world that humanists dreamed about, in which a subtle harmony of colors and light endows scenery and architecture with a serene poetry. But his inspiration stemmed not from the School of Athens, but rather from the Legend of the Cross. André Malraux has noted that he was the first to portray indifference as the prevailing expression of his figures: "his figures are like statues, and only come to life for a sacred dance...he is the very symbol of modern sensitivity, which requires the painter's expression to derive from his painting and not his figures."

THE PAZZI CHAPEL

Piero della Francesca, who left Florence at an early age and worked sometimes at Arezzo and sometimes for the Duke of Urbino, was Signorelli's master and exerted an influence over Giovanni Bellini and Antonello da Messina, forging a new link between the Florentine and the Venetian school to which Antonello da Messina, who had lived at the court of the King of Aragon, had just introduced a suggestion of Flemish art. Fra Filippo Lippi was the least intellectual of the Florentine artists. In his work we can find Masaccio's sense of space and his clarity of composition, but not his gravity. He was a marvelous colorist and his paintings are above all exquisitely graceful. This latter quality was to be developed to a high degree by his pupil Botticelli, whose works show great wisdom and a profound sense of mystery which were to win a unique place in Italian painting.

Botticelli was, in his turn, the master of Filippino Lippi, Filippo's son, who would no doubt have needed a stronger personality to free himself from the overwhelming combination of such heredity on the one hand and such teaching on the other. By a quirk of fate, it was he who was entrusted with the completion of Masaccio's frescoes, which had remained unfinished for more than fifty years. He acquitted himself of this task with obvious respect for Masaccio, but only managed to produce very feeble imitations. If Piero della Francesca, rather than Filippino Lippi, had been given the task of "tying up the loose ends" of a work from which his own was derived, he would perhaps have done it with less timidity in form, and certainly with a greater fidelity of spirit.

THE FRUITS OF A GREAT CENTURY. The fascinating interplay of relationships and influences is of course only one of the aspects of the art of the "Quattrocento." Its development was not limited to Florence, for it radiated to Umbria, to the Marches, and even as far as Rome. Mantua, Ferrara, Milan and Venice were important art centers which all left their stamp on architecture or painting. Urbino most of all, at the instance of Frederico di Montefeltro, a humanist and a patron as astonishing as the Medici family, was an admirable home of culture, whose most famous sons were Bramante and Raphael. Nor was Italy out of touch with what was happening abroad: Van der Weyden came to Ferrara, Justus of Ghent worked at Urbino, and Albrecht Dürer visited Venice in 1490.

To measure the immensity of the changes that took place, we must compare the situations at the beginning and the end of the century.

Architecture changed not only in form, through the introduction of classical elements, but in its very conception, which was linked to the philosophical conception of the world. The ideal that was proposed was that of a "uniform, limited and ordered space" which is the opposite of the Gothic aspiration toward the infinite and its enthusiasm for the vertical, which in any case Italy had never really liked.

In their search for perfection, which according to them must give man a feeling of happiness by satisfying his mind, the architects relied on a system of symbols based on figures and numbers inherited from Antiquity. Many of their churches have a circular ground plan, since the circle is "beloved of nature." Moreover, a well-proportioned human body fits perfectly into this scheme, since it fits into the square circumscribed by this circle, which is also a privileged figure. Thus harmony is intrinsically related to man, whom the Renaissance, like Plato, made the measure of all things.

Sculpture broke away from architecture for good and all, and in affirming its autonomy it won back the essential place conferred upon it by the Greeks.

Finally, painting, which had no classical tradition to draw on, embodied successively space and movement. At the end of the century Leonardo da Vinci made yet another contribution: "sfumato," or the softening of the contours by shading, which gave painting a kind of extra dimension, an illusory quality all of its own.

And he proclaimed the primacy of painting over all the arts. Because of this, and because none of his sculpture has survived, we tend to think of him essentially as a painter. But he was above all a humanist in the fullest sense of the word: a man to whom nothing human was foreign. In this he can indeed be described as the final glory of his age.

Florence, scene of one of the world's most wonderful artistic adventures, was the birthplace of the Italian Renaissance, which determined the development of Western art for several hundred years. Architects, painters and sculptors left their masterpieces in all parts of the city. One of these dominates all the others: it is the dome of the Cathedral of Santa Maria del Fiore (pages 196-197). Built by Brunelleschi, who had many taxing technical problems to solve before completing it, it seems to have been constructed not only in terms of the immense church it surmounts, but of the whole of the city over which it majestically towers. Thanks to this cathedral the capital of Tuscany takes on the aspect of a vast monument set in a ring of green hills, and which is punctuated on the right by the tower of the Palazzo Vecchio and on the left by Giotto's campanile, both built in the 14th century.

A new style is born of ardent rivalry between artists

BRUNELLESCHI (1377-1446): THE SACRIFICE OF ABRAHAM - 1401 - PALAZZO BARGELLO, FLORENCE.

A competition piece that won for the victorious young goldsmith Ghiberti the commission to make the bronze doors of the baptistery at Florence, "The Sacrifice of Abraham" (detail at left), was executed in high relief in a supple style and with a very skillful mastery of technique. The naked body of the young Isaac is classical in inspiration, while Abraham's robe still has Gothic folds. The composition is arranged on three levels (at left, the middle level) with perfect clarity.

The same theme was interpreted by Brunelleschi in a more realistic spirit. His composition is lighter than that of his rival yet has not the ease of the latter. It is closely adapted to the surrounding quadrilobe, which was modelled on those on the first set of doors by Andrea Pisano (see page 169), but here it is a true frame, not a decorative motif. Disappointed at losing to Ghiberti, Brunelleschi turned to architecture and built the dome of the cathedral.

199

GHIBERTI (1378-1455): THE SACRIFICE OF ABRAHAM (DETAIL) - 1401 - PALAZZO BARGELLO, FLORENCE.

Sculpture draws inspiration from pictorial trompe-l'œil

SVRGE ACCIPE PVERVM 7 MATREM EP 7 FVGE INEGIPTVM .MACEI. II. C.

FRA ANGELICO (1387-1455): THE FLIGHT INTO EGYPT - ABOUT 1450 - CONVENT OF SAN MARCO, FLORENCE.

Transition from Middle Ages to Renaissance is exemplified in the work of Fra Angelico, a mystic whose faith gave him a radiant and truly angelic vision of the world. Sensitive to the charms of nature, he expressed it in a truly naïve manner, by stylizing the scenery and vegetation and making them harmonize with the characters. Thus in his panel "The Flight into Egypt" (above), part of a series illustrating Old and New Testament texts painted at the top and bottom of each scene, the contour of the rock is a projection of the outline of St. Joseph.

The "Gates of Paradise," as Michelangelo called the second set of bronze doors made by Ghiberti for the baptistery of Florence, are not like the first pair. Halfway between sculpture and painting, they combine with great skill the qualities of the two media. Ghiberti took up once more the theme of Abraham's sacrifice (right). This time it is less dramatic and is imbued with a supreme grace. He set the episode in the middle of a finely modelled countryside, inspired by the harmonious Tuscan scenery that surrounded him.

200

GHIBERTI (1378-1455): THE GATES OF PARADISE - BAPTISTERY, FLORENCE.

The minor arts flourish as luxury in private life increases

Marquetry in wood, a craft raised to the status of a major art, was the creation of the fifteenth-century Italian "intarsiatori" or "maestri legnarii" (master woodworkers). They were the first to find out how to turn doors, chests and wooden panels into real pictures. They were so successful that such famous painters as Baldovinetti, Botticelli and Piero della Francesca furnished them with sketches, just as they did for the tapestry makers. They were the first artists to make still life a subject in its own right. They also excelled in their views of architecture (left) which show their respect for perspective, in which, like all the artists of this period, they were remarkably skilled, and which gives a very modern look to their work. Some of their scenes were inspired by town views, such as can still be seen in the old city of Verona, whose two banks are linked by a crenellated, three-arched bridge (below), built by the Scaligers.

THE SCALIGER BRIDGE, VERONA.

*The last expressions
of medieval
religious feeling*

The exacting talent of Donatello is
the key to the whole development of
the plastic arts in the Quattrocento
(15th century). He influenced not only
all the sculptors who followed him, but
also a number of painters, especially
Masaccio, the "father of the new painting." The latter, from his earliest
works like the Crucifixion on the right,
gave his characters, and especially the
Virgin, a sculptural volume that explains
why he has been considered a second
Giotto. But, going further, he tried to
convey a sense of space as well as
relief, and this made him the greatest
innovator of his day. He is close to
Donatello because his painting has the
"full and quiet authority of statuary"
and because the same deep and serious
feeling is at work in both of them. There
is an obvious connection between the
mute grief of the Virgin as shown here
and the striking starkness of Mary
Magdalene (left), Donatello's last work.
The sculptor, freed from the Gothic and
classical influence that had inspired
him at the outset of his career, was now
in full possession of a style that was
of his own creating. To express himself more freely he chose wood as his
material, easier to work with than stone.

DONATELLO (1386-1469):
MARY MAGDALENE - ABOUT 1460
BAPTISTERY, FLORENCE.

204

MASACCIO (1401-1428): CHRIST ON THE C
ABOUT 1420 - PINACOTECA, NAP

Biblical heroes
are henceforth represented
in the classical manner

The mysterious smile of Verrocchio's "David" (left) perhaps anticipates that of the Mona Lisa. It might be that the artist gave to the conqueror of Goliath the face of his young pupil Leonardo da Vinci. Be that as it may, he took his inspiration from another David, executed by Donatello twenty years before and which had been the first nude statue since ancient times. In contrast to his master, Verrocchio dressed his hero in a short tunic. This shows off the body and emphasizes its elegance. It is the beauty of the body that, according to the classical conception, constitutes the beauty of the whole work. But by its tense and sinuous grace it is a true product of the refined Florence of Lorenzo the Magnificent and not of Imperial Rome. Like his contemporaries, Verrocchio knew Roman statuary only in a fragmentary way, and Greek art only through books. In trying to imitate them he reinvented them.

"A warning to tyrants and a symbol of liberty" is the inscription on the base of this bronze "Judith and Holophernes." It originally stood in the Medici palace. When Piero the Unlucky left Florence to Savonarola in 1495, the people exhibited it on the Piazza della Signoria to let future tyrants know what punishment awaited them. This work, of which Donatello was so proud that he signed it, was once a fountain with water pouring out of the four corners of the cushion. Traces of gilding can still be seen. Donatello constructed it so that it can be seen to advantage from all sides.

VERROCCHIO (1435-1488): DAVID
ABOUT 1473 - PALAZZO BARGELLO, FLORENCE.

DONATELLO (1386-1469): JUDITH AND HOLOPHERNES
PIAZZA DELLA SIGNORIA, FLORENCE.

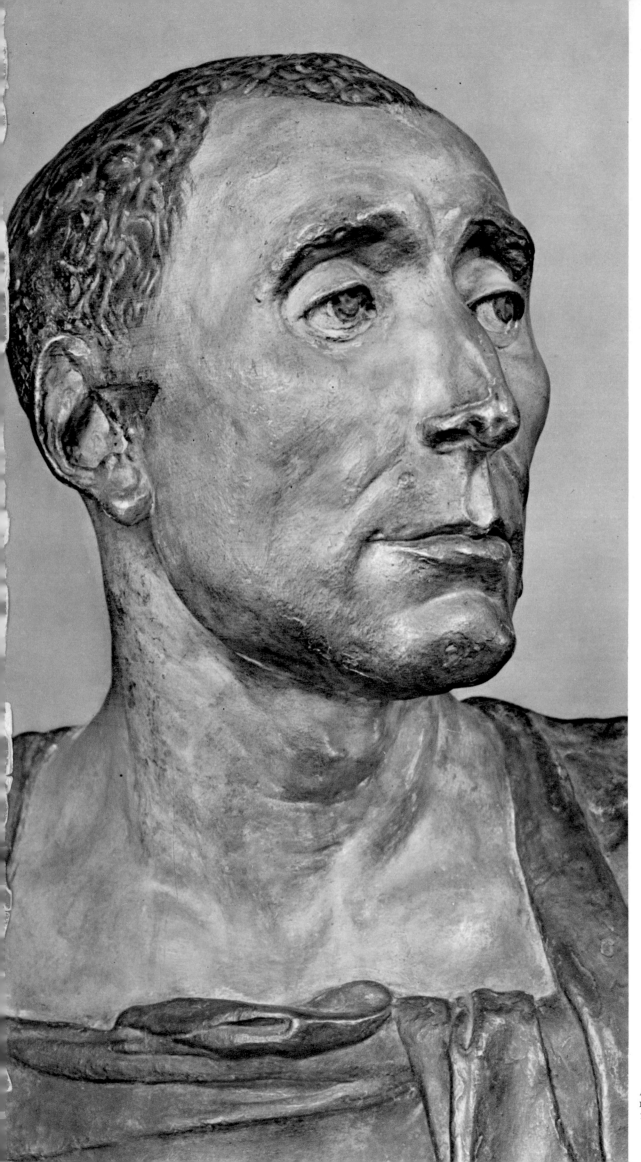

With the reawakening of individualism, the portrait appears...

Exceptionally lifelike, the bust (left) in polychrome terra cotta was long attributed to Donatello. This attribution has now been contested, but no one has contested the fact that it is a masterpiece. It reflects brilliantly the great Roman portrait tradition, itself born of Etruscan art. It probably represents Niccolo da Uzzano, the man who attempted to prevent the Medicis seizing power—and who nearly succeeded. A member of the merchant oligarchy who held the reins of command in the Florentine Republic during the last quarter of the 14th century and whose authority was imperilled by the Medicis, he became its most highly esteemed adviser. The intelligence shown in his face led him never to make a frontal attack on an adversary who had enlisted popular support. By skillful maneuvering he managed to check the progress of the Medicis, but after his death his counsels of moderation were forgotten. The conflict now came out into the open. For a short time it looked as though the oligarchy party had won, and Cosimo de Medici was exiled. Shortly after he returned in triumph and the Medicis, though they did not hold one official title, were the uncontested masters of Florence.

The thoughtful charm of the youth at right is in sharp contrast to the proud features of Niccolo da Uzzano. This difference reflects the complete transformation of Florence between the time of Cosimo de Medici and his grandson Lorenzo the Magnificent. The young man was painted by Filippino Lippi in one of those compositions so frequent at that period, in which, using religious subjects as pretexts, painters depicted contemporary figures. Filippino Lippi was the son of Fra Filippo Lippi, a monk more gifted in painting than in contemplation, who had been absolved from his vows by the intervention of Cosimo de Medici after he had run off with the pretty novice he had chosen as his model. Filippino was a pupil of Botticelli, himself a pupil of Filippo. He inherited his father's talent as a colorist, and acquired his master's virtuosity of line, but this he carried too far, and his work became mannered. His popularity shows how well he interpreted one of the traits of his day—a refinement bordering on the precious.

ATTRIBUTED TO DONATELLO:
BUST THOUGHT TO BE OF NICCOLO DA UZZA
1430 · PALAZZO BARGELLO, FLORENCE.

FILIPPINO LIPPI (1457-1504): PETER AND PAUL BEFORE THE PROCONSUL, DETAIL - 1485 - CARMELITE CHURCH, FLORENCE.

... and princesses
replace saints

Feminine beauty occupies an increasingly important place in "Quattrocento" painting as, under the
influence of Platonic ideas, a secular conception
of art develops and luxury in private life increases.
A little more than half a century and a change of
fashion separate the "Princess of Trebizond
Rescued by St. George," as shown by Pisanello
(right) from the elegant young woman painted by
Ghirlandajo (left). Both are clearly portraits.
Pisanello gave his princess that precision and
delicate relief that made him not only a painter
but also a peerless medallist. Ghirlandajo painted
a lady of Florentine high society with the quiet
charm and decorative sense so characteristic of
his talent. He put her with her companions or
ladies-in-waiting in a fresco in which he set the
scene of the "Birth of The Virgin" against the
familiar background of a palace.

GHIRLANDAJO (1449-1494):
PART OF THE FRESCO SHOWING THE BIRTH OF THE VIRGIN
1485-1490 - SANTA MARIA NOVELLA, FLORENCE.

PISANELLO (1377-1455): PART OF THE FRESCO SHOWING
SAINT GEORGE AND THE PRINCESS OF TREBIZOND
CHURCH OF SANTA ANASTASIA, VERONA.

PIERO DELLA FRANCESCA (1406-1492): THE VICTORY OF CONSTANTINE, DETAIL - 1452-1466 - CHURCH OF SAN FRANCESCO, AREZZO.

Painting combines perspective and space

PAOLO UCCELLO (1394-1475): BATTLE OF SAN ROMANO - ABOUT 1450 - UFFIZI, FLORENCE.

"Originator of one of the greatest styles known to the Western world," Piero della Francesca is one of two painters—the other is Paolo Uccello—who, after a period of relative oblivion, were rediscovered in modern times. They were chiefly preoccupied with perspective, which, for Uccello, became a true obsession. His battle scenes (above) gave him an opportunity to play with volumes and foreshortened views with such dazzling skill that experts have seen in him a forerunner of Cubism. The colors, boldly juxtaposed, reinforce an impression of unreality. On the other hand, Piero della Francesca became the master of perspective. In his fresco showing the "Victory of Constantine" (left), his horseman not only bursts through the wall, but asserts himself also by the nobility of his bearing and the quiet harmony of the colors bathing in a light that blends them with the forms. It emanates from a universe created by the painter.

213

Condottieri replace emperors

To immortalize the condottieri in the classical manner, Renaissance Italy once more gave an honored place to bronze equestrian statues. To Donatello and Verrocchio we owe two of the most magnificent ever made. The model for both of them was the Roman statue of Marcus Aurelius (page 69), but their genius led each of them to produce not a mere imitation, but one of their major original creations. They followed the Greek tradition in which the horse, noblest of all animals, deserved almost as much as man to be used as a subject for art. They thus devoted as much care to perfecting the mount as the rider. The earlier of the two, Donatello's "Gattamelata" (detail at left) is a majestic work in which the condottiere, reviewing his troops, restrains with one hand all the quivering power of his horse which he keeps at a walking pace. Verrocchio's "Colleone" has more movement: standing in his stirrups he seems at one with the caracolling steed he is riding. His intelligent and brutal face (right) is not that of one condottiere rather than another. The statue was begun several years after the death of Colleone, whom Verrocchio had probably never seen. It is the embodiment of all the condottieri, who thrived on the unceasing conflicts that set the Italian states against one another. Conflict, in all senses of the word, was their business. They administered it for their own gain, offered their services to the highest bidder and kept the combats within reasonable bounds. They killed just enough to keep up their reputation, but not so much as to reduce drastically their own numbers.

DONATELLO (1386-1466):
GATTAMELATA, DETAIL - 1453 - PADUA

VERROCCHIO (1453-1488): COLLEONE, DETAIL - 1488 - VENICE.

Gothic severity is still found in statues of the dead

The third great sculptor of the early "Quattrocento" was, after the Florentines Donatello and Ghiberti, the Sienese Jacopo della Quercia. He entered the famous competition for the doors of the baptistery, but his design, which has not been preserved, was rejected as it was not judged to be delicate enough. In effect, his style is characterized by a certain contempt for detail, the natural counterpart of a vigor and a feeling for grandeur which has caused it to be said that he was the "herald of Michelangelo." The tomb of Ilaria del Caretto was his first great work and assured him a very great reputation during his lifetime. On a sarcophagus decorated in the very latest style with "putti" freely borrowed from the classical tradition, lies the poignantly serene figure of a woman (left), Gothic in conception. Her head rests on cushions, her feet on a dog, the symbol of conjugal fidelity. Only the beauty of the figure saved it from destruction when the tomb was taken from the church by the people in revolt, on the death of the tyrant whose wife she was. Despite the strength of the Renaissance movement, the Gothic current prevailed for a long time in funerary sculpture. It survived with particular strength in Milan, kept alive by the many northern artists who had come to contribute their share to the work on the cathedral. Thus the Gothic current can also be seen in the tomb of Gaston de Foix (right), a nephew of Louis XII, who for a time was governor of Milan and who was killed at the battle of Ravenna. Yet this tomb was executed by the Milanese sculptor Bambaia more than a century after that of Caretto.

JOCOPO DELLA QUERCIA (1367-1438): TOMB OF ILARIA DEL CARETTO, DETAIL
1406 - ST. MARTIN'S CATHEDRAL, LUCCA.

BAMBAIA (1483-1548): TOMB OF GASTON DE FOIX - 1515 - CIVIC MUSEUM, MILAN.

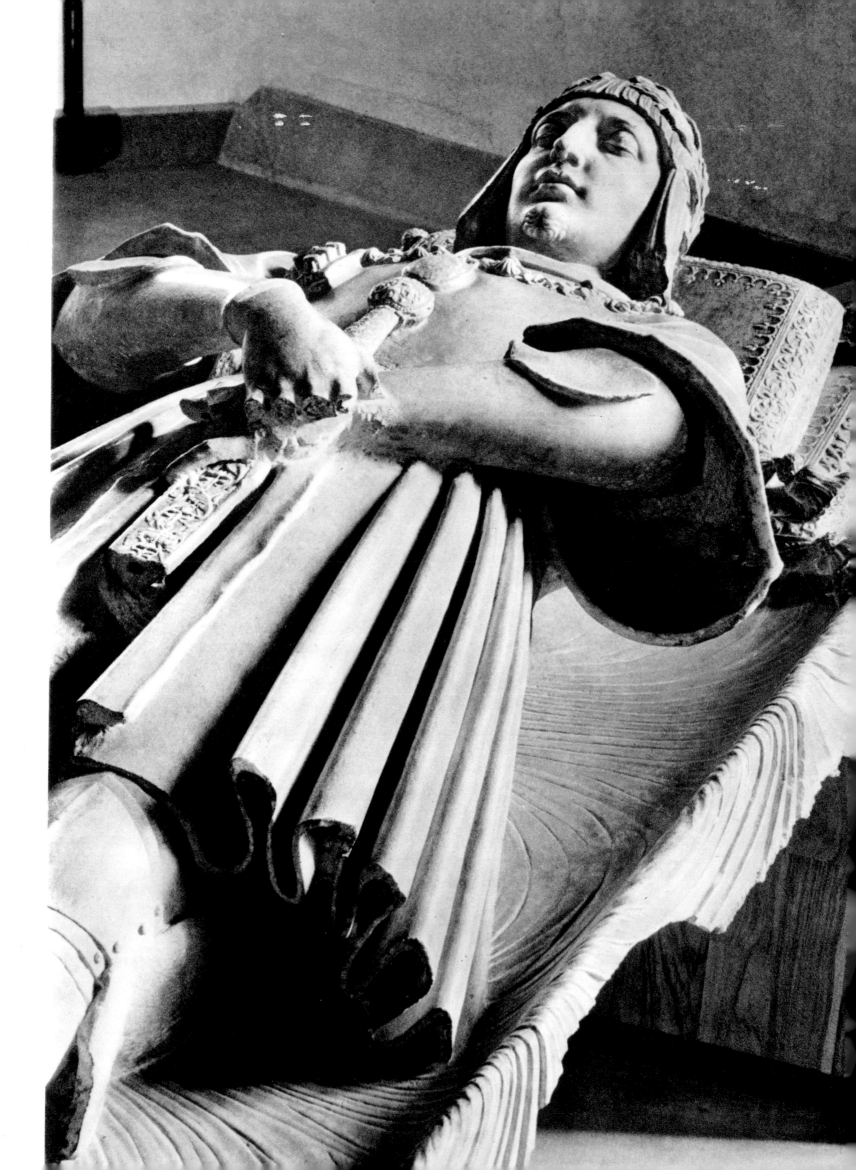

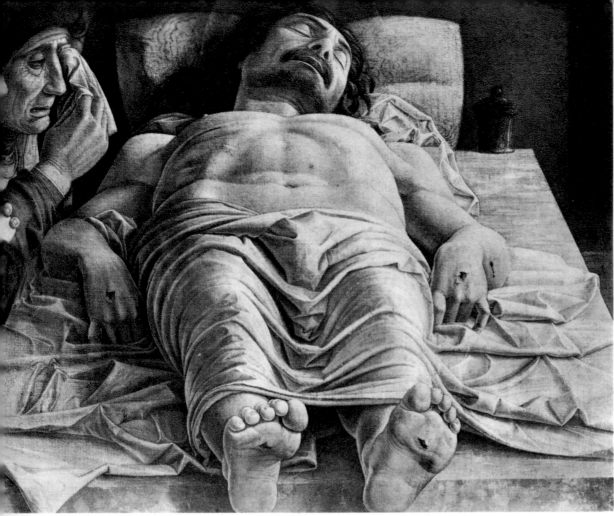

MANTEGNA (1431-1506): THE DEAD CHRIST - 1460 - BRERA MUSEUM, MILAN.

Foreshortened view, of a boldness without precedent in the history of painting, Mantegna's "Dead Christ" (above) produces an impression of singular intensity. It is very characteristic of the art of this painter, who incarnated the spirit of his times to the highest degree and was also passionately interested in perspective and the art of classical Antiquity. At first strongly influenced by Donatello, he gave his works such a peculiarly sculptural quality that they seem to be of bronze or stone. He played a most important part in the evolution of Italian painting, by acting as a link between the Florentine school from which, though a Paduan himself, he had learned much, and the Venetian school with which he was in contact through his marriage to the sister of Gentile and Giovanni Bellini. The latter was influenced by the art of Antonello da Messina who, in the South of Italy (then under the dominion of the princes of Aragon), had become acquainted with Flemish painting, a reflection of which he took back with him to Venice. In Giovanni Bellini's "Pietà" (right) there is a realism in the suffering that calls to mind Van der Weyden, while the feeling for space and the precision of the lines remind us of Mantegna. But its poignant emotion and its color are the special contributions of Giovanni Bellini himself, the master of the whole school of Venetian painting.

GIOVANNI BELLINI (1430-1516): PIETA, DETAIL - ABOUT 1470 - BRERA MUSEUM, MILAN.

Religious painting becomes more and more realistic...

FILIPPINO LIPPI (1457?-1504): VIRGIN APPEARING TO
ST. BERNARD, DETAIL - 1480 - LA BADIA, FLORENCE.

BALDOVINETTI (1427-1499):
VIRGIN, DETAIL - UFFIZI FLORENCE.

... and the Virgin assumes the appearance of the most beautiful women of the day...

FRA FILIPPO LIPPI (1406-1469): VIRGIN
AND CHILD, DETAIL - PITTI PALACE, FLORENCE.

CRIVELLI (ABOUT 1430 - ABOUT 1493): VIRGIN
AND CHILD, DETAIL - PINACOTECA, ANCONA.

BOTTICELLI (1444-1510): VIRGIN WITH POME-
GRANATE, DETAIL - 1470 - UFFIZI, FLORENCE.

COSIMO TURA (1430-1495): VIRGIN AND
CHILD, DETAIL - ACCADEMIA CARRARA, BERGAMO.

Favorite subject of all Italian painters ever since she first appeared in Byzantine art, the Virgin had been shown
to the "Trecento" (14th century) in the conventionalized pose laid down by the liturgy. Then the painters of the first
Sienese school began to give her an expression of melancholy grace, though her face remained almost impersonal.
With St. Francis of Assisi and the humanization of Christianity in the course of the "Quattrocento," painters tended
more and more to make the Virgin the symbol of the tender or sorrowful mother. They no longer tried to represent an
ideal being but wanted to give her the most beautiful face that real life offered—and that was often the face of the painter's
loved one. Each painter represented on these two pages has revealed his temperament through his interpretation of
the Virgin: whether she has, for example, the fine and intense profile of Filippino Lippi's Virgin; the melancholy and
somewhat mannered expression of Botticelli's; or the almost grimacing intensity of Tura's; the healthy peasant look
of Mantegna's, or lastly the serious face of Ghirlandajo's. If the painter sought beauty, religious feeling was far from
being excluded, and the realism was still relative.

ANDREA MANTEGNA (1431-1506): VIRGIN AND
CHILD, DETAIL - BRERA MUSEUM, MILAN.

DOMENICO GHIRLANDAJO (1449-1494): THE ADORATION OF THE
MAGI, DETAIL - 1488 - OSPEDALE DEGLI INNOCENTI, FLORENCE.

GIOVANNI BELLINI (1430?-1516): LITTLE ANGEL PLAYING A LUTE
DETAIL OF THE MADONNA DEI FRARI - 1488 - ECCLESIA DEI FRARI, VENICE.

ANDREA DELLA ROBBIA (1437-1528): BUST OF
A BOY-PALLAZZO BARGELLO, FLORENCE.

ANDREA DELLA ROBBIA (1437-1528):
MEDALLION - OSPEDALE DEGLI INNOCENTI, FLORENCE,

222

childhood are celebrated

GIOVANNI BELLINI (1330-1516): LITTLE ANGEL PLAYING A PIPE,
DETAIL OF THE MADONNA DEI FRARI - 1488 - ECCLESIA DEI FRARI, VENICE.

DESIDERIO DA SETTIGNANO (1428-1464):
BOY - PALAZZO BARGELLO, FLORENCE.

The child from birth to adolescence was frequently a subject of Alexandrine art. It was Alexandrine art that originated the "putti" which Renaissance artists had discovered on Roman sarcophagi. The theme of childhood was to become very dear to Renaissance sculptors. In this tradition one of the most important works is incontestably the "Singing Gallery" sculptured by Luca della Robbia (see detail in the center), which complemented Donatello's in the Cathedral of Florence. It shows groups of children singing, dancing and playing musical instruments, sculptured in very high relief with an intensity of life, expression and movement equalled only by Donatello. Subsequently Luca, helped by his father Agostino and his nephew Andrea, invented an economical substitute for sculpture in marble: the technique of terra cotta enamelled with white and blue, sometimes with green and yellow, to the exclusion of red, the secret of which died with them. The medallion (bottom left) is one example of this technique. But marble quarries abounded in Tuscany, and marble continued to be used for funerary sculptures and busts, among which child portraits in high relief or full relief made their appearance. They were carved by Andrea della Robbia (extreme left) and by Desiderio da Settignano (extreme right) with a grace bordering on affectation. The same subject was also taken up by painters, especially Giovanni Bellini, with his little angels in the "Madonna dei Frari" (top left.)

223

LUCA DELLA ROBBIA (1400-1481):
SINGING GALLERY, DETAIL - 1431-1438 - MUSEO DEL DUOMO, FLORENCE.

SIGNORELLI (1441-1523): PART OF A FRESCO · 1498 · MONASTERY OF MONTE OLIVETO MAGGIORE (NEAR ANCONA)

Realism of familiar everyday life is shown in one of the frescoes painted by Luca Signorelli for the Monastery of Monte Oliveto. It is part of a series of eight panels telling the story of the Olivetan Order of St. Benedict. The Blessed Bernardo Tolomei had, in 1313, chosen an austere and magnificent site which was admirably suitable for the reform he wanted to carry out in the Benedictine Order. In his fresco (above) Luca Signorelli, alluding to a certain laxity in the discipline that justified this reform, shows two monks breaking their fast by having a meal in an inn, waited on by two comely serving girls. Overlooking the desolate countryside of Ancona, the hill of Monte Oliveto stands some sixteen miles southeast of Siena. The house set up there was to become in the course of the years an immense red-brick monastery, where the same discipline is observed today (right).

224

VIEW OF THE MONASTERY OF MONTE OLIVETO MAGGIORE

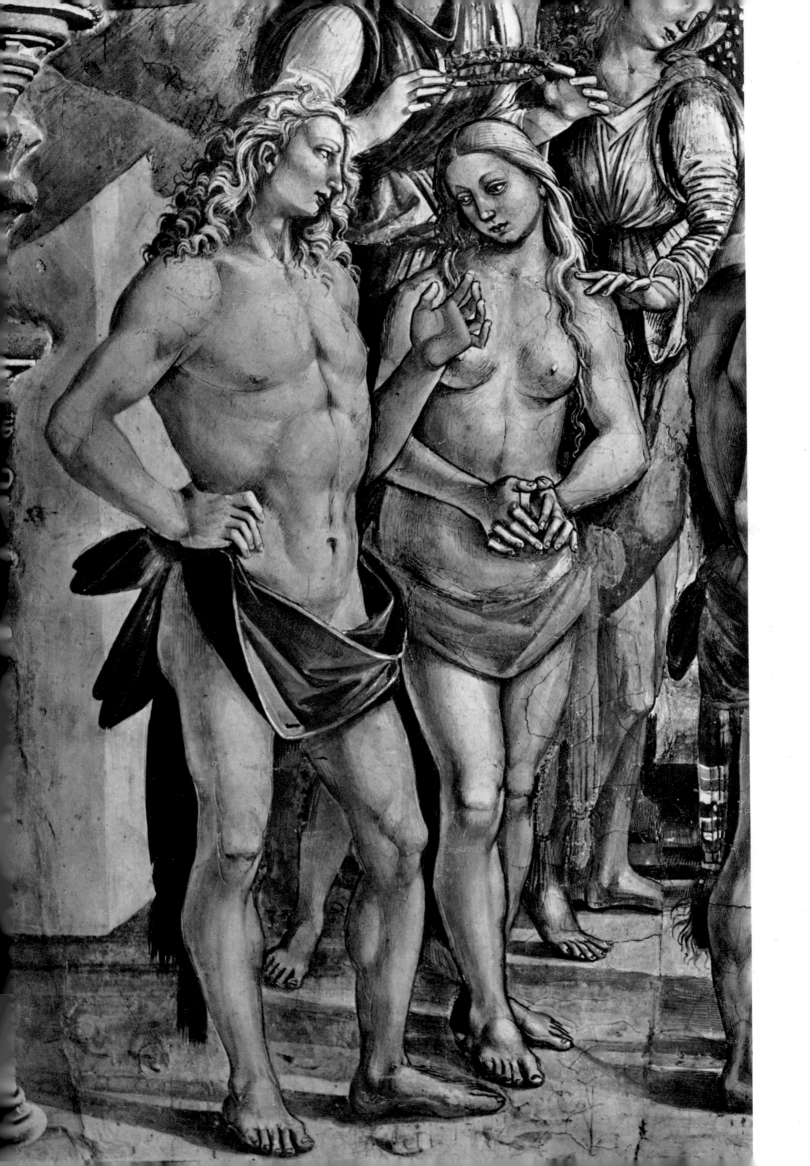

The nude figure becomes sensual...

The importance of the nude was so great to Signorelli that he considered it the essential object of his pictorial experiments. To the glory of the nude he dedicated his major work, executed at the age of fifty, for Orvieto Cathedral. The couple at left in the "Crowning of the Elect" are about to receive golden crowns from the hands of the angels. Here the human body is drawn with an anatomical precision that Signorelli learnt from Pollaiuolo, while to his master, Piero della Francesca, he owes his feeling for imposing and heavy stature. Signorelli, the last of the great Tuscan fresco-painters, was weaned on the Apocalypse of St. John and Dante's "Divine Comedy." Thus his figures, in the dramatic lighting of this end-of-the-world atmosphere, have a violent and solemn character that already heralds Michelangelo.

The first great Venetian sculptor of the Renaissance, Antonio Rizzi, was directly influenced in the statue of Eve at right, by a piece of Greek sculpture: the "Chaste Venus," from which he copied the pose and beauty of the body. This influence can be explained by the relations of Venice with the eastern Mediterranean. Certain Venetians would no doubt have discovered in the course of their business trips Hellenic works of which the rest of Italy as yet knew nothing. Rizzi, goldsmith and sculptor, is also famous for his work as an architect. He worked in the Charterhouse at Pavia, then devoted himself to Venice. There he made the Foscari Arch, flanked by statues of Adam and Eve, he designed the Giants' Stairway in the Doges' Palace, and worked at the Scuola di San Marco (see page 242).

GNORELLI (1441-1523): PART OF
HE FRESCO SHOWING THE CROWNING OF THE
LECT - 1500 - ORVIETO CATHEDRAL.

ANTONIO RIZZI : EVE (ON THE FOSCARI ARCH)
SECOND HALF OF THE 15TH CENTURY
COURTYARD OF THE DOGES' PALACE, VENICE.

... and mannerism invades art

The strange poetry and subtle grace peculiar to Botticelli reach their peak in the group of the Three Graces in his "Allegory of Spring" (right). The true meaning of this most famous of all works has never been fully discovered. The painter, enamored of Latin literature like all men of his time, may have been inspired by two lines in Lucretius and a verse by Horace. It is likely that he wanted to evoke an event in the reign of Lorenzo the Magnificent. In any case, he has caught a little of the spirit that animated Lorenzo's circle of friends, occupied with genteel festivities and the cult of beauty in all its forms. In contrast to other artists of his day, Botticelli's main concern was not for perspective. His art is distinguished by its graphic qualities and by an unrivalled handling of the arabesque. In him, the old international Gothic current, born with the first school of Siena, is given new life in an unexpected way. It spread to sculpture with Agostino di Duccio, who adorned with exquisitely delicate secular reliefs (left) the "temple" of the Malatesta family at Rimini. This was a Gothic church entirely transformed by Alberti, the great architectural theoretician who changed its façade into the form of a classical arch. It was to be the mausoleum of the beautiful Isotta degli Atti, the mistress of one of the lords of Rimini.

AGOSTINO DI DUCCIO (1418-1481): RELIEF
DECORATING THE CHAPEL OF ISOTTA
ABOUT 1450 - TEMPIO MALATESTIANO, RIMIN

BOTTICELLI (1444-151C
ALLEGORY OF SPRING, DETA
ABOUT 1487 - UFFIZI, FLORENC

The ornamental reigns supreme...

Last bastion of Orientalism, the work of the painter Carlo Crivelli has a place apart in Italian painting. A Venetian by birth, Crivelli always proclaimed his origins by signing himself "Venetus," although he left Venice after a murder in which he had been implicated. After that, he lived a solitary life in the Marches. The sumptuous gold-embroidered brocades worn by all his Virgins, and the luxuriant garlands of flowers and fruits with which he surrounds them are direct borrowings from the repertory already exploited by Byzantium and are treated as though engraved on metal. The Virgin, virtually the exclusive subject of his work, seems indifferent to her background of rich still lifes that monopolizes the whole of Crivelli's art (left). Their freedom and fancifulness compensate for any weakness in composition. Although only some ten works are assigned to him, he remains, according to Bernard Berenson, "one of the most original artists of all times and of all countries."

Dramatic intensity of expression, which is not attenuated by a certain mannerism in the poses, characterizes the work of Cosimo Tura. He founded the School of Ferrara, and his pupil and successor was the painter Francesco della Cossa, who collaborated on most of his frescoes. He was also official painter to the court of the Dukes of Este as well as the creator of costumes, festal decorations and "objets d'art." It was this last feature of his craft that very probably gave him a taste for minute detail, which often comes near to true surrealism. He could adorn the subjects of his frescoes and pictures with a symbolism understandable in his day but meaningless today to all but the initiated. The right-hand panel of an organ door (right) shows the Virgin of the Annunciation. In the middle distance a little squirrel scampering across a transversal bar is the enigmatic and distracting element in the picture.

CRIVELLI (ABOUT 1430-ABOUT 1493): MADONNA
BRERA MUSEUM, MILAN.

COSIMO TURA (1430-1495): ANNUNCIATION
DETAIL - CATHEDRAL MUSEUM, FERRARA

230

... *expressed through the most varied techniques*...

The decorated stone floor of Siena Cathedral is an extraordinary example of an art peculiar to Italy. Following in the traditions of the Cosmati family —marquetry workers who adorned the churches of medieval Rome—forty artists shared in the creation of fifty-six pictures inlaid in stone, made up of engraved flagstone and mosaics of polychrome marble, which are like a series of sumptuous carpets. Pietro del Minella created the panel below, showing the death of Absalom. Absalom, the rebel son, was defeated by his father David and fled, but was stopped in his tracks when his hair became caught up in the branches of a tree. Joab then came on the scene and finished him off with three javelins. The art of stone mosaic led to the development of the curious Florentine tables of incrusted marble in fashion during the 18th century.

The art of the illuminated manuscript owed its pre-eminence to the great Italian patrons, and in particular to the Medici family in Florence. Cosimo, the first of the Medicis, commissioned many translations of Greek and Latin texts. He sent his agents to scour Europe for ancient manuscripts. Well-paid and highly honored "servitori" copied the original works for his library. Founded in 1444, this library, enriched by all the Medicis, soon boasted two thousand volumes and was the first library in Europe to be open to the public. In 1523 Michelangelo built the house in which the collection is still kept today (see page 293). "The Birth of Eve" (right) is the work of Belbello di Pavia, the greatest miniaturist of the 15th century. The subject is treated according to traditional iconography, and is embellished with elements of fauna and flora.

SIENA - DEATH OF ABSALOM, ORNAMENTAL PAVING ON THE FLOOR OF THE CATHEDRAL - 1447.

BELBELLO DI PAVIA: THE BIRTH OF EVE - ILLUMINATED MANUSCRIPT - BIBLIOTECA LORENZIANA, FLORENCE.

... and all these transformations are owed to the great Florentine patrons

The golden age of Florence coincided with the rule of the first Medicis, fabulously rich bankers and patrons of art unequalled in their generosity. In their own palace a fresco by Benozzo Gozzoli shows them in all their splendor. The fresco supposedly represents the journey of the Magi, but recalls, against a background of Tuscan countryside, the sumptuous processions that were held in Florence in 1439 when the Emperor Michael Paleologus, last but one of the Byzantine emperors, arrived to take part in the council of the Roman and Greek churches. Paleologus and the Patriarch of Constantinople are shown as two of the Magi. The third is the young Lorenzo de Medici, shown on the right at the head of a long procession and dressed in the same clothes that he had worn for a tournament a short time before Benozzo Gozzoli painted him. Behind him, also on a white horse, we can see his grandfather Cosimo, the "father of his country." Seen full face, on another white horse, is Giuliano, brother of Lorenzo. Giuliano was murdered in Florence Cathedral in 1478 at the moment of the Elevation of the Host, by hired killers in the pay of conspirators acting at the instigation of Pope Sixtus IV. The rest of the procession is made up of a throng of Florentine personalities, among whom can be seen a few Greeks, recognizable by their beards and headdresses. They probably represent the men of letters who contributed to the dissemination of ancient philosophy.

BENOZZO GOZZOLI : JOURNEY OF THE MAGI, DETAIL - 1459 - PALAZZO MEDICI-RICCARDI, FLORENCE.

234

Meanwhile, Venice retains something of her eastern pomp...

VENICE - REGATTA ON THE GRAND CANAL.

"The finest street in the world with the finest houses," wrote Philippe de Commynes in the 15th century of the Grand Canal in Venice. Even today one could not disagree, for it has remained almost unchanged. The old wooden bridge that spanned it from the Rialto, as painted by Carpaccio (right), may have been replaced at the end of the 16th century by a stone bridge, but a great many of the palaces along its banks are the same and have lost only their old conical chimneys. The teeming crowds that throng there on feast days have not changed. When the great annual regatta takes place, if you half close your eyes you will see only the dazzling play of colors and forget for a moment the modern crowds and the changed shape of the gondolas—they are longer than they were in Carpaccio's day. The scene painted by Carpaccio shows a man possessed by evil spirits cured by a fragment of the Cross.

236

CARPACCIO (1455-1526): THE MIRACLE OF THE FRAGMENT OF THE CROSS · ABOUT 1495 · ACCADEMIA, VENICE ➤

*... stamps the
Gothic style
with her own personality.*

Swansong of Gothic art in Venice, which was a flourishing branch of the flamboyant style, the "Ca' d'Oro" (right), framed by the columns of the "Pescheria" (fishmarket) on the other side of the Grand Canal—was built between 1420 and 1440. At that time Renaissance architecture had already taken root in Florence, and Cosimo de Medici had approved Michelozzo's plans for the construction of a new palace. This was to be a large, austere building, with virtually no ornamentation, the style of which was to impose itself on all other Florentine palaces. But Venice remained attached to the Gothic style of Northern origin, to which the city had given an Eastern look by its choice of motifs and colors. Venice had also adapted this style to the traditional Veneto-Byzantine palace, with its portico and loggia (left). In addition to its ornamental lace-patterned marble, the "Ca' d'Oro" originally had a polychrome decoration heightened with gold, whence its name.

VENICE - CA' D'ORO - 1440.

VENICE - VIEW OF THE CA' D'
FROM THE FISHMARKET.

... and then leaves her mark on Renaissance art

Colorful, gay and sumptuous, Renaissance architecture finally imposed itself on Venice in the second half of the 15th century. It did not make its appearance in its original Florentine version, with its almost austere simplicity, but in a Lombardic variant, more intricate and more in keeping with the taste of the Venetian Republic for decorative effects. Nonetheless, the new style lost no time in developing in the Venetian clime. It did not culminate as it did in Lombardy in the excessive ornamentation of the Certosa di Pavia—the monument that most impressed the soldiers of Louis XII when they invaded Italy, and which determined to a great extent the French Renaissance ; instead it acquired an airy elegance. The Palazzo Dario (left) is the most perfect example of this style in private building. It was built in Venice for the city's representative at Constantinople by the architect Pietro Lombardo, whose name clearly indicates his origins.

Courtesans of Venice were long one of the city's main attractions. The remarks made about them in Michel de Montaigne's "Travel Journal"—kept by his secretary-companion—have a striking relevance to the cruel picture that Carpaccio painted of two of them (right). "He did not find there that famous beauty that people attribute to the ladies of Venice, although he saw the noblest of them that ply their trade. But he deemed this more amazing than anything else, that he saw such a great number of them, some one hundred and fifty or thereabouts, spending so much money on furniture and clothing as if they were princesses, while having no other money to keep themselves than that earned by the exercising of their trade." A splendid storyteller, Carpaccio carried narrative painting to new heights. Before him, Gentile Bellini had been the chief exponent of this style. Carpaccio's works are not only valuable documents: they also gain an exceptional charm from their skillful composition, their golden tonalities and their fascinating details.

Trompe l'oeil perspectives cover the lower part of the façade of the Scuola di San Marco (following double page), giving it an unusually charming effect. The Scuola di San Marco was not in fact a school, as its name suggests, but an association of leading Venetian citizens whose aims were both religious and humanitarian. With great wealth at their disposal, these "schools" commissioned the greatest artists of their day to build and decorate the houses where they met, which generally contained chapels and sometimes, as here, a hospital. Pietro Lombardo and his sons executed the greater part of the façade, but after a series of quarrels it was completed by Pietro Coducci, who added a crest of arched frontals, modelled on that of St. Mark's Basilica.

PIETRO LOMBARDO (1435-1515): PALAZZO DARIO - VENICE.

CARPACCIO (1445-1526): THE COURTESANS · ABOUT 1500 · CORRER MUSEUM, VENICE.

*Each city interprets
classical architecture
in its own way...*

Typically Venetian in its decorated façade of polychrome marble, the little **Church of Santa Maria dei Miracoli** (left) is a kind of religious version of the Dario Palace (see page 240). Its elegance is as elaborate, yet more noble, and its architectonic conception is more complex. On it we can see, carved in dark-colored marble, the pilasters, arches and porticoes that form the basis of every Renaissance building. The inside, like the outside, is finely carved or covered all over with marble slabs of varied colors. It is exquisite in its refinement. The love of luxury that the Venetians inherited from the East materialized in this architectural jewel, but with more reserve than previously.

Essentially Florentine, Brunelleschi's Pazzi Chapel (right) is a creation of absolute originality although it was composed of elements borrowed from Antiquity. The architect tried to achieve perfection in the harmony of the proportions of all parts of the building. We can measure his success from the feeling of unity and serenity given by the whole. His chief innovation was the portico with its Corinthian columns, which is not so heavy as those of Antiquity and which is boldly broken up by a very pure arch. The entablature and the attic it supports bring to mind Greek rather than Roman art. This shows to what extent it was an innovation, since there were no Hellenic monuments in the Renaissance. A more general feature is that the building is dominated by a preoccupation with perspective and the balance of volumes.

PIETRO LOMBARDO (1435-1515):
CHURCH OF SANTA MARIA
DEI MIRACOLI - 1481 - VENICE.

BRUNELLESCHI (1377-1446): PAZZI CHAPEL - 1430 - SANTA CROCE, FLORENCE.

... and the classical colonnade is once more given a place of honor

CRONACA (DIED 1508): COURTYARD OF THE PALAZZO STROZZI - 1507 - FLORENCE.

Rare elegance and great distinction of the inner courtyard of the Palazzo Strozzi (above), with its fine Corinthian columns supporting semicircular arches, an enclosed story and an upper loggia, are emphasized by the fine dimensions of this cortile in the greatest of Florentine palaces, begun by Benedetto da Maiano and finished by Cronaca. Faithful to their master, Brunelleschi, they worked in the classical style he had reintroduced when building the Ospedale degli Innocenti in 1419. By its clarity and brilliant harmony, the courtyard of the Strozzi Palace counterbalances the austerity of the façade, made from heavy stone bossages and surmounted by a cornice of the kind used since the Quattrocento.

The seed of all sixteenth-century architecture lies in Bramante's "Tempietto," a building as important in the history of architecture as was the Pazzi Chapel (page 245), and as was later to be the Church of La Sapienza. In the mind of its creator, the "Tempietto," as its name implies, was the reconstitution of an ancient temple. In reality, it was a new interpretation of a classical idea. Its originality lies in the treatment of volume, in the striking coherence of the whole for which it is impossible to envisage the slightest modification, and in the play of light and shade beneath the colonnade. By making it round in shape, Bramante was following the ancient theory of forms and numbers, according to which the circle is a privileged form.

BRAMANTE (1444-1514): TEMPIETTO - 1502 - ROME, SAN PIETRO IN MONTORIO.

Pomp prevails over austerity

PINTURICCHIO (1454-1510): POPE ALEXANDER VI BORGIA, PART OF A FRESCO - ABOUT 1495 - VATICAN.

Two adversaries face to face: Savonarola's struggle with the pope marked the end of the "Quattrocento", the decline of Florence and the rise of Rome. On the right we can see Savonarola the fanatical monk, as painted by Fra Bartolommeo, an artist who had been inspired to enter a monastery by Savonarola's preaching, and who excelled himself in this portrait of his master. Above, we have Pope Alexander VI, a Borgia, whose portrait can be seen in one of the frescoes that decorated his private apartments in the Vatican. The frescoes were the work of Pinturicchio, one of the painters whom his predecessor Sixtus IV had brought to Rome to work on the Sistine Chapel. Savonarola was master of Florence for four years after the banishment of Piero de Medici, known as Piero the Unlucky. He proclaimed Christ king, imposed an ascetic régime on the city, and with a mystic ardor set himself up against everything that up till then had contributed to the glory of the city: "the poetry that has brought down the wrath of God upon us," secular paintings, the love of beauty, and luxury. Then in his virtuous zeal he went so far as to denounce the morals of the supreme pontiff himself. On his election, the pope had chosen the name of Alexander in memory of the great conqueror. He had also with one deft stroke of his pen across the map of the world divided between Spain and Portugal all the newly discovered territories and those as yet undiscovered. Not a man to sit back and let himself be attacked, he excommunicated Savonarola; the Florentines, weary of austerity, abandoned him, and he was condemned to death and perished at the stake.

FRA BARTOLOMMEO (1475-1517): SAVONAROLA - ST. MARK'S MUSEUM, FLORENCE.

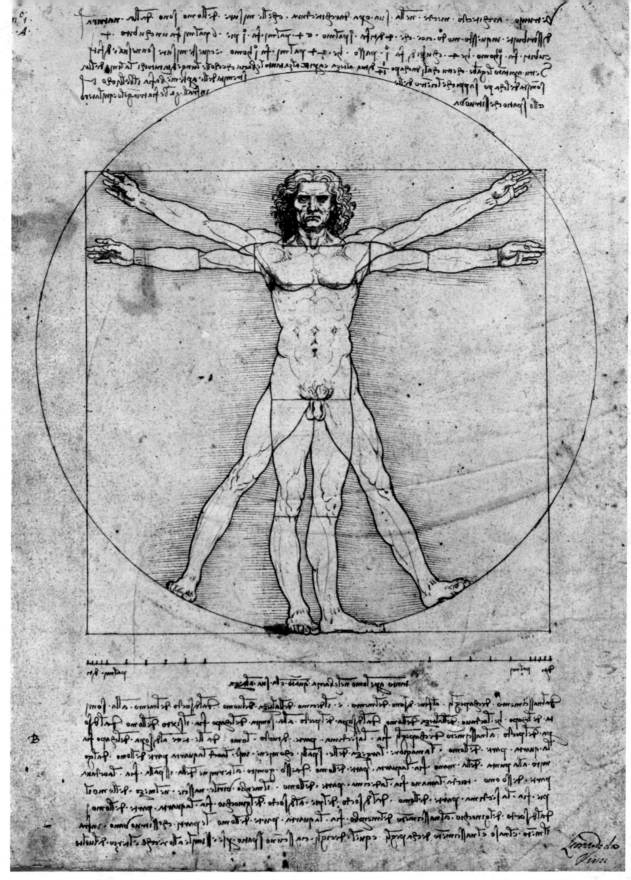

LEONARDO DA VINCI (1452-1519): THE PROPORTIONS OF THE HUMAN BODY, AFTER VITRUVIUS - 1492 - ACCADEMIA, VENICE.

The apogee of humanism

The universal genius of Leonardo da Vinci dominates all Renaissance art and expresses its quintessence. This mysterious man—scientist, inventor, philosopher, musician, sculptor, painter—placed art above science and painting above all the other arts. "Painting," he wrote, "is poetry, music, architecture and philosophy." Less than a dozen of his paintings have survived, only three of which, together with his greatly deteriorated fresco of "The Last Supper," are in Italy. Of these, the "Adoration of the Magi" (left), though unfinished, is the most revealing because of the importance of its composition. In it Leonardo departed from the traditional placing of the figures, and grouped them in a circle at the feet of Jesus with a striking vigor which for him certainly had a symbolic value. The strange scenery with its rocks, trees and ruins plays a primordial part. Instead of serving simply as a background, it links the varied elements of the painting and contributes to their fusion. This fusion is also obtained by the "sfumato," or stumped drawing of the outlines, which is one of Leonardo's great innovations. It is a subtle use of "chiaroscuro" which renders the vibration of light and creates an unexpected poetry. For Leonardo, painting was a "thing of the mind," the prolongation of his persistent search for the secrets of knowledge and beauty. This drawing (above right) is one of the countless proofs of this search. It is a study, after the theoretician Vitruvius, of the ideal proportions of the human body.

251

LEONARDO DA VINCI (1452-1519): ADORATION OF THE MAGI - 1481 - UFFIZI, FLORENCE.

Chiaroscuro
and naturalism
appear in painting

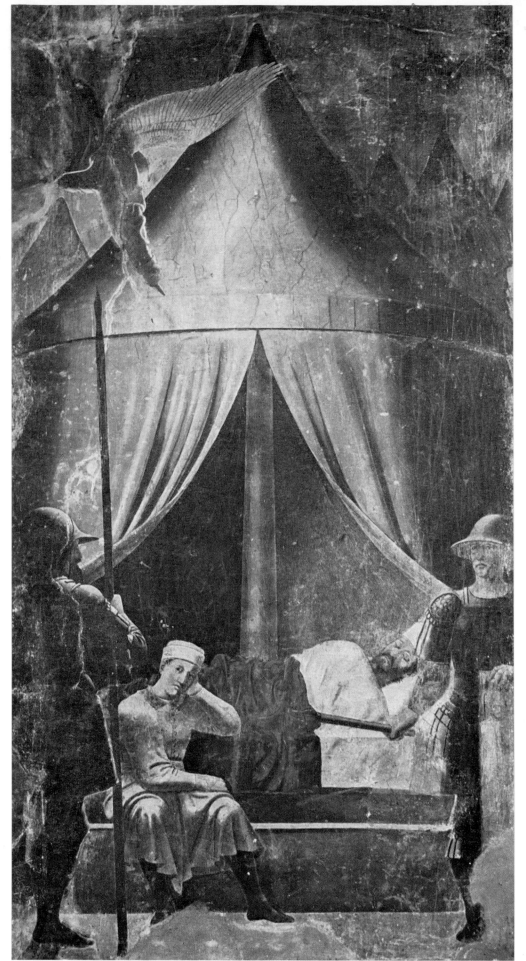

Linking the painters of Italy and Flanders, Antonello da Messina, when he was in Sicily and Naples, learned the technique by which Flemish artists gave their paintings a new transparency of colors and an impression of relief by skillful interplay of light and shade. But he was also sensitive to the art and ideas of Piero della Francesca, an influence that can be seen in the quiet authority and the nobility of his gestures. An excellent portrait painter, he gave the best of his talent in his spiritualized portrait of the "Virgin of the Annunciation" (left) whose veil casts a light shadow over her face and whose raised hand is a marvel of perspective and modelling.

First nocturnal effect in Italian painting, Piero della Francesca's "Dream of Constantine" (right) is part of the cycle "The Story of the Cross" in the Church of St. Francis at Arezzo. The Emperor Constantine, on the eve of his battle with Maxentius, whose army was larger than his own, fell into an uneasy sleep. An angel appeared to him and pointed to a cross of light with the inscription "In signo hoc confide et vinces" (Trust in this sign and you will conquer). This painting is very simple in conception and curiously impersonal. Its suggestive power does not come from the expressions of the impassive figures: it comes only from the painting itself—from its serene colors, its light, distributed with supreme artistry, and from the purity of its form.

PIERO DELLA FRANCESCA (1406-1492): THE DREAM OF CONSTANTINE, FRESCO - ABOUT 1455 CHURCH OF ST. FRANCIS, AREZZO.

The harmonious interplay of colors, which from the very first was the dominant feature of Venetian painting, found an eminently inspired master in Giovanni Bellini, under whom Giorgione and Titian were to study. All his gifts are combined with particular success in this "Allegory of Purgatory" (following double page), situated against some of the most beautiful realistic scenery possible, and in which we do not know what we should admire most: the imagination, the sense of composition, the golden light or the lyricism that Venice inspired in all its artists. It represents a stage in the pilgrimage of souls. Having been purified in Purgatory, they have assumed the shape of innocent children, and stop in the Garden of Paradise, paved with marble, where the Virgin (left), helped by St. Catherine of Siena and St. Catherine of Alexandria, will decide their fate while a child gathers the fruits of the tree of life. In the middle distance flows the river Lethe, on whose banks an ass, a sheep and a goat symbolize patience, humility and abstinence. This mingling of a religious theme with such mythological elements as Lethe renders the feeling of an age that hoped to reconcile Platonic philosophy with the teaching of the Church.

ANTONELLO DA MESSINA (1430-1479): MADONNA OF THE ANNUNCIATION - PALERMO MUSEUM.

GIOVANNI BELLINI (1430-1516): ALLEGORY - BRERA MUSEUM, MILAN.

CHAPTER VI

THE RENAISSANCE AND THE COUNTER-REFORMATION

(16th century - the "Cinquecento")

The first act of the Renaissance was staged in Florence, or rather the first two acts—those of Cosimo and Lorenzo, which set the scene and developed the action. The last act was performed in Rome. The action quickened and the characters, fewer in number, were to lead the whole movement of the previous century to its climax, and, giving it a triumphal ending, to exhaust it almost at once.

ROME IS ONCE MORE THE HOME OF ART. In 1509, in the Vatican, separated by some hundred feet of rooms and corridors, Michelangelo and Raphael were at work. The former painted alone, perched on top of rickety scaffolding in the Sistine Chapel, the latter surrounded by assistants in the neighboring chambers. On the outside, the building was one huge constructor's yard: the whole of its architecture was being transformed in accordance with plans drawn up by Bramante.

In October, 1512, Michelangelo finished his work. It was a gigantic achievement, unequaled in the history of art. He had devoted four years of his life to it: four years of frenzy and exasperation imposed on him by Pope Julius II.

The sovereign pontiff had summoned him to Rome to build a mausoleum to be set up under the dome of the new basilica of St. Peter's. Michelangelo had conceived a project for a colossal memorial of three stories adorned with forty statues, the most important of which would be larger than lifesize. He had already started work on the first statues when the pope, changing his mind, obliged him to leave this task, that suited him better than any other, in order to paint the ceiling of the Sistine Chapel. So it was with an extremely bad grace that the artist submitted to his will.

In 1513 Julius II died and his heirs decided the tomb should be built after all, but only half the size originally planned.

It was then changed and reduced in size four more times. It was, indeed, a true symbol of the life of Michelangelo, that perpetually unsatisfied genius.

Finally, at the end of this harrowing nightmare in which the tomb became smaller the nearer it reached completion, a few followers of Michelangelo built an undistinguished memorial around three of the statues executed by their master: two statues of women, and one of Moses. But the figure of this old man, larger than life and quivering with repressed energy, personifies divine power in all its glory. Never has a more impressive piece of sculpture been created.

Michelangelo and Raphael were not destined to get on with each other. Michelangelo, who was constantly struggling against the difficulties that his own nature created for him, said of himself: "I live as a happy man with an unhappy destiny. Let him who does not know what it is to live by anguish and by death join me in the fire that consumes me." Raphael knew only success and happiness: "He had to fight neither against men nor against his own heart," wrote Taine. "He was not obliged, like so many other painters, to give birth to his works by suffering, he produced them as a fine tree produces fruit. The sap was abundant and the cultivation perfect."

In their day, these two artists, so different from one another, enjoyed equal favor. Nowadays we no longer look at them in the same way.

Even those who are most irritated by Michelangelo's excesses recognize in him one of those immeasurable geniuses that humanity produces from time to time and who have the "souls of fallen gods." They readily admit that certain of his works, particularly those executed toward the end of his life or those that have remained unfinished, have an overwhelming grandeur.

Raphael's case is more complex. In his lifetime and up to the middle of the 19th century, he was infinitely praised: to Dostoievsky he was the greatest of all painters. Then certain writers began to treat him with merciless severity, considering him the father of the very worst academicism, and Jean-Paul Sartre, one of the latest, has spoken of his work as "suicide through facility."

The majority of modern critics, weighing his qualities against his defects, try to show that the former outweigh the latter, but André Malraux gave voice to a very widespread doubt when he remarked inconclusively that while the lessons of Giotto are more alive than ever, those of Raphael no longer are. And as for Raphael himself..! A hundred years ago Taine was already saying: "This painting is of another age; to understand it, the modern mind must be specially conditioned." In the light of present-day concepts of art, this must surely pass for a very harsh condemnation.

It was on the recommendation of his uncle, Bramante, with whom Michelangelo was on the worst of terms, that the young Raphael received from the pope the commission for his first fresco, in the chamber of the Vatican that was later to be called the Camera della Signatura. The fresco filled Julius II with such enthusiasm that he ordered the destruction of the works of Andrea Castagno, Piero della Francesca and others, which adorned the neighboring chambers, and entrusted Raphael with the redecoration of the whole.

At that time Michelangelo, hanging for a year from the ceiling of the Sistine Chapel, was creating those very statues that Julius II had not given him the time to carve in marble for his tomb. While painting them against the background of a vigorous, make-believe architecture, which was more in harmony with their dimensions than with those of the chapel below, he must sometimes have cast an ironical eye at the frescoes beneath him, which the extraordinary sculptural world of the ceiling would inexorably overwhelm.

These frescoes were those that Sixtus IV, the founder of the chapel, had ordered to be painted on its walls thirty years earlier by the best artists from Tuscany and Umbria, including Botticelli, Ghirlandajo and Perugino, Raphael's teacher.

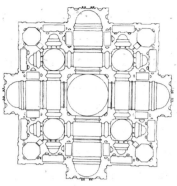

BRAMANTE'S
PLAN FOR ST. PETER'S BASILICA

The calm and spacious composition representing Christ giving the keys to St. Peter, painted by Perugino, was faithfully followed by his pupil in his "Marriage of the Virgin." Then Raphael went to Florence, where he painted madonnas of a wonderful serenity in which the practised eye can discern the influence of Leonardo da Vinci. In a few years Michelangelo was to detect his own unmistakeable influence in Raphael's fresco "The Town on Fire."

Raphael was highly receptive, a quality that made him an incomparable portrait painter. Effacing himself, he gave first place to the personality of his model and used all his talents to portray it faithfully. He was perfectly "conditioned" by the ideas of his day. He shared the humanist belief in the reconciliation of the Christian faith with classical doctrines, and illustrated this belief in his work. "As long as the world of Greece and Rome remains for us not only history but legend—the Promised Land or Paradise Lost—we shall continue," affirmed Berenson, "to see it through his eyes: a world where the song of the soul lives forever."

But Raphael was also the greatest known master of the science of representing space and of the art of composition. He showed his gift not only in his sober frescoes in the Camere, but also in those of a lighter style that he executed for the Villa Farnese and the Logge of the Vatican. These latter are surrounded by decorations in paint and stucco, a style employed by Raphael's assistant Giulio Romano in the Palazzo del Te at Mantua, and later, beyond the Alps, by Primaticcio to adorn the walls of the Château de Fontainebleau, whence it was destined to spread to the rest of France.

MICHELANGELO, THE TITAN. "Madame Bovary c'est moi," Flaubert replied to those who asked him for the key to his famous novel. Michelangelo would no doubt have given the same reply about all his figures: the Adam and Eve and the prophets and sybils in the Sistine Chapel, and the statues on the tombs of the Medici family. Even those that were supposed to represent Lorenzo and Giuliano de' Medici—"The Thinker" and "The Warrior." To those who reproached him with not having achieved good likenesses, he replied with arrogant indifference: "Who will know five hundred years from now?"

RAPHAEL'S
PLAN FOR ST. PETER'S BASILICA

Insofar as Michelangelo's work reflects his infinitely strong and tragic personality, it stands apart from its century. But it was indeed the Renaissance that gave him the form through which his art found expression: the human body. The nude body that Greece had placed at the center of art, and which Michelangelo endowed with the power to express: life and death, hope and despair.

He was also a man of his age through his work as an architect, which he began only in the second half of his long life. Nothing could be more Roman than the Corinthian pilasters and broad entablatures of the two identical palaces that he built on opposite sides of Rome's small but splendid Piazza del Campidoglio. Between them, the statue of Marcus Aurelius was finally given the setting it had lacked for more than a thousand years (see the plan on page 263).

Michelangelo died in 1564 in his eighty-ninth year. With him died the last glow of the Renaissance, but the mark of his genius has remained forever alive in the mind of man.

COUNTER-REFORMATION AND MANNERISM. A new trend manifested itself which was to characterize the second half of the "Cinquecento." It led artists to equal or surpass their more famous predecessors by adopting their methods and their "manner." Thus mannerism is to a certain extent the continuation of the Renaissance through its superficial manifestations.

For, under the pressure of events, the spirit changed. It is true that during the "Quattrocento" Italy had been divided up into states which were hostile to one another. But from time to time the complex game of coalitions made allies of adversaries, and Italian culture knew no frontiers. In the last decade of the century the wars with France began. In 1520—the year of Raphael's death—Charles V, king of Spain and Austria, claimed the kingdom of the Two Sicilies. Italy became a battlefield, and it was at Pavia that Francis I was taken prisoner by the Spaniards in 1525. Two years later, the troops of the Holy Roman Emperor entered Rome, and their German and Protestant mercenaries sacked the town with greater savagery than any of the barbarian hordes in earlier centuries.

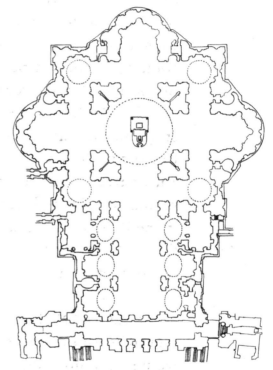

PLAN OF ST. PETER'S, ROME

St. Peter's was turned into a stable, and the Vatican into kitchens. Twenty-five years later the whole of Italy, save Venice, fell under the yoke of Spain.

The Church, for its part, reorganized itself in reaction against Protestantism. New religious orders, stricter than the old ones, were founded, in the first rank of which were the Jesuits. The Council of Trent defined the Counter-Reformation. It was the end of the great humanist illusion; there was no longer any question of a synthesis of philosophy and religion. The painter Daniele di Volterra, who adopted Michelangelo's "manner," was ordered by the pope to paint clothes on the nudes of Michelangelo's "Last Judgment" in the Sistine Chapel.

While the Church stiffened and tried to banish pagan elements from art, social life became more worldly and formal. The princes of the little Italian courts played no more than a representative role; they had to have a more spectacular setting in which to exercise their functions and to give themselves importance.

Hence the development of vast painted decorations in their palaces, and the increase in country villas where architecture and gardens formed a fitting background for ceremonial occasions.

In these villas, which were springing up everywhere—the Palazzo del Te at Mantua, the Villa Giulia and the Villa Medici at Rome, the Villa d'Este near Tivoli, and so on—the architects, without introducing any major innovation, abandoned the restraint of their predecessors and showed signs of a fantasy and exuberance perfectly in line with the Italian character.

The Mannerist painters Annibale and Agostino Carracci triumphed in the decoration of the Palazzo Farnese in Rome (now the French Embassy), the ceiling of which was taken as a model in Italy and France right up to the end of the 18th century. While the majority of their colleagues were content to imitate the style of their favorite master, these two painters concocted a more subtle recipe, claiming to take what was best in each old master: the awesome quality in Michelangelo, the movement of the Venetians, the fine feeling of Correggio, and so on.

The most fertile Mannerist trend nevertheless derives from Correggio, a contemporary of Raphael, who played a special part in the evolution of art in the "Cinquecento." A native of Parma, where he painted the greater part of his works, Correggio is preeminently a painter of feminine beauty. He had a predilection for mythological scenes in which he showed nude young goddesses against scenery lit with a soft golden light. The frescoes that are so full of movement, with which he decorated the domes of several churches in Parma, form the basis of all cupola decoration in the Baroque period.

His pupil Parmigiano took up his style, but gave it a more mannered treatment. He elongated his figures to make them more elegant, and gave them a grace that was to be interpreted with success by the sculptors Giovanni da Bologna and Benvenuto Cellini.

THE TRIUMPH OF VENETIAN PAINTING. If the "Quattrocento" was the century of Florence, the "Cinquecento" witnessed the apogee of Venetian painting.

The beginning of the century was dominated by the enigmatic Giorgione, who had taken only a few years to acquire a fame equal to that of the greatest of his elders, and who died at thirty-three, leaving behind only a small number of paintings.

From the middle of the century until its last years the indefatigable Tintoretto covered the walls of Venice with his immense fiery compositions; although he never succeeded in disarming the criticisms of his fellow citizens, he fascinates the art-lover today by his boldness, his vehemence and his way of dealing with light, in which can be found some foreshadowing of Impressionism.

Between these two can be placed Titian, Veronese and all the painters of that great school of color which, succeeding the Florentine school which was dominated by form, makes Italian Renaissance painting a perfect and superb whole.

All the painters of this school were products of the studio shared by the brothers Gentile and Giovanni Bellini, who, in the second third of the "Quattrocento," had given Venetian painting the quality of softness and warmth which was henceforward to be its main characteristic. Gentile died in 1507, and Giovanni, who had Giorgione and Titian as pupils, died in 1516.

At the time when Giorgione began to paint, Venice, taking over the place held by Florence in the previous century, had become the most advanced cultural center in Europe. But the inhabitants of this incredible city, where the reflections on the water and the sunlit mists rising from it create a dream atmosphere, were more attracted by the mysteries of Greek thought than by its logic, and more receptive to poetry than to science. Giorgione was a musician as well as a painter. He frequented the most cultured men in Venice, and must have been acquainted with the esoteric studies some of them were pursuing. We can find a hint of this in his paintings, the deeper meaning of which has remained a secret. We do not know in what strange astrological calculations (revealed recently by X-ray examination) the Magi are absorbed in his painting "The Philosophers." If we understood the ideas that inspired the painter, perhaps we could better define the strange magic of his painting. We can at least analyze its principal elements, which are the astonishing quality of his scenery, the noble and gentle bearing of his figures, and, above all, the extraordinarily subtle harmony of golden tones.

At the outset of his career Titian imitated Giorgione so well that experts cannot distinguish their paintings from one another. But Titian did not possess Giorgione's anxious sensitivity, and soon his temperament bore him off toward a more dazzling art, with more brilliant colors.

His output was immense, for he lived to a great age (till he was ninety-nine, it was believed for a long time; but it now appears that he must have been only eighty-six or seven when he died) and worked right up to the end, when the plague tore him away from the "Pietà" that he was painting for his tomb. He enjoyed a greater international reputation during his lifetime than any other painter. He was official painter to the Most Serene Republic, to popes, kings, princes and the Emperor Charles V, who summoned him to his court twice.

Titian treated religious and secular subjects with the same grandiose authority. He had a very dramatic sense of composition and was one of the most admirable portrait painters that ever lived. Toward the end of his life his painting had evolved and increased in depth. His colors became darker, and a shimmering light filled his paintings, which acquired a pathetic beauty that was lacking in his early works.

He was already at the height of his glory when Veronese, who, as his name indicates, came from Verona, arrived in Venice and won rapid success by painting the ceiling of the Church of San Sebastiano. Titian probably realized that the competition from his young colleague was not to be feared, for he complimented him and gave him his support.

Their fields of action were not, in fact, the same. With his clear tones, transparent light, lustrous textures and carefree figures, Veronese was ideally fitted to be the great painter of the pomp and ceremony of Venice. He was also a decorator, and worked in the Villa Barbaro, built by Palladio. As Venice sensed its power waning, the city tried to alleviate the situation with entertainments and festivals. We have only to compare the charming dignity of the ceremonies painted by Carpaccio with the extravagant banquet that Veronese disguised with the title "Banquet at the House of Levi," to appreciate the ground that had been covered in half a century.

But if there was room next to Titian for the happy and exuberant painting of Veronese, it was quite a different matter for the disquieting art of Tintoretto, who in his adolescence, so the story goes, had been driven from Titian's studio, where he was an apprentice, because his master found he was too talented.

Tintoretto is the most Venetian of all Venetian painters. He left his native city only once, and then went no farther than Mantua. It is only in Venice that we can come to know him properly. There, to judge by the number and size of his canvases, one might think he was the most sought-after painter of his day. Nothing is further from the truth. He had to fight for his commissions by charging low fees or by stealing a march on his competitors, thus making them his enemies. His contemporaries found that his pictures looked unfinished.

He has often been classified as a Mannerist because he is supposed to have said that he wanted to "ally Titian's color to Michelangelo's drawing," but it is not certain that this formula was his. In any event, his genius was too strong to bend for any length of time to any "manner" other than his own. This genius of light effects and stage-setting was reminiscent, as André Malraux commented, of the art of film-making, and has something of Victor Hugo's "Légende des Siècles." Malraux goes on to say that it was Tintoretto who invented perspective as it appears at ground level, and which film-makers capture by lowering their cameras.

He varied his figures and accessories with a boundless imagination, viewing them from the most unexpected angles, and he dramatized each of his effects with great splashes of light: an oblique light that makes his colors quiver and sets up reflections everywhere.

Tintoretto was the first misunderstood painter in Italy. People liked neither his dark colors—he said he preferred black and white—nor the off-hand way he lightly sketched in the figures in the shadows, nor the way he elongated some of his figures to make them more striking—a trick remembered by his pupil El Greco. But perhaps Venice also sensed that all the tragedy of her decadence was expressed through his painting, and preferred to forget, with the help of Veronese, the constant threat of Turkish aggression, and the discovery of new sources of wealth in America. In an attempt to forget these misfortunes, the city continued to develop and embellish itself.

ARCHITECTS WHO WERE BOTH INNOVATORS AND CLASSICAL. After the sack of Rome, the architect and sculptor Jacopo Sansovino, who had fled to Venice, had been commissioned to carry out an old project of town-planning that had been left in abeyance. The plan was to rebuild the whole of the city center around St. Mark's and the Doges' Palace. Opposite the latter he had built the Library, considered to be his masterpiece. In it he remained faithful both to the classical principle of superimposition of orders (Ionic upon Doric) and to the Venetian tradition of buildings resting on an arched portico. But, by accentuating the contrast of light and shade, he gave his structure an entirely new rhythm. Fifty years later (about 1580) his successor Scamozzi was inspired by it to build the Procuratie Nuove lining one side of St. Mark's Square, making it the "world's finest drawing room."

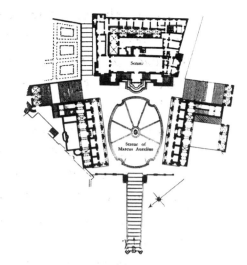

ROME, CAPITOL SQUARE

Meanwhile, two important churches had been begun: San Giorgio Maggiore and the Redentore, built to commemorate the end of the plague that had struck down Titian. Both were built from plans by Palladio, the Italian architect who was to have a most widespread and lasting influence: it was felt throughout Europe, and appeared again in the 18th century with renewed vigor.

At a time when Italian art was turning toward the Baroque, Palladio revived classical art and gave it back its prestige and purity. A humanist, as Alberti had been, he was a member of the academy of Vicenza, his home town, where he built so many monuments that he completely changed its appearance. He wrote a treatise on architecture in which he referred to classical models and the teachings of the Roman Vitruvius, whose works, that had only been discovered in the previous century, he had republished.

Of all ancient monuments, it was the temple that most inspired him. He adapted its façade to his churches with a really remarkable combination of rigor and invention. He also used the temple as the basic element of his many villas. Palladio always calculated the proportions of his buildings with extreme care, and endeavored to respect that "harmony of numbers" that it had been thought possible to deduce from the texts of Pythagoras. In any case, he found in them that "exact and unsurpassable balance of culture and of taste" that caused his constructions to be often imitated, never equaled, and he can be said to have brought to perfection the architecture of the whole of the Renaissance.

TITIAN (1477-1576): JULIUS II - PITTI PALACE, FLORENCE (A COPY OF RAPHAEL'S PAINTING IN THE UFFIZI).

Under the aegis of the popes, the new patrons...

"The century of the Popes" followed that of the Medicis, and Rome took over from Florence the rôle of artistic capital first of Italy, then of the Western World. The 16th century, or "Cinquecento," was divided into two more or less equal parts: during the first half the Renaissance reached its apogee; during the second, it continued to flourish but its spirit had changed, and gradually inspiration dwindled. Too dazzled by their predecessors' brilliance, its artists only sought to imitate them, and the result was mannerism. Four popes presided over the rapid and glorious rise that in fifty years gave back to the capital of Christendom a splendor reminiscent of that of ancient Rome. Julius II, the first of them, played a decisive rôle in bringing to Rome the three great artists of the period, Bramante, Michelangelo and Raphael. Raphael, upon whom Julius II heaped favors and commissions, left us this portrait of his patron (on the left) as well as that of his successor, Leo X (below right), who was no other than Giovanni de' Medici, son of Lorenzo the Magnificent. Raphael painted him accompanied by his two nephews. The figure on the left is Cardinal Giulio de' Medici, who was in his turn to succeed to the pontifical throne as Clement VII. Paul III, who was pope after him, was painted by Titian (below left) with his two grandsons in a cruelly revealing picture. In each of these three works the artists seem to have tried to surpass themselves. Titian, suspected at times of flattering his subjects, shows that he possesses psychological penetration equal to that of Raphael who, with his customary truth, expressed the poignant weariness of Julius II, conscious a year before his death of the failure of his power politics. Raphael, in his portrait of Leo X, used red, gold and white with as much skill as Titian, the great master of color, assembling his various reds.

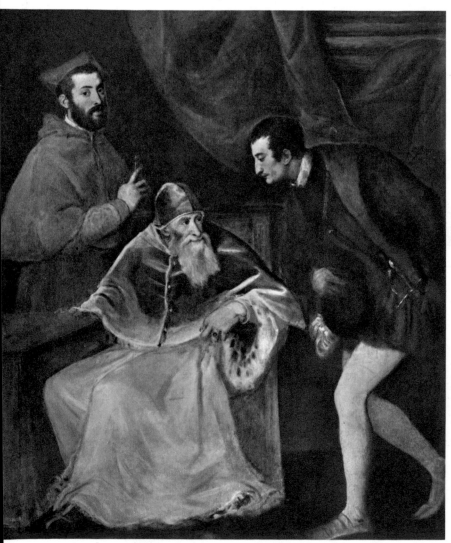

TITIAN (1477-1576): PAUL III - 1546 - MUSEO DI CAPODIMONTE, NAPLES.

RAPHAEL (1483-1520): LEO X - 1518 - UFFIZI, FLORENCE.

*... Rome
takes the lead
in the artistic
movements
of the day...*

The rebuilding of St. Peter's was the greatest event of the century. Pope Julius II commissioned Bramante to carry out this task, and work was started in 1506. When the Pope and the architect died, the one a year after the other, not much progress had been made. Work was continued by Raphael, Fra Giocondo and Giuliano da Sangallo, who modified the original ground plan in the form of a Roman cross. This was the first of a long succession of changes. Twice more the architects came back to the idea of a Greek cross and twice more to the Roman cross, which finally triumphed. Yet, among those who had favored the original plan was Michelangelo himself, the architect of the splendid dome that crowns the building, setting off the greatness of an edifice that has survived many changes, and giving it a beauty worthy of the first church in the Christian world. When we look at it, as in the photograph on the left, from the side of the apse which was redesigned by Michelangelo from Bramante's plan, we can clearly see its kinship with Brunelleschi's dome in Florence (page 196), and we are made fully aware of its great wealth of decoration.

ROME - ST. PETER'S BASILICA -
16TH CENTURY - PANORAMIC VIEW.

... while Florence continues to grow more beautiful

An open-air museum, the Piazza della Signoria, center of Florentine life, is completed by the old Loggia dei Lanzi, built in the 14th century as a shelter for public meetings, and adorned with classical statues. The square itself was embellished in the course of the 16th century by the Fountain of Neptune. A design project for this fountain had been the object of a competition in which Benvenuto Cellini, Giovanni da Bologna and Bartolomeo Ammanati had taken part. The latter was the winner in 1575, with a design full of fantasy and life, dominated by an enormous white marble Neptune. Unfortunately this did not meet with the approval of the Florentines, who preferred the nearby statue of David. Hence, the popular epigram "Ammanati, Ammanati, che bel marmo ha rovinato!" ("What fine marble he spoiled!") On the other hand, the bronze sirens and fauns (detail at left) were without a doubt delicately and finely sculptured. Some years later, in 1583, Giovanni da Bologna carved a group in marble representing the various ages of man, and which was christened the "Rape of the Sabines" (right). It was placed in the Loggia dei Lanzi, where Cellini's "Perseus" also stood. This remarkable square is today still a pole of attraction for tourists from all lands.

AMMANATI (1511-1592):
FOUNTAIN OF NEPTUNE, DETAIL
1575 - PIAZZA DELLA
SIGNORIA, FLORENCE.

GIOVANNI DA BOLOGNA (1529-1608): RAPE OF THE SABINES - 1583 - LOGGIA DEI LANZI, FLORENCE

Michelangelo
dominates his age...

"Cataclysm made man," Michelangelo's Moses (left) is the work most representative of the superhuman genius and troubled destiny of its creator. It was meant for the tomb that Julius II had commissioned from Michelangelo, and which was to be a colossal monument in the center of the new Basilica of St. Peter. But hardly had Michelangelo made the first rough models for this monument, which offered a perfect challenge to his genius and into which he threw himself wholeheartedly, than the Pope changed his mind and entrusted him with the decoration of the ceiling of the Sistine Chapel, a task that was to keep him fully occupied for four and a half years. In the course of the next twenty-five years, the projected tomb was discussed five times, and five times its size was reduced. Of four gigantic statues that were to adorn the second story, only Moses was carved. Seated, trembling with revolt, touching yet contemptuous, it embodies with a power never since equalled the "just wrath of one of God's chosen defying the world" —the very wrath to which Michelangelo was subject all his life.

"The more painting resembles sculpture the better I think it is," wrote Michelangelo, and his tremendous painting on the ceiling of the Sistine Chapel, though indeed a painting, is at the same time a work of sculpture and architecture. It is the true sum of his art and ideas: a whole world is there. The Book of Genesis is the main subject, which Michelangelo in some way balanced by an alternating series of twelve Prophets and twelve Sybils. Both hold the secrets of the future, but this gift of prophecy is given to them in varied degrees according to their origins: the pagan Sybils are less clairvoyant than the Christian Prophets. The Sybil of Cumae (right) is shown as an already old woman reading the Book of Wisdom. With her worn face and redoubtable looks, she might be the elder sister of Moses—she already has his violent expression.

MICHELANGELO (1475-1564): MOSES - TOMB
OF POPE JULIUS II, DETAIL - 1513-1516
ROME, CHURCH OF SAN PIETRO IN VINCOLI.

MICHELANGELO (1475-1564): THE SYBIL OF CUM
CEILING OF THE SISTINE CHAP
DETAIL - 1508-1512 - RO

*... and influences
all artists...*

Strength and anger incarnate can be seen in Michelangelo's "David" (left). A huge block of Carrara marble, begun and then abandoned forty years earlier by Agostino di Duccio, was one day given to Michelangelo, the son of the "Podestà" (magistrate) of Caprese. The young sculptor, then just twenty-one, had been under the patronage of Lorenzo de' Medici. He was ordered to carve a statue of David from this marble, and he was even told the proportions. He immediately produced a masterstroke, since the statue was erected in the Piazza della Signoria in 1505. Michelangelo had just returned from Rome where he had been greatly moved by the Apollo Belvedere that had been dug up before his very eyes in the gardens of the Church of San Pietro in Vincoli. The strength and anger shown in the statue were the two civic virtues greatly valued by Renaissance men, inspired —once again— by Antiquity. It is, in fact, a young god of ancient times, a "giant," as the Florentines called it. It would be hard to imagine the proportions of a Goliath by the side of this David. The anatomy is rendered with such extreme richness and exactness of detail that we can see the bones, muscles and veins under the skin. Painting was soon to yield to this naturalistic tendency, since Andrea del Sarto in 1522, in his "St. John the Baptist" painted a portrait, also in the classical style, of a young man with a naked torso, whose anatomy is shown off by skillful lighting that plays a more important rôle than the color itself. Four years later, del Sarto elaborated this subject in the frescoes in the Chiostro dello Scalzo which tell in cameo of the story in St. John.

MICHELANGELO (1475-1564): DAVID 1501-1503 - FLORENCE, THE ORIGINAL IN THE ACCADEMIA, A COPY IN THE PIAZZA DELLA SIGNORIA.

ANDREA DEL SARTO (1486-1531): ST. JOHN THE BAPTIST - 1522 - PITTI PALACE, FLORENCE.

*... but his genius
frees itself from
the bonds of matter
and form...*

Dramatic single combat between creator and matter, which was Michelangelo's whole life, can be seen in all its striking intensity in his unfinished works. From the blocks of marble that he himself lovingly chose from the quarries of Carrara, his subjects surge forth with an irresistible force as he first conceived them, and strike us all the more since they remain stylized, a fact that brings them more in line with modern sensibility. The "Waking Slave" (left), still in its rough state, is particularly impressive in that the slave is doubly a prisoner: of the solid mass of stone from which Michelangelo has not finished freeing him, and of the sleep from which he awakens with difficulty and which had helped him to forget his misery. With five other statues of slaves, the only two of which to be finished are today in the Louvre Museum in Paris, it was meant for the famous tomb of Julius II which was originally intended to have forty statues. But not one of the slaves found a place on the much smaller tomb that was finally executed, and for which only "Moses" was done by the hand of Michelangelo alone. Some years later, for the tomb of the Medicis, he carved four reclining figures symbolizing the inexorable fate that governs life, representing Dawn, Day, Twilight and Night. The tragedy that put him to the test then was not only that of a work he was not allowed to finish, but that of all Florence, his proud mother-city, besieged and then conquered by the army of Charles V, despite fierce resistance in which Michelangelo had personally taken part. The features of the figure representing Day (right) express the bottomless despair he felt at that time. It is possible that Michelangelo never intended to finish off this face, so that it would contrast more strikingly with the body, and so that the light, playing upon the marks left by the chisel, might emphasize its suffering even more.

MICHELANGELO (1475-1564):
WAKING SLAVE - 1513-1514
ACCADEMIA, FLORENCE.

MICHELANGELO (1475-1564):
DETAIL - TOMB OF GIULIANO DE' M
ABOUT 1530 - CHURCH OF SAN LORENZO, FLOR

*... while Tintoretto
follows
along the paths
he has opened up...*

Tintoretto's boldness and passion were beyond the understanding of his contemporaries and made him the first unrecognized genius of Italian art. Posterity awarded him the place of high honor he so richly deserved. One can only really get to know this astonishingly fertile painter in Venice, where the essence of his work is to be found. He might have declared that he wanted to draw like Michelangelo and paint like Titian, but he had too much personality to follow this mannerist program. Virtually by force he obtained the commission for a vast series of paintings for the Scuola di San Rocco in Venice, comparable in importance only with the decorations in the Sistine Chapel. "The Crucifixion," part of which—the crucifixion of one of the thieves—we can see here, is the most important of these paintings. In it we see all the features that make its artist a precursor not only of Baroque painting, but also of Goya, Delacroix and Manet: an inexhaustible fertility of invention, an incomparable feeling for stage-setting, an angle of vision that elongates his figures in a spectacular way, dramatic oblique strokes, and finally an extraordinary use of light that makes the colors vibrate and gives the composition an extra dimension as it lights up the human figures or casts them into shadow. It is one of his most significant works. "Ten scenes in one single scene, which balance each other to blend into one," according to Taine's definition.

TINTORETTO (1518-1594):
CRUCIFIXION, DETAIL - 1565
SCUOLA DI SAN ROCCO, VENICE.

... and renders the secret anguish of Venice

VENICE - COURTYARD OF THE DOGES' PALACE.

The courtyard of the Doges' Palace (above) which clearly influenced Tintoretto (right) had just been completely repaired after a fire which had burned down the east wing of the palace. The façade was reconstructed from designs by Antonio Rizzi and Pietro Lombardo. A magnificent stairway was built on to it, called later the "Giants' Stairway" because of the two enormous statues of Mercury and Neptune, carved by Sansovino, the architect who had just built the Library opposite the Doges' Palace (page 350). Then the less ornate east front was built; then, at the back—and with typical Venetian contempt for symmetry—the clock house; and next to this, the Doge's elegant private oratory. This ensemble harmonized with the outside of the building because of the use of ogival arches throughout.

This wonderful painting, showing the body of St. Mark being taken from Alexandria in the 9th century (right) by two Venetian merchants, who bore it in triumph to their native city where St. Mark was adopted as patron saint, is one of the first works in which Tintoretto freed himself from Titian's influence. It was part of a series of huge canvases hung in the Scuola di San Marco (page 276), and which depict different episodes in the life of the Evangelist. The highly symmetrical composition—this effect was originally much more pronounced, for a strip that had deteriorated had to be cut off the left side—the impression of depth, given by the perspective, and the dramatic storm lighting are all features that free it from the classical tradition.

278

Painter of the glory of Venice, although a native of Verona, Veronese was the great decorator of the Doges' Palace; all his works have a sumptuous, theatrical atmosphere. He enriched them with his knowledge of history and mythology, and showed a sensual delight in color and light. In the foreground of his "Victory of Lepanto" (left) the Turkish and Venetian galleys in the throes of battle recall the great year of 1571 when Venice defeated the Turkish fleet. This glorious event should have allowed Venice to keep Cyprus, its last great eastern colony, but in effect only gave the Republic one short final respite, before its commercial power collapsed for ever.

Condottiere in the service of art, Benvenuto Cellini, like no other artist of his day, applied his talents to such varied fields as music, gold and silver work, jewelry, sculpture, mechanics, literature and war. In his "Memoirs," he shows an enthusiastic partiality for his own works that is justified by some of his sculpture and in particular by the "Perseus" on the Piazza della Signoria. The base is covered with bronze bas-reliefs which have all the splendor of Ghiberti's "Gates of Paradise." On them we can see Andromeda (right) chained to a rock at the mercy of a furious sea-monster. This princess, daughter of the king of Ethiopia, had dared to dispute the prize of beauty with the Nereids. Neptune, to avenge them, created a monster that ravaged the country, and Andromeda, to redeem her pride, was delivered up to the monster. Then Perseus, son of Jupiter and Danae, arrived on his winged horse Pegasus, killed the dragon, freed the princess and married her. This bas-relief, exquisitely carved in a manner worthy of a highly-skilled silversmith, is in conception the work of a sculptor.

VENUTO CELLINI (1500-1571):
SEUS, DETAIL FROM THE BASE OF THE STATUE
- FLORENCE, PIAZZA DELLA SIGNORIA.

VERONESE (1528-1588): PART OF THE VILLA BARBARO FRESCO - ABOUT 1565 - MASER.

More a decorator than a painter, Veronese depicted all that was most superficial in Venice, a city that had always been passionately addicted to pomp and ceremony but whose love of sumptuous entertainments had increased greatly with the decline of its power. In this he is the opposite of Tintoretto, who expressed the deeper anguish of Venice. A pupil of Giulio Romano and an admirer of Raphael, he was a child of the classical tradition, which quite naturally gave him a close affinity to the humanist architect Palladio. In the elegant villa built by Palladio at Maser (page 300), Veronese painted his most original and attractive works. These are the large frescoes that decorate the main rooms, and with their "trompe-l'oeil" effects create architectural designs in the same style as those on the outside of the villa, only more fanciful and which thus create unexpected dimensions. They show scenes of astonishing freshness and "modernism," peopled by figures dressed in bright colors and painted with good-humored spirit: the two women (above), on a make-believe balcony, are looking out on the antechamber like the mistress of the house with her servant casting an eye over her guests before going down to greet them. On the right, the young man with his dogs returning from the hunt, who seems to be entering the room through a door—also in "trompe-l'oeil"—is thought to be a self-portrait of Veronese.

PARMIGIANO (1503-1540): PORTRAIT
OF ANTEA - 1535-1537 - NATIONAL MUSEUM, NAPLES.

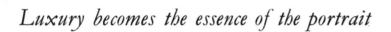

Luxury becomes the essence of the portrait

TINTORETTO (1518-1594): DOGE
ALVISE MOCENIGO - ACCADEMIA, VENICE.

First worldly painter of the Italian school, Parmigiano idealized female beauty according to a precept of his own, which was characterized by an elegant lengthening of the lines. His "Long-necked Virgin" is a famous example of this. The portrait (above left) is thought to be of Antea, a well-known Roman courtesan praised for her charm and compliancy by Aretino and Benvenuto Cellini in their writings. Here, the perfect oval of the face, the very straight long nose, the small mouth, the ear slightly out of place so that we can the better appreciate its shape, the purity of the modelling, all transcend the portrait and make for idealization of the subject.

Portraitist of Doges and eminent Venetians, Tintoretto also executed the decorations in the Doges' Palace. An admirable chapter in his work is made up of a series of portraits of old men. One of these is the portrait of Alvise Mocenigo, who was Doge from 1575-1577. In all these portraits, Tintoretto devoted his attention to the face and, above all, the expression of the eyes, preferring to play down the pose, dress and hands in order to emphasize the psychological truth of a man whose great age proves his experience of life.

Portraitist of Europe's princes, Titian divided his time between Alfonso d'Este at Ferrara, the Gonzaga family at Mantua, the Farnese family and the Popes at Rome, Charles V and Philip II in Spain. His fame was so widespread that Francis I commissioned a portrait which Titian painted from a medal, without ever having met his subject. The portrait of Francesco della Rovere, Duke of Urbino (left) fully justifies his reputation: the colors are brought out by broad brushwork and light effects that come from many different sources. Titian was one of the great portraitists of his day. In his work, the portrait held a place almost equal in importance to that of his great religious and profane compositions.

Official painter to the Medicis, whose dynasty was nearly at an end, Bronzino entered their service in 1540, after being official painter to the Duke of Urbino. With a sharpness and delicacy reminiscent of Holbein, he painted Maria de' Medici (right), daughter of Eleonora of Toledo and Cosimo I. Most often Bronzino's portraits show the subject's social position rather than his personality. In this respect he belongs to the mannerist school that marked the final days of Florentine painting.

TITIAN (1477-1576): FRANCESCO
DELLA ROVERE - UFFIZI, FLORENCE.

BRONZINO (1502-1572): MARIA DE' MEDICI - UFFIZI, FLORENCE.

*An abundance of sumptuous
fabrics, precious objects...*

The satins, velvets, and brocades that Aretino
wore when sitting for Titian were depicted by the
artist in all their splendor. Indeed, he knew the
importance his subject attached to fine clothes and
how much he wanted everyone to know of his wealth,
the product of his pen and the sign of his power. On
receiving this splendid picture, Aretino sent him a
note in which he pretended he thought the painter
would have done better work if he had been paid more.
But Titian knew him well enough to know that it was
a joke; he could not help but take the comments of
such a protector with a smile. A successful—and
notorious—author, Aretino had managed to attract
the favors of the Roman banker Chigi, then of Popes
Leo X and Clement VII, who were entertained by his
dialogues and sonnets, sometimes slanderous, sometimes licentious, but always brilliant. Nonetheless,
he carried his attacks on the papal court a little too far,
and in the end was obliged to flee Rome. He then
settled in Venice. Realizing that he could sometimes
make more money by keeping silent than by writing,
he quickly increased his fortune by blackmail or through
certain persons who paid handsomely for the privilege
of seeing their praises in print. A great lover of beautiful things, he lived in splendor and gathered all the
best artists around him. He greatly helped Titian in
his career and seemed to have sincere friendship for
the artist.

Gold and silverwork constituted the principal work
of most of the great artists of the Renaissance, including
Ghiberti, Brunelleschi and Donatello. This art was
highly appreciated by the Medicis who acquired a splendid collection. The superb cup (right), made from
Grisons jasper, is one of the most striking objects.
Its creator showed an extraordinary skill: making its
form fit the subject, he carved the struggle between
Hercules and the Lernaean Hydra. The jasper, inlaid
with pearls, is surmounted by a statuette of Hercules
in solid gold. The hero is preparing to hurl the stone
that will kill the Hydra. The head and tail of the Hydra
form the handles of the cup, attributed to Mazzafirri,
who worked for Grand Duke Ferdinand I.

ATTRIBUTED TO MAZZAFIRRI - HYDRA-SHAPED CUP - PITTI PALACE, FLORENCE

TITIAN (1477-1576): ARETINO - 1545 - PITTI PALACE, FLORENCE.

287

RAPHAEL (1483-1520): THE LADY WITH THE UNICORN - PALAZZO BORGHESE, ROME.

... and superb gems

FAIENCE PLATE FROM PESARO - DETAIL OF CENTERPIECE - NATIONAL MUSEUM, FLORENCE

Rich in talent and extremely versatile, Raphael tackled all styles of painting with equal success. As the great art critic Bernard Berenson observed, the type of woman that Raphael painted has consistently delighted Europe for four hundred years. This type is just as much that of the "Lady with the Unicorn" (left), the portrait of an unknown woman, as it is of his famous Madonnas, all different but each one with a beauty that shows, more than any other, the balance between the instincts of the heart and the more conscious requirements of art. This type of woman charmed Italy so much that the style was taken over by the popular art of "faïence," so-called after the town of Faenza, in Romagna. The plate (above) dates from the period when the quality of this work was at its highest. But Raphael could also deal with subjects in which he expressed intense emotion, as in his fresco in the Vatican showing the liberation of St. Peter (page 291), where the angel radiating light who is waking St. Peter contrasts with the unshakable torpor of the guards.

FLORENCE - A PALACE DOOR.

RAPHAEL (1483-1520): THE LIBERATION OF ST. PETER · DETAIL · VATICAN.

MICHELANGELO (1475-1564): ENTRANCE TO THE BIBLIOTECA LORENZIANA - FLORENCE - 1524.

Austere grandeur of Florentine palaces stems in great part from the predilection of their architects for large projecting bossages, usually of diamond-cut or pyramidal shape. They used them either as a superb framework for doors and windows (page 290) or as the basic element of a whole building. Their use reached its peak in the Pitti Palace, of which Taine said: "I doubt whether there is a more monumental palace in Europe; I have seen none more impressive in its grandeur and simplicity." Its construction, following plans by Brunelleschi, was soon interrupted, as it was proving too costly. Then Ammanati started work on it for Cosimo I. He added a court-yard and terraces (left), more Roman in inspiration than the rest of the building, and which overlook the Boboli gardens.

The architecture of Michelangelo is profoundly original, although based on classical elements. This originality can be most clearly seen in the Biblioteca Lorenziana. Starting with the vestibule, a small, high-ceilinged room (above), the vertical lines of which contrast with the horizontal lines of the library to which it serves as the entrance, Michelangelo wanted the reader to feel estranged and isolated from the outside world. This impression is conveyed by the articulation of the walls, broken up by twin columns which are not used to support but which are in themselves elements of force. It is as though they were imprisoned in recesses below which their volutes seem to be bulges in the stone, about to give way under their pressure. Between these recesses, false windows heighten the effect of isolation. An unusual staircase, the center part of which has been compared with a wave of lava held in check by the two lesser staircases, comes slowly down from the reading room. In contrast to Brunelleschi or Bramante's constructions, which were in harmony with human pro-portions, this building has independent dimensions and a life and power of its own.

293

ANTONIO SANGALLO (ABOUT 1483-1546) AND MICHELANGELO (1475-1564): PALAZZO FARNESE (FIRST AND SECOND FLOORS OVERLOOKING THE COURTYARD) · 1514-1560 · ROME.

Palladio blends his villas with the landscape...

PALLADIO (1508-1580): "LA MALCONTENTA" - 1551 - MIRA (VENICE).

◄ **The Farnese Palace, now the French Embassy in Rome**, was begun for Cardinal Alessandro Farnese, the future Pope Paul III, by Antonio Sangallo and continued by Michelangelo, who was responsible for the second story overlooking the courtyard (previous page) which he embellished with heavily framed windows. Contrary to the rule usually observed, that the upper floor should be lighter than the lower floor, Michelangelo made his upper floor heavier to convey a feeling of tension and energy. Vertical continuity was assured by clusters of three Corinthian pilasters superimposed on the Ionic pilasters.

The inventor of the "temple-villa" was Palladio: he created them for the aristocracy of Vicenza, who loved to meet in the country to discuss philosophy or organize family entertainments. Palladio opportunely revived architectural classicism at the very moment when it seemed to be on the wane and when the Baroque trend was beginning to make itself felt.
La Malcontenta (above), built for the Doge Foscari, was the first villa commissioned from Palladio by a Venetian. It was the consecration of the fame he had won at Vicenza, a fame that from the 18th century onwards was to become worldwide and was to win him many imitators from the United States to Russia. This villa's majestic simplicity is the result of the perfect balance of its proportions.

Most fascinating of Venetian paintings is perhaps Giorgione's "Tempesta" (detail on the right). This small painting, the true significance of which has never been made clear, shows on one side a woman feeding a child against a background of deep, warm tones, through the middle of which runs a clear river with houses and ruins on its banks. On the opposite side, an elegantly dressed young man is standing. He is dreaming or waiting, and does not seem to see the woman. It is one of the rare paintings whose attribution to Giorgione has never been contested. At the very outset of the "Cinquecento," he introduced into painting an entirely new poetry and luminosity that captivated all his contemporaries, and once and for all gave the Venetian school its reputation for exquisite color.

GIORGIONE (1478-1510): TEMPESTA (THE STORM) - DETAIL - ACCADEMIA VEN

296

*... his inspiration
is strictly classical...*

The only one of its kind to survive, Vicenza's Teatro Olimpico is a reconstitution of a Roman theater according to known data—albeit incomplete—in the 16th century. Begun by Palladio, it was completed after his death by Scamozzi, who slightly modified the original plans. It was built at the instigation of the members of the Academy of Vicenza, statues of whom were placed in the recesses on the stage. This theater bears astonishing witness to the fascination that Antiquity held for the cultured men of the Renaissance. Facing a semicircle of wooden steps, surrounded by a colonnade that gives unity to the whole, rises scenery of wood and stucco, evocative of the "frons scenae" of classical theaters (page 52). Its form was inspired by the triumphal arch. In the center and on either side are streets lined with mansions, supposedly streets in Thebes. Their perspective is enhanced by a "trompe-l'oeil" effect. Actors made their entrances through these streets which were thus given an imposing and solemn character.

PALLADIO (1508-1580): TEATRO OLIMPICO COMPLETED IN 1585 - VICENZA.

... *transposed with great elegance*

Theoretician of architecture, to which he devoted his "Four Books," long famous, Palladio displayed all his knowledge and all his art in the Villa Barbaro, built for a Venetian ambassador, who was moreover an eminent humanist deeply versed in mathematics, and an owner better able than any other to appreciate the subtleties in the construction of this dwelling and the carefully studied proportions of its different rooms. These had been established according to the Pythagorean conception of the "harmonic relationships" of numbers and they dictated the exterior proportions of the building. The Villa Barbaro is halfway between the "temple-villas" Palladio had built previously, and the "palace-villa" with two stories of colonnades, a little too ostentatious for the country, that he was to build later. Conceived to blend with the surrounding countryside, it is the most remarkable of Palladian villas, and its interior decoration (page 282) by Veronese gives it an incomparable attraction.

The façade of a classical temple, which he had previously adapted to his villas, was used by Palladio in the three churches he built in Venice, the most important of which is San Giorgio Maggiore (pages 302-303). The problem facing Palladio, made architect-in-chief to the Venetian Republic in 1566, was how to integrate this classical element into sacred architecture. This problem he solved with as much ingenuity as elegance. Two façades of different height were superimposed and blended into one single façade of harmonious grandeur. The taller, central façade gives access to the central nave of the church, and the other to the side naves. Their columns rest on a raised base, a system employed later by Longhena, the great Baroque architect, for the Church of Santa Maria della Salute (page 349).

PALLADIO (1508-1580):
VILLA BARBARO - 1566 - MASER.

300

VENICE - SAN GIORGIO MAGGIORE - 1566-1610.

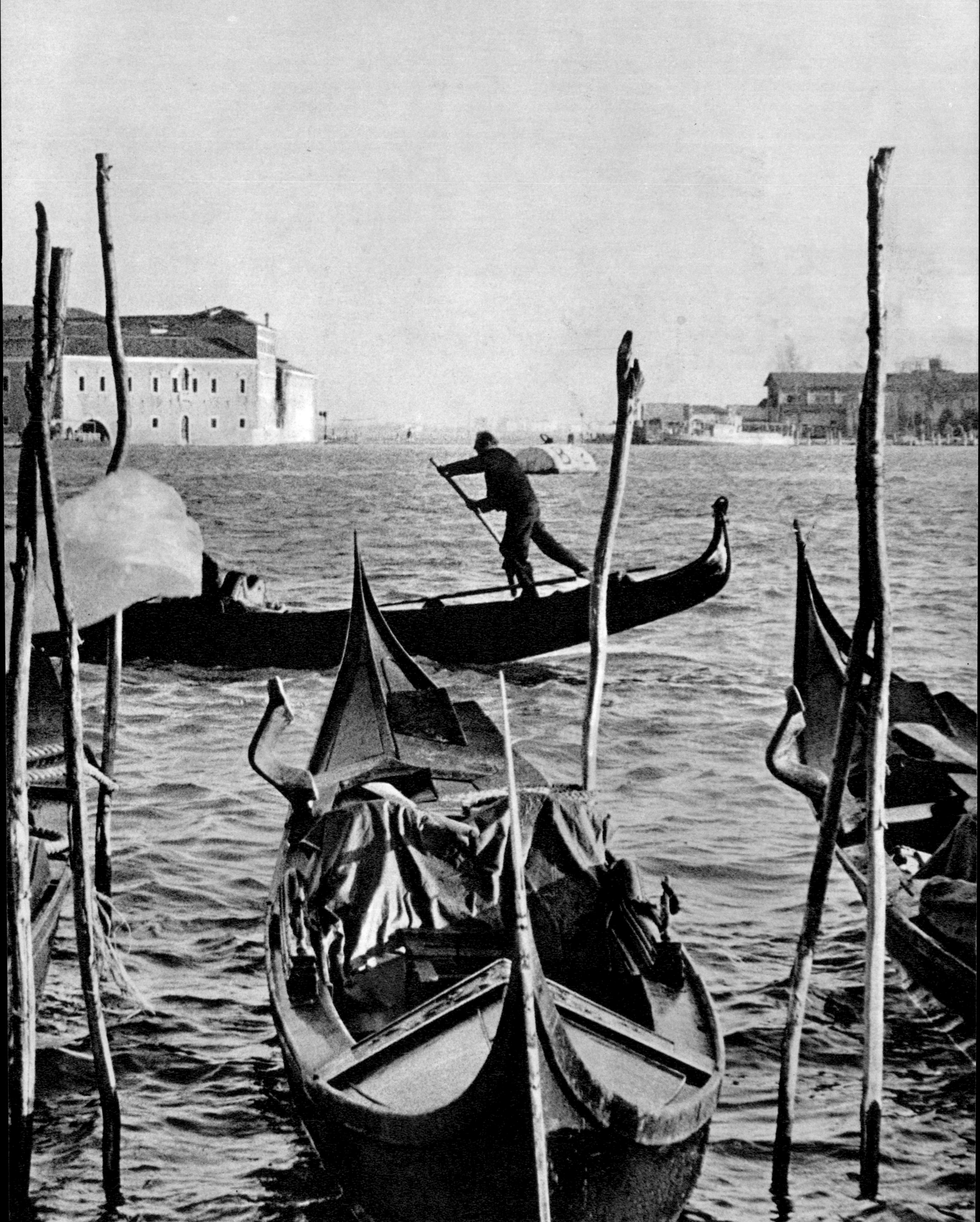

*Mannerism
imposes its law...*

The most brilliant student of the first Academy of Fine Arts, founded in Bologna by the Carracci, was Guido Reni. The theory of the school was based on imitation of the great masters of the Renaissance: its members strove to take the essential qualities of each master and combine them to achieve perfection (other "mannerist" schools took only one master and one "manner" as their inspiration). In addition to painting, the Academy taught literature and anatomy.

Samson Victorious (detail at left) is first and foremost a nude study, almost excessively graceful, in which we can see the distant influence of classical statuary. In its pose it also reminds us of Raphael's frescoes in the Villa Farnese, and classifies Guido Reni as one of the "luminous" painters.

Linking Renaissance and Baroque, the Turtle Fountain (right) was for a long time attributed to Raphael because of its grace. It is in fact the work of Giacomo della Porta. The charm of the subject and the skill of its composition enhance the supple and sinuous lines of the bodies of the four youths added by Taddeo Landini. The fountain owes its name to the four small bronze turtles which, seeming to be drinking at the edge of the basin, add a note of intimacy to the whole.

GUIDO RENI (1575-1642): SAMSON VICTORIOUS, DETAIL - ABOUT 1610 - PINACOTECA, BOLOGNA.

GIACOMO DELLA PORTA (1539-1602): TURTLE FOUNTAIN · 1585 · ROME.

... and its excesses...

Mysterious monsters all made of stone fill the gardens surrounding the four-hundred-room palace built near Viterbo by Prince Vicino Orsini in 1525. Hidden, gnawed away by vegetation, these monsters have never yielded the secret either of their creation or of their creators. There are many different rumors about them, all without foundation. One possible explanation is quite simply that anonymous crafts-men carved these fantastic figures and animals out of the rocks in the garden for some unknown lover of the gigantic who had an erotic and cruel imagination. The elephant shown on the left, harnessed and caparisoned as for some ancient battle, has caught a soldier in its trunk, while a second figure is sitting on its head. Further on an ogre's head (right) is lying on the ground. Its size is such that you can walk into its gaping mouth without having to bend, and sit down on benches around a table which is the monster's tongue. On the ogre's chops, the inscription "Ogni pensiero vo..." which might be translated as "Fly away all thought," does not help to solve the mystery. From what tortured imagination sprang these giants, dragons, lions, sphinxes and mutilated women? Perhaps Freud could have analyzed the anguish and obsession that must have haunted Prince Orsini.

BOMARZO, GARDENS OF THE
PALAZZO ORSINI - ELEPHANT.

BOMARZO, GARDENS OF THE PALAZZO
ORSINI - HEAD OF AN OGRE.

... and flourishes in ornamental fountains

TIVOLI - VILLA D'ESTE - GREAT WATERFALL.

One of the greatest sculptors of his day, Giovanni da Bologna was an Italian by adoption. Born at Douai, he went to Rome, then settled in Florence. In 1563 he was summoned to Bologna by Pope Pius IV, who commissioned him to build a fountain in the square in front of the Municipal Palace. In four years he executed the bronze figures of this monument, designed by Lauretti; its ascending composition on three superimposed levels is especially remarkable. At the base are four mermaids set into the stone (left). In the middle are four child-angels trying to fly away. On the top, nearly twelve feet high, is Neptune, who looks as though he has shaken himself free of the waters. These waters flow everywhere in Italy, and more splendidly than anywhere else in the terraced gardens surrounding the Villa d'Este, built in 1550 for Cardinal d'Este outside Rome. The great waterfall (above), recently restored, is one of the largest of the many fountains in the gardens.

GIOVANNI DA BOLOGNA (1524-1608): FOUNTAIN OF NEPTUNE - DETAIL - 1566 - BOLOGNA.

Gardens display masterpieces

Virtuosity in modelling and casting, realism in the subject, these are the characteristics of Florentine sculptors who, starting in the "Cinquecento," no longer took man as their only subject. Alongside mythological beasts like Ganymede's eagle (right), executed by Cellini, we can find various animal subjects, generally intended as garden ornaments. Giovanni da Bologna and his assistants carved a horse, a bull, an eagle and this turkey (left), incredibly lifelike; the bronze admirably suggests the smallest details of the plumage with an art that was, however, already on the point of degenerating into academicism.

BENVENUTO CELLINI (1600-1671): GANYMEDE - NATIONAL MUSEUM, FLORENCE.

GIOVANNI DA BOLOGNA (1524-1608): TURKEY-COCK, NATIONAL MUSEUM, FLORENCE.

312

The triumph of the female nude

The same full-blown, healthy sensuality is characteristic of the two beautiful young women chosen as models by Giovanni da Bologna to represent Virtue overpowering Vice (left), and by Titian to contrast "Sacred Love and Profane Love" (detail at right). Michelangelo's influence can be clearly seen in the twist of the body and the projection of lines in the piece of sculpture. In the painting there are reflections of Giorgione. It is one of Titian's early works, and one of the first in which the painter's talent can be clearly distinguished from that of his master, with whom he had at first collaborated: the landscape still has, in effect, some of Giorgione's characteristics, but the play of colors is brighter and not so soft. The exact meaning of the allegory is unknown; what is clear is that Titian wanted to sound a handsome paean to nature and beauty.

The breathtaking Venus of Urbino (pages 314-315) was the highlight of Titian's career and the epitome of his exquisite talent. Vasari declared that it was the most beautiful of the female nudes painted by Titian. He recalled that it was said to be the portrait of one of the favorites of Duke Guidobaldo della Rovere, for whom the work was painted, and who had at the same time commissioned his own portrait from Titian. It was the first time that the female body had been painted with such transparent shadow and such luminous skin, the pearly texture of which contrasts with the whiteness of the sheet. The method the artist had perfected, and which consisted in working multiple touches of color and glazing in just the right proportions and applied with a brush virtually without any preliminary sketch, was exploited here with the greatest art and success.

GIOVANNI DA BOLOGNA (1524-1608):
VIRTUE OVERPOWERING VICE
1565 - PALAZZO BARGELLO, FLORENCE.

TITIAN (1477-1576): SACRED AND PROFANE LOVE - DETAIL - 1514 - PALAZZO BORGHESE, ROME.

TITIAN (1477-1576): VENUS OF URBINO - 1538 - UFFIZI, FLORENCE.

CHAPTER VII

FROM BAROQUE TO NEO-CLASSICISM

(17th and 18th centuries)

At no period since classical times had there been in Rome such intense artistic activity as between 1590 and the first quarter of the 18th century. During this period emerged a new style, characterized by a lavish freedom, which extended over the rest of the country and even beyond its frontiers. Thanks to this new style, Italy kept her place in the forefront of European architecture and sculpture. For the whole of the Western World Italy remained the motherland of art.

Toward the middle of the 18th century, an extremely violent reaction took place. Suddenly, the sober styles of Antiquity were given a place of honor again, and in consequence all the works of the preceding period were despised as "Baroque," judged decadent and dismissed in horror.

Once again, the movement had originated in Rome, which had become the rendezvous for artists of all nationalities. But this time the movement had been launched by foreigners, the Germans and the French. It was to culminate in neo-classicism, in the development of which Italy played no more than a minor role. The era of her artistic primacy was at an end. The 19th century and the beginning of the 20th constitute a period of inactivity, and it is only in the last decade that a reawakening has become apparent.

THE BAROQUE ADVENTURE. The history of Baroque art was doubly curious. First because it has taken nearly two hundred years for it to free itself from the contempt with which the neo-classicists had overwhelmed it. Secondly, because this capricious and spectacular art, which seemed ready-made to express the joys of life and serve as a setting for festivities, was by some strange paradox used chiefly for religious ends.

At first sight, it is disconcerting that churches should be popularized by painters and sculptors using methods similar to those adopted by modern publicity to "sell" a new product. We must try to imagine ourselves back in the atmosphere of the age to understand that the ostentatious character of Baroque art does not exclude sincerity. On the esthetic plane, its qualities have been rediscovered, and today it is accorded a place equal to that of all the great styles that have followed one another in the course of the history of art. Those who know Italy well affirm that one cannot really appreciate its genius if one is not sensitive to the Baroque charm that corresponds perfectly to the effusive temperament of its inhabitants.

Paul Lechat described Baroque art as a true likeness of this Italy—turbulent, sonorous and ignorant of all understatement... the enchantment and the grace of an Italy that has found an ideal style and rhythm. Guido Piovene does not attempt to hide his predilection for Baroque Rome: "One can get to know all other styles elsewhere, but he who has not seen Rome does not know the Baroque."

ANCIENT FORMS AND NEW LIBERTY.   The majority of art historians admit that the evolution of the different styles presents certain common features: after a classical phase during which a rigorous order dictated the assemblage of forms, a stage is reached where forms break free.   Then decorative elements take on a value of their own, develop without restraint and form a whole designed to please only their creator.   Thus it was that the flamboyant succeeded the true Gothic, and the Baroque succeeded the Renaissance.

Taken as a whole, the forms used by Baroque architecture are the same as before: columns, pilasters, entablatures, domes, etc., but the spirit in which they were used changed completely.   Movement and not static perfection was sought; the boundless rather than the finite; opulence rather than purity.   Curves were preferred to straight lines, and there was a marked liking for violent contrasts of light and shade.

This change in the conception of beauty coincided in Rome with a great change in the rôle accorded to art by the Church, which was its one big client.   This explains why the new style developed with such dazzling splendor.

PRESTIGE TACTICS.   Since the old iconoclastic crisis that had divided the Byzantine Empire in the 8th century, the Church had taken a stand for the retention of images, but in practice it had left artists free to tackle religious subjects as they thought fit.

At the Council of Trent, which had ended in 1563 after leading to the Counter-Reformation, the retention of images was officially confirmed.   In the face of Protestantism, new emphasis had been placed on their educational value, and the clergy soon formulated the new doctrine of religious art, which henceforth should be clear and intelligible to all, realistic in the representation of scenes of martyrdom and in the evocation of suffering and death, and finally, capable of evoking an emotion conducive to piety.

From homage to the Lord, painting and sculpture were thus transformed into works of edification.   Whence the suppression of nudes inherited from the Renaissance, as well as all the elements that were not indispensable to the story, or which had no obvious symbolic meaning.

But the wind of austerity that the Counter-Reformation had set blowing through the Church quickly died down.   With the support of the new religious orders, whose authority and resources continued to increase, Catholicism won back a great part of the lost ground.   Beginning in the last decade of the 16th century, the Church and its orders, with renewed strength and wealth, adopted a policy of prestige through art.

Pope Sixtus V undertook to make Christian Rome a city whose splendor would surpass that of pagan Rome, and Urban VIII had dreams of being another Julius II.   In their eyes nothing was too magnificent to proclaim divine glory, and a work of art had to be done in a way that would strike and move the faithful.

In other words, art had to be popular, with all its implied exaltation and danger.

Henceforth, the great artists, liberated from classical restraint, could give free rein to their natural exuberance. But others, motivated by the desire to astonish or to captivate popular attention, in many cases descended to mere facility.

CARAVAGGIO—AN INDEPENDENT PAINTER. As a curtain-raiser to the 17th century, Caravaggio, a painter of great originality, lived his short and stormy career and accomplished the break with Mannerist painting that the Carraccis still brilliantly represented. His independence was so great that he defies all classification and can only be connected to the Baroque through his sense of the dramatic and predilection for contrasts of light and shade. He was one of the first painters whose artistic life aroused as much scandal as his private life. His many misdeeds forced him first to leave Rome, then to flee the police in city after city. His pictures, admired by some, so deeply shocked the general public by their brutality that on several occasions his religious compositions were rejected by the churches that had commissioned them.

Two features characterized his work: his violently contrasted light effects and his realism. He found his models in taverns, which was not to the liking of all his contemporaries. As Stendhal remarked, the reign of the ugly had not yet begun in Europe.

Caravaggio had several talented imitators in Italy, but his influence was greatest abroad. "Caravaggio-ism" was a movement of European importance to which Rubens, Rembrandt and the Frenchman Simon Vouet owed a great deal, and which restored a lost vigor to painting.

BERNINI'S REVOLUTION. Three artists of exceptional quality worked in Rome between 1620 and 1670—Bernini, Pietro da Cortona and Francesco Borromini. These three incarnate Italian Baroque at its apogee. Through them we can grasp its various aspects and understand that the extravagant illogicality that characterizes it is the fruit of coherent thought and not of uncoordinated inspiration.

Bernini was the greatest genius of his time, and he has often been compared with Michelangelo. Like Michelangelo, he worked for the popes and made a great name for himself, and like him he was endowed with an amazing capacity for sheer output and stupendous energy. But instead of being a solitary individual, always prey to doubt and anguish, he was a brilliant, worldly man and very self-satisfied; so much so, in fact, that his self-importance antagonized the French when Louis XIV called on him to build the east wing of the Louvre. The foundation stone was laid in his presence because his prestige demanded it. But as soon as he had gone, work stopped. (Claude Perrault was approached, and he built a colonnade in place of the monumental façade that had originally been planned.)

Sculptor, architect and painter, Bernini was a revolutionary in every one of his activities, but even more so in the way he brought together different branches of art so closely that the boundaries that separated them became indistinct. He introduced color into sculpture, gave relief to decorative painting by combining it with stucco, and made architecture into a kind of decoration. For him everything had to lead up to the final effect and to the creation of an illusion strong enough to make the beholder lose all feeling of reality.

His most significant work is the Cornaro Chapel, which contains a sculptural group known as the "Ecstasy of St. Theresa of Avila."

André Chastel described this work as so bold that the excessive pomp, the fusion of arts, the ambiguity of the pious evocation, all of which make it a model of Baroque extravagance, cannot but horrify or deeply impress, as much by the wealth of its devices as by the artist's skill of expression.

Everything about it was new: the decoration in polychrome marble and gold; the play of light directed as from a projector to give a supernatural effect; the dynamic force of the sculpture which seizes the figures at the final moment of action and accentuates their movements by billowing draperies; the combination of stucco and fresco that reinforces the "trompe-l'oeil" effect of the vault, and finally the desire to subordinate the whole building to a center of interest toward which the attention of the visitor would be automatically attracted. In the oval church of San Andrea al Quirinale, which Bernini built a little later, this desire is even more evident, and it is the architecture itself that obliges the worshipper to turn his gaze to the main altar as soon as he enters.

BERNINI AT ST. PETER'S. It is through the works that he created in St. Peter's—the baldaquin, the chair of St. Peter and the colonnade—that Bernini has become universally famous. The baldaquin was destined to cover the pontifical altar. Thus it would be under Michelangelo's gigantic dome, to which it had to be in proportion. Bernini decided to execute it in bronze, and on the orders of Pope Urban VIII (one of the Barberinis) the bronze for it was taken from the Pronaos on the Pantheon. All Rome declared that the Barberinis were doing what the Barbarians had not dared to do. But once the baldaquin was completed, no one thought any more about the Pantheon.

Bernini's creation furnished and at last gave life to the immense basilica, which had previously seemed empty. It is a monument unique of its kind, and it is impossible to say whether it is derived from architecture or sculpture. Its inspiration was the cloth baldaquin held above the pope when he was carried about in his "sedia gestatoria." Four enormous wreathed columns constitute its main feature. They contrast by their shape and color with the white pilasters of the basilica, and their function is purely decorative, since they have to support only angels and draperies.

Thirty years later, Bernini was to give them a new rôle and use them as a frame seemingly containing the Chair of St. Peter, which was placed at the end of the apse and which, though separated from it by some one hundred and fifty feet, forms a fitting complement to the baldaquin. It is a sumptuous composition covering the wooden seat, said to have been that of the Prince of the Apostles. It appears in the background of the baldaquin like an enormous picture full of life and color. All styles and materials were brought together with an extraordinary feeling for stage-setting: statues of gilt bronze, architectural forms, decorations in multi-colored marble, stucco motifs and so on.

But it is the colonnade embracing St. Peter's Square, which gives to the first church of Christendom an approach worthy of it, that is the masterpiece of Bernini, that most universal of artists. Made up of four rows of powerful Doric columns, it has great simplicity, but also great boldness. For the first time, columns were used for their sculptural value only, and not to articulate a façade or to suggest a wall with vertical openings. The effect they produce by masking and revealing themselves as the visitor walks across the square is striking and profoundly Baroque in its changing character.

TWO OTHER GREAT MEN. In a parallel direction to Bernini, whose fame somewhat eclipsed their own, Pietro da Cortona and Borromini brought Baroque art to its peak.

Pietro da Cortona, architect, painter and decorator, was the inventor of the curved church façade. In a first version, in the church of San Martino e Luca, the center part of the façade is arched as though it were squeezed between the two pilasters on each side of it. In a second version, the church of Santa Maria della Pace, the artist showed greater boldness, and the portico describes a more emphatic curve, while the wings of the building sweep away in the opposite direction, calling to mind the inside of a theater, the portico being the stage.

As a painter, Cortona was a virtuoso in the decoration of ceilings and domes. Above towering "trompe-l'oeil" architecture, he revealed a sky of apparently infinite depth, in which he painted a swirling host of dazzling figures.

It was in this type of decorative painting, perfectly in harmony with the Baroque spirit, that the 17th century in Italy was to excel. This is illustrated by Giovanni Lanfranco, the Jesuit Pozzo, the Neapolitan Luca Giordano and on occasion by Guido Reni and Guercino, all of whom showed proof of a remarkable understanding of perspective and gave free rein to their imagination. On the other hand, easel painting at that time became rather dull and unconvincing, probably because the artists tried too hard to achieve the opposite effect.

Francesco Borromini, whose achievements were exclusive to architecture, and who in this domain was Bernini's great rival, asserted himself as the grand master of the "bizarre." The sculpturesque effect of his buildings is even more delicate and intricate than their decoration. His most surprising achievement was the church of La Sapienza, the plan of which, approximately hexagonal, has been thought by some to represent a bee, the emblem of Pope Urban VIII. In this building, full of strange effects, Borromini resolved

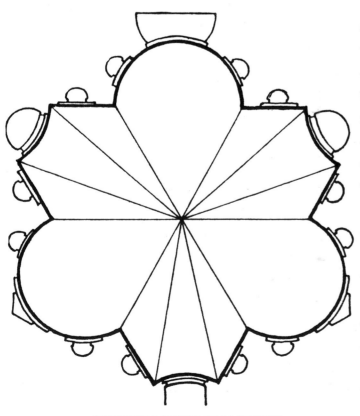

BORROMINI : CHURCH OF LA SAPIENZA

with extraordinary skill the difficulties inherent in such a complex construction and in the harmonious fusion of its different parts.

One of Borromini's followers was the Piedmontese priest and mathematician Guarini, whose Chapel of the Holy Shroud in Turin—the height of Baroque extravagance—holds fascination for anyone who can look at it without preconceived ideas. He covered his churches with unusual domes which make us wonder whether we should see in them the influence of Hispano-Moorish monuments or his own very personal interpretation of the Gothic style.

CITIES, FOUNTAINS AND GARDENS. When Baroque art broke away from the religious setting in which it had mainly developed, it found unlimited scope in the planning of towns and the embellishment of gardens. Here its theatrical qualities and fantasy produced wonders.

Rome owes to the Baroque period her greatest town-planning achievements: not only St. Peter's Square, but also the Piazza del Popolo with its twin churches, the picturesque steps of the Piazza di Spagna, and above all the captivating fountains that give this majestic city that note of gaiety that is one of its greatest charms.

In Sicily, which had been laid waste at the end of the 17th century, there remain whole towns and districts that were rebuilt in the Baroque style, from plans that afford spectacular perspectives. This is the case with the little town of Noto which shows an exceptional unity of style, as well as with a major part of Catania and Syracuse.

THE SECOND TRIUMPH OF VENETIAN PAINTING. Painting in the 17th century was—with the exception of Caravaggio and some of his followers whose merit has now been recognized—the least highly esteemed of the arts.

At the beginning of the 18th century, Venice gave painting a brilliant revival and at the same time ensured for Italy one last great artistic success. As in the great age of Titian and Tintoretto, it was a victory for color, to which seventeenth-century Venetians—especially Domenico Feti and Giovanni Lys—had remained attached, while many painters in other cities had adopted Caravaggio's theory according to which bright colors were the "poison of painting."

The painter who dominated the 18th century in Venice was Giambattista Tiepolo, who carried the art of the decorative fresco to its highest peak. Tiepolo's understanding of perspective was as profound as that of the great Romans, but he added to it a zest, a luminosity and a gaiety that are typically Venetian. Through his great compositions, with their fresh and delicate hues, we can feel all the magic and charm of this town that had become the world capital of pleasure.

The picture of life in Venice at that period was immortalized by three artists who raised styles usually regarded as minor to new and spectacular heights. These were Pietro Longhi, Canaletto and Guardi.

The first, a specialist in scenes of everyday life, full of humor, grace and delicacy, was to some extent the Goldoni of painting. The other two were essentially landscape painters, and their talents complemented each other to perfection.

Both rendered the pink and gold harmony of their native city, but Canaletto painted it with greater precision and a faultless clarity, while Guardi used a freer brush and worked with vibrant little touches that remind us of Impressionism.

POMPEII BRINGS THE CLASSICAL BACK INTO FASHION. In 1713 workers engaged in digging the foundations of a villa near Naples suddenly brought to light walls and statues—this was Pompeii. But the government, who wanted to keep the uncovered works for itself, strictly forbade any excavations. Twenty-five years later, while building a new palace for the King of Naples, another buried city was discovered. Thought at first to be Stabiae, it was in fact Herculaneum.

This time excavations were undertaken, but unfortunately without method, and the king, jealous of his rights, allowed no one near the site. For a long time it was even forbidden to make sketches of what had been found.

In spite of, or perhaps because of this secrecy, these discoveries had caused a great stir in Rome, where there were many artists from all countries, for the most part grouped in academies where they studied classical and Italian art. When the first reproductions of the works found at Herculaneum and Pompeii were finally published in 1757, people almost fought for them.

Antiquity, which had never ceased to interest Italian minds, but the attraction of which had gradually waned, again captured the imagination of all. New finds kept enthusiasm running high. In Tuscany, Etruscan remains were dug up, and immediately they were the subject of fierce debates. In Hadrian's villa were discovered the Egyptian works that the emperor had brought there. Finally, Greek works began to arouse artists' curiosity. In 1750 some adventurous travelers, one of whom was Soufflot, the future builder of the Panthéon in Paris, got as far as Paestum and saw there, for the first time, Doric temples. Toward the end of the century other "art-explorers" reached Sicily. Some Englishmen, crossing the Adriatic, visited Split. and came back full of admiration. Finally, Greece itself was reached.

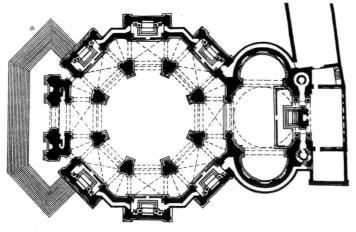

LONGHENA : CHURCH OF SANTA MARIA DELLA SALUTE

In Rome, two men expressed the new passion of the 18th century for classical art.

One of them was an Italian, the architect and engraver Piranesi, who produced many volumes of etchings of extraordinary evocative power, showing Roman remains and classical ornaments, that were to become a book of reference for architects and decorators in later years.

The other was the German Winckelmann who, in his "History of Ancient Art," expounded a new doctrine of art that provoked a ruthless reappraisal of values. He affirmed that art was great only if it sought the ideal beauty of which the Greeks had set the example. In architecture, reason was henceforth to be the sole rule; moreover, polychromy had to be banished from architecture, for it was not yet known to have existed with the Ancients.

In Italian art the Baroque was relentlessly condemned, Michelangelo was judged with severity, and only artists who had been directly inspired by the Ancients were admired. Raphael and Palladio, to name but two, were praised to the skies.

But neo-classicism enjoyed only moderate success in its country of origin. The region where it developed most fully was Venezia, where the "neo-Palladian" movement began, and where many very elegant villas were built.

At the end of the 18th century only one Italian artist won general acclaim. This was Canova, whose success seems nowadays to have been somewhat unjustified and his severe talent very academic.

There is no doubt that the Italian Renaissance was too dazzling a phenomenon for a second to have been produced on the same ground. It was the French—the architect Ledoux, the sculptor Houdon and the painters David and Ingres—and the English—the Adam brothers—who gave neo-classicism its true expression.

Italy had gradually lost her place at the forefront of Western art. But the torch had been handed on. For the last three hundred years, Europe has lived on the artistic heritage of Italy.

The 17th century belongs to Bernini...

"Perfection in art," wrote Stendhal of St. Peter's Square in Rome. "If there were any more decorations, its majesty would be diminished, any fewer, and it would look naked." The square that gives access to the first church of Christendom had to be not only of unquestionable magnificence but had also to allow for various practical necessities. A crowd of thousands had to meet there for the blessing "urbi et orbi" given by the pope from the balcony of St. Peter's, and on this occasion the supreme pontiff had to be seen by all. Moreover, processions had to take place there sheltered from rain and sun. Finally, the façade had to be improved. This façade, the work of Maderno, seems to be too low for its length, for it had not been framed, as had been planned, by the two towers which would give it height. Bernini's triumph lay in finding the solution that offered the most advantages, while at the same time being profoundly original. This was his famous quadruple colonnade (right), elliptical in shape, which to his mind symbolized the maternal embrace of the Church. Though not very high, it is impressive. By a stroke of genius its builder surmounted it not by arches as tradition dictated but by a rectilinear entablature. This, calling to mind the idea of a roof, shows that it is indeed a complete monument, not just an architectural element detached from a more important whole. The center of the square is marked by an obelisk that Pope Sixtus V had had transported there one hundred years previously. It had been brought from Heliopolis by the Emperor Caligula, who had set it up in the Circus of Nero, on the site where the first Basilica of St. Peter was partly built. Around this obelisk white stripes mark out a compass dial and frame the stairway (left) that leads up to the church.

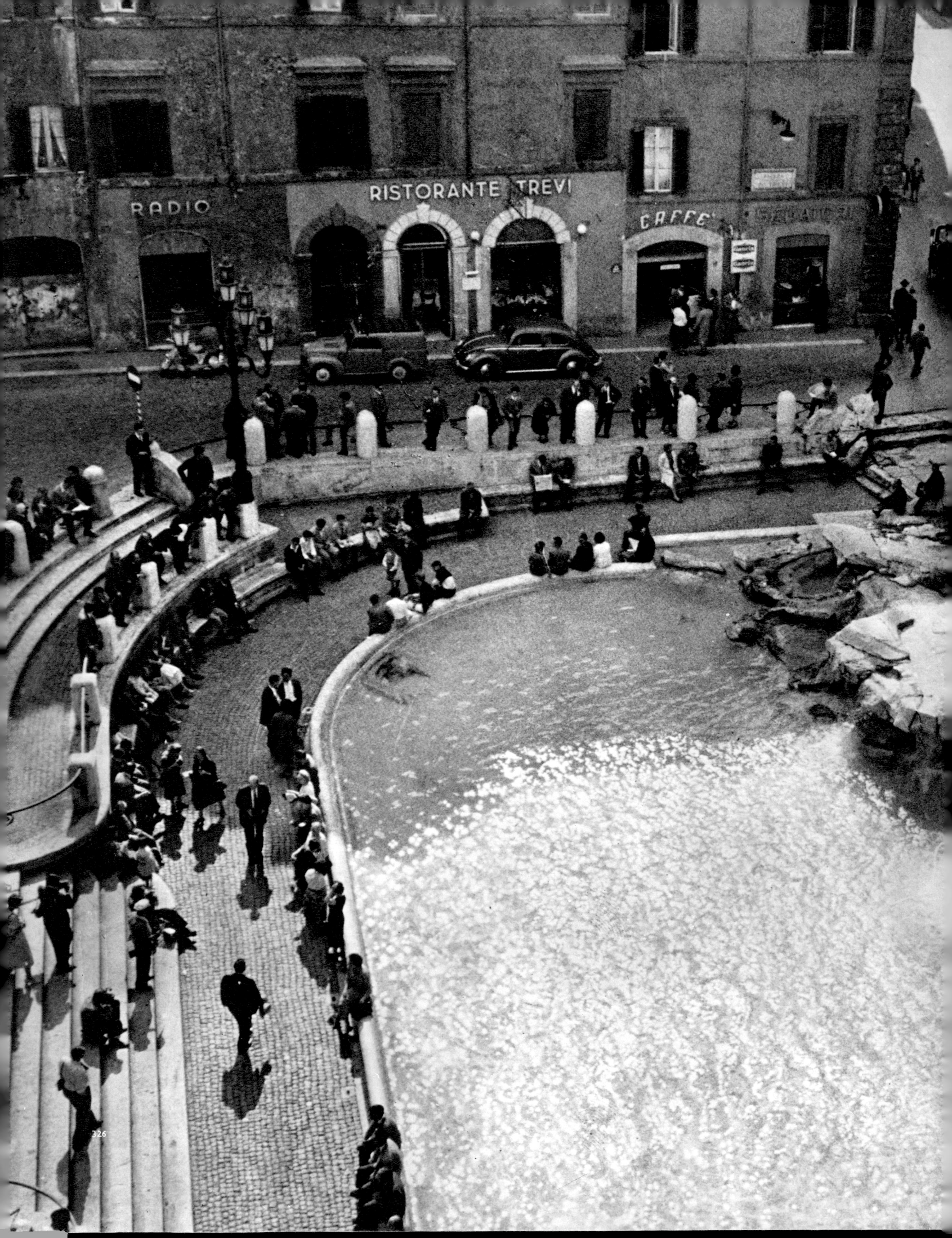
RISTORANTE TREVI
RADIO
CAFFE'

BERNINI (1598-1680): THE FOUNTAIN OF THE RIVERS - DETAIL - 1648 - PIAZZA NAVONA, ROME.

BERNINI (1598-1680): ELEPHANT BEARING AN OBELISK - 1667 - ROME, PIAZZA DELLA MINERVA.

... who sets his stamp on all Rome...

A world of figures intermingled with water sweeps from the façade of a palace to make the most sumptuous fountain in the world: the Fountain of Trevi (pages 326-327). Since Roman times there has been a fountain on this spot, sustained by the "Aqua Vergine," which, brought by canal from Salona, seven or so miles from Rome, once supplied the baths of Agrippa. It still gushes out today at the meeting point of three ways—the "tre vie" or "Trevi"—that gave the fountain its name. The present fountain was built in the 18th century by Niccolo Salvi, inspired by a design by Bernini. The conception of the whole is truly Baroque. On the one hand, the monument and the background against which it stands were conceived as complementary entities. On the other hand, it has no symmetry of composition—we can look at it from any number of angles and admire its inexhaustible richness. In the center, Neptune on his chariot is drawn by two horses. One of them, unharnessed, symbolizes the untamable sea, and the other, which is peaceful, the calmed sea. Several sculptors, including Pannini and Giambattista Maini, gave the finishing touches to this monument which, so the story goes, cost Salvi his life, since he died of exhaustion after conceiving it.

The boundless imagination of Bernini revived the design of the fountain, for centuries highly appreciated by the Italians. His masterpiece in this manner is the Fountain of the Rivers. In contrast to the Florentine fountains of the previous century, elegantly symmetrical, it is so exuberant that it seems to flaunt all the rules. But in fact, there is nothing incoherent about it: it developed from a very clear conception of the available decorative resources and of the subject to be illustrated. Its basic element is an enormous artificial rock, with an opening driven through it to give it a less heavy look, which supports an ancient obelisk. The form and dimensions of the whole work are carefully proportioned to those of the long and narrow square it adorns. Leaning against the rock are four statues, some sixteen feet high, personifying the four rivers that water the various parts of the world. The Nile, symbolizing Africa, has its head veiled, since its source was undiscovered. Beside it grows a palm tree lightly bending in the wind (left). The water, instead of spurting out in fine jets as it did in earlier fountains, flows in from all sides in full waves. On top of the obelisk, a dove, the emblem of Pope Innocent X, proclaims the worldwide power of the Church headed by this supreme pontiff. It was to the glory of his successor, Alexander VII, that Bernini erected the curious memorial (above) which represents an elephant, also supporting an Egyptian obelisk.

329

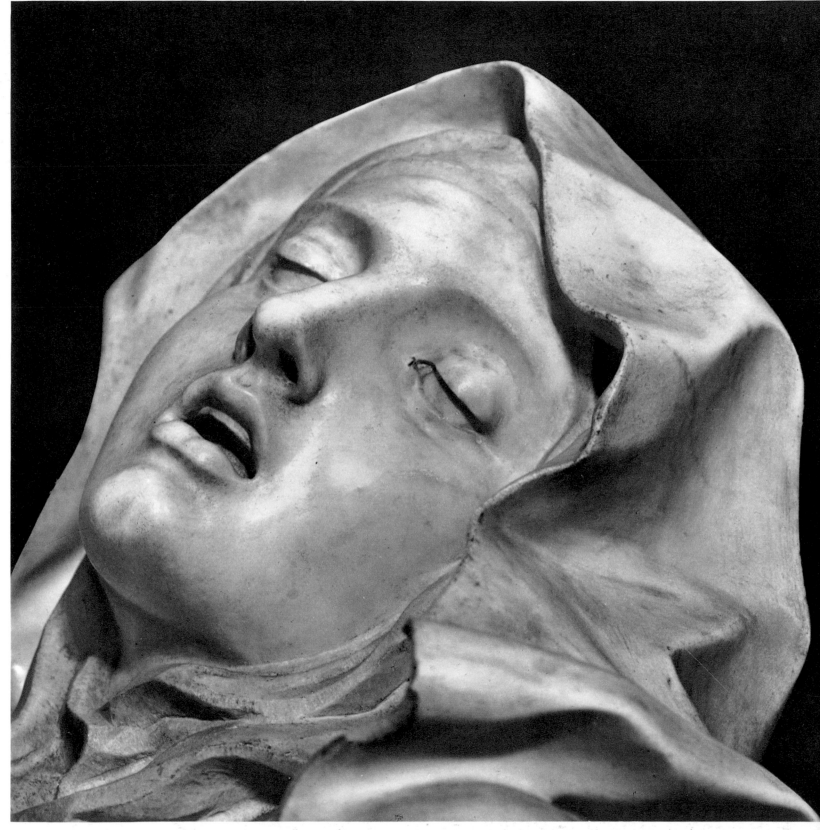

ST. THERESA - DETAIL.

Epitomizing the apogee of Baroque art, Bernini's "St. Theresa in Ecstasy" (left) is an essentially spectacular work. It is like a living tableau, cleverly lit by a hidden window, the light of which is continued and emphasized by a fan of golden rays. The saint is lying on a cloud which looks as though it is miraculously suspended in the middle of a little stage which, opening out above the altar of the chapel, is one of Bernini's most unusual creations. The sides of this altar are lit up and terminate in an arch decorated with paintings and stucco, which heightens the illusion. Bernini, a sincere believer, illustrated here St. Theresa's account of her mystical experience. Her uplifted face (detail above) reflects the suffering and joy she felt when the angel pierced her heart with the arrow of divine love. In the grouping for angel and saint (left), there is "nothing stable and tangible, all is movement or change." Sculpture lost its essential qualities and took on a pictorial character; it was intended to be seen from only one angle. The extravagant folds of St. Theresa's robes destroy any effect of continuity: everything in this work is in direct contradiction to the classical spirit.

331

BERNINI (1598-1680): ST. THERESA IN ECSTASY - CHURCH OF SANTA MARIA DELLA VITTORIA, ROME.

*Baroque complexity
succeeds
classical simplicity...*

Great works of urban planning were undertaken in Rome in the 17th and 18th centuries. The most successful of these are the steps leading from the Piazza di Spagna to the Church of Trinità dei Monti (right). Composed of elegant curves, the steps were made mainly with one object in view: to give a series of constantly changing impressions. Their many irregularities and changes of direction reserve many surprises for the visitor and continually whet his curiosity as he ascends them. While classical works were made to convey a feeling of absolute clarity—a single column breaks the monotony of the steps leading up to the Senatorial Palace at the top of the Capitol Hill (left)—the steps in the Piazza di Spagna are beautiful by their very complexity. From no point can they be absorbed at one glance. They keep that secret quality that marks the whole Baroque style.

ROME - THE DELL'ARCE STEPS
LATE 16TH CENTURY.

ROME - PIAZZA DI SPAGNA STEPS - 1723.

BORROMINI (1599-1667): CHURCH OF LA SAPIENZA - 1642 - ROME.

... and reigns over an architecture of curves and broken lines

Wholly revolutionary in concept, Borromini's architecture was declared excessively extravagant by certain of his contemporaries, particularly friends of Bernini, whose collaborator he was before becoming his rival. His masterpiece is the Church of La Sapienza, with a ground plan of such complexity that it was thought to be in the shape of a bee, the emblem of Pope Urban VIII. The exterior (above) is distinguished by a surprising succession of concave and convex curves. By way of a façade, Borromini quite simply—and quite brazenly—used the incurvated end of the courtyard built a century before by Giacomo della Porta and which is overlooked by the church. He surmounted this façade with a high drum with convex curves that hides all but the crest of the dome. Above this a very high lantern-tower is cut out in concave curves. On top of this is a spiral, unique in western architecture, which probably has some symbolic meaning that is completely unknown to us today.

Ten lively guardian angels by Bernini and his pupils look down on the ancient bridge of San Angelo (right). This bridge was built in the 2nd century by the Emperor Hadrian to give access to his mausoleum, and its three central arches have remained intact. In contrast to the majority of Bernini's sculptures, these were conceived in such a way that they could be seen by people crossing the bridge from several different angles instead of from the front alone.

ROME - BRIDGE OF SAN ANGELO - 2ND CENTURY A.D., STATUES OF THE 17TH CENTURY.

Fountains lend themselves to the sculptor's whim

ROME, PIAZZA NAVONA - FOUNTAIN OF NEPTUNE - 16TH AND 19TH CENTURIES.

Rome's countless fountains are this solemn city's main escape into fancy. Several of them were designed by Jacopo della Porta in the 16th century, including that of the Rotonda and those of the Piazza Navona, to which central figures were added several hundred years later. The detail (left) of the Rotonda fountain is formed by a pile of rocks from which rises an obelisk supported by dolphins: it was added in 1711 by Felici. So as to respect the existing harmony, the sculptor Antonio della Bitta took inspiration from a Neptune by Bernini (today in the Victoria and Albert Museum in London) to adorn the fountain (above) at one of the corners of the Piazza Navona. In the middle of the square stands Bernini's magnificent Fountain of the Rivers. Some years later Giuseppe Valadier reacted against Baroque excesses with a fountain, shaped like a shell with perfectly regular ribs (pages 338-339). This fountain was part of the reconstruction work on the Piazza del Popolo, to which Valadier gave its final unity by building an immense stone semicircle of steps leading up to the Pincio Park. The architect thus put the finishing touches, in the neo-classical style, to the great works of urban planning started in the 17th century by papal initiative.

ROME, PIAZZA DELLA ROTONDA - FOUNTAIN - 16TH AND 18TH CENTURIES.

GIUSEPPE VALADIER (1762-1839): FOUNTAIN - EARLY 19TH CENTURY - PIAZZA DEL POPOLO, ROME.

PIETRO DA CORTONA (1596-1669): PART OF A FRESCO · PITTI PALACE, FLORENCE.

Caravaggio introduces realism into painting...

CARAVAGGIO (1569-1609 ?): BACCHUS - ABOUT 1595 - UFFIZI, FLORENCE.

The same subject from mythology interpreted by two artists at the beginning of the 17th century enables us to assess the tendencies in painting at that time. On the one hand, Caravaggio in his "Bacchus" (above) renders with brutal realism man degraded by drunkenness. On the other hand, Pietro da Cortona in his "Boy with Grapes" (left) shows the lovable, playful and attractive side of the young Bacchus. This detail is from one of the frescoes he painted between 1637 and 1647 for Grand-Duke Ferdinand II in the Pitti Palace. Pietro da Cortona, who was also one of the three great Baroque architects, was a joyful painter, stately and full of imagination and wit. His somewhat fluid lines, the pearly effect he gives to flesh, his stucco frame-work, his deceptive perspectives, all herald the Louis Quatorze style. He belongs to the school of "luminous" painters, which was hostile to Caravaggio. The latter was in vogue in Italy only for the sensual realism emanating from his early works, when he preached that the study of the model should replace the study of the old masters, but he still used light colors.

341

... and spectacular chiaroscuro effects

CARAVAGGIO (1569-1609?): THE CALLING OF ST. PAUL - SANTA MARIA DEL POPOLO, ROME.

Master of light effects, famous for his use of "chiaroscuro," that he carried almost as far as to produce a monochrome effect, Caravaggio lived his life with as much violence as he put into his work—neither of which was free from scandal. His religious paintings show holy people in the most realistic poses. Thus St. Paul is shown (above) the prey to some strange attack, thrown by his horse which is about to trample him. The whole subject is subordinated to the light which comes from the upper right-hand corner, strikes the horse's right shoulder and runs right along its body down to the ground where St. Paul is lying, with decreasing effects of luminous intensity that finish in total darkness. Caravaggio, the anatomist, makes a study of man and horse at the same time in a very fine foreshortened view. This picture belongs to the great period of the painter's Roman maturity. He encloses himself more and more within the formula he created, which gave birth to a whole new school of European painters who were henceforth to be known as the "Tenebrosi."

A stage-setter of genius, Bernini, who thought of ways of flooding the Piazza Colonna, with its column of Marcus Aurelius, so that water spectacles could be held there, would have liked the modern lighting that accentuates the theatrical nature of the Fountain of Rivers. It makes the statue of the Danube loom up out of the shadows (right). The Danube has a better and smoother finish than the three others, because the figure symbolizes Europe, then considered incontestably the most civilized part of the world.

BERNINI (1569-1680): THE FOUNTAIN OF THE RIVERS - DETAIL - 1648 - PIAZZA NAVONA, ROME.

The taste
for the ornamental
and the unexpected...

Comic turns in painting, pranks of a jester of Maximilian II at his court in Prague, such are the "composite heads" attributed to a recently discovered painter—Arcimboldo. His portrait of a peasant (left) made up of carrots, turnips and onions is, when turned upside down, a pile of vegetables in a basin. The originality of the process and its drollness amused the Austrian emperor, who loved to collect curios. He ordered Arcimboldo to paint portraits of all his servants: for example, his librarian would be made up of books, his admiral of fish, etc. Certain marble mosaics are akin in spirit. The detail of the center piece of a console-table (right)—the face of a holy old man with a beard of vine-branches — marks the apogee of the ancient technique of the Cosmati family, who since the 12th century in Rome worked with great dexterity in different marbles and hard stones. In the 17th century Florence was the center of this craft. By varying the cut of the marble and choosing from a wealth of colors, true pictures could be made and widely were used to adorn palace furniture.

GIUSEPPE ARCIMBOLDO (17TH CENTURY): PEASANT - CREMONA MUSEUM.

344

DETAIL OF THE CENTERPIECE OF A MARBLE TABLE - 17TH CENTURY - PITTI PALACE, FLORENCE.

MONSÙ DESIDERIO (FIRST HALF OF THE 17TH CENTURY): TOWER OF BABEL - DUKE PIRONTÈ DI CAMPANIA COLLECTION, NAPLES.

... reaches a frenzied extravagance

The work of "Monsù Desiderio" (the Italian form of the French Monsieur Didier) is interesting from a psychological as well as an artistic point of view. In 1950 art historians discovered that this was the name that cloaked the identities of two French artists from Lorraine who had settled in Naples and who worked in collaboration. In "The Tower of Babel" (above) we can see them presenting the sketch of their painting to a figure wearing a crown. In the shadows at the foot of the violently lit tower, in the style of Caravaggio, can be found the basic motifs of their repertoire: votive steles, action statues and a "tempietto" in the classical style. Here, as in all their paintings, the architectural forms are fantastic. "The Tower of Babel" marks a stage in the career of the two painters, who at first painted palaces and temples intact, then showed them half destroyed, and finally painted whole cataclysms: stumps of columns and broken statues with apocalyptic light effects.

Spanish and Roman influence combined to give birth in Sicily to a Baroque style of exceptional richness, abundant in ornaments. In the façade of Syracuse Cathedral (right) added to the ancient Greek Temple of Athena, i.e. Minerva (interior, page 32), the truly Italian contribution predominates; this appears in the coupling and superimposition of the Corinthian columns and in the breaks in the cornices. But the sculpture of the capitals is Spanish in its exuberance.

Venice keeps a sense of proportion and allows painting a final burst of splendor...

WOOD MARQUETRY - CERTOSA DI SAN MARTINO, NAPLES.

Virtuosity invades all art and takes over inlaid woodwork, a fifteenth-century creation (page 202). The use of different kinds of wood together with perfection of technique resulted in works such as the panel above which can be counted among the masterpieces of its kind: the "studiolo" of Frederico di Montefeltro at Urbino, the whole of Gubbio's ducal palace and Pisa Cathedral. While because of the complexity of its treatment, this art risked ending in decadence, it kept all its basic qualities when it dealt with architectonic views of which the linear precision corresponded to the carving of the wood.

Superb Baroque decoration, with scrolls as its basic element, give the Church of Santa Maria della Salute, built by the Venetian architect Longhena, the grandiose and picturesque character demanded by the tastes of his day, and which was particularly fitting to its privileged position at the entrance to the Grand Canal (right). Its architectural conception is different from the baroque churches of Rome or Milan and shows a curious fidelity to local tradition. In effect its ground plan was inspired by the Church of S. Vitale, at Ravenna (pages 106-107), and its domes still have something Byzantine about them. Many Palladian elements were taken up and integrated into a whole of unquestionable originality and spectacular effect.

Light vibrant touches were used by Guardi to paint Venice. He reproduced the city's monuments with fidelity, captured with subtle brushwork the scintillating light and keenly observed the liveliness of the passers-by. Pupil and imitator of Canaletto, who had specialized in Venetian scenes eagerly sought after by foreigners (and especially the British), he surpassed his master by his freedom and his sense of color, which have led some critics to perceive a foreshadowing of impressionism in his work. In the picture on the following double page, we can see the Piazzetta, a continuation of St. Mark's Square toward the lagoon, which has not changed since the end of the 16th century. On the left of the picture is the Doges' Palace; on the right the campanile and the Loggetta by Sansovino—which by some strange whim he shows stripped of its sculptured decorations— then the Library, with its two superimposed porches, a masterpiece by the same artist.

BALDASSARE LONGHENA (1631-1681): SANTA MARIA DELLA SALUTE, VENICE

GUARDI (1712-1793): PIAZZETTA - ABOUT 1770 - CA' D'ORO, VENICE.

PIETRO LONGHI (1702-1785): THE RIDOTTO - DETAIL - ABOUT 1760 - MUSEO CORRER, VENICE.

Gambling and parlor games had gradually become the essential occupations of the aristocrats of Venice, who were slowly exhausting the fortunes amassed by their ancestors. This easy life bred less serious painters. Pietro Longhi immortalized each episode of such life in a large number of small pictures that are so many charming and delicate records of the customs of his day among the nobility and the ordinary people. The most important is the "Ridotto" (above). It shows the vestibule of the chief gaming house in Venice at a time when Casanova went there in search of adventure. In front of the table of the money-changer can be seen the men and women gamblers, wearing three-cornered hats, their faces covered with white or—not so frequently—black masks that could be worn from the first Sunday in October till Lent, then again during the greater part of spring. It was understood that this accessory assured absolute anonymity for all concerned.

The carnival of Venice provided Giandomenico Tiepolo with the subject for the frescoes with which he decorated one of the rooms in the Villa Valmarana. He placed them, as though they were easel-paintings, in a "trompe-l'œil" décor, part of which is the young Moorish page standing at the foot of a flight of make-believe stairs (right). Although for a long time he collaborated with his father, who treated only great mythological or allegorical subjects, Giandomenico had talents and tastes very different from those of Giambattista. For the latter's bold composition and airy imagination he substituted precise strokes and a lively sense of observation. He painted the everyday characters of Venetian life in preference to his father's sumptuous heroes. But, like his father, he used a fresh and subtly tinted palette. In the scene decorating the back of the wall (right), he shows us passers-by thronging around one of the fairground huts set up for the carnival.

GIANDOMENICO TIEPOLO (1727-1804): FRESCO IN THE CARNIVAL ROOM · 1757 · VILLA VALMARANA, VICENZA.

Tiepolo
is the crowning glory of this last
surge toward the spectacular...

An international decorator, Giambattista Tiepolo
traveled far and wide over Europe, leaving some of
his masterpieces behind in Spain and Germany. In
his native city of Venice, he decorated the finest aris-
tocratic villas with unequalled refinement, dash and
virtuosity. In an atmosphere of silvery light, white,
his favorite color, predominates. In the Palazzo
Labia he told the story of Anthony and Cleopatra in
a decorative painting executed entirely in "trompe-
l'oeil," which creates the illusion of a second chamber,
full of bustling activity. In the banquet scene (left)
the artist painted himself at the table next to a Moorish
slave and facing the viewer. In the Scuola dei Carmini,
the Madonna of Carmel (right) is descending from
heaven holding a scapular in her hands. The figures
are weightless, floating on air in a cloud of veils and
angels' wings. Here Tiepolo employed his favorite
pyramidal construction with magnificent freedom.

GIAMBATTISTA TIEPOLO (1696-1770): THE STORY OF ANTHONY AND
CLEOPATRA: THE BANQUET - 1745-1750 - PALAZZO LABIA, VENICE.

GIAMBATTISTA TIEPOLO (1696-1770): MADONNA OF CARM
1740-1743 - SCUOLA DEI CARMINI, VENIC

*... while his son searches
the streets for
the eternal characters
of the Commedia dell' Arte*

Tender and slightly malicious realism tinges the "Declaration of Love" (left) in which a completely natural man and woman are painted against a picturesque landscape. In this work the originality of Giandomenico Tiepolo's talent stands out clearly, and we can understand why, after father and son visited Spain, the young Goya underwent their double influence. Thanks to them, the Venetian school itself was once more internationally famous.

The Italian instinct for happiness and gay spontaneity, born of the sun in this "land where the lemon-tree blooms," is incarnated by the "pagliacci"—half clowns, half acrobats—who kept the man in the street laughing with their capers and rough fun. It was these clowns whom Giandomenico Tiepolo painted for his own pleasure on the walls of his family's country house, in a series of splendidly lively grisailles. They are so true to life that two hundred years later at Frascati, near Rome, their successors for a day instinctively adopted the same gestures and the same sprightliness (following double page). Eternal Italy, land of beauty, remains also the land of gaiety.

GIANDOMENICO TIEPOLO (1727-1804): CLOWNS - ABOUT 1753 - CA' REZZONICO, VENICE.

GIANDOMENICO TIEPOLO (1727-1804): THE DECLARATION OF LOVE, FRESCO IN THE PROMENADE ROOM - 1757 - VILLA VALMARANA, VICENZA.

FRASCATI - CLOWNS AT THE SPRING FESTIVAL.

INDEX OF ARTISTS, CITIES AND PRINCIPAL MONUMENTS CITED

ANCIENT ITALY

In ancient Italy the principal cities were founded first by the Greeks and the Etruscans, then by the Romans. The cities that played a leading rôle in the history of art can be found on the upper map on the left. After the fall of the Roman Empire many Italian cities became the centers of small states hostile to one another, and underwent many changes in fortune. Thus centers of art often moved from one city to another. On the lower map left, are the most important of these centers.

MODERN ITALY

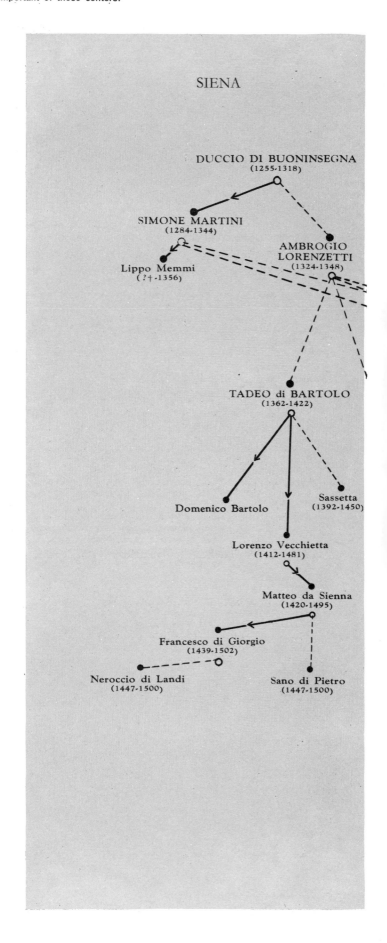

SIENA

DUCCIO DI BUONINSEGNA
(1255-1318)

SIMONE MARTINI
(1284-1344)

AMBROGIO LORENZETTI
(1324-1348)

Lippo Memmi
(?†-1356)

TADEO di BARTOLO
(1362-1422)

Domenico Bartolo

Sassetta
(1392-1450)

Lorenzo Vecchietta
(1412-1481)

Matteo da Sienna
(1420-1495)

Francesco di Giorgio
(1439-1502)

Neroccio di Landi
(1447-1500)

Sano di Pietro
(1447-1500)

The great schools of Italian painting

The deep unity of Italian painting, despite its great diversity, can be explained by the strength of the bonds between the painters of each city or state, and which were established between the various schools thanks to the travels of the artists. These bonds were of two kinds: the first are those forged directly between master and pupil in the many studios where young artists would come to work under their elders. The second were the results of the influence exerted over their contemporaries and successors by the works of certain innovators. On the chart below, the first kind of bonds are shown by continuous lines, the second by dotted lines. At the black dot above the name of each artist are joined the principal influences he underwent. From the circle underneath radiates his influence, integrating the currents that combined in his works, and which he transmitted after molding them. The painters have been grouped under the three chief schools. Those who were trained in one school but then went to work in other cities are also shown.

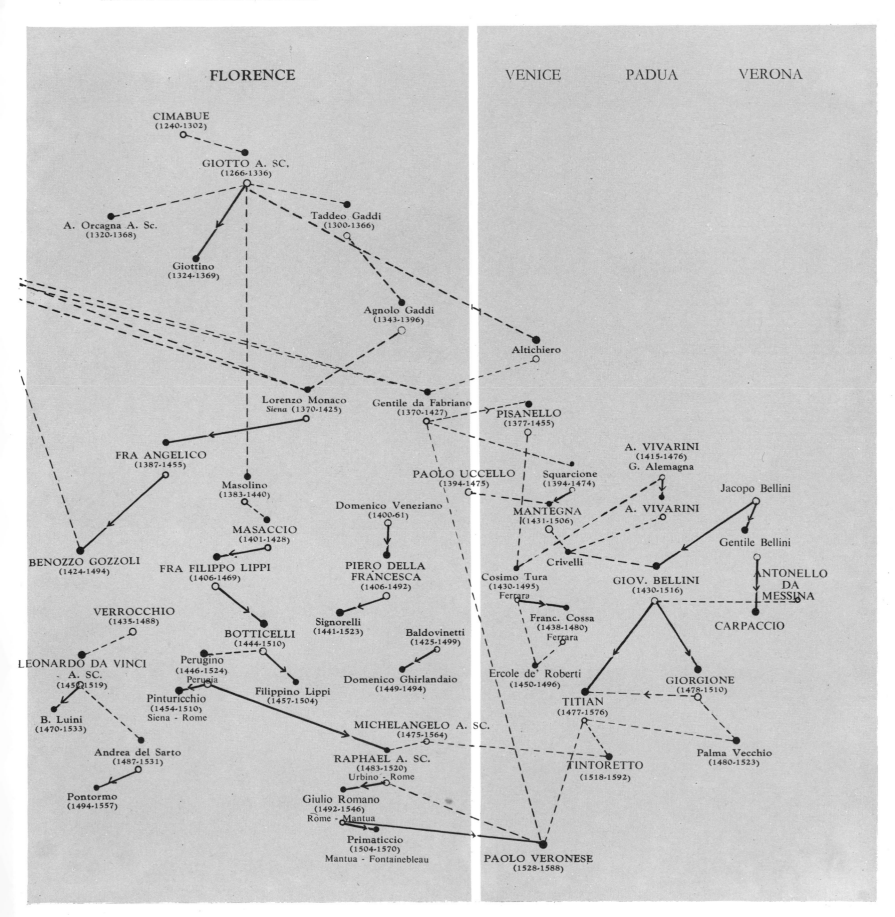

FLORENCE

VENICE   PADUA   VERONA

CIMABUE
(1240-1302)

GIOTTO A. SC.
(1266-1336)

A. Orcagna A. Sc.
(1320-1368)

Taddeo Gaddi
(1300-1366)

Giottino
(1324-1369)

Agnolo Gaddi
(1343-1396)

Altichiero

Lorenzo Monaco
Siena (1370-1425)

Gentile da Fabriano
(1370-1427)

PISANELLO
(1377-1455)

FRA ANGELICO
(1387-1455)

Masolino
(1383-1440)

A. VIVARINI
(1415-1476)
G. Alemagna

PAOLO UCCELLO
(1394-1475)

Squarcione
(1394-1474)

Jacopo Bellini

Domenico Veneziano
(1400-61)

MANTEGNA
(1431-1506)

A. VIVARINI

Gentile Bellini

MASACCIO
(1401-1428)

BENOZZO GOZZOLI
(1424-1494)

FRA FILIPPO LIPPI
(1406-1469)

PIERO DELLA
FRANCESCA
(1406-1492)

Crivelli

Cosimo Tura
(1430-1495)
Ferrara

GIOV. BELLINI
(1430-1516)

ANTONELLO
DA
MESSINA

VERROCCHIO
(1435-1488)

BOTTICELLI
(1444-1510)

Signorelli
(1441-1523)

Baldovinetti
(1425-1499)

Franc. Cossa
(1438-1480)
Ferrara

CARPACCIO

LEONARDO DA VINCI
- A. SC.
(1452-1519)

Perugino
(1446-1524)
Perugia

Filippino Lippi
(1457-1504)

Domenico Ghirlandaio
(1449-1494)

Ercole de' Roberti
(1450-1496)

GIORGIONE
(1478-1510)

B. Luini
(1470-1533)

Pinturicchio
(1454-1510)
Siena - Rome

MICHELANGELO A. SC.
(1475-1564)

TITIAN
(1477-1576)

Andrea del Sarto
(1487-1531)

RAPHAEL A. SC.
(1483-1520)
Urbino - Rome

TINTORETTO
(1518-1592)

Palma Vecchio
(1480-1523)

Pontormo
(1494-1557)

Giulio Romano
(1492-1546)
Rome - Mantua

Primaticcio
(1504-1570)
Mantua - Fontainebleau

PAOLO VERONESE
(1528-1588)